PERCEPTION AND COGNITION OF MUSIC

PERCEPTION AND COGNITION
OF MUSIC

Edited by

IRÈNE DELIÈGE

Unité de Recherche en Psychologie de la Musique (URPM)
Centre de Recherches Musicales de Wallonie
Université de Liège

JOHN SLOBODA

Unit for the Study of Musical Skill and Development
Department of Psychology
University of Keele

Psychology Press
a member of the Taylor & Francis group

Psychology Press Ltd, Publishers
27 Church Road
Hove
East Sussex, BN3 2FA
UK

British Library Cataloguing in Publication Data

A catalogue record for this book is available from the British Library

   ISBN   0-86377-452-0

Printed and bound in the United Kingdom by Biddles Ltd, Guildford and King's Lynn

Contents

Foreword and Acknowledgements

This volume is constructed from revised and expanded versions of presentations that were made at the Third International Conference for Music Perception and Cognition, organised in July 1994 at the University of Liège (Belgium) by the European Society for the Cognitive Sciences of Music (ESCOM). The editors were assisted in their selection of contributors by the views of conference delegates themselves. Each delegate was invited to indicate which of the over two hundred presentations had been the most interesting and attractive.

The editors would like to acknowledge financial support for this project from a number of sources:

The European Communities (Kaleidoscope Program of cultural events),
The Belgian Ministry of Scientific Politics,
The Belgian Ministry of Education and Scientific Research,
The Belgian Ministry of Culture and Social Affairs,
The General Commissariat of International Relations,
The National Foundation of Scientific Research,
The Council of Music of the French Communities of Belgium,
The embassies of Canada, France, Israel, Netherlands, Quebec,
The British Council,
The Centre of Music Research from Wallonia,
The Unit of Research in Psychology of Music,
and the University of Liège.

The editors gratefully acknowledge the collaboration of several colleagues who kindly agreed to review first drafts of the chapters: Rita Aiello, Simha Arom, Ian Cross, Christoph Fassbender, David Hargreaves, Ralph Krampe, Carol Krumhansl, Jean-Pierre Lecanuet, Jean-Jacques Nattiez, Richard Parncutt, Bruno Repp, Xavier Seron and Neil Todd. The editors and the authors are extremely grateful for their valuable suggestions and assistance. In addition the invaluable administrative assistance of Noémie Ziv and Marie-Isabelle Collart is also gratefully acknowledged.

Finally we would like to take this opportunity to thank Michel Imberty, ESCOM's President during its first three years (1992–94) for his contribution of a preface and epilogue chapter of the book that place the book's contents within the broad area of music cognition research. He has initiated a practice that ESCOM hopes will become a tradition in future publications arising from its tri-annual conferences.

Irène Deliège
John Sloboda
Liège and Keele
December, 1995

Contributors

Robert M. Abrams, Department of Obstetrics and Gynecology, University of Florida, College of Medicine, PO Box 100294, Gainesville, FL 32610-0294, USA

Simha Arom, LACITO CNRS, 44, rue de l'Amiral Mouchez, F - 75014 Paris, France

Klaus-Ernst Behne, Meisenweg, 7, Schloß Ricklingen, D - 30826 Garbsen, Germany

Mireille Besson, Centre for Research in Cognitive Neuroscience, CNRS - LNC, 31, Chemin J. Aiguier, F - 13402 Marseille - Cedex 20, France

Edward C. Carterette, Systematic Ethnomusicology, University of California, UCLA, 405 Hilgard Avenue, Schoenberg Hall # 2539, Los Angeles, CA 90024, USA

Dalia Cohen, The Hebrew University of Jerusalem, Department of Musicology, Jerusalem, Israel 91905

Ian Cross, Faculty of Music, University of Cambridge, 11 West Road, Cambridge CB3 9DP, UK

Lola Cuddy, Department of Psychology, Queen's University, Kingston, Ontario K7L 3N6, Canada

Irène Deliège, Unité de Recherche en Psychologie de la Musique (URPM), Université de Liège, 5, boulevard du Rectorat, B 32, Sart Tilman, B - 4000 Liège, Belgium

Kenneth J. Gerhardt, Department of Communication Processes and Disorders, The Institute for Advanced Study of the Communication Processes, University of Florida, Gainesville, FL 32610-0294, USA

John M. Hajda, Systematic Ethnomusicology, Box 951657, Los Angeles, CA 90095-1657, USA

Michael L. Harshberger, Systematic Ethnomusicology, University of California, UCLA, 405 Hilgard Avenue, Schoenberg Hall # 2539, Los Angeles, CA 90024, USA

David S. Hill, Centre for Research in Human Development, University of Toronto, Erindale Campus, Mississauga, Ontario L5L 1C6, Canada

Michel Imberty, President of the University of Paris X, 200, avenue de la République, F - 92001 Nanterre - Cedex, France

Ruth Katz, The Hebrew University of Jerusalem, Department of Musicology, Jerusalem, Israel 91905

Roger A. Kendall, Systematic Ethnomusicology, University of California, UCLA, 405 Hilgard Avenue, Schoenberg Hall # 2539, Los Angeles, CA 90024, USA

Andreas Lehmann, Department of Psychology, The Florida University, Tallahassee, FL 32306-1051, USA

Fred Lerdahl, Department of Music, Columbia University, New York, NY 10027, USA

Gilles Léothaud, Université de Paris IV - Sorbonne, 45, rue des Ecoles, F - 75006 Paris, France

Marc Mélen, Unité de Recherche en Psychologie de la Musique (URPM), Université de Liège, 5, boulevard du Rectorat, B 32, B - 4000 Liège, Belgium

Jean-Jacques Nattiez, Faculté de Musique, Université de Montréal, C.P. 61–28, Succ. Centre-ville, Montréal, Québec, Canada, H3C 3J7.

Aniruddh D. Patel, The Neurosciences Institute, 10640 John Jay Hopkins Drive, San Diego, CA 92121, USA.

Isabelle Peretz, Département de Psychologie, Université de Montréal, C.P. 6128, succursale Centre-ville, Montréal, Québec, Canada HC3 3J7

Elisheva Rigbi-Shafrir, Department of Musicology, The Hebrew University of Jerusalem, Mount Scopus, Jerusalem, 91905 Israel

E. Glenn Schellenberg, University of Windsor, Department of Psychology, Windsor, Ontario, Canada N9B 3P4

John Sloboda, Department of Psychology, University of Keele, Staffordshire, Keele, ST5 5BG, UK

Sandra Trehub, Centre for Research in Human Development, University of Toronto in Mississauga, Erindale College, 3359 Mississauga Road North, Mississauga, Ontario, Canada LSL 1C6

Takao Umemoto, Konan Women's University, Marikatcho 6-2-23, Higashinada, Kobe 658, Japan

Philippe Vendrix, Séminaire de Musicologie, Université de Liège, 7, place du Vingt Août, B - 4000 Liège, Belgium

Barry Vercoe, Head, Music Cognition, The Media Laboratory MIT, 20 Ames Street, Cambridge, MA 02139, USA

Frédéric Voisin, LACITO CNRS, 44, rue de l'Amiral Mouchez, F - 75014 Paris, France

Preface

FROM CLASSICAL EXPERIMENTATION TO MODELISATION EXPERIMENTS OF MUSICAL BEHAVIOUR IN REAL TIME

The Third International Conference on Music Perception and Cognition (ICMPC) was held at Liège in July 1994. The European Society for the Cognitive Sciences of Music (ESCOM) was honoured to be invited to host the ICMPC in its first European venue. The first ICMPC was held at Kyoto, Japan, in 1989, and the second in Los Angeles in 1992. The fourth (Montreal, August 1996) will already have taken place by the time this volume is published. The third ICMPC is the first in the series to have stimulated a book of this sort, and we hope that it may begin a tradition to be followed by our successor organisers. The present book includes but a few of the numerous conferences and lectures given during this congress. All of these presentations were made by members of the ESCOM which, together with the ICMPC, thus held its own tri-annual conference, the first of which took place at Trieste in October 1991.

As we shall see, the issues discussed in these articles are varied and cover domains and research objects which were the basic concept of ESCOM (founded at a first Triennial Conference in Trieste, and for whom the third ICMPC also served as its second Triennial Conference): treating the musical phenomenon in its full complexity, through its neurophysiological, psychological, but also cultural, historic and sociological aspects, since these may not be isolated from one another without compromising the real reach of the works, their implication for psychologists, as well as for musicians and educators. Interdisciplinarity is thus essential, even though the psychological works naturally predominate in this book. This interdisciplinarity is also associated with a diversity of methods, which may not always confer to the severity or the precision of experimentation or analysis, but which favours an opening towards more qualitative approaches, without which our works would have no bearing on music.

Naturally, my aim here is not to guide the reader in the discovery of the research presented, some of which is remarkable. However, I could propose some reference points. It seems to me that four groups of works may be distinguished, each addressing a common problem or aspect, even if the disciplinary or methodological boundaries may seem indistinct.

The first group consists of research which directly concerns cognitive psychology, and to a lesser degree music. The reason may lie, to some extent, in psychologists' consideration of music as a privileged research domain for understanding certain general cognitive processes. For a long period of time, language was considered a privileged domain, and in a sense, Chomsky changed our conceptions of mental functioning, through the modelisation and theorisation of linguistic behaviour and objects. These changes reached music as well, and the debates about *The Generative Theory of Tonal Music* put forward by Lerdahl and Jackendoff (1983) are the most direct evidence of this trend. However, almost thirty years later, and through the test of facts and scientific evolution, language now seems more complex than was imagined, since language behaviour reflects both problems concerning the organisation of knowledge, and the organisation of communication. This clustering of human behaviour around language, which Chomsky tried to avoid in order to produce the "purist" model of the specialised and defined linguistic competence, we now know to be one of the essential realities of human language; the Chomskien linguistic competence may be, at least in part, but a myth. Vendrix tests this confrontation between cognitive psychology and the complex historic and cultural status of music.

Music may fulfil this cognitivist wish—or at least certain cognitivists' wish—of providing a study field which allows the establishment of a certain number of fundamental processes without too many interferences originating from other human activities. In this regard, the neuropsychological studies on music (of which we have several examples here, and in particular the study by Patel and Peretz) demonstrate this point of view: the recognition of certain parallels between language and music allows us to better understand the modular functioning of the brain, especially as concerns complex processing systems of supra-modular integration. Likewise, the studies on auditory perceptions of the foetus and the infant, which are becoming increasingly numerous, respond to the concern raised by neurosciences which studies with musical stimuli shed a new light (Abrams and Gerhardt, Trehub). The research based on the evaluation of expectation processes in temporal musical sequences and their effect on evoked potentials are also related to this trend (Besson).

A second group of studies directly concerns music and is centred around the musical activities of composition, listening, and learning. The preoccupations are diverse, but their starting point is often the testing of models proposed by theoretical music analysis (Cross, Cuddy) or by psycho-acoustic models (Hajda, Vercoe). However, research tends more and more to examine concrete behaviours *in real time*, and to progressively construct a model of the listener, instead of persisting with the verification of what was still called at the beginning of the 1980s "the psychological reality of linguistic or musical grammars". An important contribution in this evolution is given by studies carried out on the child and the development of his musical capacities and on the pedagogic applications, since the future adult music-listener is formed at this stage and this forming also determines the future of music itself (Behne, Trehub, Umemoto). Of course, the works on musical behaviours themselves are already numerous—studies on performance (Lehmann), relations between the written text and execution or the perception of sounds, of sequences, of musical forms (Deliège, Rigbi-Shafrir).

The third group of studies also proved important in this congress: works dealing precisely with the interdisciplinary aspect that the ESCOM wanted to recognise as essential to the research on music psychology. In this respect, apart from the works of pedagogic inspiration which were not reproduced here, it seems to me that experimental research in ethnomusicology is important, both in its suggestions of hypotheses for musical cognition, and on the methodological level. We must not forget that the musical object, in its structure as well as in its perception, is eminently cultural. At the same time confrontations allow us to situate the constants of cognitive musical functioning more accurately. The example given by S. Arom on the definition of the scale (which integrates timbre for an African musician) is very indicative of this necessity of interdisciplinarity.

A final group needs to be strongly identified: the group of studies which, as we have already said, depart from behaviours *in real time*, and deal with the problem of *musical time* as such through the structural aspects of forms, whether they be short sequences or complete musical pieces taken from the repertory. The works by I. Deliège are in this regard especially significant; they are essentially based on the principle of segmentation during audition of sequences or pieces, and propose a whole series of varied experimental tasks around this principle. I would like to note that this fruitful methodological paradigm—of which all the exploration possibilities on listening-behaviour in real time are far from being exhausted—was first enunciated by European researchers, even if several American researchers use it today in a number of interesting studies. Ethnomusicologists have largely worked in this spirit—as the works of S. Arom amply show—and psychologists are clearly in their debt in this sense. All this is, again, a way to emphasise the necessary interdisciplinarity of our works.

I was probably the first to conceive and use this paradigm in my works on Brahms and Debussy, in my book from 1981, *Les Ecritures du Temps*. I subsequently reused it in a substantial paper on Debussy's *La Cathédrale*

Engloutie (1985), and later on Berio's *Sequenza III* (1987, 1991). I will cite a summary of the passage in *Les Ecritures du Temps* which formalises the essential cognitive hypotheses on which most of the works effected later are based, in a more or less explicit way. All semiological works, I wrote at the time, depart from the operation of *segmentation* of the musical flow, and we may consider, at least at an initial stage, that the structure of a musical piece emerges from this segmentation which is repeated on several levels. This structure appears through the inter-level relations between the segmented units, in a form of *hierarchy*. The hypothesis I formulated and confirmed in numerous studies, and which was taken up and developed by Deliège, is that this hierarchy has a perceptive and cognitive reality. In other words, the segmentation is not only an operation of the semiological analysis, but also a set of real psychological processes which allow the subject to decode the form with which he is presented.

We may clarify matters in three directions: (1) this segmentation is based on the perception of qualitative changes which are more or less prominent—or salient, to use Deliège's term—in the temporal musical flow; (2) this segmentation depends on "models" of reference, coded and stored in memory, which were essentially learned through acculturation processes; (3) this segmentation also depends on the piece's "deep" structure, and partly reveals it; at least, the way in which the perceptive segmentation occurs, the number of units which result from it and their duration, as well as the contrasts, the ruptures or the dynamic elements which define them, indicate the way in which a particular organisation of musical time is decoded. This process can be identified as the perceptive reality of the given piece's *style*. This last aspect, which is of a more aesthetic nature, and which in my mind is more fundamental, was not addressed by the purely cognitive works.

The first two aspects may be summarised by saying that any musical piece appears as a *perceived hierarchy of qualitative changes which are more or less salient and of the more or less identifiable and recognisable units which they define*. The strength or weakness of this hierarchy depends on the degree of differentiation between the various parts, and on the number of differentiations which are effectively perceived. In 1981, I had proposed the distinction between a strong hierarchy (a structure consisting of a small number of particularly salient changes on a given level, repeated on the next branches of the tree) and a weak hierarchy (a structure composed of a relatively high number of salient changes, without repetition on lower levels of the tree) (cf. *Les Ecritures du Temps*, p.85 onward). This distinction was used and completed by Deliège. It undoubtedly has implications on the level of the *stylistic dimension* of temporal organisation in music, as I have shown in experimental comparisons between Brahms and Debussy.

This concept of hierarchy, thus formalised through a model of the listener, has the distinct advantage of allowing us to deal both with atonal music and tonal music: the notion of qualitative change, or that of contextual prominence (which was proposed later, in 1989, by Lerdahl) are more efficient than grammatical systems formalised in the framework of a theory of tonal music which is presumed to be general, without, however, achieving a definite demonstration of this generalisability. I. Deliège (1989, 1991, 1993) and myself have undertaken experimental work on the perceptive structure of complete pieces by Berio and Boulez, which demonstrates the pertinency of the segmentation method in real time and its generalisability, particularly to atonal music.

We have thus each contributed to the enhancement of the model, through concepts which I consider as complementary, since they do not correspond to the same aspects of this hierarchic perceptive-structure which underlies any musical piece organised in the subject's memory. I. Deliège develops the concepts of cues (and cue abstraction) and of imprint, while I work on the concepts of macro-structure and of the dynamic vector.

As retiring President of ESCOM it gives me great pleasure to see the work in music perception and cognition becoming more excellent and substantial as each year passes. It gives me even more pleasure to see the particular lines of work which I find to be so important being developed here in Europe and around the world. I hope that ESCOM will continue to provide the opportunities for innovative multi-disciplinary approaches to the study of music, drawing particularly on the rich European heritage of musical master works and Europe's diverse but deep-rooted intellectual traditions.

Michel Imberty
Translated by Noémie Ziv

REFERENCES (CITED OUTSIDE THE CONGRESS)

Deliège, I. (1989). A perceptual approach to contemporary musical forms. In S. McAdams & I. Deliège, (Eds.), *Music and the cognitive sciences*. Contemporary Music Review, Harwood Academic Publishers, vol. 4, pp. 212–230.

Deliège, I. (1991). L'organisation psychologique de l'écoute de la musique. Des marques de sédimentation—indice, empreinte—dans la représentation mentale de l'œuvre. (Ph.D. dissertation, University of Liège).

Deliège, I. (1993). Mechanisms of cue extraction in memory for musical time. In I. Cross and I. Deliège (Eds), Proceedings of the 2nd International Conference on Music and the Cognitive Sciences, Cambridge, September 1990. *Contemporary Music Review*, 9, 191–207.

Imberty, M. (1981). *Les écritures du temps. Sémantique psychologique de la musique*. Paris, Dunod.

Imberty, M. (1985). La Cathédrale Engloutie de Claude Debussy: de la Perception au Sens. *Revue de Musique des Universités Canadiennes*, 6, 90–160.

Imberty, M. (1987). L'occhio e l'orecchio: "Sequenza III" di Berio. In L. Marconi & G. Stefani, (Eds.), *Il senso in musica* (pp.163–186). Bologna, CLUEB.

Imberty, M. (1991). Le concept de hiérarchie perceptive face à la musique atonale. *Communicazioni scientifiche di Psicologia Generale*. Università "La Sapienza", *Roma, 5*, 119–133.

Lerdahl, F., & Jackendoff, R. (1983). *A generative theory of tonal music*. Cambridge, Mass: M.I.T. Press.

Lerdahl, F. (1989). Atonal prolongation structure. *Contemporary Music Review, 4*, 65–88.

Musicological Approaches

1 Experimental ethnomusicology: An interactive approach to the study of musical scales

Simha Arom
LACITO-CNRS, Paris, France
Gilles Léothaud
Université de Paris-IV, France
Frédéric Voisin[1]
LACITO-CNRS and IRCAM, Paris, France

Musical scales confront us with a combination of complex natural constraints and poorly described procedural solutions, as illustrated by various cultural traditions. The discussion and design of research programmes have yet to incorporate these two aspects into one practical, integrated set of working hypotheses.

The present paper presents one such programme, defined in terms of the assumption of the primacy of psychoacoustical, perceptual measurements over physical ones. Moreover, it assumes the fruitfulness of the 'emic' versus 'etic' distinction, as exemplified in descriptions of human language.

An interactive research programme, focusing upon local specialists (musical instrument makers and/or tuners) representative of a given cultural tradition, is broadly outlined, with illustrations from recent fieldwork in Central Africa and Indonesia. The discussion focuses on three important contributions by these knowledgeable people, namely: (1) judgements of acceptance or refusal of some proposed solutions to the problem of designing a musical scale for a given musical context; (2) tuning procedures for generating or modifying such scales in a concrete manner; (3) verbal or non-verbal comments and/or reactions during a situation of confrontation, which is considered here to be an experimental context.

The availability of digital musical instruments and signal processing has been vital for the practical implementation of such a research programme, as it allows us to deal with time delays and requirements of flexibility in the design, as well as for the conduct of experimental protocols and procedures. Some theoretical conclusions about the structure of musical scales which have already been experimentally confirmed are presented, but more emphasis is given here to a methodological definition of a rigorous heuristic of interaction with the cognitive competencies that local specialists are able to display.

This approach, while retaining some aspects of a pioneering work by Klaus Wachsmann (1957), is to the best of our knowledge unprecedented in the ethnography of musical practice. It should lead to a constructive debate about the validity of interactive methods.

THE DETERMINANTS OF PITCH

Musical Scales and Musical Instruments

Before discussing the different methods of measuring musical scales, it is important to raise a methodological issue concerning the choice of musical instruments subjected to these measurements and the empirical validity of this choice from the perspective of the study of musical scales. In the field of ethnomusicology, three main scenarios can be given.

The first scenario is the case of instruments which are both situated and measured outside their cultural context, for instance instruments kept in museums. Both now and (more so) in the past, measurements have on occasions been taken from instruments out of context, upon which a variety of theories of musical scales have been based (Ellis, 1885; Hornbostel, 1927; Jones, 1971). Although access to these instruments is relatively straightforward, it must be noted that there is little guarantee of the constancy of the instrument's state of tuning during the period between acquisition by a museum and the point at which measurements are taken. The interpretation of such measurements must be carefully considered in the light of a number of factors, including the length of time elapsed between acquisition and measurement, transportation, climatic change, different states of humidity, and any constraints imposed on the instrument in order to preserve it—the latter often being more damaging in the case of organic material. At the very least, one would hope that such instruments are regularly tuned by a representative of the original tradition who possesses the relevant skill, as is more often the case nowadays, especially for the *gamelan*. Furthermore, it should also be recalled that until very recently, collectors placed less importance on the accuracy of the instrument's tuning than on its external appearance, a more accessible symbolic and explicative value. Due to the skill required and the necessary equipment, measurements from museum instruments are often carried out at the very earliest at the time of storage, which is the point at which the instrument has already been subjected to the greatest possible degree of physical constraints. It is true that one often finds musical recordings accompanying the instrument which have been carried out at the point of collection, but until recently the technology of tuning measurements has been such that interpretation or use of such documentation is rarely possible (as discussed in the next section): for example, the instrument may be heard in a polyphonic ensemble, the notes may be short, the recording situation may not be ideal, and so on.

The second scenario concerns measurements of instruments in context, which appear more acceptable but do however pose a different problem of relevance. It is often observed that the symbolic value attributed to an object is not simply a function of its intrinsic value. Thus the social or symbolic value of a musical instrument is not necessarily a guarantee of its accuracy in terms of tuning. There may indeed be a real contradiction between the social or symbolic value of an instrument and its accuracy when, as for example in Java and Bali, certain sacred instruments may not be tuned except by a divine hand. Thus although the instrument plays a full role in the cultural life of the society, this is not a reliable index of its representativeness in terms of tuning. Conformity of tuning in relation to the cultural norm must be investigated as such, and detailed investigation is still more necessary when the instruments bear an intimate relationship to the sacred values of the society.

The third scenario has become more frequent with the current promotion of concerts of traditional musics: it concerns instruments in performance which, if subjected to rigorous testing on numerous occasions, can become the object of careful scrutiny by the musicians. The "sacrilege" which is necessary for performance outside the original context, along with the number of rehearsals, enables a degree of attention to be focused upon the instruments themselves. Yet the presence of an instrument tuner during a performance, or at the very least a musician with some tuning competence, can provide an indication of the care which is taken in tuning the instruments. From questioning the instrument tuners one also finds that certain instruments of similar construction are more easily tuneable than others, both in performance and in context.

Consideration of the Relevance of Frequency Measurements

The pitch of a note is in essence related to frequency, even if this relationship is not an exclusive one[2]. Over the last two centuries in the West, the frequency of a note has been extrapolated by measuring its pitch (using a monochord, for example), but in modern ethnomusicology, with the development of new technologies, it is more common to take measurements of frequency in order to extrapolate the pitch. Ethnomusicology relies more on frequency measurements as they circumvent the subjectivity implied in the perception of systems that are foreign to the observer (see for example Castellengo, 1965). A brief survey of the diverse kinds of technology employed in ethnomusicology shows that this move from perception towards a reliance upon electronic measurements is not itself entirely problem-free.

The most commonly employed technique, the oscilloscopic procedure, involves a tape recorder and a calibrated frequency generator, connected respectively to the X and Y inputs of a cathodic oscilloscope. The generator is tuned to the note to be measured and when a Lissajous figure (i.e. a stable geometric figure) appears on the screen, the value of the required frequency is read off from the generator. In place of a calibrated generator, one can use a frequency meter which shows the value of the signal emitted by the generator[3]. Furthermore, it is sometimes desirable to insert different filters between the tape recorder and the oscilloscope, which thus enable the elements to be measured to be selected from the note (Surjodiningrat, 1993).

The Stroboconn, based upon this principle, combines the generator and the oscilloscopic procedure in a single instrument, whilst directly presenting the frequency measured in the form of an interval converted into cents related to the notes of the 12-note equal-tempered scale. This instrument has been mainly used in ethnomusicology since the 1950s and has replaced the mechanical procedures using sonometers (monochords), pitch pipes and tuning forks.

Whilst it is easy to use, inexpensive and widely found in acoustical laboratories, the oscilloscopic method does however exhibit some disadvantages: frequency measurements are recognised to be very difficult for unstable notes or notes whose spectral components mask the fundamental, and this requires notes to be both quasi-stationary and to have a duration of longer than a second. These are conditions which are extremely difficult to meet in ethnomusicology: the majority of instruments studied, whilst melodic, are also percussive, and the pieces recorded and performance techniques studied rarely present extended durations. This technology thus represents both the advantage of a direct measurement of fundamental frequency and the disadvantages of the acoustic apparatus which it replaced[4].

Spectrography, which is frequently used nowadays, enables the trace of a note to be drawn according to its three dimensions—frequency, duration and intensity—which also provides objective support for interpretations of pitch.

Analogue measurements of sound do however exhibit limitations which are not only technological (such as weak resolution of band-pass filters) but also relate to the direct reading of fundamental frequencies which is made difficult by the density of recording (related to intensity). This is a pragmatic reason why the values of the fundamental frequency are not read off directly, but extrapolated from readings of the component frequencies which are assumed to be harmonic (cf. Leipp, 1974; Rouget, 1969). In the case of complex or inharmonic tones, the frequency has often been established by calculating the mean value of the input corresponding to the fundamental frequency, resulting in gross approximations. Thus, whilst being extremely useful in ethnomusicology for demonstrating timbral phenomena and unusual performance techniques, analogue measurements of sound do not provide the necessary technical underpinning for a detailed investigation of musical scales.

Digital spectrographs do not exhibit this significant disadvantage in that where the spectral analysis is carried out according to the calculation of FFT

(Fast Fourier Transform), they attribute to a digitalized tone, for each instant t of the measurement, a precise intensity and phase value for each frequency point of the FFT: the frequency resolution (R) is thus a function of the sampling rate (Sr) of the note and the number of points (N) at which the FFT operates in the signal (R = Sr/N) (Harris, 1978; Nuttall, 1981; Ramirez, 1985). A variety of modes of representation are possible: intensity may be represented not only by the depth of the trace but by the colour, intensity and frequency represented by successive "slices" of time intervals or, better still, by means of listed values which enable data processing to be carried out. The theoretical constraints of Fourier transforms do still however apply to phenomena of limited duration (such as lack of frequency precision with short time periods, and analysis noise resulting from the segmentation of the signal and windowing) which restrict the actual sonagraphic representations[5].

Electronic methods of frequency measurement, which still have great potential in terms of their precision, have enabled researchers to focus upon the aperiodic nature, or at the very least the unstable character, of the majority of musical notes. It is rare to find an instrument which presents perfect stability from the point of view of frequency, especially in a typical performance situation. We can see that the control of frequency measurement is as tentative as the spectral structures are complex. How, then, can this control operate? How can we establish a perceptual control, in other words how can we *hear* the result of the measurements—which Jairazbhoy was attempting to achieve in the field of ethnomusicology (Jairazbhoy, 1977), and which is now possible—without taking a few steps backwards, without succumbing to the precise problem which we were attempting to circumvent, namely the subjectivity of the observer?

Psychoacoustical Measures of Pitch

Psychoacoustics has firmly established that the spectral composition of a note plays a determining role in the perception of its pitch (Moore, Glasberg & Peters, 1985; Schouten, 1938; Terhardt, 1974; Terhardt, Stoll & Seewann, 1982a). However, whilst ethnomusicology has recognised the importance of timbre in diverse musical traditions, this parameter is still rarely investigated in the application of measurement protocols (see Schneider & Beurmann, 1992 on this topic). This can be explained simply by the practical difficulties of interpreting the collection of spectral parameters, as ethnomusicology is more often confronted with complex tones, the majority of which are inharmonic (as is the case with musical instruments of no fixed pitch, namely all instruments with the exception of fretted stringed instruments and certain wind instruments)[6].

A range of experiments has shown that for the same fundamental frequencies, different inharmonic spectral structures produce different perceptions of pitch (Singh, 1989). An irregular inharmonic structure produces a blurred perception of pitch, whilst regular inharmonic structures (for example a systematic shift of frequencies) can give the impression of a precise pitch but one which differs from that which is created by the lowest frequency component of the note. Between these two extremes, there are a number of sounds which are more or less inharmonic or "noisy", but which produce a degree of ambiguity in interpretation. From this perspective, "acoustical paradoxes" are not uncommon and noise itself can produce pitches which are sufficiently precise to have a melodic nature (as is apparent in the *inganga* repertoire for whispered voices in the Burundi; see Fales & McAdams, 1994a, b).

Thus the precision of pitch measurements[7] depends upon the particular instrument measured and a method which would be entirely appropriate for an oboe is shown to be inadequate for a xylophone. We thus see that *the* pitch is primarily a *perceived* pitch. It is the ear which must act as the final judge and guarantor of the reliability of the results[8].

Psychoacoustical research has led to a partial understanding of the principal effects of the spectrum of a note upon the perception of its pitch, and has resulted in algorithmic modelling of these effects (see especially Terhardt, Stoll & Seewann, 1982b). Some new computer programmes like the ones we have used at IRCAM[9] are now able to integrate these algorithms, and enable one to objectify the possible differences between the fundamental frequency—where it exists—which is of a physical nature, and the pitch, which is of a perceptual nature. However, this kind of weighting, which is partly based upon empirical observations conducted with Western instruments, does not always prove to be effective when applied to music of other cultures. We have observed that the same musical material produces different results when analysed according to different protocols. For complex tones which are spectrally well-constituted, such as those of many central African xylophones, differences between measurements of an eighth of a tone (25 cents) have been found which, although relatively small, render any kind of interpretation impossible (Voisin, 1994a), and on occasions our research team has heard differences of over 100 cents between the results of Terhardt's algorithm[10] and the actual perceived pitch.

Methodological Consequences of the Effects of Spectral Composition on Pitch Perception

Accounting for the dimensions of timbre can take place at different stages in the study of musical scales. From the most concrete to the most abstract, from acoustical analysis to music cognition, there are different levels, and each is accompanied by its own evaluation procedures and specific types of control.

In the realm of acoustical analysis, which aims to obtain a physical measurement of pitch, it is necessary to study spectral structures in order to understand their effect upon physical measurements of pitch. For example, the localisation and the length of the sample to be measured are found to be determinants of the results obtained, and the choice of these parameters must be made in the knowledge of their causes and effects. Whilst measurements are best in the most stable parts of the note, they are less so when concerned with notes from melodic idiophones, a very common group of instruments in traditional musics. It is thus important to note in detail the structure of the spectrum (especially if the note is inharmonic), and its duration and the time of the measurements, alongside the measurements of fundamental frequency.

It is equally important to outline the protocol employed. We shall see that this practice, which was common in ethnomusicology using analogue measurements (see for example Rouget, 1969 using a sonagraph, Surjodiningrat, 1993 using oscilloscopic measurements), is less visible when digital measurements are employed, where the size and type of window of analysis adopted[11] have a significant effect upon the results obtained and their interpretation by determining the selection and treatment of digital data which define the note.

From a psychoacoustical perspective, it remains difficult to differentiate between the physiological and the cultural in pitch perception. Both are intimately linked to perception at a deep level, especially through the existence of a circuit which leads from the brain to the inner ear (Bonfils, Rémond & Pujol, 1986), and this necessitates an a priori distinction to be drawn between the pitch perceived by the researcher and that of the musicians. This phenomenon provides justification for pitch perception *experimentation in ethnomusicology* (see below) to be carried out with musicians in the field.

However, our own observations of tuning by Javanese professionals of keyboard instruments, which naturally produce quasi-harmonic notes, have not to date shown any differences from our own perception of pitch. Furthermore, we have observed that pitch perception of these keyboard instruments by Javanese professionals is entirely consistent with the pitch predicted by Terhardt's algorithm:[12] the slight rise in perceived pitch at the end of notes (4-6 seconds) where the physical frequency remains the same (resulting from both the Stevens effect and the dispersal of the harmonic components) is the subject of an explicit verbalisation by the tuners. For gongs, with inharmonic spectra, we have all observed that the tuners' intonation is the same as our own (within the limits of precision of vocal intonation). This leads to the conclusion that in Java extended experience with inharmonic notes does not necessarily imply any change in the *perception* of isolated pitches, but we should recall that here the keyboard instruments, with harmonic spectra, represent the pitch reference for the instrument makers and tuners and also for the instrumentalists (voice, *rebab*) and the puppeteer (*dhalang*) who are always situated closest to these instruments.

In Central Africa, this problem of pitch perception is of vital importance due to the fact that on the one hand very few instruments exhibit harmonic spectra (excepting the reference instrument, the xylophone), and on the other, instrument makers and musicians produce a wide variety of unisons. One can appreciate the difficulty of conducting pitch perception experiments if one realises that the structure of the musical scales of this region avoids, or allows for the avoidance of, a perfect unison in a systematic manner (see later discussion of characteristics of musical scales in Central Africa). The fact that the unison is realised in different ways in Central African musics (Voisin, 1995) does not necessarily imply that the strict unison, in a Western sense, is not relevant, nor that pitch perception is different. It is important here to differentiate the musical system from the computational processes of pitch, and this leads to a further distinction, which we will discuss later, between experiments in the field which operate within a specific musical context and those which in relating to more general cognitive processes must operate outside any direct reference to specific musical experience or practices.

This does not detract from the fact that any account of mental representations of timbre within a theory of musical scales strongly implies a cultural dimension. The theory of fusion (Helmholtz, 1877), which is still today the most widely accepted and the most explicit (see for example Chailley, 1951, 1964; Plomp & Levelt, 1965; Brailoiu, 1973; Leipp, 1974; Lerdahl, 1987), in the absence of a clearer alternative, does not aspire to any kind of universalism, as has already been noted by Ellis (1885). Spectral fusion, in the sense of the physiological phenomenon it invokes, is not a sufficient criterion for the formation of musical scales and the recognition of correctness of intervals. It should be recognised that the necessary criterion above all is that of the qualities and symbolic connotations (of a cultural nature) attributed to natural phenomena, fusion being one such, which are implied in the notion of 'consonance' (Voisin, 1994b). In order for the criterion of spectral fusion to operate within a culture, it is necessary that the culture recognises it as such, by attributing positive qualities to harmonic fusion against which all other kinds of spectral phenomena are placed in opposition. Whilst this is generally the case in the West, ethnomusicology has shown for some time that a significant number of societies have developed strikingly different timbral representations.

From the above it appears that:

1. A reliance only upon digital measurements does not represent a precision gauge nor a measure of reliability, and the accumulation of such measurements does not improve their validity;
2. In research into musical scales, it is the concept of *perceived pitch* which should be the aim of all measurement processes and not the frequency, which can be viewed as equivalent to a 'physical' event.

Ethnomusicology treats the musical scale as an object of cognitive theory, and measurements can only be interpreted once they are integrated into their cultural context, where they regain their relevance.

THE EXPLORATION OF MUSICAL SCALES

Central Africa and Java

Central Africa and Indonesia are two strikingly different geographic and cultural regions. They do however have several points in common from the viewpoint of our investigation: (1) the importance of keyboard instruments, with fixed notes and determined pitches; (2) the tuning of these instruments which represents the most common musical reference for the range of music of the cultural community (Kunst, 1934; Arom, 1991a; Dampierre, 1992); (3) the assumption of what one might call the 'mythical' existence of scales comprised of equally-spaced intervals (of 5 degrees in Central Africa and 7 degrees in Indonesia, Western Africa and South East Asia); and (4) the determinants of musical scales have proved to be problematic[13].

In Africa, the large dispersal of measurements has created the impression of a similarly large dispersal of pitches. This has given rise to explanations in terms of vast margins of tolerance in regard to the scale degrees (Tracey, 1958 & 1969) or interpretations which regard these scales as 'elastic' (Kubik, 1983).

The principal problem relates to the *ambiguity* inherent in these musical systems. On first hearing, the musics of this region give the impression of being based upon a pentatonic scale which is anhemitonic (without semitones), characterised by the division of the octave into five inequal intervals and by the *absence of the semitone interval*[14]. In such a system, the "field of realisation" of each note is so large that it is impossible to assign with certainty an unequivocal position to it.

This problem also arises with regard to Indonesia. Jaap Kunst focused for much of his life on a study of the scales of the *gamelan* orchestras in Java. He employed the monochord for this purpose[15]. He recorded measurements on a variety of *gamelan*: 46 tunings of the *slendro* system (pentatonic), and 39 of the *pelog* system (heptatonic)[16].

As has already been noted by others (Hood, 1966; Surjodiningrat, 1993), Kunst's measurements are only relevant to one single instrument—the *saron demung (slentem)*, a six-keyed instrument—and not to the entire orchestra. Moreover, there are two important constraints implied by the use of the monochord: firstly, the timbre of a vibrating string is significantly different to that of a struck metallic key, and secondly, once a unison has been achieved between the pitches of the string and the key, it can prove to be relatively difficult to specify precisely the frequency of the string. Finally, the *saron demung* is not the reference instrument for tuners of the *gamelan*, this function being performed by the *gender barung*.

In conclusion, Kunst's work achieves success through his reluctance to simply carry out measurements and his attempts to justify the results of such exercises by means of a theoretical foundation aimed at giving coherence to the values obtained. This is principally concerned with the so-called theory of "blown fifths", expounded by Erich von Hornbostel (1927), a theory which was relatively rapidly abandoned (Bukofzer, 1937).

In contrast to Kunst, Ki Mantle Hood arrived at his conclusions through examining four *gamelan* in the full range of six octaves which these orchestras span. His measurements were all taken using a stroboconn. Hood (1966) found firstly the existence of a principle of compression and stretching of octaves which was evident in the registral extremes, which for him represented one of the characteristics of the tuning pattern unique to each *gamelan*. Thus his views are in opposition to Kunst, for whom the scale was represented within a perfect octave (of 1200 cents), whatever the register[17].

Is the Javanese *slendro* an equipentatonic scale? This hypothesis, proposed by Kunst (1934), and later rejected by Hood (1966), was taken up again by Jones (1971), who was keen to find an Indonesian influence upon the scales of Central Africa. This particular hypothesis has been suggested by a number of researchers, particularly Bruno Nettl (1964).

As Hood stressed, since the different measurements have not provided any consensus level of coherence, there is still doubt as to the size and distribution of the intervals of these scales.

Thus it is important to note that after more than a century of measurements of the *gamelan*, we still do not have a clear definition of the respective structures of the *pelog* and *slendro*. But one can see, as Vetter has noted this in relation to these studies (Vetter, 1989; p.219):

> They deal only with the product of tuning and not with the individuals who do the tuning. It is not uncommon for authors in these studies to imply or say outright that the tuner's intent was to produce this or that intervallic pattern, even though the writers had no contact of communication with a tuner.

Towards a New Experimental Approach

These problems of determining the scales and intervals of Central Africa and Indonesia have been addressed since 1988 by Simha Arom's team of researchers under the auspices of the Ethnomusicology Department of LACITO (the laboratory of *Langues et Civilisations à Tradition Orale*) at the CNRS. As well as Simha Arom himself, this team included Vincent Dehoux, Suzanne Fürniss, Frédéric Voisin and Gilles Léothaud. Three research expeditions have been carried out to the Central African Republic (1989, 1990 and 1993) and two to central Java (Indonesia) (1993 and 1994).

At the current stage of our research, we consider the musical scale to be a *finite collection of discrete elements arranged along the axis of pitch, elements whose respective positions create an oppositional system amongst themselves.*

In the light of such a definition, one can note that the octave does not necessarily represent the generative module of the scale. Whilst the notion of the octave within a scalar context has been widely recognised by theorists, especially in contemporary acoustics since the time of Helmholtz, we will see that certain scales, especially those of Central Africa and central Java, are not formed within this context.

Moreover, the oppositional system formed by the discrete elements of the scale can be compared to a phonological system (Jakobson, 1932; Nattiez, 1975; Arom, 1976). Just as in a language the same phoneme is realised in many different ways, so in music the same pitch element can be realised in many ways, which together constitute a *field of realisation.* Following the concept of the phoneme, we shall call these elements "scalemes" (Voisin, 1995), referring to the abstract mental referent which only exists conceptually: the scaleme is part of the sole cognitive universe of the bearers of a particular tradition.

It is thus important to differentiate the scalemes themselves from their actualisation, i.e. from their perceived pitch and their syntactic function—the degrees—within a musical setting. Syntactic functions imply a number of rules and constraints which can affect the realisation of the scalemes. This is shown in Fig. 1.1. One can see that the direction of the arrows in the figure implies that the listener is not able to deduce the syntactic functions and the scalemes (and, in consequence, the margin of tolerance) from the only perception and measurement of notes if these two conceptual levels (functions and elements) are not known in advance.

Thus, pitches as they occur in context, whilst they may relate to their respective conceptual units, are not necessarily direct reproductions of these. They result in a dispersion of pitches, whose evaluation is not possible without prior knowledge of the implicit referents, the scalemes. It is this point which renders futile an approach based only upon acoustical measurements, even if these are collected in context in the field: a statistical analysis carried out on the field of realisation measured can provide an average pitch, but this does not take account of the value of the mental referent.

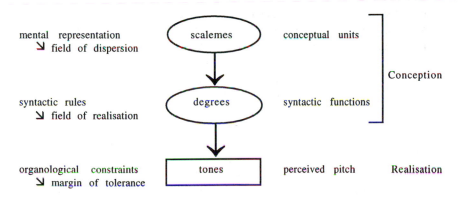

FIG. 1.1. The steps between the conception and the realisation of tone.

Methodological Premises

The issues that we have raised above result from a reorientation of the problematic which was necessary due to the shortcomings of previous theories and their inability to understand traditional musical practice as observed in the field.

This cognitivist perspective requires new methodological means of investigation and has given rise to the development of specific research tools, both methodological and technical. In the light of these issues, it follows that a complete understanding of how a musical scale is conceived demands that the research proceeds on the level of the conceptual universe; such a universe, the product of both physiological and cultural phenomena, appears for the most part to be unconscious. Thus, the diverse processes involved in auditory perception can best be discovered by means of cognitive-perceptual *experimentation*.

The analytic method of recording known as "play-back" (re-recording) which was developed by Simha Arom in the 1970s provides one solution to this constraint (Arom, 1976; Delalande, 1991). It is important to emphasise one crucial point: the aim of our programme is to research a nonverbal mental model, and not simply to verify a theory developed by the researchers themselves. From this perspective, it is essential that traditional musicians play a direct role in the analysis, by assessing judgements about the material under examination. The experimental procedure must therefore be truly *interactive*: it must allow the musicians not only to respond to the suggestions which are submitted to them, but more importantly, it must also allow them—as we shall see—to interact with the experimental procedure itself.

Interactive Experimentation

The experimental context thus situates this kind of research within a perspective of modelling musical scales or, more precisely, in that of their mental representation within a given culture. The method proceeds from this point in five stages, some of which are simultaneous: ethnographic observation and measurements in the field, interactive experimentation, modelling, validation, and formalisation. We have principally applied this method to the study of keyboard instruments of fixed pitch whose tuning is the most stable and which constitute (as we saw earlier) the tuning reference in both Central Africa and Java.

There are two different types of experiments in the field which are possible and which complement each other. One comprises *simulation* of real musical situations in order to place the instrumental players in a situation as close as possible to their traditional performance context. This represents experimentation *in the context of performance*, where traditional practice is little modified, and the musicians are in a situation close to their normal behaviour.

The other is an experimental situation *outside the context of performance*, to which the musician can be gradually accustomed, the aim of which is to collect more psychoacoustical data on the perceptual processes which operate at a more general cultural level, particularly the processes of categorisation and perception of timbre.

Simulation Within a Musical Context

In order to achieve ecological validity with respect to context, we have simulated the traditional instruments under study on digital synthesisers, these instruments being the keys of xylophones for Central Africa and of metallophones for Indonesia. A detachable device, which remains fixed to the synthesiser keyboard, enables the number and spacing of the keys which are added to the keyboard to be changed according to the requirements of the situation. Thus it is possible to simulate the 12-keyed *zanga* of the Gbeya, an orchestra of two 10-keyed *kalangba* of the Banda-Linda, or the Javanese *gender* and *saron*, no matter how many keys are used. The notes produced by the synthesisers are also simulated by means of synthesis or sampling.

A precise procedure underpins the research we have conducted into musical scales. On the basis of prior knowledge of the culture, we begin by researching the instruments which are representative and correctly maintained, with instrumentalists but also and more importantly with instrument makers and tuners, the keepers of the tradition. The latter, having practical experience and understanding of the tuning process, are the most open and effective in the experimental situation. We then construct an inventory of the vernacular expressions regarding instruments and the conception of scales, alongside an ethnographic study of the techniques of instrument making and tuning. It is very illuminating to pay close attention to the comments of the specialists on location during the experiments in order to detect how these may be contradicted by experimental conjecture or research hypotheses.

We then proceed with a classificatory and acoustical study of the instruments (using measurements of fundamental frequency and spectral analysis), which is oriented towards simulating them. Timbral and pitch analysis enable hypotheses to be generated concerning the spectral and scalar structures, these two elements being indissociable, as we have seen. These hypotheses lead on to a programming of the relevant scales by simulating the timbres of the particular instruments under investigation, which are configured on the synthesiser according to the particular topology of the instruments. Variations in the classification of instruments mean that it is practically impossible to impose a uniform experimental procedure upon each study. The procedure has to be modified in a very precise manner as a function of the specificities of each culture.

Timbre can be simulated by means of two main techniques, sound synthesis and digital sampling. Whilst digital sampling is the method which produces the closest results to reality, nonetheless it is a difficult process to carry out in the field. Sampling noise is almost always inevitable and becomes combined with the sample itself when it is played.

We will see that in a general way, the actual fidelity of the sample gives it an anecdotal character which is too concrete, contradicting the more general and desirable notion of the abstract model. Synthesis, on the other hand, by only preserving the significant elements of timbre, relates more immediately to a more conceptual level and ultimately this method proves to be more acceptable to the musicians. Thus synthesis, which is in its own way a form of modelling, will be placed at the centre of this experimental method. Sampling will be reserved for resynthesis of certain parameters (such as envelopes) as well as for comparative verifications between the model and reality.

The experiments alone consist of the musician playing, on several occasions, on the simulation device, one piece from his repertory and giving a judgement on the tunings which are presented to him, which are changed by a series of modifications of the scale and/or of the timbre. For tuners and instrument makers, playing a piece from the repertory is replaced by a traditional stereotypical sequence which enables them to provide an effective evaluation of the goodness of tuning.

The response to these models by the musician can be binary ("accepted/ refused"), or can be followed by a comparative or qualitative judgement (very good, better than, etc.). Such a response already represents a fundamental element of the confirmation or rejection of certain hypotheses, beginning with that according to which traditional instruments are always considered to be well-tuned—a hypothesis which is too often unfortunately transformed into an implicit postulate. We have often found, in both Central Africa and Java, that when we submit reproductions of the tuning of real instruments, renowned and competent tuners have two main reactions: firstly, the simulated reproduction is rejected; later, and only due to this rejection, the specialist realises that his own instrument does not match the criteria which he has used to make his judgement. Therefore he proposes a retuning of both the synthesised instrument and his own instrument. The musician can recognise and accept the difference between the instrument and the implicit norm of tuning, whilst leaving the instrument as it is. There is, thus, an apparent practical margin of tolerance, distinct from the field of realisation and the field of dispersion (see Fig. 1.1).

Video recordings carried out at the time of the research sessions enable a number of non-verbal appraisals of the situation to be made. By this means, the rigid binary values such as acceptance or refusal can be balanced by taking account of non-verbal expressions (gestures, mimicry, or hesitation), or even measured, for example by means of response times.

The possibility of action which is given to the musicians—by proposing that they themselves retune the simulatory device—provides a direct opening to cultural data within the experimental procedure which it would be impossible to collect otherwise (Arom, 1991b; Arom & Voisin, in press). However, the initial tuning suggestion, like the final result of retuning by the musicians, does not always provide sufficient data. This is why, in our last experiments in Java, we recorded on the sequencer the entire sequence of actions carried out by the musicians on the synthesisers, including the amplitude and speed of changes made using the tuning cursors and any hesitations, thus placing an emphasis not only on the final result but also on the collection of processes which are implemented in order to achieve it. Furthermore, the sequencer enables us to reproduce this sequence of operations at a later date and to analyse them, and if necessary, to synchronise them with the video recording.

The result of retunings does not in itself provide direct access to a model. There are strategies in existence which enable the musician to avoid having to restructure entirely the incriminating tunings, and to provide a retuning which, if not perfect, is at least acceptable by means of a *limited number of actions*. Results obtained from this reveal more about *intentions* than an abstract model, and must be interpreted as such. In support of this, many retunings are often themselves subject to later corrections, whether this be by their originator or by other tuners from the same culture.

Whilst it is relatively simple from a modelling perspective to simulate the notes of instruments of fixed pitch (which, we recall, are most commonly the reference instruments in a wide range of traditions), we have also attempted to apply this experimental procedure to a study of vocal polyphony and to the *rebab* fiddle. The principle consists of integrating the process of simulation within the recording technique in *play-back* which has been used extensively by Arom (Arom, 1976); examples (and counter-examples) of modelled polyphonic music (via a synthesiser and a sequencer) are played to performers or singers, and the string player or singer's own reproductions are recorded on different tracks. In the same manner as in experiments with instruments of fixed pitch, information gained directly from the performance (whether ornamented or not) or from verbalisation (in the form of comments), whilst extremely important, is not sufficient: detailed analysis of reactions, in terms of intonation, gathered from the musician by the different syntheses proposed[18] is still necessary in order to formulate sufficiently detailed hypotheses about his frame of reference.

This procedure was adopted in 1990 by the team for the study of musical scales of the *a cappella* polyphonies of the Aka Pygmies (in Central Africa), the components of the syntheses having been programmed by frequency modulation and sequencing on the basis of transcriptions carried out previously

(Arom & Fürniss, 1992). However, due to the difficulty posed by vocal synthesis using frequency modulation (the only technique which is possible in the field) and the fact that this experiment was not repeated, we have not yet been able to verify the hypotheses according to which melodic contour takes precedence over interval size (Arom, 1985; Fürniss, 1992).

The same procedure was used in Central Java in 1994 by Voisin, in order to study the scale used in the two-stringed *rebab*, accompanied by a *saron* which had been previously sampled and performed. Analysis of this data, which is still in progress, should enable new hypotheses to be generated about the model of the Central Javanese *slendro* scale which has been elaborated on the basis of experiments with instruments of fixed pitch (see above).

Outside a Musical Context

In order to verify certain cognitive aspects of the model, and particularly to gain information about the mental representations of the musician in terms of intervals, pitch or timbre and to distinguish these from effects related to the context of performance, we have also carried out a certain number of ad hoc experiments outside the musicians' habitual context of musical practice.

One of these experiments consisted of measuring the pitch perceived by the musicians, whilst asking them to alter in isolation each of the notes of the instrument. The goal of this experiment, whilst measuring the musicians' margin of precision, was to discover if the topology of the instrument, in other words the distribution of pitches, would have an effect upon perception. This type of measurement also enables us to gain values of precise and culturally significant pitches, which is difficult to obtain by any other method for sounds which are strongly inharmonic.

Other experiments aimed to reveal the emergence of the culturally relevant intervals which constitute the scale by discrimination within either a continuum or a series of micro-intervals of an eighth of a tone. For musicians, this comprised a creation of the scale *ex nihilo*, since they were not asked to retune given intervals but to construct them themselves on the continuum or by accumulating the micro-intervals provided. This kind of categorisation experiment has proved to be essential in revealing the relevant number of intervallic categories which constitute a scale and also the processes of categorisation (Voisin, 1994a).

SCALAR FEATURES IN CENTRAL AFRICA AND CENTRAL JAVA

Characteristics of Musical Scales in Central Africa

The following relates to the two most important ethnic groups of Central Africa and their principal sub-groups, namely the Banda (Banda-Gbambiya, Banda-Linda, Banda-Mbiyi, Banda-Ndokpa) and the Gbeya (Ali, Manza, Ngbaka-Manza). For all these, the xylophone, whether used alone or in combinations of two to four instruments, serves the primary function of underpinning vocal music. Ensembles are completed by different percussion instruments, such as drums, rattles or bells. What we have is a stable type of portable 5 to 14 keys xylophone, with multiple gourd resonators equipped with small buzzing membranes (the keys are distributed in a non-linear manner according to the relevant topography of each sub-group).

We came to the conclusion that there are two ways of conceiving of the structures of anhemitonic pentatonic scales: (1) as a pair of intervals which correspond approximately to our major second (about 200 cents) and our minor third (about 300 cents) (Brailoiu, 1973); or (2) as a single interval, hypothesised to be 240 cents, which has been assumed to exist in Java and Central Africa (Ellis, 1885; Wachsmann, 1957; Gottlieb, 1986)[19]. In Central Africa we find a third interval, which is approximately halfway between the two other intervals[20]. We have been able to establish that the scale is based on three constituent intervals (CIs): 200, 240, 280 cents. It appears that all the musicians are able to discriminate adjacent intervals to within +/–20 cents—closer than one tenth of a tone (Voisin, 1991, 1994a). When the musicians themselves tune the simulated xylophone according to a particular pattern of these three CIs, their precision becomes more accurate than +/–10 cents. From observation of these procedures of retuning we have been able to establish that intervals are formed by successive conjunct ascending motion, and not by simultaneous intervals through fusion (octaves or fifths, for example). We have been able to establish the number of these intervals by means of discrimination experiments (mentioned earlier) within a succession of eighths of a tone. A hundred different tuning suggestions, programmed and presented to musicians for judgement, and the successive retunings of these models carried out by the musicians, have enabled us to arrive at the precise value of the CIs. It was difficult to interpret certain rejections because they were due either to the value of one of the intervals of the tuning or to its position in the scale. Thus, for example, for the Manza, the sequence of intervals (from low to high) in cents of 200-200-240-280, whilst correct from the point of view of the size of each CI, nonetheless constitutes a poor combinatory variant, due to the presence of an interval of 280 cents between the two highest keys of the xylophone, whilst the sequence in cents of 280-200-240-200 is acceptable: similarly, the sequence 280-220-240-200 is rejected, because of the presence of a 220 cent interval. We have thus shown that, based upon the notion of conjunct constitutive intervals, we can add a collection of combinatory rules which constitute the layout and allow the permutations between CIs which are responsible for the wide fields of realisation we have observed. Thus, the sequences 280-200-240-200 and 200-240-240-240 taken from two xylophones— whether they belong to the same orchestra or not—are culturally *equivalent* despite the apparently considerable differences in location of the same degree. Thus, for instruments within the same orchestra, differences as large as 80 cents between two structurally equivalent keys (with the same name, the same function, and the same place in the scale) do however constitute a musically correct unison in the Central African musical system, *independent of any phenomenon of tolerance*. Whilst the two tunings mentioned above may be observed on two different xylophones, they can also follow one another (280-200-240-200-200-240-240-240) within one single instrument with 9 keys. In this case, the keys corresponding to the same degrees do not necessarily form perfect octaves of 1200 cents (we note that the sequence of these three ICs rarely results in such an octave interval); thus the same situation obtains for both the octaves and the unisons of a collection of xylophones.

This model of three sizes of interval leads us back, in one of its combinations, to a purely conceptual model that is the equipentatonic system which is systematically recognised and preferred by the musicians, as shown from extremely short response times (t < 3 seconds) as compared to other systems (6s < t < 30s), shown from the video recordings.

Within this equipentatonic system, the principal of equal constitutive intervals takes precedence over the size of the octave, the latter not necessarily being perfect. Thus, for example for the Banda-Linda, the instantiation of a model based on 235 cents resulting in an octave of 1175 cents is judged better than a sequence based on 240 cents which does however result in a perfect octave of 1200 cents. It is only the Gbeya who have a control procedure for the octave (although, as we have just seen, this is not necessarily a strict one), by playing it homophonically during the tuning verification procedure. Their preference for an equipentatonic system of 240 cents seems to be a consequence of this emphasis on the octave. For the Manza, it is the interval of a wide major sixth (900 to 940 cents, depending upon the combination of ICs), corresponding to the span of the five keys of the instrument, which is crucial in judgements of the conformity of a xylophone tuning (Voisin, 1994a).[21] However conjunct intervals (200, 240, 280 cents) still represent the constitutive elements of the scale. The tuning procedure continues by comparing the size of a given interval with its lower neighbour, each of these being played in ascending motion.

The abstract concept of *equality of intervals*—independent of their size— enables us to explain certain paradoxical reactions from the musicians, reactions provoked by the experimental situation, such as that of a Manza instrument maker who was unable to recognise the conformity of tuning in a "scale of tones" (a regular sequence of 200 cent intervals) on five keys of a simulated instrument. This musician normally responded to tuning suggestions within 20 seconds, yet we can understand his confusion when presented with a conceptually correct tuning (the intervals being equal) but one which covered a span smaller than he was accustomed to hearing (800 cents instead of his usual 900 to 940 cents). Similarly, a strictly equipentatonic tuning based on 240 cent intervals, resulting in a span of 960 cents (too large for the Manza) is often acceptable, whilst a combination of inequal intervals which span the same range (for example, 280-200-240-240) is refused. This demonstrates that from a conceptual perspective the equality of intervals is more important than their size.

To our knowledge, and excepting the biases of interethnic differences, there is an abstract conception of the scale in Central Africa which implies the summation of equal intervals, in an ideal state: this conception exists independently of the size of the intervals. The realisation of this conceptual model is based on three sizes of constitutive intervals (200, 240 and 280 cents), in different combinations, which must be considered as *equivalent* in order to be judged acceptable. There are rules which constrain the combination of occurrences of these three intervals in the sequence of xylophone keys. Depending on the ethnic group, we find a variable number of these rules. Thus, for the Manza, for a five-keyed xylophone the total span is between 900 and 960 cents, the intervals of 200 and 240 cents must occur once at least, the interval of 280 cents must also occur once but cannot occur in the extreme positions of the sequence. For the Gbeya, the keys can be between 9 and 12 in number, and thus the span varies proportionately; between the two highest keys, as for the Manza, large intervals are not permitted.

Detailed study of the differences between ethnic groups, either conceptually or according to the status of the octave (which is different for the Gbeya and the Banda), or according to the modalities of realisation, reflects a very complex cultural situation in Central Africa, where many migrations, for the most part little known, have played an important role in enriching the history of these societies. Comparison and corroboration of musicological data upon scales with those from linguistics (phonology, syntax, lexicon) enable us to articulate new hypotheses concerning the history of these migrations, particularly regarding the Eastern origins of the Banda groups, which have later become linked to the family of Western African languages (Voisin & Cloarec-Heiss, 1995).

Central Java

In Java[22], a critical problem arises from the fact that the discourse of musicians and tuners incorporates a range of theories formulated by Western researchers (particularly those of Kunst and Hood)—the very theories we are attempting to verify. Whilst this is difficult to control, such situations are especially interesting because the foundations of ethnomusicological theories can be readily authorised by the statements of Javanese informants who have developed their own theory in parallel.

The methodology adopted for research in Java must therefore account for the problems which may arise from Javanese tuners' recognition of the gap between theory itself and their own practice, and this also demands that the history of the oral traditions who produced written theories should be retraced and separated out as far as possible[23]. Thus, it is possible that the experiments themselves could act as a blockage to the investigation when they highlight a contradiction between the "theoretical school" and the tuner's own practice, a blockage which can only be surmounted by the tuner having a high degree of confidence in himself during the experiments. This confidence can often be regained by the simple fact that the tuner realises that he is in direct control of the information which he chooses to transmit. Furthermore, in the experimental setting the tuner may also evaluate the ethnomusicologists' own knowledge by means of the relevance of the models which are presented to him (and not by his knowledge of the researcher's hypotheses, which he must ignore at the time of the experiments). It is this last issue above all which dictates the need for adaptation of the experimental procedures of ethnomusicology; it is evident that 'ad hoc' experiments are truly hazardous in such a context because what they gain by covering a larger field of hypotheses they lose in terms of their relevance to the expectations of the tuner. Moreover, as *memory* and *speech* play an important role in societies with oral tradition, it is very difficult for the ethnomusicologist to ask the tuner to make another judgement on a model of tuning which he has already judged. After having made a judgement several days previously, the tuner is often able to recognise and distinguish a model which has already been tested, and does not always understand the experimental necessity of repeating the exercise. Thus the tuners often inform us that they have already judged this particular version, both in Central Africa and in Java.

Taking into account the effort and attention required on the part of the musicians for this type of experiment, it would be difficult to carry out studies of both scalar systems of the *gamelan*, the pentatonic scale (*laras slendro*) and the heptatonic scale (*laras pelog*). We have chosen to study the *slendro* scale because of its proximity to the scales of Central Africa.

Preparatory research consisted of sampling a number of *gamelan* stored in France, conducting acoustical analysis and synthesis of the sound of the *gender*, a bronze keyboard instrument with multiple resonators, which is the reference instrument for tuning *gamelan*[24] in Central Java. Experiments were conducted with *gamelan* makers (blacksmith-tuners), in Surakarta in 1993 and 1994 with Bpk[25] Tentrem, Bpk Sunyoto and Marjo (the main tuner from Bpk Soe Reso's workshop), and in Yogyakarta in 1994 with Bpk Trimanto (the only bronze *gamelan* maker in this town). In earlier times, we have assumed that a preliminary series of synthesis models would enable the hypotheses of Kunst, Jones and Hood to be verified, and make comparison with the tunings of different *gamelan* sampled in the field (some of which had been measured by Kunst). Yet it is the successive tunings and retunings carried out by different instrument makers as well as the models enabling validation or rejection of our attempts at modelling which constitute the essence of the tuning models submitted to the *gamelan* makers for judgement.

Our first trip revealed the complexity of the relationship between theory and practice in this region. Verbalisation, which plays an important role in these experiments, enabled us to clarify the meaning of the different explicit concepts involved in tuning, which are already well known due to earlier ethno-musicological research in this area: the octave (*gambyang*), the fifth (*kenpyung*), beats (*ombak*), the sizes of conjunct intervals, small (*kecil*) or large (*besar*), their position in the scale, and also the modes (*pathet*) and the ethos or "essence" (*rasa*) which they possess, which enable us to explain that no tuning could be considered as the same as another (a point which could only be confirmed by measurements of the *gamelan*) (Arom & Voisin, 1994).

However, these experiments also show that the mental representation which is *active* in the tuning situation is not as clear nor as flexible as the conceptualisation might suggest. During this first investigation in Central Java, a number of tuning suggestions were refused[26], thereby showing the existence of a norm. This norm could not be defined by verbalisation: even if we account for the phenomenon of beating, which is very slow in Central Java (approximately 1 Hz), or the phenomenon of "stretching" mentioned by Hood, the values of octaves and fifths did not correspond to the expected values. Similarly, the relationship between the *pathet* and the positions of conjunct intervals in the scale remained indeterminate. To the extent that tunings carried out by one of the instrument makers were systematically judged as false by another, the only reliable concept which remained appears to be that of the *rasa*.

A second visit to Yogyakarta in 1994 by Voisin has shown that at this stage of modelling three ICs are both necessary and sufficient to constitute a good *slendro* tuning: 200 +/–20 cents, 240 and 270 +/–10 cents. It was the tuning models founded on the combinatory variants of these three ICs which the instrument makers judged as constituting *a true slendro* tuning, or, to use their own terminology, as being "the *basis* for a *laras slendro*". This model is provisional, but we can understand that here not only is the "basis" close to the minimum relevant structure of the scale (in contrast to all other tunings, founded on different values, which did not receive the same appreciation: they were judged only as "*possible laras slendro*"), but also that there does exist a consensual and implicit norm—which is known by the tuners—*over and above the differences measured with different* gamelan (Kunst, 1934; Hood, 1966).

Experiments with the *gender* have shown different regional sensitivities in relation to the concepts observed at Surakarta: the influence of mode—*pathet*— on the structure of the scale is ignored here, but is replaced by that of the *embat*. According to Bpk Trimanto, the *embat* (which corresponds to the "profile" or "feel" of the tuning, and is fairly close to that of the *rasa* in meaning) determines —or is determined by—the size of the octaves[27]. According to Bpk Trimanto, the *embat larasati* has octaves which are stretched in the higher register, whilst the *embat sundari* has smaller octaves. This statement should have been at least partially validated by our experiments: the stretching of octaves is not as systematic as is suggested by statistical analysis (Hood, 1966; Carterette & Kendall, 1994), since smaller octaves of 1180 cents can alternate with larger ones of 1220 cents. Yet the opposition between small and large octaves is manifested in terms of tendencies: certain octaves, not necessarily the same ones, tend to be smaller or larger than perfect octave in the higher register of the *gender*. The implementation of a model based on this principle enables us to show that the effects of the *embat* in Yogyakarta are perceived in the same terms as the effects of the *pathet* in Surakarta: the most appropriate scalar structure— with somewhat larger octaves in the upper register—in Yogyakarta for the *embat larasati* is also the most appropriate in Surakarta for the *pathet manyora* and conversely the structure of the *slendro* with small octaves is acceptable in Yogyakarta for the *embat sundari* and is preferred in Surakarta for the *pathet sanga*.

Furthermore, our experiments have shown that the notion of the octave has not always had the same degree of pertinence in Java as it has today. When confronted with models which they judged valid in spite of non-perfect octaves, the Surakarta tuners acknowledged that their forebears did not place the same importance on the octave as nowadays, but that they employed other methods of verification which they themselves did not know any longer. It is still the case, both in experiments and in the normal practice of tuning, that the two pitches (whether from memory or using the standard keys—*bapon*) necessary to define the *rasa* of a *slendro* tuning system are those which comprise the reference of a fifth (the same found in the rebab, *nem-ro*, commonly known as 6-2).

Yet above all the observation of tuning procedures and our preliminary experimental data show that it is the values of conjunct intervals, their combinations, and the *possible values of the reference fifth which determine the different structures of the tuning system* and its *embat* or *rasa*. Furthermore, there are two classes of preferred combinations in existence today based on two values of the reference fifth, 680 cents and 720 cents, each of which corresponds either to the *embat sundari* or *larasati* and thus respectively to the *pathet sanga* and *manyora*, but also one or the other of these fifths corresponds to the one of the reference *gamelan* of Surakarta[28]. From this, the effect of stretched or compressed octaves observed in the *gamelan* of Java appears to be more dependent on the values selected for the reference fifth and the combinatory variants of the three ICs that follow from this, than from a psychoacoustical phenomenon which, although well known, remains negligible in relation to the status of the octave in the tuning traditions of Central Java. It can also be seen that we are not able to affirm that only two values of normative fifths exist, or have ever existed. On the contrary, the problematic which Kunst set out at the start of this century and the statements of instrument tuners regarding the knowledge of this period provide support for the notion that it provided a much greater combinatory potential than today[29].

Analysis of experiments conducted with the *rebab* scale has enabled us to make some suggestions which are relatively easy to verify experimentally: a detailed analysis of performance in re-recording from two *rebab* virtuosi in Yogyakarta reveals that the number of categories of conjunct intervals comprises three, or even four of the values relatively close to those obtained by modelling the instruments of fixed pitch. This study, currently in progress, shows however that if one *averages* the ICs to the following values: 210, 240 and 265 +/–10 cents, or 210, 230, 250 +/–10 cents and 275 +/–15 cents, the distance between each category can vary (by around 10 cents at the extreme) according to the modal context (*pathet*), the individual musician, or even the context (solo performances have 3 categories, accompanied performances 4 or 5 categories) (Berland, 1995). These findings must be taken into account in the development of future experimental protocols in Central Java.

CONCLUSION

In both Central Africa and Java, there is a significant difference between a scalar model obtained through experimentation and the measurements of instruments conducted in the field. Should this call into question the validity of the experimental model, even though it has been constructed through interaction with musicians? We have seen that certain data of an ethnographic nature arise as a direct result of this experimentation. This enables the local specialist to express himself in certain modalities which cannot be predicted from his thought: "It's true, my own instrument is not tuned very well, but let me show you how it should be . . .". It is at this level that the concept of *margin of tolerance* emerges, when the perception of a deviation is related to a cultural norm by means of an individual judgement, and this thus guarantees the coherence of a system of mental representation.

It seems to us that the interaction between ethnomusicologists and the bearers of a musical tradition is a paradigmatic instance of the universal and ongoing dialogue about the multiple dimensions of constructive tools. According to various assumptions, the burden of musicological proof is often abandoned to some other discipline, such as physical acoustics. However, if we are to understand anything at all of the nature of a cultural artefact, what we must address is the necessary (but too often forgotten) cross-fertilisation of various cultural practices, of which ethnological fieldwork is a decisive instance.

What our procedural experimentation does allow us is a prepared expectancy of very particular events, namely the emergence of a critical consideration by indigenous experts of their own traditional artefacts. The exercise of judgements of acceptance or rejection involves the reactivation of cultural criteria related to the complex of systematic musical features available; and these criteria are applied for the retuning of what was earlier considered an acceptable instance of intervallic distribution. We thus have a privileged opportunity to witness critical and normative competencies concretely and effectively applied to cultural devices.

Such an experimental setting may be useful in order to solve other cognitive problems. What we wish to emphasise is that the very general nature of its application to musical tuning allows us to consider the exercise of normative, systematic thinking[30].

Translated by Alexandra Lamont

NOTES

1. Frédéric Voisin would like to thank the Fyssen Foundation for the support which it has generously provided for this research.
2. We shall not consider here the effect of intensity (the Stevens effect), but we shall consider the effect of timbre (see Section 1.3 below).
3. We note that it is not possible to send the note to be measured directly to the frequency meter. This apparatus is involved in order to measure the frequencies of the notes which are themselves calibrated (sine waves, square waves, sawtooth waves) and thus entirely periodic.
4. Amongst the simplest systems which are easily transportable in the field, there are small electronic tuners frequently used by orchestral musicians, harpists, guitarists and so on. Based upon reduced electronics, these cannot achieve the precision of a Stroboconn, but do enable nonetheless some refinement of measurements to be achieved.
5. It should be noted that the recent theory of wavelets and its application by the Musical Acoustics Group led by J.-C. Risset suggests an alternative to the Fourier transform which has as yet been little investigated.
6. We note that in this respect the proportions are generally reversed between Western symphony orchestras and the majority of traditional musical ensembles.
7. Meaning principally frequency but, as we have shown above for other reasons, not simply this.
8. The notion of measuring perceived pitch is itself not a new one. In the absence of any kind of electronic technology, the only means of studying the pitch of notes was to study collections of pitch pipes (Ellis & Hipkins, 1884; Stumpf, 1901; Tracey, 1958) or sonometers (monochords) (Kunst, 1934). The principle was to match by ear the pitch produced by the instrument with that of the sonometer or one of the pitch pipes.
9. We include, for example, the analytical programmes IANA and SVP (Super Vocodeur de Phase) for the UNIX operating system, the Patchword and Audiosculpt (SVP) libraries for Macintosh, for detecting the fundamental frequency F0 and Terhardt's algorithm.
10. Analysis and resynthesis done at IRCAM using softwares IANA—Csound SVP (Super Vocoder of Phase), Patchwork, and Audiosculpt 1.0.
11. Whilst the necessary segmentation in this respect contradicts the hypotheses of Fourier's theory, it appears that it has a direct effect upon the results (Harris, 1978). Different types of segmentation (of cosine, Hamming, Hanning, Blackman and other), with correspondingly different forms of 'windows' of analysis, attempt to compensate for this contradiction, and to reduce the 'noise' of analysis. To our knowledge, in ethnomusicology the choice of type of window has remained largely an empirical question.
12. These measurements and observations were conducted by F. Voisin in 1994 using the Audiosculpt programme to analyse and extract virtual pitch.
13. It is worth stating that whilst trade contact may have existed between Africa and Malaysia (Kunst 1934; Jones 1971) this is outside the realm of our current investigation.
14. At least in melodic sequences.
15. This methodology, in relation to frequency measurements, provided the double advantage of enabling the perceived pitch to be account for and of giving values close to the tonic.
16. We should specify that the *pelog* comprises two degrees which are mutually exclusive; thus, there are only ever six degrees in use within any musical work.
17. Kunst in fact only worked on the *slentem*, an instrument which spans scarcely more than an octave.
18. Upon the basis of detailed transcriptions resulting from tracing the fundamental frequency, the frequency peaks (FFT) and/or perceived fundamentals (Terhardt, 1974). Whilst simply tracing the components itself raises a number of problems, recourse to graphical analysis is still more feasible when it is a case of files of notes which are not longer than several minutes.

19. Kunst proposed a different solution for the Javanese *slendro* scale consisting of two different intervals, of 234 cents and 264 cents respectively, which originates from the theory of blown fifths.
20. The size of this interval is approximately 240 cents, which corresponds to the division of the perfect octave (1200 cents) into five equally sized intervals.
21. A similar observation has been made in relation to the tuning of Nzakara five-stringed harps (Marc Chemillier, personal communication).
22. It should be recalled that we are writing about research in progress; the results which are discussed here are not complete and are those which are readily interpretable after only preliminary data analysis.
23. We would like to thank Florence Bodo who has been of great help in this endeavour.
24. We note that Kunst's measurements of the most prestigious Javanese gamelan were not of the *gender* but of the *slentem*, with a register of less than an octave. This choice seems to have resulted from the fact that in Western Java (the Sunda region), where Kunst carried out much of his research, the *gamelan* are lacking in *gender*.
25. 'Bpk' is an abbreviation of 'Bapak', the Javanese name for a professional or tradesman.
26. Amongst the suggestions which were accepted, we note that which Kunst called "modern *slendro*", consisting of intervals of 234 and 264 cents, but which does not match tunings carried out in the experimental situation.
27. We were able to verify directly with Bpk Trimanto that he believed he was referring to Kunst (who always considered *gamelan* octaves to be 1200 cents), whilst in fact Hood (1966), Carterette (1994), Carterette & Kendall (1994) and Surjodiningrat are the only ones to mention this phenomenon.
28. The well-known Kyai Kanyut Mesem of the Kraton Mangkunegaran, and the *gamelan* of the Radio Republika Indonesia, RRI.
29. It is likely that this confusion of terminology is a result of the necessary simplification encountered by the progressive disappearance of the Javanese instrument makers: half a century ago, there were over a hundred bronze foundries, but today there are no more than half a dozen, some of which are subsidised by the State.
30. We are grateful to Serge Pahaut for his careful reading and very pertinent comments on this chapter.

REFERENCES

Arom S. (1976). The Use of Play-back Techniques in the Study of Oral Polyphony. *Ethnomusicology, 20*(3), 483–519.

Arom, S. (1985). De L'écoute à l'analyse des musiques centrafricaines. *Analyse Musicale, 1*, 35–39.

Arom, S. (1991a). *African Polyphony and Polyrhythm: Musical Structure and Methodology.* Cambridge: Cambridge University Press.

Arom, S. (1991b). L'étude des échelles dans les musiques traditionnelles: une approche interactive. *Analyse Musicale, 23*, 21–24.

Arom, S. (1991c). A Synthesizer in the Central African Bush: A Method of Interactive Exploration of Musical Scales. *Für György Ligeti. Die Referate des Ligeti-Kongresses Hamburg 1988*, (pp.163–178). *Hamburgisches Jahrbuch für Musikwissenschaften, 11.* Hamburg, Germany: Laaber-Verlag.

Arom S., & Fürniss, S. (1992). The Pentatonic System of the Aka Pygmies of the Central African Republic. In M.-P. Baumann, A. Simon & U. Wegner, (Eds.), *European Studies in Ethnomusicology: Historical Developments and Recent Trends. Selected Papers Presented at the VIIth European Seminar in Ethnomusicology, Berlin, October 1–6, 1990* (pp. 159–173). Wilhelmshaven: Florian Noetzel Verlag.

Arom, S., & Fürniss, S. (1993). An Interactive Method for the Determination of Musical Scales in Oral Culture: Application to the Vocal Music of the Aka Pygmies of Central Africa. *Music and the Cognitive Sciences: Proceedings of the Cambridge Conference on Music and the Cognitive Sciences 1990, Contemporary Music Review*, 9, 7–12.

Arom, S. & Voisin, F. (1994). De l'Afrique à l'Indonésie: Expérimentations interactives sur les échelles musicales. In I. Delième (Ed.), *Proceedings of the 3rd International Conference Music Perception and Cognition*, pp. 99–100, Liège, Belgium: European Society for the Cognitive Sciences of Music.

Arom, S., & Voisin, F. (in press). Theory and Technology in African Music. In R. Stone (Ed.), *The Garland Encyclopaedia of African Music, II* (27 pp.). New York: Garland.

Berland, G. (1995). *L'échelle "slendro" de la vièle "rebab" à Java Central: une étude expérimentale.* (Unpublished Masters Dissertation, Université Paris IV, Paris).

Bonfils, P., Rémond, M-C., Pujol, R. (1986). Efferent Tracts and Cochlear Frequency Selectivity. *Hearing Research, XXIV.*

Bodo, F. (1991). *Etat actuel de la recherche sur les échelles "équidistantes" indonésiennes.* (Unpublished DEA dissertation, Université Paris IV, Paris).

Brailoiu, C. (1973). *Problèmes d'ethnomusicologie.* Geneva, Switzlerland: Minkoff.

Bukofzer, M. (1937). Kann die "Blasquintentheorie" zur Erklärung exotischer Tonsysteme beitragen? *Anthropos, 32,* 402 sq.

Castellengo, M. (1965). Sur la naissance du sonagraphe. *Bulletin du GAM, 8.*

Carterette, E.C., & Kendall, R.A. (1994). On the Tuning and Stretched Octave of Javanese Gamelans. *Leonardo Music Journal, 4,* 59–68.

Chailley, J. (1951/1977). *Traité historique d'analyse harmonique.* Paris: A. Leduc.

Chailley, J. (1964). *Formation et transformation du langage musical, I. Intervalles et échelles.* Paris: Centre de Documentation Universitaire.

Dampierre, E. de (1992). *Harpes Zandé.* Paris: Klincksiek.

Dehoux, V., & Voisin, F. (1992). The Determination of Scalar Systems in Xylophone Music of Central Africa. *Selected articles of the VIIth European Seminar in Ethnomusicology, October 1990,* IICTM, Berlin.

Dehoux, V., & Voisin F. (1993). An Interactive Experimental Method for the Determination of Musical Scales in Oral Cultures. Application on the Xylophone Music of Central Africa. *Music and the Cognitive Sciences: Proceedings of the Cambridge Conference on Music and the Cognitive Sciences 1990. Contemporary Music Review,* 9, 13–17.

Delalande, F. (1991). L'analyse musicale: une discipline expérimentale? *Analyse Musicale, 23,* 11–20.

Ellis, A. (1885). On the Musical Scales of Various Nations. *Journal of the Royal Society of Arts, 33,* 485–527.

Ellis, A., & Hipkins, A. (1884). Tonometrical observations on some existing non-harmonic scales. *Proceedings of the Royal Society, 37.*

Fales, C., & McAdams, S. (1994a). Tone/Noise Fusion and Timbre in African Musical Instruments. In I. Delième (Ed.), *Proceedings of the 3rd International Conference for Music Perception and Cognition* (pp. 105–106). Liège, Belgium: European Society for the Cognitive Sciences of Music.

Fürniss, S. (1992). *Le système pentatonique de la musique des Pygmées Aka (Centrafrique).* (Unpublished Ph.D. dissertation, Université Paris III, Paris).

Gottlieb, R. (1986). Musical Scales of the Sudan as Found Among the Gumuz, Berta, and Ingessana Peoples. *The World of Music, 1986(2),* 56–76.

Harris, F.J. (1978). On the Use of Windows for Harmonic Analysis with Discrete Fourier Transform. *Proc. IEEE, 66* (January), 51–83.

Helmholtz, H.L.F. von (1877/1954) *On the Sensation of Tone as a Physiological Basis for the Theory of Music,* New York: Dover Inc.

Hood, M. (1966). Slendro and Pelog Redefined. *Selected Reports in Ethnomusicology,* Los Angeles, University of California, *1.*

Hornbostel, E.M., von (1927). Musicalich Tonsystem. *Handbuch der Physik, 8*. Berlin.

Jakobson, R. (1932). Musikwissenschaft und Linguistik. *Prager Presse*, 7 XII 1932. French translation: "Musicologie et linguistique". *Musique en Jeu, 5*, 57–59.

Jairazbhoy, N. (1977). The "Objective" and Subjective View in Music Transcription. *Ethnomusicology, XXI*(2).

Jones, A.M. (1971). *Africa and Indonesia. The Evidence of the Xylophone and Other Musical and Cultural Factors*. Leiden, Netherlands: E.J. Brill.

Kubik, G. (1983). Kognitive Grundlagen afrikanischer. In A. Simon (Abteilung Musikethnologie), (Ed.). *Musik in Afrika. 20 Beiträge zur Kenntnis traditioneller afrikanischer Musikkulturen* (pp. 327–400). Berlin: Berlin Museen Preussischer Kulturbesitz.

Kunst, J. (1934). *Music in Java, Its History and Its Technique*. The Hague, Netherlands: Martinus Nijhoff (new editions: 1949, 1973).

Leipp, E. (1974). *Acoustique et musique*. Paris: Masson.

Léothaud, G. (1991). Le sens de la mesure. *Analyse Musicale, 23*, 47–49.

Lerdahl, F. (1987). Timbral Hierarchies. *Contemporary Music Review, 2*(1), 135–160.

Moore, B.C.J., Glasberg, B.R., & Peters, R.W. (1985). Relative Dominance of Individual Partials in Determining the Pitch of Complex Tones. *Journal of the Acoustical Society of America, 77*, 1853–1860.

Nattiez, J.J. (1975). *Fondements d'une sémiologie de la musique*. Paris: Plon.

Nettl, B. (1964). *Theory and Method in Ethnomusicology*. Glanco: Free Press.

Nuttall, A.H. (1981). Some Windows with Very Good Sidelobe Behavior. *Proc. IEEE Trans. Ac. Sp. and Sig. Process, ASSP 29*(1), 84–91.

Plomp, R., & Levelt, W.J.M. (1965). Tonal Consonances and Critical Bandwidth. *Journal of the Acoustical Society of America, 38*, 548–560.

Ramirez, R.W. (1985). *The FFT: Fundamentals and Concepts*. Englewood Cliffs, N.J.: Prentice-Hall.

Rouget, G. (1969). Sur les xylophones équiheptaphoniques des Malinké. *Revue de Musicologie, 55*(1), 47–77.

Schneider, A., & Beurman A. (1993). Notes on the Acoustics and Tunings of Gamelan Instruments. In B. Arps, (Ed.), *Performance in Java and Bali, Studies of narrative, theatre, music and dance* (pp. 197–218). London.

Schouten, J.F. (1938). The Perception of Subjective Tones. *K. ned. Akad. Wet. Proc., 41*.

Singh, P. (1989). *Interaction of Timbre and Pitch in Spectral Discrimination Tasks Using Complex Tones*. Paper presented to the Acoustical Society of America (manuscript).

Stumpf, C. (1901). Tonsystem und Musik der Siamesen. *Beiträge zur Akustik und Musikwissenschaft, 3*, 69–138.

Surjodiningrat, W. (1993). *Tone Measurements of Outstanding Javanese Gamelans in Jogjakarta and Surakarta*. Jogjakarta: Gadjah Mada University Press (first published 1969 in Indonesian).

Terhardt, E. (1974). Pitch, Consonance and Critical Bandwidth. *Journal of the Acoustical Society of America, 55*, 1061–1069.

Terhardt, E., & Stoll, G., & Seewann, M. (1982a). Pitch of Complex Signals According to Virtual-Pitch Theory. *Journal of the Acoustical Society of America, 71*(3), 671–678.

Terhardt, E., Stoll, G., & Seewann, M. (1982b). Algorithm for Extraction of Pitch and Pitch Salience from Complex Tonal Signals. *Journal of the Acoustical Society of America, 71*(3), 679–688.

Tracey, H. (1958). Towards an Assessment of African Scales. *African Music, II*(1), 10–20.

Tracey, H. (1969). Measuring African Scales. *African Music, IV*(3), 73–77.

Vetter, R. (1989). A Retrospect on a Century of Gamelan Tone Measurements. *Ethnomusicology, 33*(2), 217–227.

Voisin, F. (1991). La modélisation des systèmes d'accord des xylophones centrafricains. *Analyse Musicale, 23*, 42–46.

Voisin, F. (1994a). *L'accord des xylophones des Gbaya et Manza de Centrafrique: de l'expérimentation à la modélisation.* (Unpublished Masters Dissertation, EHESS, Paris).

Voisin, F. (1994b). The Status of Natural Consonances: An ethnomusicologist's perspective. *ESCOM Newsletter, 6,* 2–7.

Voisin, F. (1995). Musical Scales in Central Africa and Java: Modelling by Synthesis. *Leonardo Music Journal, 6,* 85–90.

Voisin, F., & Cloarec-Heiss, F. (1995). Echelles musicales et données linguistiques: Vers une histoire des sociétés oubanguiennes. In V. Dehoux *et al.,* (Eds.), *Ndroje Balendro. Musiques, terrains et disciplines.* (pp. 113–130). Paris: SELAF.

Wachsmann, K.P. (1957). A Study of Norms in the Tribal Music of Uganda. *Ethnomusicology Newsletter, 11,* 9–16.

APPENDIX: Hardware & software used for experimentation in the field

HARDWARE

Power generator (only in Central Africa);
1 Power and frequency regulator;
2 synthesisers (frequency modulation) Yamaha DX7, 8 voices each (Grey Mater E! extension board);
1 Akai S 1000 sampler with 16 Mb RAM;
1 Apple Macintosh SE30 computer with 16 Mb RAM (with late system 6 for low-cost memory);
MIDI interface Opcode Studio 4;
Nagra IV analogue tape recorder;
Sony TCD 10 Pro digital tape recorder;
6 microphones (2 Sennheiser MKH 415, 2 Sennheiser MKH 435, 2 Beyer M69);
8mm Sony V 200 video;
1 small black and white video monitor;
video tapes, analogue and digital audio tapes, tripods, cables, tools for electrical maintenance (soldering iron, etc.)

SOFTWARE

Alchemy 2;
SVP / Audiosculpt 1.0 (IRCAM);
DX7 Editor (Opcode);
Patchwork (IRCAM);
Text and table processing software

2 Attitudes to the time axis and cognitive constraints: The case of Arabic vocal folk music

Dalia Cohen and Ruth Katz
The Hebrew University of Jerusalem

This present paper attempts to show that regularity in musical organisation reflects both cognitive and cultural constraints. The work is based on studies of various musical cultures, analyses of various styles, and theoretical considerations, and it pays attention to various levels of musical organisation, from the unconsciously selected raw material to the immediate level of the performance. The study that will exemplify our main points is one of Arabic folk music in Israel which we have just completed.

According to our hypothesis, cultural preferences, among other factors, determine the attitude to the time axis, which may be assessed via the type of complexity and the directionality that guide the musical events. The complexity will be assessed in relation to its range, from the smallest event (such as a motive, ornament, or even the timbre of a "single" sound) to the overall composition. Directionality, which may be related to different parameters that are relevant to different levels, will be assessed by its range—short or long (like complexity)—and by the degree of clarity (i.e. the degree of predictability that results from various kinds of schemes, learned and natural). Examination of the type of directionality and complexity is possible by means of the following compound variables: (1) quantity of elements on the various levels; (2) their degree of definition; (3) their degree and kind of distinctness; (4) their dependence on or independence of context; (5) the kinds of hierarchies; (6) the levels at which schemes appear; (7) concurrence/non-concurrence among musical phenomena; and (8) the relationship between learned and "natural" parameters. All of these are subject to cognitive constraints[1].

As far as directionality is concerned, long-range directionality, like that of Western tonal music, meets the following necessary conditions at least: (1) the absence of predetermined relationships on the immediate level (which are so prevalent outside the West, as in the rhythmic patterns *mizan* in Arabic music, *tala* in Indian music, and *gongan* in *gamelan* music; or melodic motives such as the *gushe* in Persian music; predetermined relationships in Western music, such as those in scales or chords, are not on the immediate level)[2]; (2) the use of learned musical parameters (mainly an interval system) to a large extent[3], (3) the use of cognitive raw material that consists of numerous (optimal) distinct, categorised elements that can be identified even when they are far from each other on the time axis[4], (4) the overall use of systems that meet the conditions of cognitive coherence[5], and (5) the use of systems that allow for clear and complex hierarchies and a multiplicity of schemes on various levels that make a complex set of expectations possible. Tightening the hierarchical laws for the selected musical elements increases the clarity of directionality. In the classical period as compared with the Baroque, for example, the hierarchy between the selection of chords and harmonic degrees is stricter, and consequently the directionality is far clearer.

By contrast, short-range directionality depends on conditions that are, in part, the opposite of these[6]. Here we shall try to illustrate short-range directionality using performances of an oral, vocal, improvisatory folk tradition that is devoid of theoretical awareness. The material we have used (Arabic music in Israel)[7] represents a cultural preference resulting in the following possibilities, which we define as follows:

1. Embedding the music in extramusical frameworks;
2. Emphasising the text and its interpolation in the music;
3. Improvising both text and music;
4. Short-term ranges of directionality, with momentary complexity.

The last point is important on its own, but also derives from the other three.

THE CLASSIFICATION OF THE EXAMINED REPERTOIRE

Our repertoire was classified according to various criteria, musical and otherwise. The most general overall classification turned out to comprise two different frameworks that determine two types of groupings of songs: the first in accordance with the *maqām* system (which the performers use but are not able to articulate); and the second as a modal framework made up of groups of songs that are like genres, with general names—*šrūqi, mijanā, ᶜatābā, muᶜannā,* etc.— that are well known to the bearers of the culture, who are able to discuss these genres. Our findings revealed that the rules governing the *maqām* system in practise are related mainly to various aspects of pitch organisation, as in theory (although the nature of the rules differs). The rules of the second framework primarily involve rhythmicity, melismatism, text, and other extramusical factors. The second framework, however, *depends* on the *maqām* system (i.e. pitch organisation), whereas the *maqām* system is independent of the modal system. Because of the dependence of the genres on the text we termed them Musico-Textual Genres (M.T.G.).

As we shall see below, these two general frameworks already contribute to short-range directionality through the behaviour of the factors that characterise them. Let us mention at this point that the very choice of parameters that characterise these groups of songs emphasises "unlearned" parameters, the regularity of which we tried to uncover.

THE MAQĀM SYSTEM (IN PRACTICE)

The *maqāmāt* are best known from the numerous theoretical formulations of them in various periods[8]. However, when scholars have tried to find some regularity in the performance of the *maqāmāt* that would correspond to the theories concerning their intonation, they gave up and declared that there was no connection between theory and practice (Jeannin & Puyade, 1924; Lachman, 1940; Parisot, 1900; Reabours, 1906; Sachs, 1943; Villoteau, 1799).

We, however, assumed (given the consensus among the singers) that there *must* be some regularity that allows performers and listeners to classify the songs by *maqām*, albeit unwittingly. Meticulous examination with the aid of a melograph[9] revealed (as will be explained below) a latent regularity that "translates" the theoretical rules into rules governing performance practice. As we shall see, this regularity reflects the cultural preference for short-range directionality and great complexity, which, in turn, increases the possibilities for improvisation. Were we to agree with the notion that the *maqām* refers only to factors of pitch, our studies reveal that these pitch factors go beyond the standard definition of the *maqām* by scale only[10]. Our broadening of the *maqām* framework both by the complex regularity of intonation and by additional hidden factors proves to be of significance.

The following pitch factors were found to be characteristic of the *maqām* system: (1) the collection of notes; (2) the intervals; (3) the central notes; (4) the various kinds of ranges of the pitches in the songs—ambitus, tessitura, and even absolute range; (5) characteristics of the motives; (6) the intonation. These pitch factors were examined (in light of the aforementioned eight compound variables) in our extensive study of Arabic music as regards their contribution to the kinds of directionality. For example, in characterising the *maqāmāt* as performed in terms of the above six factors (a–f) and their contribution to types of directionality and complexity, the factor of "collection" (factor a in the list of factors) was defined in terms of two of the abovementioned variables of directionality, namely, quantity and hierarchy (nos. 1 and 5 in the list of variables); the interval factor (factor b) was defined in terms of quantity (no. 1), hierarchy (no. 5), concurrence among parameters (no. 7), and the relationship between the learned and the natural parameters (no. 8); the central notes (factor c) were defined in terms of the quantity (no. 1), distinguishability (no. 3), and hierarchy (no. 5); and so on.

Thus, each factor was examined in terms of various aspects that were relevant to defining the types of directionality. Below we only list the aspects involved in examining one of the pitch factors, viz. the motives, and go into some detail on the meaning of the organisation of the hidden factor of intonation (factor f) in practice. (The rules of intonation, as we have already stated, are known mainly from theory.)

In the course of our examinations, we found that the variables relevant to the characterisation of the motive were as follows: the interval bounding the motive; the structure (divisible/indivisible, short/long, etc.); the melodic contour; the tessitura; the meaning of "sameness", i.e. the degree of consistency between different performances of the same motives; the overall number of various motives in a song or group of songs and the ways in which they are grouped; and above all—the dependence of all of these on the location on the time axis (the opening, closing, or middle of the phrase or stanza). This extended list gives an idea of the complexity of such assessments without entering into their far-reaching implications. Due to the confines of this paper, we decided to list here only the major findings concerning the most important though hidden factor: intonation.

With respect to the parameter of intonation (which defied reliable examination before the age of the melograph), our findings (from analysis of various groups [Cohen, 1964, 1969; Katz 1968], including the present study) showed a large scatter in the sizes of each of the diatonic intervals, even among the average sizes. This, in fact, explains why so many scholars refrained from attempting to uncover the regularity of this music in practice. However, we were able to find regularity in intonation, once we determined the "intonation skeleton", based on the averages of the intervals in each song. (This skeleton is fleshed out by the sizes in practice.) The regularity found pertains to two factors: (1) the scatter; and (2) the "type of intonation skeleton". More explicitly: (1) The *maqām* "determines" which notes (degrees of the scale) or intervals are relatively stable and which "require" a large scatter. (2) Similarity between the skeletons of the songs in a single *maqām* is obtained by preserving the ratio between the sizes of the consecutive seconds in the scale (the ratio is expressed as "greater than", "less than", or "equal to", rather than as a precise number). This ratio determines a "type of intonation skeleton" (in practice), which can be considered a scheme, analogous to the concept of the scale in theory (see Fig. 2.1). Every intonation type may thus be realised in various intonation skeletons (Fig. 2.1b gives three examples of realisations), and each skeleton may be realised in various sizes within the bounds characteristic of the *maqām*

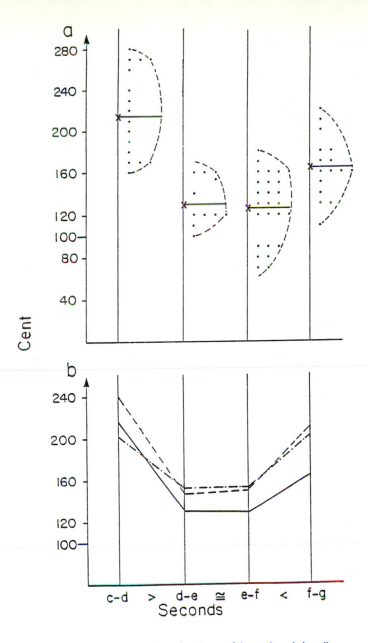

FIG. 2.1. (a & b) Stages in uncovering the "type of intonation skeleton"
On the x-axis Õ the successive diatonic seconds.
On the y-axis Õ the sizes of the seconds in cents.
a. The scatter of the seconds in a specific song in *maqām bayāt*. x denotes the average
size.
b. Three intonation skeletons, all of the same type.
  Õ the skeleton of the specific song above;
  --- the average of the skeletons in *maqām bayāt;*
  -- the scale of *maqām bayāt* in theory.

(Fig. 2.1a). All the realisations derived from a single type can thus be considered equivalent. Under these loose conditions, each second can be identified only in the immediate context. As we noted at the beginning of the paper, context-dependent components are not compatible with long-term organisation. In contrast, as we saw above, interval sizes in the West are not context-dependent and are therefore comparable even when separated from each other; this is one of the conditions for long-term organisation.

The concept of the intonation type is also found in other non-Western cultures that prefer to focus on the moment. Particularly notable is the intonation in the *gamelan*; many people have commented on its flexibility, as it appears differently in each individual *gamelan* (see, for example, Hood 1969). Careful observation, however, shows that the intonation type is preserved despite the numerous changes. Thus, the "intonation type" represents the hidden regularity that we assumed must exist. It is important to bear in mind that the concept of the scale in theory already fails to meet the conditions for long-range directionality (as specified above). Regularity in practice—i.e. the "intonation type" on which the elements are context-dependent, hinders long-range organisation even more, emphasizing the short range instead.

We should also note that the term "type" can refer to other parameters as well. The most salient example concerns the ratios of durations in poetic metres: the metre denotes the type, which can be realised with various ratios.

THE M.T.G. (MUSICO-TEXTUAL GENRES)

Most of the genres that we will discuss (those belonging to the "modal framework", i.e. the second grouping of songs) are prevalent outside northern Israel as well, especially in areas once included in Greater Syria (Syria, Lebanon, northern Jordan, and northern Israel). In general, most of the research into these genres focuses on the poetic aspects, and touches upon musical ones only marginally if at all[11]. In our detailed research we found about ten M.T.G. that are characterised by various combinations of musical and textual factors and cultural functions. For the most part their characterisation is not univalent, i.e. the definition of a genre may involve a particular factor, but that factor need not be unique to the genre. For instance, one of the *maqāmāt* may characterise a particular genre, but that *maqām* may also appear in another genre. The exception is textual structure, which is exclusive to each genre. Similarly, not all of the factors are as important in the definitions of all the genres. The way the different genres share defining factors is akin to similarity relationships in "family resemblance".

Our findings showed that the M.T.G. can be arranged on an axis stretching between two poles defined by a variety of contrasting factors: rhythmic/free; syllabic/melismatic; multiplicity versus uniformity in each of the characteristics (*maqāmāt*, motives, metres, poetic design, structures). Moreover, this axis can be seen as a scale of "ethos" (*ta`thīr* in Arabic) ranging from "calm" to "excitement". In the most general sense, the M.T.G. can be divided into two classes based on their proximity to these poles (Fig. 2.2).

The poetic structures, though they, too, can be divided into two types, do not exactly overlap with the two classes of the M.T.G. The simpler poetic type, the *qaṣīdah*, is common to both extremes of the M.T.G. axis, while the more complex structure, the *zajal*, is located in the centre, between the two extremes[12].

The examination of the relationship between the units that make up the music (motives, partial and whole phrases, a single section, and the song as a whole) and those that make up the text revealed a great deal of overlap between musical and poetic units. As a directional unit, the song as a whole is of no significance, neither from the textual nor from the musical point of view. This is because one may both extend and contract the song in the course of its renditions. Moreover, in most cases the song consists of many repetitions of the same stanza, so that their order on the time axis is of no significance. As for the stanza itself, it is defined in minimal terms—by the addition of a refrain in the text and music or some other concluding pattern.) The phrase, then, is the main musical unit that can be considered in terms of directionality, and it parallels the smallest poetic unit—the stich or line. Thus, each poetic stich or line goes with a single musical phrase. As for the characteristics of the phrase, we can distinguish between the two aforementioned M.T.G. types—rhythmic and free. The rhythmic type has a melodic unit composed of a collection of short, fairly well defined motives. The "free" type contains a well developed, indivisible motive that parallels the hemistich in poetry (Fig. 2.3).

These two types exemplify Von Forster's general law concerning two mutually exclusive options of organisation that determine the possibilities for higher levels of organisation[13]. Accordingly, in the present case, the well developed, indivisible motive type impairs the level of the melody, whereas the simple, well defined motive serves as a natural building block for the melody (Figs. 2.4 and 2.5).

Along with their differences, the two classes of M.T.G. share numerous *a priori* relationships (at the immediate level) that prevent long-range directionality. If we apply Von Forster's Law to comparison of different musical cultures, then the discussed repertoire as a whole (which contains numerous

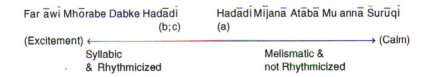

FIG. 2.2. The "ethos" axis of the principal genres and their division into two classes (the *hadādi* genre has three types: a, b, and c).

FIG. 2.3. Musical examples of the two types of genres (the transcription reflects only in part the musical practice, which is far more flexible). Type 1: unornamented, rhythmic and syllabic from the genre *babke* (melody is constituted from divisible motives; binarity governs the metre but not the organisation of measures). Type 2: ornamented, rhythmically free and melismatic from the genre *ʿatābā* (there is no melody, but complex indivisible motives; neither metre nor beat is discernable).

schemes in various parameters on the immediate level) will contrast sharply with Western music, which is almost completely devoid of complex ties on the immediate level. This absence, however, allows for extremely complex schemes on higher levels.

The most complex overall scheme is probably that expressed in the Schenkerian graphs. This scheme, which concerns only the parameters of pitch, determines both vertical and horizontal relationships between the notes. It can be used to uncover many relationships between the levels of a musical work. Schenker believed that this is responsible for the "supradirectionality" (to use our own term) that is so characteristic of Western tonal music. As is well known, however, the Schenkerian approach deliberately ignores stylistic differences, i.e. differences that result from intentional "distortions" of clear directionality within Western tonal music. These "distortions" are precisely what interests us here, since they do reflect stylistic preferences.

Poetry:

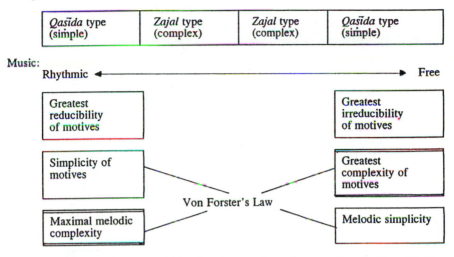

| Qasīda type (simple) | Zajal type (complex) | Zajal type (complex) | Qasīda type (simple) |

Music:

Rhythmic ⟷ Free

| Greatest reducibility of motives | | Greatest irreducibility of motives |

| Simplicity of motives | | Greatest complexity of motives |

Von Forster's Law

| Maximal melodic complexity | | Melodic simplicity |

FIG. 2.4. Simplicity and complexity in poetry and music on various levels, and Von Forster's Law

Poetic simplicity (the *qaṣīda*) is combined with musical complexity on the level of the motive or of the melody. The reverse relationship between the complexity of levels follows Von Forster's Law.

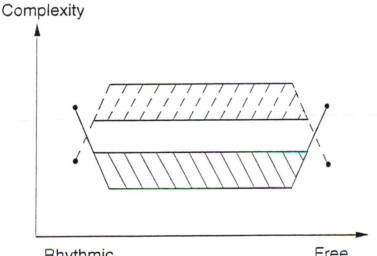

Complexity

Rhythmic   Free

FIG. 2.5. Complexity in poetry and music (without distinguishing between levels) as a function of the M.T.G. axis.

A solid line (—) denotes complexity in the music.

A broken line (--) denotes complexity in the poetic structure.

SUMMARY

In our study we tried to demonstrate, by means of the music that we studied, issues that are relevant to the study of music from a cognitive perspective. To conclude, we reiterate the three focal points of the present paper:

1. An examination of the attitude toward the flow of events on the time axis, reflecting the stylistic ideal, by means of directionality.
2. Determination of the musical factors that contribute to types of directionality and complexity, subject to cognitive constraints.
3. Determination of the desired directionality in the material that we studied and the specific factors that contribute to it. Of these many factors, we only went into detail here on the factor of intonation, while those characteristics that affect the motive were merely mentioned.

The "solution" to the cultural preference in the present case is dictated by cognitive constraints that allow for an abundance of predetermined schemes (mostly unconscious), which allow for many realisations despite the limited scope.

Based on the results of this study and other theoretical considerations, we can formulate very general principles that hold true for various categories of music and make possible the connection between cultural preferences and cognitive constraints. These principles determine the selection of rules of musical organisation, which reflect the attitude toward the time axis and can be formulated as follows:

1. The greater the connection between music and extramusical factors, the weaker the overall directionality and complexity of the music (Von Forster's Law).
2. The interrelations between directionality and complexity are by no means simple: in the short term the two are inversely related (in keeping with information theory), and in the long term they are directly related.
3. Optimal realisation of the preferred directionality and complexity must take into account a kind of "diminishing returns", that is, the ideal is always at the centre of an inverted U function.
4. There is an inverse relationship between momentary complexity and directionality and overall complexity and directionality (due to Von Forster's Law, to constraints of perception, and to cognitive constraints, largely related to the nature of attention).
5. Due to cognitive constraints, the kinds of complexity and directionality that are determined by preference restrict the possibilities for selection of the raw material, the rules of composition, and the rules of performance.

NOTES

1. These variables were selected so as to make it possible to characterise directionality and complexity in the music that we are examining, from the raw material on which it is based to the rules of the specific piece. We will not explain here the meaning of each individual variable or of various combinations of them in terms of their contribution to types of directionality and complexity that reflect the cultural ideal (Cohen, 1994). Neither shall we delve into why different composers, periods, or cultures have different preferences. However, let us emphasize that one may consider directionality and complexity to be both consequences and antecedents. It is, in fact, a two directional process that mitigates between choices and constraints (Cohen, 1994). The matter is determined largely by a universal cognitive regularity that intervenes in the musical regularity and is not self-evident (Cohen et al. 1993; Cohen and Granot 1995). For example, we know today that the choice of raw material in Western tonal music (i.e. the selection of the specific 7 and 12 in the scale system) is no accident, but derives from Western stylistic ideals (Balzano 1980, Agmon 1989). In similar fashion, the choice of raw materials in other musical cultures is dictated by their stylistic ideals. Thus it is no coincidence that the Arabic scale system has many poorly identified intervals, since such multiplicity contributes to the Arabic ideal of suspensive momentary directionality and maximum momentary complexity, with the option of maximum improvisation within the limits of the style (see below for a more detailed discussion of improvisation in intonation).

2. The simple musical metres in the West, which indicate a clear separation between rhythm and metre, serve as background for hierarchical organisation on high levels. By contrast, the prevalent predetermined non-Western rhythmic patterns do not differentiate between rhythm and metre and do not provide a simple background for further elaboration; instead, to various degrees, they form part of the foreground, which, as such, partakes in improvisation (Cohen, 1978).

3. The fact that different parameters are given priority in different musical cultures indicates a musical stylistic ideal in the sense that each parameter has several constraints on the possibilities for organisation. The interval has maximum potential for clear, complex, long-term organisation. Let us remember that the interval is considered extremely "abstract" because *distinct* intervals, not to mention interval system, do not occur in nature (at least not overtly). To obtain interval systems, people have to construct musical instruments so as to produce selected sounds with definite pitches. The rest of the parameters are known to us to different extents from their occurrences in nature. Interestingly, the earliest evidence concerning the interval as a musical parameter comes from the Babylonian tablets of the second millennium BCE (Kilmer, Crocker, and Brown 1976).

4. Some of the interval systems meet these conditions (for experiments on the existence of categories in the perception of pitches and intervals in the West, see Burns 1978 and Rakowski 1990; on the perception of intervals in the "chroma" as opposed to "height" (i.e. pitch class versus octave position) in the long term versus short term, see Deutsch and Feroe 1989, Rakowski 1989); most of the non-Western systems do not meet these conditions (for experiments that prove a lack of categorisation in the Vietnamese interval system, see Keefe et al. 1991). In systems such as the Chinese pentatonic system that meet the conditions of categorisation, there are relatively few elements. Rhythm and timbre are also identifiable without context, but they cannot be arranged on a scale in any simple way that would make possible comparison and conditions 4 and 5. (Attempts to express hierarchies of timbres [e.g. Ehresman and

Wessel 1978, Lerdahl 1987] indicate that complex possibilities exist as early as the first level of organisation of timbres.)

5. In Western tonal music not only is the interval given precedence, but the possibilities inherent in it are completely exhausted (Agmon, 1989, Babbit 1987, Balzano 1980, Brown 1981, Gauldin 1983, Makeig 1982).

6. It is worth stressing that the contrast between directionality and complexity (as obtained from information theory) exists only in the short term. Long-range directionality requires increased complexity.

7. As was mentioned above, the present article is based in part on a comprehensive study on the Arabic repertoire as actually performed. The study examines many variables that are directly or indirectly relevant to understanding the repertoire in various ways.

8. See the works of d'Erlanger (1930–1959), Farmer (1954), Shiloah (1979), Wright (1978). Also see *Recueil* (1934).

9. Note that the melograph provides continuous information on the variations in the fundamental frequency over time as well as intensity over time. The Cohen-Katz melograph, which has undergone numerous stages of development, was first created in the 1950s, around the same time as Seeger's melograph and that of Gurvin (Cohen and Katz 1960, 1967).

10. The prevailing opinion is that, on the axis that has the scale at one end and the melody type at the other, the *maqām* framework is extremely close to the scale end, while other modal frameworks, such as the *dastgah* in Persian music and the *raga* in Indian music, are near the end of the melody type (Powers 1980). Our studies of intonation and other parameters in the *maqām* join with other studies that uncover hidden regularity in improvisations of Arabic music, thereby distancing the *maqām* from the pure scale end (see, for example, Elias 1992, Nettl and Riddle 1973, Touma 1971).

11. The published studies on Palestinian folk songs can be divided into two groups: first, those published in the early part of the century, mainly by European researchers, and second, those published in the last few decades, most of them by Palestinian researchers. Most of the studies do not focus exclusively on the genres, and they consider the genres chiefly from the poetic standpoint and in terms of the setting of the performance. Prominent among the first group are the work of Dalman (1901), Grangvist (1935), Linder (1952), and Stephen (1922, 1932); and in the second group Wahiba (1952), al Asadi (1976), al - Bārgūti (1979), Ḥātir (1985), Jargy (1978), Libis (1989) and Rabiʿa (1987). To the latter group we can add the work of Shiloah, who also addresses musical aspects.

12. This conclusion was drawn after formulation of the poetic structures in general, especially the structures of Arabic poetry at its peak, i.e. the *muwaššah,* the *qasidah*, and the *zajal.* This kind of formulation makes it possible to compare the principles of poetic structures in various folk and art genres in the East and West, as well as the principles of poetic and musical structures in light of the stylistic ideal. For details on this formulation of the poetic metres, see Cohen and Katz (1994, 1995).

13. Von Forster's theory maintains that the better defined the elements in a system are, and the more "trivial" the relationships between them, the less influence they will have on the overall system. Therefore, the large number of relationships on a particular level prevents complex organisation on higher levels and vice-versa. For information on the theory, see Koppel, Atlan, and Dupoy 1987. For use of the theory in linguistics, see Shanon and Atlan 1990. For use of the theory in self-organising systems, and particularly in biological systems, see Atlan 1987. The present study demonstrates the theory in music.

REFERENCES

Agmon, E. (1989). A mathematical model of the diatonic system. *Journal of Music Theory*, *33*(1), 1–25.

Al-Asadi, S. (1979). Al - Aḡāni min al - Jalil. Nazareth

Atlan, H. (1987). Self creation of meaning. *Physica Scripta*, *36*, 563–576.

Babbitt, M. (1987). *Words about music*. Madison, Wisconsin: University of Wisconsin Press.

Al – Barḡuṭi, ᶜA. (1979). *al - Aḡāni, alᶜ – Arabiyyah al – ṣaᶜabiyah fi Falastin wal – Urdun*. Palestine: Bir-zeyt University.

Balzano, G. J. (1980). The group theoretic description of 12-fold and microtonal pitch systems. *Computer Music Journal*, *4*, 66–84.

Brown, R. (1981). Tonal implication of the diatonic set. *In Theory Only*, **6–7**, 3–21.

Burns, E. M., & Ward. W. D. (1978). Categorical perception-phenomenon or epi-phenomenon evidence from experiments in the perception of melodic musical intervals. *Journal of the Acoustic Society of America*, *63*(2), 456–468.

Cohen, D. (1964). An investigation into the tonal structure of the *maqamat*. *Journal of the International Folk Music Council*, *16*, 102–106.

Cohen, D. (1969). Patterns and frameworks of intonation. *Journal of Music Theory*, *18*(1), 69–92.

Cohen, D., & Katz, R. (1960). Explorations in the music of the Samaritans: An illustration of the utility of graphic notation. *Ethnomusicology*, *4*(2), 67–74.

Cohen, D., & Katz, R. (1967). Some remarks concerning the use of the melograph. *Yuval*, 155–168.

Cohen, D. (1978). Rhythm and Meter in Music and Poetry. *Israel Studies in Musicology*, *2*, 99–141.

Cohen, D. (1994). Directionality and Complexity in Music. *Musikometrica*, *6*, 27–77.

Cohen, D., & Katz, R. (1994). Structural aspects of musico-poetic genres in practice and of the medieval Hebrew *muwassah*. *Proceedings of the Eleventh World Congress of Jewish Studies* (pp. 227–234).

Cohen, D., & Katz, R. (1995). Musico-poetic Arabic tradition. *Proceedings of the Fifteenth Congress of the International Musicological Society at Madrid, 1992*.

Cohen, D., & Granot, R. (1995). "Constant and variable influences on stages of musical activities. *Journal of New Music Research*, *24*.

Cohen, D., Granot, R., Pratt, H., & Barneah, A. (1993). Cognitive meanings of musical elements as disclosed by ERP and verbal experiments. *Music Perception*, *11*(2), 153–184.

Dalman, G. H. (1901). *Palästinischer Diwan*. Leipzig: J.C. Hinrichsische Buchhandlung.

Deutsch, D., & Feroe, J. Pitch class and octave similarity. *Proceedings of the First International Conference on Music and Perception, 1989* (pp. 107–112).

Ehresman, D., & Wessel, D. L. (1978). *Perception of timbral analogies*. Paris: IRCAM (technical report 13).

Elias, T. (1992). Improvisation in instrumental Arabic art music in Israel: Individual and group. (Master's thesis, the Hebrew University of Jerusalem).

Erlanger, R., Baron d'. (1930–1959). *La musique arabe*, 6 vols. Paris: Libraire Orientaliste Paul Geuthner.

Farmer, H. G. (1954). Arabian music. In *Grove's dictionary of music and musicians* (5th edition), vol. 1.

Gauldin, R. (1983). The cycle-7 complex: Relations of diatonic set theory to the evolution of ancient tonal systems. *Music Theory Spectrum*, *5*, 39–55.

Grangvist, H. N. (1935). *Marriage conditions in Palestinian village*. Helsingsfors: Akademische Buchhandlung.

Ḥatir, L. (1985). *al -ʿ āḍat wal - taqālid al - lubnāniyyah*. Beirut: Mansūrāt dār Lahad Ḥatir.

Hood, M. (1969). Java. In *Harvard dictionary of music* (2nd edition). Cambridge, MA: Harvard University Press

Jargy, S. (1978). The folk music of Syria and Lebanon. *World of Music, 20,* 79–89.

Jeannin, J., & Puyade, J. (1924). *Mélodies liturgiques syriennes et chaldéennes,* vol. I. *Introduction musicale,* vol. II. *Introduction liturgique et recueil de mélodies.* Paris: Librairie Orientale.

Katz, R. (1968). The singing of *baqqashot* by Aleppo Jews: Study in musical acculturation. *Acta Musicologica, 40,* 65–85.

Keefe, O. H., Burns, E. M., & Nguen, Ph. (1991). Vietnamese modal scales of the *dan trank. Music Perception, 8*(4), 449–468.

Kilmer, A. D., Crocker, R. L., & Brown, R. R. (1976). *Sounds from silence: Recent discoveries in ancient Near Eastern music.* Berkeley, CA: Bit Enki Productions.

Koppel, M., Atlan, H., & Dupoy, J. P. (1987). Triviality and alienation in systems: Proof of Von Forster's conjecture. *International Journal of General Systems, 13,* 257–264.

Lachman, R. (1940). *Jewish cantillation and songs in the isle of Djerba.* Jerusalem: The Hebrew University.

Lerdahl, F. (1987). Timbral hierarchies. In S. McAdam, (Ed.), *Music and psychology: A mutual regard.* London & New York: Harwood Academic Publisher.

Libis, N. (1989). Al - ag̱ani al - fulkluriyyah al - nisa'iyyah. Nazareth.

Linder, S. (1952, 1955). *Palästinische Volksgesange,* 2 vols. Uppsale, Sweden: *Uppsala Universitets Arskrift, 5 and 9.*

Makeig, S. (1982). Affective versus analytic perception of musical intervals. In M. Clynes, (Ed.), *Music, mind and brain.* London & New York: Plenum Press.

Nettl, B., & Riddle, R. (1973). *Taqāsi̱m nahāwand:* A study of sixteen performances by Jihad Racy. *Yearbook of the International Folk Music Council, 5,* 11–50.

Parisot, J. (1900). Rapport sur une mission scientifique en Turquie d'Asie. In *Nouvelles archives des missions scientifiques et littéraires.* Paris.

Powers, H. (1980). In. S. Sadie, (Ed.), *The New Grove Dictionary of Music and Musicians,* vol. 12. London: Macmillan.

Rabi a, W. (1987). *Qaryat turmus iyya.* Al-Birah: Jam iyyat In as al-Usrah.

Rakowski, A. (1988). Some phonological universals in music and language. In M. G. Broda, (Ed.). *Musikometrika, 1: Quantitative Linguistics, 37,* 1–9.

Rakowski, A. (1989). Memory for pitch in music. *Proceedings of the First JCMPC, Japan.*

Rakowski, A. (1990). Intonation variants of musical intervals in isolation and in musical context. *Psychology of Music, 18,* 60–72.

Reabours, J. B. (1906). *Traité de psaltique. Théorie et pratique du chant dans l'église grecque.* Paris: Alphonse Picard et Fils.

Recueil des travaux du Congrès de musique arabe. (1934). Cairo.

Sachs, C. (1943). *The rise of music in the ancient world.* New York: W. W. Norton.

Shiloah, A. (1974). A group of Arabic wedding songs from the village of Deyr al-Asad. *Folklore Research Center Studies, 4,* 267–296.

Shiloah, A. (1979). *The theory of music in Arabic writings (ca. 900–1900).* Descriptive catalog of manuscripts in libraries of Europe and the U.S.A. Munich: G. Henle.

Shanon, B., & Atlan, H. (1900). Von Forster's theory: Semantic application. *New Ideas in Psychology, 9,* 81–90.

Stephen, St. H. (1922). Modern parallels to the Song of Songs. *Journal of the Palestinian Oriental Society, 2,* 202–279.

Stephen, St. H. (1932). Palestine nursery rhymes and songs. *Journal of the Palestinian oriental Society, 12,* 62–85.

Touma, H. (1971). The *maqām* phenomenon; an improvisation technique in the music of the Middle East. *Ethnomusicology, 15,* 38–48.

Villoteau, G. H. (1799). De l'état de l'art de musique en Egypte. In *Description de l'Egypte*, vol. IV. Paris.

Wahibah, M. I. (1952). Al-zajal-ta)rihuhu, adabuhu wai(lamuhu, qadiman wahaditan. Harisa, Lebanon.

Wright, O. (1978). *The modern system of Arab and Persian music—1250–1300*. London: Oxford University Press.

3 Radical subjectivisation of time in the music of the fin-de-siècle: An example by Max Reger

Elisheva Rigbi-Shafrir
The Hebrew University of Jerusalem
Department of musicology

AIMS AND THEORETICAL CONSIDERATIONS

The music of the fin-de-siècle (roughly 1890–1920) has most often been treated as either post/late-Romantic, or as antecedent to 20th-century "contemporary" music. Nevertheless, this music has features that make it deserving of independent historical treatment which can benefit from a consideration of the overall cultural context. The following discussion will show that some of these features are related to a changed experience of time. This makes them relevant to cognitive studies, even though they are not investigated empirically, but rather with the tools of cultural analysis. The results enjoy the support of philosophical writings of the period, and a wide range of other contemporary cultural phenomena. Due to shortage of space, the latter are mentioned here only in brief [1]. For the same reason I shall not dwell at length on the analogies between issues of fin-de-siècle philosophy, discussed below, and many recurrent themes and dilemmas of more recent cognitive science, though undoubtedly they are conspicuous [2]. The main task of this paper is to discuss the experience of time as emerging in the music of the period. Before embarking on this, however, several aspects of time organisation that are perhaps so obvious that they are taken for granted, need to be revisited.

Note: In this chapter, in references with a double date, the earlier date refers to the time of writing, and the latter to the date of publication. In double-dated references containing the letter 'R' ('*Reprint*'), the earlier date refers to the first published edition.

Whenever we speak of time organisation, we refer to patterns of intelligibility within a state of flux. This, of course, applies not only to music, but to the characterisation of processes in general. Concerning music, we normally refer to time organisation by a variety of terms implying structure or direction. Notions such as form, structure, anticipation, or direction are not separate issues, because all have in common two a-priori theoretical conditions: (1) stable and distinct identities, and (2) order.

Thus, when we speak of musical form, we are in fact speaking of a specific ordering of distinct identities, and likewise every mention of direction inevitably presupposes distinct points of reference and their stable ordering. In the extreme case, where neither identities nor orderings have any stability, there is neither form nor direction—in short: no guided intelligibility. Every discussion of time organisation therefore necessarily involves a discussion of its a-priori conditions of identity and order, which are, clearly by now, but "temporalised" version of the logical distinction between terms and relations.

In what follows, I hope to show that the very notions of both identity and order were destabilised in the fin-de-siècle, that this resulted in a new, subjectivistic conception of music, in which the listener was called upon to play a much more central role, and that this new conception and the breakdown of tonality were not causally related, but analogous manifestations of the general cultural endeavour of the period, both challenging stable identity and order as a-priori notions for the structuring of music.

The term "order" is not restricted to questions of chronology, but applies also to questions of priority and hierarchy. By "chronology" I shall refer to relations of succession and simultaneity alike, thereby relating horizontal aspects of music to vertical ones. Since the term "identity" refers to both abstract and concrete entities, I shall apply it to both music and music theory. Any discussion of style, therefore, must link the concrete acoustic phenomena with the theoretical presuppositions and propositions according to which they were identified.

In the present context this may hardly require mention. Anybody dealing today with cognition is continually faced with the difficulty of isolating perception from conception. In the fin-de-siècle, however, it was far from obvious. After almost three centuries of the Rational Paradigm, the most entrenched belief was that identity is prior to order, and thus independent of it. This is inherent in the belief in a *given*, cognitively inviolate *objectivity* as the locus and source of all reality and thus also of all true knowledge. This belief was the assumption underlying both the empiricist-positivist and the rationalist-idealist traditions in philosophy, notwithstanding the polarity of opinion as to the nature of the truly objective and the criteria of objectivity. Both induction and deduction, favoured by those traditions respectively as the road to the truth, owe to it their serial-computational nature. More importantly, this objectivism (mainly in its positivist formulation, namely that if there is to be order, any order, there must first be something objectively given to order) served as both underlying assumption and ideal of the entire cultural practice during most of the 19th century. This was true of the arts and humanities as well as of the natural sciences, whose empirical model all other disciplines sought to emulate, or at least accommodate. This objectivism was not challenged by 19th-century Romanticism, for example, because Romanticism represented a shift in attitude towards the perceived world more than the desire to re-formulate it. It was challenged, it is true, implicitly in notions developed already in the 18th-century and summarised by Kant, and more and more explicitly as the 19th century progressed, Kierkegaard and Nietzsche being two of the most notable examples. Nonetheless, the implications of these challenges were not yet fully realised, and certainly did not penetrate the public cultural domain, which continued to labour under objectivistic assumptions. Within that domain, systematic music theories, such as tonal theory in both its *Stufentheorie* and *Funktionstheorie* forms, also seem to have subscribed to such assumptions, vestiges of which are to be found in the much more recent serial and pitch-class-set theories.

The intellectual concern of the fin-de-siècle, in most spheres of culture, was precisely to move away from this world-view, into a "world of pure experience", to quote William James (1904,a,b). In that new world where nothing is truly given from without, everything, short of the infinite, must be constituted from within. There are no objects there, save those which had been *objectified* by the subject, from the matrix of subjective existence and in the form of individual subjective experience—*Erlebnis*—the only thing truly given[3]. The recognition that all objectivity is irretrievably imbued with subjectivity is the tenor of fin-de-siècle philosophical endeavours such as Neo-Kantianism, Husserl's phenomenological method with its goal of 'pre-suppositionless science', Dilthey's *Lebensphilosophie* and hermeneutic model of the *Geisteswissenschaften*, Croce's Philosophy of the Spirit, William James' Radical Empiricism, pragmatism, and pluralism, and Bergson's philosophy of pure time and intuition. No less is that recognition at the core of the new "aesthetic" model of knowledge exemplified by so much of the cultural production of the period, from Gestalt psychology to Symbolist poetry, or from cubist art to quantum physics and the theory of relativity.

All of these may be interpreted as separate forays into the "same" mind-made terrain, that all-image where subject and object interpenetrate. This interpenetration came to be regarded the *prima materia* whose parts, as such, are indistinguishable and of equal status in substantive terms, and therefore their identity is determined *only* by each other, consisting only in the *function* they may (or may not) assume towards each other. These parts, such as subject and object, substance and function, "things" and thoughts or emotions about things, or identity and order, came to be acknowledged as mutually dependent, *mutually constituent functions* of each other, neither possible without the other, both involved whenever either is established, therefore precluding all predetermination and standing to each other in no constant order of priority[4] .

In the field of music theory and aesthetics, of course, the notion of function has played an increasingly important role ever since Aristoxenus, but it was only in the fin-de-siècle that functionality became completely divorced from substantive claims, so as to be freed of any absolute or universally valid determination. Despite this, and in viewing knowledge itself, or cognition, as but a relation—or ordering—identity and order came to be regarded as the absolute prerequisites of intelligibility, which in the fin-de-siècle replaced the truth as the locus of knowledge and focus of interest. This was acknowledged not only by those who welcomed the new mode of knowledge, but also by those who at times rejected it, such as Bergson[5]. Compared to knowledge as previous generations had conceived it, the new knowledge of intelligibility was no longer a matter of possession, but of creation, and had a far greater extension. It subsumed both conception and perception within the notion and experience of activity, "life", or "change"—three fin-de-siècle synonyms for the absolute minimum and hence essence of experience. It was thus a knowledge that could never be complete.

Indeed, stated in more recent "cognitive" terms, it appears that the fin-de-siècle would *not* have viewed the computational and the more holistic, image-oriented models of cognition as mutually exclusive, or even as hierarchically related. Instead, it would have viewed them as essentially mutually constituent, inherent in each other at the most fundamental, irreducible level. The crux of this view is that the circularity it involves would be problematic only relative to objectivistic assumptions. Once these are fully expunged from knowledge, as the fin-de-siècle thinkers endeavoured to do, circularity is no longer objectionable[6].

THE MUSIC

The music of many fin-de-siècle composers such as Mahler, Richard Strauss, Reger, Busoni, Janacek, and even Debussy is most often described as combining progressive elements with traditional ones, and, as already mentioned, therefore regarded as either late-Romantic, or as a prelude to the revolution yet to come. In consequence, it has not been given enough historical attention unto itself. The only person to suggest that the fin-de-siècle be regarded as a music-historical period in its own right was Carl Dahlhaus[7]. Although he pointed out many unique features of fin-de-siècle music, which he called *die Moderne* and dated from 1889 to 1924, Dahlhaus did not get a chance to integrate his observations into a general positive formulation of a period style. It is my view that fin-de-siècle composers were dealing in their music with the same issues that concerned their contemporaries in other spheres of culture, namely the paradigmatic shift just described. Furthermore, in view of the general subjectivisation and consequent destabilisation of knowledge involved therein, combined with the extreme technical heterogeneity of the repertoire and the plurality of music-analytical and music-psychological theories emerging from the very same years, I believe that a formulation of a fin-de-siècle period style should be sought for in aesthetic terms, rather than in the more customary terms of music theory[8].

Consequently, the method employed in the following musical examples consists in the application of the results of the cultural analysis briefly sketched above, formulated in epistemological terms, as tools of music-analysis, while restricting music-theoretical terminology as much as possible to the very basic technical vocabulary that was shared by the divergent analytical attitudes spawned during the fin-de-siècle. All the examples are taken from a single piece: Max Reger's Variations and Fugue on a theme by J.S. Bach, op.81, for piano solo, composed in 1904. This should not be taken to mean that the method is based on this piece: the latter serves merely as an example of a larger period-repertoire. A demonstration of the emergence of global qualities, such as the temporal ones discussed here, and, more generally, of the fin-de-siècle view of knowledge as process rather than product requires that large portions of the music be considered. Limitations of space make it impossible to include here suitably large portions of additional pieces. Moreover, in dealing with a pre-existing "objective" musical reality (i.e. Bach's theme) these variations may well represent the spirit of their time as regards the renunciation of objectivity through the destabilisation and mutual relativisation of identity and order, and the consequently greater role of the listener. While much may be said about the piece, I shall limit my analysis to four major aspects, which together exemplify the shift in the construction of music.

The piece itself consists of a theme in b minor (Fig. 3.1, see page 52), taken verbatim, save for instrumentation, from Bach's cantata no.128. It is followed by fourteen separate variations, each beginning with a new tempo indication, metronome marking, key signature and metre, and ending with a full caesura. Finally, there is a fugue in the "tonic" key. Ostensibly, then, the piece is in the form of strophic variations, and in the first two variations there is little to make us doubt that. Reger's radical departure from traditional practice becomes evident immediately at the beginning of the third variation, and is developed throughout the remainder of the piece. It affects all levels of musical organisation, but is expressed most saliently in his attitude toward the theme.

Destabilisation of Identity and Order: The Theme Level

As is well known, in Classic-Romantic strophic variations a certain feature of the theme as a whole, most often harmonic phrase structure, is preserved in each and every variation, serving, as it were, as the theme's "nucleus of identity". In those well known examples from the repertoire where the the constant feature is other than harmonic phrase structure, the *function* of constant feature is nevertheless maintained. Here, in contrast, only five of the variations follow this practice,

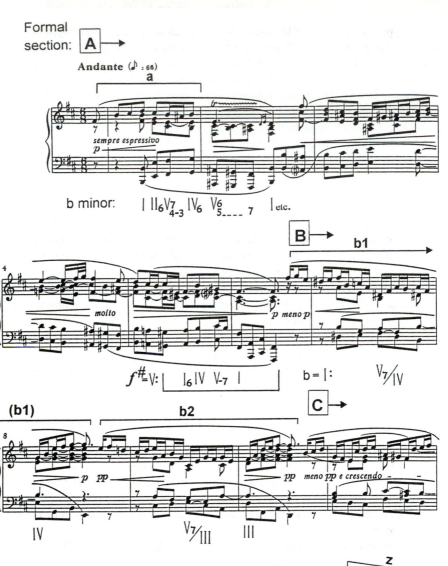

FIG. 3.1. The theme. Marked only are those aspects pertinent to the analysis of the variations.

52

notably preserving a *set* of features (harmonic phrase structure, melody and key) rather than a single one, thereby refraining from positing either as the more central to the theme's identity. In the other variations, the theme is represented through a variety of aspects other than harmonic phrase structure, none of which applies to the theme in its entirety, and this seemingly according to no consistent pattern.

Sometimes only a segment of the theme or a formal section is present in the variation. At times, it is preserved intact, as in Fig. 3.2 (see page 54), where the cadence of the *A* section, which is all that is left of it, is quoted verbatim from the theme. At other times, that segment retains only one of its original aspects, usually melody, as in Fig. 3.3 (the *z* figure; see pages 56–57), occasionally harmony or key, as at the end of Fig. 3.4 (the cadence on f# minor; see page 57). Such representative segments of the theme may also vary in size, from as large as whole formal sections, as in Fig. 3.2 (the *B* melody), to as small as single motifs or measures as in Fig. 3.3, where only the first and last measures of the theme are represented, or even smaller, as in the beginning of Fig. 3.4. Such segments may pervade the entire duration of some variations, whereas in others they appear, or disappear, among varying amounts of new material. They may occur singly, or in any assortment and combination. Thus in Fig. 3.3, *z* and *a* are combined horizontally, in a contiguous succession which is notably the reverse of the original, incontiguous one, while in Fig. 3.4, the truncated versions of the same two segments are superimposed vertically. Though contrapuntal juxtaposition of elements taken from disparate parts of the piece is an age-old procedure, here the absence of any other reference to the theme is most apparent. Lastly, it is sometimes not a concrete segment of the theme that is immanent in the variation, but some general aspect or attribute thereof, such as a formal trait, key, or general harmonic style. In Fig. 3.5 (see page 58), the possible melodic references to the theme are either not very specific, and even when they are (e.g. the partial *a* motif), they are easily subsumed within the strong b minor tonality and clearly functional harmonic style of the opening measures, which, coming after several highly chromatic variations in other "keys", becomes the most salient reference to the theme.

Already at this superficial level it is clear that to Reger, the theme is no longer the organic unity it was to Classic-Romantic composers[9], and that, instead, he conceives it as an "aggregate of images", to use a term coined by Bergson just eight years earlier[10]. As an aggregate, the theme is not governed by any unique necessary relation, and therefore all relations become contingent, i.e. subject to constant reordering and dissolution. This attitude is applied by Reger equally to all relations, whether logical or chronological, horizontal or vertical, and among its most obvious casualties are the logical relations of essential to contingent, the whole to its parts, and the abstract to the concrete. We have already seen in Figures 3.2–3.5 that the theme-aggregate has no central, or "essential" image, such as the constant feature in traditional strophic variations, and that Reger

b minor:

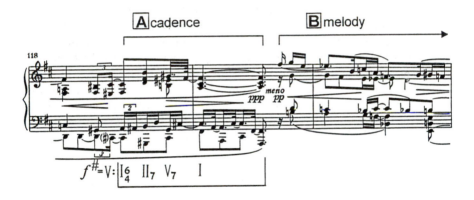

FIG. 3.2. Variation 7.

splits it into a variety of partial or constituent-images, both abstract and concrete, all of which, in isolation or in combination, he treats as *equally*, and *fully* representative of the theme[11].

It is worthwhile mentioning here that Heinrich Schenker devoted his entire 1926 essay "A Negative Example"[12] to a detailed analysis of this piece. As implied by the title, Reger's variations are his example of everything a true piece of music is *not*, precisely on grounds of its lack of organic unity[13].

The aggregate of images

Conceptual Constituent Images

Such destabilisation of order and identity does not stop at theme level. The constituent-images of the theme-aggregate are in themselves aggregates, and therefore subjected to further dissolution, along similar lines. This is true whether they are concrete segments of the theme or theoretical abstractions thereof. Reger's harmonic style well demonstrates the latter case. As often pointed out, any case of chromatic harmony, so common in the fin-de-siècle, may be interpreted as the destabilisation of the monistic hierarchy of harmonic functions, with an inevitable effect of weakening long-range connections. The extent of the literature devoted to the subject makes it superfluous to repeat the the details here. It is nevertheless noteworthy that while traditional late-19th century theorists tried to accommodate chromatic harmony within a unified overall context of tonality, explaining it through the addition of yet another (usually melodic) principle of universal validity, fin-de-siècle theorists, most notably Ernst Kurth, offered for chromatic harmony a *set* of explanations, neither of which is universal or prior to the others. Kurth's suggestion of three different referential modes for any chord (global-, local-, and self-referentiality)[14], all of which operate in the music and are not mutually compatible, is in itself an indication that the fin-de-siècle was moving away from a view of harmony itself as a conceptual organic unity towards viewing it as an aggregate, where no relation is necessary but at the same time none is impossible.

That Reger already treated harmony in this way is evident from his pluralistic harmonic style. Rather than consistently pursuing a single harmonic style, he alternates between styles ranging from the clearly functional late-Baroque style of the theme, which bespeaks a universal context, to the extreme chromaticism of his own day, bespeaking a selection of limited contexts. This alternation takes place not only between variations, but within single variations. It is manifest, in minute form, already in Fig. 3.3, where the theme-quotation *a*, retaining the original Baroque harmonic style, is embedded in a highly chromatic context, and in Fig. 3.4, where the first measure starts in quasi-modal harmonic style and continues in a highly chromatic one.

Furthermore, Reger does not restrict himself to the three harmonic referential modes suggested by Kurth for late-Romantic music (and which operate in

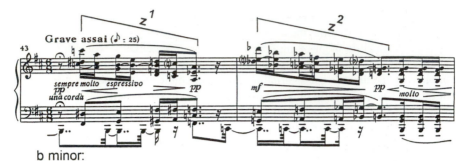

b minor:

(z contour)

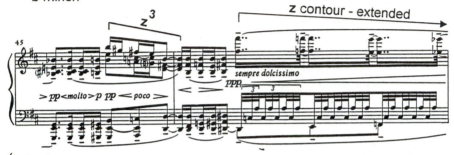

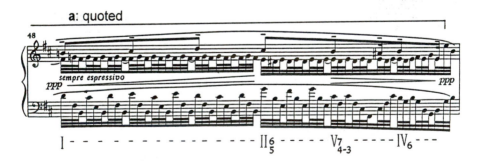

Fig. 3.3. continued on next page

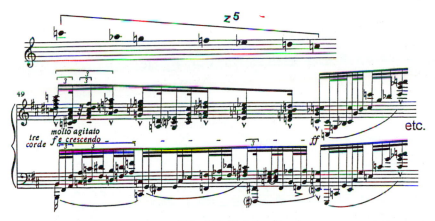

FIG. 3.3. Variation 3.

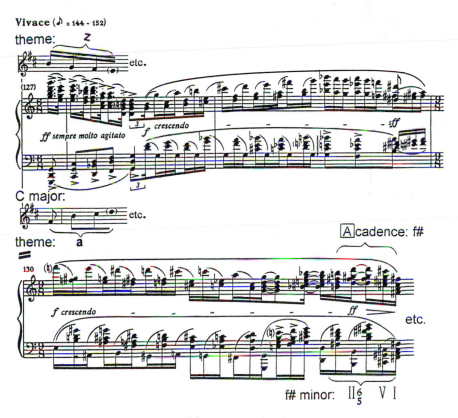

FIG. 3.4. Variation 8.

FIG. 3.5. Variation 13. Possible melodic references to the theme are subsumed within the much more salient reference through key and general harmonic style.

mutual dependence, albeit a contrasting "negative" one), but adds to them a fourth, namely the harmony of the theme itself. The result is a destabilisation of the very notion of harmony by its recategorisation as concrete, rather than as abstract or conceptual. This can be seen already in Fig. 3.4, where the cadence on f# minor, in a C major variation, represents the theme's harmony through pitch content alone, in isolation of both its original context and any context within the variation or of the cycle as a whole (whose existence is doubtful). This attitude to harmony is further evident in Fig. 3.7 (see pages 62–63), where the pitch-content of isolated chords from the theme (the *B* cadences, mm. 189 & 192) is partly reproduced, but in a completely different functional context. In its most extreme form it is to be seen in Fig. 3.6 (m. 211; see pages 60–61) where the D major chord of the second *B* cadence is reproduced verbatim, but in isolation of any context of explanation in the variation, harmonic or otherwise[15].

I have already noted that Reger's treatment of harmonic and tonal aspects of the theme as its possible but certainly not essential constituents abolishes all fixed relations of priority between aspects of music traditionally considered abstract or conceptual and those traditionally regarded as concrete. Here, however, the traditional classification itself is destabilised. The rifts in harmonic intelligibility resulting from this are not merely cases of Kurthian self-referentiality measured against a real or ideal standard of context. Instead, the concretisation of harmony, when it occurs, makes the whole issue of internal context inconsequential, irrespective of whether it is large, small, or nil. Internal relations are replaced by purely external ones to the theme, which is not immanent in the variations.

Concrete Constituent Images

Very similar results are obtained from the deconstruction and destabilisation of concrete constituent-images of the theme. A melodic image of a theme segment may be split into its determinants such as intervallic content, rhythmic grouping, structure, contour, voice-leading, and even mere length[16], all of which, in isolation or in any partial combination, are again regarded as fully representative of the theme. These determinants, originally ordered vertically, may thus be reordered horizontally, resulting in the interchangeability of internal and external relations, or in other words, of identity and order. In Fig. 3.6, the melody of the first *B*-phrase is represented rather explicitly: retaining the motivic content and structure, and consequently the length, contour and voice leading, and supported by a newly-introduced arpeggiated left-hand figuration that in the context of increasingly minute constituent images representing the theme is understood as an allusion to the *B*-cadences. The second *B*-phrase, in contrast, is represented twice: first immediately following *b1*, and the second time in mm. 210–211.The first representation retains of the original phrase only its similarity to *b1* in length and texture, its position immediately following it, and the descending second in the voice leading between the references to the two *B* cadences, all external relations. The second *b2* representation is only of the cadential arpeggio, but in melodic terms is an exact replica of the original, both structurally and in pitch-class terms, and is furthermore doubled in stretto in the left hand, and supported by an exact replica of the original harmony, although the D-major here is, as noted above, an isolated chord, totally unprepared and foreign to the local harmonic context.

B major:

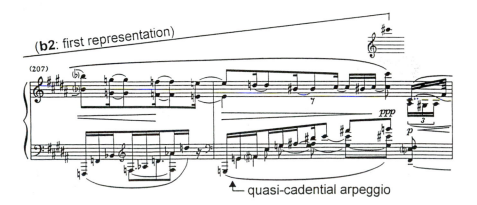

— quasi-cadential arpeggio

Fig. 3.6 continued on next page

FIG. 3.6. From Variation 12 (andante sostenuto).

References such as the first *b2* may only be described as *associations*, because they refer to the theme through relations other than the ones hitherto relating it to the variation, and in that, they also refer to it by relations other than the ones governing the rest of the variation or relating it to them, thereby precluding any long-range relations. We read a descending 2nd in the voice leading and a similarity in length and texture as references to *b2* only because of the immediate context of following *b1*, and the expectations created thereby.

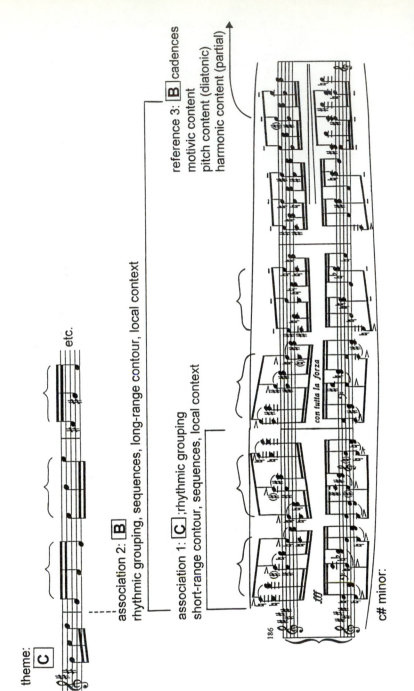

theme: **C**

etc.

association 2: **B**
rhythmic grouping, sequences, long-range contour, local context

association 1: **C** ;rhythmic grouping
short-range contour, sequences, local context

reference 3: **B** cadences
motivic content
pitch content (diatonic)
harmonic content (partial)

186

fff

con tutta la forza

c# minor:

Fig. 3.7 continued on next page

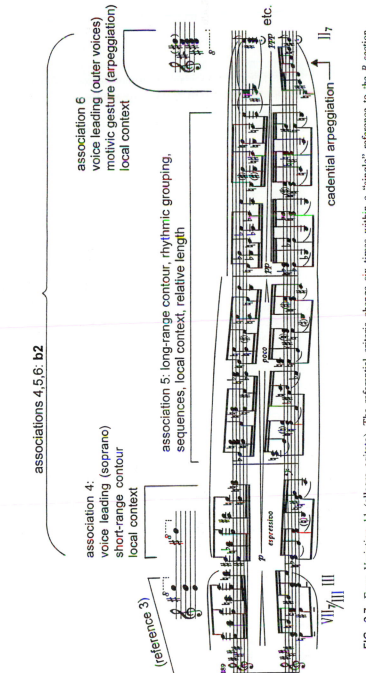

FIG. 3.7. From Variation 11 (allegro agitato). The referential criteria change six times within a "single" reference to the *B* section.

Another association to the *B*-melody can be seen in Fig. 3.7. The rhythmic grouping of eighth-note triplets (in 2/4 metre) may be regarded as recalling equally that of *A*, *B* or *C*, but the immediate horizontal context, following something that was interpreted as an *A*-reference, makes us prefer to see in it a reference to either *B* or *C*. One feels certain that this is an allusion to the theme, but is undecided as to which part of it. It is only in mm. 188–189, with an explicit reference to the *B*-cadences that reproduces almost exactly the arpeggiated motif and pitch-class content (of the first cadence), and even, on the last note, the (tonicalised and majorised) harmony, it is only then that one decides that the association referred to *b1*, after all. It is noteworthy that the association here is redetermined with the external context, and that this is done in retrospect. The reference to *b2* in the following three measures is likewise through association, because it, too, cannot be specified without the very local context, and, more importantly, because it exemplifies yet more changes in the principles of reference.

Listening to the entire *B*-representation in Fig. 3.7, it appears to exemplify six different sets of referential principles, or, in other words, six different definitions of identity. The bulk of the literature devoted over the centuries to the subject of representation attests to the fact that it is far from a simple one. It is nevertheless remarkable that Reger's procedure here complies with observations made about representation seventy years later by Max Black, namely that it cannot be defined in terms of necessary and sufficient conditions, since it is what he calls a 'range-concept', comprising a set of conditions out of which any partial set counts as valid representation[17]. Although in material terms, Reger invented no new apparatus and in this respect belongs with the Classic-Romantic composers of the Rational Paradigm, his usage of that apparatus groups him with Black, in the Post-Rational world which came into being in the fin-de-siècle.

THE EXPERIENCE OF TIME

The conception of identity as aggregate, the contingency of all relations implied thereby, and the consequent interchange of internal and external relations do not, of course, add up to an exhaustive account of the piece. They do, however, account for the new experience of time. When all identities, i.e. inner *and* outer relations are destabilised, so is all reference, in both syntactic and piece-specific semantic terms. One effect of such frequent stylistic changes is a growing awareness, on the part of the listeners, that the theme is an unordered aggregate. They therefore focus more and more on the momentary, and increasingly regard long-range considerations as irrelevant. A much more important effect, however, is that in order to preserve intelligibility in such pluralism, the listeners must constantly readjust the principles whereby they process the material. The bulk of their attention must hence focus on the processing-activity itself, which is by definition a thing of the present. The outer reality of "objective" musical "data" fades to a blur in the background. It is the inner reality of cognitive processes which precedes any objective datum—in phenomenological parlance: intentionality itself—that occupies centre stage.

Furthermore, the perpetual present of this inner reality is no longer a zero-dimensional division in a linear structure extending from a fully determinate past to a projected future. When references are constantly mobilised, determined and *redetermined* only by the momentary context of immediate contiguity, and often cued just by the very experience of change in the processing-principles, so is the past (consisting of all previous musical events). When the past is thus no longer given in substantive terms, it ceases to serve as the referent of the present. The reverse is the case. The present becomes the primary reality, engulfed by an increasingly non-linear and nebulous halo of possibilities comprising both past and future, into which the listeners may, and do project equally. If such temporal non-linearity did not ultimately nullify the possibility of direction, one could say that the listeners, moving in a constant present, project "backwards" no less than "forwards".

Such an experience of time is strikingly like the one described in the very same years by Dilthey (c. 1906/1958) as fundamental to all musical understanding:

> "earlier musical events are qualified by those that come later ... a melody moves towards its conclusion, which both conditions it and is conditioned by it. In every case all possibilities remain open. Nowhere is there a necessity ..."

This of course, is the "historistic" image of time that has been called self-contradictory (if not self-destructive) as far as "objective" historical science is concerned precisely because it ultimately abolishes both past and future, leaving only an ever-growing present. Indeed, when it is only the present that is given, reformulated in functional terms, the only stable identity left to make intelligibility possible is that of the processing activity itself. Through the process of dissolution and reformulation and *as* a process of dissolution and reformulation this activity, as ultimate content of the present, becomes increasingly synonymous with the very experience of activity which is the essence of experience and, ultimately, each listener's subjective sense of self. This is not to say that the ever-present of subjectivity is indeterminate. It comes into being only as it constitutes the piece which is its object, and it is through the ongoing creation of each other that both are determined, in an image of *"la durée réelle"*.

NOTES

1. Some such support, from the field of fin-de-siècle psychology, was presented at the 3rd International Conference on Music Perception and Cognition (ICMPC) in more detail by Albrecht Schneider, in a keynote address on "Brentano, Stumpf, and the cognitive approach to psychology".

2. In another paper presented at the 3rd ICMPC, concerned with the study of emergent global qualities, Rolf Inge Godøy treated some of the fin-de-siècle philosophical trends dealt with here, namely phenomenology and, indirectly, hermeneutics, with reference to connectionism and more recent research into categorial perception.

3. Of course, the notion of objectification originates in Hegel's Objective Spirit, but fin-de-siècle thinkers who adopted it did not posit above it any higher determining reality, such as Hegel's Absolute Spirit, which has all the immutability of objectivity. An explicit expression of the fin-de-siècle view is offered by Dilthey (1910/R1958), who notably adopted the term as well as the notion in a central section devoted to *"Die Objektivation des Lebens"*: "... the objective mind is divorced from its one-sided foundation on a universal reason (which expresses the nature of the world-spirit) and from any ideal construction ... what Hegel distinguished from objective mind as absolute mind ... also falls under this same concept", and later: "... we replace Hegel's reason by life in its totality ..." (translation: Rickman (1976). pp. 194–195). See also James (1909/R1958). Other fin-de-siècle versions of the notion of objectification are, of course, Husserl's notion of "constitution" of objects, and Croce's pure intuition.

That the primacy accorded to *Erlebnisse* collapses the entire tripartite Hegelian hierarchy of Subjective Spirit, Objective Spirit, and Absolute Spirit onto a single level of the totality has often been noted.

On the concept and term '*Erlebnis*', their history and relation to '*Leben*', see Gadamer (1975), pp.55–63.

4. See, for example, James (1904,b): "... Any kind of relation experienced must be accounted as 'real' as anything else in the system" (p. 42). In other words, order is neither less 'real' (i.e. of lower priority) than identity, as in "ordinary empiricism ... (which) has always shown a tendency to do away with the connections of things", nor more 'real' (i.e. of higher priority), as in "rationalism (which) always tends to treat them (relations) as being true in some supernal way, as if the the unity of things and their variety belonged to different orders of truth and vitality altogether." (ibid., pp. 43–44).

5. Bergson rejected it on grounds that it is unsuitable for achieving truth, which, unlike his contemporaries, he viewed in the "old" sense. Bergson (1903) accordingly says: "If there exists any means of possessing a reality absolutely, instead of knowing it relatively, of placing oneself within it instead of looking at it from outside points of view, of having the intuition instead of making the analysis: in short, of seizing it without any expression, translation or symbolic representation—metaphysics is that means. *Metaphysics, then, is the science which claims to dispense with symbols*" (pp.7–8, original italics). Of course, the union advocated here by Bergson is unlike anything considered as knowledge, either by his predecessors, or by those of his contemporaries mentioned in this paper, who either gave up metaphysics, or the old view of the truth.

6. One of the most explicit expressions of this is, of course, the notion of "hermeneutic circle" raised to methodological respectability by Dilthey and many others in his wake and upheld as not only valid, but also as central. For another statement, see, e.g. Croce (1902): "true logic ... uses a method that combines together induction and deduction, *using neither separately*, and this is to say that it uses a method that is *intrinsic* to itself ..." (p. 47, my italics), and later: "But the Aesthetic has always been at once both inductive and deductive, like any philosophical science. Induction and deduction cannot be separated, neither, separately, can they be used to characterise a science." (p. 122).

7. See Dahlhaus (1974) and, especially, (1980). Dahlhaus' suggestion is followed in Danuser (1984).

8. This is the subject of Rigbi-Shafrir (unpublished).

9. On the notion of 'organic unity' as a concretisation of the rationalist idea of 'system' see e.g. Cassirer (1950), especially pt. II: "The Ideal of Knowledge and its Transformations in Biology".

10. See Bergson (1896), esp. ch. 1: "On the Selection of Images . . .". Bergson uses the term to define Matter, which is used synonymously with "the universe as a whole". "Real" discreta are treated as a "fiction" and an "absurdity".

11. Concerning the relation of whole to parts, there is striking affinity between 'aggregate of images' and '*Erlebnis*', which although finite and definite, is nonetheless a *full* representative of the infinite and continuous '*Leben*'. The similarities between this aspect of '*Erlebnis*' and Bergson's '*durée réelle*' have been remarked by Gadamer, *op. cit.*

12. "*Ein Gegenbeispiel*", in Schenker (1926/R1974); English translation in Kalib (1973).

13. Compare e.g.:"Reger . . . only had the ear and mind for the very closest relationships; these are the only things he heard in the compositions of others, and these are the only things he composed himself. That is the way he understood the theme of Bach which he selected for a variations theme, not by any chance through its structure, through its organically connected ascent, retention, and descent, nor in the connections of voice leading; he only knew it by its individual tones with which he then dealt as he pleased in the variations as well as in the quotes." (Kalib. *op. cit.* pp. 487–488.) Schenker's Hegelian, if not outright Platonic view of organic unity as the evolvement through an all-pervasive principle of *Auskomponierung* of all foreground and middleground levels from the background, which in itself is a temporalised form of the single, immutable and essentially vertical *Naturidee* pervades his writings. For a concise formulation of it, see, for example, the preface to the first volume of *Das Meisterwerk in der Musik* (1925/R1974). See also Solie (1980).

14. In Kurth (1920/R1975). I am following the English usage in Rothfarb (1988).

15. Such concretisation of harmony may account, in part, for the fact that Reger invents in the variations (and elsewhwere) no new technical apparatus. Instead, he draws exclusively on the harmonic material of the theme, viewing it at times in a more abstract, generalised capacity, and at others as completely concrete, adhering to a strictly tertian repertory of chords, seemingly relishing the rich possibilities of ambiguity afforded by their connotations.

16. Of course, the criteria for measuring length vary. See below, my discussion of "associations".

17. Black (1972).

18. Translation from Bujić (1988), p. 371.

REFERENCES

Bergson, H. (1896). *Matière et Mémoire*. Paris: Presses Universitaires de France. English translation (1911) of 5th edition (1908), *Matter and Memory*. London: George Allen & Unwin.

Bergson, H. (1903). *An Introduction to Metaphysics*. English translation by T. E. Hulme (1913). London: Macmillan & Co.

Black, M. (1972). How do Pictures Represent? In E. Gombrich, (Ed.). *Art, Representation and Reality*. Baltimore: Johns Hopkins University Press.

Bujić, B. (1988). *Music in European Thought 1851–1912*. Cambridge: Cambridge University Press.

Cassirer, E. (1950). *The Problem of Knowledge*. New Haven & London: Yale University Press.

Croce, B. (1902). *Estetica come scienza dell'espressione e linguistica generale, parte I.* English translation of 7th edition (1941) by C. Lyas (1992), *The Aesthetic as the Science of Expression and of the Linguistic in General*. Cambridge: Cambridge University Press.

Dahlhaus, C. (1974). *Zwischen Romantik und Moderne: Vier Studien zur Musikgeschichte des späteren 19. Jahrhunderts*. München: Emil Katzbichler. English translation by M. Whittall

(1980), *Between Romanticism and Modernism: Four Studies in the Music of the Later Nineteenth Century*. Berkeley & Los Angeles: University of California Press.

Dahlhaus, C. (1980). *Die Musik des 19. Jahrhunderts (Neues Handbuch der Musikwissenschaft, VI)*. Wiesbaden: Akademische Verlagsgesellschaft Athenaion. English translation by J. Bradford Robinson (1989), *Nineteenth-Century Music*. Berkeley & Los Angeles: University of California Press.

Danuser, H. (1984). *Die Musik des 20. Jahrhunderts (Neues Handbuch der Musikwissenschaft, VII)*. Laaber: Laaber Verlag.

Dilthey, W. (c. 1906/1958). "Dans musikalische Verstehen". In B. Groethuysen (ed.). *Plan der Fortsetzung zum Aufbau der geschichtlichen Welt in der Geisteswissenschaften (Gesammelte Schriften VII, 2nd edition)*. Stuttgart: B.G. Teubner & Göttingen: Vandenhoeck & Ruprecht. English Translation by Martin Cooper and Bojan Bujić in Bujić, B. (1988). *Music in European Thought 1851–1912*. Cambridge: Cambridge University Press.

Dilthey, W. (1910/R1958). *Der Aufbau der geschichtlichen Welt in den Geisteswissenschaften (Gesammelte Schriften VII, 2nd edition)*. Stuttgart, B.G: Teubner & Göttingen, Vandenhoeck & Ruprecht. English translation of selected portions in H.P. Rickman (Ed.) (1976). *W. Dilthey: Selected Writings*. Cambridge: Cambridge University Press.

Gadamer, H.-G. (1975). *Truth and Method*. New York: The Seabury Press.

James, W. (1904a). Does Consciousness Exist? In *idem*. (1912/R1958). *Essays in Radical Empiricism*. New York & London: Longman, Green & Co.

James, W. (1904b). A World of Pure Experience. In *idem*. (1912/R1958). *Essays in Radical Empiricism*. New York & London: Longmans, Green & Co.

James, W. (1909/R1958). Hegel and his Method. In *A Pluralistic Universe*. New York & London: Longmans, Green and Co.

Kurth, E. (1920/R1975). *Romantische Harmonik und ihre Krise in Wagners "Tristan"*. Hildesheim: Georg Olms.

Rothfarb, L.A. (1988). *Ernst Kurth as Theorist and Analyst*. Philadelphia: University of Pennsylvania Press.

Schenker, H. (1925/R1974). *Das Meisterwerk in der Musik I*. Hildesheim & New York: Georg Olms.

Schenker, H. (1926/R1974). Ein Gegenbeispiel. In *Das Meisterwerk in der Musik II*. Hildesheim & New York: Georg Olms.

Solie, R.A. (1980). The Living Work: Organicism & Musical Analysis. *19th-Century Music IV/2*.

Musical sources

Reger, M. (1904). Variationen und Fuge über ein Thema von Joh. Seb. Bach, op. 81. In *Max Reger: Sämtliche Werke X*, Wiesbaden: Breitkopf & Härtel.

Unpublished material

Kalib, S.S. (1973). *Thirteen Essays from the three Yearbooks "Das Meisterwerk in der Musik" by Heinrich Schenker*. (Ph.D dissertation, Northwestern University).

Rigbi-Shafrir, E. *The Modern in Music (1890–1920) against the 'Crisis of Historicism' and the Breakdown of the Rational Paradigm: A Critical Definition of a Style*. (Ph.D. dissertation, in preparation), The Hebrew University, Jerusalem).

4 Cognitive sciences and historical sciences in music: Ways towards conciliation

Philippe Vendrix
Membre of the CNRS (Centre d'Études Supérieures de la Renaissance, Tours) and professor at the University of Liège and the École Normale Supérieure de Paris

> *"History does not need to protect itself from any foreign invasion. It need only reconcile itself with its own name"*
> Jacques Rancière, *Les mots de l'histoire* (Paris, Seuil, 1992)

The relationships between the cognitive sciences in music and history, are complex to say the least. These relationships are all the more complex for the attempt to establish them at a moment when the cognitive sciences, just like the historical sciences, are rethinking their areas of coverage, their working, their tools and their concepts. This slow process of reconstruction in knowledge is undoubtedly taking place in parallel, but following different paths. The diversity of epistemological approaches stems from the current situation within each discipline. Whilst the cognitive sciences are achieving undeniable success in academic circles, musicology is in many cases struggling to prove its legitimacy. It is confronted with an institutional crisis affecting its position as a university discipline. A second reason for the diversity of epistemological approaches lies in the relation of both these disciplines to their own tradition.

The cognitive sciences—in the manner of those disciplines which enjoy, at a given moment, an unprecedented level of interest—hesitate, even refuse, to turn back to their origins and examine their archetypal forms. Whether because they are the product of modernity or because they are resolute in their wish to be modern, the cognitive sciences in music seek pioneer status. Conversely, musicology is working in the opposite direction. In reconstructing its past, or, more accurately, its pasts, in an almost radical manner it is forging new paths and pursuing angles which have been hitherto overshadowed. In the manner of the social sciences, musicology no longer bases its dynamism upon a shared ambition, but rather upon a questioning of its canons. This upheaval is compounded by reflection on the nature of the musicological narrative linked, notably, to the return of the literary dimension of historical narrative.

Does this difference in the manner of self-analysis suggest that the lines of allegiance are irreversible? Is there a space in which cognitive musical sciences and historical sciences in music could develop their thought together? In other words, how can a musical phenomenon be read jointly by the two sciences? There is no question here of constructing a new framework, another analytical grid. That would be to fall once more into the now-contested enthusiasm which resulted from the definition of dominant paradigms rooted in marxism, structuralism or even confidence in systems of quantification. Rather, my intention is to show how the two disciplines have, whilst innocent of the other's involvement, been able to share a single objective, and how they can encourage a profound and non-exclusive mode of thought on the phenomenon of music.

THE MISSED MEETING

Cognitivists have reached a consensus on situating the origin of their work between 1935 and 1950 (Dupuy, 1994). However, music made its appearance only later as an object of study within a cognitivist perspective. Nevertheless, at the time of music's entry, general schematas for research were defined; automatically, and without being called into question, these schematas continue to serve for new research in music. On the one hand, the cognitivists work on the relationships between the mind and the computer; on the other, the connectionists are more interested in the relationships between the brain and the computer. These general principles suffice most of the time, and cognitivists, whatever their orientation, are generally content to situate themselves within this global framework.

Since the beginning of the 1980s, certain theorists have tried to draw up a geography of cognitive sciences. Of these, the most complete is undoubtedly that of Le Moigne (Fig. 4.1). This type of picture—and others would serve only to corroborate my findings—excludes any historical dimension from its field of inquiry, or relegates it to a sub-discipline. In an almost logical way, the cognitive sciences in music have dominated proceedings, and have been unable to consider the historical dimension as a pertinent parameter.

Paradoxical though it may seem, from the end of the 1950s the historical disciplines effected a process which shows many similarities. Under the influence of structuralism, historians oriented themselves towards the identification of structures and of relationships. This identification rejected the perceptions and the intentions of individuals, or turned them into independent experiences, thus separating knowledge from subjective consciousness. In parallel, the number, the series, the quantification which Carlo Ginzburg has

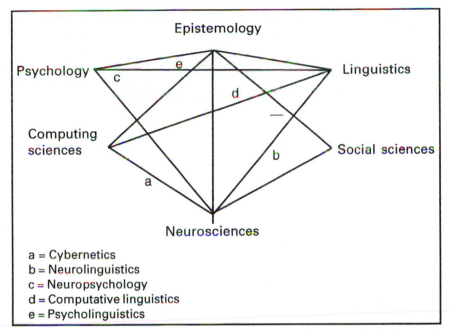

FIG. 4.1. Source: Le Moigne, J.L. (1986). "Genèse de quelques nouvelles sciences: de l'Intelligence artificielle aux sciences de la cognition". *Méchanismes de l'intelligence, intelligence des mécanismes*. Paris: Fayard, pp. 15–54.

called "Galilei's paradigm", drove history towards a rigorous formulation of structural relationships, the establishment of whose laws became its mission.

THE COMMON OBJECT

To say that the cognitive sciences in music and the historical sciences of music have a common object might appear tautological. The assertion thus merits some explanation. The position which I shall defend here considers that the cognitive sciences treat the processes inherent in a musical representation whilst the historical sciences study the genesis of such representations. The key element, whose outlines demand definition, is "musical representation". Is it the idea of music? The score? Perception? Practices? The question is complex in the extreme, and turns out to pose problems now which are much more intricate than certain systems thought to claim. If we limit ourselves to the area of Western culture, the element which renders complex any definition of a musical representation can be identified with the aesthetic object. It is primarily because the nature of the object poses problems that cognitive sciences and historical sciences in music experience a certain number of difficulties in finding common ground.

Undeniably, there is an antinomical position between these two disciplines as to the nature of the aesthetic object. Is it defined by itself or by transcending its nature as object? Historians adopt the second solution, because it implies inscription in time. It conditions all musicological discourse from, broadly speaking, the end of the eighteenth century, and achieves its realisation in manifestations of historicism. The transcendence of music's nature as object is directly related to the principle of mutation which, in turn, suggests the relativity of a truth, a fundamental principle of historical discourse.

The cognitive sciences are rather quiet on the nature of the musical object, considered as a means of living an aesthetic experience. In general, building from the silences of cognitivists, it seems that the first definition—the object is defined by itself—underpins cognitive research. In that, it would be legitimate to draw up a parallelism between the postulations of analytical aesthetic (Goodman & Elgin, 1990; Levinson, 1980) and the practices of the cognitive sciences, even if the first have often reiterated their wish to work only within a purely theoretical framework. The reification of the musical object presents itself as a necessary condition for any scientific treatment of a cultural object. And it is broadly from this angle that most of the work in the cognitive science of music can be read.

If there is no consensus on the nature of the aesthetic object, there is, on the other hand, a common interest in the phenomenon of the representation—a phenomenon which is also perilously difficult to define. At this point a backwards glance at the genesis of systems of musical representation can enhance our understanding of the hiatus which separates cognitive and historical sciences, but also of a link between the two disciplines which should allow us to envisage a common strategy.

THE GENESIS OF MUSICAL REPRESENTATIONS

The history of the concept of musical representation has yet to be written. Nevertheless, its broad outlines can be touched upon here, with a few summaries and elisions intended to bring to the fore the elements which will be pertinent to my project.

When Heidegger, in *The era of conceptions of the world*, writes, "that the being becomes a being in and through representation; this is what makes each era which eventually arrives a new era in comparison with that which preceded it", he agrees that the concept of representation can be historically confined. Generally speaking, historians of philosophy consider that Descartes played the role of founding father. He inaugurated the modern era by giving the term "representation" meaning and by defining the conditions of its existence. For Descartes, there is no representation until the moment when thought, conscious of acting as such, renders the object present, gives the object its shape and content, realises its objectivity. Therefore the representation, of whatever nature, is produced only by and for a subject.

The musical representation, in the manner of all other phenomena, saw fundamental upheavals at the beginning of the seventeenth century. The entire system of musical knowledge turned upside down, since it was no longer the object which was primordial, but the thought. Music becomes an object because it is represented by the subject. The process is not stated so explicitly in the texts of Descartes or Marin Mersenne. It is only incipient, but this simple beginning is indicative of a radical change. It coincides with the abandonment or the marginalisation of conceptions relating to the immutable (the music of the spheres, universal harmony), and of magic (the fantastical) etc.

If the first reflections on understanding go back to Aristotle and Plato, it nonetheless remains true that the first system explaining mental musical representations in the human dimension goes back to Descartes. Critical of Zarlino and Galilei, Descartes attempts to show that emotion is an non-intentional state (i.e. not linked essentially to its object) and that the relationship between emotion and its physiological, behavioural and psychic manifestations is contingent (Neuberg, 1990). For the philosopher, emotion results, certainly, from a judgement, but it reaches the soul having already been evaluated by the brain, as a result of bodily reactions. Descartes does not develop this theory strictly in relation to music. However, from the time of his *Compendium musicae*, he had sensed a part of this process in his interpretation of the awareness of rhythmic figures. Borrowing from Salinas, who had highlighted a logical order running in parallel with the activity of the senses and the memory, Descartes affirms that the memory records rhythmic orders perceived by the ear and functions as a referent which is exploitable at every hearing. This process permits it to review the status of the memory which, to use the terms of Frédéric de Buzon, passes "from the state of buried and rediscovered memory to that of consciousness of time as constituting a present" (Buzon, 1990).

It is possible to establish a first perceptual chain taking the rhythmic figure as a given and pleasure as a result. The sense and the intellect (which is affected simultaneously by the external object and the thinking subject) combine to produce pleasure. The advantage of this process resides in a conciliation between the sense and the intellect, but also in the importance accorded to the experience by the role of memory (Fig. 4.2).

The approach put forward by Descartes derives from a cognitive model to the extent that the physiological processes are subordinated to the subject's

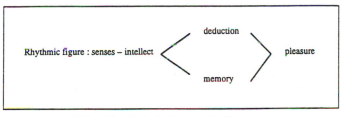

FIG. 4.2. Musical pleasure for Descartes.

evaluation of the object of emotion. Thus, after various unsuccessful attempts in the sixteenth century (Frangeburg, 1991), which failed for lack of knowledge and because of their implication in a system of knowledge which excluded the individual factor, Descartes introduced a cognitive schema for the explanation of the emotions: that they derive from the metaphysical domain or from a more material domain, such as pleasure in music (Vendrix, 1993).

The detailed study of phenomena relating to musical cognition, to use today's vocabulary, can be traced back to Marin Mersenne. The Minim's ambition was not located specifically in the search for an explanation of music's perceptual and interpretive functions by humanity. His project in musical cognition worked within a larger context of reflection on knowledge (Dear, 1988).

On various occasions, from the *Traité de l'harmonie universelle* (Paris, 1627) to the *Harmonie universelle* (Paris, 1636), Marin Mersenne called into question the traditional system of classifications in music, which Johannes Kepler had reiterated forcefully in his *Harmonices mundi.* (Linz, 1619). In this work, the physicist sets out the notion of 'archetypal harmony' in order to explain the intellectual origin of the judgement which human beings bring to bear on perceptible harmonies. This archetypal harmony does not constitute merely a simple potentiality of the soul; it is an act present in it, an innate knowledge, or an instinct. It is, in a way, the paradigm for perceptible harmonies, whether for the eye or for the ear. In other words, and in more general terms, this archetypal harmony must be understood as a geometry expressing the mathematical proportions of the body; it precedes the creation of bodies, coeternal with the divine soul, and present in the human soul.

Mersenne does not reject the notion of archetypal harmony as defined by Kepler. In contrast to his predecessor, Mersenne does not wish to relegate music to a subordinate position within the science of number, but rather to make it the exemplary model of an omnipresent order and a psychagogic technique conceived like a language capable, within limits, of expressing creation itself. The Minim achieves his objectives in 1636 when he develops a theory of consonances and dissonances resting on a physical component susceptible to rigorous experimentation, and when he attempts to eliminate the principle of innateness in the archetypal harmony: "Some imagined with Plato, that the proportions of harmony and chords were etched into the spirit of man from his creation, and that the soul rejoiced in being able to perceive the sounds which awaken and recall its ideas and respond to its proportions." (*Harmonie universelle*, 1636) Mersenne does not reject the notion of archetypal harmony. He displaces the concept. Archetypal harmony is not, strictly speaking, innate: the arithmetic used to describe it is contained in the capacities of the soul. By contrast, the innateness of the criteria of consonance and of dissonance cannot, according to him, be considered as an intellectual criterion to the extent that experience proves that its functioning works entirely independently of prior mathematical knowledge.

Up to this point, Mersenne traces the contours of a cognitivist approach to music which allows him to avoid touching upon metaphysical and ideological questions. He takes stock of the phenomenon of the musical representation as a non-preexistent process which demands, for its understanding, to be analysed from the outset according to the psychological and physiological reactions of the listener. However, for several reasons which cannot be elaborated upon here, Mersenne cannot prevent the intrusion of a metaphysical dimension. This dimension intervenes from the moment when Mersenne attempts to discover music's divine essence, which reveals its ideal form in the unison. Two factors condition the choice of the unison: firstly, it presents itself as the least significant interval in the musical discourse (moreover, it was often omitted from theoretical discussion during the Renaissance); secondly, the unison is the end of music, for all music can be brought to form a unison, in the same way that, according to the system of analogies, the virtues are nothing other than love (*Harmonie universelle*, 1636):

> It is easy to conclude that one can represent everything that exists in the world, and consequently all the sciences through the means of sound, for since all things consist of weight, in number and measure, and since sounds represent these three properties, they can signify anything one might wish, except Metaphysics, which separates the propositions of perceptible and intellectual matter, and which purifies them to the point where they make us envisage the sovereign goodness of the being of beings.

In his uninterrupted quest for a mechanistic understanding of music's functionings, Mersenne does not escape the clutches of metaphysics, and it is precisely on this point that he can be of interest to today's new cognitive sciences in music. Mersenne's explanations incontrovertibly evoke the propositions of Baily as reported by Cross (1992): cognitive science's *parti pris* of trying to discover an explanation of the abstract levels of the cognitive phenomenon. There is real danger in such an attitude, and Mersenne's working method brilliantly demonstrates at what point any metaphysical explanation can engender a totalitarian system. However, Mersenne avoids the pitfall by seeking to define a parameter which might take account of the phenomena of a musical representation without implying a pre-established order. Putting aside the question of harmony for the moment, the Minim father turns towards unfoldings, towards temporality. For these two parameters, which Descartes had also emphasised in his *Compendium musicae*, work within an ontological dimension: they refer directly to the experience of hearing. By this device, Mersenne locates his inquiry at the level of systems of musical representation, since he allows the principle of revelation, which had hitherto predominated, to be brushed aside.

The introduction of the concept of representation, aside from its influence on systems of knowledge, on the nature of the relationships between the being and nature, between subject and object, has also had the consequence of subdividing the objects of musical knowledge into three orientations. Firstly, there was the emergence of a philosophical aesthetic based upon the analysis of the conditions of the subjectivity of taste. There followed the slow affirmation of a concept of the work which would emerge in analysis inasmuch as it attempted to define musical strategies. Finally, there was an approach to the nature of the musical phenomenon as object, one of whose most familiar manifestations remains Rameau's principle of the sonorous body. Without excluding each other in an irrevocable fashion, these categories of knowledge have informed and continue to inform modes of approach to musical phenomena (object, work, judgement). Imposing itself like the canons of apprenticeship, in diverse forms, this structure has, for twenty years, had people reading across its grain. Yet despite it all, the cleavages remain visible, well or ill concealed, and explain, notably, the chasm which distinguishes the cognitive approach from the historical one.

If one restricts oneself to the relationships between cognitive sciences and historical sciences in music, there are obstacles in the way of a reading which might reconcile the two. The music historian must call traditional ways into question by trying to apprehend the epistemological stakes within the cognitive sciences in music. Unfortunately, this epistemological discourse hardly exists. A cognitivist must accept the principle of variable truth and must therefore question the universal dimension accorded to experiment, and deny themself any universalist research.

A REFORMULATED HERMENEUTIC

I have already shown, above, that there exists in effect a territory common to cognitive and historical sciences in music, i.e. the musical representation. Asserting the existence of common ground which is in itself difficult to define does not provide the element by which it might be possible to envisage a common strategy. If one turns towards other disciplines which have for some time given musicology interdisciplinary status, one reaps very little. Thus, even though progress in the neurosciences regarding vision can claim to yield probing and precise results, art history has not managed to bring together history and the cognitive sciences. The most striking example is undoubtedly the work of Jean-Pierre Changeux (1994), whose normative conclusions do not proceed from the elaboration of a logic common to the two approaches, but, more seriously, pose real problems of the ethics of artistic creation.

Within musical sciences during the last decade, historical musicology has undoubtedly submitted its canons to scrutiny to the greatest extent. It has done so by making apparent the symbolic phenomena which reveal the differences between bodies of knowledge within a single culture (Tomlinson, 1993), between the sexes (McClary, 1991), between modes of communication. On the one hand, musicology displays its intention to open itself up explicitly to the question of the musical representation. On the other, it maintains its discourse in an epistemological environment which does not readily risk an encounter with the most recent investigations of the cognitive sciences in music. Thus, Tomlinson's reflections relate almost exclusively to an historical discourse as already defined outside the field of musicology. As for work in "gender studies", historical musicologists are hesitant, and with good reason, about integrating cognitivist approaches on femininity and masculinity.

Cognitive research is also experiencing a period of self examination. The limitations of experiment arise (Richard, 1994), sometimes in brutal fashion, to drive home the point that the notion of relativity plays an undeniable role. This relativity, whether perceived as a dialectic between the conceptual and the perceptual (Godøy, 1994), between psychic apparatus and the organisation of musical parameters, emphasises the individual dimension (Kleinen & Kreutz, 1994). In a certain way, there exists a common heritage in the evolution of the two disciplines. And if this evolution works in an identical manner for each, the reason implies a need to research a territory whose contours remain undefined.

The place which seems the most appropriate for a (re)conciliation of the two approaches seems to be that of the aesthetic experience. Talking of aesthetic experience does not make the development of a system—which is clearly not my objective—any easier, in that this experience differs according to the conditions of its existence and its function, of the physical or the psychological experience as this extract from Seel (1993) makes clear:

> The aesthetic experience resides in the experience of the fact of having had given experiences, experiences which are determinants for the present life of the person who experienced them, or which, on account of the aesthetic experience, become determinants for his/her present life. Its relationship with the universe of experience integrates the experience into the domain of the lived world, at the same time as it determines its specific place within the context of the various types of experience. In their aesthetic experiences, men do not sever their links with their modes of life; they place themselves before objects, or interest themselves in objects through which they learn to know—and to experience—that which, given the experience which they have, engages their attention and causes them to act now.

The territory of aesthetic experience allows us to integrate that which the canons of musicology had been able to push aside for various reasons. For all objects which arouse aesthetic interest become aesthetic objects, without the intervention of any element of evaluation.

Of course, working on the aesthetic musical experience slows down a study of the symbolic constitution of musical works, because this study has meaning only from the moment when one is capable of saying what distinguishes the aesthetic presentation from the representation. Which comes back to determining what distinguishes musical representation from the representation of states of fact within the world. This postulation is unmistakably oriented towards a redefinition of the autonomy of the musical work, an autonomy which, from the 1960s, the historical sciences in music had cast into doubt, and which had been pushed aside in the reflections of cognitivists.

In that it concerns the creative and the perceptual acts simultaneously, the project of studying the aesthetic experience brings together different points of view. Above all, it allows us to glimpse the possibility of a double-pronged approach already defined by Dewey (1934, p. 83):

> If literal reproduction is signified by 'representative' then the work of art is not of that nature, for such a view ignores the uniqueness of the work due to the personal medium through which scenes and events have passed (. . .) But representation may also mean that the work of art tells something to those who enjoy it about the nature of their own experience of the world: that it presents the world in a new experience which they undergo.

If an investigation into the nature and conditions of the musico-aesthetic experience constitutes the first stage in bringing together the cognitive and the historical dimensions, it does not, however, constitute the sole condition. Effectively, the concept of the aesthetic experience obliges the subject's return. And we know to what degree the placing of the subject in analytical philosophy or in the philosophy of mind becomes problematic. In fact, the subject can be regarded as the stumbling block of the cognitivist edifice in that it prevents us from explaining the signification or the content of a musical representation without using other significations or other contents. This situation renders complex any attempt at conciliation. On the one hand, the historian works on a collection of sources which contain presentations (a musical work) and/or evidence of representations (theoretical texts, critical reviews, etc.). On the other, from these presentations or this evidence of representation the historian, once more, constructs an interpretation which may be considered as the manifestation of his/her own system of the representation. Revealing this chain is in some way to show to what extent the hermeneutic project becomes caught in its own snare. It is now no longer a question of imagining conciliation between cognitive sciences and historical ones, since it would require entrusting to the cognitive sciences the task of deconstructing the historian's process of representation.

However, whatever their process of representation, the historian's mission remains oriented towards the truth (Chartier, 1994). This is certainly the case for any historical discipline and thus, *a fortiori*, for historical musicology. Working within the confines of a knowledge which is both controllable and verifiable, how can we take account of a past aesthetic experience? How, for example, can we take account of the experience of the tragic in Josquin des Près when he composes the *Nymphe des bois*? The project appears audacious, unrealisable due to the psycho-linguistic factor which sits like an opaque window between

Josquin and the historian, and between the historian and the cognitivist. However, far from affirming that any conciliation seems unrealisable, I would say that the cognitive sciences can bring hope of transparency to the project undertaken by the historical sciences. Nevertheless, this transparency undergoes a double journey: the relocalisation of musical discourse through a realisation of the nature of the aesthetic experience as a particular and complex phenomenon; evaluation, among cognitivists, of the subjective dimension of the presentation and the representation of the aesthetic experience.

REFERENCES

Aiello, R., & Sloboda, J.A. (Eds.), (1993). *Musical Perceptions*. Oxford: Oxford University Press.

Buzon, F. de (1990). Fonctions de la mémoire dans les traités théoriques au XVIIe siècle. *Revue de musicologie*, 76(2), 163–172.

Changeux, J.P. (1994). *Raison et plaisir*. Paris: Odile Jacob.

Chartier, R. (1994). L'histoire) entre récit et connaissance. *MLN*, *109*, 583–600.

Cross, I. (1992). Musique, culture et action. *ESCOM Newsletter*, *1*, 31–34.

Dear, P, (1988). *Mersenne and the Learning of the Schools*. Ithaca-London: Cornell University Press.

Dewey, J, (1934). *Art as Experience*. New York: G.P. Putman's Sons.

Dupuy, J.P. (1994). *Aux origines des sciences cognitives*. Paris: Editions de la découverte.

Frangenberg, T, (1991). *Auditus visu prestantio*. Comparisons of Hearing and Vision in Carles de Bovelles's *Liber de sensibus. The Second Sense. Studies in Hearing and Musical Judgment from Antiquity to the Seventeenth Century*. London: The Warburg Institute.

Godøy, R. I. (1994). Shapes and spaces in musical thought. In I. Deliège, (Ed.), *Proceedings of the 3rd International Conference on Music Perception and Cognition* (pp. 177–178). Liège, Belgium: European Society for the Cognitive Sciences of Music.

Goodman, N. & Elgin, C. (1990). *Esthétique et connaissance. Pour changer de sujet*. Paris: L'Eclat.

Imberty, M. (1992). Quelques réflexions et orientations pour une apporce interdisciplinaire de la musique et des sciences cognitives. *ESCOM Newsletter*, *1*, 8–15.

Kleinen, G., & Kreutz, G. (1994). Music, metaphor, and imagination. In I. Deliège, (Ed.), *Proceedings of the 3rd International Conference on Music Perception and Cognition* (pp. 201–202). Liège, Belgium: European Society for the Cognitive Sciences of Music.

Le Moigne, J.L. (1986). Genèse de quelques nouvelles sciences: de l'Intelligence artificielle aux sciences de la cognition. In *Mécanismes de l'intelligence, intelligence des mécanismes* (pp. 15–54). Paris: Fayard.

Levinson, J. (1980). What a Musical Work is. *Journal of Philosophy*, *77*, 5–28.

McClary, S. (1991). *Feminine Endings: Music, Gender and Sexuality*. Minneapolis: University of Minnesota Press.

Neuberg, M. (1990). Le traité des passions de l'âme de Descartes et les théories modernes de l'émotion. *Archives de philosophie*, *53*, 479–508.

Rastier, F. (1991). *Sémantiques et recherches cognitives*. Paris: Presses Universitaires de France.

Richard, D.M. (1994). Name that tune: The Turing test revisited. In I. Deliège, (Ed.), *Proceedings of the 3rd International Conference on Music Perception and Cognition* (pp. 175–176). Liège, Belgium: European Society for the Cognitive Sciences of Music.

Seel, M. (1993). *L'art de diviser. Le concept de rationalité esthétique* (pp. 148–149). Paris: Armand Colin.

Tomlinson, G. (1993). *Music in Renaissance Magic*. Chicago: The University of Chicago Press.

Vendrix, Ph. (1993). L'augustinisme musical en France au XVIIe siècle. *Revue de musicologie*, 78(2), 237–255.

Developmental Approaches

5 Some aspects of the foetal sound environment

Robert M. Abrams, Ph.D.
Department of Obstetrics and Gynecology, Department of Pediatrics, University of Florida, Gainesville, Florida
Kenneth J. Gerhardt, Ph.D.
Department of Communication Processes and Disorders, The Institute for the Advanced Study of the Communication Processes, University of Florida, Gainesville, Florida

INTRODUCTION

Studies in pregnant humans (Querleu, Renard, Versyp, Paris-Delrue, & Crepin 1988; Querleu, Renard, Bontteville, & Crepin, 1989) and sheep (Armitage, Baldwin, & Vince, 1980; Gerhardt, Abrams & Oliver, 1990) leave little doubt of the existence of a varied foetal sound environment, heavily dominated by mother's voice and other internal noises and permeated by rich and diversified rhythmic and tonal surrounding sounds. Interest in the foetal sound environment has come from diverse groups, some uneasy over the potential harmful effects of excessive noise levels on development and function of foetal hearing, others utilising a prenatal response to sound in the development of tests designed to assess foetal well-being.

Environmental health and safety experts are concerned about the possibility that excessive noise could place the foetus at risk for hearing loss. Pregnant women working in noisy industrial settings or otherwise exposed to intense sounds can protect themselves by wearing ear protection; however, the foetus cannot be easily protected from the direct effects of these sounds. Noise levels and durations exceeding the limits specified in several international occupational safety and health guidelines occur during non-working conditions, such as during amplified music concerts (Henderson & Hamernik, 1986). A period of susceptibility to noise trauma has been correlated with the stage of inner ear development when the cochlea in experimental animals acquires its exquisite properties of sensitivity and frequency selectivity (Pujol,

Lavigne-Rebillard & Uziel, 1990). Effects of intense noise are generally classified as either temporary or permanent shifts in the threshold for hearing. Griffiths, Pierson, Gerhardt, Abrams & Peters, (1994b) recorded auditory brainstem responses (ABR) *in utero* from chronically instrumented foetal sheep prior to and following exposure of pregnant ewes to intense broadband noise (120dB SPL for 16 hours) (Fig. 5.1). In Griffiths' experiments, ABRs were elevated by clicks and tone bursts delivered through a bone oscillator secured to the foetal skull. Latency-intensity functions for most of the four vertex positive waves (labelled I-IV) were prolonged and ABR thresholds were temporarily elevated by an average of 8dB following the noise exposure. Twenty-four to ninety-six hours after exposure the absolute wave latencies decreased to pre-exposure levels. Whether or not the shifts in auditory function are accompanied by histopathologic changes in the cochlea is currently under evaluation. The sheep is an excellent animal model for studies of this type because it is affected minimally by the surgical procedures required to place intrauterine transducers and because hearing develops prenatally as it does in the human foetus. Furthermore, sheep have an auditory sensitivity similar to that of humans (Wollack, 1963).

A second group interested in the foetal sound environment is comprised of obstetricians who use a brief noise exposure to induce foetal heart rate accelerations which are predictive of foetal well-being. Research with the most common stimulator, the electronic artificial larynx (EAL), showed extremely high intrauterine sound pressure levels (SPL) when the EAL was placed on the abdominal skin of pregnant sheep (Gerhardt et al., 1990) and of pregnant women (Nyman, Arulkumaran, Hsu, Ratman, Till, & Westgren, 1991). The spectral features of commercial EALs are quite similar (Fig. 5.2).

By the 24th week of intrauterine life, the cochlea and peripheral sensory end organs have reached their normal development (Pujol et al., 1990). By 26 weeks' gestational age, most foetuses will respond to vibroacoustic stimulation with an increase in foetal heart rate (Gagnon, Hunse, Carmichael, Fellows, & Patrick, 1987). Some modification of the response that occurred as gestation proceeded led Gagnon et al. to infer a continued functional maturation of the autonomic nervous system (1987). Other indexes of foetal perception of sounds during EAL stimulation included foetal body movements and breathing movements, both easily visualised during ultrasonography.

Widespread clinical interest in foetal acoustic stimulation is evidenced by the appearance in the English language literature of over 125 papers, abstracts and reviews on the subject (Abrams, Gerhardt, Richards, & Peters, 1995b). The test is practised by numerous obstetricians in spite of apprehension by some about its safety (Gagnon, 1989; Visser, Mulder, Wit, & Prechtl, 1988) and ambivalence over its efficacy in the assessment of foetuses in the course of clinical practice (Richards, 1990).

The literature generated by scientists in these two groups has directed the interests of our team at the Perinatology Research Laboratory to the study of the

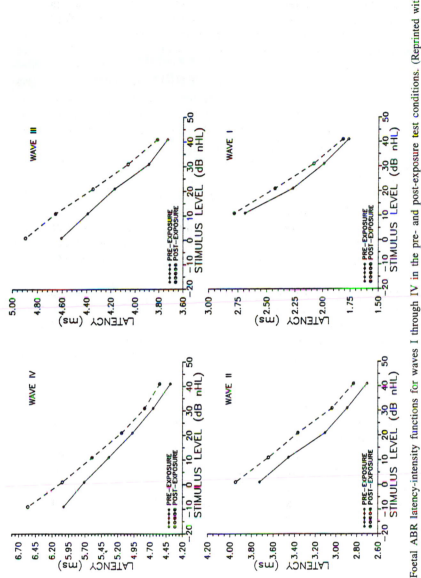

FIG. 5.1. Click-evoked Foetal ABR latency-intensity functions for waves I through IV in the pre- and post-exposure test conditions. (Reprinted with permission Griffiths et. al., 1994a)

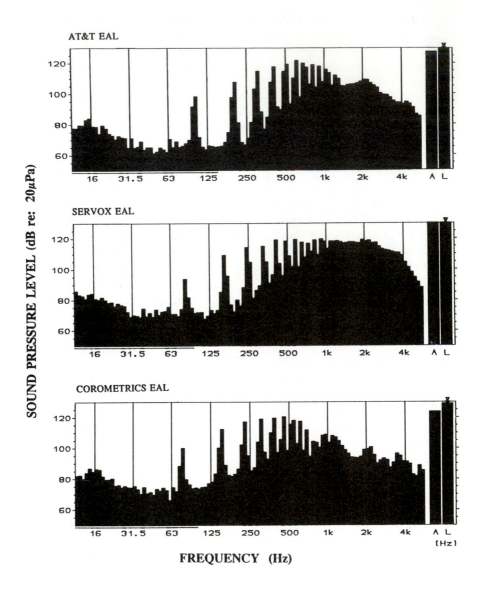

FIG. 5.2. One-twelfth octave band spectra of intrauterine sound pressure levels created during abdominal wall stimulation with an AT&T and Servox EAL, a Corometrics Foetal Acoustic Stimulator. L = linear measurement (total sound pressure produced by energy at all frequencies). A = weighted sound pressures (low frequency energy has been filtered and do not contribute to the measurement). (Reprinted with permission, Abrams et al. 1995)

biophysical and physiological bases for foetal hearing. The following account reviews these accomplishments including results of experiments on transmission of sound and vibration into the uterus. A section on the general foetal response to sounds is followed by a description of recent studies of vibroacoustic stimulation with a double bass and brief commentary on the foetal perception of airborne music.

TRANSMISSION CHARACTERISTICS OF SOUND

There have been scores of articles in which foetal responses have been evaluated following stimulation with continuous airborne and vibroacoustic noise (Abrams et al., 1995b). Synthesised pulsed sounds have also been used as stimuli (Abrams et al., 1993). The abdomen and uterus filter these externally generated sounds before they reach the foetal head (Gerhardt et al., 1990). Sound pressures below 200Hz pass through to the foetus more or less unattenuated. The importance of frequency in determining the sound pressure level in the uterus has been underscored in studies in humans (Visser et al., 1988; Walker, Grimwade & Wood, 1971) and in several recent studies in sheep by the Gainesville group (Gerhardt et al., 1990; Graham, Peters, Abrams, Gerhardt, & Burchfield, 1991; Peters, Abrams, Gerhardt, & Burchfield, 1991a; Peters, Abrams, Gerhardt, & Longmate, 1991b; Peters, Abrams, Gerhardt, & Griffiths, 1993a; Peters, Gerhardt, Abrams, & Longmate, 1993b).

Gerhardt et al. (1990) summarised the results of his studies in sheep and compared them with earlier studies showing the high transmissibility of airborne sounds in low frequencies with progressive attenuation above frequencies of 200–300Hz (Fig. 5.3). In fact, in some experiments with calibrated hydrophones implanted in the uterus of pregnant sheep (Gerhardt et al., 1990; Vince, Billing, Baldwin, Toner, & Moore, 1985) and pregnant women (Richards, Frentzen, Gerhardt, McCann, & Abrams, 1992), an unexplained enhancement of SPL in frequency bands below 250Hz was noted.

In a carefully planned study of transmission of airborne sound from 50–20,000Hz into the abdomen of sheep, Peters et al. (1993a) found sound attenuation to vary inversely as a function of stimulus level for low frequencies (50–125Hz) and for high frequencies (7,000–20,000Hz). At higher stimulus levels (110dB SPL recorded in air), attenuation was greater than the attenuation at lower stimulus levels (90dB). The trend downward in attenuation progressed at a rate of 10dB per octave from a high of 25dB at 12,500Hz. Thus, the stimulus level had a significant effect on sound attenuation for both low and high frequencies (Fig. 5.4). In the mid-frequency range (200–4,000Hz), no effect of stimulus level was found.

Clear illustrations of the importance of signal frequency were given in the reports by Peters et al. (1991b); Peters et al. (1993b) (Figs. 5.5 & 5.6). The

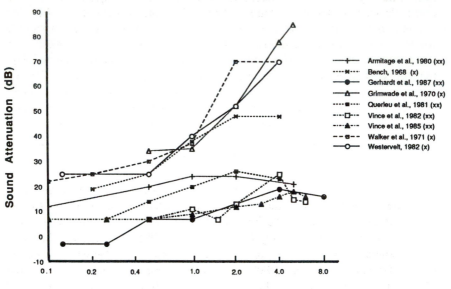

FIG. 5.3. Data from this report are included with the results of eight other studies of sound attenuation in humans and sheep. Earlier studies used microphones covered with rubber sleeves(x) and current studies used calibrated hydrophones(xx). (Reprinted with permission, Gerhardt et al., 1990).

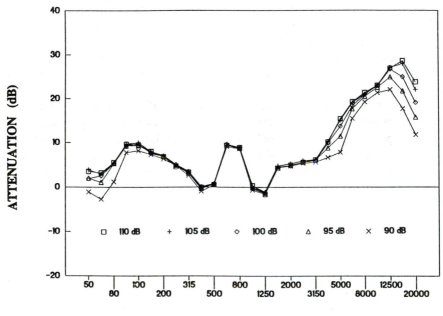

abdominal segments of sheep were stimulated by different frequencies delivered either through a shaker or loudspeaker and recorded with the indwelling hydrophones. During vibroacoustic stimulation with the vibration source applied directly to the abdomen and generating 10 and 100Hz tones, the isosound pressure contours in the abdomen were fairly flat as illustrated in Fig. 5.5. Higher frequencies (2000Hz) produced curved isopressure contours. During airborne sound exposure with a loudspeaker, the contours were much more circular, presenting a somewhat "wrap-around" effect (Fig. 5.6). The maximum attenuation tended to be centrally located, at least at frequencies of 1000Hz and greater. In these studies sine wave stimulation was used, but presumably the same patterns would be produced when one dissected out the frequency bands comprising complex sounds, including music.

In addition to the influence of signal frequency and mode of stimulation (airborne vs. mechanical vibration) on the transmission of sound to the foetus, other factors are important and include: the static force with which the sound generator is placed on the body (Graham et al., 1991); the distance between sound generator and the target, in this case the foetal head (Gerhardt, Abrams, Kovaz, Gomez, & Conlon, 1988); and the dynamic force developed by the vibrator (Peters et al., 1991a). Increasing dynamic force, with static force held constant, significantly increases the generated SPL.

In the experiments just described, the SPL was measured either in the abdominal cavity or in the uterine cavity next to the foetal ear. But what is the degree to which these sounds actually stimulate the hearing of the foetus? Querleu and his colleagues (1989) hypothesised that sound energy in the amniotic fluid passes without resistance through fluids filling the external canal and middle ear cavities into the fluids of the inner ear. A case can be made, however, for bone conduction as the primary route of sounds to the inner ear in conditions where the head is submerged in fluid (Hollien & Feinstein, 1975).

Gerhardt, Otto, Abrams, and Oliver, (1992) quantified the extent to which the foetal auditory system was isolated from sounds produced outside pregnant ewes by comparing cochlear microphonic (CM) amplitudes evoked by airborne external sounds to CM evoked from lambs. The CM is an electrical response generated at the level of the inner ear hair cells and mimics the acoustic stimulus in amplitude and frequency. Thus, the CM can function as a "microphone" located in the inner ear. Sound attenuation was clearly correlated with the signal frequency, with the least isolation (6–17dB) occurring at 125 Hz rising to 27–56dB at 2000 Hz (Fig. 5.7).

FIG. 5.4. Facing page, bottom. Average sound attenuation curves for sheep (n=5) abdomen at five different stimulation levels: 90, 95, 100, 105, and 110dB SPL (L value). Spectrum levels at different frequencies are in 1/3-octaves (re: dB). (Reprinted with permission, Peters et al., 1994a)

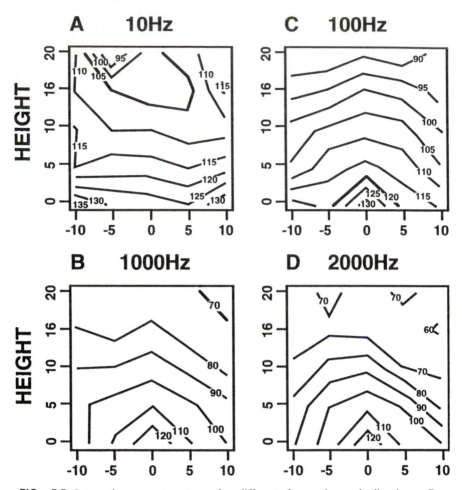

FIG. 5.5. Isosound pressure contours for different frequencies and directions. Cross sectional plane (20 × 20 cm) through the point of vibration on the abdominal midline (reference point, 0). (Reprinted with permission, Peters et al., 1991b)

Acoustic information from external sources is only available to the foetus if the sound levels exceed the noise floor already present in the uterus. The measured noise floor is determined by the sensitivity and dynamic range of the hydrophone. Sound pressures in fluids cannot be measured with microphones normally used to measure pressures in air, because an impedance mismatch prevents calibration to a recognised reference standard that is constant over frequency. Noise sources in the mother include maternal respiratory, cardiovascular, intestinal and laryngeal activity and physical movements (Benzaquen, Gagnon, & Hunse, 1990; Gerhardt et al., 1990; Querleu et al., 1988; Vince et al., 1985) as well as foetal cardiovascular pulsations (unpublished

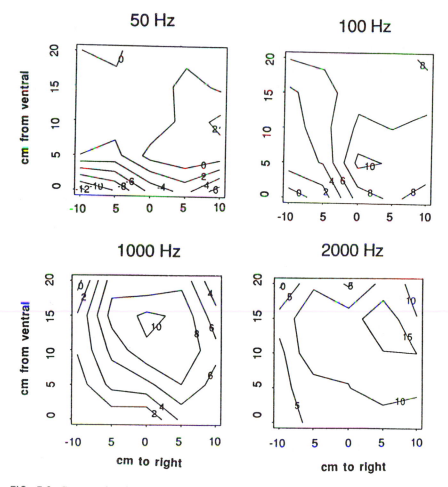

FIG. 5.6. Cross-section isoattenuation contours within sheep abdomen. Airborne broadband noise was delivered to left flank and recorded intraabdominally. Attenuation contours of four selected frequencies are displayed. Contour lines connect points of equal sound attenuation. (Reprinted with permission, Peters et al. 1993b)

observations). The point has been made by Querleu et al. (1988) that all sound data from humans has been gathered after rupture of the membranes, thus potentially overestimating the importance of the background noise.

The noise floor varies slightly with frequency. Higher SPLs (70–80dB), which can be noted in the lower frequency range (<50Hz), result mainly from vibrations normally present in buildings. This raised noise floor is present in intraabdominal recordings in subjects which are not isolated from building vibrations. Reduction in low-frequency noise (up to 10dB) can be achieved by placement of subjects on a platform separated from a concrete floor by a heavy

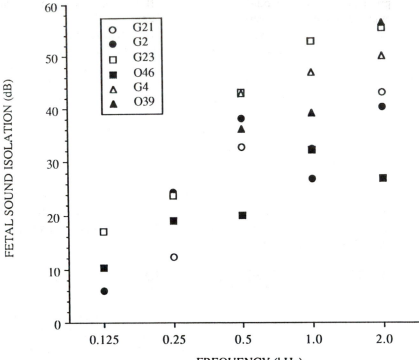

FIG. 5.7. Foetal sound isolation. The average differences between the SPLs in decibels necessary to produce equal cochlear microphonic functions for each frequency recorded from the foetus and the newborn (ex utero CM minus in utero CM). Data points represent values from six animals. (Reprinted with permission, Gerhardt et al. 1992)

steel plate resting on several layers of carpet liner (Peters, Abrams, Gerhardt & Burchfield, 1991a).

FOETAL VESTIBULAR AND MECHANORECEPTOR STIMULATION

The preceding discussion has dealt primarily with the transmission of acoustic information to the foetus. The other important sensory modality subserved by the eighth cranial nerve is vestibular. The vestibular nuclei have exceedingly high rates of glucose utilisation during foetal life (Abrams et al., 1984). This fact, together with the finding of a marked reduction in foetal cerebral glucose utilisation of both vestibular and auditory pathways following mechanical entry into the osseous labyrinth (Abrams , Hutchison, McTiernan, & Merwin, 1987) implies a functional significance of both systems in foetal perception. Foetal movements produced by loud musical sound, a common observation among many pregnant women, would likely evoke fluid movement in foetal semicircular canals and, thus, vestibular nerve activity.

In light of recent measurements of relatively high acceleration levels (m/sec^2) of the foetal skull during vibration of the abdominal wall with an electronic artificial larynx (Abrams et al., 1994), one needs to consider also the participation of cutaneous mechanoreceptors which mature early in development (Hooker, 1952). Another example of the ease with which vibrations in the audible range are transmitted after mechanical stimulation of the abdominal wall is given in Fig. 5.8 at the first overtone the acceleration levels at the head exceeded 300mm/sec^2, while sound pressure levels were about 110dB. These observations prove the existence of good mechanical coupling in the abdominal segment.

It is obviously very important to understand the several features of the transmission of sensory information to the foetus from the uterine environment before proceeding to the more complicated study of perception and cognition of speech and music by foetuses *in utero*.

PERCEPTION OF SPEECH SOUNDS RECORDED WITHIN THE UTERUS

As a result of experimental work, much of it with pregnant sheep, the characteristics of the intrauterine sound environment are now fairly well understood. The determination of the intelligibility of speech sounds recorded in utero has added a further dimension to the understanding of the abundant and changing acoustic surroundings of the foetus. In studies by Querleu and his associates (1988), subjects were asked to reproduce what they could hear when listening to the voices of pregnant women and other male and female speakers recorded with a microphone positioned by the foetal ear. Subjects were able to recognise 30% of 3120 tokens of French phonemes.

Griffiths et al. (1994a) determined the intelligibility of speech stimuli recorded within the uterus of a pregnant sheep using a group of untrained judges (Fig. 5.9). Two separate lists, one of meaningful and one of non-meaningful speech stimuli were delivered to the side of the ewe through a loudspeaker and were simultaneously recorded with an air microphone located 15cm from the flank and with a hydrophone previously sutured to the neck of the foetus. Perceptual test tapes generated from these recordings were played to 102 judges. A male talker's voice was more intelligible than a female talker's voice when recorded from within the uterus, but not so when recorded in the air. An analysis of the feature information from recordings inside and outside the uterus revealed that voicing information was better transmitted *in utero* than place of articulation (e.g. bilabial) or manner of articulation (e.g. plosive) information.

Querleu et al. (1981, 1988) inferred from their earlier analysis of intrauterine sounds that foetuses, like newborn infants, are better able to discriminate intonational patterns compared to linguistic meaning, and that both perception

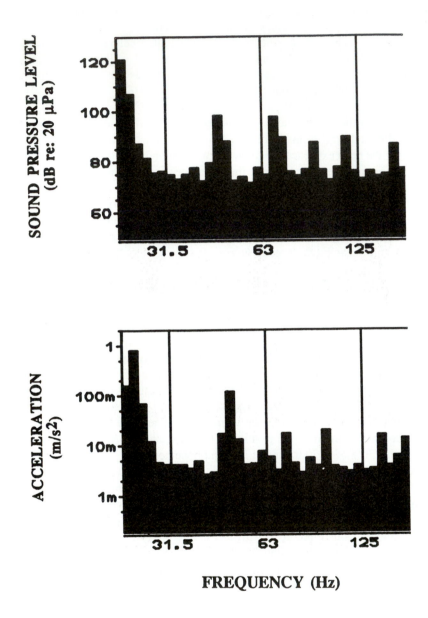

FIG. 5.8. Sound pressure level (dB) recorded with a hydrophone positioned by the sheep foetal head and acceleration levels (mm/s²) of the head during vibration of the maternal abdominal surface with an electric toothbrush.

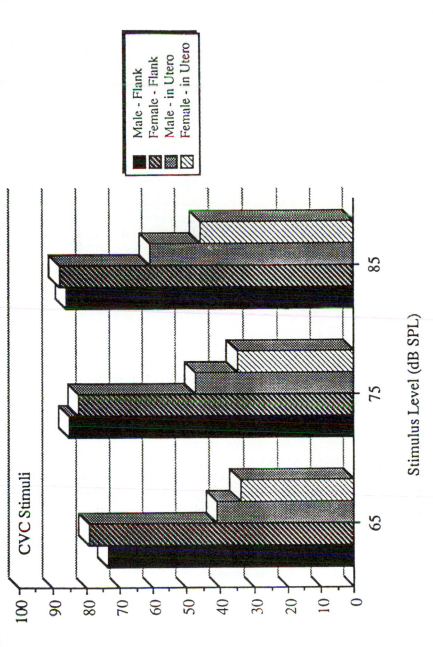

FIG. 5.9. Mean percent intelligibility of CVC words spoken by a male and a female talker recorded at the flank and within the uterus of the sheep at three stimulus levels. (Reprinted with permission, Griffiths et al. 1994a)

95

and discrimination abilities relied on prosodic contours of speech, that is on pitch, stress and rhythm. Clearly, this "thesaurus" of common intonational patterns (Querleu et al., 1988) developed by the foetus would also include those derived from the melodic and rhythmic features of music. As Griffiths, Brown, Gerhardt, Abrams and Morris (1994a) also observed, phonetic information available to the foetus may be much higher than heretofore thought.

TRANSMISSION OF MUSICAL SOUNDS

Vibroacoustic Stimulation with a Double Bass

At the recent meeting of the European Society for the Cognitive Sciences of Music, we presented research in which the transmission of musical sounds was demonstrated (Abrams & Gerhardt, 1994). A pregnant ewe carrying a singleton foetus at 128 days gestation was anaesthetised and a calibrated miniature hydrophone was sutured on the skin overlying the temporal bone. Thirteen days later the pregnant ewe was moved into a large open area in the laboratory and restrained in a stanchion fitted loosely about the neck. The wool on the right side of the abdominal segment and flank was sheared. The back of an upright double bass was placed against this side of the ewe while four open strings of the instrument were bowed in succession.

The output of the hydrophone (Bruel and Kjaer [B&K], model 8103) was conditioned and amplified with a charge amplifier (B&K, type 2635). The signal was fed through a high-pass filter, (Khron-Hite, model 3550) with a low-frequency cutoff at 60Hz and into a frequency analyser (B&K, type 2123) which uses constant percentage bandwidth filters. The air-borne SPL of the instrument was recorded using a sound level meter (B&K, type 2203) and a 1/2 inch microphone. Both hydrophone and microphone signals were also simultaneously recorded on a multichannel FM tape recorder (B&K, type 7006).

Plots of four intrauterine and four airborne spectra were acoustically evaluated. An example of the spectra developed from bowing an open "G" string is given in the Fig. 5.10. The intrauterine sounds were above the intrauterine noise floor at all frequencies studied (46–8000Hz). When the open A and G strings were bowed, the linear value of the intrauterine sound pressure was slightly greater than that in air. The fundamental frequencies were clearly evident as spikes in all the spectra at the known frequencies of the vibrating open strings. In the case of the G string, the spike was seen in the 1/12 octave band centered at 97Hz. A number of overtones were evident in the spectra from airborne sound, but were reduced considerably in spectra recorded with the hydrophone.

Airborne Stimulation with Classical Music

In other experiments in pregnant sheep we recorded both the foetal cochlear microphonic level and *in utero* sound pressure with a hydrophone during a brief period of exposure to the well known theme of the first movement of

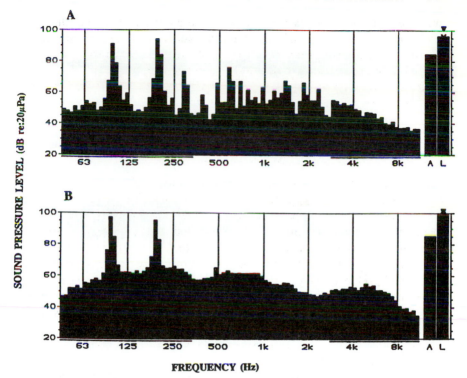

FIG. 5.10. One-twelfth octave band spectra in response to bowing an open G string of a double bass held against the flank of a standing ewe. A. Spectrum recorded in air 0.5m from the bridge of the instrument. B. Spectrum recorded *in utero* with a miniature hydrophone attached to the head of the foetus.

Beethoven's Fifth Symphony. As described earlier, the ewe was anaesthetised and supine, and the foetus was exteriorised through a midline incision. An incision was made over the foetal bulla caudal and posterior to the pinna, and the round window was located using an operating microscope. Electrode placement and CM signal recording methods have been described by Gerhardt et al. (1992). A miniature hydrophone was positioned next to the foetal head. The bulla was closed and the head was replaced in the uterus. A loudspeaker was positioned one meter from the side of the operating table. CMs were recorded during 20 seconds of this music and were compared in time with SPLs recorded from the hydrophone and a microphone situated in air 2 inches over the umbilicus.

A panel showing the time course of the three signals is presented in Fig. 5.11. The time waveforms give not only a comparison of the relative attenuation of the sound as it passes first through the abdominal wall, abdominal contents, uterus and fluid, but also the information content of the signal in the two intrauterine locations. Playback of both hydrophone and CM recordings leave no doubt in listeners' minds of the specific piece being played.

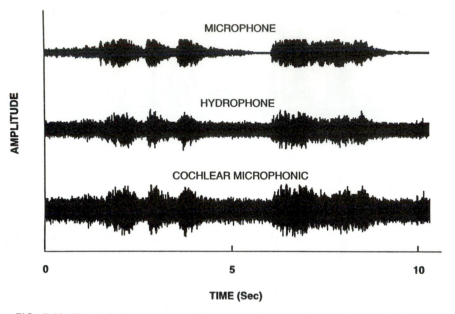

FIG. 5.11. Electrical signals generated by a microphone in air, a hydrophone in the uterus and cochlear microphonic of a foetal sheep in utero during a segment of the first movement of Beethoven's Fifth Symphony.

Whether or not the foetus is capable of detecting airborne musical stimuli depends upon a number of factors including: the sensitivity of the auditory system; the internal noise floor; the extent to which the signal is filtered as it passes through tissues and fluids surrounding the foetal head and into the inner ear; and the signal level. The foetal inner ear is well developed and fully functional during the later stages of pregnancy (last trimester) (Pujol et al., 1990). The magnitude of the external signal that produces a response threshold is dependent upon the energy level that reaches the inner ear. The noise floor in the uterus is quite high (80dB SPL) for frequencies below 60Hz. This is roughly equivalent to the lowest note on the piano. Above this frequency, the noise floor is fairly constant at about 60dB SPL. Thus, an external signal must exceed these levels before detection can occur. Filtering is another significant process that influences the detectability of external signals.

Airborne musical stimuli that reach the foetal peripheral system are filtered first by the tissues and fluids surrounding the foetus and a second time by the structures that conduct the sound into the inner ear. The results from a study of CM input-output functions obtained from foetuses and lambs suggest that airborne signals are low-pass filtered with a high frequency cut-off between 500–1000Hz and a rejection rate of greater than 10dB/octave. We can conclude from this study, (and ignoring for a moment the influence of the noise floor) that the foetus probably will not be privy to frequency information above 500–1000Hz unless it is presented to the mother at an uncomfortably loud level. On the other hand, low frequencies, those carried in the bass register, will be easily detected by the foetus when presented to the mother at normal listening levels.

Now, let us consider the levels of the musical stimulus that can be detected by the foetus given both the internal noise floor effects and sound filtering effects. We can assume that for frequencies below 60Hz that airborne signal levels must exceed 80dB SPL before threshold is reached. From 60 to 250Hz the noise floor is relatively low (<60dB) and foetal sound isolation is less than 20dB. Consequently, in this frequency region, the foetus can probably detect musical sounds when present to the mother at about 80dB SPL. For frequencies of 500Hz and above, foetal sound isolation is quite high, exceeding 40dB. Airborne signals would have to exceed 100dB in order to reach the threshold of hearing for these higher frequencies. From this, we conclude that the foetus is probably detecting only the fundamental frequencies of a musical passage. Very little high frequency information would be detected.

CONCLUSION

Sound pressure levels as well as vibration levels can be well above the intrauterine noise floor. The degree to which airborne music is heard by the foetus depends on the attenuation features of the abdominal surface (high frequency sound is attenuated considerably), the distance to the foetal head and the low pass features of bone conduction. Music produced by mechanical vibrators against the skin is transmitted more effectively and with less attenuation to the amniotic fluid. The profile of intrauterine sound pressures differs from that produced by airborne sound. Sound pressure levels are determined also by the static and dynamic forces of vibrators.

In sheep, as in humans, the peripheral and central components of the auditory system are formed and functional prior to birth. Reflex responses to touch stimuli, present early in pregnancy (Bradley & Mistretta, 1975), indicate that mechanoreception may be a second source of stimulation by musical vibrations. Mechanical vibrations of the abdominal surface results in acceleration levels well above background at the foetal head.

REFERENCES

Abrams, R.M., & Gerhardt, K.J. (1994). Fetal Sound Environment. In I. Deliège, (Ed.), *Proceedings of the Third International Conference for the Perception and Cognition of Music* (pp. 95–96). Liège, Belgium: European Society for the Cognitive Sciences of Music.

Abrams, R.M., Gerhardt, K.J., Peters, A.J.M., & Rosa, C. (1995a). Fetal Acoustic Test: Stimulus features of three artificial larynges recorded in sheep. *American Journal of Obstetrics and Gynecology, 173*, 1372–1376.

Abrams, R.M., Gerhardt, K.J., Richards, D.S., & Peters, A.J.M. (1995b). Foetal vibroacoustic stimulation test: Features of the stimulus. *Fetal and Maternal Medicine Review, 7*, 87–97.

Abrams, R.M., Hutchison A.A., McTiernan M. J. & Merwin, G.E. (1987). Effects of cochlear ablation on local cerebral glucose utilization in fetal sheep. *American Journal of Obstetrics and Gynecology, 157,* 1438–1442.

Abrams, R.M., Ito, M., Frisinger J.E., Patlak C.S., Pettigrew, K.D. & Kennedy, C. (1984). Local cerebral glucose utilization in fetal and neonatal sheep. *American Journal of Physiology, 246,* R608–R618.

Abrams, R.M., & Peters, A.J.M. (1993). Foetal response to vibroacoustic stimulation in sheep: Effect on behavioral state. *International Congress of Physiological Sciences, 236A.*

Abrams, R.M., Peters, A.J.M., & Gerhardt, K.J. (1994). Effect of abdominal vibroacoustic stimulation on acceleration levels at the fetal head in sheep. *The Physiologist, 34,* A–13.

Armitage, S.E., Baldwin, B.A., & Vince, M.A. (1980). The foetal sound environment of sheep. *Science, 208,* 1173–1174.

Benzaquen, S., Gagnon, R., & Hunse, C. (1990). The intrauterine sound environment of the human fetus during labor. *American Journal of Obstetrics and Gynecology, 163,* 484–490.

Bench, R.J. (1968). Sound transmission to the fetus through the maternal abdominal wall. *Journal of Genetic Psychology, 113,* 85–87.

Bradley, R.M., & Mistretta, C.M. (1975). Fetal sensory receptors. *Physiological Reviews, 55,* 352–382.

Gagnon, R. (1989) Stimulation of human fetuses with sound and vibration. *Seminars in Perinatology, 13,* 393–402.

Gagnon, R., Hunse, C., Carmichael, L., Fellows, F., & Patrick, J. (1987). Human fetal responses to vibratory acoustic stimulation from twenty-six week to term. *American Journal of Obstetrics and Gynecology, 157,* 1375–1384, 1987.

Gerhardt, K.J., Abrams, R.M., Kovaz, B.M., Gomez, K.J., & Conlon, M. (1988). Intrauterine noise levels in pregnant ewes produced by sound applied to the abdomen. *American Journal of Obstetrics and Gynecology, 159,* 228–232.

Gerhardt, K.J., Abrams, R.M., & Oliver, C.C. (1990). Sound environment of the fetal sheep. *American Journal of Obstetrics and Gynecology, 162,* 282–287.

Gerhardt, K.J., Otto, R., Abrams, R.M., Colle, J.J., Burchfield, D.J., & Peters, A.J.M. (1992). Cochlear microphones recorded from fetal and newborn sheep. *American Journal of Otolaryngology, 13,* 226–233.

Graham, E.M., Peters, A.J.M., Abrams, R.M., Gerhardt, K.J., & Burchfield, D.J. (1991). Intraabdominal sound levels during vibroacoustic stimulation. *American Journal of Obstetrics and Gynecology, 164,* 1140–1144.

Grimwade, J.C., Walker, D.W., & Wood, C. (1970). Sensory stimulation of the human fetus. *Australian Journal of Mental Retardation, 2,* 63–64.

Griffiths, S.K., Brown, W.S., Gerhardt, K.J., Abrams, R.M., & Morris, R.J. (1994). The perception of speech sounds recorded within the uterus of a pregnant sheep. *Journal of Acoustical Society of America, 96,* 2055–2063.

Griffiths, S.K., Pierson, L.L., Gerhardt, K.J., Abrams, R.M., & Peters, A.J.M. (1994). Noise induced hearing loss in fetal sheep. *Hearing Research, 74,* 221–230.

Henderson, D., & Hamernik, R.P. (1986). Impulse noise: A critical review. *Journal of Acoustical Society of America, 80,* 569–584.

Hollien, H. & Feinstein, S. (1975). Contribution of the external auditory meatus to auditory sensitivity underwater. *Journal of the Acoustical Society of America, 57,* 1488–1492.

Hooker, D. (1952). *The prenatal origin of behavior.* Lawrence, KS: University of Kansas Press.

Nyman, M., Arulkumaran, S., Hsu, T.S., Ratman, S.S., Till, O., & Westgren, M. (1991). Vibroacoustic stimulation and intrauterine sound pressure levels. *Obstetrics and Gynecology, 78,* 803–806.

Peters, A.J.M., Abrams, R.M., Gerhardt, K.J., & Burchfield, D.J. (1991a). Vibration of the abdomen in non-pregnant sheep: effect of dynamic force and surface area of vibrator. *Journal of Low Frequency Noise and Vibration, 10,* 92–99.

Peters, A.J.M., Abrams, R.M., Gerhardt, K.J., & Longmate, J.A. (1991b). Three dimensional sound and vibration frequency response of the sheep abdomen. *Journal of Low Frequency Noise and Vibration, 10,* 100–111.

Peters, A.J.M., Abrams, R.M., Gerhardt, K.J., & Griffiths, S.K. (1993a). Transmission of airborne sound from 50–20,000 Hz into the abdomen of sheep. *Journal of Low Frequency Noise and Vibration, 12,* 16–24.

Peters, A.J.M., Gerhardt, K.J., Abrams, R.M., & Longmate, J.A. (1993b). Three-dimensional intraabdominal sound pressures in sheep produced by airborne stimuli. *American Journal of Obstetrics and Gynecology, 169,* 1304–1315.

Pujol, R., Lavigne-Rebillard, M., & Uziel, A. (1990). Physiological correlates of development of the human cochlea. *Seminars in Perinatology, 14,* 275–280.

Querleu, Q., Renard, X., Bontteville, C., & Crepin, G. (1989) Hearing by the human fetus? *Seminars in Perinatology, 13,* 409–420.

Querleu, Q., Renard, X., & Crepin, G. (1981). Perception auditive et réactivité foetale aux stimulations sonores. *J. Gynecol Obstet Biol Reprod, 10,* 307–314.

Querleu, Q., Renard, X., Versyp, F., Paris-Delrue, L., & Crepin, G. (1988). Fetal hearing. *European Journal of Obstetrics and Gynecology and Reproductive Biology, 29,* 191–212.

Richards, D.S. (1990). The fetal vibroacoustic stimulation test: An update. *Seminars in Perinatology, 14,* 305–310.

Richards, D.S., Frentzen, B., Gerhardt, K.J., McCann, M.E., & Abrams, R.M. (1992). Sound levels in the human fetus. *Obstetrics and Gynecology, 80,* 186–190.

Vince, M.A., Billing, A.E., Baldwin, B.A., Toner, J., & Moore, B.C.J. (1982). The sound environment of the fetal sheep. *Behaviour, 81,* 296–315.

Vince, M.A., Billing, A.E., Baldwin, B.A., Toner, J., & Weller, C. (1985). Maternal vocalizations and other sounds in the fetal lamb's sound environment. *Early Human Development, 11,* 179–190.

Visser, G.H.A., Mulder, H.H., Wit, H.P., & Prechtl, H.F.R. (1988). Vibroacoustic stimulation of the human fetus: effect on fetal well-being. *Obstetrics and Gynecology, 71,* 781–786.

Walker, D., Grimwade, J., & Wood, C. (1971). Intrauterine noise: A component of the fetal environment. *American Journal of Obstetrics and Gynecology, 109,* 91–95.

Westervelt, P.J. (1982). Prenatal effects of exposure to high level noise. In *Committee on Hearing, Bioacoustics, and Biomechanics. Assembly of Behavioral and Social Sciences. Report of working group 85. National Research Council.* Washington, D.C.: National Academic Press.

Wollack, C.H. (1963). The auditory acuity of the sheep (ovis aries). *Journal of Auditory Research, 3,* 121–132.

6 The origins of music perception and cognition: A developmental perspective

S. Trehub
Centre for Research in Human Development, University of Toronto, Canada
G. Schellenberg
Department of Psychology, University of Windsor, Canada
D. Hill
Centre for Research in Human Development, University of Toronto, Canada

The abilities of infants and young children may seem largely irrelevant to the consideration of musical abilities in general. Aside from isolated instances of precocity (e.g. Wolfgang Amadeus Mozart, Michael Jackson), the music production capabilities of young children are rather limited. It is conceivable, however, that perceptual competencies in early life play a substantial role in music perception and cognition later in life. Nevertheless, music processing by adult listeners is generally believed to depend, for the most part, on long-term exposure to particular musical styles (e.g. Bharucha, 1987; Lerdahl & Jackendoff, 1983; Krumhansl, 1990). For example, Lerdahl and Jackendoff's (1983) influential theory applies largely to Western tonal music and to expert listeners. Empirical research tends to indicate, moreover, that knowledge of the principal structures of Western music (i.e. its scales and harmonies) develops throughout childhood (Krumhansl & Keil, 1982; Trainor & Trehub, 1994), becoming especially evident in adults with musical training (Krumhansl & Kessler, 1982; Krumhansl & Shepard, 1979).

Because structurally important tones in Western tonal music are characterised by a higher frequency of occurrence and by longer durations than structurally unimportant tones, listeners could progressively extract such regularities (Krumhansl, 1990) and construct implicit theories, or schemas, that guide future listening experiences (Jones, 1982; Schmuckler, 1989, 1990). Such schemas have been called extra-opus influences (Narmour 1990, 1992), insights brought to a musical piece on the basis of previous exposure to the style in question; intra-opus influences result from regularities within a particular piece of music. One apparent consequence of long-term exposure to a musical style is that adults' processing of musical passages is maximally efficient for passages that conform to the extra-opus schemas such as those involving scale structure (Cuddy, Cohen & Mewhort, 1981; Cuddy, Cohen & Miller, 1979).

Although some researchers acknowledge that music processing builds on fundamental principles of auditory pattern perception (Bregman, 1990; Handel, 1989), they have not attempted to delineate the relative contributions of primitive and higher-order strategies to music listening. The music theorist Eugene Narmour (1990, 1992) is a notable exception in this regard, but he would be the first to concede that the task is daunting. In the case of adult listeners, it is difficult, if not impossible, to disentangle primitive, or natural, strategies of pattern processing from learned or habitual strategies (see Schellenberg, 1996, for one such attempt). Musically untrained adults do not present a *tabula rasa*; they have had years of informal exposure to the music of their culture. There are suggestions, in fact, that music perception is fundamentally similar in listeners with varying degrees of musical sophistication (Cuddy & Badertscher, 1987; Bharucha & Stoeckig, 1986, 1987), presumably because of common learning opportunities, whether formal or informal.

The skills of very young listeners, however, would be unconfounded with extended exposure to a particular style of music. Indeed, infants' limited intellectual capacity and even more limited experience would qualify them as suitably naive listeners, such that their music processing skills could be appropriately attributed to biological predispositions (see Trehub & Trainor, 1993; Trehub & Unyk, 1991). In other words, adult-infant similarities in music processing would provide suggestive evidence of contributions from nature, shedding light, perhaps, on the origin of musical structures. We do not deny the possibility of some effects of exposure in the prenatal (e.g. DeCasper, Lecanuet, Busnel, Granier-Deferre & Maugeais, 1994) or early postnatal (Kuhl, Williams, Lacerda, Stevens & Lindblom, 1992) period. Nevertheless, such effects would be consistent with the notion of biologically based attentional or learning preferences (Marler, 1990).

Although a developmental inquiry into the rudiments of music listening is potentially valuable, is such an enterprise feasible? Obviously, infants cannot make aesthetic judgements nor can they name familiar tunes. What they can do, however, is to indicate their differentiation of one pattern from another by means of nonverbal responses. When infants hear auditory patterns or melodies, for example, they exhibit characteristic attentional responses such as heart rate deceleration (e.g. Chang & Trehub, 1977) or turning toward the sound source (Trehub, 1985). We can encourage them to respond reliably (e.g. head turning) to audible changes in such patterns by providing visual rewards (e.g. animated toys) for "correct" responses. By experimentally familiarising infants with various auditory patterns and selectively altering particular features, we can determine which aspects of musical patterns are salient and discriminable for infants and which are not. The typical procedure, a variant of the same-different task, involves presenting infant subjects with repetitions of a background, or standard, stimulus and training them to turn when a comparison stimulus replaces one of the background stimuli (for details see Trehub, Bull & Thorpe, 1984; Trehub, Thorpe & Morrongiello, 1987). The assumption is that infants' mental representation of the standard stimulus will affect their responses to the comparison stimulus.

INFANTS ARE MUSIC LISTENERS

Before getting immersed in a sea of hypotheses and data from music theory, ethnomusicology, and empirical research, it is reasonable to establish that the principal questions of interest are relevant to infants. If music is viewed essentially as organised sound (Cook, 1990; Sloboda, 1985; Trehub & Schellenberg, 1995) and music listening as the perception of form or structure in sound (Budd, 1985; Francès, 1958/1988), then it is not a foregone conclusion that infants are bona fide music listeners. One way of translating this abstract query into concrete terms is to ask whether infants perceive a musical passage as a coherent pattern or, instead, as a series of discrete, unrelated events.

Fortunately, there is a growing body of evidence that confirms infants' disposition to structure or organise the elements of auditory patterns in adult-like ways (Trehub, 1985, 1987, 1993). For example, infants, like adults, categorise complex tones (tones with multiple overtones) on the basis of pitch (Clarkson & Clifton, 1985), and they group the component tones of auditory sequences on the basis of similarity in pitch, timbre, or loudness (Demany, 1982; Thorpe & Trehub, 1989; Thorpe, Trehub, Morrongiello & Bull, 1988). Moreover, they recognise multi-tone patterns across variations in tempo (Trehub & Thorpe, 1989) and pitch level (Trehub et al., 1987), and they perceive the timbral similarity of complex tones across variations in pitch, loudness, and duration (Trehub, Endman & Thorpe, 1990). In short, factors that promote the temporal coherence or connectedness of auditory sequences for adult listeners (Bregman, 1990, 1993) do likewise for infant listeners (Trehub, 1990). Our consideration of music listening and its origins in the remaining pages focuses primarily on pitch relations and secondarily on harmonic relations.

INFANTS ARE SENSITIVE TO MELODIC CONTOUR

Many music theorists consider the shape or curve of a melody line to be fundamental to the aesthetic appeal of a musical passage (Hindemith, 1937/1942; Salzer & Schachter, 1969) and an important indicator of style (Gjerdingen, 1988; Jeppesen, 1931/1939). Indeed, empirical research with adult listeners has confirmed that the most prominent feature of an unfamiliar melody is its melodic contour (see Dowling, 1978, 1982a), leading some scholars to speculate that sensitivity to melodic contour is a musical universal (Dowling & Harwood, 1986; Harwood, 1976).

After hearing a novel melodic fragment for the first time, musically untrained adults are likely to remember little more than its contour (Bartlett & Dowling, 1980; Dowling, 1978). When the structure of the fragment is unfamiliar, even trained listeners have difficulty remembering its component intervals although they may encode their relative size (i.e. which are smaller, larger) (Dowling & Fujitani, 1971). After a brief lapse of time, however, neither trained nor untrained listeners have access to the exact pitch levels of familiar or unfamiliar melodies recently presented to them (Deutsch, 1975), except for the very few trained listeners who have absolute pitch (see Takeuchi & Hulse, 1993; Ward & Burns, 1982). What this means is that the starting note of a song is irrelevant to its identity. What matters, instead, are the relations between successive tones. For novel melodies, then, changes in intervals that preserve the contour of a melody largely go unnoticed. For well known materials, however, or for melodies conforming to familiar musical principles, adults readily detect interval changes (Bartlett & Dowling, 1980; Dowling & Fujitani, 1971; Cuddy et al., 1981) and may even notice slight tuning deviations (Watkins, 1985).

Could relational pitch processing be a product of experience? Because songs are freely transposed in everyday life, we might be inclined to ignore absolute pitch levels, focusing instead on relations among pitches. Thus, typical tune processing strategies need not reflect fundamental difficulties in absolute pitch processing but rather a reasonable adaptation to prevailing conventions. The evidence, for the most part, points to difficulties. For example, adults are unable to recall or recognise the exact pitch level of a three-tone sequence heard thousands of times at the same pitch level over an extended period (Attneave & Olson, 1971).

If adults have difficulty encoding and retaining absolute pitch information, should one expect anything different from infants? Perhaps. Possessors of absolute pitch (for a review see Takeuchi & Hulse, 1993) have generally had extensive music exposure or training in childhood, raising the possibility that absolute pitch processing precedes relational pitch processing. In the usual developmental course of events, the more mature strategy (relational pitch processing) would supersede the less mature strategy (absolute pitch processing). For some musically experienced children, however, relational pitch processing, once instituted, would co-exist with absolute pitch processing. Interestingly, non-human species are inclined to respond non-relationally to complex stimuli (Premack, 1983). For example, differential responding to contrasting tunes on the part of rats, songbirds, and monkeys is based on the absolute pitch of one or more tones (D'Amato, 1988; Hulse & Page, 1988).

The human developmental findings on absolute pitch are also consistent with the possibility that absolute and relational pitch processing are simultaneously present in early life, and that extensive exposure or training within some critical time frame (e.g. before 6 years of age) is necessary for the maintenance of absolute pitch processing. Nevertheless, these alternative strategies do not generate mutually exclusive predictions about infants' processing of melodies. Suffice it to say that if melody perception in infancy is like that in adulthood, it would be dominated by contour processing. Adults' processing of novel melodies is obviously most relevant here, because all melodies are novel for infant listeners, except for the specific lullabies and play songs that regularly accompany caregiving activities for particular infants (Trehub & Schellenberg, 1995).

Indeed, the available evidence indicates that infants' mental representation of melodies is based primarily on melodic contour. When 8-month-old infants are presented with repeating melodic fragments such as those in Fig. 6.1, their discrimination of contour changes is significantly better than their discrimination of key changes (i.e. transpositions) or interval changes that preserve the contour of the original melody (Trehub et al., 1984, Experiment 1). When the task is made more difficult by increasing the silent interval between pattern repetitions (e.g. from 0.8 seconds to 2.6 seconds) and filling it with distractor tones (see Fig. 6.1b and c), infants are no longer able to detect the key and interval changes but they readily detect the contour changes (Trehub et al., 1984, Experiment 2). The representation of contour information is so robust that 5-month-old infants can detect contour changes even when standard and comparison atonal melodies are separated by 15 seconds (Chang & Trehub, 1977). Furthermore, infants detect contour changes resulting from the displacement of a single tone of a six-tone melody (Trehub, Thorpe & Morrongiello, 1985) or from simply reordering the component tones (Trehub et al., 1984), but they are often unable to detect changes in three or more tones when such changes preserve the contour (Trehub et al., 1984).

Because the standard and comparison melodies in the aforementioned studies were presented at the same pitch level, infants could have performed the discriminations on the basis of absolute pitch cues. If absolute pitch processing functioned as the primary strategy, however, infants should have performed best when the standard melody was transposed, the only change that involved all new tones. Instead, transpositions led to the poorest performance levels, implying that the relations between tones were of greatest relevance to infant listeners, as they would be for adults. In a further study (Trehub et al., 1987), the standard five-tone melodies were repeated at different pitch levels on successive presentations, either with the same intervals (i.e. transpositions, see Fig.6. 2a) or with altered intervals but the same contour (Fig. 6.2b). Infants readily detected contour changes in both contexts, even though absolute pitch cues were no longer available. Because performance did not differ in the context of key or

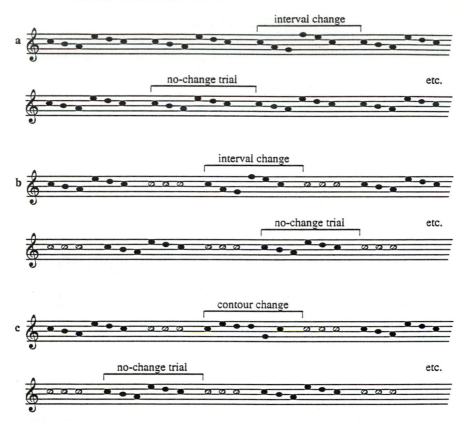

FIG. 6.1. Sample change and no-change trials used with infants in Trehub et al. (1984). Note that standard and comparison patterns are presented at the same pitch level. The addition of interpolated tones (highlighted) between the standard and comparison melodies in examples b and c increases the difficulty of the task.

key-plus-interval variations, it is reasonable to conclude that infants were focusing largely on contour. In short, infants' processing of tone sequences seems much like adults' processing of novel melodies, with melodic contour dominating over exact pitch and interval information.

Pitch level is not entirely irrelevant to melodic processing in infancy. When the pitch range of the comparison melody differs substantially from that of the standard melody, infants readily differentiate same-contour melodies (Trehub et al., 1984). Thus, infants encode crude information about pitch range along with information about melodic contour. In some contexts, however, infants go beyond global processing strategies related to contour and pitch range. For example, they selectively attend to the first and last tones of a sequence and to the points of contour change (Schellenberg & Trehub, 1994b; Trainor & Trehub, 1993b), also known as contour reversals or corners (Dyson & Watkins, 1984).

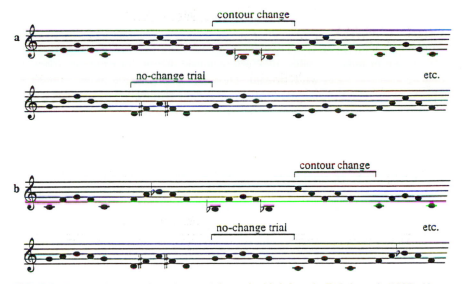

FIG. 6.2. Sample change and no-change trials used with infants in Trehub et al. (1987). Note that successive patterns are presented at different pitch levels. Repetitions of the standard pattern are transposed in example a; repetitions in example b alter the component intervals but maintain the contour.

When the melodies are relatively simple and are not transposed, infants encode more precise information about absolute pitch, detecting small changes to one tone of a melody (Lynch & Eilers, 1992; Lynch, Eilers, Oller & Urbano, 1990; Trehub, Cohen, Thorpe & Morrongiello, 1986). Moreover, even though intervals are less salient for infant listeners than is contour, especially when melodies are presented in transposition, there are circumstances in which infants successfully encode interval information (see Trehub & Trainor, 1993). In such instances, however, it is apparent that not all intervals are created equal.

INFANTS AND YOUNG CHILDREN ARE SENSITIVE TO OCTAVES

Dowling and Harwood (1986) identify octaves and the subdivision of octaves into five to seven discrete pitches as musical universals. Moreover, they consider octave equivalence (i.e. the similarity or equivalence of tones an octave apart) to be virtually the only property of intervals that is a direct consequence of the structure of the auditory system. By contrast, constraints on the number of discrete pitches per octave probably stem from cognitive limitations (Miller, 1956). Thus, although the tonal material within an octave may be constrained by cognitive processing resources, octave equivalence makes it possible to use the same pitch classes in successively higher or lower octaves, thereby increasing the number of available tones without substantially increasing the cognitive demands (Krumhansl, 1990).

In this manner, octave equivalence provides the psychological scaffolding for the use of musical scales. In Western music theory, for example, tones an octave apart (i.e. tones with the same chroma) are considered to be similar and more closely related than other tone combinations (Aldwell & Schachter, 1989). This similarity is reflected in their common designation (e.g. C, D, E, etc.; *doh*, *re*, *mi*, etc.), and the fact that intervals greater than an octave (i.e. compound intervals) are considered to have the same musical properties as those smaller than an octave (i.e. simple intervals) as long as the pitch classes of the two component tones remain the same (Aldwell & Schachter, 1989).

Exposure to complex tones, such as those of speech and music, could provide opportunities for learning about octave relations relatively early in life (Terhardt, 1984), because the first overtone of a harmonic complex tone is an octave above its fundamental frequency. Such early learning could reflect innate attentional preferences (Marler, 1990) for speech-like stimuli (Fernald, 1992), as Terhardt (1984) has proposed. Although this view does not implicate hard-wiring specifically for octave relations, it piggybacks on other predispositions and is consistent with the notion of octave universality. Alternatively, the octave may have favoured status by virtue of being the only interval for which all overtones of the higher tone are also overtones of the lower tone (Burns & Ward, 1982). Yet another possibility concerns the simple relations between the frequencies of tones an octave apart, which stand in a ratio of 2:1. Thus, a tone whose fundamental frequency is 200Hz is one octave above a tone with a 100Hz fundamental. Although some scholars have speculated that the simple pattern of two such tones sounded simultaneously and in phase (i.e. two cycles of the higher tone for every cycle of the lower tone) creates a pleasant sensation for listeners because of regularity in the pattern of neuronal firing (Boomsliter & Creel, 1961; Patterson, 1986; Roederer, 1979), evidence in support of this hypothesis is lacking (Burns & Ward, 1982).

Adding to the credence of octaves as natural features is their presence in virtually all musical cultures (Dowling & Harwood, 1986). As Dowling (1982b) notes, however, musical cultures would not necessarily capitalise on the special perceptual status of octaves (see also Lerdahl & Jackdendoff, 1983). Some scholars consider octaves to be absent in Javanese gamelan music because of the tendency for tunings of slendro and pelog scales to differ slightly from octave to octave (Hood, 1969; Lentz, 1965). Nevertheless, tones a near-octave apart are treated as musically "equivalent" and are given the same note name or number in Javanese notation (Sutton, 1991).

Tuning variations in Javanese octaves may stem from the prevalence of brass, gong-like instruments whose overtones are not exact integer multiples of one another (Burns & Ward, 1982). Alternatively, octaves, perhaps even identical pitches across instruments, may be deliberately mistuned to add depth to sonorities by virtue of the amplitude oscillations that result from tones that are close but not identical in pitch (Hood, 1971). Indeed, this principle of slight mistunings is used systematically in Balinese gamelan ensembles to produce a "shimmering" sound quality (Hood, 1971, p. 38). Mistuning of octaves is not limited to Javanese (or Balinese) music. Western piano tunings have slightly stretched octaves (Dowling & Harwood, 1986), but these stretched octaves retain their special status. Moreover, when listeners attempt to adjust two pure tones so that they are an octave apart, the resulting "octaves" are slightly larger than a 2:1 frequency ratio (see Burns & Ward, 1982), a phenomenon that is not limited to listeners from Western musical cultures (Dowling & Harwood, 1986). These findings imply that processing predispositions would not be restricted to exact 2:1 frequency ratios but rather to ratios closely approximating 2:1.

Oddly enough, empirical support for enhanced processing of octave relations by adult listeners is equivocal. For one thing, octave equivalence is by no means absolute. For example, octave displacements of tones interfere with the recognition of familiar melodies (Deutsch, 1972), especially if the displacements alter the contour of a melody (Dowling & Hollombe, 1977; Idson & Massaro, 1978). Octave displacements of tones can even interfere with infants' recognition of experimentally familiarised melodies (Trehub et al., 1984). In some studies, moreover, only musically trained adults rate tones an octave apart as more similar than tones slightly less than or slightly more than an octave apart (Allen, 1967; Kallman, 1982). There are indications, however, that methodological factors are implicated in the apparent absence of octave equivalence in untrained listeners (Schellenberg & Trehub, 1994a, 1994b, Smith, Kemler Nelson, Grohskopf & Appleton, 1994). In any case, octave similarity would seem to be a more appropriate designation than octave equivalence for the phenomenon in question.

To examine possible processing advantages for octaves on the part of 6-year-olds who had never taken music lessons, we evaluated their ability to detect changes to sequential tones an octave apart (Schellenberg & Trehub, 1996a). The children heard three successive five-tone patterns, each pattern consisting of two different pure tones (low-high-low-high-low), with the second and third patterns transposed two semitones higher relative to the preceding pattern (see Fig. 6.3). For the first two patterns, the distance between the low and high tones was always an octave. On experimental (change) trials, the octave interval was altered by displacing the top tone by one semitone from an exact transposition (forming a major seventh—11 semitones, or a minor ninth—13 semitones). On control (no-change) trials, the third pattern was also an octave. Children were simply required to indicate whether or not the interval in the third pattern had changed. Another group of children were tested on their ability to detect changes from major sevenths or minor ninths to octaves.

For some children, then, the octave was the standard pattern, and the major seventh or minor ninth were comparison patterns (see Fig. 6.3a). For other

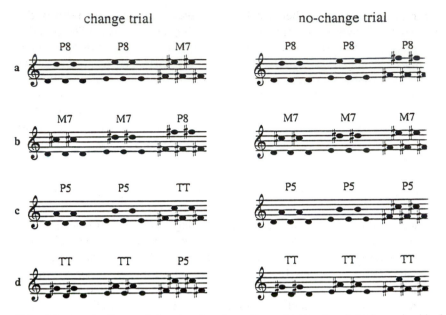

FIG. 6.3. Sample change (left column) and no-change (right column) trials used with 6-year-old children in Schellenberg and Trehub (1996a). Ascending transpositions were used on successive presentations of the patterns on all trials.

children, the major seventh or minor ninth served as standard patterns and the octave was the comparison pattern (see Fig. 6.3b). More efficient encoding of octaves compared to other large intervals (e.g. major sevenths, minor ninths) should result in greater ease of detecting changes to the octave standard. This prediction was confirmed. Children performed significantly better on changes to octave intervals than to the other intervals. In fact, they performed at chance levels on these other intervals. Thus, 6-year-old children with no musical training showed a processing advantage for octaves relative to major sevenths and minor ninths. In a related study with infant listeners, Demany and Armand (1984) demonstrated greater perceptual similarity for tones an octave apart than for tones a seventh or ninth apart. In short, the available developmental evidence is consistent with the view that the special perceptual status of octaves has a biological basis and, consequently, that the octave is a natural feature of music.

INFANTS AND YOUNG CHILDREN ARE SENSITIVE TO SIMPLE FREQUENCY RATIOS

Innate processing advantages for octaves should result in the universality or near-universality of musical scales (see Dowling, 1982b). If tones an octave apart are equivalent in some sense, then the intervals in a given octave should also appear in successively higher and lower octaves. This property reflects the universality of "logarithmic pitch scales" (Dowling & Harwood, 1986, p. 238), or the characterisation of musical intervals by frequency ratios rather than differences. For example, two pure tones of 300 and 200Hz have a 3:2 frequency ratio; the same two tones transposed an octave higher, 600 and 400Hz, also stand in a ratio of 3:2, and represent the same interval. Although the interval of an octave seems to have special perceptual status for human listeners, it is unclear whether any other intervals have favoured status. If they do, then scales would not only be universal but also similar, because the favoured intervals should be universal (or near universal), appearing in scales across disparate musical cultures.

An enduring conception in the history of Western music is the description of fifths and fourths, in addition to octaves, as perfect consonances (i.e. particularly pleasant sounding). But is such "perfection" biologically based or is it a product of cultural conventions? Pythagoras (6th century BCE) and his followers considered these intervals to be consonant because of the simple ratios between the lengths of string required to produce them; the correspondence to simple frequency ratios was discovered several centuries later (17th century) by Galileo (Dostrovsky, 1980). The fundamental frequencies of octaves, perfect fifths, and perfect fourths are related by simple, or small integer, ratios: 2:1, 3:2, and 4:3, respectively. Boethius (circa 480–524 CE), who included the study of music in the Quadrivium, the four essential disciplines of mathematics (arithmetic, music, geometry, and astronomy), introduced ancient Greek music theory to Western Europe. Like the Pythagoreans, Boethius considered consonance to be a product of the ratio between two sounds; the simpler the ratio, the greater the consonance (Bower, 1980). Indeed, from the Greek period through the middle of the 13th century CE, perfect intervals were the only fully accepted consonances (Hill, 1986).

The relatively recent discovery of a love song from the ancient Middle East (written in cuneiform signs on clay tablets) also bears on this issue. The Sumerian song, dated around 1400 BCE, is the oldest known song by a margin of "at least a thousand years" (Kilmer, Crocker & Brown, 1976, p.5). Reaction to its first documented performance since 1400 BCE, which occurred on March 15, 1974 (Fosburg, 1974; Schonberg, 1974), was unexpected but uniform; instead of sounding strange, it sounded highly familiar (like a lullaby, hymn, or folk song) because its structure was virtually identical to that of Western diatonic scales, which are based, of course, on simple frequency ratios between component tones. Thus, several hundred years prior to Pythagoras' "discovery" of the consonance of simple ratios, the scales in use reflected comparable implicit knowledge. The endurance of virtually identical scale structures over thousands of years is consistent with the notion that some properties of such structures are biologically determined. As Taruskin (1994) muses, the diatonic scale "was in people's heads three and a half milleniums ago. And as we all know from experience, it's there still" (p. 28).

Virtually all theorists of Western tonal music consider intervals with simple frequency ratios to be more consonant than those with more complex ratios. Empirical research reveals, moreover, that the judgements of musically trained listeners regarding the stability of individual tones in musical contexts are in accord with predictions from music theory (Krumhansl & Kessler, 1982). These judgements are also highly correlated with the simplicity of the frequency ratios between each test tone and the tonic of the stimulus context (Schellenberg & Trehub, 1994b). According to Rameau's (1683-1764) tonal theory, the key of a piece is delineated by the chords built on the tonic, dominant (a fifth above the tonic), and subdominant (a fifth below the tonic, or a fourth above the tonic). These three chords remain the essential harmonies of tonal music (e.g. see Aldwell & Schachter, 1989).

Music theorists, beginning with Heinichen (1728/1966), consider keys whose tonics are a perfect fourth or fifth apart to be closely related. The psychological validity of this claim can be seen in the judgements of musically trained listeners (Bharucha & Krumhansl, 1983). Presentation of a musical chord also primes listeners to expect closely related chords (Bharucha & Stoeckig, 1986, 1987). In melodic-interval discrimination tasks, moreover, adults recognise recently heard intervals more readily if these intervals have simple rather than complex ratios (Schellenberg & Trehub, 1994a); 6-year-old children who have never taken music lessons do likewise (Schellenberg & Trehub, 1996a). Specifically, adults and children are significantly more accurate at detecting semitone changes to perfect fifths and perfect fourths (Fig. 6.3c) than to tritones (Fig. 6.3d). In fact, the most parsimonious account of the available data (from several laboratories) on the perception of musical intervals has its basis in the relative simplicity of frequency ratios (Schellenberg & Trehub, 1994b). Nevertheless, a number of scholars (e.g. Cazden, 1962) reject the notion of natural intervals, arguing instead that musical conventions account for the processing advantages that have been observed.

Support for the special status of intervals with simple frequency ratios also derives from their prominence cross-culturally. The scales of three of the world's major non-Western musical systems are similar to Western scales, exhibiting the influence of perfect consonances (Burns & Ward, 1982). For example, the pitch classes of the most common pentatonic scale in Chinese music (Koon, 1979; Laloy, 1909/1979) can be formed by starting with any tone, then adding a second tone a perfect fifth higher than the first, a third tone a fifth higher than the second, and so on, assembling five different tones or pitch classes in this manner. The resulting scale corresponds to the black keys of the piano and is also the basis of many Western folk melodies. In the case of musical scales from India, the two most important tones are a perfect fifth apart. These tones are typically played as a "drone" throughout a musical piece, around which a musician improvises using other tones from the scale (Capwell, 1986; Jairazbhoy, 1971). Indeed, there are "many musical traditions where the melodic line is accompanied by a drone, which is invariably pitched on the tonic and/or dominant" (Lerdahl & Jackendoff, 1983, p. 295). Scottish bagpipe music provides one such example (Marcuse, 1964).

Some musical cultures are reputed to be free of the influence of simple frequency ratios, the most commonly cited example being Javanese music (Ellingson, 1992). Javanese (and Balinese) slendro and pelog scales have tunings that can vary quite dramatically from one gamelan ensemble to another, and even between octaves within a single ensemble (Hatch, 1986; Hood, 1969; Lentz, 1965). Do such findings rule out any influence of simple frequency ratios? Perhaps it is useful to bear in mind that, since the early 18th century, perfect fifths in Western music have not been tuned to exact 3:2 ratios, and that skilled musicians and singers from Western and other musical cultures deviate substantially from exact small-ratio intervals in their performance of musical pieces (see Burns & Ward, 1982). Nevertheless, we do not conclude that simple frequency ratios are irrelevant to Western musical structure. Even in Javanese melodies, tones that are approximately a perfect fifth apart are structurally significant (Hood, 1954; Lentz, 1965), functioning as reference points in melodies (Hood, 1954, 1969); modulations to scales an approximate fifth higher or lower are also common (Hood, 1969). As noted previously, Javanese intervals may be relatively more mistuned from exact ratios than Western intervals as a consequence of instruments with enharmonic partials (Burns & Ward, 1982).

Perhaps the most compelling counter-example regarding the naturally privileged status of simple frequency ratios comes not from Javanese music but from the music of Thailand. Thai scales are constructed from an octave that is divided into seven intervals of equal or near-equal size (Ellingson, 1992; Morton, 1980). The intervals of the resulting scale do not correspond to Western intervals, except for two that are very similar to fourths and fifths (Morton, 1980). Interestingly, the tone that is a "fifth" above the tonic is structurally significant: "Thai music places special emphasis on 5th relationships" (Morton, 1980, p. 719). On balance, then, cross-cultural evidence supports the hypothesis that the special status of simple frequency ratios is biologically based.

More potent evidence for inherent processing advantages for some intervals (i.e. those with simple frequency ratios) over others (i.e. those with more complex frequency ratios) necessitated the evaluation of infant listeners. Accordingly, we tested 6-month-old infants on their ability to detect changes in melodic intervals with frequency ratios of 3:2 (perfect fifth, 7 semitones), 45:32 (tritone, 6 semitones), or 4:3 (perfect fourth, 5 semitones) (Schellenberg & Trehub, 1996b). Our assumption in this instance, as in our discrimination studies with adults (Schellenberg & Trehub, 1994a) and children (Schellenberg & Trehub, 1996a), was that the ease of detecting changes in a tone sequence would reflect its relative ease of processing. We presented an alternating series of pure tones (low-high-low-high-low-high-low-high, etc.) that was transposed upward or downward by two semitones after every eight tones (four low tones and four high tones). On change trials, the second and sixth tones (the first and third high tones) were displaced downward by a semitone; on no-change trials, the alternating series continued as before (see Fig. 6.4). Infants' discrimination performance was significantly better in the perfect fifth and perfect fourth conditions than in the tritone condition, replicating the pattern of findings obtained with adult (Schellenberg & Trehub, 1994a) and child (Schellenberg & Trehub, 1996a) listeners. In fact, performance was well above chance levels in the two simple-ratio conditions, but only at chance levels in the complex-ratio (tritone) condition. We are confident, then, that melodic intervals with simple frequency ratios are inherently easier to process than those with more complex ratios. Our use of pure-tone stimuli and intervals a perfect fourth or larger makes it possible to rule out alternative explanations that are not based on the simplicity of frequency ratios (e.g. overlapping critical bands, see Plomp & Levelt, 1965).

The notion of inherent processing advantages for intervals with simpler frequency ratios can account for several previous findings with infant listeners. For example, infants' success in detecting changes in the context of melodies based on the major triad (ratio of 4:5:6) coupled with their failure in the context of melodies based on the augmented triad (ratio of 16:20:25) (Cohen, Thorpe & Trehub, 1987) or other complex-ratio intervals (Trehub, Thorpe & Trainor, 1990) can be explained in terms of the greater ease of processing simple compared to complex frequency ratios. Similarly, infants' superior

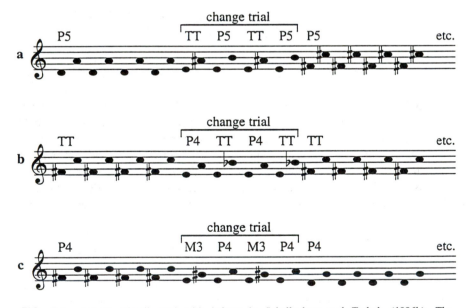

FIG. 6.4. Sample stimuli used with infants in Schellenberg and Trehub (1996b). The alternating high and low tones are transposed by 2 semitones after every 8 tones. The perfect fifth standard changes to a tritone in example a. The tritone standard changes to a perfect fourth in example b. The perfect fourth standard changes to a major third in example c. In each case, the altered pattern is preceded and followed by the repeating background pattern.

discrimination performance in the context of melodies transposed to closely related keys rather than distantly related keys (Trainor & Trehub, 1993b) can also be explained in terms of processing advantages for successive melodies related by simple frequency ratios (i.e. the most closely related keys stand in a ratio of 3:2 or 4:3). Moreover, the perfect fifth, or 3:2 ratio, may serve as a perceptual anchor, making it possible for infants to encode and retain melodies that incorporate other "less natural" intervals (Trainor & Trehub, 1993a). Finally, the special perceptual status of octaves throughout ontogeny and across widely disparate cultures may reflect the octave's status as the interval with the simplest frequency ratio (other than the unison, of course). These findings allow us to reject the oft-stated notions that the composition of scales is arbitrary and that musical consonance is primarily a matter of convention (e.g. Blacking, 1992; Cazden, 1962; Serafine, 1983). Equally untenable is the claim that sensory consonance depends solely on the frequency distance between tones (Plomp & Levelt, 1965). Although conventional notions of sensory consonance involving critical bands (Kameoka & Kuriyagawa, 1969a, 1969b; Plomp & Levelt, 1965) are applicable to simultaneously presented complex tones (i.e. harmonic intervals consisting of naturally occurring tone complexes), they fail to account for the influence of simple ratios on the perception of melodic intervals consisting solely of pure tones.

INFANTS ARE SENSITIVE TO SOME, BUT NOT TO OTHER, PROPERTIES OF HARMONY

The aforementioned demonstrations of sensitivity to frequency ratios by infant listeners involved melodies or sequences of tones. This emphasis on melody as opposed to harmony (simultaneous combinations of tones) is reasonable in the search for processing predispositions because, without exception, all musical systems have rules governing the structure of melodies (e.g. adherence to a scale structure). Western music differs from many other musical cultures, however, by also having an elaborate system of rules governing combinations of simultaneous tones. These rules may be less likely to reflect natural processes because of their relative uniqueness. Indeed, the available developmental evidence largely supports the view that properties of Western harmony are learned by exposure to Western music.

For example, one study (Trainor & Trehub, 1992) evaluated the ability of adults and 8-month-old infants to detect alterations to a standard 10-tone sequence that implied a typical tonic-dominant-tonic (I-V-I) harmonic change (See Fig. 6.5a). Some of these alterations were inconsistent with the implied harmony and outside the key of the melody (Fig.6.5b); others were within the key and consistent with the harmonic implications (Fig. 6.5c). Not surprisingly, adults found it easier to detect a one-semitone change with a non-key note than a four-semitone change that remained within the key and harmony. Infants, by contrast, detected both changes equally well. What was especially remarkable was that infants' absolute level of performance exceeded that of adults on changes that were within the key and harmony. These results are consistent with the notion that much of listeners' knowledge of Western harmony is based on learning and exposure rather than predispositions. For infants, the issue was simply one of detecting changes—contour-preserving changes in this case. Their discrimination of the target changes, one-semitone or four-semitones, was probably facilitated by the structure of the standard melody, whose principal tones (i.e. those at contour reversals) were related by simple frequency ratios. For adults, however, informal exposure to music resulted in implicit knowledge that

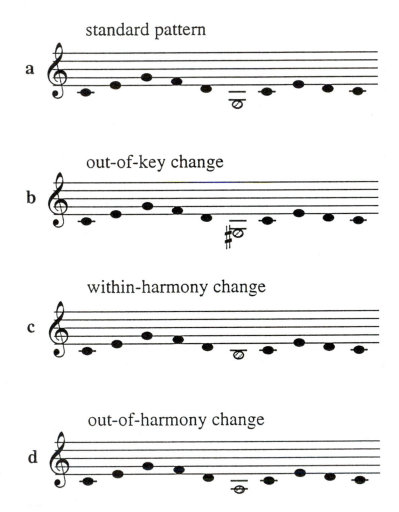

FIG. 6.5. Sample stimuli used with infants, children, and adults in Trainor and Trehub (1992, 1994). The repeating standard pattern was presented in transposition such that the first tone was C4, E4, or G4. The sixth (potentially altered) tone is highlighted in each case.

obscured some highly conventional changes, notably those within the implied harmony of the standard melody.

A subsequent study (Trainor & Trehub, 1994) examined children's as well as adults' sensitivity to three types of changes: (1) those outside the key of the same 10-note standard melody (Fig. 6.5b), (2) those consistent with the key and the implied harmony (Fig. 6.5c), and (3) those consistent with the key but not with the implied harmony (Fig. 6.5d). The 5-year-old participants performed significantly better on the out-of-key changes than on the two other changes, for which performance was at chance levels. By contrast, 7-year-olds and adults performed similarly on changes that violated the key or the harmony, and both performed significantly more poorly on changes within the implied harmony. Moreover, the extent of musical training (i.e. years of lessons) on the part of adult participants was correlated with performance on the two within-key changes but not the out-of-key change. These two studies (Trainor & Trehub, 1992, 1994) jointly indicate that: (1) implicit knowledge of key membership, although absent in 8-month-old listeners, is present by 5 years of age, (2) knowledge of implied harmony is evident in 7-year-old listeners, and (3) this knowledge continues to be refined with further exposure and training.

If exposure to Western music did not enable infants to distinguish out-of-key from within-key changes (Trainor & Trehub, 1992), then such exposure is unlikely to have been responsible for infants' enhanced performance on tasks involving melodic patterns that conform to Western musical structure (Cohen et al., 1987; Trehub et al., 1990; Trainor & Trehub, 1993a, 1993b) or that contain intervals with simple frequency ratios (Schellenberg & Trehub, 1996b).

Although biological influences are irrelevant to implied harmony in particular, they may be relevant to some rules of Western harmony and counterpoint. One such rule involves a prohibition against consecutive perfect fifths and octaves, which are considered to compromise the integrity of individual voices (e.g. Salzer & Schachter, 1969). This rule may stem from the structure of the overtone series of complex tones, because the fundamental frequencies of two tones separated by an octave could also be the first and second harmonics of a single tone complex, the fundamentals of tones separated by a fifth could be the second and third harmonics, and so on. Evidence from adult listeners indicates that tones are more likely to fuse (DeWitt & Crowder, 1987; Moore, Glasberg & Peters, 1986) or blend smoothly (see Schellenberg & Trehub, 1994b) if they are related by simple frequency ratios such as those between the components of harmonic tone complexes. In a setting with multiple melodic lines, rules of voice leading specify that each line should be distinct (unfused) until the end, when the final combination of tones should be a perfect consonance, signalling oneness, or completion (fusion) of the melodic line (e.g. Salzer & Schachter, 1969).

These rules may reflect innate sensitivity to the overtone series, such that simultaneous combinations of tones related by simple frequency ratios are more likely to be perceived as a single percept than combinations related by more complex ratios. As noted, however, rules of harmony and voice leading are less applicable to non-Western musical cultures, which place less emphasis on harmonic relations. In India, however, the simultaneous sounding of two tones a perfect fifth apart throughout a musical piece is suggestive of inherently special status for this interval in harmonic as well as melodic contexts.

In principle, simultaneous tones (i.e. harmonic intervals) that are related by simple frequency ratios are more likely to be perceived as organised or unified events (gestalts) than are tones related by complex ratios. Accordingly, mistunings of harmonic intervals with simple ratios might be inherently more salient than mistunings of intervals with complex frequency ratios. A recent study with 9-month-old infants (Schellenberg & Trehub, 1996b) bears directly on this issue. Infants heard repeated presentations of harmonic intervals consisting of simultaneous pure tones in phase. The comparison patterns mistuned the higher component tone downward by one-quarter of a semitone. As predicted, infants detected the change when the standard pattern was an equal-tempered perfect fifth or fourth, but not when the standard was a tritone. These findings are consistent with the possibility that music-theoretic proscriptions of parallel perfect consonances are based, in part, on processing predispositions. Indeed, the music-theoretic dictum of ending on a perfect consonance may also have its basis in natural processing tendencies.

INFANTS HAVE MUSICAL PREFERENCES

If infants are sensitive to melodic contour, simple frequency ratios, and some aspects of harmony, then they might have preferences for some musical forms over others. Prelinguistic listeners could express such preferences by greater attentional or affective responsiveness for one pattern compared to another.

In two related studies (Jusczyk & Krumhansl, 1993; Krumhansl & Jusczyk, 1990), 4- and 6-month-old infants heard contrasting renditions of simple piano minuets that Mozart composed as a child. In one rendition, designated natural, the investigators added two-beat pauses between phrases. In the other, designated unnatural, they added comparable pauses within phrases. For any infant listener, the natural rendition was presented consistently over a loudspeaker on one side (e.g. right) and the unnatural rendition was presented on the other side (e.g. left). These two versions of the test materials were presented on a series of alternating trials during which infants' visual fixation toward the relevant loudspeaker was monitored. A comparison of the duration of visual fixations or looking times revealed a significant attentional "preference" for the natural over the unnatural version, which was considered to reflect infants' sensitivity to aspects of musical phrase structure.

The young Mozart, adhering to music-theoretic rules, tended to end his phrases with perfect consonances, typically octaves. In fact, the occurrence of octave intervals before pauses was correlated with infant looking times (Jusczyk

& Krumhansl, 1993; Krumhansl & Jusczyk, 1990), a finding that is consistent with a natural basis for such endings, as suggested previously. Because Mozart's phrases also tended to end with drops in pitch height and with tones of relatively long duration, both of which were also correlated with looking times, it is impossible to assess the separate contributions of these factors.

Perhaps it is more appropriate to consider infant preferences in terms of musical genres that are more directly relevant to infants. In every culture and historical period, adults have invariably sung to infants in the course of caregiving (for reviews, see Trehub & Schellenberg, 1995; Trehub & Trainor, in press; Trehub, Trainor & Unyk, 1993). The most common type of caregiving song, the lullaby, is defined primarily by its goal, that of soothing infants or promoting sleep. Lullabies from diverse cultures share a number of common features including repetition, contour simplicity, and a preponderance of descending intervals (Unyk, Trehub, Trainor & Schellenberg, 1992). Such features may underlie adults' ability to differentiate foreign lullabies from non-lullabies that are matched on tempo and performing style (Trehub, Unyk & Trainor, 1993a). Adult listeners can also distinguish contextually appropriate performances, those sung in the presence of an infant, from contextually inappropriate instances, notably those sung in the infant's absence (Trehub et al., in press; Trehub, Unyk & Trainor, 1993b).

Trainor (1996) used the Krumhansl and Jusczyk (1990) procedure to evaluate the possibility of infant attentional preferences for one of two recorded versions of particular songs. One version had been sung by mothers to their infants; the other version (same song) had been sung without the infant present. Infants "preferred" the infant-directed version, as indicated by significantly greater visual attention to the loudspeaker from which it was presented. Adult listeners, without knowledge of the context in which the songs were performed, rated the infant-directed versions as significantly more "loving" than the others. Thus, infants exhibited a preference for the more natural (i.e. contextually appropriate) and more emotionally expressive of the two performances.

An alternative procedure has been used to assess infants' affective as opposed to attentional responsiveness during contrasting performances of songs (Trehub & Henderson, 1994). This procedure involved videotaping infants as they listened to pairs of recorded musical samples and, subsequently, having adults judge, from soundless videotapes, the segment in which each of several infants exhibited greater enjoyment. Such judgements indicated that infants "enjoyed" lullabies more than adult songs or play songs (same singer in both comparisons), and that they enjoyed mothers' singing more than fathers' singing. Across all comparisons, infants revealed a preference for the more universal musical form, the lullaby, and for the more conventional performing style within this genre, that of a mother singing to her infant.

In short, infants are active listeners, deploying their attention selectively to particular musical genres, such as lullabies, to particular performing styles, such as those associated with maternal singing, and to particular features that signal conventional phrase endings. Nevertheless, we are a long way from a complete understanding of the contribution of various melodic, rhythmic, and timbral features to infants' attentional and affective responses.

IMPLICATIONS

We indicated, at the outset, that adult-infant similarities would reflect nature's contribution to music processing, on the one hand, and to musical structures, on the other. On the basis of the developmental data presented, infants and adults appear to perceive novel melodies in fundamentally similar ways. Surprisingly, dramatic differences in processing capacity and cumulative exposure between infancy and adulthood are not matched by qualitative leaps in musical processing but rather by subtle quantitative changes. As a result, we are inclined to concur with Meyer (1994) that "the central nervous system, acting in conjunction with motor systems, predisposes us to perceive certain pitch relationships, temporal proportions, and melodic structures as well shaped and stable" (p. 289). In the absence of developmental data, such as we have presented here, Meyer's pronouncement could be dismissed as speculative, pompous, even ethnocentric. In the context of the current evidence, however, his position seems incontrovertible.

Meyer (1994) did not claim that special intervals (e.g. octave, fifth, fourth) or durational proportions (e.g. 1:1, 1:2, 1:3, 2:3) were necessary elements of a musical style but rather that their presence facilitated, and their absence impeded, perception and learning. Indeed, these musical information-processing constraints seem to have functioned as selection restrictions across musical systems. "Despite the enormous variety of musics, the ways in which people everywhere have chosen to make music are more restricted than the boundaries of the imaginable" (Nettl, 1983, p. 43).

Some listeners consider atonal music to approach, perhaps even to go beyond, such boundaries. On the other side of the fence, however, are those who believe that a lifetime of experience with tonal music is the principal barrier to the acceptance of atonal music, a barrier that could be readily overcome by early exposure. (e.g. Adorno, 1948/1973). The foregoing developmental perspectives suggest otherwise. Avant-garde composers, by abandoning the tonal system, particularly its melodic, harmonic, and metrical-rhythmic constraints, may have created musical forms that are inherently difficult for human listeners, forms requiring deliberate, effortful learning for their understanding and appreciation. Such composers and their compositions may remain perpetually elite, because music-theoretic, cross-cultural, and empirical perspectives provide converging support of Taruskin's (1994) view that nature calls the tune.

ACKNOWLEDGEMENTS

The preparation of this chapter was assisted by grants from the Natural Sciences and Engineering Research Council and the Social Sciences and Humanities Research Council of Canada.

REFERENCES

Adorno, T. W. (1973). *The philosophy of modern music*. English translation by A. G. Mitchell & W. V. Bloomster. London: Sheed & Ward. (Original work published 1948).

Aldwell, E., & Schachter, C. (1989). *Harmony and voice leading* (2nd ed.). San Diego, CA: Harcourt Brace Jovanovich.

Allen, D. (1967). Octave discriminability of musical and non-musical subjects. *Psychonomic Science, 7*, 421–422.

Attneave, F., & Olson, R. K. (1971). Pitch as a medium: A new approach to psychophysical scaling. *American Journal of Psychology, 84*, 147–166.

Bartlett, J. C., & Dowling, W. J. (1980). Recognition of transposed melodies: A keydistance effect in developmental perspective. *Journal of Experimental Psychology: Human Perception and Performance, 6*, 501–515.

Bharucha, J. J. (1987). Music cognition and perceptual facilitation: A connectionist framework. *Music Perception, 5*, 1–30.

Bharucha, J. J., & Krumhansl, C. L. (1983). The representation of harmonic structure in music: Hierarchies of stability as a function of context. *Cognition, 13*, 63–102.

Bharucha, J. J., & Stoeckig, K. (1986). Reaction time and musical expectancy: Priming of chords. *Journal of Experimental Psychology: Human Perception and Performance, 12*, 403–410.

Bharucha, J. J., & Stoeckig, K. (1987). Priming of chords: Spreading activation or overlapping frequency spectra? *Perception & Psychophysics, 41*, 519–524.

Blacking, J. (1992). The biology of music-making. In H. Myers, (Ed.), *Ethnomusicology: An introduction* (pp. 301–314). New York: Norton.

Boomsliter, P., & Creel, W. (1961). The long pattern hypothesis in harmony and hearing. *Journal of Music Theory, 5*, 2–31.

Bower, C. (1980). Boethius, Anicius, Manlius Severinus. In S. Sadie, (Ed.). *The new Grove dictionary of music and musicians* (Vol. 2, p. 844). London: Macmillan.

Bregman, A. S. (1990). *Auditory scene analysis*. Cambridge, MA: MIT Press.

Bregman, A. S. (1993). Auditory scene analysis: Hearing in complex environments. In S. McAdams & E. Bigand, (Eds.), *Thinking in sound: The cognitive psychology of human audition* (pp. 10–36). Oxford: Oxford University Press.

Budd, M. (1985). *Music and the emotions: The philosophical theories*. London: Routledge & Kegan Paul.

Burns, E. M., & Ward, W. D. (1982). Intervals, scales, and tuning. In D. Deutsch, (Ed.), *The psychology of music* (pp. 241–269). New York: Academic Press.

Capwell, C. (1986). South Asia. In D. M. Randel, (Ed.), *The new Harvard dictionary of music* (pp. 778–787). Cambridge, MA: Belknap Press.

Cazden, N. (1962). Sensory theories of musical consonance. *Journal of Aesthetics and Art Criticism, 20*, 301–319.

Chang, H. W., & Trehub, S. E. (1977). Auditory processing of relational information by young infants. *Journal of Experimental Child Psychology, 24*, 324–331.

Clarkson, M. G., & Clifton, R. K. (1985). Infant pitch perception: Evidence for responding to pitch categories and the missing fundamental. *Journal of the Acoustical Society of America, 77*, 1521–1528.

Cohen, A. J., Thorpe, L. A., & Trehub, S. E. (1987). Infants' perception of musical relations in short transposed tone sequences. *Canadian Journal of Psychology, 41*, 33–47.

Cook, N. (1990). *Music, imagination, and culture*. Oxford: Oxford University Press.

Cuddy, L. L., & Badertscher, B. (1987). Recovery of the tonal hierarchy: Some comparisons across age and levels of musical experience. *Perception & Psychophysics, 41*, 609–620.

Cuddy, L. L., Cohen, A. J., & Mewhort, D. J. K. (1981). Perception of structure in short melodic sequences. *Journal of Experimental Psychology: Human Perception and Performance, 7*, 869–883.

Cuddy, L. L., Cohen, A. J., & Miller, J. (1979). Melody recognition: The experimental application of musical rules. *Canadian Journal of Psychology, 33*, 148–156.

D'Amato, M. R. (1988). A search for tonal pattern perception in cebus monkeys: Why monkeys can't hum a tune. *Music Perception, 5*, 453–480.

DeCasper, A. J., Lecanuet, J-P., Busnel, M-C., Granier-Deferre, C., & Maugeais, R. (1994). Fetal reactions to recurrent maternal speech. *Infant Behavior and Development, 17*, 159–164.

Demany, L. (1982). Auditory stream segregation in infancy. *Infant Behavior and Development, 5*, 261–276.

Demany, L., & Armand, F. (1984). The perceptual reality of tone chroma in early infancy. *Journal of the Acoustical Society of America, 76*, 57–66.

Deutsch, D. (1972). Octave generalization and tune recognition. *Perception & Psychophysics, 11*, 411–412.

Deutsch, D. (1975). The organization of short-term memory for a single acoustic attribute. In D. Deutsch & J. A. Deutsch, (Eds.). *Short-term memory.* New York: Academic Press.

DeWitt, L. A., & Crowder, R. G. (1987). Tonal fusion of consonant musical intervals. *Perception & Psychophysics, 41*, 73–84.

Dostrovsky, S. (1980). Physics of music, 1: to Mersenne. In S. Sadie, (Ed.). *The new Grove dictionary of music and musicians* (Vol. 14, pp. 664–665). London: Macmillan.

Dowling, W. J. (1978). Scale and contour: Two components of a theory of memory for melodies. *Psychological Review, 85*, 341–354.

Dowling, W. J. (1982a). Melodic information processing and its development. In D. Deutsch, (Ed.), *The psychology of music* (pp. 413–429). New York: Academic Press.

Dowling, W. J. (1982b). Musical scales and psychophysical scales: Their psychological reality. In R. Falck & T. Rice, (Eds.), *Cross-cultural perspectives on music* (pp. 20–28). Toronto: University of Toronto Press.

Dowling, W. J., & Fujitani, D. (1971). Contour, interval, and pitch recognition in memory for melodies. *Journal of the Acoustical Society of America, 49*, 524–531.

Dowling, W. J., & Harwood, D. L. (1986). *Music cognition.* San Diego, CA: Academic Press.

Dowling, W. J., & Hollombe, A. (1977). The perception of melodies distorted by splitting into several octaves: Effects of increasing proximity and melodic contour. *Perception & Psychophysics, 21*, 60–64.

Dyson, M. C., & Watkins, A. J. (1984). A figural approach to the role of melodic contour in melody recognition. *Perception & Psychophysics, 35*, 477–488.

Ellingson, T. (1992). Transcription. In H. Myers, (Ed.), *Ethnomusicology: An introduction* (pp. 110–152). New York: Norton.

Fernald, A. (1992). Human maternal vocalizations to infants as biologically relevant signals: An evolutionary perspective. In J. H. Barkow, L. Cosmides, & J. Tooby, (Eds.), *The adapted mind: Evolutionary psychology and the generation of culture* (pp. 345–382). Oxford: Oxford University Press.

Fosburgh, L. (1974, March 6). World's oldest song reported deciphered: Near-east origin. *The New York Times*, pp. 1, 18.

Francès, R. (1988). *The perception of music.* English translation by W. J. Dowling. Hillsdale, NJ: Lawrence Erlbaum. (Original work published 1958).

Gjerdingen, R. O. (1988). *A classic turn of phrase: Music and the psychology of convention.* Philadephia: University of Pennsylvania Press.

Handel, S. (1989). *Listening: An introduction to the perception of auditory events.* Cambridge, MA: MIT Press.

Harwood, D. L. (1976). Universals in music: A perspective from cognitive psychology. *Ethnomusicology, 20*, 521–534.

Hatch, M. (1986). Southeast Asia. In D. M. Randel, (Ed.), *The new Harvard dictionary of music* (pp. 787–800). Cambridge, MA: Belknap Press.

Heinichen, J. D. (1966). *Thorough-bass accompaniment.* English translation by G. J. Buelow. Berkeley, CA: University of California Press. (Original work published 1728)

Hill, C. C. (1986). Consonance and dissonance. In D. M. Randel, (Ed.), *The new Harvard dictionary of music* (pp. 197–199). Cambridge, MA: Belknap Press.

Hindemith, P. (1937/1942). *The craft of musical composition.* English translation by A. Mendel. New York: Associated Music Publishers.

Hood, M. (1954). *The nuclear theme as a determinant of patet in Javanese music.* Groningen, Netherlands: J.B. Wolters.

Hood, M. (1969). Java. In W. Apel, (Ed.), *Harvard dictionary of music* (2nd ed.) (pp. 435–440). Cambridge, MA: Belknap Press.

Hood, M. (1971). Slendro and pelog revisited. In D. P. McAllester, (Ed.), *Readings in ethnomusicology* (pp. 35–56). New York: Johnson Reprint Corporation.

Hulse, S. H., & Page, S. C. (1988). Toward a comparative psychology of music perception. *Music Perception, 5,* 427–452.

Idson, W. L., & Massaro, D. W. (1978). A bidimensional model of pitch in the recognition of melodies. *Perception & Psychophysics, 24,* 551–565.

Jairazbhoy, N. A. (1971). *The rags of North Indian Music.* London: Faber & Faber.

Jeppesen, K. (1939). *Counterpoint: The polyphonic vocal style of the sixteenth century.* English translation by G. Haydon. Englewood Cliffs, NJ: Prentice-Hall. (Original work published 1931)

Jones, M. R. (1982). Music as a stimulus for psychological motion: Part II. An expectancy model. *Psychomusicology, 2,* 1–13.

Jusczyk, P. W., & Krumhansl, C. L. (1993). Pitch and rhythmic patterns affecting infants' sensitivity to musical phrase structure. *Journal of Experimental Psychology: Human Perception and Performance, 19,* 1–14.

Kallman, H. J. (1982). Octave equivalence as measured by similarity ratings. *Perception & Psychophysics, 32,* 37–49.

Kameoka, A., & Kuriyagawa, M. (1969a). Consonance theory part I: Consonance of dyads. *Journal of the Acoustical Society of America, 45,* 1451–1459.

Kameoka, A., & Kuriyagawa, M. (1969b). Consonance theory part II: Consonance of complex tones and its calculation method. *Journal of the Acoustical Society of America, 45,* 1460–1469.

Kilmer A. D, Crocker, R. L., & Brown, R. R. (1976). *Sounds from silence: Recent discoveries in ancient Near Eastern music.* Berkeley, CA: Bit Enki Publications.

Koon, N. K. (1979). The five pentatonic modes in Chinese folk music. *Chinese Music, 2*(2), 10–13.

Krumhansl, C. L. (1990). *Cognitive foundations of musical pitch.* New York: Oxford University Press.

Krumhansl, C. L., & Jusczyk, P. W. (1990). Infants' perception of phrase structure in music. *Psychological Science, 1,* 70–73.

Krumhansl, C. L., & Keil, F. C. (1982). Acquisition of the hierarchy of tonal functions in music. *Memory and Cognition, 10,* 243–251.

Krumhansl, C. L., & Kessler, E. J. (1982). Tracing the dynamic changes in perceived tonal organization in a spatial representation of musical keys. *Psychological Review, 89,* 334–368.

Krumhansl, C. L., & Shepard, R. N. (1979). Quantification of the hierarchy of tonal functions within a diatonic context. *Journal of Experimental Psychology: Human Perception and Performance, 5,* 579–594.

Kuhl, P. K., Williams, K. A., Lacerda, F., Stevens, K. N., & Lindblom, B. (1992). Linguistic experience alters phonetic perception in infants by 6 months of age. *Science, 255,* 606–608.

Laloy, L. (1979). *Chinese music.* English translation by N. Karel. Paris: Henri-Laurens. (Original work published 1909)

Lentz, D. A. (1965). *The gamelan music of Java and Bali*. Lincoln, NB: University of Nebraska Press.

Lerdahl, F., & Jackendoff, R. (1983). *A generative theory of tonal music*. Cambridge, MA: MIT Press.

Lynch, M. P., & Eilers, R. E. (1992). A study of perceptual development for musical tuning. *Perception & Psychophysics, 52*, 599–608.

Lynch, M. P., Eilers, R. E., Oller, D. K., & Urbano, R. C. (1990). Innateness, experience, and music perception. *Psychological Science, 1*, 272–276.

Marcuse, S. (1964). *Musical instruments: A comprehensive dictionary*. Garden City, NY: Doubleday

Marler, P. (1990). Innate learning preferences: Signals for communication. *Developmental Psychobiology, 23*, 557–568.

Meyer, L. B. (1994). *Music, the arts and ideas: Patterns and predictions in twentieth-century culture*. Chicago: University of Chicago Press.

Miller, G. A. (1956). The magical number seven, plus or minus two: Some limits on our capacity for processing information. *Psychological Review, 63*, 81–97.

Moore, B. C. J., Glasberg, B. R., & Peters, R. W. (1986). Thresholds for hearing mistuned partials as separate tones in harmonic complexes. *Journal of the Acoustical Society of America, 80*, 479–483.

Morton, D. (1980). Thailand. In S. Sadie, (Ed.), *The new Grove dictionary of music and musicians* (Vol. 18, pp. 712–722). London: Macmillan.

Narmour, E. (1990). *The analysis and cognition of basic melodic structures: The implication-realization model*. Chicago: University of Chicago Press.

Narmour, E. (1992). *The analysis and cognition of melodic complexity: The implication-realization model*. Chicago: University of Chicago Press.

Nettl, B. (1983). *The study of ethnomusicology*. Urbana: University of Illinois Press.

Patterson, R. D. (1986). Spiral detection of periodicity and the spiral form of musical scales. *Psychology of Music, 14*, 44–61.

Plomp, R., & Levelt, W. J. M. (1965). Tonal consonance and critical bandwidth. *Journal of the Acoustical Society of America, 38*, 548–560.

Premack, D. (1983). The codes of man and beast. *Behavioral and Brain Sciences, 6*, 125–167.

Roederer, J. G. (1979). *Introduction to the physics and psychophysics of music* (2nd ed.). New York: Springer-Verlag.

Salzer, F., & Schachter, C. (1969). *Counterpoint in composition*. New York: McGraw-Hill.

Schellenberg, E. G. (1996). Expectancy in melody: Tests of the implication-realization model. *Cognition, 58*, 75–125.

Schellenberg, E. G., & Trehub, S. E. (1994a). Frequency ratios and the discrimination of pure tone sequences. *Perception & Psychophysics, 56*, 472–478.

Schellenberg, E. G., & Trehub, S. E. (1994b). Frequency ratios and the perception of tone patterns. *Psychonomic Bulletin & Review, 1*, 191–201.

Schellenberg, E. G., & Trehub, S. E. (1996a). Children's discrimination of melodic intervals. *Developmental Psychology, 32*.

Schellenberg, E. G., & Trehub, S. E. (1996b). Natural musical intervals: Evidence from infant listeners. *Psychological Science, 1*, 272–277.

Schmuckler, M. A. (1989). Expectation in music: Investigation of melodic and harmonic processes. *Music Perception, 7*, 109–150.

Schmuckler, M. A. (1990). The performance of global expectations. *Psychomusicology, 9*, 122–147.

Schonberg, H. C. (1974, March 6). World's oldest song reported deciphered: Out of prehistory. *The New York Times*, pp. 1, 18.

Serafine, M. L. (1983). Cognition in music. *Cognition, 14*, 119–183.

Sloboda, J. A. (1985). *The musical mind: The cognitive psychology of music*. Oxford: Clarendon Press.

Smith, J. D., Kemler Nelson, D. G., Grohskopf, L. A., & Appleton, T. (1994). What child is this? What interval was that? Familiar tunes and music perception in novice listeners. *Cognition, 52*, 23–54.

Sutton, R. A. (1991). *Traditions of gamelan music in Java*. Cambridge, UK: Cambridge University Press.

Takeuchi, A. H., & Hulse, S. H. (1993). Absolute pitch. *Psychological Bulletin, 113*, 345–361.

Taruskin, R. (1994, September 18). Classical view: Does nature call the tune? *The New York Times, Sec: 2*, p. 28.

Terhardt, E. (1984). The concept of musical consonance: A link between music and psychoacoustics. *Music Perception, 1*, 276–295.

Thorpe, L. A., & Trehub, S. E. (1989). Duration illusion and auditory grouping in infancy. *Developmental Psychology, 25*, 122–127.

Thorpe, L. A., Trehub, S. E., Morrongiello, B. A., & Bull, D. (1988). Perceptual grouping by infants and preschool children. *Developmental Psychology, 24*, 484–491.

Trainor, L. J. (1996). Infant preferences for infant-directed versus non-infant-directed playsongs and lullabies. *Infant Behavior and Development, 19*, 83–92.

Trainor, L. J., & Trehub, S. E. (1992). A comparison of infants' and adults' sensitivity to Western musical structure. *Journal of Experimental Psychology: Human Perception and Performance, 18*, 394–402.

Trainor, L. J., & Trehub, S. E. (1993a). Musical context effects in infants and adults: Key distance. *Journal of Experimental Psychology: Human Perception and Performance, 19*, 615–626.

Trainor, L. J., & Trehub, S. E. (1993b). What mediates infants' and adults' superior processing of the major over the augmented triad? *Music Perception, 11*, 185–196.

Trainor, L. J., & Trehub, S. E. (1994). Key membership and implied harmony in Western tonal music: Developmental perspectives. *Perception & Psychophysics, 56*, 125–132.

Trehub, S. E. (1985). Auditory pattern perception in infancy. In S. E. Trehub & B. A. Schneider, (Eds.), *Auditory development in infancy* (pp. 183–195). New York: Plenum.

Trehub, S. E. (1987). Infants' perception of musical patterns. *Perception & Psychophysics, 41*, 635–641.

Trehub, S. E. (1990). The perception of musical patterns by human infants: The provision of similar patterns by their parents. In M. A. Berkley & W. C. Stebbins, (Eds.), *Comparative perception: Vol. 1. Basic mechanisms* (pp. 429–459). New York: Wiley.

Trehub, S. E. (1993). Temporal auditory processing in infancy. *Annals of the New York Academy of Sciences, 682*, 137–149.

Trehub, S. E., Bull, D., & Thorpe, L. A. (1984). Infants' perception of melodies: The role of melodic contour. *Child Development, 55*, 821–830.

Trehub, S. E., Cohen, A. J., Thorpe, L. A., & Morrongiello, B. A. (1986). Development of the perception of musical relations: Semitone and diatonic structure. *Journal of Experimental Psychology: Human Perception and Performance, 12*, 295–301.

Trehub, S. E., Endman, M., & Thorpe, L. A. (1990). Infants' perception of timbre: Classification of complex tones by spectral structure. *Journal of Experimental Child Psychology, 49*, 300–313.

Trehub, S. E., & Henderson, J. (1994, July). Caregivers' songs and their effect on infant listeners. In I. Deliège, (Ed.), *Proceedings of the 3rd International Conference on Music Perception and Cognition* (pp. 47-48). Liège, Belgium: European Society for the Cognitive Sciences of Music.

Trehub, S. E., & Schellenberg, E. G. (1995). Music: Its relevance to infants. *Annals of Child Development, 11*, 1–24.

Trehub, S. E., & Thorpe, L. A. (1989). Infants' perception of rhythm. Categorization of auditory sequences by temporal structure. *Canadian Journal of Psychology, 43*, 217–229.

Trehub, S. E., Thorpe, L. A., & Morrongiello, B. A. (1985). Infants' perception of melodies: Changes in a single tone. *Infant Behavior and Development, 8*, 213–223.

Trehub, S. E., Thorpe, L. A., & Morrongiello, B. A. (1987). Organizational processes in infants' perception of auditory patterns. *Child Development, 58*, 741–749.

Trehub, S. E., Thorpe, L. A., & Trainor, L. J. (1990). Infants' perception of good and bad melodies. *Psychomusicology, 9*, 5–15.

Trehub, S. E., & Trainor, L. J. (1993). Listening strategies in infancy: The roots of language and musical development. In S. McAdams & E. Bigand, (Eds.), *Thinking in sound: Cognitive perspectives on human audition* (pp. 278–327). London: Oxford University Press.

Trehub, S. E., & Trainor, L. J. (in press). Singing to infants: Lullabies and play songs. In C. Rovee-Collier & L. Lipsitt (Eds.), *Advances in Infancy Research*. Norwood, NJ: Ablex.

Trehub, S. E., Trainor, L. J., & Unyk, A. M. (1993). Music and speech processing in the first year of life. *Advances in Child Development and Behavior, 24*, 1–35.

Trehub, S. E., & Unyk, A. M. (1991). Music prototypes in developmental perspective. *Psychomusicology, 10*, 31–45.

Trehub, S. E., Unyk, A., Kamenetsky, S. B., Hill, D. S., Trainor, L. J., Henderson, J. L., & Saraza, M. (in press). Mothers' and fathers' singing to infants. *Developmental Psychology*.

Trehub, S. E., Unyk, A. M., & Trainor, L. J. (1993a). Adults identify infant-directed music across cultures. *Infant Behavior and Development, 16*, 193–211.

Trehub, S. E., Unyk, A. M., & Trainor, L. J. (1993b). Maternal singing in cross-cultural perspective. *Infant Behavior and Development, 16*, 285–295.

Unyk, A. M., Trehub, S. E., Trainor, L. J., & Schellenberg, E. G. (1992). Lullabies and simplicity: A cross-cultural perspective. *Psychology of Music, 20*, 15–28.

Ward, W. D., & Burns, E. M. (1982). Absolute pitch. In D. Deutsch, (Ed.), *The psychology of music* (pp. 431451). New York: Academic Press.

Watkins, A. J. (1985). Scale, key, and contour in the discrimination of tuned and mistuned approximations to melody. *Perception & Psychophysics, 37*, 275–285.

7 Developmental approaches to music cognition and behaviour

Takao Umemoto
Konan Women's University, Kobe, JAPAN

The developmental approach is gaining its significance in recent researches into the psychology of music. Though there were already systematic contributions by Gardner (1973), Hargreaves (1986), and Sloboda (1985) and solid experimental contributions by Imberty (1969) and Zenatti (1969), the fields of research in developmental music psychology in this period were rather limited. A recent surge of interest in the developmental approach permeates almost all fields of music psychology. In the third ICMPC at Liège, 1994, about fifteen percent of all papers read at the conference treated some aspects of developmental problems, from prenatal musical environment to musicality in adolescence. Traditionally, the developmental approach has been an important method to assess the relative weight of environmental factors to innate dispositions on music perception, cognition and music behaviour. Today the significance of the developmental approach is found not only in the broader contexts of biological and comparative studies, but also in cognitive studies for assessment of the relative contribution of knowledge or experience as compared to maturational factors like age, to say nothing of its significance in educational contexts.

SINGING, SPEECH AND IMPROVISATION

Singing behaviour as a root of musicality has been an important target of research requiring developmental or comparative approaches in musicology and psychology since the nineteenth century. Papousek (1994) has proposed an evolutionary theory of musicality, which stresses the biological meaning of singing behaviour. According to Papousek, playfulness is an important aspect of human culture. Musicality has its origin in vocal play in early infancy. The vocal tract, he says, functions very early as a vehicle for vocal play and/or as the first musical instrument for vocal music. These functions are connected with intrinsic motivation for exploration, concept formation, and playful modification of existing concepts. Thus Papousek integrated and condensed many psychological variables and topics such as speech development, vocal communication, play, concept formation, creativity, and social inputs of care givers into one early singing behaviour, and put the problem of musicality on a large scale of evolution.

Infants also have special sensitivity to lullabies sung by care givers, according to Trehub and Henderson (1994) and Unyk, Trehub, Trainor, and Schellenberg (1992). Across cultures, these songs have smooth pitch contours, a strong tonal centre, repetitive rhythms, and a distinct vocal style. The investigators found that infants enjoyed lullabies more than adult songs and more than play songs, and they also enjoyed mothers' singing more than fathers' singing. Thus they stressed the implications of these studies that detailed analyses of lullabies and maternal performances may yield important clues to as yet unknown musical universals.

Dowling (1988), has stressed the importance of environmental factors based on his findings that children as young as three and four years old displayed the ability to respond to the degree of tonality of the stimuli. Nursery songs in the environment of infants usually emphasise the pitch content of the basic scales in the culture, without shifts of key or the introduction of altered pitches foreign to the key, and this should best facilitate perceptual learning involving the scale invariant. Dowling (1988) also showed that 208 melodies of 223 nursery songs (93%) remained in the initial key throughout, while only 220 (69%) out of 317 folk songs, and 2 (5%) of out of 44 Schubert songs remained in the initial key. Growing in such a musical environment, children acquire knowledge of pattern structure and tonality schema, becoming sensitive to atonal melodies by the ages of three or four.

The study of early singing behaviour as a critical activity in understanding the roots of musical behaviour is also emphasised by Dowling (1994). He acknowledges the common roots of speech and singing, but his model of the development of singing behaviour is more elaborative. He says that "There are at least two forms of early babbling: patterns of proto-syllables and vocal play, often exploring the extremes of the pitch, timbre, and loudness ranges of the voice. Between the ages of 9 and 12 months the first of these babbling patterns leads to speech, while both patterns lead to spontaneous singing." Differences between singing and speech which were clearly identified by Dowling were the sustaining of vowels on steady, discrete levels of pitch, and the superimposing of complex rhythms on a more steady beat.

Environmental factors that determine the development of singing in early infancy were studied with three infants from different musical environments (Kelly & Sutton-Smith, 1987); one from a professionally musically oriented home, the second from a non-professional but musically oriented home, and the third from non-musically oriented home. The mother-infant context, instruments, media and instruction were observed, and development of body movement and song were analysed in terms of melodic and rhythmic features. There were remarkable differences in the progress of singing between the three infants.

In a study of improvised singing with children from 5 to 10-years old, where children were required to sing songs improvising on given short texts which had different emotional meanings of pleasant, unpleasant and neutral, Umemoto (1994) found that the first feature which differentiated their songs from simple recitation of the text was rhythmic regularity. There was little movement of pitch level in the improvised songs of younger children, but rhythmic arrangement in regular duple metre appeared from the beginning. The most popular rhythm for them was skip one. Triple beat metre did not appear until 10-years old. From further observations on improvised singing, he showed that the concept of song in children develops from something that is first different from speech in rhythmic aspect, then in pitch aspect with larger intervals than in speech, sung at a higher register than speech, then through more intense emotional expression, with happy mood expressed by louder level and fast tempo, and sad mood expressed by quieter level and slow tempo.

An extensive study on the development of song was described by Davidson (1994). The data were earliest songs of preschoolers, the singing of musically untrained adults, and the perceptual changes in tonal relationships that a student undergoes in music school. He showed that a girl, at age three, already knew several important things about singing—for instance that pitches in the melody should be distinct from one another. Learning to sing songs is a complex task which involves (1) singing articulate pitches that reflect an underlying scale or tonal structure; (2) performing both surface and underlying rhythmic patterns regulated by a common pulse; (3) mastering the canons of song form; (4) forming structures that make possible the use of internal reference. Development of song proceeds further to the stages of collecting songs and forming a database, constructing the first boundaries of tonal space, and meeting the culture in middle childhood.

To regard development of singing behaviour not only as a limited topic in music psychology but as a representative topic within the framework of Piagetian tradition was the aim of Stadler-Elmer's (1994) study. According to her interpretation, musical development is an active construction of structures that serve the subject to experience, perceive, interpret, and produce music. Based on the theory of Fetz (1982), which considers imitation and play as central promoters in development, she distinguished two different types of singing:

songs by imitation of given song-models and singing by improvising or inventing. They are functionally interdependent. She tried to prove her interpretation by a longitudinal and cross-sectional study of 40 children from 4 to 6 years old.

Improvisation is the most primitive form of musical creativity. Mialaret (1994) tried to find regularities in the course of improvisation, not of singing but of playing on a metallophone, with 11 children of 2 years 10 months through 3 years 5 months. He found five types of pattern of trial-and-error-based musical explorations out of 289 productions. There were some regularities and irregularities in the repetition of their musical activities, which shows that children tried to make sensory-motor connections between the structure of their activities and sound qualities. At this age, however, children could not use sensory information for proper control of their activities, by interruption or modification of initial actions. In another article (1994) Mialaret analysed the dynamic aspect of development of musical creativity.

PERCEPTUAL AND COGNITIVE DEVELOPMENT AND MUSICOLOGY

Modern musicology, like modern linguistics, has a cognitive flavour. The current paradigm change in contemporary psychology from behaviourism to cognitive psychology has stimulated many researchers in related fields to produce interesting psycho-musicological researches. The work of Lerdahl and Jackendoff (1983) has been one of the most influential, but was not concerned with developmental problems. In the 1960s developmental studies on musicological concepts like cadence, tonality, modulation have been intensively studied by Imberty (1969) and Zenatti (1969), in relation to the problem of acculturation. More recently Serafine (1988) made an intensive study of the development of music cognition. She categorised music cognition into temporal processes and nontemporal processes; her studies on temporal processes include four experiments on understanding the successive dimension and three experiments on the simultaneity dimension, and studies on nontemporal processes include an experiment on tonal closure, four experiments on transformations, two experiments on abstraction and an experiment on hierarchical levels. It was a cross-sectional study of 6 groups of 15 subjects each, aged five, six, eight, ten, eleven and adults. Serafine found that the correlation between the closure task (discrimination between finished melody and unfinished melody) and a Piagetian conservation task was most significant (r=0.65, p<.005) at 8 years old. Performance on understanding similarity and difference among transformed melodies was 78% for the children of 10 and 11 years old. It seems that her results show that eight is one of the critical ages in the development of music cognition.

Deliège (1994), influenced by the ideas of cognitive psychologists like Neisser (1987), Fodor (1983) and Rosch (1978), has developed through her studies on musical cognition the notion that categorisation processes in music listening are comprised of two distinct steps: the first—cue extraction—is peripheral and perceptual, while the second—access to the evaluation of items during listening—is central. She tried to relate music listening process to the module hierarchy of the human mind as proposed in the modularity thesis of Fodor (1983). Comparing the performances of classification, frequency judgement and similarity rating in music listening in adults, children, and autistic children, she proved the validity of modular hypotheses. In an experiment (Deliège & Dupont, 1994) for normal children, subjects were of age 9 to 11 years old and composed of two groups of musical and non-musical children. Three pieces of Schubert, Diabelli and Bach, each containing 2 motives, were presented to the children and they then took three different tests on the frequency of appearance of two motives, classification of motives and similarity ratings. Results showed that the abstraction of cues was already possible in children aged between 9 and 11 years, but judgement of similarity was not. The influence of music training was significant, especially for the categorisation test. The results for the autistic children showed that their performance for frequency judgement and similarity was poor, but they had no difficulty with the classification task. From these results Deliège (1994) concluded that the idea of a hierarchy within the architecture of the modular system for music listening is justified.

The significance of developmental research that closely relates to musicology was stressed in a substantial body of studies on music perception by Trehub and her collaborators (1993,1994). Her fundamental theory is that there are good musical patterns innately matched to natural processing abilities. In assessing these patterns separately from the influence of Western music infants are the best subjects, because the pervasive influence of Western music makes it unlikely that researchers will find adult listeners who are unaffected by Western musical forms. Her method of experimentation was a modified habituation-dishabituation paradigm based on head turning responses of infants toward a loudspeaker. She found many important results which were relevant to music theory; e.g. infants detected intervallic change in the context of conventional melodies but not of unconventional melodies; children's ability to detect melodic changes is, by five years of age, influenced by key membership but not by implied harmony, however by seven years implicit understanding of implied harmony is clearly evident. Schellenberg and Trehub (1994) showed that it was easier for six year old children to detect change in melodic intervals with simple frequency ratios than intervals with more complex ratios. These findings help us to comprehend the relative contributions of innate and cultural factors in the development of chord, scale, key, intervals and other musical concepts.

The question of whether connotational discrimination of major and minor mode is innate or acquired is one of the most controversial topics in the psychology of music. Crowder and Kastner (1989) tested 38 children from ages of 3 to 12 with 12 tunes taken from original folk songs on the preference for major and minor. The tunes were arranged in four different versions of major, minor, with and without harmonic accompaniment. Children were asked to match each of tunes against one of four schematic facial expressions of happiness, contentment, sadness and anger. The results expressed as the sum of hits minus false alarms were significantly different from chance in all age groups of subjects. Even the youngest children—three-years old—showed significant responses. However, when the study was extended (Crowder, Reznick & Rosenkrantz, 1992) to infants of approximately six months of age, and tested with the method of contingent head-turning, there were no significant differences in looking time of infants. Since they found significant difference in infant's preference for dissonant and consonant chords, they concluded that the negative result cannot be ascribed to an insensitive experimental technique. It seems difficult to integrate the opposite hypothesis on the one hand that connotational meaning of scales and chords are mostly historical and culturally bound, and on the other hand, that they are inherent in the structure of tonality.

That melodic contour is an important feature in melody perception from early infancy has been stressed repeatedly by Dowling (1982,1986,1988). As infants grow they acquire knowledge of melodic schemata present in Western culture. Development of perception and cognition of music takes up various aspects and each aspect proceeds at its own rate which is domain specific. Focusing attention on hidden melodies amid distracter tones has been reported (Andrews & Dowling, 1991) to develop between 5 to 12 years. In a study by Andrews, Dowling, Bartlett and Halpern (1994), listeners at three levels of expertise and in three age ranges from 18 to 80-years old were tested. It was found that the relation of pitch range of distracter tones to the target tones and synchronising of metronome clicks to the target beat had significant effects. Performance did not decline with age for highly experienced listeners.

The problem studied by Lamont and Cross (1994) concerns the tonal hierarchy of children ranging in age between six and eleven. The method used was a probe tone technique with two contrasting context-types, one being a cadential sequence, and the other consisting of different randomisations of the diatonic collection. Children also participated in a game-playing experiment using chime bars. Results showed that the variables of age, gender, context-type and interaction between age and context-type were all significant. Response profiles from randomised diatonic context shows that even at an early age, a diatonic scalar/non-scalar distinction is evident. They concluded from the results that the sensitivity to diatonic structure which emerges can be claimed to constitute a product of enculturation rather than formal training.

The critical age in tonality acquisition is one of the most disputed topics in cognitive development related to enculturation. Children 7- and 8-years old were tested on their tonality and meter representation by Wilson, Wales and Pattison (1994). There were 20 melodic pairs consisting of tonal and atonal stimuli, and 20 rhythmic pairs consisting of metrical and non metrical stimuli. Children made three separate judgements of same/different, normal/strange and likableness rating. Results showed that 9-year old children were significantly more likely to categorise the tonal melodies as "normal" than 7-year old children. For the rhythmic pairs, both 7-year and 9-year old children were significantly more likely to categorise the metrical stimuli as "normal" compared to the non metrical stimuli. It seems that internal representation of tonality develops with age, but that there is some décalage between development of tonality and metricality concepts.

Melody categorisation methods were also used by Schwarzer (1994) to assess the development of learning strategies of melodies. The problem is whether children perceive melodies as an unanalysable whole (holistically) or attend selectively to single melodic attributes (analytically). Subjects were three groups of 6- to 7-year olds, 9- to 10-year olds, and adults. Their task was to classify short melodies varying systematically in melody-related attributes (contour, rhythm, and tonality) or non melody-related attributes (pitch level, tempo, instrument, and loudness). The results showed that both children and adults preferred to categorise melodies analytically rather than holistically, but the types of attributes chosen by different age groups changed from melody-unrelated to melody-related attributes; children preferred attributes that were not melody-related, especially loudness and timbre, whereas adults focused on melody-related attributes, particularly melody contour.

Integration of several attributes is a typical feature of cognitive development. Demorest (1994) tested the Information Integration Theory (Anderson, 1982) with a Pitch Rhythm Integration Measure (PRIM). The PRIM requires the subject to rate the degree of difference between a four measure theme, which is heard each time, and eight systematic variations of pitch and rhythm. Subjects were five groups of grades 1, 5 and 8, college adults and experts. The results showed a significant pitch x rhythm interaction for all novice groups. The expert pattern was more parallel and significantly differed from patterns of novices. The results suggest there is a an age-related increase in the perceptual response to rhythm variation.

In a study by Adachi and Carlsen (1994) the development of melodic expectancy was measured by the sung continuation method, in which subjects were required to continue a melody where the beginning two tones were given by an experimenter. Subjects were recruited from three age levels from 4 years 6 months old to 11 years 11 months old. The interval between the second pitch of the given melodic beginning and first sung pitch was coded as the expectancy. In the expectancy patterns obtained, there were scale patterns, chordal patterns, gap-fills, and octave completions. The melodic patterns demonstrated in children's expectancies were commonly observed in Western tonal music, and developmental trend and influence of cultures were not clear.

The development of musical cognition is studied not only by musical performance or musical judgement directly, but also indirectly by children's drawings or invented notation. It has been found by many researchers (Bamberger, 1991; Davidson & Scripp, 1988; Uptitis, 1987; Gromko,1994) that when children were asked to draw something to a given music, their drawings were not random but related to their levels of musical cognition. Bamberger (1991) analysed drawings of rhythm by children from ages four to twelve, and of college students. She classified drawings into two types; figural and metric, and found a development of drawing from conventional to hierarchical which represented their multiple hearing. She generalised that children's drawing of music reflects their development of musical intelligence. Uptitis (1987) also found significant developmental trends in accuracy and sophistication of description to rhythm by children. Davidson and Scripp (1988) analysed the song drawing of children from ages five to seven, concerned with the relationship of representational development to perceptual and performance development. They found developmental trends in their use of symbols, the level of sophistication of their notation, and their selective attention to musical features depending on the context. They expressed children's musical drawing as 'windows on music cognition'.

Are children's drawings really representing their musical cognition? To investigate the validity of the drawing, Gromko (1994) tried to assess the relation between measures of drawing and musical cognition independently. Principal component analysis was performed on the five variables: ages of sixty children (from four to eight years), tonal and rhythmic accuracy in their singing and playing, and two measures from Primary Measure of Musical Audiation by Gordon (1979). Children's invented notations were judged on the measures of tonal and rhythmic awareness. By principal component analysis on all variables, one factor was extracted, which was named as music understanding factor, and assigned a factor scores to each subject. ANOVA on factor scores on each subjects showed that higher the factor score of subjects, the more likely it was that their notation reflected pitch and rhythm awareness. The author concluded that the results confirmed the validity of children's invented notations as a measure of their musical understanding.

DEVELOPMENTAL PROCESS IN BECOMING AN EXPERT

Studies on experts contribute not only to professional music education, but also to theoretical development in recent cognitive psychology. Richardson (1994) studied the verbal protocols of 31 children in grades 1 to 8, while listening to ten short recorded musical examples. 1805 statements were coded into 10 categories of knowledge, imaginative use of language, sensitivity, expectation, comparison, prediction, evaluation, outer statement, metacognising and recognition. From the results she described three distinct levels of expertise; identifying and evaluation at the first level, expectation, comparison and prediction at the second level, and metacognition at the third level.

Acquisition of absolute pitch with systematic training by the Yamaha method was reported by Ogawa and Miyazaki (1994). The subjects were 104 children from 4 to 10-years old and a cross-sectional rate of correct response showed a remarkable growth by the age of seven.

The problem of domain specificity of musical knowledge has set some intriguing research targets. Oura and Hatano (1988) did three experiments with 3 groups of subjects differing in age and experience in music. They were 4th grade children and college students, both with experience of about 5 years of piano training, and musically inexperienced college students. They were required to learn an unfamiliar short CM song and reproduce it by singing. The results were that experienced subjects, even 4th grade children, were far superior to inexperienced college students. However, in an additional experiment, when subjects were required to learn a poem, the performance of older subjects was better than that of the children. In the third experiment, when subjects were required to learn a Japanese melody which has no tonality, there were no significant differences between the experienced and the inexperienced. They concluded that the superb memory of the children was restricted to the domain of tonal music, and that the domain-specific knowledge supporting memory of melodies must at least in part be highly specific to tonal music.

A number of studies on the development of expert musicians have been carried out recently. Manturzewska's (1990) biographical study of professional musicians was one of the most extensive. A group of 165 Polish professional musicians ranging in age from 21 to 89 was interviewed for a longitudinal study of life-span development. From content analysis of biographic data, she found that the family environment and intrinsic motivation for musical activity are the factors most influencing musical development.

Studies by Ericsson, Krampe and Tesch-Römer (1993) and by Sloboda and Howe (1991) suggest that the best predictor for level of expertise is the cumulated time spent in effortful practice by the age of 21. These studies, however, have shortcomings in that they do not include data from low achieving subjects and reliability and validity of retrospective reports. Sloboda, Davidson, Moore and Howe (1994) tried to find reliable data to assess this prediction. Their subjects were 257 children divided into 5 groups according to their musical careers. Among five groups there were children who attended specialist music schools, children who had applied for but failed to enter the specialist music schools, and children who were currently learning musical instruments at non-specialist schools or had given up such study. Average daily practice time was estimated for each instrument learned, and they were also asked to estimate time spent on improvisation, playing through previously learned pieces, and unstructured informal activities. Results showed that at every age tested, the subjects who attended specialist music schools did most practice and those who had been relatively unsuccessful at instrumental music did least.

To analyse the relations between children's implicit theories of ability as stable or malleable and progress in their instrumental music tuition, 51 children aged 6 to 11 were longitudinally studied by O'Neill (1994). Results showed that majority of children made internal attributions after the success condition, but that this changed to external attributions after the failure condition. While studies on the role of motivation in musical development are few, this longitudinal study will contribute to the understanding of relations between musical self-concept and expertising.

Is it true that the most important factors contributing towards a child's persistence with music lessons are support and stimulation from family and teacher? This is suggested by an intensive study of Davidson, Sloboda and Howe (1994). They collected interview data from five groups of young people and their parents. The groups were selected to reflect different levels of musical competence and success. Results were analysed in terms of parental involvement in lessons, motivation to practice, parental involvement in supervising practice, parents' own involvement in music, siblings' influence on musical interest, and teacher qualities. In all of these items the hypotheses were supported.

Studies on music appreciation are few, but Behne (1994) reported an important longitudinal study concerned with the development of music appreciation during the years of adolescence. By way of cluster analysis of 39 items on appreciation, he identified 9 styles of listening such as compensational, vegetative, concentrated, emotional, distancing, sentimental, associative, stimulative and diffuse listening. With repeated measurements of listening style with children aged 11 and a half years old, he found two main trends: the more cognitive components (concentrated and distancing) tend to weaken, while more body-orientated components (vegetative, stimulative) gain greater intensity over time.

In all of these works the authors did not confine their viewpoint to a specific theory of musical activities. They referred to more general theory of development, either biological or cognitive like Piaget or Bruner. In this respect, Parncutt's proposal (1994) on the genesis of music is also relevant. He discussed the genesis of music from the emergence of symbolic skill and sensitivity of prenatal auditory system, and concluded that all humans are motivated to take part regularly in musical activities.

A grand theory of musical development or developmental model has also been proposed by Gardner (1973) and Swanwick and Tillman (1985). Gardner (1973) schematised aesthetic development into three periods or six stages in the term of symbolic use. From ages 0 to 1 is a period of presymbolic activity, 2 to 7 is a period of symbol use, and from eight years there is a period of later artistic development. The second period involves three stages each of which has characteristics of immersion in symbolic media, exploration and amplification of the symbol, and forming familiarity with culture's aesthetic code.

Another model of musical development by Swanwick and Tillman (1985) schematised the developmental processes into eight stages of sensory and manipulative (0–4), personal expressiveness and the vernacular (4–9), the speculative and the idiomatic (10–15), and the symbolic and the systematic (16+). The model is re-examined by cross-cultural data (Swanwick, 1994) and supported. The model has practical implications for music curricula.

Thus findings obtained through developmental approach to the study of musical cognition and behaviour are not isolated facts or topics in music psychology, but rather recent examples of themes which exhibit typical problems contributing to the progress of psychology in general.

REFERENCES

Adachi, M., & Carlsen, J.C. (1994). Melodic expectancy development in musical children. In I. Deliège, (Ed.), *Proceedings of the 3rd International Conference on Music Perception and Cognition* (pp. 143–144). Liège, Belgium: European Society for the Cognitive Sciences of Music.

Anderson, N.H. (1982). *Methods of information integration theory.* NY: Academic Press.

Andrews, M.W., & Dowling, W.J. (1991). The development of perception of interleaved melodies and control of auditory attention. *Music Perception, 8,* 349–368.

Andrews, M.W., Dowling, W.J., Bartlett, J.C., & Halpern, A. (1994). Attentional focus in the perception of rapid tone sequences by young and elderly musicians and non musicians. In I. Deliège (Ed.), *Proceedings of the 3rd International Conference on Music Perception and Cognition* (pp. 145–146). Liège, Belgium: European Society for the Cognitive Sciences of Music.

Bamberger, J. (1991). The mind behind the musical ear. Cambridge: Harvard University Press.

Behne, K.E. (1994). The development of music appreciation in adolescence. In I. Deliège (Ed.), *Proceedings of the 3rd International Conference on Music Perception and Cognition* (pp. 383–384). Liège, Belgium: European Society for the Cognitive Sciences of Music.

Crowder, R.G., & Kastner, M.P. (1989). Emotional connotations of the major/minor distinction in young children. *Proceedings of the 1st International Conference on Music Perception and Cognition* (pp. 389–394).

Crowder, R.G., Reznick, J.S., & Rozenkrantz, S.L. (1992). Perception of the major/minor distinction: V. Preferences among infants. *Program of the 2nd International Conference on Music Perception and Cognition* (p. 80).

Davidson, L. (1994). Songsinging by young and old. A developmental approach to music.In Aiello,R., & Sloboda, J.A. (Eds.), *Musical perceptions* (pp. 99–139). Oxford: Oxford University Press.

Davidson, J.W,. & Scripp, L. (1988). Young children's musical representation: windows on musical cognition. In J.A. Sloboda, (Ed.), *Generative processes in music* (pp. 195–230). Oxford: Clarendon Press.

Davidson, J.W., Sloboda, J.A., & Howe, M.J.A. (1994). The role of family and teachers in the success and failures of music learners. In I. Deliège (Ed.), *Proceedings of the 3rd International Conference on Music Perception and Cognition* (pp. 359–360). Liège, Belgium: European Society for the Cognitive Sciences of Music.

Deliège, I. (1994). The two steps of the categorization process in music listening. An approach of the cue extraction mechanism as modular system. In R.Steinberg (Ed.), *Music and the mind machine. The psychophysiology and psychopathology of the sense of music* (pp. 61–73). Berlin: Springer-Verlag.

Deliège, I., & Dupont, M. (1994). Extraction d'indices et catégorisation de la musique chez l'enfant: effet de l'âge, de la formation et du style musical sur la capacité à identifier, classer et comparer des structures musicales. In I. Deliège (Ed.), *Proceedings of the 3rd International Conference on Music Perception and Cognition* (pp. 287–288). Liège, Belgium: European Society for the Cognitive Sciences of Music.

Demorest, S.M. (1994). The integration of pitch and rhythm in musical judgment: a paradigm for research in musical development. In I. Deliège (Ed.), *Proceedings of the 3rd International Conference on Music Perception and Cognition* (pp. 149–150). Liège, Belgium: European Society for the Cognitive Sciences of Music.

Dowling, W.J. (1982). Melodic information processing and its development in D. Deutsch (Ed.), *The psychology of music* (pp. 413–429). New York; Academic Press.

Dowling, W.J., & Harwood, D.L. (1986). *Music cognition.* New York: Academic Press.

Dowling, W.J., (1988). Tonal structure and children's early learning of music. In J.A. Sloboda (Ed.), *Generative processes in music* (pp. 113–128). Oxford: Clarendon Press.

Dowling, W.J. (1994). The development of melodic perception and production. In I. Deliège (Ed.), *Proceedings of the 3rd International Conference on Music Perception and Cognition* (pp. 253–254). Liège, Belgium: European Society for the Cognitive Sciences of Music.

Ericsson, K.A., Krampe, R.T., & Tesch-Römer, C. (1993). The role of deliberate practice in the acquisition of expert performance. *Psychological Review*, 363–406.

Fetz, R.L. (1982). Nachahnung, Spiel und Kunst. Fragen einer genetischen Aesthetik. *Freiburger Zeitschrift für Philosophie und Theologie, 29,* 489–508.

Fodor, J.A. (1983). *The modularity of mind.* Cambridge, MA: MIT Press.

Gardner, H. (1973). *The arts and human development.* New York: John Wiley.

Gordon, E.E. (1979). Primary measures of music audiation and the intermediate measures of music audiation. Chicago: G.I.A. Publications.

Gromko, J.E. (1994). Children's invented notations as measures of musical understanding. *Psychology of Music, 22,* 136–147.

Hargreaves, D.J. (1986). *The developmental psychology of music.* Cambridge: Cambridge University Press.

Imberty, M. (1969). *L'acquisition des structures tonales chez l'enfant.* Paris: Klincksieck.

Kelly, L., & Sutton-Smith, B. (1987). A study of infant musical productivity. In J.C. Peery, I.W. Peery & T.W. Draper (Eds.), *Music and child development* (pp. 35–53). Berlin: Springer-Verlag.

Lamont, A., & Cross, I. (1994). Mental representations of musical pitch. A developmental study. In I. Deliège (Ed.), *Proceedings of the 3rd International Conference on Music Perception and Cognition* (pp. 131–132). Liège, Belgium: European Society for the Cognitive Sciences of Music.

Lerdahl, F., & Jackendoff, R. (1983). *A generative theory of tonal music.* Cambridge, MA: MIT Press.

Manturzewska, M. (1990). A biographical study of the life-span development of professional musicians. *Psychology of Music, 18,* 112–139.

Mialaret, J.P. (1994). Régularités au cours de tâtonnements musicaux exploratoires chez le jeune enfant. In I. Deliège (Ed.) *Proceedings of the 3rd International Conference on Music Perception and Cognition* (pp. 155–156). Liège, Belgium: European Society for the Cognitive Sciences of Music.

Mialaret, J.P. (1994). La créativité musicale. In A. Zenatti (Ed.), *Psychologie de la musique* (pp. 223–258). Paris: Presses Universitaires de France.

Neisser, U. (1987). From direct perception to conceptual structure. In U. Neisser (Ed.), *Concepts and conceptual development. Ecological and intellectual factors in categorization* (pp. 11–24). Cambridge: Cambridge University Press.

Ogawa, Y., & Miyazaki, K. (1994). The process of acquisition of absolute pitch by children in Yamaha music school. In I. Deliège (Ed.), *Proceedings of the 3rd International Conference on Music Perception and Cognition* (pp. 135–136). Liège, Belgium: European Society for the Cognitive Sciences of Music.

O'Neill, S.A. (1994). Factors influencing children's motivation and achievement during the first year of instrumental music tuition. In I. Deliège (Ed.), *Proceedings of the 3rd International Conference on Music Perception and Cognition* (pp. 123–124). Liège, Belgium: European Society for the Cognitive Sciences of Music.

Oura, Y., & Hatano, G. (1988). Memory of melodies among subjects differing in age and experience in music. *Psychology of Music, 16*, 91–109.

Papousek, H. (1994). To the evolution of human musicality and musical education. In I. Deliège (Ed.), *Proceedings of the 3rd International Conference on Music Perception and Cognition* (pp. 13–14). Liège, Belgium: European Society for the Cognitive Sciences of Music.

Parncutt, R. (1994). A scenario for the genesis of music. In I. Deliège (Ed.), *Proceedings of the 3rd International Conference on Music Perception and Cognition* (pp. 93–94). Liège, Belgium: European Society for the Cognitive Sciences of Music.

Richardson, C.P. (1994). The music listening process of the child connoisseur: a developmental model. In I. Deliège (Ed.), *Proceedings of the 3rd International Conference on Music Perception and Cognition* (pp. 153–154). Liège, Belgium: European Society for the Cognitive Sciences of Music.

Rosch, E. (1978). Principles of categorization. In E. Rosch & B.Lloyd (Eds.), *Cognition and categorization* (pp. 28–49). Hillsdale, NJ: Erlbaum.

Schellenberg, E.G., & Trehub, S.E. (1994). Processing advantages for simple frequency ratios: Evidence from young children. In I. Deliège (Ed.), *Proceedings of the 3rd International Conference on Music Perception and Cognition* (pp. 129–130). Liège, Belgium: European Society for the Cognitive Sciences of Music.

Schwarzer, G. (1994). Development of analytic and holistic modes of melody apprehension. In I. Deliège (Ed.), *Proceedings of the 3rd International Conference on Music Perception and Cognition* (pp. 141–142). Liège, Belgium: European Society for the Cognitive Sciences of Music.

Serafine, M.L. (1988). *Music as cognition. The development of thought in sound.* New York: Columbia University Press.

Sloboda, J.A. (1985). *The musical mind. The cognitive psychology of music.* Oxford: Oxford University Press.

Sloboda, J.A., & Howe, M.J.A. (1991). Biographical precursors of musical excellence: an interview study. *Psychology of Music, 19*, 3–21.

Sloboda, J.A., Davidson, J.W., Howe, M.J.A., & Moore, D. (1994). Formal practice as predictor of success and failure in instrumental learning. In I. Deliège (Ed.), *Proceedings of the 3rd International Conference on Music Perception and Cognition* (pp. 125–126). Liège, Belgium: European Society for the Cognitive Sciences of Music.

Stadler-Elmer, S. (1994). Children's acquisition and generation of songs. In I. Deliège (Ed.), *Proceedings of the 3rd International Conference on Music Perception and Cognition* (pp. 119–120). Liège, Belgium: European Society for the Cognitive Sciences of Music.

Swanwick, K. (1991). Further research on the musical development sequence. *Psychology of Music, 19*, 22–32.

Swanwick, K., & Tillman, J. (1986). The sequence of musical development. *British Journal of Music Education, 3*.

Trehub, S.E. (1994). Developmental perspectives on music perception. In I. Deliège (Ed.), *Proceedings of the 3rd International Conference on Music Perception and Cognition* (pp. 15–16). Liège, Belgium: European Society for the Cognitive Sciences of Music.

Trehub, S.E,. & Trainor, L.J. (1993). Listening strategies in infancy: the roots of music and language development. In S. McAdams & E. Bigand (Eds.), *Thinking in sound. The cognitive psychology of human audition* (pp. 278–327). Oxford: Oxford University Press.

Trehub, S.E, & Henderson, J. (1994). Caregivers' songs and their effect on infant listeners. In I. Deliège (Ed.), *Proceedings of the 3rd International Conference on Music Perception and Cognition* (pp. 47–48). Liège, Belgium: European Society for the Cognitive Sciences of Music.

Umemoto, T. (1994). Children's knowledge about song. In I. Deliège (Ed.), *Proceedings of the 3rd International Conference on Music Perception and Cognition* (pp. 121–122). Liège, Belgium: European Society for the Cognitive Sciences of Music.

Unyk, A.M., Trehub, S.E., Trainor, L.J., & Schellenberg, E. G. (1992). Lullabies and simplicity: A cross-cultural perspective. *Psychology of Music, 20*, 15–28.

Uptitis, R. (1981). Toward a model for rhythm development. In J.C. Peery, I.W. Peery, & T.W. Draper (Eds.), Music and child development. (pp. 54–79), Berlin: Springer-Verlag.

Wilson, S.J., Wales, R.J., & Pattison, P. (1994). The representation of tonality. In I. Deliège (Ed.), *Proceedings of the 3rd International Conference on Music Perception and Cognition* (pp. 151–152). Liège, Belgium: European Society for the Cognitive Sciences of Music.

Zenatti, A. (1969). Le développement génétique de la perception musicale. *Monographie Française de Psychologie, 17.*

8

The development of "Musikerleben" in adolescence: How and why young people listen to music

Klaus-Ernst Behne
Hochschule für Musik und Theater Hannover, Germany

MUSICAL EXPERIENCE, MUSIKERLEBEN AND MUSIC APPRECIATION

Musikerleben is a common experience, but a German term which is perhaps impossible to translate into English. It can be defined as the sum of psychic processes which accompany the experience of music in situations when music is in the focus of interest: When a person is not only hearing, but listening to and appreciating music. The nearest English equivalent would be "music appreciation", but with its "awareness of salient characteristics"[1] the definition of this term seems to be more restricted than Musikerleben. In comparison with Musikerleben, music appreciation tends to be a more intellectual approach to music based on knowledge that can be acquired in college classes. By using this knowledge the listener is able to trace the structure of the music and recognise its salient characteristics. Music appreciation in this sense corresponds to the idea of "strukturelles Hören", a concept of the ideal listening style Adorno (1968/ 1976) developed in his writings on music aesthetics. Neither is Musikerleben identical with musical *experience,* which is a much broader concept (including activities such as playing an instrument, singing, remembering or reading about music). Musikerleben has nothing to do with taste or preferences, but a positive attitude towards music is certainly a precondition. Furthermore, Musikerleben is also part of aesthetic experience, but it is not necessarily an "intense subjective and personal experience", as this term is described by the American colleagues of the SRIG (Price, 1986). On the contrary, in a perceptual world determined by the omnipresence of various audio and audiovisual media, Musikerleben must be thought of as varying in intensity on different levels of attention. "Strong experiences with music" as discussed by Gabrielsson and Lindström (1994) have their counterpart in "diffuse listening", when music receives almost no attention, reducing Musikerleben to a minimum.

RELATED LITERATURE

Research in music psychology has focused mainly on the cognitive aspects of Musikerleben, though some research has attempted to answer the question of how and why people enjoy music.

Vernon (1930) tackled this problem with a methodologically unusual approach: he organised special concerts for his subjects who stated their thoughts and feelings while listening to music in an elaborate questionnaire and in free comments. Using those quantitative as well as qualitative data, he developed the idea of "true visualisation" as "essentially an emotional response" (p.52), "a kind of day-dream stimulated directly and continuously by the music as it proceeds" (p.57). With regard to the empirical data he had gathered (but did not report), he found that "true visualisers" are comparatively rare but "wholly absent among the most musical" (p.63). Visualising is interpreted positively, because it adds to the fascination of music and can be viewed as a desirable aspect of music appreciation. The unusual and surprising aspect of Vernon's approach is the assumption that there may be desirable components of music appreciation experienced mainly by non-musicians and that the musical experts' listening styles must not necessarily be a model for music lovers and amateurs!

Yingling (1962) has also worked with qualititative and quantitative methods. He hypothesised four reactions in listening to music: "associative", "emotional", "intellectual", and "sensory". These may constitute various different patterns. All four dimensions were found in unstructured verbal descriptions as well as in the questionnaire data, with students in "appreciation" courses showing a dominantly "intellectual" response more often than other students. "Physical sensing of music" seems to him to be "important for its apprehension" (p.119)—a very rare point of view.

In contrast to Vernon (and his "true visualisers"), Crickmore (1968) had the idea that music appreciation should, among other features, be characterised by the absence of mental pictures. As a British author with a "Gestalt" approach, his use of the term "music appreciation" may perhaps come a bit closer to Musikerleben. He developed a special questionnaire to ascertain a priori defined patterns of reaction, which involve both an "active and a passive element" (p.239). His idea of musical experience comes close to what later has been discussed as "flow" (Csikszentmihalyi, 1975).

Hedden (1973) used a more elaborate multivariate design in developing his 20-item "music listening reaction scale" to gather information "about how subjects said they reacted when they listened to orchestral music" (p.226). Using factor analysis, Hedden found five different dimensions of response to music: "associative", "cognitive", "physical", "involvement" and "enjoyment". In this study, as well as in a later one by Lewis and Schmidt (1991), correlations with selected aspects of personality were found. By summing up the individual ratings for the different items the last named authors reduced the reaction scale to a single dimension.

TYPOLOGIES

In addition to this handful of empirical studies, other authors have investigated Musikerleben in a more introspective, philosophical manner. Alt (1935) and Müller-Freienfels (1936) reviewed the work of numerous authors who developed concepts of different dimensions of Musikerleben, especially dimensions constructed by opposites, such as "Stoff-Form", "pathetisch-ästhetisch", "Abstraktion-Einfühlung" or "appollinisch-"dionysisch". Alt was one of the first German authors whose (typological) ideas were based on empirical data (texts written by students), although today some methodological aspects of his study appear outdated. Following a philosophical tradition, he developed two typologies of "musikalisches Genießen" and "musikalisches Werten" and attempted to find out which of these ideas could be verified in the verbalisations of musically interested students.

Some decades later, in his "Einleitung in die Musiksoziologie", Adorno (1968/1976) published a brilliant but strongly biased essay about "Typen musikalischen Verhaltens". He developed the idea that except for the musical expert's highly intellectual, structural way of listening to music, there are only inferior listening styles, such as "emotionale Hörer", "Ressentimenthörer" or "Jazzfans". What is most remarkable about this text is that although it lacks any empirical evidence it is generally accepted in Germany—with questionable effects on music education! In most of the studies cited the authors try to differentiate between different types of Musikerleben, but unfortunately they usually do so in an evaluative manner. Most of them not only disagree about what should constitute Musikerleben, but also fail to give reasons for their biased evaluation of its different components.

Vernon searched for "true visualisers", but what is it that makes other visualisers not "true"? Crickmore, referring to the ideas of Wing, searched for one special pattern of music appreciation, but failed to explain why only one such pattern should exist. Finally, Yingling's conclusion that "as a result of instruction in Music Appreciation, the *sensory, emotional* and *associative* aspects of the music are largely obliterated by the intellectual aspect" (p.116) raises the question of why such a modification would be desirable.

At this point it is perhaps evident that the study of Musikerleben should be free of normative ideas. People develop different ways of listening to and of "using" music. If we try to understand music as a human phenomenon, we must be aware of these differences, even though we can neither precisely describe nor understand them so far. With this in mind, we began a longitudinal study in 1991 on the development of Musikerleben. First results are discussed in the following sections.

DEVELOPMENT OF THE QUESTIONNAIRE

Taking into account the evidence from the previously mentioned studies, a set of 40 items was constructed to ask for habitual aspects of Musikerleben. They all began with: "When I listen to music,..." and were then continued by a statement, such as: "..., I like to hum and sing" or "..., it makes me feel better", for which respondents were asked to rate their agreement on a 5-point scale. Subjects were encouraged to think of music they liked, music they often listened to. One special problem emerged in formulating aspects of structural listening in a way that children aged 11 would understand. After discussions with music teachers and music majors this first set was reformulated and reduced to 26 items, which were then used in a pilot study (n=118 students aged 11 to 13). Subjects were invited to write down additional items if they felt that there were relevant aspects not mentioned in the questionnaire. We then formulated a final version with 32 items which were used in a study with a sample of n=1224 students aged 11 to 20 ("Hörertypologien", Behne, 1986a).

Searching for the different dimensions of Musikerleben in such data can be done in two ways, by using either factor analysis or cluster analysis. Factor analysis is normally used to find orthogonal dimensions. Given our scanty knowledge of Musikerleben we decided to use variable cluster analysis (Schlosser, 1976) to avoid violations of orthogonality associated with factor analysis. Variable cluster analysis yielded 8 variable clusters (including 26 of the 32 items).[2]

A slightly enlarged version of this questionnaire ("habitual music listening patterns") was used in a crosscultural investigation by Lehmann (1994a), who gathered data in the USA and in Germany. For a subsample in his study he found a retest-reliability (after 3 months) of = 0.886, which seemed of acceptable magnitude.

To date, several other studies have been conducted using this type of questionnaire (with slightly varying numbers of items). The comparability of results is problematic as variable cluster analyses of different sets of data seldom yield exactly the same structures. However, there is usually great convergence of findings. Each study can therefore only be interpreted in its own right, considering the unique composition of its synthetic variables. Nine variable complexes (listening styles) emerged from the first data of the longitudinal study (1991), such as "compensating listening" (consisting of 5 items, see Table 8.1[3]) or "emotional listening".

TABLE 8.1
Clustering of Items Creating the 9 Listening Styles in the Longitudinal Study
(data gathered in 1991, subjects aged 11)

When I listen to music, ...

Compensating	..., *it changes my mood.* ..., *it really calms me down, if I was excited before.* ..., *it is possible that I can find my own moods and feelings in the music.* ..., *I feel less lonely.* ..., *it makes me feel better.*
Concentrated	..., *I like to close my eyes.* ..., *I like to follow the various themes.*
Emotional	..., *I pay attention to what types of feelings are expressed through the music.* ..., *it is for me above all a matter of sentiment.*
Distancing	..., *I like to identify the musical style (to say whether it is Folk music or Modern Jazz or baroque music).* ..., *I try to understand the words of the vocal part.* ..., *I follow the musical lines of a special instrumental part.* ..., *I try to grasp the structure of a piece of music (repetitions, variations).*
Vegetative	..., *it really gets under my skin.* ..., *I assume a different body position.* ..., *it can happen that I am captivated by the rhythm.* ..., *I sometimes feel my heart beat faster, my skin prickling, butterflies in my stomach.*
Sentimental	..., *I like to dream.* ..., *I remember things of the past.* ..., *it makes me think about myself.* ..., *I sometimes want to cry.* ..., *I'd like to be far, far away.*
Associative	..., *I have pictural images.* ..., *I invent a story, as if I were watching a movie.*
Stimulative	..., *I like to play it very loud.* ..., *it makes me feel excited, even aggressive.*
Diffuse	..., *my attention is divided.* ..., *I like to do other things besides just listening.*

FIRST RESULTS

This first study (Behne, 1986a) was cross-sectional. It yielded a very clear trend for most components of Musikerleben: For the ages 10 to 13, a moderate decline of the originally already low level of acceptance for the respective items could be observed. But after age 13, most components of Musikerleben showed a dramatic increase. The greatest increase was found for the "vegetative" and the "emotional" listening style, with the youngest showing the least and the oldest the most pronounced acceptance. At first glance these results suggest that Musikerleben develops in the late years of adolescence, predominantly after the peak of puberty. For reasons of methodology, however, such a conclusion is not possible, because cross-sectional studies do not take into consideration factual changes in the lives of individuals. They can be interpreted only in the sense of differences between persons of different ages. This drawback was the main motivation for conducting a longitudinal study.

In the cross-sectional study it was, for the first time, possible to search for correlations between different ways of Musikerleben (listening styles) and music preferences. We differentiated between verbal ("Do you like Jazz?") and sounding preferences ("Do you like this music?", followed by an unlabelled music example). Verbal and sounding music preferences are far from being identical. These discrepancies and their possible explanations are very interesting and are discussed elsewhere (Behne, 1986a). Table 8.2[4] gives correlations $> = 0.20$ (all significant at 0.001%) between three listening styles and the various music preferences. Like many other authors we expected

TABLE 8.2
Highest Correlations (> = 0.20) Between Listening Styles and Two Sorts of
Music Preferences

Listening styles:	*Sounding Preferences:*	*Verbal Preferences:*
distancing	Beethoven Ex.1 (0.22) Mozart Ex.1, Vivaldi , Dufay (0.20)	Klass.Konzertmusik (0.28) Oper (0.21) Chor (0.20)
emotional	Beethoven Ex.1 (0.37) Brahms (0.32) Corelli (0.26) Mozart Ex.2 (0.25) Mozart Ex.1, Bach, Vivaldi (0.23) Hindemith (0.22) Simon & Garfunkel (0.21) Beethoven Ex.2 (0.20)	Klass.Konzertmusik (0.27) Reggae (0.26) Musicals, Liedermacher (0.22) Operette (0.21)
vegetative	Beethoven Ex.1 (0.27) Simon & Garfunkel (0.21) Brahms (0.20)	Reggae (0.26) Liedermacher (0.21)

correlations to be high between a "distancing" listening style and classical music and between an "emotional" listening style and popular music.

As can be seen in the first section of the table, "distancing" listening does indeed correlate with classical preferences, especially with the category "Klassische Konzertmusik". "Emotional" and "vegetative" listening, however, both correlate positively not only with popular music but unexpectedly also with various other preferences, nearly all of them examples of high culture music (e.g. Beethoven). No negative correlations between any kind of listening style and any kind of preferred music could be found. One explanation for this astonishing result may be that the "emotional" listeners are also those with the greatest musical curiosity. A greater contrast between expected and actual results cannot be imagined. It is obvious how misleading such unfounded expectations concerning the complex relations between preferences and Musikerleben can be for music educators whose aim it is to motivate adolescents.

A similar questionnaire was used by Lehmann (1994a) in his cross-cultural study. Using the same items he asked for the habitual aspects of Musikerleben and for reactions to three sounding music examples. This was done to reveal habitual patterns, formed during individual development, and to see how stable these behavioural patterns prove to be when the listeners are confronted with unknown music. The author found that the components of the habitual listening patterns generally showed a greater intensity than the situational ones. A remarkable effect was found for those groups who either preferred or disliked the music very strongly: to like or to reject certain music is closely related to great differences in the intensity of the listening styles. The intensity of music preferences seems to be a mirror of the intensity of Musikerleben.

RESULTS OF THE LONGITUDINAL STUDY

I will now present the initial results of the longitudinal study concerned with the development of Musikerleben during the years of adolescence (11 to 17). The main objective of this study is to look for processes of change in the development of Musikerleben, i.e. how the listening styles and their interaction with different aspects of music preferences can be interpreted in the context of individual biographical events. For example, will adolescents with problems in school develop a more intense compensating listening style than students without such problems? Up to now 155 children have been surveyed four times, at ages eleven years and eight months, eleven years and ten months, twelve years and thirteen years. The sample reflects the social structure in the city of Hannover, Germany (population 600,000). The children take part voluntarily, although their motivation to cooperate is reinforced by a small payment, and by a living-room-type atmosphere with sweets and soft drinks offered to them. The children are asked to rate the different aspects of their Musikerleben on the described questionnaire (39 items). In an additional questionnaire they are asked for their music preferences (verbal and sounding) and for several other aspects of their daily lives (how and how often they use different media, musical activities, problems they may have etc.). As shown in Table 8.1, 28 of the 39 items could be bundled to nine listening styles using variable cluster analysis. Fig.8.1 gives the changes of the nine listening styles over time: L1 refers to the beginning of the study (children aged 11.5), L3 refers to the third investigation after 7 months, and L4 to the last after 19 months.[5] The centrepoint of the scale (ranging form 1 to 5) is 3.0. The asterisks in the graph indicate levels of significance (* $p<0.05$, ** $p<0.01$ and *** $p<0.001$). Asterisks on the left indicate significant MANOVAs with repeated measures, those on the right represent special contrasts between first (L1) and third (L4) measurement point. Significance between adjacent points (asterisks between L1 and L3, L3, and L4, respectively) are computed as nonorthonormalized contrasts using transformed variables (instead of repeated measures).

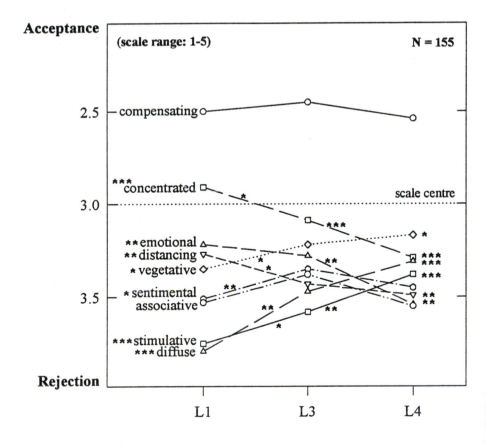

FIG. 8.1   Variations for nine listening styles over time

It can be seen that the majority of the listening styles show only slight intensity, with means below 3.0. This coincides with the early cross-sectional study mentioned above, i.e. components of Musikerleben are only weakly developed at the beginning of the second decade. To use music for mood-management ("compensating" listening), is by far the most important listening style at this point. This is in agreement with other results of our study, showing that already at this early age children have definite and distinctive ideas of what kind of music they would like to hear in a sad, angry or happy mood. Of the other listening styles, the "concentrated" and "emotional" style show a medium intensity, while the "diffuse" and "stimulative" are poorly developed.

With the exception of "compensating", "sentimental" and "associative" listening there is a general tendency for components with initially higher intensity to decrease over time, while those that were the least intense at the beginning show a clear tendency to increase. Although at first (L1) all components (with the exception of "compensating" listening) are well differentiated at low intensities, 1.5 years later (L4) they are nearly all similar. There are two main trends: The more cognitive components ("concentrated" and "distancing") tend to weaken while more body-orientated components ("vegetative", "stimulative") gain greater intensity over time. "Diffuse" listening—the weakest component at the youngest age—shows the greatest increase, with an associated proportional decrease of "concentrated" listening.

Now to the possible correlations between Musikerleben and the problems adolescents may experience. Subjects (in L3, at the age of 12) were asked to indicate how frequent (often=2, seldom=1, never=0) they had problems concerning school, boredom, family, outward appearance, depression, friends, health, loneliness, fear, worries about the future. A problem index was computed for the weighted frequency of problems, summing up a "2" for any "often" answer and a "1" for any "seldom" answer. This way the sample could be divided into three nearly equally sized groups (n = 53 + 47 + 54) with low, medium, and high frequency of problems.

A MANOVA with the nine listening styles as dependent variables and weighted frequency of problems as a factor with three levels was computed. The analysis yielded a significant multivariate effect (F=2.06, p=0.01 Pillais). Fig. 8.2 shows the means for those variables with significant univariate effects. For the two extreme groups (with low and high problem frequency) asterisks indicate whether the contrasts (in relation to the mean of the whole sample) were significant.

As could be expected, there is an effect on "compensating" listening, but it is only the weakest effect, showing that children with many problems tend to listen in a slightly more compensating manner. More pronounced, however, is the effect on "sentimental" listening: it is significantly lower for those with few problems and significantly higher for those with many problems. The third effect indicates that children with few problems have habitually "vegetative"

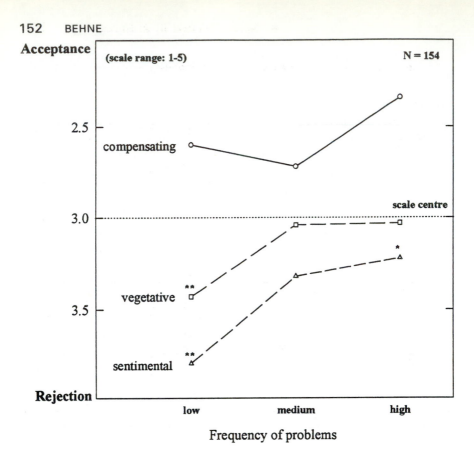

FIG. 8.2 Listening styles and frequency of problems

concomitants while listening to music in only a modest degree. In a general sense our hypothesis that "compensating" listening corresponds with the frequency of problems was confirmed by a multivariate effect. Unexpectedly an even stronger effect was found for "sentimental" listening. A "compensating" listening style is an active strategy of mood management, whereas "sentimental" listening shows a more passive tendency. "Sentimental" listening is another way to cope with problems by escaping into dreams and into the past.

So far we have only considered the frequency, not the quality of problems. Can we suppose that worrying about the future will have the same consequences on music listening styles as depression or trouble in school? Extreme groups were formed for each of the ten potential problem areas mentioned above by considering only those who gave "often" or "never" as an answer (neglecting those who indicated "seldom" in the questionnaire). With two exceptions (loneliness, fear) the so constructed subsamples were large enough (> 15) to compute ANOVAs for the nine listening styles as dependent variables, and the remaining eight types of problems as independent variables. Table 8.3 gives an overview of the significant effects and shows the corresponding means.

TABLE 8.3

Relations Between the Experience of Specific Problems and Listening Styles

Listening style (dependent var.)	Problems (independent var.)	"often"	"never"	F	p
Compensating	Depression	2.26[1]	2.71	4.23	.04
Concentrated	Depression	2.92	3.50	5.58	.02
Emotional	Worries about the future[2]	3.24	3.81	6.44	.01
	Depression	3.12	3.72	5.68	.02
Distancing	Outward appearance	3.88	3.30	9.06	.00
	School	3.74	3.20	6.43	.01
Vegetative	Depression	2.63	3.47	15.74	.00
	Worries about the future	2.81	3.38	8.87	.00
	Friends	2.84	3.34	6.19	.02
	Outward appearance	2.92	3.37	5.21	.03
	Family	2.91	3.30	4.30	.04
Sentimental	Depression	2.87	3.83	23.26	.00
	Worries about the future	3.15	3.70	8.64	.00
	Health	3.15	3.67	6.12	.02
	Friends	3.13	3.59	5.16	.03
	Outward appearance	3.23	3.66	4.93	.03
Associative	Depression	3.12	3.99	11.88	.00
Stimulative	Family	2.93	3.61	9.31	.00
	Boredom	2.93	3.50	4.86	.03
	School	3.07	3.62	4.47	.04
Diffuse	Boredom	3.81	3.21	5.14	.03

[1]Lower values of means (boldfaced) indicate a higher intensity of the respective listening strategy.

[2]The "problems" are ranked for each listening style in the order of significance level.

As can be seen, "depression" (in the sense of sadness) is the most dominant problem: it influences six of the nine listening styles and for most of them it has the greatest effect compared to the other problems. For this age group experiencing depressive moods is the most effective reinforcer of the habitual components of Musikerleben. With two exceptions, the sub-groups with frequent problems show greater intensity ratings on all respective listening styles. This trend has already been documented in the first step of our analysis.

We can now see that *certain* problems intensify *certain* styles of listening. Children with different problems chose different coping strategies and, consequently, develop specific ways of Musikerleben: "Sentimental" and "stimulative" listening are two examples of highly specified problem-profiles with not a single problem having effects on both listening styles. Subjects who are having trouble in the family and at school and suffer from boredom show high ratings on "stimulative" listening. Depression, worrying about the future and problems concerning health, friends, and outward appearance are experienced by subjects with a preference for "sentimental" listening. An almost identical problem-profile was found for "vegetative" listening differing only in one out of five problems.

The great number of problems having an effect on these three listening styles suggests that "compensating" listening may not be the only means of coping with problems. Results indicate that we have to differentiate between psychological ("sentimental") and physiological ("vegetative", "stimulative") coping strategies. This raises the question of how far these differences are due to personality traits. "Vegetative" listening, for instance, may be linked to a higher sensitivity for problems caused by the outer world as well as to physiological sensations of the inner world. But further investigations into the causal relations between problem experience and listening styles would be necessary to back up these assumptions.

Regarding four further listening styles ("compensating", "concentrated", "emotional" and "associative") we find that ratings support the above made statement that frequently having certain problems tends to intensify the different listening styles. But a reversed effect emerged for the two remaining listening styles, for "distancing" listening and even more so for "diffuse" listening. In the case of "distancing" this reverse effect is easily explained: Students with such an intellectual approach to music are "good" students who seldom have problems with school. They also seem to have hardly any problems with their outward appearance, perhaps because they place greater importance on academic achievement.

The reversed effect for "diffuse" listening may be seen as the consequence of a coping strategy: if music is used as a medium of mood or problem management, it cannot be just an unimportant part of the background. Together with other details of Table 8.3 not mentioned here, we can conclude that individual characteristics of music appreciation must be interpreted in the context of individual history as individual ways of coping with life.

USING MUSIC AS GRATIFICATION

Several aspects of Musikerleben change over time, but we do not know why. So far, there is no definite theory to explain these changes, but perhaps the "uses and gratification" approach (Katz et al., 1974), a concept from media theory, may be applicable to the field of music behaviour (Wells & Hakanen, 1991). The results reported concerning the experience of individual problems may be interpreted as evidence that adolescents *use* certain music because they expect certain *gratifications*, i.e. it may help them cope with their problems. Everyday experience tells us that people use different music in different ways in different situations. How can we demonstrate these diversities, and how can we find possible patterns in this behaviour? Some selected results of an earlier questionnaire study (Behne, 1986b) may help to structure this complex field.

A sample of n=391 students (ages 13 to 15) were asked to imagine different emotional situations, for example, a situation of anger: "Imagine you had a fierce quarrel with your best friend and you are terribly angry. If in this situation you chose a piece of music, what would it sound like?" A list of eight pairs of opposites (see the semantic differential in Fig.8.3 for the original and the translated adjectives) describing the preferred music were given. Students rated their "situative preferences", gave concrete musical examples and tried to explain why they chose them. Besides anger, they were also asked for music preferences in situations of joy, sadness, and contentment.

The results showed clear differences between the four situations. In a joyful mood, students would like to listen to music which can be described as happy and gay, lively and fast. In a contented mood they would prefer a music with similar but slightly less pronounced attributes. For the two negative situations, however, there were no clearcut preferences, because students disagreed on which music they would most like to hear. When high variances result in questionable means (regression toward the mean), cluster analysis can help find groups of individuals who show similar response patterns while maximally differing from other groups. To give an impression of how different individual preference patterns can be, I will confine myself to some selected patterns of these analyses.

Cluster analysis of the music preferences in a situation of anger yielded 12 different clusters (Fig.8.3, for three examples). Cluster 1 (n=77) preferred a very

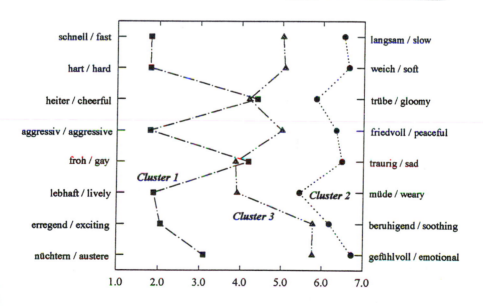

FIG. 8.3 Three ways of coping with anger with the help of music

fast, hard, aggressive, and lively music. This preference may be interpreted as a specific coping strategy, lustily living out all feelings of anger, wanting to keep up this mood for a while, but not reflecting the cause of the anger.

The subjects of Cluster 2 (n=25) chose in most cases attributes opposite to their imagined mood state: when angry, they would prefer very slow, soft, peaceful, emotional, and sad music. These students seek consolation in music, they would like to be sad and stay in a sad mood for a while, perhaps because they perceive themselves as being the losers in an imagined quarrel. Cluster 3 (n=70) is characterised by a slight tendency to the middle of the scale, but nevertheless showing a preference for calming and emotional music. It may be interpreted as less intensive "comfort-seeking", but in contrast to Cluster 2, there is no desire for sadness. One of the other profiles tends to be very close to the centre of the scales and could be interpreted as a desire for no music at all. The choice of music varied similarly when another negative emotion—sadness—was to be imagined.

So far the results of this study are exemplary (for further details see Behne, 1986b). The outlined examples of findings show that children at this early age have already developed differentiated strategies of coping with moods, especially bad moods, resulting in distinguishable music preferences in mood-induced situations. Hopefully the results of this longitudinal study will enable us to answer the question of how stable these patterns will prove to be. Gembris (1991) replicated our study with adults using a different method for cluster analysis. Despite these alterations he found similar characteristic cluster profiles. So we may say that generally individual differences in music preferences reflect the diversity of coping strategies.

DISCUSSION

In the last ten years the described questionnaire for different aspects of Musikerleben has been used in several studies and has proved to be a reliable instrument to differentially describe the development of Musikerleben. This developmental process has to do with coping, or to be more exact, with different coping strategies. The most pronounced listening style at the age of 11 to 13 is "compensating" listening. Evidently there are various ways of compensating as can be shown by the dramatic differences in listening strategies with respect to imagined situations of anger (Fig. 8.3) and sadness. "Stimulative" and "sentimental" listening can alternatively be interpreted as compensating, as they seem to reflect different problem experiences (Table 8.3). "Stimulative" listening is more pronounced for boys, "sentimental" listening for girls, suggesting possible gender-specific coping strategies. The tendency toward more body-oriented ways of Musikerleben at the beginning of puberty was anticipated and confirmed.

It is quite obvious that even the youngest children of our sample already have clear strategies of how to use music for mood-management. The changes over time appear like communicating tubes: the dramatic increase in intensity of the initially weakest components ("diffuse", "stimulative" listening) is synchronous with the decline observed for the two cognitive components ("concentrated", "distancing" listening). The significant decrease of "emotional" listening at the beginning of puberty may be attributed to other reasons; such as a growing self-consciousness regarding emotional issues.

Results show surprisingly clearly how strongly individual listening styles are connected with the experience of individual problems, depression appearing to be the most important experience in this context. In most cases plausible explanations for the interrelations between problem experience and listening style are possible.

Musical experts tend to think of a "compensating" listening style as an inappropriate behaviour towards a piece of music as a work of art. As members of a cultural upper class they think of such a plebeian way of using music as a misuse which should be restricted to trivial music, to pop-songs, "Schlager", musical "Kitsch" and to products of low culture in general. But there is no empirical support for this attitude. In a study of concert audiences in Germany Dollase, Rüsenberg, and Stollenwerk (1986) found that visitors of so-called high-culture concerts (classics by Beethoven or serious entertainment) reported having more problems in their everyday lives than those who attended more popular events. The first rated themselves higher than the latter for using music as a means of consolation. Our own results support this view: having problems seems to enhance the intensity of Musikerleben. Adolescents use Musikerleben to help them cope with their problems and this, perhaps, is why for very many adolescents music is one of the most important things in the world.

Several questions pertaining to the methods used remain unanswered. How many dimensions does Musikerleben really have, and how can we compare the results of different studies? Which items should be bundled to form listening style constructs? Should this decision be based on the data structure at the beginning of the study (age 11) or at the end (age 17)? Is Musikerleben connected with personality traits, and if so, can individual ways of listening to music be interpreted as aspects of personality?

In a recent study, Lehmann (1994b) tested the hypothesis that the intensity of habitual listening is correlated with general "affect intensity" (a construct of Larsen & Diener, 1987). That such a consistency was not found suggests that intensity of Musikerleben could also be interpreted as "musical sensitivity" in a wider sense. In a very special sense, musical sensitivity is part of a concept of musical ability in Gordon's "Music Aptitude Profile" (1965). In a more general sense this idea is part of the somewhat old-fashioned concept of musical ability of Révész: "Unter Musikalität im allgemeinen sind das Bedürfnis und die Fähigkeiten zu verstehen, die autonomen Wirkungen der Musik zu erleben, . . ."[6] (Révész, 1946/1972, p.163). Given that Musikerleben is probably one of the core aspects of musical ability and the strongest motivating factor for human interest in music, we have to ask why it has not received far more attention in the field of psychology of music.

NOTES

1. As defined by the "Affective Response Special Research Interest Group (SRIG)" (Price, 1986).
2. For further details of this process, including the question at what point in the dendrogram the analysis should stop, see Behne (1986a).
3. See Lehmann (1994a) for translations of the most relevant dimensions. More detailed information may be obtained from the author.
4. In column 2 of this table the respective music examples of the sounding preferences are shortly mentioned.
5. The second step of the survey (L2) is not mentioned here because it dealt with different aspects of Musikerleben.
6. "Musicality is generally understood as the need and the ability to experience the autonomous effects of music . . .".

REFERENCES

Adorno, T.W. (1968). *Einleitung in die Musiksoziologie*. Frankfurt/M. English translation: "Introduction to the sociology of music". New York: Seabury Press, 1976.

Alt, M. (1935). *Typen des musikalischen Genießens und Wertens*. Leipzig.

Behne, K.-E. (1986a). *Hörertypologien*. Regensburg: G.Bosse.

Behne, K.-E. (1986b). Die Benutzung von Musik. *Jahrbuch Musikpsychologie*, Wilhelmshaven: Noetzel, *3* (1986), 11–31.

Crickmore, L. (1968). An Approach to the Measurement of Music Appreciation (I). *Journal of Research in Music Education, 16(3)*, 239–253.

Csikszentmihalyi, M. (1975). *Beyond Boredom and Anxiety —The Experience of Play in Work and Games*. San Francisco: Jossey-Bass.

Dollase, R., Rüsenberg, M., & Stollenwerk, H.J. (1986). *Demoskopie im Konzertsaal*. Mainz: Schott.

Gabrielsson, A., & Lindström, S. (1994). On Strong Experiences of Music. *Jahrbuch Musikpsychologie*, Wilhelmshaven: F.Noetzel, *10* (1993), 118–139.

Gembris, H. (1991). Situationsbezogene Präferenzen und erwünschte Wirkungen von Musik. *Jahrbuch Musikpsychologie*, Wilhelmshaven: Noetzel, *7* (1990), 73–95.

Gordon, E.E. (1965). *Musical aptitude profile manual*. Boston: Houghton Mifflin Comp.

Hedden, S.K. (1973). Listeners' Responses to Music in Relation to Autochthonous and Experiential Factors. *Journal of Research in Music Education, 21(3)*, 225–238.

Katz, E., Blumler, J.G., & Gurevitch, M. (1974). Utilization of mass communication by the individual. In J.G. Blumler & E. Katz, (Eds.), *The uses of mass communication*.(pp. 19–32). London.

Larsen, R.J., & Diener, E. (1987). Affect intensity as an individual difference characteristic: A review. *Journal of Research in Personality, 21*, 1–3.

Lehmann, A.C. (1994a). *Habituelle und situative Rezeptionsweisen beim Musikhören: eine einstellungstheoretische Untersuchung*. Frankfurt/M: P.Lang.

Lehmann, A. C. (1994b). The Personality construct of affect intensity and its relation to music listening experience. In I. Deliège, (Ed.), *Proceedings of the 3rd International Conference on   Music Perception and Cognition* (pp. 385–386). Liège, Belgium: European Society for the Cognitive Sciences of Music.

Lewis, B.E., & Schmidt, C.P.   (1991). Listeners' Response to Music as a Function of Personality Type. *Journal of Research in Music Education, 39(4)*, 311–321.

Müller-Freienfels, R. (1936). *Psychologie der Musik.* Berlin: Chr. Friedrich Vieweg.

Price, H.E. (1986). A proposed glossary for use in affective response literature in music. *Journal of Research in Music Education, 34 (3)*, 151–159.

Révész, G. (1972). *Einführung in die Musikpsychologie.* Bern & München: Francke. (Original work published 1946).

Schlosser, O.T. (1976). *Einführung in die sozialwissenschaftliche Zusammenhangsanalyse.* Reinbek: Rowohlt.

Vernon, P.E. (1930). The Phenomena of Attention and Visualization in the Psychology of Musical Appreciation. *British Journal of Psychology, 21*, 50–63.

Wells, A., & Hakanen, E.A. (1991). The emotional use of popular music by adolescents. *Journalism Quarterly, 68(3)*, 445–454.

Yingling, R.W. (1962). Classification of Reaction Patterns in Listening to Music. *Journal of Research in Music Education, 10(2)*, 105–120.

The acquisition of expertise in music: Efficiency of deliberate practice as a moderating variable in accounting for sub-expert performance

9

Andreas C. Lehmann
Florida State University, Tallahassee, Florida

The reason for studying expert performance in expertise research is similar to that for investigating adult cognition in developmental psychology as stated by Siegler (1986, p. 361): "Knowledge of the adult cognitive system is useful for studying changes in children's thinking. It is much easier to study development when we know where the development is going." Likewise, the study of the acquisition and structure of expert performance allows us to investigate the adaptations and changes that appear in individuals who perform in a certain domain at a level that typically exceeds the average level of performance expected from an adult in the population. Rather than emphasising developmental changes, expertise research focuses on formal training and the mechanisms that mediate superior performance.

By showing that estimates of amounts of deliberate practice are predictive of levels of expert performance, Ericsson, Krampe, & Tesch-Römer (1993) have suggested an alternative explanation for attained performance to that provided by the talent perspective. However, at the sub-expert level, the relation between performance and amount of practice is not as clear-cut (Sloboda & Howe, 1991; Sloboda, Davidson, Moore, & Howe, 1994). The purpose of this paper is to try to extend the practice account to sub-expert levels of performance and discuss some of the factors that are likely to influence the relation between training and performance at this level. Throughout, I will illustrate the importance of early training, optimisation of practice in general, and supervised practice in particular.

The first half of the paper will start with a more general overview on the development of expert performance in music, and I will differentiate three levels of expertise in music. The next section will review findings regarding the initial stages of the acquisition of instrumental music skills and discuss some of the issues associated with early starting ages. After that, I will talk about deliberate practice, which can be seen as the central mediating behaviour in the acquisition of music skills. In the second half of the chapter, I will first present evidence suggesting that estimates of amounts of deliberate practice have been used successfully to account for expert levels of performance. Then, I will review findings relating sub-expert performance to indicators of music aptitude and indicators of skill acquisition such as practice and instruction. Following some considerations regarding general factors such as developmental changes, deliberate efforts, goal-setting and supervision that may influence the efficiency of practice, an analysis of data from biographies of famous prodigies will serve as evidence for the central claim that supervised practice is a prerequisite for early exceptional achievements. Finally, I will suggest that increased efficiency of practice—especially through supervision—may facilitate optimal progress which ultimately leads to a competitive advantage; once practice is optimised, its quantity may also be used as an indicator of individual differences among experts.

LEVELS OF EXPERTISE

As Sloboda (1991) points out, everybody in our culture possesses a great deal of knowledge and cognitive skills with regard to music. What makes the domain of music special compared to other domains of expertise commonly investigated, such as chess, computer programming, sports or expert decision making, is that in most cultures people engage in music-related activities every day. They acquire an extensive implicit musical knowledge and at least some basic performance skills through informal as well as formal learning experiences. While one can view expertise as a continuum, there are theoretical considerations to restrict the definition of expertise to being more than mere experience. One reason for this is that experts develop specific mechanisms to overcome limitations that usually constrain the performance of novices (see Salthouse, 1991, for an elaboration). For simplification, I propose three levels of expertise, the first of which represents mere experience which culminates in what one would call an average adult performance without formal training (see Fig. 9.1). The second and third levels take into account the effects of formal training with the third level representing the achievements of professionals.

Basic Level of Experience

Developmental studies in music typically investigate this category of expertise, which culminates in the average performance displayed by adult non-musicians. Most children reach this level of proficiency some time during puberty. This

FIG. 9.1. A three-level model of experience and expertise in music.

basic level of experience is described well in developmental literature and is not central to this paper. Suffice it to say that similar to expertise in reading, basic musical expertise is the result of developmental changes, facilitated by the learning opportunities offered by home environment and public schooling. While developmental models (Bamberger, 1991, rhythm; Behne, 1986, music listening; Moog, 1976, singing; Tighe & Dowling, 1993; melody and rhythm; Zenatti, 1981, acculturation) describe the basic mechanisms of music perception and cognition, they cannot explain differences among individuals with regard to highly developed cognitive and perceptual-motor skills such as those needed to play an instrument at a professional level.

Sub-Expert Levels of Expertise

The sub-expert or novice level of expertise is characterised mainly by the issues surrounding the acquisition of relevant performance skills and the decision to make music a career. Often, researchers capture the difference between this category and the basic level by asking for more formal instrumental music experience, thereby distinguishing between incidental and active involvement in music. A number of researchers have studied the acquisition of expertise within this level by testing and interviewing young subjects who showed exceptional promise in music (Bastian, 1989; Howe & Sloboda, 1991; Sloboda, Davidson, Howe & Moore, 1996; Sloboda & Howe, 1991). This category of aspiring experts allows the researcher to track developments which are already completed in experts. Although these subjects are more experienced compared to individuals without formal instruction, it is clear that only a very few of them will ultimately qualify as expert performers according to some established criteria. Most of the sub-experts will remain amateurs of varying degrees of proficiency. A recurring problem in research on skill acquisition is that at this level, developmental changes and musical skill acquisition are often confounded. For example, Gruson (1988) found a correlation of 0.75 between age and skill level. Because music instruction is normally initiated during childhood—a prerequisite for prodigies—it is sometimes difficult to generalise findings about younger ages to later starting ages.

Expert Performance Level

Depending on the definition, experts are usually individuals who perform at a high level, are recognised in their domains and even make innovative contributions, in which case they can be termed eminent performers (Krampe & Ericsson, 1995). This level of performance is the end-state of a skill acquisition process that starts in early childhood and requires at least ten years of training (Ericsson et al. 1993). A more constrained definition suggests that experts are individuals who display superior performance on representative tasks in their domain compared to other individuals with similar training (Ericsson & Smith, 1991, for an overview).

Research in expert performance uses a recommended methodology, which evolved from the first studies in chess to more recent studies in all areas of expertise (see Ericsson & Charness, 1994; Ericsson & Lehmann, 1996; Ericsson & Smith, 1991, for a review). Expert performance research requires well-defined laboratory tasks that mirror the real-life task requirements of the domain as closely as possible under controlled conditions (Ericsson & Smith, 1991). Otherwise, only the transfer of real-life skills to some related laboratory task is tested, a transfer which might be due to other variables than those that mediate expert performance. In order to account for superior performance and the mediating cognitive processes, the expert's performance can later be related to acquisition variables such as the number of hours of practice (Ericsson et al. 1993), size of repertoire (Ericsson & Lehmann, 1994a), or biographical data (Sloboda & Howe, 1991; Sosniak, 1985). Although most biographical information can be reliably assessed, validation of information is especially important for very early memories (Loftus, 1993) and time estimates.

By using expert subjects, one can investigate the physiological, cognitive, and perceptual-motor adaptations that occur as a result of extensive training (see Ericsson et al. 1993; Ericsson & Kintsch, 1995, for a review; Ericsson & Lehmann, 1996, for a review in the context of expert performance). These adaptations are always very localised and meet the specific requirements of representative tasks in a domain. For example, accomplished brass players were found to have significantly larger vital and total lung capacities (Tucker, Faulkner & Horvath, 1971) than a matched control group. Similar findings were reported for singers (Sundberg, 1987). Pianists and violinists differed significantly in the range of motion (supination vs. pronation) of their forearms (Wagner, 1988). It is unlikely that these physiological changes are innate. Instead, it is more plausible that they are normal adaptations of the human body to habitual usage (Ericsson et al. 1993; Ericsson & Lehmann, 1996, for an extensive discussion).

Expert music performers show high levels of conscious motor control. For example, they are able to reproduce reliably timing and force variations on repeated renditions of the same piece of music (Gabrielsson, 1987; Krampe, 1994; Palmer, 1989; Shaffer, 1982). Compared to novices or lesser experts they also have superior memory for domain-related information such as melodies (Kauffman & Carlsen, 1989) or music notation (Halpern & Bower, 1982). Finally, experts seem to encode larger chunks of material when sight-reading (Goolsby, 1994; Sloboda, 1974), take advantage of meaningful musical structure (Clifton, 1986), and use their knowledge base to make inferences and build up expectations (Sloboda, 1985). These adaptations are specific to the domain of music performance but they are consistent with similar adaptations in other domains (see Ericsson & Lehmann, 1996).

In sum, while the level of basic expertise in music is acquired in response to the surrounding culture, the sub-expert levels of expertise involve formal training, and, in few cases, culminate in expert skills. Superior expert performance in music is accompanied by specific adaptations concerning physiological, cognitive and perceptual-motor abilities, which allow the individual to overcome basic limitations of human information processing capabilities. Admittedly, the evidence is mostly correlational and the experts are a self-selected population. But unless one believes that the observed adaptations are innate, the selection is more likely triggered by aspects of motivation, instruction, and practice, and those factors are related to the acquisition of the skill rather than to initial predispositions.

DEVELOPMENT OF EXPERTISE

There is certainly an overlap among the mechanisms that are involved in acquiring the basic level of experience as well as the higher levels of performance. In addition, higher-level developments of expertise require the early initiation of formal instruction and specially designed practice (Ericsson et al. 1993). While involvement in a domain is characterised in the beginning by the acquisition of relevant skills, such as learning to play the piano, later contact with the domain includes other aspects, such as concertising and teaching, and the maintenance of the skill. While the acquisition of a skill is likely to be a continuum, several authors have tried to divide the development of expertise into characteristic periods. General models of expertise that are independent from the life-span will not be considered here (see Dreyfus & Dreyfus, 1986; vanLehn, 1989).

Phases of Skill Development

Generally, the life-span models in music (Ericsson et al. 1993; Krampe & Ericsson, 1995; Manturzewska 1986, 1990; Sosniak 1985) allow for a pre-instruction phase, during which an individual comes into contact with the domain through play and incidental exposure but does not receive formal instruction. The next period comprises the early phases of skill acquisition before the transition is made to a full-time commitment to the domain. This transition is associated with the decision to make music a career. These later phases are characterised by instruction and training that are explicitly meant to lead to expert performance. A later phase contains the career peak of the performer and the possible innovations that this expert contributes to the field. Ensuing phases fall in later years of a musician's career and can sometimes even be considered a change in profession from performer to teacher and adjudicator. It is important to note that the development of expert performance is specific to the domain and that in other domains, such as medicine or science, trajectories may be very different. The next section outlines the beginning of skill acquisition and raises some issues related to the alleged role of talent and the veridicality of anecdotal evidence.

"Marks of Genius" and Early Start

There has to be an incentive for parents to seek lessons for their child. While some children themselves might voice their desire to play an instrument, as Menuhin did, the majority of children are coaxed into formal instruction by well-meaning parents (Bastian, 1989, for examples; also Sloboda & Howe, 1991, 1992). Parents are reported to have responded, in some cases, to their children's musical behaviours, such as singing or picking out notes on a piano. These behaviours are often interpreted as interest, potential, or talent. Yet, the actual achievements that are reported of the children are rather modest and unspectacular (Bastian, 1989, p. 71) or even extra-musical, such as playing make-believe instruments in the case of Haydn (Ingman & Brett, 1978) or wiggling fingers as an infant, as did Glenn Gould (Friedrich, 1989; see also Scheinfeld, 1939, cited in Ericsson & Charness, 1994).

Howe, Davidson, Moore, and Sloboda (1995) investigated early indicators and their possible relation with musical activities of the home environment and found that singing had occurred about 6 months earlier for the more competent musicians. The results are consistent with reports by parents of high achievers who repeatedly mention early singing as a sign of talent (Bastian, 1989) and with anecdotal evidence (e.g. Rubinstein, 1973).

Although appealing, anecdotal evidence may be unreliable. The parents' retrospective reports can be altered by their knowledge about the child's later progress, and in the absence of veridical information about the quality and exact date of these signs, these accounts are difficult to verify (Lehmann & Ericsson, 1995). Contrary to the rare cases of children who play chess or perform mental calculations at early ages, all children engage in some music-related behaviours, such as singing or dancing, hence making it difficult to use such behaviour as a distinct predictor for future success.

Absolute pitch (AP) has also been viewed traditionally as a gift, but recent research suggests that it can be acquired (Takeuchi & Hulse, 1993, for a review) or may be a result of early training (Sergeant, 1969). A number of instrumental music education methods have successfully taught AP (cf. Ogawa & Miyazaki, 1994). Anecdotal evidence from biographies suggests that although AP might precede formal training, playful interactions with the domain (e.g. pitch naming games) are typically associated with its "discovery" (see biographies by Friedrich, 1989; Rubinstein, 1973).

For those who think that musical ability runs strongly in families, Coon and Carey's (1989) results come as a disappointment. Although there seems to be some genetic aspect (expressed as h^2), the shared environment (c^2) appears more important than shared genes with regard to similarity of musical skills in twins. Especially when formal instruction took place, heritability coefficients went down, indicating that whatever is inherited may wash out as training is initiated. The data did not allow to assess how much training was necessary to cover up completely the shared genes. In sum, behaviour genetics does not support the notion of innate talent once individuals engage in formal training[1].

Krampe, Tesch-Römer and Ericsson (1991) found that the start of systematic practice, years of training, or age at first public performance did not differentiate among expert groups of violinists (not world class). Yet, reliably earlier starting ages were found for expert pianists compared to amateurs, as well as for world-famous violinists compared to other violin experts (Ericsson et al. 1993; Howe et al. 1995 and Manturzewska's, 1979, 1990; Krampe & Ericsson, 1995) found similar results concerning early signs of talent. Evidence suggests that expert performers indeed tend to start practising earlier and at higher levels than do lesser experts (Sloboda et al. 1996).

In order to achieve the level of technical proficiency necessary to play a demanding repertoire around mid-teens when students start to compete, an early starting age may be advantageous for string players (Heaney, 1994; Manturzewska, 1990, for pianists). On the contrary, low performance at early adolescence may lead to lack of motivation and drop-out (Heaney, 1994). The individuals who show early promise and high levels of performance are likely to gain access to better teachers and the other scarce resources society can offer (Ericsson et al. 1993).

In sum, early signs of talent, which appear in the context of playful interaction with the domain, are usually quite modest achievements, but they prompt some parents to initiate formal instruction and associated practice. The resulting superior achievements at the end of childhood of some individuals compared to their peers may lead to subsequent allocation of support and resources to those who excel.

PRACTICE AS A MEDIATING FACTOR OF PERFORMANCE

Deliberate Practice

The insight that practice improves performance is not new, nor is the observation that musicians spend huge amounts of time engaging in it. Ericsson et al. (1993) proposed the concept of "deliberate practice" as a mediating mechanism of expert performance and tried to relate expert performance to time estimates of accumulated past practice. Deliberate practice is not inherently enjoyable, requires effort, and its goal is to improve performance. Thus, not all time spent at the instrument necessarily qualifies as deliberate practice. For it to be sustained for the extensive periods of time necessary to reach high levels of performance in a domain, deliberate practice is constrained by different factors, such as motivation (Csikszentmihalyi, Rathunde & Whalen, 1993; Ericsson et al. 1993; Sosniak, 1985). Sloboda et al. (1996) adopt a similar construct termed "formal practice", emphasising the difference between the effortful striving for improvement compared to less formal interactions ("informal practice") of individuals with their domain of expertise, such as playing a previously learned repertoire or improvising[2].

Although motivational issues and the management of motivation are very important for the long-term commitment to a domain, not much is known about them, and it is still unclear why a large majority of children stop playing their instruments (Manturzewska, 1979; Mawbey, 1973; Scheuer, 1988), while a few continue practising at various rates, and some even burn out from over-practice. It appears that parental support, which I will discuss later, initially plays an important role in children's progress (see Sloboda, Davidson, & Howe, 1996; Freyhof, Gruber & Ziegler, 1993; Lassiter, 1981; Sloboda & Howe, 1991; Breamer 1985). Later, it is conceivable that comparisons with other peers through public performances and competitions may, for some music students, be a motivation to continue or even to increase their intensity of practice. For less proficient students this comparison may result in the decision to drop out. (The motivations of adult beginners for initiating and continuing practice may be somewhat different; see Adler, 1994). Siegler (1986) summarises his review of evidence of early learning experiences and motivation by stating that "early-developing interests, formed for quite idiosyncratic reasons, may snowball into significant factors in children's lives" (p. 376). This statement is probably also true for music.

Development of Practice throughout the Life-Span

The start of formal instruction usually entails the teaching and practising of basic technical skills, and students are encouraged to continue at home what they have experienced during the lesson. Generally, a great number of teachers indicate that they convey practice skills as part of their beginning instruction (Barry & McArthur, 1994).

Younger children have to get used to regular practice and the time spent practising appears to increase with years of study. In his qualitative study, Harnischmacher (1993) finds an increase in practice times up to the time of study at a conservatory or university. Quantitative data of middle-school age violin students is reported by Doan (1973) who found a correlation of 0.43 between years of private violin instruction and practice times per week. It is interesting to note that the increase of practice times for future experts is much higher than that for amateurs (Freyhof, Gruber & Ziegler, 1993; Krampe, 1994). Sloboda et al. (1996) found similar results for childhood through the teenage years with high-achievers increasing their practice times much more than low-achievers. Similarly, the lessons gained significantly in length (Sloboda et al. 1994). Although the increase in practice time could be attributed to developmental changes, it has also been shown in other domains of expertise, where individuals start much later than is typically the case in music (Starkes, Deakin, Allard, Hodges, Hayes, 1996). Thus, increase in practice time appears to be a characteristic of skill acquisition that is independent from the age at which training is initiated.

Skill maintenance seems to require less practice time than skill acquisition, and duration of regular practice decreases after entrance in the profession (Harnischmacher, 1993). Krampe (1994) found that older experts reported 30% less practice time, due to conflicting activities such as teaching, rehearsing, or judging performances. It is possible that this decrease leads to anecdotes about little practice by famous musicians (Lehmann & Ericsson, 1995). Yet, the same pattern of increase and decrease of practice times was not found for amateurs, who typically do not increase their practice schedules and remain at the same low level (Krampe, 1994). The next sections will relate practice activities to observed performance, first in experts and then in sub-experts.

ACCOUNTING FOR EXPERT AND
EXCEPTIONAL PERFORMANCE

There are at least two possible ways to account for performance (cf. Ericsson et al. 1993; Ericsson and Charness, 1994). The talent explanation implies that differential aptitudes, along with practice, will allow individuals to reach certain levels of performance. More gifted students would progress faster, reach higher final levels, and need less practice. The alternative account assumes acquisition of skills through practice and basically does not imply any domain-specific innate limitations to the final level of performance. Given similar motivation and practice times, the slopes of the learning curves should be equal.

Since the ground-breaking laboratory study in which a college student was trained to increase his digit span from 7 to over 80 digits in about 230 hours (Ericsson & Chase, 1982), we know that exceptional performance can be accounted for by the cognitive adaptations accompanying increases in performance with practice. Recent studies were able to show that the amount of practice accumulated during life by three expert groups of musicians correlated highly with their respective levels of performance on domain-relevant tasks (Ericsson et al. 1993; Krampe, 1994; Krampe & Ericsson, 1995).

Other exceptional feats by great musicians of the past, such as Mozart's transcription of Allegri's "Miserere" after one hearing or frequently cited sight-reading feats, are usually attributed to talent but can be accounted for alternatively by lack of veridical information or by historical changes related to expertise and training (Ericsson & Lehmann, 1994b; Ericsson, 1996). Even such exceptional feats as those displayed by musical savants do not seem to emerge without training and large amounts of time spent engaging in relevant activities. Ericsson and Faivre (1988) suggest that savants are encouraged from an early age to develop their highly specialised abilities (also Charness, Clifton & MacDonald, 1988; Ericsson & Charness, 1994; Sloboda, Hermelin & O'Connor, 1985). Furthermore, many savants' abilities fall in domains that are not usually very well developed in the average population, hence making their performance appear even more impressive.

We have seen that empirical evidence exists which accounts for experts' high levels of performance. The question arises whether or not we can also account for the performance of younger musicians or amateurs.

ACCOUNTING FOR SUB-EXPERT PERFORMANCE

To my knowledge there exists no study investigating the variability in level of performance among adult beginners. Therefore, all evidence presented below stems from studies with child beginners, in which age and skill level are confounded. Compared to the correlations between practice and performance found among experts, those among sub-experts are somewhat lower due to a larger variability in observed performance. We have to ask why this variability may be greater. In an attempt to answer this question, I will report studies relating assessments of musical aptitude to performance and other predictors and discuss the relation between practice and instruction or performance.

Talent and Performance.   If talent played an important part in a young musician's performance, one would expect a relatively low correlation between reported practice times and achievements, but a relatively high association between measures of achievement and those of musical talent or aptitude. However, the correlation between scores on music aptitude tests and performance achievements are usually low (see Shuter-Dyson & Gabriel, 1981, for examples; also Stivers, 1972).

Interestingly, one reasonably good predictor of music aptitude—especially at younger ages—is academic achievement and IQ scores (Doxey & Wright, 1990; Hedden, 1982; Rowntree, 1970). Shuter-Dyson and Gabriel (1981, p. 234) state that "many students with no formal musical training achieve higher scores on musical ability tests than do some subjects with considerable training," but present no conclusive evidence for this statement. We would suggest that variability observed at initial testing of younger children is due to informal training, which is hardly ever assessed.

Shuter-Dyson and Gabriel (1981) also review evidence of influence of training on various musical abilities and measures of music aptitude and conclude that subjects who have had formal instruction prior to testing tended to score higher. For example, Rowntree (1970) showed impressive effects of practice on the improvement of 7 to 10-year-olds' scores on Bentley's aptitude test, where improvement on the practised sub-tests even transferred to related sub-tests. Wright (1928) found a 0.45 correlation between the scores of college freshmen on the entrance exam (audition) and the composite score for the Seashore measure. The study of Flohr (1981) shows that scores on Gordon's PMMA for the experimental group, receiving a total of 600 minutes of music instruction, increased significantly at post-test after 12 weeks compared to a control group. Similar training effects were shown for college musicians for Gordon's AMMA (Estrella, 1992).

The only exception to these findings are Gordon's own results. He reported a high predictive correlation between music aptitude scores and instrumental performance skills after two years (Gordon, 1967). However, there are several inconsistencies: while one study (Gordon, 1967)[3] involving intensive music training did not result in scores higher than the norm data (even somewhat less than the norm), another study showed that music instruction does seem to increase aptitude scores (Gordon, 1979).

In sum, the scores on aptitude measures do not explain much of the variance observed in performance. Furthermore, at early ages they seem to be affected by intellectual achievements and at all ages by prior musical training—formal as well as informal. In this they are comparable to measures of intelligence (Kurtz,

1990, for a review of related findings). The next section reviews the importance of acquisition variables such as practice and instruction for attained level of achievement.

Predicting Performance from the Acquisition Variables Practice and Instruction

Based on his extensive experience as a Suzuki teacher working with standardised educational material, Donner (1987) suggests a positive, linear relation between increase in performance level and associated weekly practice times. Of a sample of over one thousand music students participating in a German national music competition, those who won a prize reported higher regular and pre-performance practice times per week (Deutscher Musikrat, 1993). Sloboda, Davidson, Moore, and Howe (1994) found a 0.30 and 0.37 correlation between teacher ratings of performance level and accumulated amounts of formal practice at ages 8 and 13 respectively. All subjects were instrumental music students of varying levels of proficiency, some of whom had stopped playing. Thus, these correlations are underestimating the correlation between practice and performance for those who continue. In fact, the accumulated amounts of practice for the more successful groups were significantly higher at all age levels investigated (8, 12, 15; also Manturzewska, 1979). Most compellingly, Sloboda et al. (1996) did not find any indication consistent with the common belief that "talented" children practice less in order to achieve a given level of performance. Data on the development of practice times is also reported by Krampe (1994), and the correlation between skill level (amateur vs. experts) and accumulated practice times before age 20 was 0.63. Note that the amount of practice explained the level of performance among experts but not among sub-experts.

One important piece of evidence is still missing, namely a controlled study of beginners, in which the amount of practice and musical aptitude will have been measured at the onset of instruction and after some time of instruction. Only a longitudinal study of this type would shed light on the relation between music aptitude, practice, and achievement. Given the literature reviewed in this chapter, we would anticipate a positive correlation between practice and achievement and a low or no correlation between the residuals and initial musical aptitude as well as a positive correlation between practice times and the increase in musical aptitude scores at the end. We will now turn to the relation between level of performance and duration of instruction.

In a cross-skill sample of 20 instrumental music students, Brennan (1927) found a 0.65 rank correlation between the measured performance and the number of hours of instrumental instruction. A reanalysis of the data in Cramer (1958) by myself indicated a significant correlation of 0.34 between months of instrumental music instruction and performance of 4th through 8th graders. However, Cramer's sample comprised different instruments, for which practice times seem to vary (Bastian, 1989; Madsen & Geringer, 1981). A reanalysis of Watkins' (1942) data for cornet beginners reveals a correlation between number of months of instruction and scores on the performance scale of 0.56 over the first three years (data for this analysis were extracted from a published graph).

In assessing duration of practice and instruction, we often have to rely on retrospective reports, which may not always be valid. For example Doan (1973) found a correlation between hours of practice per week and the scores on a performance test of 0.25 for violin students from public schools. It is not clear whether all subjects had only group instruction in school, or if some had additional individual instruction with a private teacher, which might yield a higher correlation (Bloom, 1984). Furthermore, performance preparation was not supervised by the experimenter, and some students might not have given accurate estimates of their practice of the assessment piece. Finally, the reliability of the weekly estimates of practice are questionable since they were obtained from the parents, who may not have had any basis for their estimates or might have asked their children. Furthermore, individuals tend to overestimate their practice times (Krampe, 1994), while underestimating the time they spend with leisure (Ericsson et al. 1993). Especially young musicians may find it difficult to distinguish between efficient and inefficient practice when giving retrospective estimates of their practice times. Hence, not only social desirability may play a role in assessing the role of talent or practice, but simply the inability of individuals to accurately access and recall certain information.

Although far from perfect, the correlation between practice or instruction and performance are more strongly related to performance than measures of aptitude usually are. Therefore, the somewhat lower correlations between practice and performance observed at the sub-expert level have to be attributed to other factors than alleged differences in talent. One source of error is obviously the accuracy of the practice estimate. The next section attempts to provide an explanation beyond the accuracy of estimates and extend the framework of "deliberate practice" to account for sub-expert performance.

OPTIMISATION OF PRACTICE

There is a large body of empirical literature concerning specific problems of practice (Barry, 1990; Gellrich, 1993, for a historical perspective on piano practice; Harnischmacher, 1993, for reviews; Kopiez, 1990); but also professional journals and master teachers' writings address specific problems and give tips on how to learn and improve performance with regard to unique performance problems. Rarely are more general problems addressed. More specifically, time spent at the instrument and deliberate practice are not completely overlapping; is it possible that different kinds of sub-optimal practice might account for differences in progress between children who indicate similar amounts of practice?

The fact that practice is effortful can be inferred from the limited amount of time per day that it can be sustained (see Ericsson et al. 1993). Some students may be more willing or able than others to maintain the high level of attention necessary in order to profit from practice. This is where motivational aspects come in; given the difficulty to assess motivation directly, amount and intensity of practice have to be viewed as indicators of motivation. As I will show, sustained effort may be necessary but not sufficient to make practice work. Some general factors such as the acquisition of effective practice skills and habits, developmental changes in children that facilitate efficient practice, the "Flow" state, and the setting of challenging goals with subsequent evaluation of practice outcomes may optimise practice—not only in music. It is noteworthy that these factors are not specifically musical in the sense that one could view them as indicators of musical talent.

Factors Influencing Practice Efficiency

Musicians have to learn how to practice and practice appears to change with skill and age. Based on the qualitative analysis of 100 middle and high school students' essays, Harnischmacher (1994) observed a gradual decrease of the playful aspects in instrumental music practice, while an increase in complexity of practice strategies was noted. Gruson (1988) investigated practice strategies of pianists of varying skill levels and found that practice behaviour differed more across skill levels than across consecutive practice sessions devoted to the acquisition of a new piece. It was noted that more skilled performers tended to repeat longer sections, reached performance tempo earlier and verbalised more in the initial stages of practice (see also Miklaszewski, 1989). Gruson (1988) and Harnischmacher (1994) both found that with increased age and experience subjects were able to verbalise their practice behaviour more fluently and with more complexity. The change in the structure of practice appears to be accompanied by a metacognitive awareness of one's own practising. Likewise, this occurs at a general intellectual level.

Developmental changes in children's cognition, which develop through interaction with their social environment, play an important role when learning everyday tasks (Siegler, 1986, for a review). Since most successful performers start their training early, these changes should also impact on early stages of learning an instrument. Initially, young children might not be able to manage their attention, plan, and monitor their practice, thus requiring an external agent. As they get older, they learn how to deploy their cognitive resources, disregard irrelevant stimuli, and develop metacognitive skills which allow them to optimise their learning time and efficiency. In this, they are usually helped by parents who model for them and verbalise (Moss, 1992; Siegler, 1986).

A broader knowledge base may facilitate learning independent of age. Chi (1978) unconfounded age and skill level in the domain of chaos and found that content knowledge in chess facilitated memory for chess-related material and that strategy use was linked to knowledge in the domain. Oura and Hatano (1988) replicated Chi's results in music, showing that musically experienced children outperformed adults without formal training in recalling a tonal melody. Some of the naturally occurring changes during development can be greatly accelerated (Siegler, 1986). Yet, some of these effects have been found to be temporary when the intervention is discontinued (Behne, 1974, cited in Ribke, 1979, for early music training; Nielsen, 1989, for IQ; Wagner & Rashotte, 1993, for reading). However, in cases where a child continues to practice at optimal levels in a competitive setting with optimal societal support, one would expect the advantage to persist at least for the critical period until recognition is reached and excellent teachers consulted. The fact that experts find their teachers earlier and have fewer teachers than lesser experts (Ericsson et al. 1993) may confirm this point.

Well-defined goals such as getting louder at a given point in a piece of music or the memorisation of a phrase can be objectively evaluated as opposed to the general goal of improving performance, which is ill-defined (cf. Ericsson, 1996, for a general discussion). The process of setting goals (Ericsson et al. 1993) and the subsequent evaluation of outcomes in relation to those goals is tantamount to deliberate practice (also Heaney, 1994; Mantel, 1987). The information about how and how well an individual performed on a task can be provided through various forms of augmented feedback (Magill, 1993, p. 193, for athletes). Mere repetition (à la Kalkbrenner or Fields) with the general goal of improving performance is not efficient and most teachers advise against it (e.g. Gat, 1965; Powell, 1986). Unlike laboratory studies, in which practice is usually designed to maximise the outcome using distributed practice, feedback, and incentives to elicit differential effects of treatments, real-life situations are far less controlled. Also unlike in sports, where beginners are usually coached, most novice musicians work by themselves outside their lessons. Even advanced instrumental music students may be able to improve their practice by increasing their attentiveness and on-task behaviour (Madsen & Geringer, 1981). In sum, goal-setting and feedback during practice sessions may, in many cases, be sub-optimal in beginning musicians.

Finally, the Flow state—although predictive of teenagers' commitment to the development of talent (Csikszentmihalyi et al. 1993)—causes the "cessation of the monitoring activities that normally accompanies the higher levels [of mental activities]" (Dreyfus & Dreyfus, 1986, p. 40). Given that flow and some other activities that require less than maximum effort do not seem specifically aimed at the improvement of skills, they come closer to play, which is by definition distinct from deliberate practice (Ericsson et al. 1993). However, those activities could serve motivational purposes and alternate with more effortful activities throughout the course of practice to help manage physical and psychological resources, such as muscular strength and attention.

Given optimal levels of energy and motivation, which may themselves be subject to particular management techniques, there are many factors that influence the efficiency of practice. Foremost are the setting of goals and the subsequent or concurrent evaluation of the performance with regard to these goals. Although developmental changes may facilitate the self-guidance and self-monitoring of the child at a general level, domain-specific metaknowledge is also necessary. In order to avoid inefficient trial-and-error practice strategies, the beginner has to be provided with knowledge about "what works in practice and what doesn't."

Domain-Related Activities with Practice Character

While practice is often associated with solitary confinement and the playing of scales, this is not necessarily so, and some domain-related activities, such as accompanying, can gain quasi-practice character by providing adequate challenges along with the opportunity for evaluation. Sight-reading is rarely systematically practised, yet pianists of comparable skill differ in their ability to sight-read. Prospective accompanists have been found to sight-read significantly better than young piano performers (Lehmann & Ericsson, 1993), and sight-reading ability was predicted by relevant accumulated experience in accompanying and the size of the pianists' accompanying repertoire (Ericsson & Lehmann, 1994a). While the accompanying experience consisted of regular (sometimes paid) accompanying and sight-reading opportunities, most repertoire was built up outside these events by the accompanists in response to frequent repertoire demands of instrumental performers or singers for such works as complete song cycles and standard string or clarinet sonatas. While this self-imposed regimen might lead to some degrees of performance improvement, mere playing opportunities may not be conducive to overcoming specific weaknesses. For example, uncommon key signatures might not occur in the pieces required and therefore will not be mastered; on the contrary, instructional material designed by experts (e.g. Spillman, 1990) offers all known problems in isolation and variation. This example stands for many others where incidental experience leads to an initial increase in performance, but only the performers' deliberate attempts to remedy weaknesses and impose challenges on themselves can lead to long-term improvement.

Supervised Practice in the Home Environment

The influence of the home environment has long been acknowledged as an important factor in the development of skills in various domains of expertise (Bloom, 1985), but how exactly it contributes to this development is less clear. Two main influences seem to exist, one of which is immediately music-related while the other exerts a more general effect.

Musicological evidence from past centuries indicates that some parents forced their children to work as musicians and frequently exploited them, regardless of their "talent", while others carefully paced their children's development (cf. Wehmeyer, 1983). Sloane (1985) stated that parents of talented children were active, hard-working individuals with a "work-ethic," who prevented waste of time and excessive leisure. Bastian (1989) found the parents of his musically successful interviewees to be characterised as strict and demanding, although the students retrospectively legitimated the parents' behaviour (Lassiter, 1981 for a similar finding). This might help explain why successful young musicians do not necessarily have parents with extensive expertise in music (Sloboda & Howe, 1991). Parents of successful musicians seem to offer contingencies and a good understanding of the motivational and personality structure of their children, which enables them to keep their children at their instruments and motivated.

There are also music-related influences of the home environment (Doan, 1973, for examples), which should be most beneficial when associated with practice activities. In Sosniak's (1985) sample, the parents of all pianists monitored at least the quantity, if not the quality, of daily practice; half of the parents fell in the latter category. Similar results were found for members of the string sections of the Philadelphia Orchestra (Heaney, 1994), and for successful music students (Bastian, 1989; Sloboda & Howe, 1991). Davidson et al. (1996) found that successful young musicians' parents were more likely than parents of less successful music students to sit in on the lesson and assist in daily practice.

A number of famous musicians have had several lessons per week, some even had one every day—at least initially (e.g. Mendelssohn, C. Schumann, Liszt). Increasing the numbers of lessons per week for beginning students might have similar effects to those of monitoring in that more immediate evaluation of the student's progress can take place and new detailed assignments given. Conversely, Sloboda and Howe (1991) found exceptionally promising students to have had fewer formal lessons than average students. These results may just reflect that better students work with master teachers who are often under severe time constraints. Also, the boundary between formal and informal instruction is not as clear-cut as it appears when a child is taught at home or receives supervised practice.

Supervised Practice among Past Prodigies

Ericsson and Lehmann (1994b) proposed that close monitoring of practice by a "live-in teacher" was a good indicator of early exceptional performance. In the following, evidence from an ongoing analysis of a number of historical prodigies will be reported. By cross-referencing a large pool of names of piano prodigies in history given in Stevens (1982) with Fisher (1973) and Ingman and Brett (1978), a sample was extracted (see Table 9.1), and biographical information gathered for each individual. In all cases the children were taught by

TABLE 9.1
Starting ages, early teachers and practice environments of
famous piano prodigies.

Starting age	Supervised practice	First teacher	Duration of instruction	Parent is performer*	Student lives with teacher	Subsequent teacher**
G.F. Händel (1685–1759)						
7	?	F. Zachau	3 years	N	N	—
J.S. Bach (1685–1760)						
<10	Y	father/ uncle	?	Y	Y	J.C. Bach (11)†
W.A. Mozart (1756–1791)[h]						
<4	Y	father	—	(Y)[violin]	Y	—
L.v. Beethoven (1770–1827)[m o]						
4	Y	father	4–6 years	(N)[singing]	Y	v.d. Eeden (10)
F. Mendelssohn (1809–1847)[d]						
<6	Y	mother	?	N	Y	L. Berger (6)
F. Chopin (1810–1849)[g]						
4	Y	sister/ mother	2 years	N	Y	W. Zywny (6)
F. Liszt (1811–1886)[f]						
<7	Y	father	3 years	N	Y	C. Czerny (9)
C. Schumann (1819–1896)[n p]						
5	Y	father	—	(N)[piano]	Y	—
Anton Rubinstein (1830–1894)[k]						
5	Y	mother	?	N	Y	Villoing (7)
T. Carreño (1853–1917)[j]						
<6	Y	father	>2 years	N	Y	Gottschalk (8)
I. Albéniz (1860–1909)[c]						
>1	Y	sister	3 years	N	Y	N. Oliveras (5)
C. Debussy (1862–1918)[d l]						
9	Y	Mauté/ Cerutti	1 year	N	?	Durand (10)
Arthur Rubinstein (1886–1982)[e]						
<3	Y	sister	>2 years	N	Y	A. Prechner (5)
R. Slencznska (1925–)[i]						
2	Y	father	>2 years	(N)[violin]	Y	A. S.-Kennedy (4)

Note. General biographical information was obtained from The New Grove (1980), Baker's (1992), and supplemented by additional sources indicated in superscript letters. *Y/N = yes/no, (Y/N) = a parent was professional music teacher for instrument indicated in superscript. **The age at which student started taking lessons with this teacher is indicated in parentheses. †J.S. Bach's eldest brother Johann Christoph. [c]Istel, 1929. [d]Ingman & Brett, 1978. [e]Rubinstein, 1973. [f]Walker, 1990. [g]Wierzynski, 1949. [h]Langegger, 1978. [i]Slenczynska, 1957. [j]Milinowski, 1977. [k]Bowen, 1939. [l]Lockspeiser, 1962. [m]Tienot, 1975. [n]Litzmann, 1902. [o]Schiedermair, 1970. [p]Reich, 1985.

a caretaker, and supervised practice would have been likely or is even explicitly reported. Händel seems to present an exception, but his biographical data is lacunary and known to be unreliable. Further counter examples may be found. Admittedly, the presence of supervised practice and early achievements are correlational, and we cannot be sure whether the musician would have succeeded equally without this support. Also, most children were taught by a relative, and one could argue that genetic factors play a role, although as indicated earlier, instruction seems to wash out the effect of shared genes.

By no means were all parents accomplished musicians (see Table 9.1). Most live-in teachers were only able to initially support the skill acquisition, implying that the child soon exhausted the first teacher's own playing capabilities. Only in those cases where the parent was a professional performer or music teacher was the transfer of skill done without subsequent teachers (e.g. Bach, Mozart, Schumann). Most first teachers are valued for their motivational influence, their enthusiasm, and understanding for the child (Bastian, 1989; Howe & Sloboda, 1991) rather than for their performance skills. In addition, the first teacher's main function could be the formation of good practice habits. Practising is a skill in itself, and since it mediates performance, it should be optimised to achieve the maximum level of performance given a limited amount of time. Various factors contribute to the efficiency of practice and it appears that supervised practice, preferably by a live-in teacher, can create optimal conditions for deliberate practice and the resulting skill acquisition. The historical prodigies investigated here satisfied this condition.

In the remaining part of the paper, I propose an explanation for the observed variability in performance at the sub-expert or amateur level by taking into account individual differences in practice efficiency, and I argue that home instruction and supervised practice may lead to faster optimisation of time spent practising.

CONCLUSIONS REGARDING OPTIMISED PRACTICE AND PERFORMANCE

While even younger students tend to spend a fair amount of time at the instrument, the outcome is not in all cases proportional to the time invested or indicated. Differences in the progress of beginners during skill acquisition for seemingly same amounts of practised time are therefore frequently attributed to differences in talent. However, expecting high correlations between practice and performance at younger ages and sub-expert levels means disregarding influences that impact on all children, such as maturation, as well as those that are individualised, such as quality of teaching and supervision, metaknowledge of practice, motivation, and prior experience. I realise that both sets of effects may interact in a fashion unknown to us at this point.

The model proposed by Ericsson et al. (1993) explains that an early start will invariably lead to a higher level of performance earlier in life, because a skill advantage early in life makes it more likely that an individual, when compared in performance to other individuals of the same age group, will gain access to better teachers and other facilitating resources earlier. Therefore, a late starter may never catch up to or reach the level of a musician with an extremely early start. The authors assume that individuals practice at the optimal level in terms of time and efficiency, an assumption that results in a high correlation between accumulated hours of practice hours and level of performance later in life. While this model appears to apply to optimal conditions like those in the sample of piano prodigies described above, the same conditions may not be met in most samples available to researchers, who therefore find low to moderate correlations between practice and levels of performance.

Growing up in an environment in which metaknowledge about practice and practice skills are available through relatives or other people could lead from initial sub-optimal practice activities to those behaviours that meet the definition of deliberate practice. Subsequent improvement would be faster, especially when informal learning experiences have taken place prior to the onset of formal instruction (see Fig. 9.2). Supervised practice should facilitate the faster optimisation of practice, not only in children but also in late starters

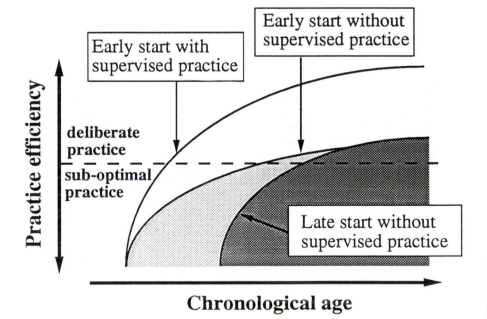

FIG. 9.2. Hypothetical relations between the onset of formal instruction and optimisation of instrumental music practice with and without supervision.

(not shown in graph). Due to age, motivation, or environmental factors, instrumental music beginners may vary considerably in their mastery of self-monitoring skills and the implementation of efficient practice strategies. A later start of instruction should benefit optimisation of practice in this respect, but important time has been lost. Although there is evidence that individual differences in the attentiveness during practice exist even in more advanced students (Madsen & Geringer, 1981), conclusive empirical evidence is missing to ascertain the above hypothesis that children optimise their practice at a varying pace depending on their environment (support, motivation, quality of instruction, etc.).

My analysis of data from past musicians revealed that in virtually all cases conditions for supervised practice were present—often explicitly stated. It seems possible that a live-in teacher—especially a parent—with moderate or even no performance skills can facilitate initial progress of a child (see Table 9.1). We can only speculate about the musical careers of early as well as late instrumental music beginners who fail to reach a level of practice efficiency that would qualify as "deliberate practice" (see Fig. 9.2). They will not be able to compete with their peers, may even give up, and thus contribute to a selection process, which in the end promotes those individuals who started early and soon optimised the efficiency and amount of their practice activities.

More joint research efforts between (music) educators and (music) psychologists will be necessary to uncover the mechanisms that govern the macro and micro structure of practice. Not only controlled studies of practice times and prior experience of instrumental beginners—children and adults alike—are needed, but also more careful investigations into the attentional and motivational processes underlying the long-term commitment of individuals who play an instrument. In this line of research, investigating those individuals who fail to sustain the necessary high level of involvement in the domain may prove to be as interesting as looking at those who succeed—the traditional subjects of research in expert performance.

Ericsson et al's (1993) initial explanation of individual differences in level of performance among experts is open to the argument that talent may still play a role at lower levels of proficiency, and that it is through selection that only the most talented reach the expert levels. This would explain why amount of deliberate practice correlates with performance at the highest levels—where talent is controlled for—but not at the sub-expert level. Based on the evidence presented, however, this chapter maintains that quantity and quality of sub-expert practice, rather than innate talent, offer sufficient explanation for individual differences in performance at the sub-expert level.

ACKNOWLEDGEMENTS

This chapter is dedicated to my mentor and friend, K. Anders Ericsson, who encouraged me to work in the area of expertise and expert performance. Chloe Casella was of invaluable help in assembling biographical information about the prodigies. Neil Charness, Ralf Krampe, Rolf Zwaan, Phillip Spurgeon and Peter Delaney have given helpful comments on earlier versions of this chapter. Finally, I thank the editors for including my paper in this volume.

NOTES

1. It is unlikely that Coon and Carey's (1989) twin sample contained many expert musicians. Thus, we can stipulate that even modest amounts of training appear to lower the heritability component considerably.
2. Practising improvisation or deliberately maintaining previously learned repertoire may of course qualify as deliberate practice when it is done with the goal of further improvement rather than for recreation or leisure.
3. This study does not contain enough details regarding frequencies of played instruments, age means, out-of-school activities, and pre-experimental training to be evaluated objectively in this context.

REFERENCES

Adler, G. (1994). *Wege Erwachsener zum Instrumentalspiel.* (Unpublished Ph.D. dissertation, Hochschule für Musik und Theater Hannover, Germany).

Baker, T. (1992). *Baker's biographical dictionary of musicians.* New York: Schirmer (8th ed., rev. N. Slonimsky).

Bamberger, J. (1991). *The mind behind the musical ear: how children develop musical intelligence.* Cambridge, MA: Harvard University Press.

Barry, N. H. (1990). *The effects of practice strategies, individual differences in cognitive styles, and sex upon technical accuracy and musicality of student instrumental performance.* (Unpublished dissertation, Florida State University, Tallahassee, FL).

Barry, N., & McArthur, V. H. (1994). Teaching practice strategies in the music studio: A survey of applied music teachers. *Psychology of Music, 22,* 44–55.

Bastian, H. G. (1989). *Leben für Musik. Eine Biographie-Studie über musikalische (Hoch-Begabungen.* Mainz, Germany: Schott.

Behne, K. E. (1986). *Hörertypologien: Zur Psychologie des jugendlichen Musikgeschmacks.* Regensburg, Germany: Bosse.

Bloom, B. S. (1984). The 2-sigma problem: The search for methods of group instruction as effective as one-to-one tutoring. *Educational Researcher, 13,* 4–16.

Bloom, B. S. (1985). Generalizations about talent development. In B. S. Bloom, (Ed.), *Developing talent in young people* (pp. 507–549). New York: Ballantine.

Bowen, C. D. (1939). *Free artist: The story of Anton and Nicholas Rubinstein.* Boston, MA: Little.

Breamer, S. (1985). The parent-child relationship: The right kind of nurturing will aid in promoting practise. *Suzuki World, 4*(1), 2–3.

Brennan, F. M. (1927). The relation between musical capacity and performance. *Psychological Monographs, 36,* 190–248.

Charness, N., Clifton, J., & MacDonald, L. (1988). Case study of a musical "mono-savant": A cognitive-psychological perspective. In L. K. Obler & D. Fein, (Eds.), *The exceptional brain* (pp. 277–293). New York: Guilford.

Chi, M. T. H. (1978). Knowledge structures and memory development. In R. S. Siegler, (Ed.), *Children's thinking: What develops?* (pp. 73–96). Hilsdale, NJ: LEA.

Clifton, J. V. (1986). Cognitive components in music reading and sight-reading performance (Ph.D. dissertation, University of Waterloo, Ontario, 1986). *Dissertation Abstracts International, 47,* 2203A.

Coon, H., & Carey, G. (1989). Genetic and environmental determinants of musical ability in twins. *Behavior Genetics, 19*(2), 183–193.

Cramer, W. F. (1958). *The relation of maturation and other factors to achievement in beginning instrumental music performance a the fourth through eighth grade levels.* (Unpublished Ph.D. dissertation, Florida State University, Tallahassee).

Csikszentmihalyi, M., Rathunde, K., & Whalen, S. (1993). *Talented teenagers: The roots of success or failure.* Cambridge, MA: Cambridge University Press.

Davidson, J. W., Sloboda, J. A., Howe, M. J. A. (1996). The role of practice and teachers in the success and failure of instrumental learners. *Bulletin of the Council for Research in Music Education, 127,* 40–44.

Deutscher Musikrat (1993). *Gute Noten mit kritischen Anmerkungen. Erste Ergebnisse einer Umfrage unter den Teilnehmern der Regionalwettbewerbe "Jugend musiziert" 1992.* Augsburg, Germany.

Doan, G. R. (1973). An investigation of the relationship between parental involvement and the performance ability of violin students. *Dissertation Abstracts International, 34*(08), 5226A. (University Microfilm No 7403150).

Donner, N. (1987). The effect of daily practise. *Suzuki World, 6*(5/6), 5.

Doxey, C., & Wright, C. (1990). An exploratory study of children's musical ability. *Early Childhood Research Quarterly, 5,* 425–440.

Dreyfus, H. L., & Dreyfus, S. E. (1986). *Mind over machine: The power of human intuition and expertise in the era of computer.* New York: Free Press.

Ericsson, K. A. (1996). The acquisition of expert performance: An introduction to some of the issues. In K. A. Ericsson, (Ed.), *The road to excellence: The acquisition of expert performance in the arts and sciences, sports and games* (pp. 1–50). Mahwah, NJ: LEA.

Ericsson, K. A., & Charness, N. (1994). Expert performance. Its structure and acquisition. *American Psychologist, 49,* 725–747.

Ericsson, K. A., & Chase, W. A. (1982). Exceptional memory. *American Scientist, 70,* 607–615.

Ericsson, K. A., & Faivre, I. A. (1988). What's exceptional about exceptional abilities? In I. K. Obler & D. Fein, (Eds.). *The exceptional brain: Neuropsychology of talent and special abilities* (pp. 436–473). New York: Guilford.

Ericsson, K. A., & Kintsch, W. (1995). Long-term working memory. *Psychological Review, 102,* 211–245.

Ericsson, K. A., Krampe, R. T., & Tesch-Römer, C. (1993). The role of deliberate practice in the acquisition of expert performance. *Psychological Review, 100,* 363–406.

Ericsson, K. A., & Lehmann, A. C. (1994a). The acquisition of accompanying (sight-reading) skills in expert pianists. In I. Deliège, (Ed.), *Proceedings of the 3rd International Conference on Music Perception and Cognition* (pp. 337–338). Liege, Belgium: European Society for the Cognitive Sciences of Music.

Ericsson, K. A., & Lehmann, A. C. (1994b). *Marks of genius? Re-interpretation of exceptional feats by great musicians.* (Paper presented at the 35th Annual Meeting of the Psychonomic Society, St.Louis, Missouri, November 11–13, 1994).

Ericsson, K. A., & Lehmann, A. C. (1996). Expert and exceptional performance: Evidence of maximal adaptation to task constraints. *Annual Review of Psychology, 47,* 273–305.

Ericsson, K. A., & Smith, J. (1991). Prospects and limits of the empirical study of expertise: An introduction. In K. A. Ericsson & J. Smith, (Eds.), *Toward a general theory of expertise* (pp. 1–38). Cambridge: Cambridge University Press.

Estrella, S. G. (1992). Effects of training and practice on Advanced Measures of Music Auditiation scores. *Dissertation Abstracts International, 53*(04), (University Microfilm No AAG9227456).

Fisher, R. B. (1973). *Musical prodigies: Masters at an early age.* New York: Association Press.

Flohr, J. W. (1981). Short-term music instruction and young children's developmental music aptitude. *Journal of Research in Music Education, 29*(3), 219–223.

Freyhof, H., Gruber, H., & Ziegler, A. (1993). *Anfänge des Expertiseerwerbs bei Berufs- und Laienmusikern* (Paper 7/1993). München, Germany: Max Planck Institut für psychologische Forschung.

Friedrich, O. (1989). *Glenn Gould: A life and variations.* New York: Random House.

Gabrielsson, A. (1987). Once again: The theme from Mozart's piano sonata in a major (K. 331). In A. Gabrielsson, (Ed.), *Action and perception in rhythm and music,* (pp. 81–103). Stockholm, Sweden: Royal Swedish Academy of Music, No. 55.

Gat, J. (1965). *The technique of piano playing.* London: Collet's.

Gellrich, M. (1993). Üben. In C. Richter. (Ed.), *Handbuch der Musikpädagogik: Vol. 2. Instrumental- und Vokalpädagogik* (pp. 439–470). Kassel, Germany: Bärenreiter.

Goolsby, T. W. (1994). Profiles of processing eye-movements during sight-reading. *Music Perception, 12,* 97–123.

Gordon, E. E. (1967). *A three-year longitudinal predictive validity study of the musical aptitude profile.* Iowa City: University of Iowa Press.

Gordon, E. E. (1979). Developmental music aptitude as measured by the Primary Measures of Music Audiation. *Psychology of Music, 7,* 42–49.

Gruson, L. M. (1988). Rehearsal skill and musical competence: does practise make perfect? In J. A. Sloboda, (Ed.), *Generative processes in music* (pp. 91–112). Oxford, England: Clarendon.

Halpern, A. R., & Bower, G. H. (1982). Musical expertise and melodic structure in memory for musical notation. *American Journal of Psychology, 95,* 31–50.

Harnischmacher, C. (1993). *Instrumentales Üben und Aspekte der Persönlichkeit. Eine Grundlagenstudie zur Erfassung physischer und psychischer Abweichungen durch Instrumentalspiel.* Frankfurt, Germany: Lang.

Harnischmacher, C. (1994). Grundlegende Dimensionen, Progression und Entwicklungsstufen des instrumentalen Übens von Kindern und Jugendlichen. In H. Gembris, R. D. Kraemer & G. Maas, (Eds.), *Musikpädagogische Forschungsberichte* 1993 (pp. 481–483). Augsburg, Germany: Wissner.

Heaney, M. F. (1994). *The components of a string education: A qualitative study of selected members of the Philadelphia Orchestra string section.* (Unpublished Ph.D. dissertation, Florida State University, Tallahassee).

Hedden, S. K. (1982). Prediction of music achievement in the elementary school. *Journal of Research in Music Education, 30,* 61–68.

Howe, M. J. A., Davidson, J. W., Moore, D., & Sloboda, J. A. (1995). Are there early childhood signs of musical ability? *Psychology of Music, 23,* 162–176.

Howe, M. J. A., & Sloboda, J. A. (1991). Young musicians' accounts of significant influences in their early lives. 1. The family and the musical background. *British Journal of Music Education, 8,* 39–52.

Ingman, N., & Brett, B. (1978). *Gifted children of music. The young lives of great musicians.* London: Ward Lock.

Istel, E. (1929). Isaac Albeniz. *Musical Quarterly, 15,* 117–141.

Kauffman, W. H., & Carlsen, J. C. (1989). Memory for intact music works: The importance for musical expertise and retention interval. *Psychomusicology, 8,* 3–19.

Kopiez, R. (1990). *Der Einfluß kognitiver Strukturen auf das Erlernen eines Musikstücks am Instrument.* Frankfurt, Germany: Lang.

Krampe, R. T. (1994). *Maintaining excellence: Cognitive-motor performance in pianists differing in age and skill level* (Studien und Berichte/MPI für Bildungsforschung 58). Berlin, Germany: Sigma.

Krampe, R. T., & Ericsson, K. A. (1995). Deliberate practise and elite musical performance. In J. Rink, (Ed.), *The practise of performance* (pp. 84–102). Cambridge, MA: Cambridge University Press.

Krampe, R. T., Tesch-Römer, C., & Ericsson, K. A. (1991). Biographien und Alltag von Spitzenmusikern. *Musikpädagogische Forschung, 12,* 175–188.

Kurtz, B. E. (1990). Cultural influences on children's cognitive and metacognitive development. In W. Schneider & F. E. Weinert, (Eds.), *Interactions among aptitudes, strategies, and knowledge in cognitive performance* (pp. 177–199). New York: Springer.

Langegger, F. (1978). *Mozart. Vater und Sohn: Eine psychologische Untersuchung.* Zürich, Switzerland: Atlantis.

Lassiter, D. G. (1981). *A survey of parental involvement in the development of professional musicians.* (Unpublished master's thesis, Florida State University, Tallahassee).

Lehmann, A. C., & Ericsson, K. A. (1995). Talent und Übung: Ohne Übung geht es nicht, aber geht es ohne Talent? *Üben und Musizieren, 15*(2), 9–14.

Lehmann, A. C., & Ericsson, K. A. (1993). Sight-reading ability of expert pianists in the context of piano accompanying. *Psychomusicology, 12*(2), 182–195.

Litzmann, B. (1902). *Clara Schumann, ein Künstlerleben nach Tagebüchern und Briefen.* Leipzig, Germany: Breitkopf & Härtel.

Lockspeiser, E. (1962). *Debussy: His life and mind. Vol. 1.* New York: Macmillan.

Loftus, E. F. (1993). Desperately seeking memories of the first few years of childhood: The reality of early memories. *Journal of Experimental Psychology: General, 122,* 274–277.

Madsen, C. K., & Geringer, J. M. (1981). The effects of a distraction index on improving practice attentiveness and musical performance. *Council for Research in Music Education, 66/67,* 46–52.

Magill, R. (1993). Augmented feedback in skill acquisition. In R. N. Singer, M. Murphey & L. K. Tennant, (Eds.), *Handbook of research on sport psychology* (pp. 193–212). New York: Macmillan.

Mantel, G. (1987). *Cello üben: Eine Methodik des Übens für Streicher.* Mainz, Germany: Schott.

Manturzewska, M. (1979). Results of psychological research on the process of music practicing and its effective shaping. *Council for Research in Music Education, 59,* 59–61.

Manturzewska, M. (1986). Musical talent in the light of biographical research. In E. Rohlfs, (Ed.), *Musikalische Begabung finden und fördern* (pp. 86–92). Regensburg, Germany: Bosse.

Manturzewska, M. (1990). A biographical study of the life-span development of performing musicians. *Psychology of Music, 18,* 112–139.

Mawbey, W. E. (1973). Wastage from instrumental classes in schools. *Psychology of Music, 1,* 33–43.

Miklaszewski, K. (1989). A case study of a pianist preparing a musical performance. *Psychology of Music, 17,* 95–109.

Milinowski, M. (1977). *Teresa Carreno. By the grace of god.* New York: Da Capo.

Moog, H. (1976). *The musical experience of the pre-school child.* London: Schott (published in German, 1968).

Moss, E. (1992). Early interactions and metacognitive development of gifted preschoolers. In P. S. Klein & A. J. Tannenbaum, (Eds.), *To be young and gifted* (pp. 278–320). Norwood, NJ: Ablex.

Nielsen, W. L. (1989). The longitudinal effects of project Head Start on students' overall academic success: A review of the literature. *International Journal of Early Childhood, 21*(1), 35–42.

Ogawa, Y., & Miyazaki, K. (1994). The process of aquisition of absolute pitch by children in Yamaha music school. In I. Deliège, (Ed.), *Proceedings of the 3rd International*

Conference on Music Perception and Cognition (pp. 135–136). Liege, Belgium: European Society for the Cognitive Sciences of Music.

Oura, Y., & Hatano, G. (1988). Memory for melodies among subjects differing in age and experience in music. *Psychology of Music, 16*, 91–109.

Palmer, C. (1989). Mapping musical thought to musical performance. *Journal of Experimental Psychology: Human Perception and Performance, 15*, 331–346.

Powell, M. C. (1986). Ten thousand times! *Suzuki World, 5*(6), 14–15.

Reich, N. B. (1985). *Clara Schumann: The artist and the woman.* Ithaca, NY: Cornell University Press.

Ribke, J. (1979). *Musikalität als Variable von Intelligenz, Denken und Erleben.* Hamburg, Germany: Wagner.

Rowntree, J. P. (1970). The Bentley "Measures of Musical Abilities"—a critical evaluation. *Council for Research in Music Education, 22*, 25–32.

Rubinstein, A. (1973). *My younger years.* New York: Knopf.

Salthouse, T. A. (1991). Expertise as the circumvention of human processing limitations. In K. A. Ericsson & J. Smith, (Eds.), *Toward a general theory of expertise* (pp. 286–300). Cambridge, MA: Cambridge University Press.

Sergeant, D. (1969). Experimental investigation of absolute pitch. *Journal of Research in Music Education, 17*, 135–43.

Scheuer, W. (1988). *Zwischen Tradition und Trend. Die Einstellung Jugendlicher zum Instrumentalspiel.* Mainz: Schott.

Schiedermair, L. F. (1970). *Der junge Beethoven.* Wilhelmshaven, Germany: Heinrichshofen.

Shaffer, H. L. (1982). Rhythm and timing in skill. *Psychological Review, 89*, 109–122.

Shuter-Dyson, R. & Gabriel, C. (1981). *The psychology of musical ability.* London: Methuen (2nd ed.).

Siegler, R. S. (1986). *Children's thinking.* Englewood Cliffs, NJ: Prentice-Hall.

Slenczynska, R. (1957). *Forbidden Childhood.* Garden City, NY: Doubleday.

Sloane, K. D. (1985). Home influences on talent development. In B. S. Bloom, (Ed.), *Developing talent in young people* (pp. 439–476). New York: Ballantine.

Sloboda, J. A. (1974). The eye-hand span: An approach to the study of sight-reading. *Psychology of Music, 2*, 4–10.

Sloboda, J. A. (1985). *The musical mind.* New York: Oxford University Press.

Sloboda, J. A. (1991). Musical Expertise. In K. A. Ericsson & J. Smith, (Eds.), *Toward a general theory of expertise* (pp. 153–172). Cambridge, MA: Cambridge University Press.

Sloboda, J. A., Davidson, J. W., Howe, M. J. A., & Moore, D. (1996). The role of practise in the development of expert musical performance. *British Journal of Psychology, 87*, 287–309.

Sloboda, J. A., Davidson, J. W., Moore, D., & Howe, M. J. A. (1994). Formal practise as a predictor of success and failure in instrumental learning. In I. Deliège, (Ed.), *Proceedings of the 3rd International Conference on Music Perception and Cognition* (pp. 125–126). Liege, Belgium: European Society for the Cognitive Sciences of Music.

Sloboda, J. A., Hermelin, B., & O'Connor, N. (1985). An exceptional musical memory. *Music Perception, 3*, 155–170.

Sloboda, J. A., & Howe, M. J. A. (1991). Biographical precursors of musical excellence: An interview study. *Psychology of Music, 19*, 3–21.

Sloboda, J. A., & Howe, M. J. A. (1992). Transitions in the early musical careers of able young musicians: Choosing instruments and teachers. *Journal of Research in Music Education, 40*, 283–294.

Sosniak, L. A. (1985). Learning to be a concert pianist. In B. S. Bloom, (Ed.), *Developing talent in young people* (pp. 19–67). New York: Ballantine.

Spillman, R. (1990). *Sight-reading at the keyboard.* New York: Schirmer.

Starkes, J. L., Deakin, J. M., Allard, F., Hodges, N. J., & Hayes, A. (1996). Deliberate practice in sports: What is it anyway? In K.A. Ericsson (Ed.), *The road to excellence: The acquisition of expert performance in the arts and sciences, sports and games* (pp. 81–106). Mahwah, NJ: LEA.

Stevens, G. H. (1982). *Das Wunderkind in der Musikgeschichte.* (Unpublished Dissertation, University of Münster, Germany).

Stivers, J. D. (1972). A reliability and validity study of the Watkins-Farnum performance scale. *Dissertation Abstracts International, 34*(02), 815A. (University Microfilm No 7317440).

Sundberg, J. (1987). *The science of the singing voice.* Dekalb, IL: Northern Illinois University Press.

Takeuchi, A. H., & Hulse, S. H. (1993). Absolute pitch. *Psychological Bulletin, 113,* 345–361.

The New Grove dictionary of music and musicians (1980). London: Macmillan.

Tienot, Y. (1975). *Beethoven: l'homme a travers l'œuvre.* Paris: Lemoine.

Tighe, T. J., & Dowling, W. J. (1993). *Psychology and music: The understanding of melody and rhythm.* Hillsdale, NJ: LEA.

Tucker, A., Faulkner, M. E., & Horvath, S. M. (1971). Electrocardiography and lung function in brass instrument players. *Archives of Environmental Health, 23,* 327–334.

vanLehn, K. (1989). Problem solving in cognitive skill acquisition. In M. I. Posner, (Ed.), *Foundations of cognitive science* (pp. 527–79). Cambridge, MA: Bradford/MIT Press.

Wagner, C. (1988). The pianist's hand: anthropometry and biomechanics. *Ergonomics, 31,* 97–131.

Wagner, R,. & Rashotte, C. A. (1993). *Does phonological awaress training really work? A meta analysis.* (Paper presented at the Ann. Meetg. of the American Educational Reasearch Association, April 1993, Atlanta).

Walker, A. (1990). *Franz Liszt. Vol. 1.* New York, NY: Knopf.

Watkins, J. G. (1942). *Objective measurement of instrumental performance.* New York: Teachers College.

Wehmeyer, G. (1983). *Carl Czerny und die Einzelhaft am Klavier.* Kassel, Germany: Bärenreiter.

Wierzynski. C. (1949). *The life and death of Chopin.* English translation by N. Guterman with a foreword by A. Rubinstein. New York: Simon & Schuster.

Wright, F. A. (1928). The correlation between achievement and capacity in music. *Journal of Educational Research, 17,* 50–56.

Zenatti, A. (1981). *L'enfant et son environnement musical: Etude expérimentale des mécanismes psychologiques d'assimilation musicale.* Issy-les-Moulineaux, France: EAP.

Biological Approaches

10 Is music autonomous from language? A neuropsychological appraisal

Aniruddh D. Patel[1]
Department of Organismic and Evolutionary Biology,
Harvard University, USA
Isabelle Peretz
Département de Psychologie, Université de Montréal, Canada

INTRODUCTION

Music and language are universal among humans, and both employ richly structured auditory and motor patterns. Since music and language are the two primary acoustic communicative systems of our species, their similarities and differences as cognitive domains have long interested scholars. (e.g. Aiello, 1994; Albert, Sparks & Helm, 1973; Besson, Faïta, & Requin, 1994; Bernstein, 1976; Blacking, 1976; Clarke, 1989; Darwin, 1871; Handel, 1989; Judd, Gardner & Geschwind, 1983; Lerdahl & Jackendoff, 1983; Levman, 1992; Nettl, 1956; Rousseau, 1761; Selkirk, 1984; Sergent, 1993; Sloboda, 1985; Sundberg & Lindblom, 1976; Sundberg, Nord & Carlson 1991; Trehub & Trainor, 1993). These contributions highlight the diversity of fields which have addressed this issue, from philosophy to the social, psychological, and biological sciences.

This chapter focuses on aspects of the music-language relation which are amenable to empirical study. We assume that the mental domain of "music" is not an indivisible whole, but rather a confluence of interacting cognitive processes. In keeping with this view, each section of the chapter treats a selected aspect of musical structure, reviewing evidence which suggests whether this aspect engages domain-specific processes or processes which might be shared with language. The topic of music reading and its relation to linguistic reading is not covered here, as it has been treated at length by other authors (the interested

---

[1]Now at The Neurosciences Institute, San Diego, CA, USA.

reader is referred to Judd et al. 1983; Fasanaro, Spitaleri, & Valiani, 1990; Sergent, Zuck, Terriah, & MacDonald, 1992; Signoret, Van Eeckhart, Poncet, & Castaigne, 1987; Stanzione, Grossi, & Roberto, 1990). Finally, we note that this chapter emphasises perceptual processes. This reflects a decision to dwell more fully on selected topics, rather than a belief that production processes are less deserving of study.

Because neuropsychology provides empirical evidence regarding the fractionation of cognitive processes via patterns of dissociation and association after brain damage, data from this field play a prominent role in this review. In this light, two types of neurologic disorder are particularly relevant: amusia and aphasia. "Amusia" refers to an acquired disorder of music perception or production following brain damage, while "aphasia" refers to certain disorders of language secondary to neurological damage. In both cases, the problems are not a consequence of peripheral neuropathy, but of damage to central processing mechanisms.

In the past, cases of amusia without aphasia and aphasia without amusia have been cited as evidence that music and language have little cognitive overlap (Marin, 1982; Sergent, 1993). Yet such a conclusion is likely to be premature. First, the claim makes no reference to the processing subcomponents of music and language. Second, cases of aphasia without amusia are generally exceptional individuals such as conductors and composers (e.g. Basso & Capitani, 1985; Luria, Tsvetkova, & Futer, 1965), whose musical talents may not be representative of musical abilities shared by musicians and non-musicians. Third, diagnosis of "amusia without aphasia" does not rule out language deficits, because "aphasia" does not include all disorders of language processing. For example, the Boston Diagnostic Aphasia Examination (Goodglass & Kaplan, 1983) does not examine prosodic perception, and accordingly, disorders of prosody are not classified as aphasia.

Amusic subjects can teach us a great deal about the organisation of music cognition and its neural substrates, and about the relation of music to other cognitive domains. It must be remembered, however, that tests for dissociations between music and other domains can only reflect the particular tasks administered to subjects. In this light, testing musically (or linguistically) impaired subjects on maximally comparable musical and linguistic tasks has dual benefits: it can yield greater specificity in the characterisation of a particular subject's deficit(s), and sharpen our understanding of the role of implicated neural regions in both musical and linguistic processing.

AUDITORY SCENE ANALYSIS

In most natural circumstances, acoustic elements reach the ear in a disordered mixture. Assigning each element to a particular sound source is a necessary part of auditory perception. Grouping mechanisms akin to the Gestalt principles of organisation seem to help solve this parsing problem. In this early analysis, currently referred to as primitive auditory scene analysis (Bregman, 1990), sounds that share certain properties or regularities are grouped together in a single stream or auditory object. Higher level schemas (or knowledge of the typical properties of the perceptual elements) may assist scene analysis by confirming or restoring the possible organisation. This conceptualisation is intended to apply universally: that is, to voices, music, and speech sounds alike (Bregman, 1990).

This general account of auditory perceptual organisation has been seriously questioned by researchers working on speech signals (Liberman & Mattingly, 1989; Remez, Rubin, Berns, Pardo, & Lang, 1994). They argue, on the basis of substantial empirical evidence (see Remez et al. 1994, for a recent review), that perceptual organisation of speech depends on sensitivity to time varying acoustic patterns that are specific to phonologically governed sources of sounds. Perceptual organisation of speech appears autonomous from that involved in non-speech sounds.

Thus, despite its parsimony and simplicity, the generalisability of the mechanisms involved in auditory scene analysis may not be warranted. Neuropsychological data should be particularly enlightening in this area. However, to our knowledge, auditory scene analysis has never been addressed in brain-injured patients or normal subjects by way of brain imaging techniques or laterality paradigms. The only exception of which we are aware used evoked potentials (Alain & Woods, 1994) and basically confirmed the biological relevance of auditory scene analysis mechanisms. In this study, only unnatural simple sound patterns were used. Thus, the question of neural specificity of speech and non-speech domains remains open for future investigations.

MELODY

Melody, the perceptually coherent patterning of pitch over time, has many distinct aspects (Meyer, 1973; Narmour, 1991a), only three of which will be considered in this chapter: melodic contour, the use of discrete pitch categories, and the Western European system of tonality.

MELODIC CONTOUR

Melodic contour is the general shape of a melodic line (its patterns of ups and downs in pitch direction over time), without regard to exact pitch intervals. The relevance of contour to musical organisation is evident in diverse musical traditions. In Bach, the melodic subject introduced at the beginning of a fugue is soon repeated at a higher or lower register. This repetition of the theme need not be an exact transposition: it can be a "tonal answer", which preserves the contour but not the precise intervals. In American folk ballads of the English tradition, variants of a tune can be divided into families, with contour as a prominent classifying feature (Seeger, 1966). Among the Wopkaimin of Central Papua New Guinea, songs that share a particular theme (e.g. sacred initiation songs) often share similar contours (Roberts, 1996). In fact, the role of contour in the organisation of melody is one of the few features of music to appear cross-culturally (Harwood, 1976).

Over the past 25 years, Dowling and others have demonstrated that contour is a salient feature in melodic perception, whose importance relative to exact interval patterns depends on multiple factors such as memory load, tonality, familiarity and length of the melody (Dowling, Kwak, & Andrews, 1995; Edworthy, 1985). Another line of research has focused on the processing of musical contour by young infants. In an operant same-different discrimination paradigm, infants are able to treat transposed versions of a melody as similar as long as the contour is preserved, despite changes in interval structure, while discriminating melodies on the basis of contour changes (Trehub, Thorpe & Morrongiello, 1987 and Trehub, Schellenberg & Hill, this volume). While the above research suggests the importance of contour to the *structure* of musical organisation and perception across ages, there is also research suggesting that musical contour may convey an *emotional* message to a listener (e.g. Clynes & Nettheim, 1982; Gerardi & Gerken, 1995).

In speech, the pattern of fundamental frequency (Fo) over time is a basic part of the organisation and perception of spoken language. This pattern is referred to as "intonation" rather than "contour", and contributes to marking the boundaries of structural units, distinguishing pragmatic categories of utterance (e.g. statement, question, command), and signalling focus (Beckman & Pierrehumbert, 1986; Bolinger, 1989; Lehiste, 1973; Price, Ostendorf, Shattuck-Hufnagel, & Fong, 1991). Intonational marking of phrase boundaries in speech appears to be perceptually significant for infants (Jusczyk, Hirsh-Pasek, Kelmer-Nelson, Kennedy, Woodward, & Piwoz, 1992), and the similarity to phrase boundary cues in music (pitch drop, slowing) has been noted (Jusczyk & Krumhansl, 1993).

Intonation also communicates intention and affect. In infant directed speech (known informally as "motherese"), highly salient intonational patterns are used to recruit the pre-verbal infant's attention and communicate approval, disapproval, soothing, etc. (Fernald, 1985, 1993; Fernald & Kuhl, 1987). Since infants must process intonation from speakers of different ages and sexes, their sensitivity to this signal is likely to be independent of the absolute frequency at which it occurs, just as infants show generalisation of contour across different pitch registers in music (Trehub et al. 1987). Sensitivity to intonation as an intentional and affective cue remains part of speech perception throughout life, and has been empirically studied by Ladd, Silverman, Tolkmitt, Bergmann, & Scherer (1985) and others.

Given the similarities of melodic contour and intonation, it seems reasonable to expect that their processing shares some cognitive and neural resources. While neuropsychological deficits in the processing of musical contour (Peretz, 1990) and linguistic intonation (Heilman, Bowers, Speedie, & Coslett, 1984) have been reported independently, the association between the two types of processing has not been studied in a systematic fashion.

Amusics with melodic perception deficits provide an opportunity to test this issue. Specifically, one can examine the ability of amusic but non-aphasic patients to distinguish between sentences that differ only in their intonation, and between musical phrases derived from the intonational patterns of these sentences. A purely musical deficit should manifest itself in difficulty on the musical task, but success on the linguistic one: this would argue for the separability of melodic contour and speech intonation. On the other hand, a similar breakdown pattern across domains would suggest common processing.

We recently conducted an experiment which addressed this issue (Patel, Peretz, Tramo, & Labreque, in press). Thirty-four sentence pairs were recorded in French: each pair represented two lexically identical versions of a sentence, but differed in linguistic prosody. Twelve pairs constituted statement-question pairs (e.g. Il parle Français. / Il parle Français? He speaks French./He speaks French?). Twelve pairs constituted focus-shift pairs, involving a shift in the word which bore the focus of the sentence (e.g. Allez DEVANT la banque, j'ai dit. / Allez devant la BANQUE, j'ai dit. Meet me IN FRONT OF the bank, I said. / Meet me in front of the BANK, I said.). Ten additional sentence pairs were used to study the perception of timing (these "timing-shift" sentences will be discussed in the section on Grouping below).

In order to ensure that discrimination was based on intonation, all the statement-question pairs and half of the focus-shift pairs were acoustically adjusted to equalise patterns of syllable timing and loudness within each pair, yielding natural-sounding sentence pairs in which fundamental frequency was the only salient cue for discrimination. The other half of the focus-shift sentence pairs were left unmanipulated: here focal words were marked not only by pitch accents but by intensity and duration as well. These unmanipulated sentences served as controls, to determine if discrimination problems occurred in contrasting sentences of natural speech, where focus is signalled by multiple prosodic cues.

For the acoustically-controlled sentences, the fundamental frequency patterns of each sentence pair were used to generate two melodic sequences in which tones had the durational characteristics and pitch values of their parent syllables (tone amplitudes were set at a fixed value). Although the fundamental frequency of spoken language typically moves up and/or down within each syllable, the pitch of each tone was fixed at its parent syllables' mean F_0 (plus two harmonics), giving the resulting melodic analogues a discrete intervalic structure. This made the melodic analogues sound much less speech-like than the original intonation patterns. No melodic analogues were made from the acoustically-uncontrolled focus-shift pairs, since the analogues, like their parent sentences, would have differed in parameters other than intonation (e.g. timing), thus compromising the specificity of the test for pitch discrimination. It should be noted that no attempt was made to make the pitches or intervals of the melodies correspond to the Western musical scale. This precluded the experiment from addressing the perception of tonality, but allowed it to address the perception of contour versus intonation in a precise fashion.

The linguistic and musical phrases were administered in separate parts of the experiment. The task was always to listen to a pair of phrases and classify the members of the pair as sounding the same or different (pairs could appear in either configuration, and replicates were included). The subjects, CN and IR, were female French-speakers with bilateral cortical lesions (due to stroke and surgery for aneurysms) and no aphasic problems: they were 40 and 37 years old and 7 and 9 years post-surgery, respectively. Both were raised in musical households, and were classified as amusic based on personal reports of post-surgical deficits in music perception and on performance on neuropsychological tests of music processing (Peretz, Kolinsky, Tramo, Labrecque, Hublet, Demeurisse, & Belleville, 1994). At the time of testing, CN's problems appeared to be primarily with music recognition, while IR had more basic melodic and rhythmic discrimination problems (Peretz, 1994 and forthcoming).

The results for CN, IR, and 8 age-and-education-matched controls can be seen in Figure 10.1. For the sake of clarity, the focus-shift category for language is represented only by focus-shift pairs that had musical analogues.

The Fisher exact probability test revealed that for both CN and IR, the proportions of correct responses on analogous linguistic and musical tasks was not significantly different across domains (statistical comparisons used raw scores, not percentages; controls also showed no significant difference across domains). Overall, the pattern of results suggests an association between

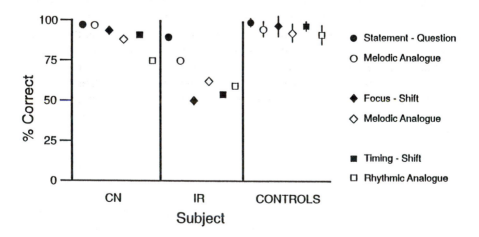

FIG. 10.1   Scores on analogous linguistic and musical tasks for CN, IR, and 8 controls, represented as percentages. Error bars on control scores represent standard deviation.

performance on musical contour and linguistic intonation tasks, arguing for some common neural contribution to both types of task.

The most surprising result of the study is IR's difficulty in discriminating focus-shift pairs in language (statistically she performed at the level of random guessing), a linguistic deficit which did not emerge in standard aphasia testing. Her difficulty cannot be attributed to artificiality in the stimuli, since her performance on "control" focus-shift pairs (not equalised for duration and intensity patterns) was just as poor. Neither can it be attributed to a failure to encode pitch: she performed well on statement-question discrimination in language and music, where she reported concentrating on the final pitch in the sequence. The focus-shift task, however, had the critical pitch located *within* the sequence. It is worth noting that IR performed well above chance on an additional task in which she listened to focus-shift sentences one at a time and identified the accented word. Thus, she can perceive sequence-internal pitch, but performs poorly on the focus-shift task and its musical analogue, both of which require pitch patterns to be maintained in memory. In other words, IR seems to have a deficit in mechanisms involved in the short term retention of musical contour and intonation (she also appears to have a deficit in the retention of temporal patterns in language and music: c.f. the section on 'Grouping', below).

CN, who performed well on the musical and linguistic discrimination tasks, has bilateral damage to the rostral and middle third of the superior temporal gyri, the middle temporal gyri, the temporal poles, and the right insula, with limited extension into the right inferior frontal gyrus, and the sparing of primary auditory cortex (Peretz et al. 1994). IR has more widespread temporal lobe damage on the left side (including primary auditory areas), and damage to the right inferior frontal cortex, suggesting that these regions may play an important role in the retention and comparison of pitch and temporal patterns in both musical and linguistic domains (details of CN's and IR's lesions, including CT scan images, can be found in Patel, Peretz, Tramo, and Labreque, in press). Details of IR's lesions are interesting in light of previous evidence that the right hemisphere plays a crucial role in musical contour perception (Peretz, 1990; Peretz and Babaï, 1992), and in light of recent metabolic neuroimaging data (from normal subjects) implicating right frontal circuits in the retention and comparison of pitches in both melodic phrases (Zatorre, Evans, & Meyer, 1994) and syllables (Zatorre, Evans, Meyer & Gjedde, 1992). However, it should be kept in mind that IR had bilateral lesions, suggesting the interaction of brain regions in different hemispheres in prosodic and musical processing.

Of course, as with any case of functional association, the possibility exists that the processes in question are in fact neurally and functionally distinct, but are disrupted by the same lesion: this issue can only be resolved by further testing. We are aware of one previous report where right fronto-temporal damage (atrophy) led to deficits in musical and prosodic perception, but the relation between melodic and intonational processing was not studied in a controlled fashion (Confavreux, Croisile, Garassus, Aimard, & Trillet, 1992). It is also possible that the association between prosodic and musical processing seen in our subject IR is due to a general auditory short-term memory deficit which disrupts the retention of auditory patterns of any kind. Another study (Belleville & Peretz, forthcoming) reveals that IR has short-term memory deficits in a wide variety of musical and verbal tasks (including digit spans). Only further testing can reveal whether the resources used in short-term storage of prosodic and musical patterns are also relevant to other kinds of patterns of sound (e.g. environmental sounds).

One way to address the specificity of the prosody-music link is to test subjects known to have prosodic deficits (but no short-term memory problems) for their musical perception abilities. Cases of prosodic perception deficits following brain damage come to light much more frequently than cases of amusia. "Aprosodia" can be due to damage to the right or left hemisphere (Blonder, Bowers, & Heilman, 1991; Cancelliere & Kertesz, 1990; Ross, 1981) or to subcortical regions (Brådvik, Dravins, Holtås, Rosén, Ryding & Ingvar, 1991), but its relation to perception of music has yet to be investigated. Most of the studies to date focus on aprosodia as a deficit of affective perception, but recent work suggests that there may be a more basic underlying deficit in the perception of pitch and temporal cues (Van Lancker & Sidtis, 1992). This is supported by the finding that certain aprosodic subjects have problems with *linguistic* prosody (Baum, Daniloff, Daniloff, & Lewis, 1982; Emmorey, 1987; Heilman et al. 1984; Weintraub, Mesulam, & Kramer, 1981), suggesting that they can be fruitfully tested with the types of stimuli and tasks discussed here. An association between prosodic and musical processing in these subjects would provide further evidence for common neural resources in the processing of prosodic and musical pitch contours.

DISCRETE PITCH CATEGORIES

To avoid confusion, a distinction should be drawn at once between perception in terms of discrete categories and Categorical Perception (capitalised here for clarity). The latter refers to a particular psychophysical phenomenon in which stimuli lying along a physical continuum are perceived in discrete perceptual classes, *and* stimulus pairs of a given physical difference along this continuum are easily discriminated when they straddle a category boundary, but poorly (or not at all) discriminated when they lie within a category (Repp, 1984). However, it is important to note that perception in terms of categories does not require Categorical Perception: for example, the Thai language (and many others) makes a phonemic distinction between long and short vowels, implying that vowels are conceived and perceived in terms of discrete categories of length: yet Thai listeners do not show Categorical Perception for variation in vowel duration (Repp, 1984).

In music, pitch categories are of three basic kinds: pitch classes, pitch intervals, and chords. Absolute pitch possessors are able to label isolated pitches with respect to pitch class (Miyazaki, 1988), but recent detailed research (Burns & Campbell, 1994) suggests that this does not reflect Categorical Perception. On the other hand, Categorical Perception for intervals (Burns & Campbell, 1994; Burns & Ward, 1978) and for chords (Repp, 1984) has been demonstrated in musicians. The perception of musical pitch in terms of categories, however (as opposed to Categorical Perception per se) is likely to be shared by both musicians and non-musicians (Smith, Nelson, Grohskopf, & Appleton, 1994).

Pitch categories are not unique to music. Over half of the world's languages are "tone languages" (Crystal, 1987; Pike, 1948), meaning that the relative pitch of a syllable can change the lexical meaning of a word (e.g. the syllable "ma" in Mandarin Chinese can mean "horse", "hemp", "mother", or "scold", depending on its tone). In a tone language, a tone is specified by its relative height (e.g. *high, low*), inflection (e.g. *falling, falling-rising*), or both (e.g. *high-rising, low-rising*). The number of tones in a tone language varies between two (many African languages) and at least nine (Southern coastal Cantonese: Yung, 1991). Evidence for Categorical Perception of linguistic tones is mixed (Repp, 1984), yet logically tones *must* be conceived and perceived in discrete categories in order to accomplish their function.

Musical and linguistic pitch categories differ in at least one crucial respect: organisation with respect to a scale. In many cultures, musical pitches divide frequency space into discrete steps, separated by prescribed intervals. To our knowledge, no tone languages have been reported to show this feature. The greater rigidity of musical pitch relations could reflect the fact that musical pitches are used to make melodies, in which the relations between pitches over extended sequences is of central importance. Linguistic tones, in contrast, act as localised semantic and grammatical signals, and their pattern over extended sequences is fortuitous, rather than explicitly structured.

Whether pitch categorisation in music and language share any cognitive mechanisms is unknown. Indeed the issue is rarely, if ever, discussed in the literature. Yet there is neuropsychological evidence suggesting that the issue merits study. Specifically, a left-hemisphere bias has been found for the processing of categorical pitch information in both music and language. In music, the evidence includes ear asymmetries in the use of pitch interval information (Peretz & Babaï, 1992; Peretz & Morais, 1987), and significantly enhanced neuroanatomical asymmetries in the area of the planum temporale in absolute pitch possessors (Schlaug, Jäncke, Huang, & Steinmetz, 1995). In tone languages, the evidence comes from aphasia, in which deficits of tone perception in aphasia are associated with left-hemisphere damage (Gandour & Dardarananda, 1983). Crucially, this is not a generalised consequence of brain damage, as right-hemisphere damage in tone-language speakers spares the perception and identification of linguistic tones (Hughes, Chan, & Su, 1983).

Furthermore, right-hemisphere damage can impair the perception of affective prosody and yet leave the perception of linguistic tones intact (Hughes et al. 1983).

Thus, there is an intriguing suggestion that discrete categories of pitch, whether serving linguistic or musical functions, are especially reliant on left-hemisphere circuits. However, as noted above, differences between musical and linguistic pitch categories (notably, the presence of scales in the former) suggest that these two forms of pitch may be processed separately within the left hemisphere. The cognitive relation between music and language in this area awaits exploration.

TONALITY

"Tonality" can be defined as "a system of organising pitch in which a single pitch (the *tonic*) is made central." (Randel, 1978). Tonality has been a prominent aspect of Western European art and popular music, and rests on several structural features. Octaves are divided into twelve discrete pitches, separated by logarithmically equal steps, creating a system of 12 *pitch classes* (named a,a#,b,c,...g#). Subsets of this group of pitch classes form the scales and chords of tonal music, which are organised in compositions in such a way that at most points in the music there is structurally most central pitch class and chord (the tonic, and tonic triad, respectively), with other pitch classes and chords forming a hierarchy of structural importance in relation to these. In addition, shifts from one subset of pitch classes to another (modulation) are not random, but follow a particular logic of key relatedness (see Piston, 1978 for more details). These compositional regularities become internalised by listeners as "tonal schemata" or "tonal knowledge", which in turn influence the perception of music. Empirical evidence for the reality of tonal knowledge has been provided by a variety of perceptual studies (Krumhansl 1990).

Tonality has a fundamental role in the dynamic and expressive qualities of music. Different pitches and chords, via their network of structural relations in a musical context, take on the ability to imply continuation or closure, movement or rest. These perceptions are part of the dynamic experience of music (Bigand, 1993; Francès, 1988; Meyer, 1956; Narmour, 1991b; Schmuckler, 1989; Schumckler & Boltz, 1994). Furthermore, tonal schemata appear to provide a basis for some of music's emotional power: Sloboda (1991) reports that appoggiaturas occurred significantly more often than chance in musical passages identified as "tear-evoking" by subjects. An appoggiatura is a tone on an emphasised beat which forms a dissonance with the prevailing harmony, before resolving to a "harmonically correct" note. This illustrates one of the interesting aspects of stable tonal schemata: they provide a background against which departures are salient, and thus can be used to aesthetic and emotional effect.

None of the principal features of tonality appear to be part of any other domain. Although tonality has been referred to as musical "syntax", attempts to find deep parallels to linguistic syntax (e.g. Bernstein, 1976) have foundered on the fundamentally different structural categories of tonal versus linguistic grammar (Keiler, 1978). Tonal and linguistic syntax can be compared at a very general level: both involve orderly structural relations, embodied in the implicit knowledge of an experienced listener. However, we are not aware of any convincing evidence for structural overlap at more detailed levels. On the contrary, there is good evidence for considering the tonal encoding of pitch as specific to music (Balzano, 1982; see Peretz & Morais, 1989, for a more complete treatment of this issue; Shepard, 1982; Sloboda, 1985). There are serious indications that translation of pitch onto tonal scales is subserved by a modular system in Fodor's (1983) sense. This system seems to operate mandatorily and to be cognitively impenetrable (Shepard & Jordan, 1984); it corresponds to an early ontogenic development (see Trehub et al. this volume) and, above all, appears associated with neural specialisation (Peretz, 1993).

The critical neuropsychological property of a modular system is its potential to exhibit selective breakdown after brain damage. Recently, we had the opportunity to document a detailed analysis of a single case, G.L., who showed a true disturbance in tonal interpretation of pitch, as opposed to difficulties from other sources (such as an impairment in short term memory, contour or interval processing and comprehension of speech). Interestingly, at the time of testing, G.L. was no longer experiencing language difficulties (Peretz et al. 1994). For instance, G.L. obtained a normal score on the Token test (DeRenzi & Faglioni, 1978), which is considered to be a sensitive measure of phonological, syntactic and semantic aspects of spoken language comprehension.

In five different experimental settings, involving judgements of melodic closure, discrimination abilities and preferences, G.L.'s results converged on a lack of sensitivity to tonal melodic cues. This absence of tonal sensitivity stood in sharp contrast with his consistent and recurrent reliance on contour and, to some extent, on interval cues for performing the same tasks (Peretz, 1993). In this respect, G.L. represents the reverse dissociation of that reported earlier by Tramo, Bharucha & Musiek (1990). These authors described a patient who also suffered from bilateral brain damage but who could still use tonal knowledge despite severely degraded pitch discrimination abilities. This patient and G.L., when considered together, constitute a double dissociation for the encoding of pitch intervals and of tonal pitch. This should, however, be taken cautiously, for the two patients were tested with different procedures. Nevertheless, the available data argue in favour of the existence of a tonal module which is dedicated to music. As such, tonal encoding of pitch does not constitute a good candidate for probing shared processes between music and speech.

RHYTHM

There is no universally accepted definition of rhythm, yet rhythmic organisation is acknowledged as an essential feature of both music (Gabrielsson, 1993) and language (Cutler, 1991; Lehiste, 1991). To avoid confusion, we adopt the following definition for the discussion below: "rhythm" means the temporal and accentual patterning of sound ("accentual" means "perceptually salient in some way"). While rhythm has many aspects, we will only treat three of its subsidiary concepts here: *tempo*, which refers to the rate of events, *grouping*, referring to the clustering of adjacent elements into larger units, and *metre*, referring to a periodic temporal-accentual scheme. In music, grouping boundaries, which are influenced by melodic and harmonic structure, are not predictable from the metrical scheme. In other words, metre and grouping are separate, though interacting, aspects of rhythm (see Lerdahl & Jackendoff, 1983, for one discussion of this issue). Thus, we will treat grouping and metre separately with regard to their specificity (or lack thereof) to music.

TEMPO

In music, dynamic modulation of rate can have a significant role in musical communication: Gabrielsson (1987) documents a systematic pattern of speeding up and slowing down to mark melodic phrases in piano performance. In speech, modulation of rate can serve multiple functions, from the communication of emotion (Murray & Arnott, 1993) to pragmatic purposes such as avoiding interruption via increases in rate (Schegloff, 1982). The control of rate would appear to be a good candidate for processing overlap between language and music.

To our knowledge, the relationship between the control of tempo in music and speech has not been investigated, but is amenable to neuropsychological investigation. Specifically, subjects with disorders of speech rate due to neurologic damage can be tested for their ability to modulate tempo in non-verbal musical tasks. However, one caveat must be observed. Abnormal speech rate characterised by *slowing* may be secondary to a disorder of articulation or speech planning (Kent & Rosenbek, 1982; Rosenbek, Kent, & La Pointe, 1984), rather than a problem with the control of tempo *per se*. Thus it is more promising to study neurologic subjects with abnormally *fast* speech (tachylalia), where the tempo problem is less likely to be secondary in nature. Tachylalia is a rare symptom which has been observed in conjunction with different neurologic syndromes (Dordain, Chevrie-Muller, & Guidet, 1978), but its relation to non-verbal timing skills awaits investigation.

GROUPING

In both performance and perception, musical elements tend to be grouped into larger units, which may be informally referred to as "phrases" (the term is used somewhat variably between researchers). One notable feature of phrasing in both music performance (Gabrielsson, 1987; Repp, 1992a; Shaffer & Todd, 1987; Todd, 1985) and perception (Repp, 1992b) is that ends of phrases appear to be associated with slowing, or ritardando, with the degree of slowing reflecting the structural importance of the phrase boundary. This fact, combined with explicit representations of grouping structure and a metric for relating ritardando to boundary strength, has been used to model phrasal timing patterns in actual piano performances with reasonable success (Todd, 1985, 1989).

Grouping of elements in production and perception appears to be an important part of speech as well. Research on read speech in English has revealed that boundaries between groups of words are often marked by local slowing, called "preboundary lengthening", with the degree of lengthening significantly related to the extent of the subjective decoupling between groups (Wightman, Shattuck-Hufnagel, Ostendorf, & Price, 1992). The similar nature of constituent marking in speech and music has been noted by researchers involved in speech and music synthesis (Carlson, Friberg, Frydén, Granström, & Sundberg, 1989), though they caution that preboundary lengthening is not a linguistic universal. In fact, other mechanisms exist for marking boundaries in speech (Wightman & Ostendorf, 1994) and in music.

Given the empirical similarities between grouping in music and language, the possibility of shared cognitive mechanisms would be interesting to pursue. Some data from our study of amusic subjects CN and IR addresses this issue. Our study included 10 sentence pairs in which a change in timing pattern created a difference in meaning (e.g. Henri, le petit mange beaucoup./ Henri, le petit, mange beaucoup. Henry, the child eats a lot./ Henry, the child, eats a lot). For each of these "timing-shift" pairs, the durational characteristics of syllables was used to create a pair of rhythmic patterns (tone sequences with no frequency variation). These rhythmic patterns did not conform to any metric scheme, but reflected the temporal patterning of the original sentences, which grouped their syllables differently according to the meaning of the sentence.

The sentence pairs and rhythmic pairs were presented separately for same/ different discrimination (pairs could appear in either configuration, and replicates were included). The results for CN, IR, and 8 controls can be seen in Figure 10.1. The Fisher exact probability test revealed that the level of performance across domains was not significantly different for either subjects or controls. IR was at chance in discriminating the timing-shift sentences as well as their rhythmic analogues. Her performance cannot be attributed to a general consequence of brain damage, as CN did quite well at this task (CN's performance was not significantly different from controls). Thus the pattern of results is consistent with some common mechanisms for grouping in language and music, though clearly more work is needed.

METRE

Metrical organisation is a prominent feature of musical traditions in diverse cultures: periodic temporal-accentual structures occur in the xylophone music of Zaire (Merriam, 1982), the tabla drumming of northern India (Kippen, 1988), and in many other traditions. In Western European music, metrical organisation tends to follow patterns based on multiples of two or three beats, with roughly even timing between those beats. Psychological investigations with westerners have confirmed the relevance of such metrical schemes in perception and performance (Clarke, 1985; Lee, 1991; Palmer & Krumhansl, 1990; Sloboda, 1983). One notable feature of recent theoretical treatments of metre in Western music has been the notion of a hierarchy of beat strength, with equal timing between beats at different levels of the metrical hierarchy (Lerdahl & Jackendoff, 1983).

A metrical scheme, once established, tends to create a stable pattern in the mind of the performer or listener. This in turn allows for meaningful deviations, such as syncopation, in which salient musical events occur on metrically weak positions. Syncopation illustrates the crucial fact that metrical patterns have a psychological reality apart from phenomenal accentual patterns.

The idea that metrical patterns are relevant to linguistic organisation has inspired both empirical and theoretical research. The notion of periodicity in speech production was formalised by Pike (1945) and Abercrombie (1967), who proposed that certain languages, such as English, produce stresses at roughly equal temporal intervals ("stress" is inconsistently defined in the speech literature: here we mean perceptual prominence, signalled by duration, intensity, pitch, vowel quality, or some combination of these). These "stress-timed" languages were contrasted with "syllable-timed" languages, such as French, which produce syllables at roughly equal intervals. Empirical research has not supported this notion (Roach, 1982). Rather, it has been suggested by Dauer (1983) that the temporal differences between these categories reflect different patterns of vowel reduction, syllable structure, and other phonetic and phonological factors. Dauer also provides data showing a general tendency to separate stresses in *both* "stress-timed" and "syllable-timed" languages, as well as in "unclassified" languages. Why so many languages should have this tendency is not conclusively known, although facilitating articulation may be one reason.

Although phonetics has not provided evidence for metrical patterning in ordinary speech, several theoretical treatments of linguistic rhythm have abandoned any concern with timing per se and focused on the patterning of syllabic stress in spoken utterances. Theories of stress patterning have shared two notable features with theories of musical metre: hierarchical patterns of "metrical weight" (stress), and a tendency to alternate between stronger and weaker "beats" (syllables) (e.g. Liberman & Prince, 1977; Martin, 1972). Some of the earlier work in this area posited a quasi-metrical scheme for speech in order to derive observed stress patterns (Hayes, 1984; Selkirk, 1984). However, subsequent work, examining a greater variety of languages, has shown that a theoretical system based mainly on *avoiding* strong stress adjacency is likely to have more explanatory and predictive power than one founded on metrical principles (Nespor & Vogel, 1989). Congruent with this idea, a tendency to avoid stress "clashes" has been documented empirically for English (Shattuck-Hufnagel, Ostendorf, & Ross, 1994).

Thus, the "metricality" of language can probably be considered a result of a primarily negative tendency (avoidance of juxtaposed stress), whereas musical metre represents the active shaping of sound based on an underlying temporal-accentual scheme. An intuitive appreciation for this difference can be gained by considering the lack of a possibility for syncopation in speech. Before considering metre as an inherent difference between language and music, however, it is important to note that metrical organisation is neither universal in music, nor particular to it. Many European folk ballads (Seeger, 1966) and contemporary musical works lack significant metrical organisation, as do certain styles of North Indian classical instrumental music: similar examples from other traditions could doubtless be found. On the other hand, many forms of communication outside music can have quite regular metrical organisation, including some forms of poetic verse (Gross, 1979; Lerdahl & Halle, 1991). This suggests that metre is not an inherent property of any communicative domain, but an organisational principle which is optionally applied across domains (e.g. in music, language, dance, etc.). This in turn suggests that if processes subserving metrical organisation are disrupted, any behaviour relying on such processes should be disrupted, whether the behaviour is musical, linguistic, both, or neither.

In order to treat this question in a neuropsychological perspective, one needs first to demonstrate that metric organisation can be selectively disrupted after brain damage. The question of generalisation across domains can then be addressed in a meaningful way. Evidence for dissociating metre from rhythm has been found in a study where perceptual aspects of temporal processing were assessed (Peretz, 1990). In that study, two tasks were used: a standard "same-vs.-different" classification task and a "waltz-vs.-march" decision task. In the former, subjects were induced to rely on rhythm, for this was the only cue available for discrimination. In the other task, a "waltz-vs.-march" interpretation for each musical excerpt was used to promote metrical organisation, for it might be close to what listeners do implicitly when hearing the first bars of a musical piece in order to get ready for dancing. Both patient groups (left or right hemisphere lesion) were found to be impaired on the rhythmic task (as in Reitan & Wolfson, 1989). However, the metric test was successfully accomplished by most patients. The fact that metre judgement was spared in presence of disrupted rhythmic discrimination suggests that meter is not only distinct but also is not derived from rhythmic organisation.

The empirical evidence for generalisation of metrical processes across domains is scarce. There are, however, a few interesting suggestions. Cross-modal disruption of temporal processing (affecting both rhythm and metre, in both perception and production) has been described by Mavlov (1980) in a professional musician who sustained a lesion in the left posterior parietal hemisphere. The loss of rhythmic abilities in this patient affected temporal pattern reproduction regardless of whether the stimuli were presented in the auditory, visual or tactile modality. The patient's linguistic abilities were described as having returned to normal, though no mention was made of the temporal aspect of his speech. In contrast, Fries & Swihart (1990) describe an amateur musician who could no longer tap along in beat with a metronome or with music but who was still able to reproduce rhythmic patterns after having sustained a stroke in the right temporal lobe and the right basal ganglia (the patient was a left-hander). The deficit was modality specific in being restricted to audition. However, the metre deficit was described as affecting most motor behaviours, including articulation and speech rate. Although no systematic effort was made to compare performance on analogous musical and linguistic material, this study provides the first hint for the existence of a common mechanism governing metrical organisation in both domains.

SONG

Song is a universal form of auditory expression in which music and speech are intrinsically related. Song thus represents an ideal case for assessing the separability or commonality of music and language. Although songs may be created independently by two artists, the composer and the poet (or librettist), the two usually work in concert to integrate their respective contributions. For example, Palmer & Kelly (1992) have shown that linguistic prosodic structure and musical metre are generally aligned in Western art song, although these factors have independent effects on sung syllable durations, suggesting that they contribute separately to song performance. In memory, however, melody and text appear inseparable (Morrongiello & Roes, 1990; Serafine, Crowder, & Repp, 1984; Serafine, Davidson, Crowder, & Repp, 1986; Samson & Zatorre, 1991; but see Crowder, Serafine, & Repp, 1990 who admit the possibility of independent representations). In song memory, the musical and the linguistic component may be represented in some combined or common code.

Empirical evidence for this idea relies on the use of a memory recognition paradigm where novel songs are first studied and then presented with a forced-choice procedure. Subjects are required to recognise the melody, the lyrics, or both, of the songs that they had previously heard: among the alternatives are excerpts in which the melody of one song and the lyrics of another song are combined (mismatch songs). Integration effects are revealed by the systematic superiority of recognition scores for match songs over mismatch songs. Listeners behave as though they cannot access the melody without having access to the text, and vice-versa, of the studied song. This is a recurrent finding, which has been documented in normal adults (Serafine et al. 1984, 1986; Crowder et al. 1990), in preschool children (Morrongiello & Roes, 1990) and in epileptic patients after unilateral temporal lobe resections (Samson & Zatorre, 1991).

It should be pointed out, however, that all these data are derived from the use of the same paradigm. Thus, it is plausible that the integration effects are task-bound or material-specific. Given unfamiliar, interfering material among the response choices, subjects may form integrated representations of melody and text in memory in order to facilitate recognition. Such a strategy might not be efficient for the recognition of well-known songs, which are typically built around a few melodic lines, each of which can carry different lyrics. Consequently, encoding melody and text independently in normal situations might be more parsimonious and efficient. There is a particular need here for both diversity in experimental tasks and systematic neuropsychological investigations before we can draw any firm conclusions about the relation of musical and linguistic mental codes in song.

There are studies in the available neuropsychological literature that do suggest separability between melody and text. However, none can yet be considered conclusive. The first suggestion comes from an earlier study done by Goodglass & Calderon (1977) who obtained opposite laterality effects (and by inference opposite cerebral hemispheric superiorities) in the recall of musical and linguistic content of the same sung digits. The evidence relied on musicians only: thus, separability between melody and digits could be the product of a highly flexible and trained auditory system. The second suggestion comes from the dissociated behaviour of our amusic patients (notably CN) who is able to quickly and accurately recognise the lyrics of familiar tunes even though she is unable to recognise the corresponding melody (Peretz et al. 1994). Yet this dissociated behaviour is compatible with an interpretation of integration. CN's intact language system may be able to compute a correct sentence representation which can achieve contact with the stored song representation, while the impaired music system may no longer do so. The stored song representation may still correspond to a single entity where melody and text are integrated. To demonstrate separability, we need to (1) combine music and lyrics in songs (and not assess each component separately as in Peretz et al., 1994) and (2) obtain evidence of a double dissociation; that is, not only evidence for the selective loss of the music but also for the text. Such work is being actively pursued by the second author.

Finally, it should be noted that subjects with non-fluent aphasia have been known to sing the melodies (and sometimes the words) of previously learned songs, a phenomenon that has been documented for over 200 years (Dalin, 1736, cited in Benton & Joynt, 1960). However, the significance of this behaviour to the relation of melody and text representation in the brain is not clear. Studies of aphasic singing have been primarily descriptive (e.g. Yamadori, Osumi, Masuhara, & Okubo, 1977). One group has developed a speech therapy for aphasics based on melodically-intoned sentences (Albert, Sparks, & Helm, 1973, Helm-Estabrooks & Albert, 1991), but systematic research into the cognitive basis of aphasic singing has yet to be done. Another source of data on text and tune processing may be Alzheimer's disease, where intriguing hints of dissociations of memory for words and melody of songs have been reported (e.g. Swartz, Hantz, Crummer, Walton, & Frisina, 1989). Further research with both aphasic and Alzheimer's subjects could help elucidate the relation between linguistic and musical representation in memory.

CONCLUSION

The evidence reviewed in this chapter suggests that "music" and "language" are not independent mental faculties, but labels for complex sets of processes, some of which are shared and some different. Neuropsychology allows the empirical delineation of the boundaries between these domains, as well an exploration of their overlap. Accordingly, such research helps define the boundaries of "modularity" in language and music (Fodor, 1983; Gardner, 1983; Jackendoff 1987). For example, neuropsychological evidence suggests that the processing of pitch contour employs some of the same neural resources in music and language, while the processing of tonality appears to draw on resources used uniquely by music.

Numerous other areas of convergence and divergence between music and language await more thorough investigation. One benefit of such studies is a refined understanding of the functional and neural architecture of both domains. More generally, studying language and music in parallel offers a chance to understand human auditory communication and cognition in a broader perspective than is possible by studying either domain alone.

ACKNOWLEDGMENTS

We thank Evan Balaban, Jennifer Burton, Claus Heeschen, Michael Kelley, Bruno Repp, Stefanie Shattuck-Hufnagel, Kay Kaufman Shelemay, Irene Vogel, and Edward O. Wilson for their valuable comments and help. This chapter was prepared with support from a grant from the Arthur Green Fund of the Department of Organismic and Evolutionary Biology, Harvard University to the first author, and from the National Sciences and Engineering Research Council of Canada to the second author.

REFERENCES

Abercrombie, D. (1967). *Elements of General Phonetics*. Edinburgh: Edinburgh University Press.

Aiello, R. (1994). Music and language: Parallels and contrasts. In R. Aiello & J. Sloboda (Eds.), *Musical Perceptions*. Oxford: Oxford University Press.

Alain, C. & Woods, D.L. (1994). Signal clustering modulates auditory cortical activity in humans. *Perception and Psychophsics, 56*, 501–516.

Albert, M., Sparks, R. & Helm, N. (1973). Melodic intonation therapy for aphasia. *Archives of Neurology, 29*, 130–131.

Balzano, G. (1982). The pitch set as a level of description for studying musical pitch perception. In M. Clynes (Ed.), *Music, Mind, and Brain: The neuropsychology of music*. New York: Plenum Press.

Basso, A. & Capitani, E. (1985). Spared musical abilities in a conductor with global aphasia and ideomotor apraxia. *Journal of Neurology, Neurosurgery, and Psychiatry, 48*, 407–412.

Baum, S., Daniloff, J.K. Daniloff, R., & Lewis, J. (1982). Sentence comprehension by Broca's aphasics: effects of some suprasegmental variables. *Brain and Language, 17*, 261–271.

Beckman, M., & Pierrehumbert, J. (1986). Intonational structure in Japanese and English. *Phonology Yearbook, 3*, 255–309.

Benton, A.L, & Joynt, R.J. (1960). Early descriptions of aphasia. *Archives of Neurology, 3*, 205–222.

Bernstein, L. (1976). *The Unanswered Question*. Cambridge, Mass: Harvard Univ. Press.

Besson, M., Faïta, F. & Requin, J. (1994). Brain waves associated with musical incongruities differ for musicians and non-musicians. *Neuroscience Letters, 168*, 101–105.

Bigand, E. (1993). The influence of implicit harmony, rhythm and musical training on the abstraction of "tension-relaxation schemas" in tonal musical phrases. *Contemporary Music Review, 9*(1–2), 123–137.

Blacking, J. (1976). *How Musical is Man?* Seattle: University of Washington Press.

Blonder, L.X., Bowers, D. & Heilman, K.M. (1991). The role of the right hemisphere in emotional communication. *Brain, 114*(3), 1115–1127.

Bolinger, D. (1989). *Intonation and its Uses: Melody in Grammar and Discourse*. Stanford: Stanford University Press.

Brådvik, B., Dravins, C., Holts, S., Rosén, I., Ryding, E. & Ingvar, D.H. (1991). Disturbances of speech prosody following right hemisphere infarcts. *Acta Neurologica Scandanavica, 81*, 133–147.

Bregman, A. (1990). *Auditory Scene Analysis: The Perceptual Organisation of Sound*. Cambridge, Mass: MIT Press.

Burns, E.M. & Campbell, S.L. (1994). Frequency and frequency-ratio resolution by possessors of absolute and relative pitch: Examples of categorical perception? *Journal of the Acoustical Society of America, 96*(5), 2704–2719.

Burns, E.M., & Ward, W.D. (1978). Categorical perception—phenomenon or epiphenomenon: Evidence from experiments in the perception of melodic musical intervals. *Journal of the Acoustical Society of America, 63*(2), 456–468.

Cancelliere, A.E.B. & Kertesz, A. (1990). Lesion localisation in acquired deficits of emotional expression and comprehension. *Brain and Cognition, 13*, 133–147.

Carlson, R., Friberg, A., Frydén, L., Granström, B. & Sundberg, J. (1989). Speech and music performance: parallels and contrasts. *Contemporary Music Review, 4*, 389–402.

Clarke, E. (1985). Structure and expression in rhythmic performance. In P. Howell, I, Cross & R. West (Eds.), *Musical Structure and Cognition*. London: Academic Press.

Clarke, E.F. (1989). Issues in language and music. *Contemporary Music Review, 4*, 9–22.

Clynes, M. & Nettheim, N. (1982). The living quality of music: neurobiologic basis of communicative feeling. In M. Clynes (Ed.), *Music, Mind, and Brain: The neuropsychology of music*. New York: Plenum Press.

Confavreux, C., Croisile, B., Garassus, P., Aimard, G. & Trillet, M. (1992). Progressive amusia and aprosody. *Archives of Neurology*, *49*, 971–976.

Crowder, R.G., Serafine, M.L. & Repp, B. (1990) Physical interaction and association by contiguity in memory for the words and melodies of songs. *Memory & Cognition*, *18*, 469–76.

Crystal, D. (1987). *The Cambridge Encyclopedia of Language*. Cambridge: Cambridge University Press.

Cutler, A. (1991). Linguistic rhythm and speech segmentation. In J. Sundberg, L. Nord, & R. Carlson (Eds.), *Music, Language, Speech and Brain*. London: MacMillan.

Darwin, C. (1871). *The Descent of Man, and Selection in Relation to Sex*. (2 volumes). London: John Murray

Dauer, R.M. (1983). Stress-timing and syllable-timing reanalyzed. *Journal of Phonetics*, *11*, 51–62.

DeRenzi, E. & Faglioni, P. (1978). Normative data and screening power of a shortened version of the token test. *Cortex*, *14*, 41–48.

Dordain, M., Chevrie-Muller, C. & Guidet C. (1978). Les tachylalies: étude clinique et acoustique de 149 sujets [Tachylalia: clinical and acoustic study of 149 subjects]. *Acta Neurologica Belgica*, *78*(6), 354–72.

Dowling, W.J., Kwak, S., & Andrews, M.W. (1995). The time course of recognition of novel melodies. *Perception and Psychophysics*, *57*(2), 136–149.

Edworthy, J. (1985). Interval and contour in melody processing. *Music Perception*, *2*(3), 375–388.

Emmory, K. (1987). The neurological substrates for prosodic aspects of speech. *Brain and Language*, *30*, 305–320.

Fasanaro, A.M., Spitaleri, D.L.A. & R. Valiani. (1990). Dissociation of musical reading: A musician affected by alexia without agraphia. *Music Perception*, *7*(3), 259–272.

Fernald, A. (1985). Four-month-old infants prefer to listen to motherese. *Infant Behavior and Development*, *8*, 181–195.

Fernald, A. (1993). Approval and disapproval: Infant responsiveness to vocal affect in familiar and unfamiliar languages. *Child Development*, *64*(3), 657–674.

Fernald, A., & Kuhl, P.K. (1987). Acoustic determinants of infant preference for motherese speech. *Infant Behavior and Development*, *10*, 279–293.

Fodor, J.A. (1983). *The modularity of mind*. Cambridge, Mass: MIT Press.

Francès, R. (1988). *The Perception of Music*. (Translated by W.J. Dowling). Hillsdale, NJ: Erlbaum.

Fries, W. & Swihart, A. (1990). Disturbance of rhythm sense following right hemisphere damage. *Neuropsychologia*, *28*,(12), 1317–1323.

Gabrielsson, A. (1987). Once again: The theme from Mozart's Piano Sonata in A Major (K.331). In A. Gabrielsson (Ed.), *Action and Perception in Rhythm and Music*. Stockholm: Publication issued by the Royal Swedish Academy of Music, No. 55.

Gabrielsson, A. (1993). The complexities of rhythm. In T.J. Tighe & W.J. Dowling (Eds.), *Psychology and Music: The Understanding of Melody and Rhythm*. Hillsdale, NJ: Erlbaum.

Gandour, J. & Dardarananda, R. (1983). Identification of tonal contrasts in Thai aphasic patients. *Brain and Language*, *18*, 98–114.

Gardner, H. (1983). *Frames of mind. The Theory of Multiple Intelligences*. New York: Basic Books.

Gerardi, G.M. & Gerken, L. (1995). The development of affective responses to modality and melodic contour. *Music Perception*, *12*(3), 279–290.

Goodglass, H. & Calderon, M. (1977). Parallel processing of verbal and musical stimuli in right and left hemisphere. *Neuropsychologia*, *15*, 397–407.

Goodglass, H. & Kaplan, E. (1983). *Boston Diagnostic Aphasia Examination Booklet*. Malvern, PA: Lea and Febiger.

Gross, H. (Ed) (1979). *The Structure of Verse: Modern Essays on Prosody*. (Revised edition) New York: Ecco Press.

Handel, S. (1989). *Listening: An Introduction to the Perception of Auditory Events*. Cambridge, Mass: MIT Press.

Harwood, D.L. (1976). Universals in music: A perspective from cognitive psychology. *Ethnomusicology*, *20*(3), 521–533.

Hayes, B. (1984). The phonology of rhythm in English. *Linguistic Inquiry*, *15*, 33–74.

Heilman, K.M., Bowers, D., Speedie, L. & Coslett, H.B. (1984). Comprehension of affective and nonaffective prosody. *Neurology*, *34*, 917–921.

Helm-Estabrooks, N. & Albert, M. (1991). *Manual of Aphasia Therapy*. Austin, Texas: Pro-ed.

Hughes, C.P., Chan, J.L., & Su, M.S. (1983). Aprosodia in Chinese patients with right cerebral hemisphere lesions. *Archives of Neurology*, *40*, 732–736.

Jackendoff, R. (1987). *Consciousness and the Computational Mind*. Cambridge, Mass: MIT Press.

Judd, T., Gardner, H. & Geschwind, N. (1983). Alexia without agraphia in a composer. *Brain*, *106*, 435–457.

Jusczyk, P.W. & Krumhansl, C.L. (1993). Pitch and rhythmic patterns affecting infants' sensitivity to musical phrase structure. *Journal of Experimental Psychology: Human Perception and Performance*, *19*(3), 627–640.

Jusczyk, P.W., Hirsh-Pasek, K., Kelmer-Nelson, D.G., Kennedy, L.J., Woodward, A. & Piwoz, J. (1992). Perception of acoustic correlates of major phrasal units by young infants. *Cognitive Psychology*, *24*, 252–293.

Keiler, A. (1978). Bernstein's *The Unanswered Question* and the problem of musical competence. *The Musical Quarterly*, *64*(2), 195–222.

Kent, R.D. & Rosenbek, J.C. (1982). Prosodic disturbance and neurologic lesion. *Brain and Language*, *15*, 259–291.

Kippen, J. (1988). *The Tabla of Lucknow: A cultural analysis of a musical tradition*. Cambridge: Cambridge University Press.

Krumhansl, C.L. (1990). *Cognitive Foundations of Musical Pitch*. Oxford: Oxford University Press.

Ladd, D.R., Silverman, K.E.A., Tolkmitt, F., Bergmann, G. & Scherer, K. (1985). Evidence for the independent function of intonation contour type, voice quality and Fo range in signaling speaker affect. *Journal of the Acoustical Society of America*, *78*(2), 435–444.

Lee, C. (1991). The perception of metrical structure: Experimental evidence and a model. In P. Howell, R. West, & I. Cross (Eds.), *Representing Musical Structure*. London: Academic Press.

Lehiste, I. (1973). Phonetic disambiguation of syntactic ambiguity. *Glossa*, *7*(2), 107–121.

Lehiste, I. (1991). Speech research: An overview. In J. Sundberg, L. Nord, & R. Carlson (Eds.), *Music, Language, Speech and Brain*. London: MacMillan.

Lerdahl, F. & Halle, J. (1991). Some lines of poetry viewed as music. In J. Sundberg, L. Nord, & R. Carlson (Eds.), *Music, Language, Speech and Brain*. London: MacMillan.

Lerdahl, F. & Jackendoff, R. (1983). *A Generative Theory of Tonal Music*. Cambridge, Mass: MIT Press.

Levman, B. (1992). The genesis of music and language. *Ethnomusicology*, *36*(2), 147–170.

Liberman, A. & Mattingly, I. (1989). A specialization for speech perception. *Science*, *243*, 489–494.

Liberman, M., & Prince, A. (1977). On stress and linguistic rhythm. *Linguistic Inquiry, 8,* 249–336.

Luria, A., Tsvetkova, L. & Futer, D.S. (1965). Aphasia in a composer. *Journal of Neurological Science, 2,* 288–292.

Marin, O. (1982). Neurological aspects of music perception and performance. In Diana Deutsch (Ed.), *The Psychology of Music.* Orlando: Academic Press.

Martin, J.G. (1972). Rhythmic (hierarchical) versus serial structure in speech and other behavior. *Psychological Review, 79,* 487–509.

Mavlov, L. (1980). Amusia due to rhythm agnosia in a musician with left hemisphere damage: a non auditory supramodal defect. *Cortex, 16,* 321–338.

Merriam, A.P. (1982). African musical rhythm and concepts of time-reckoning. In A.P. Merriam (Ed.), *African Music in Perspective.* New York: Garland.

Meyer, L.B. (1956). *Emotion and Meaning in Music.* Chicago: University of Chicago Press.

Meyer, L.B. (1973). *Explaining Music: Essays and Explorations.* Berkeley: University of California Press.

Miyazaki, K. (1988). Musical pitch identification by absolute pitch possessors. *Perception and Psychophysics, 44*(6), 501–512.

Morrongiello, B. & Roes, C. (1990). Children's memory for new songs: Integration or independent storage of words and tunes? *Journal of Experimental Child Psychology, 50,* 25–38.

Murray, I.R. & Arnott, J.L. (1993). Toward the simulation of emotion in synthetic speech: A review of the literature on human vocal emotion. *Journal of the Acoustical Society of America, 93*(2), 1097–1108.

Narmour, E. (1991a). *The Analysis and Cognition of Basic Melodic Stuctures: The Implication-Realization Model.* Chicago: University of Chicago Press.

Narmour, E. (1991b). *The Analysis and Cognition of Melodic Complexity: The Implication-Realization Model.* Chicago: University of Chicago Press.

Nespor, M. & Vogel, I. (1986). *Prosodic Phonology.* Dordrecht: Foris Publications.

Nespor, M. & Vogel, I. (1989). On clashes and lapses. *Phonology, 6,* 69–116.

Nettl, B. (1956). *Music in Primitive Culture.* Cambridge, MA: Harvard University Press.

Palmer, C. & Kelly, M. (1992). Linguistic prosody and musical meter in song. *Journal of Memory & Language, 31,* 525–542.

Palmer, C. & Krumhansl, C.L. (1990). Mental representations for musical meter. *Journal of Experimental Psychology: Human Perception and Performance, 16*(4), 728–741.

Patel, A., Peretz, I., Tramo, M. & Labreque, R. (in press). Processing prosodic and musical patterns: A neuropsychological investigation. *Brain and Language.*

Peretz, I. (1990). Processing of local and global musical information by unilateral brain-damaged patients. *Brain, 113,* 1185–1205.

Peretz, I. (1993). Auditory atonalia for melodies. *Cognitive Neuropsychology, 10,* 21–56.

Peretz, I. (1994). Amusia: Specificity and multiplicity. In I. Deliège, (Ed.), *Proceedings of the 3rd International Conference on Music Perception and Cognition* (pp 37–38). Liège, Belgium: European Society for the Cognitive Sciences of Music.

Peretz, I. & Babaï, M. (1992). The role of contour and intervals in the recognition of melody parts: Evidence from cerebral asymmetries in musicians. *Neuropsychologia, 30*(3), 277–292.

Peretz, I. & Morais, J. (1987). Analytic processing in the classification of melodies as same or different. *Neuropsychologia, 25,* 645–652.

Peretz, I. & Morais, J. (1989). Music and Modularity. *Contemporary Music Review, 4,* 279–293.

Peretz, I. & Morais, J. (1993). Specificity for music. In F. Boller & J. Grafman (Eds.), *Handbook of Neuropsychology, Vol. 8.* Amsterdam: Elsevier Science Publishers.

Peretz, I. Kolinsky, R., Tramo, M., Labrecque, R., Hublet, C., Demeurisse, G. & Belleville, S. (1994). Functional dissociations following bilateral lesions of auditory cortex. *Brain, 117,* 1283–1301.

Pike, K. (1945). *The Intonation of American English*. Ann Arbor: University of Michigan Press.

Pike, K. (1948). *Tone Languages: A Technique for Determining the Number and Type of Pitch Contrasts in a Language, with Studies in Tonemic Substitution and Fusion*. Ann Arbor: University of Michigan Press.

Piston, W. (1978). *Harmony* (4th ed.). (Revised and expanded by Mark DeVoto). New York: Norton.

Price, P.J., Ostendorf, M., Shattuck-Hufnagel, S. & Fong, G. (1991). The use of prosody in syntactic disambiguation. *Journal of the Acoustical Society of America, 90*(6), 2956–2970.

Randel, D.M. (Ed.). (1978). *Harvard Concise Dictionary of Music*. Cambridge, Mass: Harvard University Press.

Reitan, R. & Wolfson, D. (1989). The seashore rhythm test and brain functions. *The Clinical Neuropsychologist, 3*, 70–78.

Remez, R.E., Rubin, P.E., Berns, S.M., Pardo, J.S. & Lang, J.M. (1994). On the perceptual organization of speech. *Psychological Review, 101*, 129–156.

Repp, B. (1984). Categorical perception: Issues, methods, findings. In N.J. Lass (Ed.), *Speech and Language: Advances in Research and Practice, Vol. 10*. New York: Academic Press.

Repp, B. (1992a). Diversity and commonality in music performance: An analysis of timing microstructure in Schumann's "Träumerei". *Journal of the Acoustical Society of America, 92*(5), 2546–2568.

Repp, B. (1992b). Probing the cognitive representation of musical time: Structural constraints on the perception of timing perturbations. *Cognition, 44*, 241–281.

Roach, P. (1982). On the distinction between "stress-timed" and "syllable-timed" languages. In D. Crystal (Ed.), *Linguistic Controversies: Essays in linguistic theory and practice in honour of F.R. Palmer*. London: Arnold.

Roberts, C.G. (1996). *Music of the Star Mountains*. Taipei, Taiwan: Yuan-Liou Publishing Co.

Rosenbek, J.C., Kent, R., & LaPointe, L.R. (1984). Apraxia of speech: An overview and some perspectives. In J.C. Rosenbek, M.R. McNeil & A.E. Aronson (Eds.), *Apraxia of Speech: Physiology, Acoustics, Linguistics, Management*. San Diego: College Hill Press.

Ross, E.D. (1981). The aprosodias: Functional-anatomic organization of the affective components of language in the right hemisphere. *Archives of Neurology, 38*, 561–569.

Rousseau J-J. (1761). Essay on the Origin of Languages (Essai sur l'origine des langues). In Victor Gourevitch (Ed. and tr.), *Jean-Jacque Rousseau. The First and Second Discourses and Essay on the Origin of Languages*. 1986. New York: Harper and Row.

Samson, S. & Zatorre, R.J. (1991). Recognition for text and melody of songs after unilateral temporal lobe lesion: Evidence for dual encoding. *Journal of Experimental Psychology: Learning, Memory and Cognition, 17*, 793–804.

Schegloff, E.A. (1982). Discourse as an interactional achievement: some uses of "uh uh" and other things that come between sentences. In D. Tannen (Ed.), *Georgetown University Roundtable on Languages and Linguistics: Texts and Talk*. Washington, D.C.: Georgetown University Press.

Schlaug, G., Jäncke, L., Huang, Y. & Steinmetz, H. (1995). In vivo evidence of structural brain asymmetry in musicians. *Science, 267*, 699–701.

Schmuckler, M.A. (1989). Expectation in music: Investigation of melodic and harmonic processes. *Music Perception, 7*(2), 109–150.

Schmuckler, M.A. & Boltz, M.G. (1994). Harmonic and rhythmic influences on musical expectancy. *Perception and Psychophysics, 56*(3), 313–325.

Seeger, C. (1966). Versions and variants of 'Barbara Allen' in the Archive of American Folk Song in the Library of Congress. *Selected Reports, Institute of Ethnomusicology, University of California, Los Angeles, 1*(1), 120–167. (Reprinted in C. Seeger (1977), *Studies in Musicology 1935–1975*. Berkeley, University of California Press).

Selkirk, L. (1984). *Phonology and Syntax: The Relation Between Sound and Structure*. Cambridge, Mass: MIT Press.

Serafine, M.L., Crowder, R.G. & Repp, B. (1984) Integration of melody and text in memory for song. *Cognition, 16*, 285–303.

Serafine, M.L., Davidson, J, Crowder, R.G., & Repp, B. (1986) On the nature of melody-text integration in memory for songs. *Journal of Memory and Language, 25*, 123–35.

Sergent, J. (1993). Mapping the Musician Brain. *Human Brain Mapping, 1*, 20–38.

Sergent, J., Zuck, E., Terriah, S. & MacDonald B. (1992). Distributed neural network underlying musical sight-reading and keyboard performance. *Science, 257*, 106–109.

Shaffer, L.H. & Todd, N. (1987). The interpretive component in musical performance. In A. Gabrielsson (Ed.), *Action and Perception in Rhythm and Music*. Stockholm: Publication issued by the Royal Swedish Academy of Music, No. 55.

Shattuck-Hufnagel, S., Ostendorf, M. & Ross, K. (1994). Stress shift and early pitch accent placement in lexical items in American English. *Journal of Phonetics, 22*, 357–388.

Shepard, R. (1982). Geometrical approximations to the structure of musical pitch. *Psychological Review, 89*, 305–333.

Shepard, R.N., & Jordan, D.S. (1984). Auditory illusions demonstrating that tones are assimilated to an internalized musical scale. *Science, 226*, 1333–4.

Signoret, J.L, Van Eeckhout, P., Poncet, M. & Castaigne, P. (1987). Aphasie sans amusie chez un organiste aveugle: Alexie-agraphie verbale sans alexie-agraphie musicale en braille [Aphasia without amusia in a blind organ player: Verbal alexia-agraphia without musical alexia-agraphia in braille]. *Revue Neurologique* (Paris), *143*, 172–81.

Sloboda, J.A. (1983). The communication of musical metre in piano performance. *Quarterly Journal of Experimental Psychology, 33*, 377–96.

Sloboda, J.A. (1985). *The Musical Mind: The Cognitive Psychology of Music*. Oxford: Clarendon Press.

Sloboda, J.A. (1991). Music structure and emotional response: Some empirical findings. *Psychology of Music, 19*, 110–120.

Smith, J.D., Nelson, D., Grohskopf, L.A., & Appleton, T. (1994). What child is this? What interval is that? Familiar tunes and music perception in novice listeners. *Cognition, 52*, 23–54.

Stanzione, M., Grossi, D. & Roberto, L. (1990). Note-by-note music reading: A musician with letter-by-letter reading. *Music Perception, 7*(3), 273–284.

Sundberg, J.D. & Lindblom, B. (1976). Generative theories in language and music descriptions. *Cognition, 4*, 99–122.

Sundberg, J., Nord, L. & Carlson, R. (Eds.). (1991). *Music, Language, Speech and Brain*. Wenner-Gren Center International Symposium Series, Vol. 59. London: MacMillan.

Swartz, K.P, Hantz, E.C., Crummer, G.C., Walton, J.P & Frisina, R.D. (1989). Does the melody linger on? Music cognition in Alzheimer's disease. *Seminars in Neurology, 9*(2), 152–158.

Todd, N. (1985). A model of expressive timing in tonal music. *Music Perception, 3*(1), 33–58.

Todd, N. (1989). A computational model of rubato. *Contemporary Music Review, 3*, 69–88.

Tramo, M.J., Bharucha, J.J. & Musiek, F.E. (1990). Music perception and cognition following bilateral lesions of auditory cortex. *Journal of Cognitive Neuroscience, 2*(3), 195–212.

Trehub, S.E. & Trainor, L.J. (1993). Listening strategies in infancy: the roots of music and language development. In S. McAdams & E. Bigand (Eds.), *Thinking in Sound: The Cognitive Psychology of Human Audition*. Oxford: Clarendon Press.

Trehub, S.E., Thorpe, L.A., & Morrongiello, B. (1987). Organizational processes in infants' perception of auditory patterns. *Child Development, 58*, 741–9.

Van Lancker, D., & Sidtis, J.J. (1992). The identification of affective-prosodic stimuli by left- and right-hemisphere-damaged subjects: all errors are not created equal. *Journal of Speech and Hearing Research, 35,* 963–970.

Weintraub, S., Mesulam, M.-M., & Kramer, L. (1981). Disturbances in prosody: a right-hemisphere contribution to language. *Archives of Neurology, 38,* 742–745.

Wightman, C.W. & Ostendorf, M. (1994). Automatic labeling of prosodic patterns. *IEEE Transactions on Speech and Audio Processing, 2*(4), 469–481.

Wightman, C.W., Shattuck-Hufnagel, S., Ostendorf, M. & Price, P.J. (1992). Segmental durations in the vicinity of prosodic phrase boundaries. *Journal of the Acoustical Society of America, 91*(3), 1707–1717.

Yamadori, A., Osumi, Y., Masuhara, S. & Okubo, M. (1977). Preservation of singing in Broca's aphasia. *Journal of Neurology, Neurosurgery, and Psychiatry, 40,* 221–224.

Yung, B. (1991). The relationship of text and tune in Chinese opera. In J. Sundberg, L. Nord, & R. Carlson (Eds.), *Music, Language, Speech and Brain.* London: MacMillan.

Zatorre, R.J., Evans, A.C. & Meyer, E. (1994). Neural mechanisms underlying melodic perception and memory for pitch. *Journal of Neuroscience, 14*(4), 1908–1919.

Zatorre, R.J., Evans, A.C., Meyer, E. & Gjedde A. (1992). Lateralization of phonetic and pitch discrimination in speech processing. *Science, 256,* 846–849.

11 Electrophysiological studies of music processing

Mireille Besson
Centre for Research in Cognitive Neuroscience
National Centre for Scientific Research
Marseille, France

INTRODUCTION

In this chapter I will review experiments on music perception that have been conducted using brain imaging technics. However, as work in our laboratory is based on the analysis of Event-Related Potentials (ERPs), specific emphasis will be given to this approach. Furthermore, several points should be kept in mind. First, the electrophysiology of music processing is a relatively new research area. Most of the studies conducted in the last few years have been aimed at finding electrophysiological markers of music processing. This can be considered a first step. Once components of the ERPs have been demonstrated to relate to certain aspects of music processing, specific hypotheses can be tested that will help develop models of music perception. Second, research in this field has benefitted from parallel research on language processing and some examples of this will be provided. Finally, while the comparison between Western tonal music and other types of music, using brain imaging technics, will certainly provide important insights into music perception and cognition, I am unaware of any cross-cultural studies using ERPs. Therefore, this review will be restricted to research focusing on Western tonal music.

Reviewing research on the electrophysiology of music processing, I will first focus on the study of the changes in the electroencephalogram (EEG) which are synchronised with the occurrence of specific events (ERPs). After providing a brief methodological and historical background, I will describe the results of several experiments in which ERPs have been used to test different aspects of music processing, such as the analysis of the physical characteristics of sounds (timbre and pitch) or the higher cognitive processes involved in the perception of melody and harmony. The second part of this chapter is devoted to the analysis of the EEG in relation to music processing. I will describe these studies and try to illustrate how ERPs and EEG analysis can be combined to provide a more complete image of what the brain is doing while listening to music.

Methodology

Since Berger (1929) first described the EEG in humans, one of the main aims of researchers using this method has been to analyse the time structure of the differences in electrical potentials (i.e. voltage) between two recording sites, and to correlate these voltage changes with behavioural changes. In order to record variations in the brain electrical activity from electrodes placed on the scalp, a large number of neurons have to be activated simultaneously. The occurrence of specific sensory or cognitive events will elicit evoked potentials that can be recorded from the scalp electrodes (the ERPs) if the recording period is time-locked to stimulus presentation. The change in the EEG to a particular event is usually of small amplitude, and several trials have to be averaged in order to discern the ERP from the background noise of the on-going EEG. ERPs are described by several features including polarity, amplitude, the time course of shifts in polarity relative to stimulus onset, and the distribution of these shifts across a number of scalp locations (for reviews, see Hillyard, 1993; Hillyard & Kutas, 1983; Hillyard & Picton, 1987). These shifts are often referred to as components[1]. Spontaneous activation of neural assemblies will also generate oscillations in the EEG record. These oscillations are characterised by their frequency bands, ranging between 0.5Hz and 60Hz, and their amplitude usually decreases with increasing frequency (Singer, 1993). Interest in these oscillatory patterns (specifically in the 40Hz frequency activity) has been growing over the past decade, because it may reflect important interactions between neural assemblies (Lowel & Singer, 1992; Singer, 1993).

HISTORICAL REVIEW

One of the first studies in which ERPs were recorded to musical stimuli was conducted by Besson & Macar (1987). This experiment was not, however, directly aimed at studying music processing, rather the aim was to compare the brain's response to unexpected stimuli in two contexts: language and music. Kutas & Hillyard (1980) analysed ERPs when people read sentences with incongruous endings such as "He takes coffee with cream and dog". The word "dog" elicited a specific ERPs component, of negative polarity relative to the baseline activity, that peaks around 400ms post-terminal word onset (the N400). Further studies then demonstrated, however, that semantic incongruity per se is neither sufficient nor necessary to elicit the N400. Indeed, the N400 decreases in amplitude with one repetition and completely vanishes with two repetitions of the same sentence (Besson, Kutas & van Petten, 1992; Van Petten, Kutas, Kluender, Mitchiner & McIsaac, 1991). Furthermore, Kutas & Hillyard (1984; Kutas, Lindamood and Hillyard, 1984) found an inverse relationship between N400 amplitude and the probability of occurrence of the sentence terminal word, operationally measured in terms of Cloze probability[2] (Taylor, 1953). Note also that N400 amplitude is smaller for incongruous words that are semantically related to the best sentence completion, such as the word "drink" in the sentence, "the pizza was too hot to", than for unrelated incongruous words ("cry"; see Fig. 11.1). Thus, the N400 was interpreted as reflecting semantic priming and expectancy processes.

The discovery of the N400 opened new perspectives in language research and has proven useful in testing models of word recognition and sentence processing (see Fischler & Raney, 1991, and Kutas & Van Petten, 1988; 1994, for reviews). Importantly, the N400 component is not tied to the visual modality but may be generated by spoken words as well as written words (Holcomb & Neville, 1990; 1991; McCallum, Farmer & Pocock, 1984).

Our experiment (Besson & Macar, 1987) was designed to test whether an N400 component would also be found with non-linguistic stimuli (see also, Katayama & Yagi, 1993; Paller, McCarthy & Wood, 1992; Nigam, Hoffman, & Simons, 1993; Polich, Vanasse, & Donchin, 1981; Polich 1985; Stuss, Sarazin, Leech & Picton 1983). We compared the ERPs elicited by semantically congruous and incongruous terminal words of sentences with those elicited in response to correct, expected notes and to "wrong" terminal notes of well-known french melodies (e.g. "Sur le pont d'Avignon"). Wrong notes were harmonically (out of key) and melodically (out of the melodic contour) incongruous. The timbre of the terminal note was also incongruous relative to the timbre of the other notes. In each condition, 25% of the trials ended with an incongruous stimulus.

Only incongruous words elicited N400 components. Incongruous notes, in contrast, were associated with large late positive components (LPCs; see Fig. 11.2). Thus, while these results suggested that the N400 was restricted to linguistic processing, they also demonstrated that the LPC was associated with violations of musical expectancy.

A further attempt to elicit an N400 component using simple, well-known musical phrases ending incongruously was conducted by Paller, McCarthy & Wood, (1992). They used a design similar to the one used by Besson & Macar (1987), but terminal congruous and incongruous notes were equiprobable and delayed by 800ms in one condition. This manipulation was introduced in order to provide subjects more time to generate a specific expectancy for the final note. Nonetheless, as in Besson & Macar's experiment, large LPCs were associated with the incongruous terminal notes, with no evidence of an N400.

Verleger (1990) designed an experiment in a somewhat different perspective. His main interest was to further understand the functional significance of one of

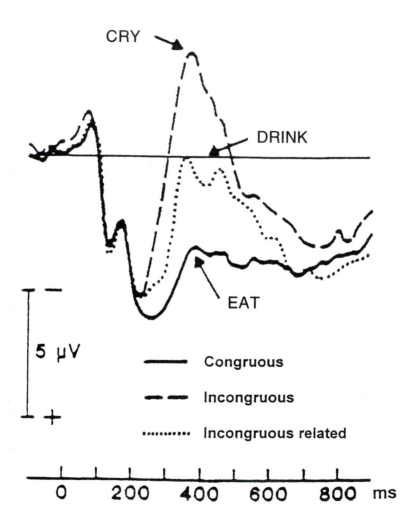

FIG. 11.1. ERPs elicited by sentence-final words at central site (Cz) for the best sentence completions (solid line), for incongruous endings (dashed line), and for incongruous endings that are semantically related to the best completions (dotted line). In this and subsequent Figs, amplitude (uV) is represented on the ordinate, and time (ms) on the abscissa. Negative voltage is up. [From Kutas et al (1984).]

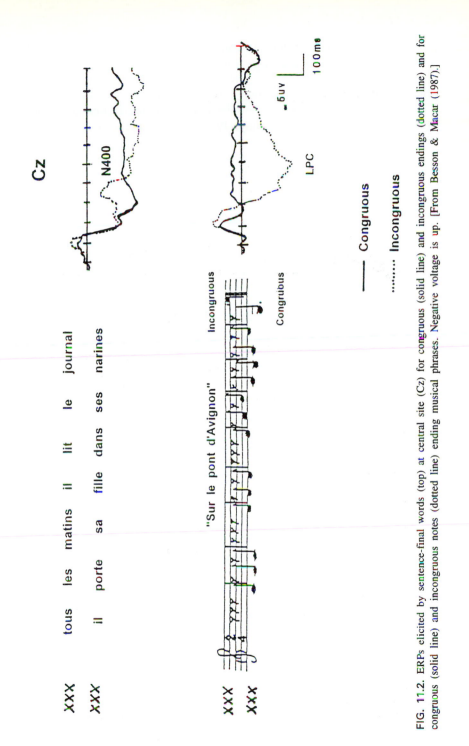

FIG. 11.2. ERPs elicited by sentence-final words (top) at central site (Cz) for congruous (solid line) and incongruous endings (dotted line) and for congruous (solid line) and incongruous notes (dotted line) ending musical phrases. Negative voltage is up. [From Besson & Macar (1987).]

the most studied ERPs component, namely the P300. The P300 component, often referred to as a family of potentials, is elicited by any task-relevant stimulus. Its amplitude and latency are modulated by the difficulty of the decision to be made. P300 amplitude is also particularly sensitive to stimulus probability and to the degree of confidence a subject has in his/her decision[3] (Hillyard, Squires, Bauer, & Lindsay, 1971; Sutton, Braren, Zubin, & John, 1965). Traditionally, the P300 has been interpreted as reflecting stimulus evaluation and its latency would correspond to the time at which the decision is made (for reviews, see Donchin & Coles, 1988; Johnson, 1986; 1988; McCarthy & Donchin, 1981; Pritchard, 1981; Verleger, 1988). In contrast, Verleger proposed that the P300 reflects perceptual closure: P300s are elicited when a stimulus signals unambiguously the end of a sequence, like terminal words of sentences or terminal notes of musical phrases (see also Friedman, Simon, Ritter & Rapin, 1975; Verleger, 1988). Consequently, congruous terminal notes should elicit P300 components. Besson & Macar's (1987) results, showing a P300-type response to incongruous notes only, did not fit with this hypothesis. Verleger's explanation was that since incongruous notes always occurred at the end of the musical phrases, they served as unambiguous markers of closure. This was not the case for congruous notes since subjects may not have been aware that they were the last notes[4].

In order to test this hypothesis, Verleger designed an experiment in which congruous and incongruous notes were presented at the end of musical excerpts chosen either from the beginning or the ending of the musical pieces. He hypothesised that P300 components would be elicited in all conditions except the congruous, opening condition, because only in this case did some ambiguity exist regarding whether or not the terminal note signals the end of the sequence. However, these predictions were not supported. Incongruous notes elicited large late positive components, and congruous notes did not, independently of whether the notes ended beginning or ending parts of the musical pieces.

ERPS TO THE "BUILDING BLOCKS" OF MUSIC PERCEPTION

Timbre

In contrast with the studies reviewed above, Hantz and his collaborators have used ERPs with the explicit aim of studying the neural mechanisms involved in music processing (Crummer, Hantz, Chuang, Walton & Frisina, 1988; Frisina, Walton & Crummer, 1988; Hantz & Crummer, 1988; Hantz, Crummer, Wayman, Walton & Frisina, 1992; Walton, Frisina, Hantz, Swartz & Crummer, 1988; Wayman, Frisina, Walton, Hantz & Crummer, 1992). Their first experiment was designed to test the effect of musical expertise in a timbre discrimination task (Crummer et al, 1988). They used a task typically known to elicit P300 components: the oddball task, in which infrequent stimuli (the "oddballs") are intermixed with frequent stimuli. In this particular task, subjects were asked to detect infrequent timbre of the violin among frequent timbre of the C trumpet. Discrimination difficulty was also manipulated and, in a different condition, subjects had to discriminate the timbre of two trumpets (e.g. B-flat versus E-flat trumpet). Both the musicians and non-musicians were perfect in discriminating the timbre of the C trumpet from the violin, tuba and trombone. On the more difficult discrimination, both groups performed poorly (around 60% correct responses) with the musicians performing better than the non-musicians. Only the P300 component of the ERPs was analysed in this experiment[5]. For both musicians and non-musicians, P300 amplitude was largest to infrequent stimuli in each condition except the most difficult discrimination condition. In this condition, P300s were larger for musicians than non-musicians. Finally, for both musicians and non-musicians P300 latency was longest in the most difficult discrimination condition. These latency results should be considered with caution, however, since, as mentioned by the authors, no P300 could be identified in this condition for some subjects. The most interesting finding is that when the discrimination is difficult and requires a "musical ear", P300 amplitude differs between musicians and non-musicians. These results thus seem to indicate that P300 amplitude is sensitive to musical expertise.

Interval Progressions

Hantz et al (1992) conducted an experiment in which musicians and non-musicians had to discriminate melodic intervals. In the first session, target and standard intervals were easily discriminated on the basis of the melodic progression (up or down). In the second session, the discrimination was more difficult. Four semi-tone intervals were used as standard and had to be discriminated from similar three-tone target intervals. In both sessions, discrimination performance was better for musicians than for non-musicians. In the second session, non-musicians performance was not different from chance. ERPs results showed that while P300 components were elicited to the target intervals for both musicians and non-musicians in the first session, with larger P300s for musicians than non-musicians, only musicians generated P300s in the second session. Thus, both behavioural and ERPs data seem to indicate that musical expertise is necessary to perform the most difficult discrimination and that P300 amplitude correlates with musical expertise. Another interpretation of these data is proposed in the discussion section.

Pitch

Cohen and collaborators (Cohen & Eretz, 1991; Cohen, Granot, Pratt & Barneah, 1993) have focused on the ERPs to the changes in pitch within short musical sequences. Within a trial, a five tone reference pattern was initially presented, followed by a five tone comparison pattern. The reference and comparison patterns could either be identical or different. When different, two notes in the sequence were presented in reverse order. Tone patterns were either presented at a fast rate with a 75ms tone duration and no interval between tones, or at a slow rate with a 100ms tone duration and a 650ms interval between two successive tones. Furthermore, while the comparison pattern was always presented in the auditory modality, the reference pattern could either be presented visually, by means of musical notation, or auditorily. Half of the subjects could read music and the other half could not. They were asked to decide whether the tones patterns were identical or different.

Results showed that in both the fast and slow rate conditions, larger P300 components were elicited in the different than identical pattern conditions. Note that because each tone was presented for only 75ms in the fast rate condition, the P300 effect emerged at the end of the 375ms five-tone sequence and can not be directly related to the position of the change in the tone sequence. This comparison is, however, possible in the slow rate condition in which the time interval between two notes is long enough (750ms SOA) to allow for the P300 to develop. Interestingly, P300 amplitude increased when the pitch shift occurred late in the sequence. This may reflect that as the tone sequence develops, expectancy for a change increases (see Fig. 11.3).

When the reference pattern was presented visually, the early N1-P2 components elicited to the first tone of the comparison pattern were larger than when both the reference and comparison patterns were presented auditorily. This finding reflects the fact that continuous auditory stimulation is associated with a decrease in cortical neurons excitability (the "refractory period", Gastaut, Gastaut, Roger, Corriol & Naquet, 1951). This refractoriness effect is not present when the reference pattern is visually presented. Finally, no clear differences were found between music readers and non-readers, when both the reference and comparison patterns were presented auditorily.

Wayman et al (1992) used an oddball task in which infrequent 1000Hz target tones were intermixed with frequent 500Hz tones. ERPs to the target tones were compared between non-musicians, musicians and musicians with absolute pitch. Results showed that while neither P300 amplitude or latency differed between musicians and non-musicians, P300 amplitude was smaller for musicians with absolute pitch (Fig. 11.4; see also Klein, Coles, & Donchin, 1984 and Evers, Grotemeyer, & Suhr, 1994 for differences in P300 latency between subjects with and without absolute pitch). This P300 amplitude differences need not reflect musical training since the two groups of musicians had comparable training. The authors offer two hypotheses. First, the brain pathways that evoke the P300 component may be different for musicians with absolute pitch than for other subjects. Alternatively, the task may require less attention for subjects with absolute pitch.

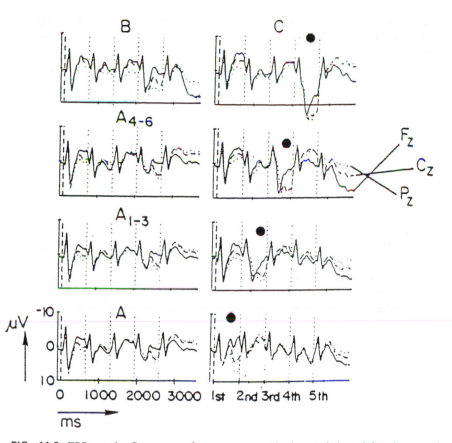

FIG. 11.3. ERPs to the five tones reference patterns (A, A_{1-3} and A_{4-6}; left column) and comparison patterns when identical (B, left column) or different (C) from the comparison patterns (right column). Results are for the slow rate condition when both the reference and comparison patterns are presented auditorily. The vertical dotted lines mark the beginning of the tones. The places where different tones were introduced are indicated by filled circles. ERPs recorded at three midline sites: Frontal (Fz, solid line), Central (Cz, dashed line) and Parietal (Pz, dotted line) are overlapped. Negative voltage is up. [From Cohen & Eretz (1991).]

ERPS TO VIOLATIONS OF MUSICAL EXPECTANCIES

Chord Progressions

Janata (1995) tested musicians on a harmonic expectancy task, based on the concept of tonal hierarchy described by Krumhansl & Shepard (1979), using ERPs and EEG analysis. An incomplete cadence composed of the tonic (I), the sub-dominant (IV) and the dominant (V) chords was followed, with an equal

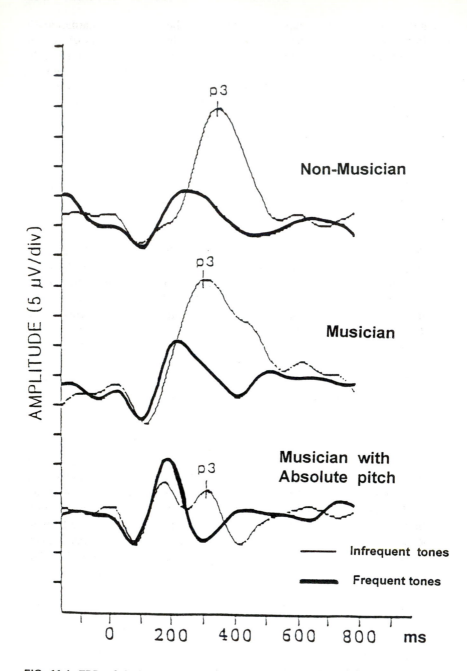

FIG. 11.4. ERPs of single subjects elicited by infrequent target tones (thin lines) and frequent standard tones (thick lines). ERPs were recorded at the parietal (Pz) electrode. Positive voltage is up. [From Wayman, Frisina, Walton, Hantz & Crummer (1992).]

probability, by the most expected resolution (the tonic), an harmonically plausible but ambiguous resolution (tonic of the relative minor), or an unexpected, dissonant resolution (tonic of a distant tonality). Each chord of the cadence was presented for one second followed by one second silence, during which subjects had to imagine the best resolution. The resolution chord was then presented for two seconds and subjects were asked to decide whether it provided the best possible resolution or not. In one condition this decision was associated with a motor response while in the other condition it was not.

ERP results showed that large N1-P2 components were elicited by each chord of the cadence at fronto-central sites and were followed by negativities that developed between chords. This negativity did not, however, increase in amplitude over the course of the cadence, as found by Cohen & Eretz (1991), but rather was larger between the first and second chord than between the second and third (see Fig. 11.5). The fact that the presentation of the resolution was always delayed by one second, while subjects had to imagine the best possible resolution may account for the discrepancy between the two studies. A negative-positive biphasic complex (an "emitted potential") was then generated in the one second interval during which subjects were asked to imagine the best plausible resolution. As pointed out by Janata, while these ERP effects can be linked with sound imagery, they may also reflect the temporal disruptions in the chord sequence. This second interpretation would fit with our results obtained when terminal notes of musical phrases were delayed by 600ms (see below). An emitted potential, similar to the one found by Janata (1995), was observed at the time when the terminal note should have been presented. However, our subjects had not been instructed to imagine the best possible completion of the musical phrase.

Reaction times and accuracy results showed that the ambiguous resolution was categorised more slowly and less accurately than either the expected or unexpected completions. Furthermore, ERPs to the resolution chord showed that P300 amplitude was largest to the dissonant, intermediate to the minor and smallest to the tonic resolution. P300 latencies were somewhat longer (35ms) to the minor chord than either of the other conditions. These results were independent of whether or not subjects had to give a motor response. Janata distinguishes between the P300 component mentioned above (to which he refers to as P3b) and an earlier positivity (P3a). In contrast to P3b, P3a amplitude was larger in the response than no-response condition, and largest to the dissonant, intermediate to the tonic and smallest to the minor. No clear effect was found with the latency data. Thus, somewhat different effects were found for the P3a and P3b components. Of most interest, however, is that for both components, the incongruous/dissonant resolution elicited the largest positivities. Stimulus probability can not account for this result since the three types of resolution were equiprobable. These results thus provide evidence that some components of the ERPs (P3a and P3b) are sensitive to harmonic expectancy as determined by tonal

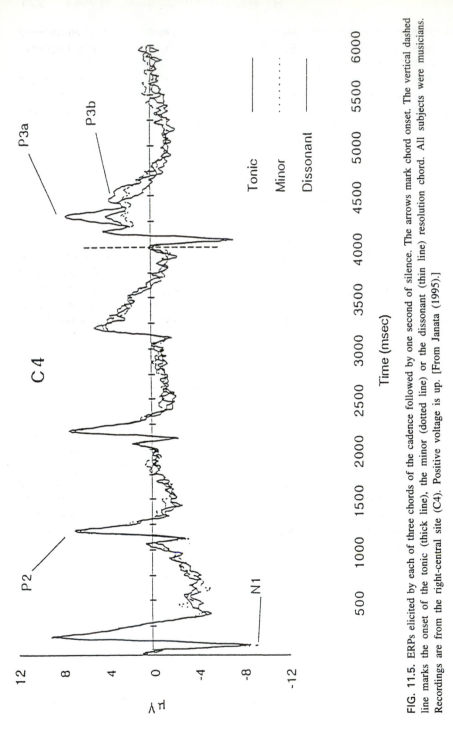

FIG. 11.5. ERPs elicited by each of three chords of the cadence followed by one second of silence. The arrows mark chord onset. The vertical dashed line marks the onset of the tonic (thick line), the minor (dotted line) or the dissonant (thin line) resolution chord. All subjects were musicians. Recordings are from the right-central site (C4). Positive voltage is up. [From Janata (1995).]

hierarchy. It is important to note that similar results have recently been reported by Beisteiner, Menze, Erdler, Huter, & Deecke, (1994) using magneto-encephalographic recordings.

Levett & Martin (1992) also used chord sequences and compared the performance of musicians and non-musicians. The sequences were more musical, including phrases from Bach's harmonised chorals. Each phrase was composed of eight chords and was musically correct in 60% of the trials. In the remaining 40% of the trials, either a mordent (trill) or an harmonic error (semitone pitch alteration) was added within one chord of the sequence. Both the mordent and harmonic error were equiprobable and occurred randomly within the 3rd, 4th, 5th, or 6th chord of the sequence. Subjects had to press a key as soon as they detected a "note that sounded wrong or out of place".

Different patterns of results were obtained for the early and late positive components. The amplitude of the early positivity (P300E) was largest to chords including mordents, intermediate to harmonically wrong chords and smallest to correct chords (see Fig. 11.6). Furthermore, the latency of the P300E was longer to chords including mordents than to the other chords. Neither the amplitude or the latency of the P300E differed between musicians and non-musicians. On the other hand, the late positive component (P300L) elicited by the harmonically incongruent chord was larger for musicians than non-musicians. No difference in P300L amplitude or latency was found between the two groups for chords including mordents.

The interpretation of these data is not straightforward, however. First, the mordent and harmonic error are physically/perceptually different. While only one note of the chord is altered (semitone change) to produce an harmonic error, several notes are added to the chord to create the mordent. Thus, these differences may account for the effects found. Second, while a response was required to both the mordent and the harmonic error trials, no response was required on correct trials. Thus, the three types of chords can not be directly compared. Finally, while the alteration (harmonic or mordent) could occur at different positions within the chord sequence, this factor was not taken into account in the analyses. It is likely that an expectancy developed as the musical phrase unfolded, and that this factor might alter the ERP results.

Effects of Expertise and Familiarity of the Musical Phrases

In a series of experiments, we directly manipulated two factors known to influence musical expectancy, musical expertise and familiarity of the musical phrases (Besson, Faïta & Requin, 1994; Besson & Faïta, 1995). Musicians and non-musicians were asked to listen to familiar, well-known pieces of classical music, and to unfamiliar musical phrases, composed for the experiment. Familiar and unfamiliar musical phrases were equiprobable and ended with either the

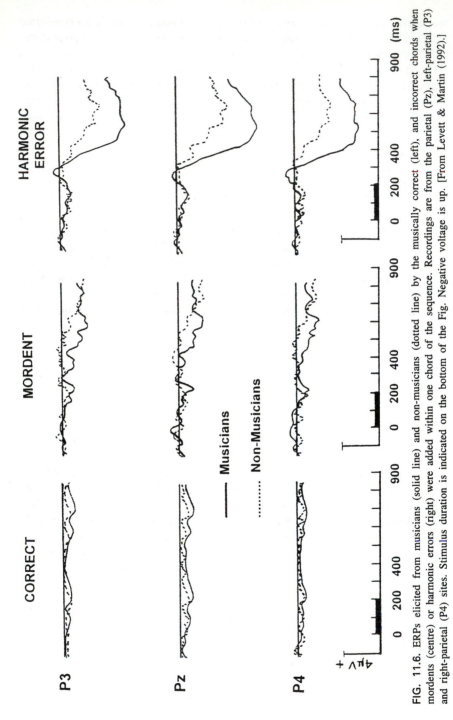

FIG. 11.6. ERPs elicited from musicians (solid line) and non-musicians (dotted line) by the musically correct (left), and incorrect chords when mordents (centre) or harmonic errors (right) were added within one chord of the sequence. Recordings are from the parietal (Pz), left-parietal (P3) and right-parietal (P4) sites. Stimulus duration is indicated on the bottom of the Fig. Negative voltage is up. [From Levett & Martin (1992).]

230

correct, expected final note, or with an unexpected note. For the latter condition, the deviation could be nondiatonic, diatonic or include a rhythmic change in the temporal structure. The nondiatonic change, with the last note out of key, violated the rules of tonal structure. The diatonic change, with the note in key, respected tonal structure, but did not provide a sense of closure. For the rhythmic change, a 600ms delay was inserted before the last note, thus creating a violation of the rules of temporal structure. Subjects were asked to determine whether each melody was familiar or unfamiliar and to categorise the ending (congruous, nondiatonic, diatonic or rhythmic). Percentage of correct responses was analysed in Experiment 1 and ERPs were recorded in Experiments 2 and 3.

Results in Experiment 1 showed that familiar melodies were better recognised by musicians than by non-musicians. Furthermore, when identification of the incongruity was independent of specific musical knowledge (rhythmic incongruity) or could be based on an episodic memory trace (nondiatonic incongruity, familiar fragments), non-musicians performed as well as musicians. On the other hand, when knowledge of musical rules was necessary to perform the task (nondiatonic incongruity, unfamiliar fragments; diatonic incongruity), musicians out performed non-musicians (see Fig. 11.7).

Since familiarity judgements were obtained for each musical phrase in Experiment 2, ERPs were averaged as a function of whether or not familiar melodies were correctly recognised, and unfamiliar melodies correctly identified (Besson & Faïta, 1995). Analyses were conducted on the ERP data associated with correct recognition and identification only. Results of Experiment 2 showed that LPCs were elicited in response to musical incongruities that were sensitive to the different manipulations. Specifically, the LPCs were larger and had a shorter onset latency for musicians than non-musicians, for familiar than unfamiliar phrases, and for nondiatonic than diatonic incongruities (Fig. 11.8). For the rhythmic incongruities, emitted potentials were elicited when the terminal note should have been presented. The amplitude of the emitted potentials was not different for musicians and non-musicians but was larger for familiar than unfamiliar melodies (see Fig. 11.9).

Subjects in this experiment were not asked to give a motor response to indicate which category the terminal note belonged to. They were, however, asked to mentally categorise the terminal notes. Consequently, decision-related processes that are known to influence the amplitude of late positive components, such as the P300 or LPC (see Donchin & Coles, 1988 for a review), may have influenced the effects found in Experiment 2. In order to reduce the potential influence of decision-related processes, this categorisation requirement was eliminated in Experiment 3. Subjects were simply asked to listen to the musical phrases in order to answer some general questions. ERPs were thus recorded in close-to-natural listening conditions.

The results of this experiment largely replicated those found in the previous one: the LPC was larger and had a shorter latency for familiar than unfamiliar

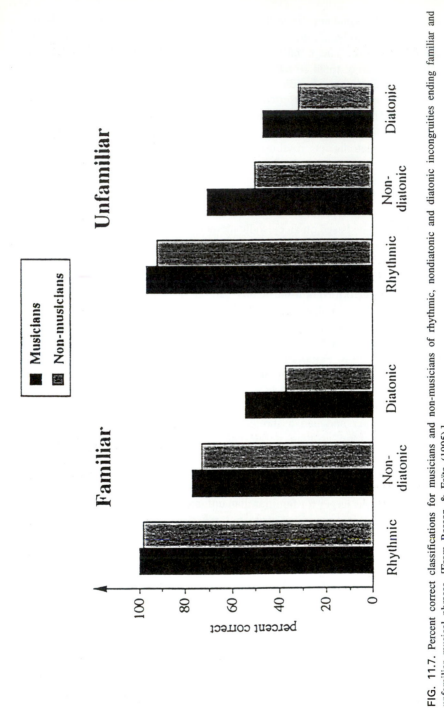

FIG. 11.7. Percent correct classifications for musicians and non-musicians of rhythmic, nondiatonic and diatonic incongruities ending familiar and unfamiliar musical phrases. [From Besson & Faïta (1995).]

232

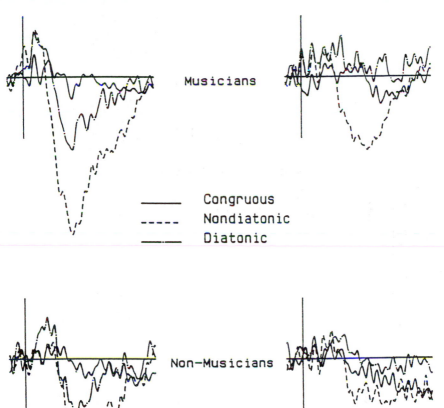

FAMILIAR UNFAMILIAR

Musicians

——— Congruous
- - - - - Nondiatonic
——·—— Diatonic

Non-Musicians

-5 μv

0   400   800   0   400   800   ms

FIG. 11.8. ERPs elicited by congruous notes (solid line), nondiatonic (dashed line), and diatonic (dotted-solid line) incongruities ending familiar (left) and unfamiliar (right) melodies. Results are for musicians (top) and non-musicians (bottom). Recordings are from the parietal (Pz) site. Negative voltage is up. [Modified from Besson & Faïta, 1995.]

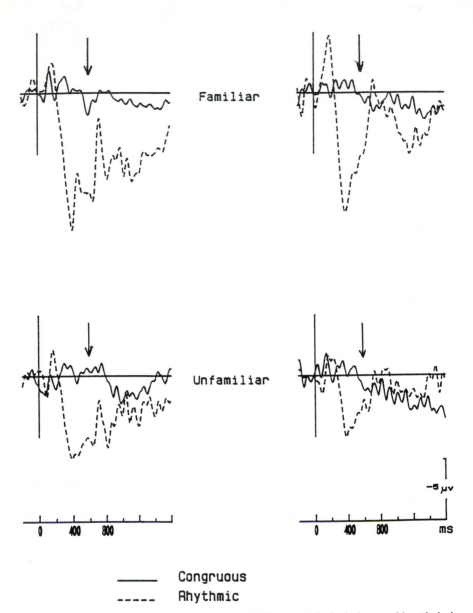

MUSICIANS   NON-MUSICIANS

Familiar

Unfamiliar

$-5 \mu v$

0   400   800   0   400   800   ms

———— Congruous
- - - - - Rhythmic

FIG. 11.9. ERPs elicited by congruous notes (solid line) and rhythmic incongruities (dashed line), ending familiar (top) and unfamiliar (bottom) melodies. Results for the musicians are on the left and for non-musicians on the right. The vertical lines mark the onset of the terminal congruous notes; the arrows mark the onset of the delayed terminal notes. Recordings are from the parietal (Pz) site. Negative voltage is up. [Modified from Besson & Faïta, 1995.]

melodies and for nondiatonic than for diatonic incongruities. Therefore, these effects cannot be interpreted as solely reflecting the decision-related aspects of processing. There was one main difference between the two experiments. Whereas the effect of terminal note interacted with the effects of expertise in Experiment 2, this interaction was not significant in Experiment 3. Since the LPCs differences between musicians and non-musicians were only found when a decision was required from the subjects, it seems that expertise influences the decisional aspects rather than the purely perceptual aspects of music processing.

In conclusion, results of Experiment 3 are important in showing different patterns of ERP effects for familiar and unfamiliar melodies and for nondiatonic, diatonic and congruous terminal notes when subjects are passively exposed to musical excerpts and have no explicit demands made of them. Note that Vanoorbeek and Timsit-Bertier (1994) have also reported ERPs differences when subjects listen to familiar (preferred) and unfamiliar musical pieces. ERPs can thus provide an useful tool to study the perceptual aspects of music processing, while reducing the influence of post-perceptual decision-related processes.

Repetition

In order to further explore the effects of musical expectancy on the amplitude and latency of the LPC, repetition was manipulated in a second series of experiments (Faïta & Besson, 1994, in preparation). Repetition effects in music are important for at least three reasons. First, music theorists have argued that repetition is the basic building block of musical representations; the main motive or musical theme is often repeated within the musical piece. Furthermore Lerdhal & Jackendoff (1983; Jackendoff & Lerdhal, 1982) have proposed that "prolongational reduction", that is the successive movements of tension and relaxation, is a strong component of music perception, and repetition of a musical event is considered a strong prolongation. The classical musical form of sonata, for instance, perfectly illustrates the compositional use of repetition and transformation of thematic materials (Sloboda, 1985).

Second, musical preference seems to increase with familiarity (Meyer, 1956; 1967a and b; Narmour, 1989; 1991: Pollard-Gott, 1983). Following Narmour (1991), musical emotions emerge from the opposition between two expectations systems, a bottom-up system based on innate, parametrical implications, and a top-down system, based on learned, stylistic implications (Bigand, 1991; 1994). The surprise effects in music would emerge from the conflict between expectations based on bottom-up and top-down systems. While such conflicts may become expected and anticipated with repeated exposures, they do not disappear with repetition.

Finally, repetition effects in music can be used to further track the functional significance of the LPC. If the LPC reflects aspects of musical expectancy, its amplitude and latency should be modulated by repetition, when an unexpected event, such as a nondiatonic change ending a musical phrase, becomes expected due to repetition. Specifically, if the LPC is a sensitive marker of musical expectancy, its amplitude should decrease with repetition.

In order to test this hypothesis, we conducted two sessions with the same musicians. Familiar musical phrases were presented in the first session and unfamiliar musical phrases in the second session[6]. In both sessions, half of the melodies ended with the expected congruous note and the other half with a nondiatonic change. Melodies were presented in short blocks of 12 melodies and each block was repeated 4 times. Subjects were only asked to listen to the musical phrases in order to answer general questions afterwards.

The pattern of results differed for the familiar and unfamiliar melodies. For familiar melodies, the amplitude of the LPC to nondiatonic changes progressively decreased with repetition (see Fig. 11.10). Thus, these results support the interpretation that the LPC is a good index of musical expectancy: its amplitude decreases when the terminal incongruous notes become expected with repetition. In this respect, the LPC is functionally similar to the N400 component elicited by unexpected words, which amplitude decreases with repetition (Besson et al, 1992: Van Petten et al, 1991). For unfamiliar melodies, this attenuation was not observed in the LPC amplitude, but the latency of the LPC was shortened after 4 repetitions. The fact that no effect was found on LPC amplitude may result from the summation of two opposite effects. An effect similar to that found with familiar melodies may be taking place for unfamiliar melodies, with a decrease in the LPC when the terminal incongruous notes became expected. However, we also know from the results of our earlier experiments that nondiatonic changes elicit larger LPCs when presented at the end of familiar than unfamiliar melodies. Thus, it may be that unfamiliar melodies become familiar with the repeated presentations and that the amplitude of the LPC consequently increases with repetition. The LPC decrease with musical expectancy and the LPC increase with familiarity may both be operative, resulting in no net change. Finally, the decrease in LPC latency with the repetition of unfamiliar musical phrases may reflect changes in the time course of the mental operations associated with music processing. Incongruous notes may be detected more rapidly when the melodies become more familiar with repetitions.

DISCUSSION OF ERPS STUDIES

An overview of the experiments in which ERPs have been used to study music processing reveals that musically incongruous or unexpected events are generally associated with an increase in the amplitude of late positive components. This increased positivity is found for tones that differ in timbre (Crummer et al, 1988) and pitch (Cohen & Eretz, 1991), for notes that are unexpected within the tonality or within the melodic contour (Besson & Faïta,

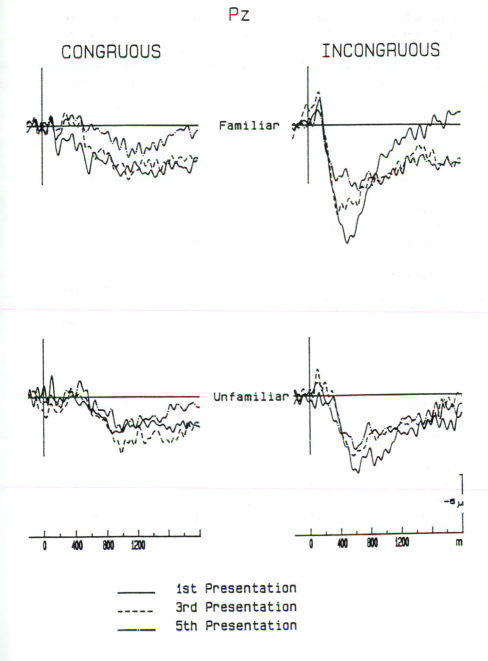

FIG. 11.10. ERPs elicited by the first, third and fifth presentations of congruous and incongruous notes ending familiar (top), and unfamiliar (bottom) melodies. Recordings are from the parietal (Pz) site. Negative voltage is up. [Modified from Faïta & Besson, 1994]

1995; Besson, Faïta & Requin, 1994; Besson & Macar, 1987; Faïta & Besson 1994) and for chords that are dissonant within the musical context or progression (Janata, 1995; Levett & Martin, 1992). Furthermore, results of several experiments have shown that the amplitude of the late positive components is larger for musicians than for non-musicians (Besson & Faïta, 1995; Besson, Faïta & Requin, 1994; Crummer et al, 1988; Levett & Martin, 1992). Finally, the amplitude of the LPCs has also been shown to be larger for violations within familiar than unfamiliar musical phrases (Besson & Faïta, 1995; Besson, Faïta & Requin, 1994). The interpretation of these robust findings is not obvious, however. Several questions can be asked. To what extent are the positive components observed in response to musical violations specific to music processing? Are these components similar across music experiments? Are there other ERPs components that are sensitive to music processing? While additional experiments are obviously needed to answer these questions, some answers are already provided by examining the extant literature.

While it would be exciting to consider that the late positive components described above are specific to the processing of unexpected musical events, other interpretations must be considered. First, let us consider the effects of stimulus probability. In several experiments (Besson & Macar, 1987; Crummer et al, 1988; Levett & Martin, 1992), the probability of violations was lower than the probability of the expected musically correct events. As mentioned previously, numerous results have demonstrated that stimulus probability exerts a powerful influence on the amplitude of late positive components, such as the P300, regardless of the actual stimulus used. Decreases in stimulus probability are typically associated with increases in P300 amplitude (Donchin, 1981; Duncan-Johnson & Donchin, 1977; Johnson, 1986; 1988; Kutas, McCarthy & Donchin, 1977; Squires, Wickens, Squires & Donchin, 1976; Verleger, 1988). In other words, finding larger late positivities to infrequent than frequent musical events cannot be taken as evidence that the positivity reflects some aspects of music processing per se. It may also be a consequence of the probability manipulation. In order to avoid such effects of probability, it is necessary to use an equal number of incongruous and congruous musical events. If larger positivities are still found in response to incongruous than congruous events, the difference can no longer be attributed to difference in probability. In fact, this pattern of results has been observed in several experiments (Cohen & Eretz, 1991; Faïta & Besson, 1994; Janata, 1995; Paller et al, 1992; Verleger, 1990). There is one additional complication, however. Even if the objective probabilities of occurrence of incongruous and congruous stimuli are the same, the subjective probability may be different because of prior knowledge of musical rules or of specific musical pieces. Listeners are usually expecting congruous rather than incongruous events and Squires et al (1976) have demonstrated that the subjective probability of an event also influences P300 amplitude. Thus, the differences found in the studies mentioned above may reflect the effect of subjective rather than objective probability. Note, however, that differences in subjective probability are precisely the building blocks of learning and expectancy processes, and thus the object of study. Therefore, the fact that violations always have a lower subjective probability than congruous events in an experimental design is not necessarily a problem.

Finally, it is important to keep in mind that probability manipulations are useful in producing an effect, but once the effect has been obtained, it is necessary to dissociate the effect of the probability manipulation from the effect of interest. For instance, let's imagine an experiment designed to test the psychological validity of the concept of tonal hierarchy described by Krumhansl & Shepard (1979), following which some chords are more expected than others within the tonal system. In one condition, the best resolution is presented on 80% of the trials and the most unexpected resolution on 20% of the trials. In another condition, the best resolution is again presented in 80% of the trials, but an ambiguous resolution is presented on 20% of the trials. Both infrequent resolutions will elicit P300 components. However, results showing differences in P300 amplitude or latency between the most unexpected and the ambiguous resolution, would provide an argument in favour of the importance of tonal hierarchy, uncontaminated by objective probability. Subjective probability may differ for the unexpected and ambiguous resolutions but this would be a direct consequence of the hierarchical organisation of the tonal system.

A second problem in trying to determine whether or not the late positive components are specific to music processing stems from data analysis. Consider the finding that the amplitude of the positivity is larger for musicians than non-musicians (Besson, Faïta & Requin, 1994; Besson & Faïta, 1995; Crummer et al, 1988; Levett & Martin, 1992). While this difference may reflect the effect of musical expertise, none of the experiments conducted so far support this interpretation unambiguously. In the Crummer et al's (1988)'s experiment, for example, behavioural analyses indicated that musicians are better than non-musicians in discriminating the timbre of a B-flat from an E-flat trumpet. In this condition, P300 was larger for musicians than non-musicians. Because the results are based on the analysis of averaged ERPs, a methodological bias may account for this finding. Assume that both musicians and non-musicians elicit P300s of similar amplitude when the infrequent B-flat trumpet timbre is detected, but no P300 when it is not detected. Since behavioural results showed that musicians detected the difficult target more often than non-musicians, a larger number of trials in which detection occurred (and therefore a positive component was generated) would have contributed to the averaged ERPs for the musicians than for the non-musicians. This could explain the larger amplitude of the P300 for musicians. One way to avoid this possible biais is to include ERPs to correct responses only. If the increase in positivity reflects musical expertise, the positivity should still be larger for musicians than non-musicians. Note that this potential confound arises whenever all trials are averaged and there are different levels of performance.

Finally, a third problem in assessing the specificity of the late positivities to music processing is to determine the extent to which LPC differences reflect perceptual or less specific decision-related processes. As mentioned previously, several experiments have shown that late positive components such as the P300 are elicited in any task requiring a decision (Donchin, 1981; Hillyard et al, 1971; Johnson, 1986, 1988; Squires, Squires & Hillyard, 1975; Sutton, Ruchkin, Munson, Kietzman & Hammer, 1982). Furthermore, its amplitude and latency are modulated by the difficulty of the decision. Thus, it may be that some of the results described above, showing smaller P300s to ambiguous than dissonant chord resolutions (Janata, 1995), to the mordent than to the harmonic error (Levett & Martin, 1992), to the infrequent B-flat trumpet than to the infrequent violin (Crummer et al, 1988) or to the nondiatonic than diatonic change (Besson & Faïta, 1995), reflect general differences in decision difficulty rather than specific differences linked to the manipulations of interest. One solution to this problem would be to take advantage of one of the most appealing characteristics of the ERP methodology; namely, that ERPs can be recorded without any motor task such as when subjects are asked simply to listen to musical sequences. If differences still persist under these conditions, it would be difficult to associate them with decision-related processes. Interestingly, the results of Besson & Faïta (1995, Experiment 3) demonstrated that the effect of musical expertise on LPC amplitude reflected decisional aspects of processing. In contrast, the effects of type of terminal note and familiarity on LPC amplitude were still present when no decision was required from the participants and thus did not reflect decision-related processes.

To summarise, results of the various experiments reviewed in this chapter have consistently shown that the latency and the centro-parietal distribution on the scalp of the late positivities were similar across experiments. Therefore, we can conclude that the late positivities are sensitive indicators of musical expectancy: they are modulated, in amplitude and latency, by the extent to which expectations are disconfirmed. In this respect, they are not functionally different from the N400 component described in ERPs and language experiments.

Another point deserves comment. While most of the experiments described above have focused on the analysis of the late positive components, one may expect that manipulations of the physical characteristics of the sounds, such as timbre or pitch, would also affect the earlier sensory ERPs components, such as the P100, N100 and P200. One advantage of the ERP methodology is that the brain's response to every tone can be recorded within a few milliseconds and for as long as necessary. It is thus possible to observe the manner in which a tone is processed on-line and to gain information about early sensory and perceptual processes as well as later cognitive processes. One may thus assess the many operations that lead from the perception to the representation of real musical pieces.

Using reaction times measures, Bharucha and Stoeckig (1986, 1987) have shown that target chords, harmonically related to a prime chord, are identified more quickly than unrelated chords. Furthermore, they demonstrated that this priming effect was equally strong when the chords did not overlap in their frequency-spectra, thus pointing to a cognitive rather than to a purely sensory priming effect. It would be very interesting to use such a paradigm in an ERP study and precisely determine the time course of the priming effects. More generally, several designs that have been successfully used in cognitive psychology and psycholinguistic research, such as priming, categorisation, recognition, cued-recall and free-recall can now be transposed to study the perceptual as well as the memory aspects of music processing (see also, Clarke, 1989; Hantz & Crummer, 1988; McAdams, 1987; 1989; Peretz & Morais, 1989; Schmuckler, 1989).

EEG AND MUSIC PROCESSING

Petsche and collaborators have conducted a number of experiments aimed at determining whether or not specific parameters used to quantify the EEG are correlated with music processing (Janata & Petsche, 1993; Petsche, Lindner, Rappelsberger and Gruber, 1988; Petsche et al, 1993). In their first experiment (Petsche et al, 1988), EEG at rest was compared with EEG recorded while musicians and non-musicians subjects listened to the beginning of the first movement of Mozart's string quartet KV 458. EEG was recorded for several 1 minute periods. For each frequency band (theta, 4-7.5Hz, alpha, 8-12.5Hz, beta 1, 13-18Hz, beta 2, 18.5-24Hz, and beta 3, 24.5-31.5Hz), two EEG parameters were analysed: power and coherence. Power represents the intensity of the EEG at a given frequency. Coherence is an estimate of the degree of similarity (computed through cross-correlations) between oscillations recorded at two scalp locations at a given frequency. The results showed differences in EEG power and coherence between the rest and listening conditions, as well as between musicians and non-musicians and between male and female listeners. A decrease in EEG power in the alpha frequency band was found in the listening relative to the rest condition. This decrease was more pronounced and extended over the scalp for musicians than for non-musicians. While decreases in EEG power were restricted to the alpha band for female musicians, small decreases in Theta, Beta 1 and Beta 2 power were found for both male musicians and non-musicians. Insofar as EEG power is generally reduced with increased attention, the finding of alpha blocking was interpreted as reflecting the fact that musically trained subjects payed more attention to the musical piece. Increase in interhemispheric coherence between the temporal posterior and parietal regions was also found in the beta 2 frequency band during the listening condition, but this was only true for female musicians. As the authors point out results of coherence analysis are difficult to interpret. Higher coherence may reflect higher functional connection between two brain regions. It remains unclear, however, why such changes in coherence are only found for female musicians and between the temporo-parietal regions of the brain. Furthermore, changes in inter-hemispheric coherence were also found as a function of musical training and sex in the rest condition. This makes it difficult to determine the extent to which these changes are specific to music processing or to musical training.

In a second experiment, Petsche et al. (1993), improved their measures of coherence by analysing all possible correlations between the 19 different electrodes and extended the method to single case studies. Their aim was to further study lateralisation of music processing and to explore whether the effects were dependent on musical style. Results showed no clear-cut lateralisation effects. While listening to Mozart's string quartet KV 458, coherence increased at the temporal electrodes on both hemispheres relative to the rest condition, but such increases differed across frequency bands and were most frequent in the beta 2 and beta 3 bands. Furthermore, differences also emerged as a function of the style of the musical excerpts (Bach, Beethoven, jazz or Schönberg). While changes in coherence were found in the right temporal region in the alpha frequency band independent of musical style, changes linked to style occurred primarily in the beta 2 and beta 3 frequency bands.

Taken together these studies open interesting perspectives in the study of music processing. Analyses of the coherence patterns between the two hemispheres may reveal how information is transmitted between brain regions and in which frequency bands such transmission is likely to occur. However, data interpretation is complicated by the fact that the measures themselves, EEG power and coherence, can not yet be interpreted unequivocally. Nevertheless, this approach could be used to test models of music perception. Consider Narmour's (1991) model of musical expectancy. The basic concept of implication/realisation could be tested empirically. If alpha blocking reflects an increase in attention, it should occur more often when the musical structure implies tension/implications. Conversely increases in the alpha band should be found when the musical structure implies relaxation/realisation.

Finally, a study by Janata & Petsche (1993) is important in that it provides the first attempt to correlate ERPs and EEG analysis. EEG and ERPs were recorded in the same experiment. As mentioned above, incomplete harmonic cadence of three chords were ended with the tonic, the minor or a dissonant resolution. The EEG analysis was conducted to determine whether violations of harmonic expectancies would be associated with changes in EEG power and coherence and to localise such effects.

The results showed that in the delta frequency band, amplitude and coherence were lowest for the tonic, intermediate for the the minor and largest for the dissonant resolutions. These changes were larger over the right temporal location. Thus, specific EEG parameters seem sensitive to the degree of context violation. Furthermore, it is interesting to note that the relationship found in the delta frequency band is similar to the relationship found for the P300b component with the largest amplitude for the dissonant and the smallest amplitude to the tonic. These results are encouraging in that they demonstrate how different measures can be combined to provide important information about the cognitive dynamics of music perception as well as the functional coupling of local and distant cortical areas.

CONCLUSION

Through the studies described above, I hope to have shown that music processing is now amenable to electrophysiological scrutiny. Research is at an exciting stage with some important clues emerging about what the brain is doing when we listen to music. Changes in brain electrical activity can be observed when subjects are listening to musical pieces in close to normal listening conditions. Thus, the marriage of cognitive and electrophysiological approaches to music processing has been consumated and is giving birth to new approaches and ideas.

It should be noted that I did not review results of experiments that have investigated the lateralisation of music processing. While it has been argued that music is preferentially processed by the right hemisphere, the evidence gained from ERP studies is mixed and no clear picture has emerged from this literature (see also Walton et al, 1988). However, sophisticated approaches are now being developed to localise the generators of the ERPs components (see Dale & Sereno, 1993; Gevins et al, 1994); in combination with other brain imaging technics such as Positron Emission Tomography, Functional Magnetic Resonance Imaging and Magnetoencephalography (Beisteiner et al, 1994; Fox & Woldorf, 1994; Posner & Raichle, 1994; Posner, Petersen, Fox & Raichle, 1988; Sergent, Zuck, Terriah & MacDonald, 1992; Zatorre, 1994), and important breakthroughs should soon be made.

To conclude, I would like to emphasise again the importance of comparing language and music processing. There are several differences between language and music[7]. For instance, while the essential purpose of language is communication, the functional importance of music is less clear. More specifically, an important characteristic of language is that words are assigned meaning by convention (form to meaning mapping). In contrast, music is not tied down to specific meanings and functions (Jackendoff & Lerdhal, 1982). In other words, while meaning in language is often understood by reference to an extra-linguistic designated space, music seems to be more self-referential (see also Chew, Larkey, Soli, Blount & Jenkins, 1982). The same idea was developed by Meyer (1956): "That is, one musical event (be it a tone, a phrase, or a whole section) has meaning because it points to and makes us expect another musical event" (p.35). Thus, if music represents itself, the "meaning" conveyed by a musical piece may very well be "understood" differently by the various listeners. As shown in this chapter, the study of music allows us to assess the effects of specific experience. This comparison may, in turn, highlight which aspects of music are immediately available to a naive listener, and which aspects require training.

On the other hand, several authors have emphasised the similarities between language and music (Dowling, 1978; Krumhansl 1991; Meyer, 1956; 1967b; Peretz & Morais, 1989, Sloboda, 1985; Tan, Aiello & Bever, 1981; Zatorre, 1984; Zatorre & Halpern, 1979). Both are highly organised, indigenous to humans, and composed of sequential events that extend in time. Tan et al (1981) pointed to the role of harmonic structure in the "understanding" of music: "Harmony provides the structural framework of a musical "language" and, thus, functions as a part of a musical "grammar" (p. 533)". In his book *Music alone: Philosophical reflections on the purely musical experience* Peter Kivy (1990) also argued for a musical syntax, and thus for structural similarities between language and music: "For unlike random noise or even ordered, periodic sound, music is quasi-syntactical; and where we have something like syntax, of course, we have one of the necessary properties of language" (p.8). It is important to note in this respect that psycholinguists have recently started using ERPs to investigate the syntactic structure of language. In several experiments, the effects of different types of syntactic violations have been compared (Hagoort, Brown & Groothusen, 1993; Kutas & Hillyard, 1983; Münte, Heinze & Mangun, 1993; Osterhout & Holcomb, 1992). This research has shown that syntactic violations are generally associated with large late positive components that resemble the LPC/P300 described in response to violations of musical expectancies. We have conducted an experiment in which the effects of syntactic and musical violations are compared within the same subjects (Patel, Gibson, Ratner, Besson & Holcomb, submitted). Similar ERP effects were found in response to harmonic and syntactic violations. These types of studies will provide further insights into the similarities of language and music processing. Finally, I would like to emphasise the striking similarity of the results illustrated in Figs 11.1 and 11.8. Irrespective of polarity (positive for music and negative for language), the same relationship can be seen between the amplitude of the LPC and of the N400 and the degree of expectancy: the amplitude of both components is largest to the highly unexpected endings, intermediate to the less unexpected endings and smallest to the highly expected endings. Further research will demonstrate the extent to which these effects are similar or different.

ACKNOWLEDGEMENTS

Part of the work presented in this chapter was supported by two grants from the Ministère de la Recherche et de la Technologie (90.V.0011 and 92.C.0420) to Mireille Besson, Joël Pynte and Pierre Courrieu. I am grateful to Rich Ivry, Joël Fagot, Marta Kutas and Jean Requin for helpful comments on an earlier draft of this chapter, and to Elisabeth Fonteneau and Jean-Philippe Guillard for assistance with the illustrations. The experiments reported from our own laboratory were conducted in collaboration with Frédérique Faïta.

Correspondence concerning this article should be addressed to Mireille Besson, CNRS-CRNC, 31 Chemin Joseph Aiguier, 13402 Marseille cedex 20.

NOTES

1. For a discussion of the concept of component, see Allison, Wood & McCarthy, 1986; Donchin, Ritter & McCallum, 1978.
2. That is, the probability for a word to be given as completion for a sentence context.
3. The late positive components found by Besson & Macar (1987) and Paller et al (1992) in response to musical violations did probably belong to the P300 family. The question of whether or not late positive components are P300 components will be addressed in the discussion. In this review, I use the terms P300 or LPC depending upon which terms were chosen by the authors.
4. A set of familiar French melodies were used by Besson & Macar (1987). Although the melodies were not presented in their entirety, they were nevertheless chosen so as to provide a sense of closure or completion.
5. This is a problem insofar as P300 amplitude was measured relative to the preceding negative peak. Results can thus reflect differences in the amplitude of the negative component that preceded the P300 as well as differences in P300 amplitude itself.
6. Familiar and unfamiliar musical phrases were a subset of those used in the previous series of experiments.
7. I am thankful to David Kirsh for fruitful discussion on these matters.

REFERENCES

Allison, T., Wood, C.C., & McCarthy, G. (1986). The central nervous system. In M.G.H. Coles, S.W. Porges & E. Donchin, (Eds.), *Psychophysiology: systems, processes, and applications* (pp. 5–25). New York : Guilford.

Beisteiner, R., Menze, A., Erdler, M., Huter, D., & Deecke, L. (1994). Objective testing of harmonic processing capabilities by magnetoencephalography. In I. Deliège, (Ed.), *Proceedings of the 3rd International Conference for Music Perception and Cognition* (pp. 437–438). Liège, Belgium: European Society for the Cognitive Sciences of Music.

Berger, H. (1929). Uber das Elektrenkephalogramm das menchen. *Archiv für Psychiatrie, 87,* 527–570.

Besson, M., & Faïta, F. (1995). An event-related potential (ERP) study of musical expectancy: comparison of musicians with non-musicians. *Journal of Experimental Psychology: Human Perception & Performance, 21,* 1278–1296.

Besson, M., & Macar, F. (1987). An event-related potential analysis of incongruity in music and other non-linguistic contexts. *Psychophysiology, 24,* 14–25.

Besson, M., Faïta, F., & Requin, J. (1994). Brain waves associated with musical incongruities differ for musicians and non-musicians. *Neuroscience Letters, 168,* 101–105.

Besson, M., Kutas, M., & van Petten, C. (1992). An event-related potential (ERP) analysis of semantic congruity and repetition effects in sentences. *Journal of Cognitive Neuroscience, 4,* 132–149.

Bharucha, J.J., & Stoeckig, K. (1986). Reaction time and musical expectancy: priming of chords. *Journal of Experimental Psychology: Human Perception and Performance, 12,* 403–410.

Bharucha, J.J., & Stoeckig, K. (1987). Priming of chords: Spreading activation or overlapping frequency spectra? *Perception & Psychophysics, 41*, 519–524.

Bigand, E. (1991). La perception de schémas de tensions et détentes musicales dans une phrase musicale. *Analyse musicale* (special issue), 144–146.

Bigand, E. (1994). Contributions de la musique aux recherches sur la cognition auditive humaine. In S. McAdams & E. Bigand (Eds.), *Penser les sons. Psychologie cognitive de l'audition* (pp. 249–292). Paris: Presses Universitaires de France.

Chew, S.L., Larkey, L.S., Soli, S.D., Blount, J., & Jenkins, J.J. (1982). The abstraction of musical ideas. *Memory & Cognition, 10*, 413–423.

Clarke, E.F. (1989). Considérations sur le langage et la musique. In S. McAdams & I. Deliège (Eds.), *La musique et les sciences cognitives* (pp. 23–43). Liège, Belgium: Pierre Mardaga.

Cohen, D. & Eretz, A. (1991). Event-Related Potential measurements of cognitive components in response to pitch patterns. *Music Perception, 8*, 405–430.

Cohen, D., Granot, R., Pratt, H., & Barneah, A. (1993). Cognitive meanings of musical elements as disclosed by Event-Related Potential (ERP) and verbal experiments. *Music Perception, 11*, 153–184.

Crummer, G.C., Hantz, E.C., Chuang, S.W., Walton, J.P., & Frisina, R.D. (1988). Neural basis for music cognition : initial experiment findings. *Psychomusicology, 7*, 117–126.

Dale, A.M. & Sereno, M.I. (1993). Improved localization of cortical activity by combining EEG and MEG with MRI cortical surface reconstruction: a linear approach. *Journal of Cognitive Neuroscience, 5*, 162–176.

Donchin, E., (1981). Surprise!. . . Surprise? *Psychophysiology, 18*, 493–513.

Donchin, E. & Coles, M.G.H. (1988). Precommentary. Is the P300 component a manifestation of context updating? *Behavioral and Brain Sciences, 11*, 357–374.

Donchin, E., Ritter, W., & McCallum, W.C. (1978). Cognitive psychophysiology: The endogenous components of the ERP. In E. Callaway, P. Tueting & S.H. Koslow (Eds), *Event-related potentials in man* (pp. 349–412). New York: Academic Press.

Dowling, W.J. (1978). Scale and contour: Two components of a theory of memory for melodies. *Psychological Review, 85*, 341–354.

Duncan-Johnson, C.C., & Donchin, E. (1977). On quantifying surprise: the variation in event-related potentials with subjective probability. *Psychophysiology, 14*, 456–467.

Evers, S., Grotemeyer, K.H. & Suhr, B. (1994). Effect of absolute pitch ability on visual evoked potentials. In I. Deliège (Ed.), *Proceedings of the Third International Conference for Music Perception and Cognition* (pp. 429–430). Liège, Belgium: European Society for the Cognitive Sciences of Music.

Faïta, F. & Besson, M. (1994). Electrophysiological index of musical expectancy: Is there a repetition effect on the event-related potentials associated with musical incongruities? In I. Deliège (Ed.), *Proceedings of the Third International Conference for Music Perception and Cognition* (pp. 433–435). Liège, Belgium: European Society for the Cognitive Sciences of Music.

Fischler, I. & Raney, G., (1991). Language by eye: Behavioral and Psychophysiological Approaches to Reading. In J.R. Jennings & M.G.H. Coles (Eds), *Handbook of cognitive psychophysiology* (pp. 511–574). New York: John Wiley and Sons.

Fox, P.T. & Woldorf, M.G. (1994). Integrating human brain maps. *Current Opinion in Neurobiology, 4*, 151–156.

Friedman, D., Simon, R., Ritter, W. & Rapin, I. (1975). The late positive component (P300) and information processing in sentences. *Electroencephalography and Clinical Neurophysiology, 38*, 255–262.

Frisina, R.D. , Walton, J.P. & Crummer, G.C. (1988). Neural basis for music cognition: Neurophysiological foundations. *Psychomusicology, 7*.

Gastaut, H., Gastaut, Y., Roger, A., Corriol, J & Naquet, R. (1951). Etude éectroencéhalographique du cycle d'excitabilité cortical. *Electroencehalography and Clinical Neurophysiology, 3*, 401–428.

Gevins, A., Cutillo, B., DuRousseau, D., Le, J., Leong, H., Martin, N., Smith, M.E., Bressler, S., Brickett, P., McLaughlin, J., Barbero, N. & Laxer, K. (1994). Imaging the spatiotemporal dynamics of cognition with high-resolution evoked potential methods. *Human Brain Mapping, 1*, 101–116.

Hagoort, P., Brown, C. & Groothusen, J. (1993). The syntactic positive shift (SPS) as an ERP measure of syntactic processing. *Language and Cognitive Processes, 8*, 439–483.

Hantz, E.C., & Crummer, G.C. (1988). Neural basis for music cognition: psychophysical foundations. *Psychomusicology, 7*, 109–115.

Hantz, E.C., Crummer, G.C., Wayman, J.W., Walton, J.P. & Frisina, R.D. (1992). Effects of musical training and absolute pitch on the neural processing of melodic intervals: a P3 event-related potential study. *Music Perception, 10*, 25–42.

Helmholtz, H.L.F. (1954). On the sensations of tone (A.J. Ellis, trans.). New York: Dover. (Re-issue of the last English edition, 1885).

Hillyard, S.A. (1993). Electrical and magnetic brain recordings: contributions to cognitive neuroscience. *Current Opinion in Neurobiology, 3*, 217–224.

Hillyard, S.A., Squires, K.C., Bauer, J.W., & Lindsay, P.H. (1971). Evoked potential correlated of auditory signal detection. *Science, 172*, 1358–1360.

Hillyard, S.A. & Kutas, M. (1983). Electrophysiology of cognitive processing. *Annual Review of Psychology, 34*, 33–61.

Hillyard, S.A. & Picton, T.W. (1987). Electrophysiology of cognition. In *Handbook of Physiology: The nervous system V*, chapter 13, 519–584.

Holcomb, P., & Neville, H. (1990). Auditory and visual semantic priming in lexical decision: a comparison using event-related brain potentials. *Language and Cognitive Processes, 5*, 281–312.

Holcomb, P.J. & Neville, H.J. (1991). Natural speech processing: an analysis using event-related brain potentials. *Psychobiology, 19*, 286–300.

Jackendoff, R., & Lerdahl, F. (1982). A grammatical parallel between music and language. In M. Clynes (Ed.), *Music, mind and brain* (pp. 83–117). New York and London: Plenum Press.

Janata, P. (1995). ERP measures assay the degree of expectancy violation of harmonic contexts in music. *Journal of Cognitive Neuroscience, 7*(2), 153–164.

Janata, P. & Petsche, H. (1993). Spectral analysis of the EEG as a tool for evaluating expectancy violations of musical contexts. *Music Perception, 10*, 281–304.

Johnson, R., Jr. (1986). A triarchic model of P300 amplitude. *Psychophysiology, 23*, 367–384.

Johnson, R., Jr. (1988). The amplitude of the P300 component of the event-related potential: review and synthesis. In P.K. Ackles, J.R. Jennings & M.G.H. Coles (Eds.), *Advances in psychophysiology* (Vol. 3, pp. 69–137). Greenwich, CT: JAI Press.

Katayama, J. & Yagi, A. (1992). Negative brain potentials elicited by an unexpected color patch or word. *Electroencephalography and Clinical Neurophysiology, 83*, 248–253.

Klein, M., Coles, M.G.H. & Donchin, E. (1984). People with absolute pitch process tones without producing a P300. *Science, 223*, 1306–1309.

Kivy, P. (1990). *Music alone. Philosophical reflections on the purely musical experience*. Ithaca and London: Cornell University Press.

Krumhansl, C.L. (1991). Melodic structure: theoretical and empirical descriptions. In Sundberg, Nord, Carlson (Eds.), *Music, language, speech and brain* (pp. 269–283). London: MacMillan.

Krumhansl, C.L., & Shepard, R.N. (1979). Quantification of the hierarchy of tonal functions within a diatonic context. *Journal of Experimental Psychology: Human Perception and Performance, 5*, 579–594.

Kutas, M., & Hillyard, S.A. (1980). Reading senseless sentences: brain potentials reflect semantic incongruity. *Science, 207*, 203–205.

Kutas, M. & Hillyard, S.A. (1983). Event-related brain potentials to grammatical errors and semantic anomalies. *Memory & Cognition, 11*, 539–550.

Kutas, M. & Hillyard, S.A. (1984). Brain potentials during reading reflect word expectancy and semantic association. *Nature, 307*, 161–163.

Kutas, M., Lindamood, T., & Hillyard, S.A. (1984a). Word expectancy and event-related brain potentials during sentence processing. In S. Kornblum and J. Requin (Eds), *Preparatory states and processes* (pp. 217–237). Hillsdale: Lawrence Erlbaum.

Kutas, M., & Van Petten, C., (1988). Event-related brain potential studies of language. In P.K. Ackles, J.R. Jennings & M.G.H. Coles (Eds.), *Advances in Psychophysiology* (Vol. 3, pp. 139–187). Greenwich, Connecticut: J.A.I. Press.

Kutas, M., & Van Petten, C. (1994). Psycholinguistics electrified: Event-Related brain Potential investigations. In M. Gernsbacher, (Ed.), *Handbook of Psycholinguistics* (pp. 83–143). New York: Academic Press.

Kutas, M., McCarthy, G. & Donchin, E. (1977). Augmenting mental chronometry: The P300 as a measure of stimulus evaluation time. *Science, 197*, 792–795.

Lerdahl, F. & Jackendoff, R. (1983). *A generative theory of tonal music.* Cambridge, Mass: MIT Press.

Levett, C., & Martin, F. (1992). The relationship between complex music stimuli and the late components of the event-related potential. *Psychomusicology, 11*, 125–140.

Lowel, S. & Singer, W. (1992). Selection of intrinsic horizontal connections in the visual cortex by correlated neuronal activity. *Science, 255*, 209–212.

McAdams, S. (1987). Music: a science of the mind? In S. McAdams (Ed.), *Music and Psychology: a mutual regard.* London: Gordon & Breach Science Publishers.

McAdams, S. (1989). Les nombreux visages de la cognition humaine dans la recherche et la pratique musicale. In S. McAdams & I. Deliège (Eds.), *La musique et les sciences cognitives* (pp. 11–20). Liège, Belgium: Pierre Mardaga.

McCallum, W.C., Farmer, S.F., & Pocock, P.V. (1984). The effects of physical and semantic incongruities on auditory event-related potentials. *Electroencephalography and Clinical Neurophysiology, 59*, 477–488.

McCarthy, G. & Donchin, E. (1981). A metric for thought: a comparison of P300 latency and reaction time. *Science, 211*, 22–80.

Meyer, L.B. (1956). *Emotion and meaning in music.* Chicago: University of Chicago Press.

Meyer, L.B. (1967a). On rehearing music. In L.B. Meyer (Ed.), *Music, the arts, and ideas.* Chicago: University of Chicago Press.

Meyer, L.B. (1967b). Meaning and music in information theory. In L.B. Meyer (Ed.), *Music, the arts, and ideas.* Chicago: University of Chicago Press.

Münte, T.F., Heinze, H.J. & Mangun, G.R. (1993). Dissociation of brain activity related to syntactic and semantic aspects of language. *Journal of Cognitive Neuroscience, 5*, 335–344.

Narmour, E. (1989). Le "code génétique" de la mélodie: structures cognitives engendrées par le modèle de l'implication-réalisation. In McAdams & I. Deliège (Eds.), *La musique et les sciences cognitives* (pp. 75–101). Liège, Belgium: Pierre Mardaga.

Narmour, E. (1991). The top-down and bottom-up systems of musical implication: building on Meyer's theory of emotional syntax. *Music Perception, 9*, 1–26.

Nigam, A., Hoffman, J.E. & Simons, R.F. (1992). N400 to semantically anomalous pictures and words. *Journal of Cognitive Neuroscience, 4*, 15–22.

Osterhout, L., & Holcomb, P.J. (1992). Event-related brain potentials elicited by syntactic anomaly. *Journal of Memory and Language, 31*,1–22.

Paller, K.A., McCarthy, G. & Wood, C.C. (1992). Event-related potentials elicited by deviant endings to melodies. *Psychophysiology, 29*, 202–206.

Patel, A.D., Gibson, E., Ratner, J., Besson, M. & Holcomb, P.J. (submitted). Overlapping neural response to linguistic and musical syntactic processing.

Peretz, I. & Morais, J. (1989). Music and modularity. *Contemporary Music Review, 4*, 227–191.

Petsche, H., Lindner, K., Rappelsberger, P. & Gruber, G. (1988). The EEG: An adequate method to conretize brain processes elicited by music. *Music Perception*, *6*, 133–160.

Petsche, H., Richter, P., von Stein, A., Etlinger, S.C. & Filz, O. (1993). EEG coherence and musical thinking. *Music Perception*, *11*, 117–151.

Polich, J. (1985). N400 from sentences, semantic categories, number and letter strings? *Bulletin of the Psychonomic Society*, *23*, 361–364.

Polich, J., Vanasse, L. & Donchin, E. (1981). Category expectancy and the N200. *Psychophysiology*, *18*, 142–146.

Pollard-Gott, L. (1983). Emergence of thematic concepts in repeated listening to music. *Cognitive Psychology*, *15*, 66–94.

Posner, M.I. & Raichle, M.E. (1994). *Images of mind*. Scientific American Library, New York.

Posner, M.I., Petersen, S.E., Fox, P.T. & Raichle, M.E. (1988). Localization of cognitive operations in the human brain. *Science*, *240*, 1627–1631.

Pritchard, W. (1981). Psychophysiology of P300. *Psychological Bulletin*, *89*, 506–540.

Schmuckler, M.A. (1989) Expectation in music: investigation of melodic and harmonic processes. *Music perception*, *7*, 109–150.

Sergent, J., Zuck, E., Terriah, S. & MacDonald, B. (1992). Distributed neural network underlying musical sight-reading and keyboard performance. *Science*, *257*, 106–108.

Singer, W. (1993). Synchronisation of cortical activity and its putative role in information processing and learning. *Annual Review of Physiology*, *55*, 349–374.

Sloboda, J.A. (1985). *The musical mind: the cognitive psychology of music*. Oxford: Clarendon Press.

Squires, N.K., Squires, K.C., & Hillyard, S.A. (1975). Two varieties of long-latency positive waves evoked by unpredictable auditory stimuli in man. *Electroencephalography and Clinical Neurophysiology*, *38*, 387–401.

Squires, K.C., Wickens, C., Squires, N.K., & Donchin, E. (1976). The effect of stimulus sequence on the waveform of the cortical event-related potential. *Science*, *193*, 1142–1146.

Sutton, S., Braren, M., Zubin, J. & John, E.R. (1965). Evoked potential correlates of stimulus uncertainty. *Science*, *150*, 1187–1188.

Sutton, S., Braren, M., Zubin, J. & John, E.R. (1967). Information delivery and the sensory evoked potential. *Science*, *155*, 14–36.

Sutton, S., Ruchkin, D.S., Munson, R., Kietzman, M.L., & Hammer, M. (1982). Event-related potentials in a two-interval forced-choice detection task. *Perception and Psychophysics*, *32*, 360–374.

Stuss, D.T., Sarazin, F.F., Leech, E.E. & Picton, T.W. (1983). Event-related potentials during naming and mental rotation. *Electroencephalography and Clinical Neurophysiology*, *56*, 133–146.

Tan, N., Aiello, R. & Bever, T.G. (1981). Harmonic structure as a determinant of melodic organization. *Memory & Cognition*, *9*, 533–539.

Taylor, W.L., (1953). "Cloze" procedure: a new tool for measuring readability. *Journalism Quarterly*, *30*, 415–420.

Van Petten, C., Kutas, M., Kluender, R., Mitchiner, M. & McIsaac, H. (1991). Fractionating the word repetition effect with event-related potentials. *Journal of Cognitive Neuroscience*, *3*, 131–150.

Vanoorbeek, R. & Timsit-Bertier, M. (1994). Approche psychophysiologique de l'écoute musicale à l'aide des potentiels évoqués endogènes. In I. Deliège (Ed.), *Proceedings of the Third International Conference for Music Perception and Cognition* (pp. 431–432). Liège, Belgium: European Society for the Cognitive Sciences of Music.

Verleger, R. (1988). Event-related potentials and cognition : a critique of the context updating hypothesis and an alternative inerpretation of P3. *Behavioral and Brain Sciences*, *11*, 343–427.

Verleger, R. (1990). P3-evoking wrong notes: unexpected, awaited, or arousing? *International Journal of Neuroscience, 55,* 171–179.

Walton, J.P., Frisina, R.D., Swartz, K.P., Hantz, E.C. & Crummer, G.C. (1988). Neural basis for music cognition: future directions and biomedical implications. *Psychomusicology, 7,* 127–138.

Wayman, J.W., Frisina, R.D., Walton, J.P., Hantz, E.C. & Crummer, G.C. (1992). Effects of musical training and absolute pitch ability on event-related activity in response to sine tones. *Journal of the Acoustical Society of America, 91,* 3527–3551.

Zatorre, R.J. (1984). Musical perception and cerebral function: a critical review. *Music Perception, 2,* 196–221.

Zatorre, R.J. (1994). Musical processing in the nonmusician's brain: Evidence for specialized neural networks. In I. Deliège (Ed.), *Proceedings of the 3rd International Conference for Music Perception and Cognition* (pp. 39–40). Liège, Belgium: European Society for the Cognitive Sciences of Music.

Zatorre, R.J., & Halpern, A.R. (1979). Identification, discrimination, and selective adaptation of simultaneous musical intervals. *Perception and Psychophysics, 26,* 384–395.

IV Acoustical and Computational Approaches

12 Methodological issues in timbre research

John M. Hajda, Roger A. Kendall, Edward C. Carterette and
Michael L. Harshberger
Department of Ethnomusicology & Systematic Musicology
University of California, Los Angeles

INTRODUCTION

> *"We should here recognize that timbre as a fourth attribute*
> *of tone is by far the most important aspect of tone and*
> *introduces the largest number of problems and variables"*
> *(Seashore, 1938/1967, p. 21).*

Three-score years after Seashore's seminal work, timbre continues to be a poorly understood attribute of music. There are several reasons for this state of affairs: (1) In comparison to the other perceptual attributes—especially pitch and loudness—timbre has received little attention in the experimental literature; (2) because of its multidimensional nature, it is difficult to manipulate timbre in a controlled scientific fashion; and (3) there is no single widely-accepted operational or constitutive definition of timbre from which researchers can build empirical methods and models.

We believe the third reason will prove to be the most lasting obstacle to a better understanding of timbre. In the last thirty years, technological advances in digital signal processing and nonparametric statistical methods have helped to spur a number of important studies related to timbre. However, many of these studies have paid no explicit attention to first-order methods, namely, assumptions and working definitions of what it is that is being studied. Though nonparametric statistics may aid the researcher in uncovering previously hidden perceptual structures, some have generalised these findings beyond the scope of their original study with neither replication nor corroboration by standard hypothesis testing.

253

The purpose of this chapter, then, is to bring to light some of the most crucial empirical, methodological and statistical issues which—in the spirit of technological advancement and "user-friendly" data analysis—have been often de-emphasised and sometimes flouted by researchers in the field. This will be done through an overview of research literature which has focused on the contribution of musical tone constituents. As a foundation for a critical analysis of earlier and current timbre research, a brief discussion of the nature of timbre follows.

The Perceptual Nature of Timbre

Carterette and Friedman (1974) define perception as "the way in which the organism transforms, organises, and structures information arising from the world in sense data or memory" (p. xiii). Those who study music perception, therefore, study the way(s) in which the mind transforms, organises, and structures information which comes from the physical, physiological or psychological frame of reference. The physical and physiological frames can be considered as external to the mind, while the psychological is internal. The psychological frame consists of both implicit and explicit knowledge structures—called "schemata" by some psychologists (Bartlett, 1932; Neisser, 1976)—that enable humans to make predictions regarding what might (or might not) happen next in a musical sequence. For example, trained Western listeners will, in a major key context, expect the fourth note of the scale, *fa*, to resolve to the third, *mi*. Timbre, like pitch, is an artefact of perception.

In essence, the field of music theory in traditional Western schools of music is a series of models built on explicit structures based on musical notation. The field's ability to explain, however, is limited by its capacity to notate. If we consider perception to be a necessary condition for musical behaviour, then—unless one assumes that all mental transformations, organisations and structures of composers, performers and listeners, are represented by notation—the musical score, which is the basis for traditional music theory, is not sufficient to tell us *everything* about musical processes. This insufficiency is especially evident when it comes to timbre. Pitch, time values and dynamics are represented by at least ordinal scales in traditional notation: C4 is higher (greater) in pitch than C3; a quarter note is longer than an eighth; *f* is louder than *p*. The same cannot be said of timbre or orchestration; a clarinet is not greater or less than a trumpet. Although families of instruments can be represented within their relative positions in an orchestral score, the notation does not show us the *relationships* among these categories. Because the explication of relationships between observations is a necessary condition for any theory, one could say that a model for timbre does not exist in traditional music theory.

Nevertheless, the manipulation of timbre has proved to be an increasingly important facet of musical style in the West. Treatises of orchestration have been disseminated since at least the time of Berlioz (1844/1856) and composers, arrangers and orchestrators have been trained since the mid-19th century to become masters of timbral manipulation. The fact that such manipulation takes place regularly in the real world mandates that, in order to understand music in an ecological sense, we must strive to understand timbre. If timbral structures, such as those posited by Wessel (1979), Lerdahl (1987), Kendall and Carterette (1991), McAdams and Cunibile (1992) and others cannot be uncovered by traditional notational methods, we must turn to another method.

For music psychologists, of course, the method of choice is empiricism. But before any experiments can be designed, we must first ask ourselves the following: What is timbre? How can it be measured? How can we isolate timbre as an experimental variable such that we can control and manipulate it? To answer these questions, we must consider fundamental issues concerning the definition of variables in behavioural research.

Timbre as an Experimental Variable

All behavioural research is guided by certain principles and assumptions regarding the nature of what is being studied. These considerations allow us to build models of expected behaviour and generalise findings, when appropriate, to a properly determined population. An excellent source for the discussion of fundamental issues in behavioural research is Kerlinger (1973). In fact, much of the following discussion in this section is an encapsulation of Kerlinger's (1973) chapter 3 and Hajda (1995, pp. 5–6).

We have stated that, in order to understand timbre using empirical methods, we must be able to define timbre as an experimental variable. To create a variable, we must first have a concept of it, an abstraction formed by generalisation from particulars. Thus, we can conceive of timbre as an attribute—along with pitch, loudness, and duration—of a musical tone. Timbre does not exist orthogonally to these attributes, nor can it exist in their absence. Once this concept has been explicated for a scientific purpose, such as when we hypothesise that timbre is dependent on spectrum, it is known as a construct. This construct becomes a variable when it can be measured by assignment of number or value.

How do we define a variable, then? Kerlinger (1973) identifies two ways: constitutively and operationally. Constitutive definitions are statements which define one variable in terms of its relationships to other variables. As we stated before, these relationships are central to scientific theory. Operational definitions delineate the manners by which a variable is to be measured.

The standard psychophysical definition of timbre is: "Timbre is that attribute of auditory sensation in terms of which a subject can judge that two sounds similarly presented and having the same loudness and pitch are dissimilar" (*American national standard: Psychoacoustical terminology*, 1973, p. 56). Such a definition has several problems. First, the variable is defined by the absence of relationships with other variables; Ward (1970, p. 409) calls it a "wastebasket category." Second, if a listener is presented with two successive sounds in which the musical instrument, pitch, and loudness are different, it follows intuitively that this listener will be able to distinguish between the tone quality of musical instruments as well as the differences in pitch and loudness. In recognising this inconsistency, Pratt and Doak (1976, p. 317) proposed a modified definition of timbre: "That attribute of auditory sensation whereby a listener can judge that two sounds are dissimilar using any criteria other than pitch, loudness or duration." This definition, although it ignores the interactions between pitch, loudness and duration with timbre, is more representative of musical perception.

Finally, most definitions of timbre such as the ones above suggest operations such as (dis)similarity judgement; thus it is no surprise that this method is used widely in modern timbre research. Phenomenological definitions of timbre such as "the perceptual qualities of objects and events; that is, 'what it [sic] sounds like' " (Handel, 1995, p. 426), may communicate to a naive person an experiential description of timbre perception. They are not, however, scientifically useful, since they do not explicate a relationship between variables. To our knowledge, a truly constitutive definition of timbre has yet to be posited.

The historical development of timbre as a psychophysical variable highlights the difficulties that the field has had in identifying which signal attributes should and should not be considered to play a role in timbre perception. To Helmholtz (1877/1954), the "quality of tone" (*Klangfarbe*, A.J. Ellis, English translator preferred this term to "timbre"; see p. 24*ff*) referred only to the steady-state portion of a tone, or "the peculiarities of the musical tone which continues uniformly" (1877/1954, p. 67). Although he recognised the role of transients in differentiation between the characteristic sounds of classes of instruments, it was only the harmonic structure of the "musical part of the tone" (1877/1954, p. 68) which he considered.

Seashore (1938/1967) defined timbre as "that characteristic of a tone which depends upon its harmonic structure as modified by absolute pitch [frequency] and total intensity" (p. 97); timbre corresponded physically to only a single cycle of a periodic signal. The overall quality of tone which resulted from the "fusion of changing timbre, pitch, and intensity [loudness]" (p. 95) was called "sonance." Seashore, therefore, considered timbre to be a representative "snapshot" of the steady-state portion of the musical signal. Although the notion of a static timbre is still evident in some common acoustical measurements (long-time-average spectrum, steady-state centroid, etc.), many researchers in the last twenty years have also considered time-varying aspects of steady-state frequency components as physical attributes which influence timbre.

In the early 1960s, transients—especially the attack—became a prominent variable in timbre-related studies. In fact, all of the above signal attributes are mentioned in a footnote to the American National Standards Institute definition (1973, p. 56): "Timbre depends primarily upon the spectrum of the stimulus, but it also depends upon the waveform, the sound pressure, the frequency location of the spectrum, and the temporal characteristics of the stimulus." The above physical variables, however, are also confounding factors in the perception of pitch, loudness, and duration. To further complicate the issue, in contemporary studies the term "timbre" has also referred to the label (i.e., instrument name) given to a class of musical sounds and the tonal qualities of monophonic and homophonic musical passages.

Further Discussion

Based on just noticeable differences (JND) within the human range of hearing, the average person can detect about 1500 distinct pitches and 325 levels of loudness (Lundin, 1967). But how many different timbres can the average person hear? The answer is unknown, because timbre depends on a number of factors; it is truly a multidimensional variable. In its operational definitions, timbre has been conceived of as categorical—as in the assignment of a verbal label (e.g. flute, guitar)—as continuous—as in the assignment of a value to a number along a verbal adjective scale—or as a categorical/continuous hybrid (e.g. Grey, 1975, pp. 58-69; Martens, 1985; Hajda, 1995; and McAdams, Winsberg, Donnadieu, De Soete & Krimphoff, 1995). Because of its unique and complex features, we cannot expect that timbre is representable mentally by a single set of schemata, as is the case with the major diatonic scale with its series of resting and leading tones. Any structures that might be uncovered will be primarily descriptive, although recent research has suggested that certain timbral features can be predicted (Ehresman & Wessel, 1978; Kendall & Carterette, 1991; McAdams & Cunibile, 1992).

COMMON METHODS FOR MEASURING MUSICAL TIMBRE

Because concepts of timbre continue to broaden and new research questions, methods and technologies are being developed, a plethora of operational definitions are used. This section highlights some of the methods of musical timbre research used in the past 30 years (see also McAdams, 1993, pp. 158-166). In addition, various modes of statistical analysis are discussed.

Identification

Identification is the verbal labelling of a stimulus by class or category. In the case of musical timbre experiments, subjects attempt to name the instrument category which most closely represents the sound that they hear. Listeners can be subjected to (1) a free identification task in which no instrument choices are provided (e.g. Wedin & Goude, 1972), (2) a forced-choice identification with distracters in which all of the instruments aurally represented are listed along with other non-represented instruments (e.g. Saldanha & Corso, 1964), and (3) a forced-choice identification without distracters (e.g. Clark, Robertson & Luce, 1964). Identification was a common procedure in many of the earlier timbre studies (e.g. Clark, Luce, Abrams, Schlossberg & Rome, 1963; Berger, 1964; Saldanha & Corso, 1964). Identification procedures generally produce frequencies of hits and misses per instrument per condition; these frequencies are often presented in the form of a confusion matrix (e.g. Clark et al., 1963). Of this early group, only Saldanha and Corso (1964) conducted inferential analysis of variance (ANOVA).

Categorisation

Categorisation is the grouping of comparison stimuli with the members of a set of standard stimuli (referred to as primes or models). It has advantages over identification because it does not require the verbalisation of relationships between stimuli nor does it require a priori knowledge of verbal labels for specific sound events. It has been utilised effectively by Kendall, Carterette and Hajda (1995) in the comparison of stimuli generated by commercial synthesisers to their natural counterparts. As in identification, categorisation scores are nominal, consisting of hits and misses. They can be presented in the form of a confusion matrix and can be subjected to repeated-measures ANOVA.

Matching

Matching is the subjective pairing of a single comparison stimulus to a single model. Identification, by this definition, is a subset of matching. Both are, in essence, subsets of categorisation, which allows for the pairing of multiple comparisons to each standard. In most timbre studies that utilise matching paradigms, both the comparison and standard stimuli are sonic. Kendall (1986) used a matching paradigm in which subjects were asked to pair "choice" stimuli with "model" stimuli. This procedure allowed nonmusicians, who may not be familiar with conventional labels for classes of instrument sounds, to make nonverbal judgements. The methods of data analysis for matching are the same as those for categorisation.

The method of adjustment is similar to matching in that the subject manipulates the comparison stimuli until it is the same as the model along some attribute. In the case of Lichte (1941), subjects were asked to match the perceived "brightness" of a pure (sine) tone to that of a complex tone by altering the frequency of the pure tone. Kendall, Carterette and Hajda (in preparation) used an adjustment procedure in which subjects adjusted the loudness of tones in a stimulus set until they were equal to that of a model. A related method of equalisation was used by Grey (1975, p. 41*ff*) for pitch, loudness and duration.

Verbal Attributes

A verbal attribute rating is the forced projection of an adjectival (or adverbial) schema onto a specified set of sounds. One of the earliest set of studies of this nature was conducted by Lichte (1941), who asked subjects to judge the second stimulus in a paired comparison of spectrally-altered synthetic tones as "brighter" or "duller" than the first. After scaling, the subjects' ratings were plotted against the independent physical variable, although a Pearson correlation would have been an appropriate quantitative measure of the relationship between perceptual and physical attributes.

A common verbal rating technique in more recent studies is to utilise a scale at the extremes of which an adjective and its purported opposite, e.g. *bright–dull* are placed. This technique is known as the semantic differential (Osgood, Suci & Tannenbaum, 1957) and has been utilised by, among others, von Bismarck (1974), Pratt and Doak (1976), and Kendall and Carterette (1993a). In delimiting the number and type of adjective scales, each of these studies first asked subjects to rate the suitability of a large set of adjectives in describing timbre in general (von Bismarck, 1974) or the timbre of a specified set of stimuli (Pratt & Doak, 1976; Kendall & Carterette, 1993a). The subject then listens to a tone and rates it along each of the remaining bi-polar adjective scales.

Kendall and Carterette (1993a) discovered that the use of a subset of von Bismarck's (1974) adjective pairs did not differentiate among their natural stimuli (von Bismarck's tones were synthetic with static steady states). They modified the semantic differential method so that subjects rated the amount of a single verbal attribute; this method, verbal attribute magnitude estimation (VAME), used an adjective and its negation as the extremes of the scale. This improved somewhat the interpretability of the subject data. The VAME procedure has also been utilised by Harshberger (1992), Harshberger, Kendall and Carterette (1994) and Lakatos and McAdams (1995).

Several data analysis options are available for verbal attribute data, including factor analysis and principal components analysis (PCA). In general, ANOVA can be used to compare means of groups of subjects, individual subjects if repeated measures are used, or between instruments. Crossed-correlation matrices can also be generated by correlating the subject ratings across stimuli, thus yielding a quantified relationship between each of the verbal attributes (Harshberger, 1992; Harshberger, Kendall & Carterette, 1994; Kendall & Carterette, 1993b). The elements of these matrices (correlations) can be treated as proximity measurements and subjected to either multidimensional scaling (MDS) or hierarchical clustering in order to determine a structural representation for the correlated items (Harshberger, 1992; Harshberger, Kendall & Carterette, 1994; Kendall & Carterette, 1993b).

Proximity Rating

Proximity rating is a measure of similarity or dissimilarity between all pairs of a set of objects. It has been a method of choice for a considerable number of timbre studies in the past 25 years (e.g. Grey, 1975, 1977, etc.; Iverson & Krumhansl, 1993; Kendall & Carterette, 1991; Kendall, Carterette & Hajda, 1995; Krumhansl, 1989; McAdams et al., 1995; Miller & Carterette, 1975; Plomp, 1970, 1976; Wedin & Goude, 1972; Wessel, 1973). The proximity data can be stored as a triangular matrix and analysed by a multidimensional scaling (MDS) algorithm such as Kruskal (1964). Alternatively, individual proximity matrices can be preserved by an individual differences scaling (INDSCAL) algorithm so that a given subject's weighting along each dimension can be explicated (Carroll & Chang, 1970). We recommend Kruskal and Wish (1978) and Arabie, Carroll and DeSarbo (1987) to anyone wishing to learn more about the basic concepts and techniques of MDS.

There are several techniques by which proximity data suitable for MDS can be generated. The most common in timbre research is *similarity scaling*. All possible pair-wise comparisons are presented from a set of n stimuli to the subject. The subject then rates along a scale the degree d to which the stimuli i and j were similar or dissimilar. If only d_{ij} is tested (assumed to be equal to d_{ji}), the number of presentations is $n(n \pm 1)/2$, depending on whether or not identities are to be tested. A less common nonverbal scaling technique, *triadic comparisons* (employed by Plomp, 1970), requires the comparison of three non-identical stimuli, i, j, and k. For all $n(n-1)(n-2)/6$ triads, the subject must rate which pair of stimuli is the most similar and which is the most dissimilar. The most dissimilar pair is assigned two points, the second most dissimilar pair one point, and the third pair zero points. The proximity scores are tallied across subjects. A given stimulus, therefore, is compared to each other stimulus $n-2$ times. Finally, rectangular data can also be transformed into triangular proximity matrices, as suggested in our discussion of verbal attributes (see above). If, for example, the rows of a matrix represent instruments and the columns represent the magnitude of some perceptual attributes—verbal or nonverbal—for each instrument, correlations can be calculated among all pairs of instruments (see discussion of verbal attributes above).

The techniques mentioned to this point have proven effective for $8 < n < 25$ stimuli. However, even for brief stimuli, large stimulus sets demand a heavy cognitive load on subjects. For example, a similarity scaling of 25 stimuli would require at least 300 rating comparisons. Triadic comparisons of these same 25 would require *2300 sets* of comparisons. An additional method, *sorting* (categorisation without primes or models), has not been utilised in the most widely-reported timbre research, yet is useful for stimulus sets of 50 or even 100 elements (Kruskal & Wish, 1978, p. 10). Subjects are allowed to audition each stimulus as many times as they require before they group the stimuli into mutually exclusive and exhaustive categories. The number of common groupings between every possible pairing of stimuli can be tallied across subjects and treated as proximity data.

Discrimination

Discrimination is the subjective differentiation between stimuli or sets of stimuli. It is a fundamental procedure in psychophysical determinations of JND but has been used sparingly in the examination of musical sounds or their synthetic emulations. Grey (1975) and Grey and Moorer (1977) utilised an AAAB procedure in order to evaluate the discriminability of original recorded signals and signals with various levels of synthetic simplification. Subjects were told that one tone in a set of four (paired into twos) was different from the other three. However, subjects were not asked to discriminate between timbres; instead, they were directed to listen for differences in the "perceived quality of articulation or playing style" (Grey & Moorer, 1977, p. 459). As Grey and Moorer note, "generally, the different forms of a note did not appear to change in terms of instrumental source, but rather exhibited small qualitative alterations that resembled differences that may occur in playing the same note on an instrument with slightly different styles."

Further Discussion

The discussion above confirms that timbre is an extremely complex phenomenon which is partially described by numerous perceptual strategies and schema. Of the methods described thus far, we feel that only discrimination can uncover minute differences in timbre between stimuli. In fact, discrimination-related tasks are the norm in psychophysical studies in which synthetic steady-state spectra are carefully manipulated by the experimenter (e.g., Green, 1988; Kendall, 1980; Seashore, 1919; Singh & Hirsh, 1992). However, it has been our experience that natural stimuli recorded in an ecologically-valid environment (such as an auditorium) can be discriminated based on extraneous factors such as background noise, or, in Grey's (1975, p. 30-37) case, tape hiss. For instance, we have attempted timbre discrimination among organ tones recorded with different microphone pickup patterns. Almost invariably, noise signatures from the recording environment contaminate the process. Therefore, although discrimination-related tasks work well in contrived synthetic conditions, it is unclear how they can be used effectively in musical situations (i.e. time-variant musical signals recorded in a reverberant performance space).

Equalisation of Pitch, Loudness and Duration

It has been proposed that timbre is that attribute of a musical tone which is not pitch, loudness, or duration (e.g. Pratt & Doak, 1976). In a traditional psychophysical frame of reference, then, it is assumed that stimuli should be equalised for pitch, loudness, and duration. To our knowledge, only Grey (1975) reports the results of a formal perceptual empirical method for the control of each of these variables. However, for natural sustained tones recorded in a reverberant space, the perceptual equalisation of these variables may be extremely difficult if not impossible. This is because real musical signals are complex and time-variant. It is often the case that a single tone has variable pitch and loudness. The duration of a tone may be masked by conditions of the environment such that the cessation of reverberation is unclear. Even in conditions in which performers have played the steadiest tone possible, it has been our experience that for trained musical listeners there will not be great consistency in the equalisation values for these attributes. Final equalisation values are determined, therefore, by group consensus (Kendall & Carterette, 1991; McAdams et al., 1995) rather than a constant value across individuals. This means, of course, that what is "equal" for the group will not be for an individual.

At this time, it is unknown to what extent pitch, duration and loudness confound timbre judgements. Miller and Carterette (1975) found that, for synthetic emulations of horn, string and trapezoidal envelopes, fundamental frequency (200, 400 and 800Hz) had such high saliency that timbral differentiations could not be reliably mapped. However, Robinson and Patterson (1995) found that instrument types (synthesised brass, flute, harpsichord, and strings) could be identified better for extremely short durations (a few cycles) of extracted steady-state signal than could pitch chroma or octave. In addition, Hajda (1995) found that the inclusion of wrong-octave synthetic xylophone and tubular bell signals did not affect timbral relationships among impulse instrument classes when the octaves were corrected. Kendall, Carterette and Hajda (in preparation) did not find a significant correlation between long-time average fundamental frequency of natural orchestral continuant tones and any dimension of a timbral space, even though these tones were noticeably of slightly different pitch (range of about 10Hz). In fact, many studies use natural stimuli which have been informally equalised for pitch during performance and recording (e.g. Berger, 1964; Elliott, 1975; Kendall & Carterette, 1991; Saldanha & Corso, 1964; Wedin & Goude, 1972; Wessel, 1973). Although small deviations in pitch must have been present in these studies, we suspect that these had no confounding on either the identification or similarity scaling tasks.

We are not aware of any systematic studies that investigate the confounding effects or relative salience of loudness in comparison to timbre for musical tones. Part of this is due to the failure thus far to derive an empirical model which can predict a priori from acoustical information the perceptual loudness of *complex time-variant tones* (Moorer, 1975). In many instances (Berger, 1964; Elliott, 1975; Iverson & Krumhansl, 1993; Wedin & Goude, 1972;), researchers have made equalisations of loudness based on a priori methods which were proposed for complex tones *with no time-variance*. However, a host of studies cited by Moorer (1975, p. 10) show that "there is a variation in perceived loudness of a tone with the duration of the tone, to some extent with its rise time, and with what precedes or follows it." At best, the use of current a priori methods only yields an approximation of equal loudness. At worst, the researcher has no way of measuring the confounding effect on the relative timbres of tones with unequal loudness. Based on the facts that (1) the perceptual loudness of complex time-variant tones varies by listener, and (2) we have found extremely high correlations (> 0.9) in timbral similarity judgements between subjects (Kendall, Carterette & Hajda, 1994, 1995), it is possible that minute differences in loudness do not significantly confound with timbre in the case of perceptual scaling. However, until more is known, a perceptual matching procedure with a sufficiently large sample is the most ecologically valid method for equalising loudness.

The salience of duration (perceived length) with respect to timbre for musical tones also has not been formally studied. As with pitch, many researchers attempt to control for duration at the time of performance and recording (Berger, 1964; Kendall & Carterette, 1991; Saldanha & Corso, 1964; Wedin & Goude, 1972). Iverson and Krumhansl (1993) and Kendall, Carterette and Hajda (in preparation) report no effect of different signal lengths on timbral relationships for continuant signals. However, Hajda (1995) reported signal length as one of the salient acoustical attributes for the timbral relationships of a set of impulse signals. For sustained continuant signals of at least one second, we suspect that timbre is not confounded by slight deviations in duration; however, in the case of staccato and impulse tones, the salience of duration increases. This conclusion is supported by evidence from psychophysical studies on the JND for duration (Woodrow, 1951).

To summarise, variability among listeners means that stimuli *never* will be perceptually equal for every subject. Grey (1975, pp. 45-55) plots standard deviations of signal length, intensity, and frequency with respect to duration, loudness, and pitch. In most instances these standard deviations well exceed the psychophysical JND for these variables. Therefore, the results of equalisation paradigms are misconstrued; actually researchers *minimise* pitch, loudness and duration variability, not *equalise*. The effect of this minimisation on timbre will depend on the uniqueness of the stimuli (impulse versus continuant, sustained versus staccato, different classes of generators, resonators, etc.) as well as the experimental task. Furthermore, the influence of musical context on perceptual attributes such as pitch, loudness and duration of non-synthetic sounds, is unknown. For example, it is unclear just what procedure would equalise the loudnesses of musical phrases. As for impulse signals, loudness is largely undefined.

Methodology Reconsidered

Fashions or the prominence of particular methods or techniques may lead to a rash of studies of similar ilk, often without regard to the requirements of the research. For example, we question the reasoning behind the presentation of long-time average spectra of impulse signals, which fail to resolve envelope and spectral trajectories. Such measurements are especially objectionable if they do not relate in any manner to perception or physical attributes of the vibrating system. We reiterate that methods and techniques must be guided by the research question(s), rather than the converse. Of course, technology will limit to some extent the parameters of the research.

The foremost point in this discussion is that no operational definition of timbre is superior to another; each method has its strengths and weaknesses. No single method, therefore, can uncover the salient attributes of musical timbre. Kendall and Carterette (1992, p. 116) have stated that "what we learn is dependent on what we ask and how we ask it." Experimenters must be willing to engage in convergent methods in order to arrive at an answer to their research question. "It is not that one particular approach is inherently 'true' to the exclusion of another, but rather that different methods produce different aspects of, and converge upon, the truth" (Kendall & Carterette, 1992, p. 118).

THE PERCEPTUAL AND PHYSICAL CORRELATES OF MUSICAL TIMBRE

Any model or theory of timbre must explicate relationships between variables in the perceptual *and* physical frames of reference. In the discussion below, we will consider research findings and theories regarding both the perceptual and physical attributes related to musical timbre.

The Source and Interpretative Models of Timbre

Handel (1995, p. 426) postulates that there are two possible explanations for the subjective identification of timbre. The first explanation involves the observer's perception of the physical mechanisms and actions involved in the sound production. As Handel points out, such a view is analogous to the source-filter model of speech production (Fant, 1960). In a musical instrument system, the source is the generator (e.g. string, reed) which is excited by a driver (e.g. bow, air flow). This source is coupled to a filter (resonant box or cavity). Because the acoustic signal that emanates from a musical instrument is determined by the method of excitation (the physical process), the generator and the resonator (the physical materials and their shapes), and the couplings among these, we should be able to perceive each of these factors. Thus we can distinguish between struck metal bars, plucked nylon strings, bowed strings, and air-blown lip reeds, edge-tone mechanisms, etc. This explication is essentially identical to Balzano's (1986) view of timbre as the perception of "underlying dynamics of physical processes (p. 312)" and is analogous to theories involving the relation of the perception of articulation and articulatory mechanisms of speech (Liberman, Cooper, Shankweiler & Studdert-Kennedy, 1967). The advantage of such a view, which we shall call the "source" mode of timbre perception, is that it allows for physical invariants that would prevail regardless of the range of performance characteristics, including the skill of the performer, pitch range of the instrument, the dynamic range, long versus short tones and tones played with or without vibrato. McAdams (1993), using a term from ecological psychology, refers to these as "structural invariants", since they are based on the physical structure of the vibrating system and its excitation. Indeed, the mechanics and materials of the vibrating system and the methods of driving the generator are the bases for the traditional Western musical instrument families as well as world instrument classification systems (e.g. von Hornbostel & Sachs, 1914/1961).

Handel's (1995) second explanation for timbral object identification is based on the traditional view (Helmholtz, 1877/1954) that timbre is due to the input from a real-time frequency analysis conducted along the basilar membrane of the inner ear. The connection from these acoustic properties and the sound object itself is learned by experience; we shall hereafter refer to this connection as the "interpretative" mode of perception. The difficulty in accepting this analytical perspective rests in the fact that a given musical instrument produces markedly different spectra throughout its pitch and dynamic range. In addition, certain physical invariants may not be decipherable in the frequency-time domain due to the inherent trade-off in Fourier-based procedures: finer frequency resolution leads to coarser time resolution and vice versa. Finally, there does not appear to be any spectral invariant that would delineate a specified musical instrument system. Nevertheless, the traditional model of the ear as a frequency analyser through time provides a reliable and valid foundation for several recently developed methods for the high-fidelity reproduction of significantly compressed digital music signals (Houtsma, 1992; Tsutsui, Suzuki, Shimoyoshi, Sonohara, Akagiri & Heddle, 1992). Handel concludes that, "most probably, identification results both from the apprehension of acoustical invariants and from cognitive inferences" (1995, p. 426).

But what about timbral structures? Whether one considers the dynamic "wave equations" postulated by Balzano (1986) or the time-varying spectra of various vibrating systems, any spatial relationships between these physical outputs (i.e. Where does Timbre A fit in relationship to Timbre B and Timbre C?) must be shown to hold in the perceptual domain. Therefore, we must find the perceptual structures of timbre and then map these to the physical domain. It may well be that physical invariants are crucial for the identification and categorisation of musical instrument sounds, but there is conflicting evidence at this point that these nominal invariants can be transformed into any sort of ordinal structure that could be represented in a geometric space; e.g. Grey's (1977) analysis showed a highest-strength clustering between such physically disparate continuant stimuli as flute-cello *sul ponticello* and trumpet-bassoon, whereas Hajda (1995) and Lakatos and McAdams (1995) found that, for the most part, impulse stimuli cluster based on shared physical properties of the generator and resonator and manners of excitation. In addition, physical invariants may be discernible in acoustically-isolated, monophonic contexts, but there is no model for understanding how these physical processes are perceived in more complex, more musical contexts.

We feel that the source and interpretative modes of perception contribute uniquely to identification and timbral relationships. Indeed, both physical modelling and signal analysis are effective bases for the synthesis of natural instruments. But the relationship of the constituents of physical models to perceptual attributes has not been widely pursued. On the other hand, a vast majority of psychophysical research in timbre has relied on two principle signal characteristics: the *envelope* and the *time-varying spectrum*. Based on their distinct treatment in the research literature, we will consider each of these characteristics separately.

The Influence of Envelope Constituents on Timbre

The envelope is traditionally defined as the RMS amplitude by time graph of a signal. In the case of a continuant, or nonpercussive, isolated musical tone, the envelope can be parsed into three segments: the attack, steady state and decay. The attack can be thought of acoustically as the time from onset during which the vibrating system achieves stability in the form of a standing wave; it is marked in a signal graph by a rising amplitude. The steady state is that portion during which the standing wave is reinforced by a more-or-less continuous supply of energy to the vibrating system; it is generally, but not always, marked by periodicity (the English translation of Helmholtz, 1877/1954, p. 68, refers to the "musical part of the tone . . . which corresponds to a uniformly sustained and regularly periodic motion of the air"). The decay is that segment after which energy is no longer being supplied to the system. The standing wave is damped by friction; the decay, therefore, is marked by a steady decline in amplitude.

The Partitioning of Isolated Single Tones

A battery of studies during the 1960s and 1970s (Berger, 1964; Clark et al., 1963; Elliott, 1975; Saldanha & Corso, 1964; Wedin & Goude, 1972) attempted to isolate the salience of the attack, steady state, and decay by the parsing and permutation of the signals of isolated nonpercussive musical tones. The dependent variable in these experiments was the number of correct identifications of the source instrument.

At no time did the researchers in these particular studies operationally define the envelope segments in terms of the evolution of the physical signal, although an operational definition of attack was given as early as the mid-1960s (Luce & Clark, 1965). Instead, it was assumed that removing a certain portion of the initial segment of the signal achieved the desired result of removing the attack (Clark et al., 1963; Saldanha & Corso, 1964). Part of the steady state would also be removed, of course. But given the assumption that the steady state was a relatively stable portion of the tone, this loss of data was not considered to be significant. By converse reasoning, the removal of a certain portion from the end of the signal constituted the removal of the decay (Clark et al., 1963). The results from various conditions could be compared against the control condition (entire signal unaltered) to determine which alterations affected identification. Table 12.1 presents composite results expressed as mean percent correct (averaged across subjects and instruments) by editing condition.

Overall, conditions in which attack transients were removed produced increased confusion and poorer identification than conditions in which attack transients were present (Berger, 1964; Clark et al., 1963; Elliott, 1975; Saldanha & Corso, 1964; Wedin & Goude, 1972). On the other hand, the removal of decay transients did not substantially affect identification (Clark et al., 1963; Saldanha & Corso, 1964). And, although vibrato was not controlled as an experimental variable, Wedin and Goude (1972) noted that the identification of continuant instruments which were played with vibrato was not affected by the removal of the attack transient.

Saldanha and Corso (1964) systematically investigated a number of conditions in addition to the presence or absence of transients. These included instrument, pitch, vibrato, length of steady state, and re-testing effects. They found main effects for all of these variables; for example, the percentage of correct identifications at F4 (43%) was significantly higher than those at either C4 (37%) or A4 (38%). This study provides convincing evidence that identification is, in fact, a complex cognitive task which involves much more than a preordained, specified amount of acoustical data. Rather, the listener must also utilise musical knowledge (i.e. the playing range of certain instruments, whether or not they are commonly played with vibrato, etc.) in order to make an informed judgement.

The issue of musical signal partitioning has been re-introduced recently by Iverson and Krumhansl (1993), who produced three multidimensional scalings of sixteen digitally sampled natural sounds (Figs. 12.1A, 12.1B and 12.1C) from the McGill University Master Samples Library (Opolko & Wapnick, 1989). The pair-wise similarity data was collected under the following conditions: (1) unaltered signals, (2) constant onset transients (first 80msec) only, and (3) signals with onsets (first 80msec) removed. Iverson and Krumhansl (1993) correlated the mean subject ratings for each group with the following results: $r_{1,2} = .74$; $r_{1,3} = .92$; $r_{2,3} = .75$. The authors concluded (p. 2599) that "the salient attributes for complete tones can not be isolated to either onsets or remainders."

TABLE 12.1

Average Correct Identification Results by Editing Conditions for Five Studies Cited Above. (Results are collapsed across instruments and subjects.)

Reference	Unaltered signal	Attack alone	Steady state alone	Other signal edits
Clark, Luce, Abrams, Schlossberg, & Rome (1963); varying number of instruments; unknown pitches; unknown signal lengths; Experiment I: chance = 7.7%; Experiment II: chance = 7.1%; Experiment III: chance = 7.1% no distracters unless noted	Experiment I: 70%; 2 distracters	Experiment I: 150 msec: 69% Experiment II: 60 msec: 80%; 90 msec: 83%; 120 msec: 81%; 150 msec: 87%; 300 msec: 86%; 600 msec: 85%	Experiment I: 600 msec steady state or whole tone minus the first 150 msec (data collapsed): 61%; 3 distracters. 150 or 250 msec steady state (data collapsed): 62%; 2 distracters.	Experiment III (Decays only): last 500 msec: 41%; no distracters. last 200 msec: 29%; (only partial results published). last 1 sec: 39%; (only partial results published).
Berger (1964); 10 instruments; chance = 10%	59%; F_4 (349 Hz); 5 sec		35%; middle 4 sec	Backward: 42% Low-pass filter, fundamental only: 18%
Saldanha & Corso (1964); 10 instruments; chance = 2.5%, (29 distracters)	41%; C_4, F_4, or A_4 (261, 349, or 440 Hz); 9 sec		32%; 3 sec	Attack, short steady state, no decay (first 3 sec): 47% Attack, short steady state, decay (3 sec total length): 44% Short steady state, decay, no attack (final 3 sec): 32%
Wedin & Goude (1972); 9 instruments; undefined chance, (free identification)	33%; A_4 (440 Hz); 3 sec		20%; middle 2 sec	
Elliott (1975); 9 instruments; chance = 11%	75%; E_4 (330 Hz); 7 sec		44%; middle 6 sec	

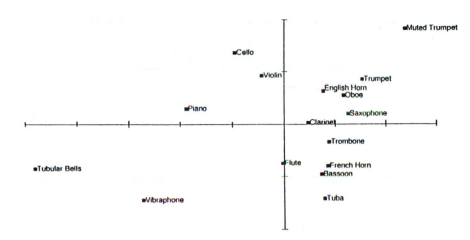

FIG. 12.1A. MDS solution for similarity judgements on 16 original tones. (From Iverson & Krumhansl, 1993; used by permission of American Institute of Physics).

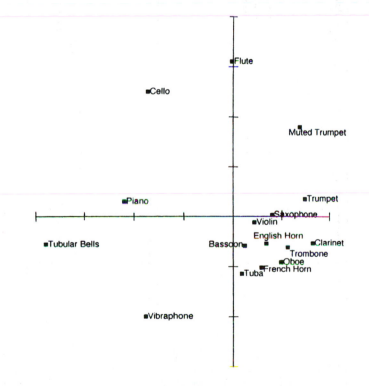

FIG. 12.1B. MDS solution for similarity judgements on 16 "onsets" (first 80 msec). (From Iverson & Krumhansl, 1993; used by permission of American Institute of Physics.)

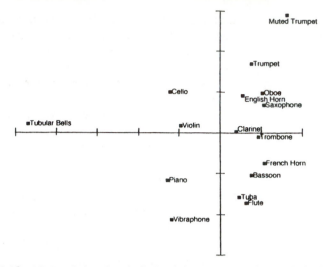

FIG. 12.1C MDS solution for similarity judgements on 16 "remainders" (original tone minus first 80 msec). (From Iverson & Krumhansl, 1993; used by permission of American Institute of Physics.)

However, we have grave concerns about the results and conclusions of Iverson and Krumhansl (1993). The sixteen stimuli utilised in the three experiments were generated from 13 continuant and 3 impulse instruments. Based on our viewing of the MDS solutions, the three impulse instruments—tubular bell, vibraphone and piano—are outliers in the two-dimensional spaces generated for each of the three experimental contexts. We suspect that the great dissimilarity between the impulse and continuant instruments created an artificially high correlation between experimental conditions. In addition, Iverson and Krumhansl acknowledge (p. 2602) that the extreme salience of envelope shape along dimension 1 may have precluded the interpretation of less striking factors that may be salient among the continuant signals. Such an effect has been pointed out by Miller and Carterette (1975), who found that the presence of fundamental frequency (pitch) differences among stimuli prevented them from determining the relative perceptual effect of less salient envelope and spectral features. The predominance of the impulse-continuant envelope dimension has been noted in other scaling studies (Kendall, Carterette & Hajda, 1994; Krumhansl, 1989; McAdams et al., 1995). Kendall, Carterette and Hajda (1994) used this data as a justification for dividing their stimuli into two sets: impulse and continuant (Hajda, Kendall & Carterette, 1994; Kendall, Carterette & Hajda, 1994). It is entirely possible and would be beneficial to reanalyse the Iverson and Krumhansl (1993) data with the impulse signals removed.

Our second concern with the Iverson and Krumhansl (1993) study regards the definition of onset transient as the first 80msec for *every* signal; of course, similar constant transient definitions have been used before (Campbell & Heller, 1978,

1979; Clark et al., 1963; Saldanha & Corso, 1964) in order to control for duration effects. The authors chose this time frame so that they could account for the time until maximal amplitude for all of the signals. Such an approach runs counter to previously-established methods for physical attack-time measurements of Luce and Clark (1965) and Kendall (1986) and the perceptual attack times determined by Gordon (1987). In fact, of the instruments used by Iverson and Krumhansl (1993), only the flute, cello and violin have physical attack times that approach 80msec based on the measurements of Luce and Clark (1965).

Iverson and Krumhansl (1993, p. 2598) concede that "the more percussive tones had attacks shorter than 80msec, so these edited tones had brief steady states." Given the above discussion, it is likely that *most* of the signals contained post-attack segments. In fact, based on the extreme repositioning of the flute and cello from the MDS solutions in Experiments 1 and 2, one might conjecture that only these signals had attack times which approached 80msec. Therefore it is, at best, inconclusive as to whether "the attributes that are salient for timbral similarity judgements are present throughout tones" (p. 2602). We do agree that the high correlation of the onsets-removed condition with the unaltered signal condition in Iverson and Krumhansl (1993) confirms the earlier findings of Wedin and Goude (1972). But the role of attack transients in timbral similarity judgements remains unknown.

Neither do we concur with Handel's (1995, p. 441) reasoning that "acoustic properties cut across the traditional segmentation of the sound (e.g. attack, steady state, decay) and can lead to the same perception using just part of the sound." He bases his conclusion on early identification studies (Berger, 1964; Saldanha & Corso, 1964; Wedin & Goude, 1972) which, he claims, showed that "the attack transient and part of the steady state or the true steady state alone can provide enough acoustic information for identification" (p. 441). But this statement contradicts what these experimenters found regarding the steady state alone. Finally, Handel's (1995, Figure 7, p. 442) rendering of Iverson and Krumhansl (1991) should be considered with great caution. The superimposed two-dimensional configurations appear to be identical to those in Iverson and Krumhansl (1993), however the amplitude by time graphs for selected instruments are certainly incorrect in both the indicated signal lengths (about 186msec!) and the envelope plots themselves.

The Influence of Melodic Context

A new condition, the legato transient, was introduced by Campbell and Heller (1978, 1979). They tested the identification of six instruments playing two-note legato phrases (F_4 at 349.2Hz to A_4 at 440Hz). The legato transient was operationally defined as an independent variable of the 110, 70, 40 and 20msec portions before the second steady state. This introduced a quasi-musical context to the isolated tone studies of the earlier researchers. These researchers found that the legato transient alone condition yielded superior identification overall—the published results were collapsed across all instruments—to the attack transients alone (defined as 110, 70, 40 and 20msec from onset of the F_4 tone) and steady state alone (defined as 300, 110, 70, 40 and 20msec beginning 150msec from onset of the F_4 tone) conditions. However, the same difficulties with operational definitions of the acoustical variables mentioned above were evident in this study: a constant time from onset is assumed for all attacks and the legato transients are all of equal duration. This is especially problematic when one considers that Campbell and Heller (1978, 1979) included an impulse instrument—a piano—with the continuant instruments.

Kendall (1986) addressed the relative salience of these envelope features by comparing the role of transients (attack and legato) and steady state across single-note and legato musical phrase contexts. His three-part hierarchical operational definition of attack and legato transients took into account signal characteristics as opposed to an arbitrary time segment imposed across stimuli. Because he used musical training as a blocking factor, he instituted a matching procedure instead of identification; in other words, subjects were not required to give an instrument name to the stimuli. In the musical (melodic) contexts, he found that steady state alone conditions were matched as well as the unaltered signal conditions; each of these conditions resulted in significantly higher mean matches than the transient alone conditions. Kendall (1986, p. 210) concluded that "the perceptual importance of transients in defining the characteristic sounds of instruments has been overstated." Collapsed results for the various editing conditions of Campbell and Heller (1978) and Kendall (1986) are given in Table 12.2.

Further Discussion

In general, we question the generalised conclusions from studies which employ a single method, such as identification tasks. For most of the studies mentioned above, correct identification scores—although above chance—are still low when one considers the reported musical expertise of the subjects. Wang and Gossick (1978), in a pre-test for musical subjects, found 15 musicians who were able to identify correctly 75% or more orchestral tones in which the attacks and decays had been removed. Unfortunately, the details of this identification task are not reported.

McAdams (1993) mentions a caveat concerning the validity of studies in which transients are excised from isolated tones. He suggests that the removal of an attack segment does not leave the edited signal without an onset transient; it replaces the natural attack with an artificial impulse. "The new attack may be considered strong perceptual evidence *against* [emphasis his] the instrument in question and so a reduction in identifiability is not surprising" (p. 166). We point out that the editing of analogue tape could cause additional anomalies in the perceptual onset of attack-removed tones. McAdams suggests that masking the attack, rather than the introduction of a new (artificial) attack might better

TABLE 12.2

Average Correct Identification Results by Editing Conditions for Campbell and Heller (1978) and Kendall (1986). (Results are collapsed across instruments and subjects.)

Reference	Unaltered signal	Attack alone	Steady state alone	Other signal edits
Campbell & Heller (1978); 6 instruments; chance = 16.7%	96%; two-note legato sequence, F$_4$ to A$_4$ (349 to 440 Hz); 4 sec total length	Extracted from first tone of sequence: 72%; 110 msec 71%; 70 msec 65%; 40 msec 49%; 20 msec	Signal length, beginning 150 msec after onset of the first tone: 55%; 300 msec 50%; 110 msec 48%; 70 msec 52%; 40 msec 49%; 20 msec	Legato transient length: 81%; 110 msec 73%; 70 msec 74%; 40 msec 61%; 20 msec
Kendall (1986); 3 instruments; chance = 33.3%, (matching task of instrument type)	54%; extracted single tones: Eb_5 (622 Hz), 510 msec; E$_4$ (510 Hz), 330 msec	51%; 20 to 60 msec from onset (refer to article)	50%; refer to article	Steady state, artificial attack (single-period): 48% Attack, single-period steady state: 41% Single-period steady state, no attack: 46%
Kendall (1986); 3 instruments; chance = 33.3%; (matching task of instrument type)	84%; varying phrase lengths and frequencies		81%; refer to article	Steady state, no legato transients, artificial (repeated single-period) attacks and decay: 80% Attack, legato and decay transients only: 57% Transients, single-period steady states: 52% Single-period steady states, no transients: 47%

isolate the salience of onset transients. To our knowledge, no formal study of this nature has been conducted with musical tones, although there is precedence in the psycholinguistic literature.

Additionally, Saldanha and Corso (1964) conducted one of the few studies of this era which utilised inferential statistics in order to determine the statistical significance of a number of variables. The fact that every independent variable (instrument, pitch, vibrato, length of steady state, and re-testing) produced a main effect in identification suggests that the perceptual process involves complex strategies dependent upon information from a variety of sources.

Reverse Playback

The effect of playback reversal on identification also merits further investigation, based on both informal (George, 1954, 1962; Houtsma, Rossing & Wagenaars, 1987, p. 67) and formal (Berger, 1964) experiments. In a reversed playback condition, the long-time average frequency and amplitude properties of recorded instrument sounds are preserved but temporal trajectories are not. In spite of this fact, identification of stimuli such as the piano (George, 1954, 1962; Houtsma, Rossing & Wagenaars, 1987) and flute, tenor saxophone, and trumpet (Berger, 1964) are significantly reduced. However, the identification of oboe, clarinet, alto saxophone, cornet, French horn, baritone, and trombone does not appear to be greatly affected by reversed playback (Berger, 1964). Informal listening studies conducted in the UCLA Music Perception, Cognition, and Musical Acoustics laboratory suggest that there is a differential effect due to reverse playback with sustained (greater than 1-sec) continuant tones as opposed to impulse or staccato tones. We have noticed too that continuant tones with the onsets removed sound virtually indiscriminable forwards and backwards.

The Operational Definition of Envelope Constituents

Due to the overall lack of appropriate operational definitions, we feel that the issue of the timbral contribution of envelope constituents is far from resolved, especially for identification and musical contexts. As we have noted, signals for which the attack is defined as a constant segment truncated from onset are most likely to be contaminated by the presence of a portion of the steady state. Operational definitions of attack based on rise time fail to uncover the point in time at which the standing wave is developed in the vibrational system. In fact, to our knowledge, only Kendall (1986) used signal periodicity as a condition for the demarcation of a transient/steady-state boundary. An alternative basis for the operational definition of envelope constituent boundaries follows.

To this point, global temporal and spectral characteristics of the acoustical signal have been considered as separate and mutually exclusive variables. Beauchamp (1982) has pointed out that RMS amplitude and centroid (he uses the term "brightness") are mathematically independent, and their perceptual counterparts, "loudness" and "brightness," are almost independent. However, in isolated acoustical signals produced by a wind instrument, it is common to find that the time-variant characteristics of RMS amplitude and centroid share a strong monotonic relationship during the steady-state portions (Beauchamp, 1982, 1993).

Figure 12.2 shows a plot of RMS amplitude and centroid by time for an imaginary signal. We identify four regions by the apparent relationship between amplitude and centroid. Region 1: Attack—amplitude increases rapidly from onset, while centroid progresses from an early local maximum towards a minimum; Region 2: Attack/Steady-State Transition—amplitude and centroid increase concurrently in a monotonic relationship to the point in time at which the amplitude reaches a significant local maximum; Region 3: Steady State—amplitude and centroid maintain their monotonic relationship, but they covary around their respective average values; Region 4: Decay—amplitude and centroid both decrease although, depending on the amount of noise in the signal, the centroid may deviate from the general amplitude pattern. Beauchamp (1993, p. 6) conceives of the concurrent evolution of RMS amplitude and centroid beginning 100msec from onset as a "trajectory." In our hypothetical model, we operationally expand this concept, which we call *Amplitude (RMS)/ Centroid Trajectory (ACT)*, to include the concurrent evolution of the principal envelope and spectral features, which begins on the order of tens of milliseconds after onset and determines the beginning of the attack/steady-state transition.

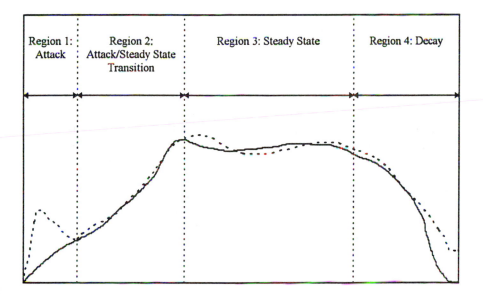

FIG. 12.2.   RMS amplitude (——) and centroid (------) by time for an imaginary signal. The time axis has been expanded to show details for Regions 1 and 2.

Figure 12.3A plots RMS amplitude and centroid versus time for a sustained oboe tone, played at C4 (ca. 262Hz). The tone was performed *piano* with a crescendo to *forte* and a decrescendo back to *piano*. Figure 12.3B plots centroid versus RMS amplitude (ACT) for the same signal. Note that the ACT holds throughout the dynamic variations.

We believe that ACT may be an unexplored salient feature of both timbre identification and timbral relationships in musical contexts. In studies in which signals are truncated to the first 100msec or so from onset, it is feasible that both identification and similarity ratings will not be greatly affected as long as the first region of the ACT—the attack/steady-state transition—is preserved, in spite of the fact that long-time average spectral features have been removed. This is because ACTs with a steep slope will imply a higher centroid than ACTs with a shallow slope. Conversely, in studies in which the first 100msec or so from onset are removed, the long-time average spectral features are preserved but the first region of the ACT is removed. It is possible that identification is impaired not because of the removal of the attack transient, as reported in numerous identification studies, but instead because of the removal of attack/steady-state transition. One might hypothesise that, for the identification of isolated continuant signals, the attack and the attack/steady-state transition (first region of the ACT) may be both necessary and sufficient; for timbral relationships, the transition or steady-state alone may be sufficient. This alternative explanation is consistent with the analyses of Wedin and Goude (1972), and the analyses (but not the conclusions) of Iverson and Krumhansl (1993) and other researchers who partitioned the acoustic signals of isolated musical tones. However, Hajda (1996) has collected preliminary data which suggest that the steady-state—as defined by the ACT model—is necessary and sufficient even for the identification of isolated, sustained continuant tones.

Impulse Tones

Much of the discussion to this point has centred around continuant tones. A different set of principles might exist for impulse tones, since these signals contain attacks followed by immediate decays. Although there is no steady state, a standing wave does develop on the generator (e.g. vibrating string, plate, bar, membrane). It is also extremely difficult for many of this class of instruments to emulate legato performance. Impulse instruments with slower rates of decay, such as the vibraphone or piano can give the illusion of a legato style, even though the second tone in such a series has an impulse attack. But instruments such as xylophone and marimba can only emulate this effect through a tremolo performance. To our knowledge, only Clark et al., (1963) and Iverson and Krumhansl (1993) have attempted to partition the signals generated by impulse instruments. However, Clark and his colleagues did not conduct a formal investigation, and Iverson and Krumhansl combined impulse signals with continuant (see our earlier discussion). Therefore, it is impossible to ascertain the

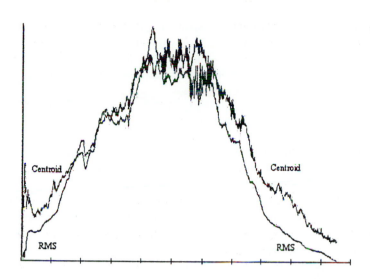

FIG. 12.3A. RMS amplitude and centroid versus time for a sustained oboe tone, played at C$_4$ (ca. 262Hz). Amplitude and centroid (ordinate) are on a standardised scale; time divisions on the abscissa are 500msec. The tone was performed *piano* with a crescendo to *forte* and a decrescendo back to *piano*. (Courtesy of James Beauchamp, University of Illinois.)

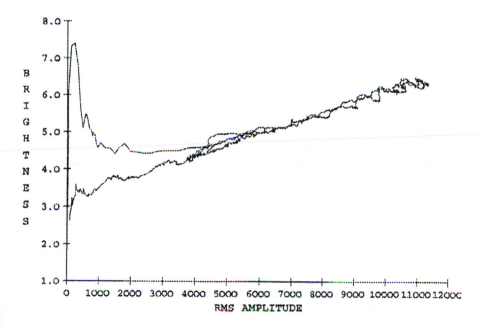

FIG. 12.3B. Centroid ("brightness") versus RMS amplitude for the entire duration of the oboe tone described in Figure 12.3A. (Courtesy of James Beauchamp, University of Illinois.)

salience of the attack and decay segments, but the phenomenological results of Clark et al. (1963) indicate that the removal of the attack transients of impulse tones may not be discriminable. Clearly, this is still an avenue for further exploration.

THE COMPARATIVE INFLUENCE OF SPECTRAL AND TEMPORAL CHARACTERISTICS ON TIMBRE

A spectrum is the amplitude by time graph for each frequency component of a signal. We include time, because it has proven to be an integral part of most analyses of musical stimuli. A number of studies, however, have used synthetic or altered synthetic signals in which the variability through time of individual components has been simplified or altogether removed. This is especially the case in many traditional psychophysical studies. Because we are concerned here with perceptual principles and acoustical correlates for musical sounds, we will continue to limit our discussion to research which is based on the manipulation or emulation of musical tones.

The Experimental Manipulation of Spectral and Temporal Features

Several studies have investigated the relative salience of spectral and temporal characteristics through the interchange of spectral and/or temporal envelopes. Strong and Clark (1967a, 1967b) used this technique in a comparison of natural, synthetic, and altered (interchanged spectral and temporal envelopes) versions of nine orchestral wind instruments. The authors concluded, from a comparison of identification ratings for the synthetic and altered tones, that the spectral envelope—created by averaging the analyses of the same instrument at several pitches—is a predominant perceptual feature over the temporal envelope where the spectral features are unique. These results held for the oboe, clarinet, bassoon, tuba, and trumpet. On the other hand, where the spectral envelope is not unique, the spectral envelope is equal or subordinate to the temporal one in perceptual significance. This was the case for the flute, trombone, and French horn.

The effect of spectral envelope modifications on the positions of stimuli within a perceptual MDS space has been investigated by Grey and Gordon (1978) and Wessel (1979). Spectral hybrids were created from four synthetic emulations generated in Grey (1975). The pairings were trumpet-trombone, oboe-bass clarinet, bassoon-French horn, and two celli (played normal and *sul ponticello*). These eight spectrally-modified tones were included with either the eight other original line-segment re-synthesised tones (Grey & Gordon, 1978) or all sixteen original tones (Wessel, 1979) and subsequently subjected to pair-wise similarity ratings. Grey and Gordon compared the hybrid three-dimensional MDS analysis to the MDS solution obtained from similarity scalings of the original 16 tones (Grey, 1975, 1977). For every pair, instruments exchanged order on the axis related to spectral envelope; they also shifted slightly on the remaining two dimensions. Wessel (1979) found a two-dimensional solution interpretable for 24 stimuli; we note that he was the lone subject. Three of the four modified pairs exchanged positions on the centroid (Wessel uses the term "brightness") axis, while the fourth—cello played normal and cello played *sul ponticello*—moved to almost identical positions in the MDS space. These interpolations have provided evidence of the structural possibility for timbral analogies (Ehresman & Wessel, 1978; Wessel, 1979), which have been investigated further using FM synthetic emulations (Krumhansl, 1989; McAdams & Cunibile, 1992) of natural instruments and hybrid timbres (see our discussion of Krumhansl, 1989 which follows).

Uniqueness, defined by Strong and Clark (1967b) as a spectral or temporal feature which is not shared among instruments, is an important aspect that may influence the identification of certain instruments. In fact, a unique feature may be invariant across the pitch and dynamic range of a musical instrument (such as the inharmonicity of a tubular bell). The relative uniqueness of an instrument will depend on the features of the other instruments with which it is being considered. A violin, for example, may have unique characteristics in comparison to wind instruments, but not in comparison to other members of the string family.

For timbral relations, traditional MDS analyses seek solutions which emphasise the commonalities among stimuli. Hence, uniqueness does not appear to be a factor in similarity studies of Grey and Gordon (1978) and others. More recently, however, a subjective correlate for uniqueness has been developed in the form of MDS models (Winsberg & Carroll, 1989, Winsberg & De Soete, 1993). These models allow individual stimuli to have dimensions of their own in combination with dimensions which are common to all stimuli (see Krumhansl, 1989; McAdams et al., 1995). These unique dimensions are referred to as "specificities." From an interpretative perspective, these specificities still must be related to a physical parameter. However, traditional analyses will not suffice here, since a specificity is a single point along a dimension, not a linear set of points which can be correlated with a unidimensional variable. A specificity may be the result of a unique feature of the stimulus or it may include additional continuous dimensions of variation (McAdams, 1995).

The Dimensions of Timbre

A dimension is, simply, an attribute of perception which can be represented by a perceptual scale. In most instances, it is assumed that this scale is continuous in nature. Once such a scale is applied to a set of stimuli, the researcher must interpret the scale in terms of the positions of the stimuli and their perceptual and physical attributes. As we have discussed above, the relative salience of spectral and temporal features will depend on the experimental context and the methods.

The following discussion of similarity studies is organised by the use of similar or identical stimuli. The findings, discussed primarily in terms of the interpretations of perceptual dimensions and the physical attributes, are compared within and between groups of studies.

Early Similarity Studies

There are three classic studies in the early similarity literature which have appeared in numerous citations: Plomp (1970, 1976), Wedin and Goude (1972), and Wessel (1973). A detailed comparative analysis of these studies is revealing, since they incorporate similar instruments and methods, but differ in stimulus conditions and results.

Plomp (1970, 1976) used synthesised continuant stimuli generated from a single period taken from the steady-state portion of 9 natural stimuli: 3 brass (trumpet, French horn, trombone), 3 woodwinds (oboe, bassoon, clarinet) and 3 bowed strings (violin, viola, cello). We note a discrepancy in fundamental frequencies reported in the 1970 and 1976 entries; the correct frequency is 349Hz (R. Plomp, personal communication, November 24, 1995) which corresponds to a concert pitch of F_4. The stimuli were subjected to triadic comparisons and MDS. Plomp (1976) found a 0.86 correlation between the three-dimensional perceptual space and a three-dimensional physical space derived from the differences in SPL outputs of a 1/3-octave band filter (taken as a model of critical bandwidth).

We scaled both the perceptual and acoustical data matrices of Plomp (1970) with a monotonic (nonmetric) MDS paradigm (Kruskal, 1964) and found that one-dimensional, two-dimensional, and three-dimensional analyses yielded stresses of 0.208, 0.060, and 0.021, respectively, for the perceptual distances and 0.226, 0.063, and 0.008, respectively, for the acoustical distances (stress is a measure of goodness-of-fit of the data to the configuration). We then correlated (Pearson r) the perceptual and acoustical MDS inter-stimulus distances for one, two, and three dimensions. We found that the acoustical and perceptual one-dimensional solutions yielded $r = 0.193$, the two-dimensional solutions yielded $r = 0.866$, and the three-dimensional solutions yielded $r = 0.842$. Based on the minimal reduction in stress from the two-dimensional to the three-dimensional solution and the correlations between acoustical and perceptual configurations, we conclude that a two-dimensional, rather than three-dimensional, solution is feasible for Plomp's data. We present our solution of the two-dimensional perceptual configuration in Figure 12.4. Here and later, quantitative relations among categories are shown by a tree generated from a hierarchical clustering algorithm (Johnson, 1967).

Wedin and Goude (1972) subjected matrices derived from the similarity scaling of continuant tones played at A_4 (about 440Hz) with and without transients to factor analysis. Their choice of instruments was identical to Plomp (1970) with the exception of flute instead of viola. The two editing conditions,

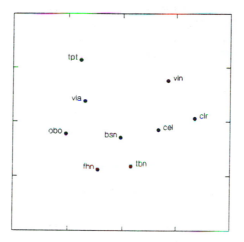

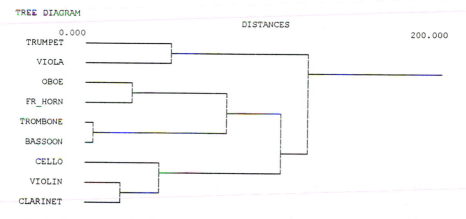

FIG. 12.4 Two-dimensional MDS solution and complete linkage hierarchical clustering of proximity ratings for nine steady-state tones generated by replicating single periods (Plomp, 1970, 1976). Solution has been rotated so that positions of points relative to the page are consistent with those of Plomp. bsn = bassoon; cel = cello; clr = clarinet; fhn = French horn, obo = oboe, tbn = trombone; tpt = trumpet; vla = viola; vln = violin.

however, yielded virtually identical mean dissimilarity matrices (McAdams et al., 1995 report a correlation of 0.92). Wedin and Goude (1972) identified three principle factors which accounted for at least 72% of the variance in each context. Each factor corresponded to the energy distribution in the steady-state portions of the tones: (1) generally high-level energy across components, (2) successively decreasing intensity of the upper components, and (3) low

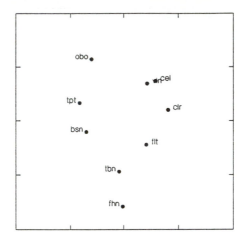

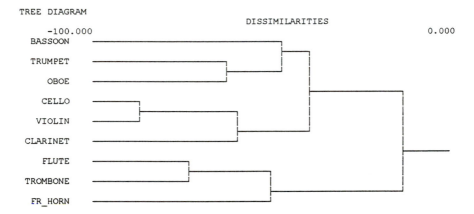

FIG. 12.5A. Two-dimensional MDS solution and complete linkage hierarchical clustering of similarity ratings for nine natural signals with transients (Wedin & Goude, 1972). Solution has been rotated so that positions of extreme points relative to the page are consistent with those of Wessel (Figure 12.6). Abbreviations are the same as in Fig. 12.4 except for flt = flute.

fundamental intensity and an increasing intensity of the next few components (p. 239). The three physical factors correlated 0.92, 0.81, and 0.66 with the perceptual factors for signals with transients removed and 0.93, 0.77, and 0.58 for the unaltered signals. We have scaled the data from both signal-editing conditions of Wedin and Goude and present the two-dimensional configurations

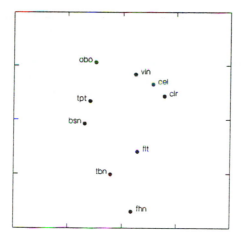

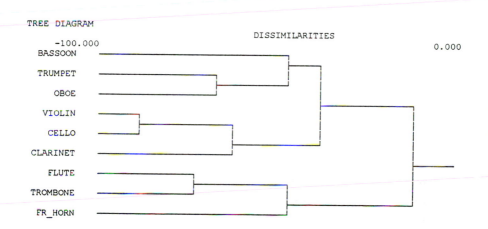

FIG. 12.5B. Two-dimensional MDS solution and complete linkage hierarchical clustering of similarity ratings for nine natural signals without transients (Wedin & Goude, 1972). Solution has been rotated so that positions of extreme points relative to the page are consistent with those of Wessel (Figure 12.6). Abbreviations are the same as in Fig. 12.4 except for flt = flute.

and hierarchical clustering categories in Figs. 12.5A and 12.5B. We note that the three factors reported by Wedin and Goude are represented by the hierarchical relationships in both figures: Factor I, violin, cello, and clarinet; Factor II, trombone, French horn, and flute; Factor III, trumpet, oboe, and bassoon.

Wessel (1973) used the same type of instruments as Plomp (1970, 1976) with isolated sustained tones played at a lower pitch, about 311Hz, or concert Eb_4. He obtained a two-dimensional interpretable analysis from the proximity data (Fig. 12.6). The primary dimension, which distinguished the relative onset characteristics of low and high frequency components, separated the brass, woodwinds and strings. The secondary dimension was distinguished by spectral centroid, called "brightness" by Wessel (1973). We find no reasonable replication of either of Wessel's dimensions in our two-dimensional Plomp configuration (Fig. 12.4).

The analyses of Plomp (1976), Wedin and Goude (1972), and Wessel (1973) are not consistent. As mentioned, Wessel's primary dimension separated the instruments by family and onset characteristics; Wedin and Goude's and Plomp's configurations did not. Wessel also reported an informal study in which the onset and decay transients were removed from his stimuli. He noted (p. 1) that "the reduction in perceived dissimilarity between the strings, oboe, and trumpet was quite noticeable while the perceived dissimilarities within the class of brass instruments remained about the same as when the transients were present." This does not agree with Wedin and Goude who found virtually no change in perceived dissimilarities between editing conditions.

To summarise, these three studies each reported a strong correlation (qualitative or quantitative) between some aspect of the perceptual configurations and a long-time average spectral characteristic. However, the relative positions of instrument types across analyses was not consistent. In the case of the Plomp (1970, 1976) tones, this is not surprising, since all transient and time-variant steady-state elements were removed. The discrepancies between Wedin and Goude's (1972) and Wessel's findings (1973) are less easy to explain. The Wedin and Goude tones are a tritone above those of Wessel; A_4 is in the upper register for bassoon, trombone and, to some extent, cello. Wedin and Goude's tones—3 sec with transients, and 2 sec without—are also longer in duration than Wessel's—about 1.5 sec. There may be salient factors other than timbre which could induce clustering. One such factor, vibrato, was reported by Wedin and Goude. However, the four instruments which were played with vibrato—violin, cello, flute and oboe—do *not* cluster. Finally, the amusical nature of the stimuli, the recording conditions, the degrees of freedom (the manners in which a tone can be manipulated) of the instruments, and the variability in tonal quality among performers may have all contributed to the differences in instrument positions.

The Grey Studies

Grey (1975, 1977) and Grey and Moorer (1977) conducted one of the most thorough and widely-cited series of investigations of timbre to date. The stimuli from these studies have become a canonical set of sounds for a host of more recent studies on the perceptual characteristics of musical tones (e.g. Gordon,

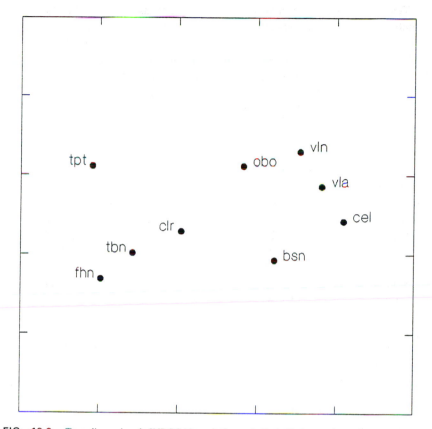

FIG. 12.6.   Two-dimensional INDSCAL solution of dissimilarity ratings for nine natural signals (Wessel, 1973). Abbreviations are the same as in Fig. 12.4 (Adapted by permission of David Wessel, University of California, Berkeley.)

1987; Grey & Gordon, 1978; Sandell, 1995; Wessel, 1979). In actuality, the canonical stimuli were line-segment re-syntheses of 16 brief (about 300msec) tones played at concert Eb_4 (311Hz): two oboes (different instruments and players), English horn, bassoon, Eb clarinet, bass clarinet, flute, two alto saxophones (one instrument and one performer, played at p and mf), soprano saxophone, trumpet, French horn, muted trombone, and three celli (one instrument and performer, played normally, muted *sul tasto*, and *sul ponticello*).

In a first attempt at uncovering salient characteristics of the stimuli, Grey (1975) compared original (recorded), complex synthesis and data reduced versions of the 16 stimuli. Discrimination scores for the comparison of the complex syntheses with the line-segment approximations (4 to 8 line segments per component) ranged from 0.477 to 0.805 with a mean discrimination of 0.627. According to Grey (1975, p. 40), "this finding suggests that the highly complex microstructure in the time-variant amplitude and frequency functions given by the analysis is not absolutely essential to the timbral quality of the tone." We note that chance for the forced discrimination procedure is 0.500, however neither inferential nor receiver-operating characteristics (ROC) analysis were conducted in Grey's (1975) dissertation or a subsequent article (Grey & Moorer, 1977). In essence, the line-segment approximations were considered to be ecologically-valid representations of the original recorded signals.

Grey (1975, 1977) obtained a three-dimensional INDSCAL solution (Fig. 12.7) based on the analysis of similarity scaling data. The first dimension, which distinguished the muted trombone and oboes from the French horn and cello *sul tasto*, corresponded to the relative distribution of energy in high and low frequency components. This physical parameter, centroid, was defined by Grey and Gordon (1978) in several fashions and applied to multiple analyses of perceptual data; we report here the most salient results for the Grey (1977) configuration. One measure of centroid was calculated as the midpoint (mean) of spectral energy distribution determined from a line spectrum of mean amplitudes for each component. In a second measure, the line spectrum was converted to a loudness function for steady-state tones (Zwicker & Scharf, 1965), and a new centroid value was calculated. Correlations between classes of centroid values (treated as points along a unidimensional scale) and Grey's primary perceptual dimension were then calculated. For the loudness function centroid, a correlation of 0.94 was found, although a marginal improvement was found by a slight ($<10°$) rotation of the perceptual axis ($r = 0.95$). However, this correlation is only slightly higher than the linear time-averaged spectrum not modified by Zwicker and Scharf's model ($r = 0.93$); in fact, most versions of centroid do not account for psychophysiological variables (c.f. Beauchamp, 1993; Kendall, Carterette, & Hajda, in preparation; McAdams et al., 1995).

Grey's (1975, 1977) second dimension, which distinguished the flute and bowed strings from the saxophones and clarinets, corresponded to the relative synchronicity in the transient portions of the upper harmonics (these tones had very brief, if any, steady state). The second dimension, with a few notable exceptions, also separated the woodwinds, brass, and strings. The third dimension, which distinguished the brass, bassoon, and English horn from the clarinets, strings, flute and alto saxophone, was related to the presence of low-amplitude, high-frequency energy near the onset of the signal.

The physical interpretations of Grey's three-dimensional solution more or less corroborate Wessel's (1973) interpretation (Fig. 12.6 above). However, the relative positions of instruments in the two configurations have clear differences. For example, trumpet and bassoon are adjacent in Grey's configuration and maximally distant in Wessel's; another discrepancy can be found with the oboe, which groups with the muted trombone in Grey's configuration, but with the strings in Wessel's.

The Krumhansl, Wessel, and Winsberg Stimuli Studies

Krumhansl (1989)—with the help of Wessel and Winsberg—performed a similarity scaling of 21 timbres (from Wessel, Bristow & Settel, 1987) which were synthesised on a Yamaha TX802 FM Tone Generator. Fourteen of the tones were simulations of natural instruments: bassoon, cor anglais (English horn), clarinet, guitar, harpsichord, French horn, harp, oboe, piano, sampled piano, unidentified bowed string, trombone, trumpet, and vibraphone. Seven hybrid stimuli combined temporal envelopes of one instrument with the spectral envelope of a second: guitarnet (guitar/clarinet), obochord (oboe/harpsichord), oboleste (oboe/celeste), bowed piano, striano (string/piano), trumpar (trumpet/guitar), and vibrone (vibraphone/trombone). As reported by McAdams and Cunibile (1992), the tones were at Eb_4 (311Hz) and *mf* (midi velocity 70) with a nominal duration of 300msec. We note that these durations and pitches were essentially the same as those of Grey (1975, 1977). However, Krumhansl's primary dimension of the three-dimensional solution (Fig. 12.8) separated

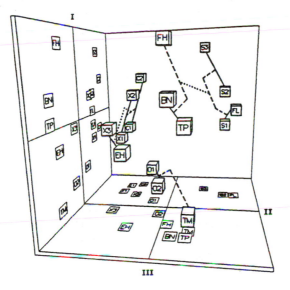

FIG. 12.7 Three-dimensional INDSCAL solution of similarity ratings for 16 line-segment re-synthesised tones (from Grey, 1977). Note that the primary dimension is vertical in this configuration. Hierarchical clustering is represented by connecting lines, decreasing in strength in the order: solid, dashed, dotted. Two-dimensional projections appear on the wall and floor. Abbreviations for stimulus points: O1, O2 = oboes; C1 = E*b* clarinet; C2 = bass clarinet; X1 = alto saxophone (played *mf*); X2 = alto saxophone (played *p*); X3 = soprano saxophone; EH = English horn; FH = French horn; S1 = cello (*sul ponticello*); S2 = cello (normal bowing); S3 = (muted *sul tasto*); TP = trumpet; TM = muted trombone; FL = flute; BN = bassoon. (Used by permission of American Institute of Physics.)

impulsive and continuant tones in a categorical fashion; she interpreted this dimension as "rapidity of attack" and "temporal envelope". She interpreted the second and third dimensions of her configuration to be centroid ("brightness" and "spectral envelope") and spectral flux, respectively. Spectral flux was qualitatively defined (p. 48) as the "temporal evolution of the spectral components." Of the three dimensions identified by Krumhansl, only the second—spectral centroid—was shared by Grey (his primary dimension). We note that, for common instrument types, the Grey and Krumhansl centroid dimensions corresponded loosely; in both spaces the oboe and English horn (high centroid) oppose the French horn, but Grey's French horn and bassoon have a low centroid in comparison to Krumhansl's.

Quantitative relationships between the perceptual dimensions of Krumhansl (1989) and certain physical parameters were initially reported by Krimphoff, McAdams & Winsberg (1994) and included in McAdams, et al. (1995). The Krumhansl tones were analysed with a modified phase-vocoder algorithm developed by Beauchamp (1993). Krumhansl's first dimension correlated very

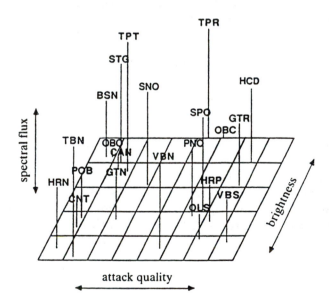

FIG. 12.8. Three-dimensional MDS solution of dissimilarity ratings for 21 FM signals (Krumhansl, 1989). BSN = bassoon, CAN = cor anglais (English horn); CNT = clarinet; GTN = guitarnet (GTR/CNT); GTR = guitar; HCD = harpsichord; HRN = French horn; HRP = harp; OBC = obochord (OBO/HCD); OBO = oboe; OLS = oboleste (OBO/celeste); PNO = piano; POB = bowed piano; SNO = striano (STG/PNO); SPO = sample piano; STG = string; TBN = trombone; TPR = trumpar (TPT/GTR); TPT = trumpet; VBN = vibrone (VBS/TBN); VBS = vibraphone. (From McAdams & Cunibile, 1992; used by permission of Oxford University Press.)

strongly ($r = 0.99443$) with log rise time ("logarithme du temps de montée"), or LRT, operationally defined as the time from the perceptual onset threshold (taken as 2% of maximum amplitude) to maximum amplitude. Log rise time is mathematically expressed as follows (Krimphoff et al., 1994, translations ours):

$$LRT = \log_{10}(t_{max} - t_{thresh}).$$

Krumhansl's second dimension yielded a high correlation ($r = 0.9359$) with long-time centroid ("centre de gravité spectrale"), defined as:

$$C = \frac{\sum_{k=1}^{N} kA_k}{\sum_{k=1}^{N} A_k},$$

where k is the harmonic, A_k is the amplitude of the kth harmonic, and the values are summed up to the 30th harmonic and averaged across time windows of approximately 12msec. The third dimension correlated strongly ($r = 0.8539$) with spectral irrégularité (" irrégularité du spectre"), defined as:

$$IRR = \log_{10}$$
$$\left(\sum_{k=2}^{n-1} \left| 20\log_{10}(A_k) - \frac{20\log_{10}(A_k+1) + 20\log_{10}(A_k) + 20\log_{10}(A_k-1)}{3} \right| \right).$$

Briefly, spectral irregularity is a measure of deviation across three successive components of a static (long-time averaged) spectrum. However, we note that the formula above yields an undefined value for a "flat" spectral distribution in which the amplitudes of all components are equal. We have found that a linear measure of spectral irregularity, in which the "$20\log_{10}$" arguments are removed, rectifies this discrepancy (Kendall & Carterette, 1996).

McAdams et al. (1995) used 18 of the 21 Wessel, Bristow and Settel (1987) instrument types (without oboe, bowed piano, and sampled piano) with longer signal lengths—mean of 673msec, ranging from 495 to 1096msec (equalised for perceptual duration!)—than Krumhansl (1989). They found a three-dimensional configuration to be most interpretable (Fig. 12.9). In a quantitative comparison of solutions McAdams et al. (1995) found that their primary and second dimensions yielded correlations of $r = 0.98$ and 0.95 with the primary and second dimensions of Krumhansl. However, McAdams et al. (1995) found no strong correlate between their third perceptual dimension and any dimension of Krumhansl, nor were they able to replicate Krumhansl's "spectral flux" dimension.

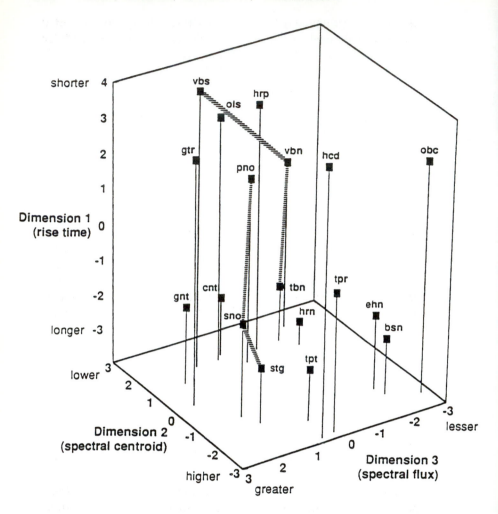

FIG. 12.9. Three-dimensional MDS solution of similarity ratings for 18 FM signals (McAdams, Winsberg, Donnadieu, De Soete, & Krimphoff, 1995). Abbreviations are the same as in Figure 12.8 except for EHN = English horn. (Used by permission of Springer-Verlag.)

As expected, log rise time and spectral centroid correlated highly with the first two dimensions of the McAdams et al. (1995) perceptual space, respectively ($r = 0.94$ in both instances). In addition, a physical measurement of duration correlated $r = -0.82$ with the primary perceptual dimension. For the signals used by McAdams et al. (1995) the physical duration correlated $r = +0.82$ with rise time; this is not surprising, given that tones with impulsive attacks tend to decay faster. However, spectral irregularity did not correlate strongly with the third dimension ($r = 0.13$). A separate acoustical measure (Krimphoff, 1993) described by McAdams et al. (1995) calculated "spectral flux" as "the average of the correlations between amplitude spectra in adjacent time windows." This parameter correlated moderately with the third perceptual dimension ($r = 0.54$).

The Kendall and Carterette Studies

Kendall and Carterette (1991, 1993a, 1993b, 1993c) conducted a convergent series of studies (outlined in Kendall & Carterette, 1992) with wind-instrument dyads. The dyads were generated through the recording of simultaneous performances of pairings of the following instruments—alto saxophone, oboe, flute, trumpet and clarinet. The following contexts were used: unisons (Bb_4, approximately 466Hz); unison melodies (D_5, Eb_5, F_5 and D_5, corresponding to 587, 622, 698 and 587Hz played successively); major thirds ($B b_4$ and D_5); and harmonised melodies (Bb_4-D_5, G_4-Eb_5, A_4-F_5, Bb_4-D_5). In the harmonised contexts, each instrument was used as the soprano. All or some of the two unison and four harmonised contexts, containing ten dyads each, were subjected to similarity scaling (1991), identification of constituent instruments and ratings of blend (1993c), and semantic differential and a magnitude estimation of verbal attributes (1993a, 1993b). Overall, it was found that the canonical two-dimensional configuration of similarity scalings could be interpreted as *nasal* versus *not nasal* for the principal dimension and *rich* versus *brilliant* for the second dimension. A third dimension of *simple* versus *complex* was postulated, although the limited number of stimuli precluded conclusive results. The data points in the two-dimensional canonical solution yielded a circumplicial configuration (Fig. 12.10). The extremes of the primary dimension were oboe (nasal) and clarinet (not nasal); of the second, trumpet (brilliant) and alto saxophone (rich). Overall, oboe dyads produced the lowest blend ratings and the highest number of correct identifications. In other words, *nasal* combinations blended less well than *brilliant* or *rich*.

In their verbal attributes magnitude estimation procedure (VAME), Kendall and Carterette (1993a) found that the MDS configuration generated from a crossed-correlation matrix of von Bismarck (1974) adjectives mapped poorly into the canonical configuration generated from similarity ratings. A final VAME experiment was conducted (1993b) with adjectives that were used to describe the timbre of orchestral instruments by Piston (1955) in his orchestration treatise. The VAME configuration based on the principle components analysis of the ratings for Piston's "musical" adjectives showed a higher correlation with the canonical similarity configuration than did the VAME configuration based on the von Bismarck adjectives.

A preliminary acoustical analysis (Kendall & Carterette, 1993b) revealed that (1) the relative amount of steady-state energy in the upper partials as compared to the lower separated the *nasal* oboe dyads from the others. This acoustical parameter, a version of harmonic distortion was defined as:

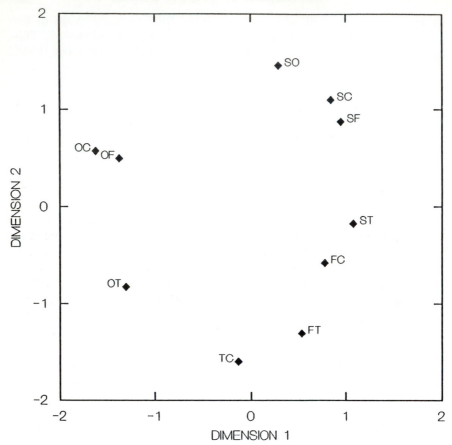

FIG. 12.10. Two-dimensional composite MDS solution of similarity ratings for 10 wind-instrument dyads played under six contexts: Bb_4 unison; major third; inverted major third; unison melody; harmonised melody; inverted harmonised melody. Dimension one, left to right, is "nasal" to "not nasal;" dimension two, top to bottom, is "rich" to "brilliant." OC = oboe-clarinet; OF = oboe-flute; OT = oboe-trumpet; SO = alto saxophone-oboe; SC = alto saxophone-clarinet; SF = alto saxophone-flute; ST = alto saxophone-trumpet; FC = flute-clarinet; FT = flute-trumpet; TC = trumpet-clarinet. (From Kendall & Carterette, 1991; used by permission).

$$HD = \frac{\sum\limits_{k=6}^{9} a}{\sum\limits_{k=1}^{3} a},$$

where a is the linear amplitude of the kth component. (2) The degree of time variance separated the *tremulous* alto saxophone dyads from the others. Time variance was quantified by the mean coefficient of variation:

$$CV_\mu = \frac{\sum_{k=1}^{n} \frac{\sigma}{\mu}}{n}$$

The standard deviation, σ, and the mean, μ, are calculated for each component k across 35 time frames. We suspect that, for these stimuli, harmonic distortion will correlate strongly with spectral centroid and mean coefficient of variation with spectral flux. Overall, the interpretation of dimensions in Kendall and Carterette seems to corroborate at least partially the findings of the studies cited above. However, once again, the positions of instrument labels within the MDS configuration only maps weakly onto configurations generated in other studies.

Kendall, Carterette and Hajda (1994, 1995, in preparation) conducted a comparative study across different tone generation methods as programmed in commercial synthesisers. A natural instrument set of eleven stimuli was recorded in a moderately reverberant concert auditorium (r.t. about 1.6 sec) at Bb_4, around 466Hz. The instruments were alto saxophone, bassoon, Bb clarinet, English horn, flute, French horn, oboe, soprano saxophone, tenor saxophone, Bb trumpet, and *arco* violin. Synthetic counterparts were generated by three commercial synthesisers: Yamaha DX7 (FM synthesis), Roland D-50 (hybrid, combinations of synthetic sources and stored acoustic samples), and the Emax II and Proteus/2 sound modules by E-mu Systems (primarily processed digital samples). These units were chosen for their ubiquity in advertisements, popular and film music and home and university music studios. Commercial and commonly-available third-party patches were digitally stored by a Hollywood synthesist and played back and acoustically recorded in the same reverberant space as the natural stimuli (n.b. emulations were not available for every instrument on every synthesiser). Two sets of stimuli were recorded: long (sustained) signals at about 3sec and short (staccato) signals at about 600msec. For the long signals, a battery of similarity scalings were conducted: natural only, synthetic only, natural with synthetic. In total, ten contexts were investigated. A canonical configuration was generated for the natural stimuli by comparing the ratings for musicians and nonmusicians in mono and stereo in the natural-only contexts and extracting the natural comparisons out of the natural versus synthetic contexts (seven contexts altogether). The Pearson correlations of group dissimilarity matrices (identities removed) were moderately high (mean $r = 0.836$) and an INDSCAL analysis treating each group as a subject indicated that the weightings on a two-dimensional solution were virtually identical for each group. The canonical configuration and hierarchical clustering tree are shown in Fig. 12.11.

The long-time mean centroid correlated strongly with every experimental context (r ranged from 0.924 to 0.990) although some configurations required rotations of up to 35 degrees in order to obtain a maximal correlation. The mean coefficient of variation correlated $r = 0.752$ with the canonical natural

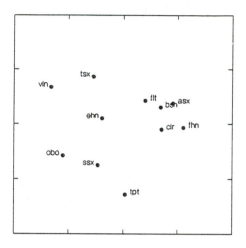

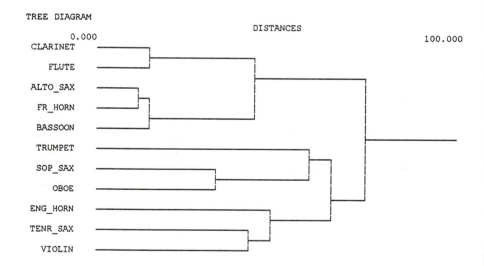

FIG. 12.11. Two-dimensional canonical MDS solution and complete linkage hierarchical clustering of similarity ratings for 11 natural instruments (Kendall, Carterette, & Hajda, in preparation). asx = alto saxophone; bsn = bassoon; clr = clarinet; ehn = English horn; fhn = French horn; flt = flute; obo = oboe; ssx = soprano saxophone; tsx = tenor saxophone; tpt = trumpet; vln = violin.

configuration almost orthogonally (70 degrees) to the principal centroid dimension. The E-mu configuration correlated strongly with mean coefficient of variation ($r = 0.904$) but at a rotation of only 53 degrees to the centroid axis. This indicates that, for the E-mu signals, emulations with high centroids tend to have high variation and vice versa. We were unable to interpret the second dimension of the Roland and Yamaha configurations. Identification and categorisation tasks did confirm clusterings found in the perceptual spaces. Overall, the canonical natural configuration corroborated the composite configuration generated by the similarity scaling of dyads by Kendall and Carterette (1991) (Fig. 12.10 above), but no single emulator produced a consistent replication of all of the natural tones. For example, for the seven instruments common to all four methods of tone generation, the natural signals were correctly identified 75% of the time, the E-mu 58%, Yamaha 45%, and Roland 42%, averaged across long- and short-tone contexts. A complete rendering of the identification results for Kendall, Carterette and Hajda (1994, 1995, in preparation) is shown in Table 12.3.

Discussion

Studies which use canonical sets of stimuli tend to reach conclusions based on convergent evidence. Although results are somewhat consistent within groups of studies, it is equally clear that conclusions diverge between groups of studies. In the case of similarity studies using continuant signals, vast differences are noted in perceptual structure in terms of physical parameters and the relative positions of instruments in the perceptual configuration. For continuant synthetic signals with durations of less than one second (Grey, 1975; Krumhansl, 1989; etc.), the attack becomes perceptually salient, perhaps because it provides information in the absence of a long steady state. In addition, in studies using both impulse and continuant tones (Iverson and Krumhansl, 1993; Krumhansl, 1989; McAdams et al., 1995), attack time also will become salient. However, for studies using sustained continuant tones, characteristics of the steady state have predominated (for an exception, see Wessel, 1973). With the exception of centroid, no other physical factor can be identified as a consistent dimensional attribute of timbre. Depending on the context, temporal/attack characteristics, time-variant features of the steady state, or long-time spectral features other than centroid contribute to the interpretation of perceptual dimensions.

Dimensional Studies of Impulse Timbres

Dimensional studies which include only impulse tones as members of their stimulus sets have not been as numerous as those which include continuant tones. Although centroid is a contributing factor in some impulse timbre research, other, more salient features often predominate. The first work of which

TABLE 12.3

Average Correct Identification Results by Method of Tone Generation for Kendall, Carterette, & Hajda (in preparation). (Results are collapsed across instruments and subjects.)

Context	Natural	E-mu EMAXII and Proteus/2	Yamaha DX7	Roland D-50
Long tones, 11 instruments; Bb_4 (466 Hz); ca. 3 sec signal length; chance = 9.1%	52%; 11 instruments; no distracters	53% 8 instruments; 3 distracters	50%; 7 instruments; 4 distracters	35%; 10 instruments; 1 distracter
Long tones, 7 common instruments; results calculated from same data set as above; chance = 9.1%, (4 distracters)	71%	52%	50%	41%
Short tones, 11 instruments; Bb_4 (466 Hz); ca. 600msec signal length; chance = 9.1%	56%; 11 instruments; no distracters	58% 8 instruments; 3 distracters	39%; 7 instruments; 4 distracters	31%; 10 instruments; 1 distracter
Short tones, 7 common instruments; results calculated from same data set as above; chance = 9.1%, (4 distracters)	79%	64%	39%	43%

we are aware is in two informal explorations reported by Martens (1985), the first in which the author made similarity judgements for eight "plucked" timbres produced by the Yamaha DX7, and the second in which four subjects rated similarities for five "struck" timbres. The first study intimated that synthetic impulse timbres could be distinguished based on phenomenological observations—e.g. the "flabby" attack of the electric guitar, plucked bass and classical guitar versus the "cleaner" attack of the lute, koto, banjo and harp. The latter study showed qualitatively that judgement and ensuing perceptual analyses are consistent across subjects.

Freed (1990) collected perceptual data for the sounding of struck metal pans by rating perceived mallet hardness. Four different pans and six mallets were used for a total of 24 stimuli; each subject completed two sessions of four repeated measures of the rating paradigm. Freed determined informally that much of the relevant acoustical information relating to mallet hardness was in the first 325msec of the signal. All 24 stimuli were evaluated along four acoustical parameters for this 325msec window: mean of the spectral level (log of the area under the spectrum), slope of the spectral level (rate of change of the spectral level per unit time), mean of the spectral centroid (in barks), and the time-weighted average of the centroid of the spectrum (in msec). Informal analysis indicated that pan features did not, on the whole, affect mallet hardness ratings. Even though the four physical parameters were not highly inter-correlated across stimuli, multiple regression analysis derived a four-predictor function which was capable of predicting the perceived mallet hardness rating with acceptable accuracy (multiple R-squared = 0.725). Spectral centroid mean was the strongest predictor.

In Harshberger (1992) and Harshberger, Kendall and Carterette (1994), subjects were able to resolve several of the acoustical features of 12 Javanese gongs, which spanned nearly two octaves (40.04Hz for the largest gong to 155.3Hz for the smallest). Similarity and VAME ratings from two groups (blocked by level of gamelan training) were analysed by principal-components, cluster, and MDS. A two-dimensional solution (Fig. 12.12) was interpreted as *pitch* and *ombak* (beating, vibrato). The acoustical complexity of the gongs suggested several diverse interpretations including the presence of a third dimension, *volume* (*spaciousness*). The salience of frequency and amplitude modulation, however, predominated.

The analyses indicated that: (1) Pitch was associated with octave-related axisymmetrical vibration modes; (2) An original finding identified the source of amplitude modulation (*ombak* rate) as the frequency difference (beating) between the octave partial and the third highest-amplitude partial in close proximity to it, in gongs where *ombak* is observed. Subjects appeared to possess correlative mappings between the acoustical and perceptual frames of reference for Indonesian gongs tones, wherein: (1) fundamental and octave axisymmetrical modes map to pitch; (2) octave and third partials in close

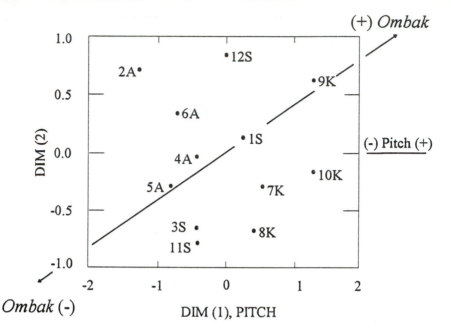

FIG. 12.12. Two-dimensional MDS solution of similarity ratings for 12 Javanese gong tones judged by listeners with gamelan training (Harshberger, 1992). A = *Ageng*, S = *Suwukan*, K = *Kempul*.

proximity to the octave map to *ombak*; (3) spectral envelopes map to perceptual identity. Gamelan training had no statistically-significant effect.

Serafini (1993), examined the dimensional attributes of Javanese percussion sounds. Subjects rated the dissimilarities of pairs of either single notes or melodies; the ratings were analysed with INDSCAL. Serafini interpreted a two-dimensional perceptual solution as (1) spectral centroid in the attack and (2) the mean amplitude level in the "resonant" portion of the tone. She concluded that the primary dimension was timbral and the second was more properly characterised as loudness-related.

Hajda, Kendall and Carterette (1994) and Hajda (1995), in an associated study of Kendall, Carterette and Hajda (in preparation, see discussion above), compared perceptual and physical attributes of impulse tones generated acoustically and by synthetic emulation. A canonical MDS configuration and hierarchical clustering analysis among the natural stimuli—classical guitar, marimba, piano, pizzicato violin, tremolo marimba, tremolo xylophone, tubular bell and xylophone—separated the idiophones from the chordophones (Fig. 12.13), regardless of experimental context or subjects' level of musicianship. The acoustical attributes which correlated best with the primary dimension of the two-dimensional MDS configurations were (1) percent change in spectral

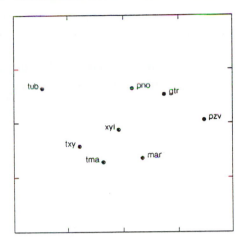

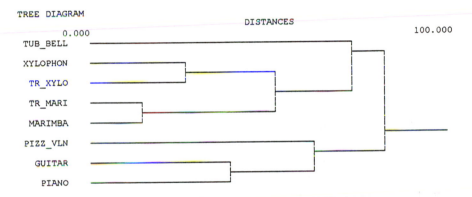

FIG. 12.13. Two-dimensional MDS solution and complete linkage hierarchical clustering of similarity ratings for eight natural impulse tones (Kendall, Carterette, & Hajda, in preparation). gtr = 3D classical guitar; mar = 3D marimba; pno = 3D piano; pzv = 3D pizzicato violin; tma = 3D tremolo marimba; tub = 3D tubular bell; txy = 3D tremolo xylophone; xyl = 3D xylophone.

centroid during the first 100msec, (2) inharmonicity at 100msec, and (3) total signal length.

Further Discussion

The relative results of musicians and nonmusicians is of primary interest in many empirical studies. However, level of musicianship has been utilised as a blocking variable in only a handful of studies. In similarity scalings with isolated tones, musicians and nonmusicians yield highly consistent data (Hajda, 1995; Hajda, Kendall & Carterette, 1994; Harshberrger, 1992; Harshberger, Kendall, & Carterette, 1994; Kendall, 1986; Kendall, Carterette, & Hajda, 1994, in preparation; Serafini, 1993; Wedin & Goude, 1972), although nonmusicians' data tend to contain more variance (Hajda, 1995; Kendall, 1986; Kendall & Carterette, 1991). This conclusion is supported by recent evidence, in which McAdams et al. (1995) utilised an extended version of MDS (Winsberg & De Soete, 1993) that estimates the number of latent classes of subjects. The classes are determined by the analysis of individual subject weightings along both common and specific dimensions. Although the model obtained a solution of five classes, the class structure had an ambiguous relation to the degree of musical training and activity. In other words, subjects with varying levels of musicianship were present in every class. However, as the musicality of the stimulus and/or the task increases, results between musicians and nonmusicians diverge in both interpretation and ease of interpretability (Kendall & Carterette, 1991; Miller & Carterette, 1975; Serafini, 1993).

CONCLUSIONS

We have argued that musical timbre is the product of a dynamic system. A truly ecological definition, therefore, must take into account the perceptual attributes of time-variant musical objects, which may themselves be horizontal and vertical combinations of constituent musical objects. Each of these temporally varying objects is a perceptually-bounded event which possesses cohesive characteristic properties, or its perceptual "persona." One goal of research is to connect these perceptual objects to the generator-resonator production systems from which they physically originate. Another goal is to understand the relationships among perceptual objects. Our approach to timbre is both an embracing and expansion of the source and interpretative modes of perception. This object-oriented approach, however, has its origins in the writings of Schaeffer (1966).

An Object Metaphor for Timbre

The *objets musicaux* of Schaeffer (1966) arose from his view that recording technology has caused all sounds—those of music, animals, or the environment—to be experienced in the same way so that they may be treated as *objets sonores*, distinct and separate from their original sources. Schaeffer's phenomenology of sound objects, "solfège des objects musicaux," is a classification under seven criteria: mass, dynamic, harmonic, timbre, profile (of melody and of mass), grain and inflection. An essential feature is the notion of reduced hearing wherein only the properties of the sound are considered. This mode of hearing Schaeffer contrasts with the common mode of response where a sound is identified by its source, e.g. "that's a soprano saxophone." From our perspective, there are several problems with Schaeffer's typology of musical objects. His scheme is highly phenomenological and subjective. Sound objects are categorised by *masse* (essentially a spectral ordering) and by *treatment*, which has three major divisions: continuous, impulsive and discontinuous. Schaeffer's ordering of properties implies a metric ordering when it is in fact nominal and is based on some dubious perceptual experiments. Also, his taxonomies often mix frames of reference, for example spectral complexity is confounded with variability.

An object metaphor yet may be useful in understanding the nature of timbre. Any two musical objects are distinct when they have mutually exclusive properties. A minimal distinction for objects occurs when all properties are shared but one. Timbral objects which share perceptual characteristics become members of the same class. The strength of membership can be quantified in terms of the number and perceptually salient nature of the shared properties.

Consider as an example, the piano, guitar and tubular bell. In the physical frame of reference, piano and guitar share the property "string", but not the method ("plucked" vs. "struck"). Tubular bell shares the method "struck" with the piano, but tubular bell belongs to the class of "idiophone", piano to "chordophone". The interaction of method with property produces, in the vibrational frame, the property of impulsive envelope shared by the three. Harmonic spectra are properties shared by piano and guitar but not by tubular bell. Perceptually, we ask about the mapping of these physical domain properties and methods onto those of perception, and find that piano and guitar are more similar as composite timbral objects to each other than to tubular bell (Fig. 12.13). We also find that, along a primary perceptual dimension, piano is in an intermediate position in relation to the tubular bell and guitar. Perceptual properties for impulse tones might include, among others, the amount of ringing, pitch ambiguity, and brightness or nasality. For continuant tones, nasality (Kendall & Carterette, 1993a, 1993b), richness, brilliance, and reediness may predominate. In any empirical study, the salience of these perceptual properties will depend on (1) the degree to which sound objects possess these properties, and (2) the contexts in which they are presented.

Our structural, hierarchical approach differs substantially from Schaeffer's (1966) schemes in a number of ways. In particular we have based a *metric* dimensionality, for example *nasality* and *centroid*, on a considerable number of experiments (those of our own and others) and great care is taken to map objects and their properties among frames of reference. Schaeffer's variables were arrived at through his personal listening and introspection; our model is based on empirical observations and measurements of acoustical signals and a quantitative effort to map the relationships among frames of reference. Most importantly, we give equal status to both the source mode and interpretative mode of perception.

The Definition of Timbre Revisited

At this point, some words must be said about developing a constitutive definition of timbre. Based on research findings and definitions which have been posited to this point, it is clear that timbre has two principle constituents: (1) It "conveys the identity of the instrument that produced it" (Butler, 1992, p. 238), and (2) It is representable by a palette or family of palettes (see Martens, 1985) in which tones from different sources can be related along perceptual dimensions. The first constituent is nominal or categorical in nature: the clarinet has a characteristic to its sound, regardless of the pitch, loudness, etc. The second constituent is a hybrid of categorical and ordinal organisation: the clarinet is not nasal and is therefore differentiated from the oboe, which is nasal. On the other hand, the clarinet has attributes which make it unique.

Although much more is known in the mid-1990s than was known 35 years ago, timbre *as a musical variable* still remains, for the most part, a mystery. What are the salient attributes of a symphony, a gamelan, or a big-band jazz ensemble? How does the mind transform, organise, and structure the timbral development of a work by Berlioz, Debussy, or Ravel? How can we take advantage of what we know about timbre to help contemporary composers explicitly develop and utilise new—and old—sound structures? These are the types of questions that must guide our inquiry into the "most important" aspect of tone (Seashore, 1938/1967).

REFERENCES

American national standard: Psychoacoustical terminology. (1973). Timbre. ANSI S3.20-1973 (p. 56). New York: American National Standards Institute.

Arabie, P., Carroll, J. D., & DeSarbo, W. S. (1987). *Three-way scaling and clustering.* Newbury Park, Calif: SAGE Publications.

Balzano, G. J. (1986). What are musical pitch and timbre? *Music Perception, 3*(3), 297–314.

Bartlett, F. C. (1932). *Remembering.* Cambridge: Cambridge University Press.

Beauchamp, J. W. (1982). Synthesis by spectral amplitude and "brightness" matching of analyzed musical instrument tones. *Journal of the Audio Engineering Society, 30*(6), 396–406.

Beauchamp, J. W. (1993). Unix workstation software for analysis, graphics, modification, and synthesis of musical sounds. Paper presented at the 94th Convention of The Audio Engineering Society Preprint, Berlin, Germany. *Audio Engineering Society Preprint 3479,* L1–7.

Berger, K. W. (1964). Some factors in the recognition of timbre. *Journal of the Acoustical Society of America, 36*(10), 1888–1891.

Berlioz, H. (1856). *A treatise on instrumentation and orchestration.* English translation by Mary Cowden Clarke. London: Novello. (Original work published in 1844)

Bismarck, G. von (1974). Timbre of steady sounds: A factorial investigation of its verbal attributes. *Acustica, 30,* 146–159.

Butler, D. (1992). *The musician's guide to perception and cognition.* New York, NY: Schirmer Books.

Campbell, W. C., & Heller, J. J. (1978). The contribution of the legato transient to instrument identification. In E. P. Asmus, Jr., (Ed.), *Proceedings of the research symposium on the psychology and acoustics of music, 1978*, pp. 30–44). University of Kansas, Lawrence.

Campbell, W., & Heller, J. (1979). Convergence procedures for investigating music listening tasks. *Bulletin of the Council for Research in Music Education, 59*, 18–23.

Carroll, J. D., & Chang, J. J. (1970). Analysis of individual differences in multidimensional scaling via an N-way generalization of "Eckart-Young" decomposition. *Psychometrika, 35*, 283–319.

Carterette, E. C., & Friedman, M. P. (Eds.) (1974). Foreword to *Handbook of perception: Vol. 1: Historical and philosophical roots of perception*. New York: Academic Press, xiii.

Clark, M., Jr., Luce, D., Abrams, R., Schlossberg, H., & Rome, J. (1963). Preliminary experiments on the aural significance of parts of tones of orchestral instruments and on choral tones. *Journal of the Audio Engineering Society, 11*(1), 45–54.

Clark, M., Jr., Robertson, P., & Luce D. (1964). A preliminary experiment on the perceptual basis for musical instrument families. *Journal of the Audio Engineering Society, 12*(3), 199–203.

Ehresman, D., & Wessel, D.L. (1978). *Perception of timbral analogies*. IRCAM Report 13/78. Paris, France: Centre de Georges Pompidou.

Elliott, C. A. (1975). Attacks and releases as factors in instrument identification. *Journal of Research in Music Education, 23*, 35–40.

Fant, G. C. M. (1960). *Acoustic theory of speech production*. The Hague, Netherlands: Mouton.

Freed, D. J. (1990). Auditory correlates of perceived mallet hardness for a set of recorded percussive sound events. *Journal of the Acoustical Society of America, 87*(1), 311–322.

George, W. H. (1954). A sound reversal technique applied to the study of tone quality. *Acustica, 4*, 224–225.

George, W. H. (1962). Musical acoustics today. *New Scientist, 311*, 256–259.

Gordon, J. W. (1987). The perceptual attack time of musical tones. *Journal of the Acoustical Society of America, 82*(1), 88–105.

Green, D. M. (1988). *Profile analysis: Auditory intensity discrimination* (Oxford psychology series, no. 13). New York: Oxford University Press.

Grey, J. M. (1975). *An exploration of musical timbre*. (Report STAN-M-2). Stanford, Calif: CCRMA, Department of Music, Stanford University.

Grey, J. M. (1977). Multidimensional perceptual scaling of musical timbres. *Journal of the Acoustical Society of America, 61*(5), 1270–1277.

Grey, J. W., & Gordon, J. W. (1978). Perception of spectral modifications on orchestral instrument tones. *Computer Music Journal, 11*(1), 24–31.

Grey, J. M., & Moorer, J. A. (1977). Perceptual evaluations of synthesized musical instrument tones. *Journal of the Acoustical Society of America, 62*(2), 454–462.

Hajda, J. M. (1995). The relationship between perceptual and acoustical analyses of natural and synthetic impulse signals. (Master's thesis, University of California, Los Angeles, 1995). *Masters Abstracts International, 33*(6). (University Microfilms International Publications No. 13–61,681)

Hajda, J. M. (1996). The effect of reverse playback and signal partitioning on the identification of percussive and nonpercussive musical tones. In B. Pennycook & E. Costa-Giomi, (Eds.), *Proceedings of the 4th International Conference on Music Perception and Cognition* (pp. 25–30). Montreal, Canada: Faculty of Music, McGill University.

Hajda, J. M., Kendall, R. A., & Carterette, E. C. (1994). Perceptual and acoustical analyses of impulse tones. In I. Deliège, (Ed.), *Proceedings of the 3rd International Conference on Music Perception and Cognition* (pp. 315–316). Liège, Belgium: European Society for the Cognitive Sciences of Music.

Handel, S. (1995). Timbre perception and auditory object identification. In B. C. J. Moore, (Ed.), *Handbook of perception and cognition* (2nd ed.), (*Hearing*, pp. 425–461). San Diego, Calif: Academic Press,

Harshberger, M. L. (1992). *Acoustics and comparative psychoacoustics of Indonesian gong tones.* (Unpublished master's thesis, University of California, Los Angeles).

Harshberger, M. L., Kendall, R. A., & Carterette, E. C. (1994). Comparative psychoacoustics and acoustics of Indonesian gong tones. In I. Deliège, (Ed.), *Proceedings of the 3rd International Conference on Music Perception and Cognition* (pp. 313–314). Liège, Belgium: European Society for the Cognitive Sciences of Music.

Helmholtz, H. L. F. von (1877). *Die Lehre von den Tonempfindungen als physiologische Grudlage für die Theorie der Musik.* F. Vieweg & Sohn, Braunschweig. English translation by A. J. Ellis, "On the Sensations of Tone as a Physiological Basis for the Theory of Music" (2nd ed., 1885), reprinted by Dover Publications, New York, 1954.

Hornbostel, E. M. von, & Sachs, C. (1961). Classification of musical instruments. [Translated from the original German by A. Baines & K. Wachsmann]. *Journal of the Galpin Society, 14,* 3–29. (Original work published 1914)

Houtsma, A. J. M. (1992). Psychophysics and modern digital audio technology. *Philips Journal of Research, 47,* 3–14.

Houtsma, A. J. M., Rossing, T. D., & Wagenaars, W. M. (1987). Demonstration 29: Effect of tone envelope on timbre. *Auditory demonstrations. Philips Compact Disc #1126–061 booklet* (p. 67). Eindhoven, Netherlands: Institute for Perception Research.

Iverson, P., & Krumhansl, C. L. (1991). Measuring the similarity of musical timbres. *Journal of the Acoustical Society of America, 89*(S2), 1988.

Iverson, P., & Krumhansl, C. L. (1993). Isolating the dynamic attributes of musical timbre. *Journal of the Acoustical Society of America, 94*(5), 2595–2603.

Johnson, S. (1967). Hierarchical clustering schemes. *Psychometrika, 32,* 241–254.

Kendall, R. A. (1980). *Difference thresholds for timbre related to amplitude spectra of complex sounds.* (Unpublished master's thesis, University of Kansas, Lawrence).

Kendall, R. A. (1986). The role of acoustic signal partitions in listener categorization of musical phrases. *Music Perception, 4*(2), 185–214.

Kendall, R. A., & Carterette, E. C. (1991). Perceptual scaling of simultaneous wind instrument timbres. *Music Perception, 8,* 369–404.

Kendall, R. A., & Carterette, E. C. (1992). Convergent methods in psychomusical research based on integrated, interactive computer control. *Behavior Research Methods, Instruments, & Computers, 24*(2), 116–131.

Kendall, R. A., & Carterette, E. C. (1993a). Verbal attributes of simultaneous wind instrument timbres: I. von Bismarck's adjectives. *Music Perception, 10*(4), 445–468.

Kendall, R. A., & Carterette, E. C. (1993b). Verbal attributes of simultaneous wind instrument timbres: II. Adjectives induced from Piston's *Orchestration. Music Perception, 10*(4), 469–502.

Kendall, R. A., & Carterette, E. C. (1993c). Identification and blend of timbres as a basis for orchestration. *Contemporary Music Review, 9*(1 & 2), 51–67.

Kendall, R. A., & Carterette, E. C. (1996). Difference thresholds for timbre related to spectral centroid. In B. Pennycook & E. Costa-Giomi, (Eds.), *Proceedings of the 4th International Conference on Music Perception and Cognition* (pp. 91–95). Montreal, Canada: Faculty of Music, McGill University.

Kendall, R. A., Carterette, E. C., & Hajda, J. M. (1994). Comparative perceptual and acoustical analyses of natural and synthesized continuant timbres. In I. Deliège, (Ed.), *Proceedings of the 3rd International Conference for Music Perception and Cognition* (pp. 317–318). Liège, Belgium: European Society for the Cognitive Sciences of Music.

Kendall, R. A., Carterette, E. C., & Hajda, J. M. (1995). Perceptual and acoustical attributes of natural and emulated orchestral instrument timbres. *Proceedings of the International*

Symposium on Musical Acoustics, July 2–6, 1995, Le Normont, Dourdan, France, (pp. 596–601). Paris: Société Française d'Acoustique.

Kendall, R. A., Carterette, E. C., & Hajda, J. M. (in preparation). Perceptual and acoustical features of natural and synthetic orchestral instrument tones.

Kerlinger, F. N. (1973). *Foundations of behavioral research* (2nd ed.). New York: Holt, Rinehart and Winston.

Krimphoff, J. (1993). *Analyse acoustique et perception du timbre.* (Unpublished DEA thesis. Université du Maine, Le Mans, France).

Krimphoff, J., McAdams S., & Winsberg, S. (1994). Caractérisation du timbre des sons complexes. II. Analyses acoustiques et quantification psychophysique. *Journal de Physique IV,* Colloque C5, supplément au Journal de Physique III, *4*, 625–628.

Krumhansl, C. L. (1989). Why is musical timbre so hard to understand? In S. Nielzén & O. Olsson, (Eds.), *Structure and perception of electroacoustic sound and music: Proceedings of the Marcus Wallenberg symposium held in Lund, Sweden, on 21–28 August 1988* (pp. 43–53). Amsterdam, Netherlands: Excerpta Medica.

Kruskal, J. B. (1964). Nonmetric multidimensional scaling: A numerical method. *Psychometrika, 29*, 115–129.

Kruskal, J. B., & Wish, M. (1978). *Multidimensional scaling.* Newbury Park, Calif: SAGE Publications.

Lakatos, S., & McAdams, S. (1995). Scaling of harmonic and percussive timbres: Perceptual spaces and verbal attributes. *Program and Abstracts for Society for Music Perception and Cognition, Conference '95, June 22–25, 1995, University of California, Berkeley* (p. 10). Berkeley, Calif: Society for Music Perception and Cognition.

Lerdahl, F. (1987). Timbral hierarchies. *Contemporary Music Review, 2*, 135–160.

Liberman, A. M., Cooper, P. S., Shankweiler, D. J., & Studdert-Kennedy, M. (1967). Perception of the speech code. *Psychological Review, 74*(6), 431–461.

Lichte, W. H. (1941). Attributes of complex tones. *Journal of Experimental Psychology, 28*, 455–480.

Luce, D., & Clark, M. (1965). Durations of attack transients of nonpercussive orchestral instruments. *Journal of the Audio Engineering Society, 13*(3), 194–199.

Lundin, R. (1967). *An objective psychology of music* (2nd ed.). New York: Ronald Press.

Martens, W. L. (1985). *Palette:* An environment for developing an individualized set of psychophysically scaled timbres. *Proceedings of the 1985 International Computer Music Conference* (pp. 355–365). San Francisco, Calif: Computer Music Association.

McAdams, S. (1993). Recognition of sound sources and events. In S. McAdams & E. Bigand, (Eds.), *Thinking in sound: The cognitive psychology of human audition* (pp. 146–198). Oxford: Oxford University Press.

McAdams, S., & Cunibile, J. (1992). Perception of timbral analogies. *Philosophical Transactions of the Royal Society, London, Series B*, 383–389.

McAdams, S., Winsberg, S., Donnadieu, S., De Soete, G., & Krimphoff, J. (1995). Perceptual scaling of synthesized musical timbres: Common dimensions, specificities, and latent subject classes. *Psychological Research, 58*, 177–192.

Miller, J. R., & Carterette, E. C. (1975). Perceptual space for musical structures. *Journal of the Acoustical Society of America, 58*(3), 711–720.

Moorer, J. A. (1975). *On the loudness of complex, time-variant tones.* Report No. STAN-M-4, Center for Computer Research in Music and Acoustics, Department of Music, Stanford University.

Neisser, U. (1976). *Cognition and reality.* San Francisco: Freeman.

Opolko, F., & Wapnick, J. (1989). *McGill University Master Samples User's Manual.* Montreal, Canada: McGill University Faculty of Music.

Osgood, C. E., Suci, G. H., & Tannenbaum, P. H. (1957). *The measurement of meaning.* Urbana, Illinois: University of Illinois Press.

Piston, W. (1955). *Orchestration*. New York: Norton.

Plomp, R. (1970). Timbre as a multidimensional attribute of complex tones. In R. Plomp & G. F. Smoorenberg, (Eds.), *Frequency analysis and periodicity detection in hearing* (pp. 397–411). Leiden, Netherlands: A. W. Sijthoff.

Plomp, R. (1976). *Aspects of tone sensation*. London: Academic Press.

Pratt, R. L., & Doak, P. E. (1976). A subjective rating scale for timbre. *Journal of Sound and Vibration, 45*(3), 317–328.

Robinson, K., & Patterson, R. D. (1995). The duration required to identify the instrument, the octave, or the pitch chroma of a musical note. *Music Perception, 13*, 1–15.

Saldanha, E. L., & Corso, J. F. (1964). Timbre cues and the identification of musical instruments. *Journal of the Acoustical Society of America, 36*, 2021–2026.

Sandell, G. J. (1995). Roles for spectral centroid and other factors in determining 'blended' instrument pairings in orchestration. *Music Perception, 13*, 209–246.

Schaeffer, P. (1966). *Traité des objets musicaux*. Paris: Éditions du Seuil.

Seashore, C. E. (1919). *Seashore measures of musical talent*. Chicago: C. H. Stoelting.

Seashore, C. E. (1967). *The psychology of music*. New York: Dover. (Original work published in 1938)

Serafini, S. (1993). *Timbre perception of cultural insiders: A case study with Javanese gamelan instruments*. (Unpublished Master's thesis, University of British Columbia, Vancouver).

Singh, P. G., & Hirsh, I. J. (1992). Influence of spectral locus and *F*0 changes on the pitch and timbre of complex tones. *Journal of the Acoustical Society of America, 92*(5), 2650–2661.

Strong, W., & Clark, M. (1967a). Synthesis of wind-instrument tones. *Journal of the Acoustical Society of America, 41*, 39–52.

Strong, W., & Clark, M. (1967b). Perturbations of synthetic orchestral wind instrument tones. *Journal of the Acoustical Society of America, 41*(2), 277–285.

Tsutsui, K., Suzuki, H., Shimoyoshi, O., Sonohara, M., Akagiri, K., & Heddle, R. M. (1992). ATRAC: Adaptive transform acoustic coding for MiniDisc. *Audio Engineering Society* Preprint No. 3456 (U–2).

Wang, C. C., & Gossick, B. (1978). Relation between timbre perception and tonal duration. In E. P. Asmus, Jr., (Ed.), *Proceedings of the research symposium on the psychology and acoustics of music, 1978* 1–13. University of Kansas, Lawrence.

Ward, W. D. (1970). Musical perception. In J. Tobias, (Ed.), *Foundations of modern auditory theory, Volume I* (pp. 407–447). New York: Academic Press.

Wedin, L., & Goude, G. (1972). Dimension analysis of the perception of instrumental timbre. *Scandinavian Journal of Psychology, 13*(3), 228–240.

Wessel, D. L. (1973). Psychoacoustics and music: A report from Michigan State University. *PACE: Bulletin of the Computer Arts Society, 30*, 1–2.

Wessel, D. L. (1979). Timbre space as a musical control structure. *Computer Music Journal, 3*(2), 45–52.

Wessel, D. L., Bristow, D., & Settel, Z. (1987). Control of phrasing and articulation in synthesis. *Proceedings of the 1987 International Computer Music Conference* (pp. 108–116). San Francisco, Calif: Computer Music Association.

Winsberg, S., & Carroll, J. D. (1989). A quasi-nonmetric method for multidimensional scaling via an extended Euclidean model. *Psychometrika, 54*, 217–229.

Winsberg, S., & De Soete, G. (1993). A latent class approach to fitting the weighted Euclidean model, CLASCAL. *Psychometrika, 58*, 315–330.

Woodrow, H. (1951). Time perception. In S. S. Stevens, (Ed.), *Handbook of Experimental Psychology* (pp. 1224–1236). New York: Wiley.

Zwicker, E. & Scharf, B. (1965). A model of loudness summation. *Psychological Review, 72*, 3–26.

13 Computational auditory pathways to music understanding

Barry Vercoe
Media Laboratory, MIT, Cambridge, Massachusetts, USA

When we listen to the radio we can easily distinguish the music from the talking. But could a machine? Music and speech are both structured audio, and our telling them apart stems from interpreting the audio signals at some stage of representation. If we could fully describe the interpreted representation to some other human, we could possibly describe it to a machine. Conversely, if we could instruct a machine to tell music and speech apart, and did so using only those elementary processes we believe operate in humans, we would be close to accounting for how humans apparently do it.

Telling music apart from speech is not a very high-level goal, and we might like to imbue a machine with more sophisticated musical power. We might want it to "name that tune", or identify some rhythmic style given only the acoustic signal as input. We could go further by insisting that it do this in realtime, that it take only microphone input (for ears) and need no internal audio storage (like us). If it can pitch-track and follow a score, and its response is itself a musical signal (it sings or plays), then we would have a surrogate performer, able to participate in chamber ensembles with some degree of musicianship. It might even be able to improve its performance by learning from rehearsals.

Lest the above ideas sound like fantasy, we should point out that each has already been demonstrated to varying degrees in various contexts (Large & Kolen, 1994; Richard, 1994; Todd & Lee, 1994; Vercoe & Puckette, 1985). The computational methods that made them work have taught us something about how human music cognition appears to operate, but they are all based on different abstractions of what music is (some are scores, some are just points in time). The purpose of this chapter is to suggest how to bring many different methodologies into a single environment, to start from an original acoustic signal and proceed to the many elements of music processing in a sequence of stages. Some stages concern auditory-peripheral information processing, where the acoustic signal finds its first multiple representations and its first pre-attentive interpretations. Others concern mental representations and associated processes that are often highly attentive and prone to being driven by emotion and affect.

The approach we will use is two-fold. We will first look at the problem from the standpoint of the Auditory Experience, surveying what we know about neural representation of music data and associated information processing, with occasional forays into computational representations of both. We will then examine Computational Representations in practice using a realtime software environment for modelling acoustic and music data processing, one that will enable us to implement our existing knowledge in realtime and then use it as a substrate for constructing and testing new theories about how music cognition appears to work.

THE AUDITORY EXPERIENCE

It takes only a few moments contemplating any music to realise that there are so many shapes and gestures in simultaneous motion that they must keep a large set of sensors and interpretors in continuous parallel work. We can see physiological evidence of this in the cochlea, in the mass of auditory nerve fibres going from it to one way-station after another. A first reaction might be one of disbelief: surely the brain cannot be coping with all that data! What we first need to understand is the nature of the parallelism, the degree to which the parallel information is sifted and simplified, and how the complex acoustic surface is reduced to a few parallel strands of semi-interpreted information. We will begin by taking a closer look at the what the cochlea apparently does.

Spectral Sensors

The human ear probes the external world with some 2,000 hair-cell sensors, each sending different firing patterns along its 20 or so attached nerve fibres. The distribution of hair cells is roughly logarithmic with frequency, save for clustering in the middle-high registers that leads to increased frequency sensitivity. It was once believed that each hair cell acted independently, sending its own report for the brain to arbitrate and sort out as best it could. Recent research has shown that much of the simplification happens right in the cochlea, and that the information passed on is already reduced to a few elements.

An example is seen in some data analysis reported by Secker-Walker and Searle (1990). When a simple speech sound was sent to the ear of a cat, and about 200 of its auditory nerve fibres were monitored for their response, a time-domain analysis revealed the patterns shown in Fig. 13.1. (The case for humans would be similar.) In the diagram the nerve fibres are aligned by their characteristic frequency (CF, shown left in KHz), which is the frequency to which each fibre is individually most responsive. Time proceeds from left to right, and is measured in milliseconds. In response to the stimulus, the neural firing rate for each fibre (summed over dozens of repetitions) is seen to exhibit periodic bursts of activity. The period for the low fibres (CF around 250Hz) is about 8.3 milliseconds, corresponding to a speech fundamental of 120Hz. Medium-low fibres (around 700Hz) peak collectively about every 2 milliseconds (500Hz), and medium fibres (around 1600Hz) peak collectively about every 0.7 milliseconds (1400Hz). There is also collective peaking every 0.4 milliseconds (2500Hz) as well as every 8.3 milliseconds (120 Hz) in the high CF fibres.

We can interpret this data for some facts relevant to our musical needs. First, it is apparent that auditory nerve fibres do not restrict their concerns to just their CF ratings. Most of them are willing to "vote as a block" if it concerns something in their vicinity, and some blocks collectively send two or more reports when these will not be confused. The latter is interesting: the 120Hz period sent by the high CF fibres is identical to the fundamental period reported by the low CF fibres. The high CF report is due to the "beating" that occurs when two or more harmonics of the fundamental fit within a single critical band (about 1/3 octave for most filters in this region), and this will be the case for all harmonics above the sixth. What Fig. 13.1 tells us is that if we are listening to an instrument with almost no energy at the fundamental (such as the bassoon), that will be just fine since, even though the low CF fibres will have nothing to report, the high CF fibres will send a loud and clear pitch message anyway.

Of most relevance, and perhaps most surprising, is the "block voting" effect. It appears that the natural harmonics of the glottal speech stimulus have almost no representation in the cochlea reports. Instead of 120Hz being supported by 240, 360, 480, etc. we see only 500, 1400 and 2500. What are these? They are the frequencies of the speech formants (resonances), here being encoded temporally for transmission and later processing. Not only are they not coincident with the simple harmonics, but on closer inspection the three formants are slowly changing their periods in two different directions while the fundamental remains stationary. Far from sending a mass of Fourier transformed audio data for the brain to worry about, the 40,000 fibres are sending just 4 pieces of information: the perceptual fundamental (whether or not present), and the three resonant frequencies that characterise a particular vowel quality (this one being the short a).

The lesson learned here is that the essence of both pitch and musical timbre is already determined in this early processing, and we would be safe in basing our computer pitch detectors and timbral recognisers on processing of this form. The key lies in the method used to process the data, for the information sent on by the cochlea does not take the form of Fig. 13.2a, but that of Fig. 13.2b. Figure 13.2a

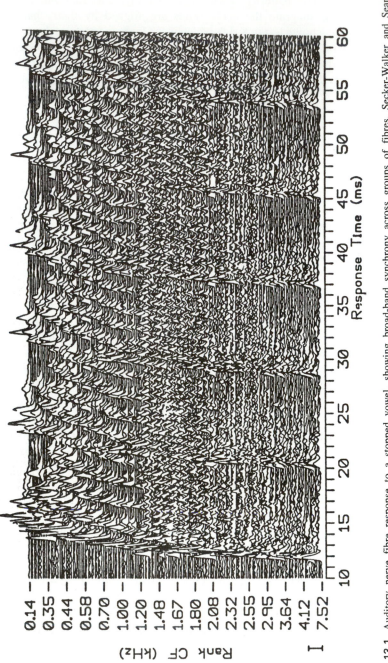

FIG. 13.1. Auditory nerve fibre response to a stopped vowel, showing broad-band synchrony across groups of fibres. Secker-Walker and Searle (1990). Used by permission.

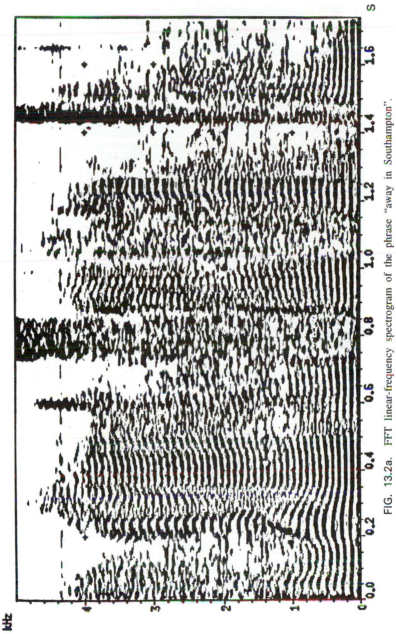

FIG. 13.2a. FFT linear-frequency spectrogram of the phrase "away in Southampton".

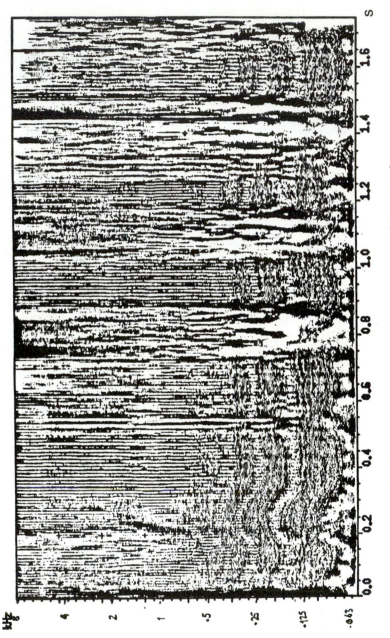

FIG. 13.2b. Constant Q log-frequency spectrogram of the same phrase.

312

is a mathematically convenient view of the utterance "away in Southampton". It is a computer representation, obtained via a Fast Fourier Transform (FFT) which has computational elegance and gets the job done in record time. This kind of "spectrogram" is often still seen in texts and in legal proceedings, yet it does not represent what the cochlea reports: it has linearly spaced filter bins (y-axis) with the same bandwidth at all frequencies, while the cochlea has near logarithmic spacing of hair cell frequencies with roughly proportional bandwidths (constant ratio to the CF). The FFT gives poor frequency resolution in the lower octaves, and too much in the upper, and since its bandwidths are constant it entirely misses the "beating" that can make up for a missing fundamental.

Figure 13.2b is a logarithmic analysis of the same speech phrase. The filters are log spaced in frequency (see the KHz on the left) and constant Q (bandwidths have constant ratio to the CF). This means that medium- to high-frequency filters are broad-band, which makes them quick to respond to changes; they will also exhibit "beating" above the sixth harmonic, which accounts for the vertical striations visible in the figure. A closer view is seen in Fig. 13.2c, which shows a similar analysis of the word "spoil". The constant Q filters give separate resolution to the lower six harmonics, above which the "oi" formant motion is being pulse-modulated by the vertical striations of the broadband higher filters. (Comparison with Fig. 13.1, though upside down in frequency, is informative here.) Mammals have an abundance of broad-band filters; the fast response is ideal for sensing data where precision timing is critical. In mid-range this helps a binaural system sense the direction of a sound. At higher frequencies the pulse-time perturbations would help collect all the harmonics emanating from a soft, life-theatening footstep into a single percept. In music we have learned to capitalise on fast-acting filters. An effective time-marking percussion instrument is one with a predominance of high frequencies. And the violin is successful because its broad spectral nuances are gathered aurally into a single meaningful note-event. A computer with broad-band high-frequency filters would have full access to this timing and integrating information.

Spectral Separators

In addition to sensing the musical structure of a single line, humans also experience the extra dimension of polyphonic music. Because of the low conscious effort seemingly required to do multivoice audio tracking, most human musical cultures have developed complex polyphonic or polyrhythmic traditions. They have developed instruments (like the piano) whose apprehension depends on skilful signal separation, and composers and orchestrators have felt free to punctuate their melodic lines with rhythmic chords and percussive effects. Yet we know very little about how the auditory system does multi-source signal separation. From where amongst the mass of mixed partials does it find the grouping cues? One clue stems from the work of McAdams

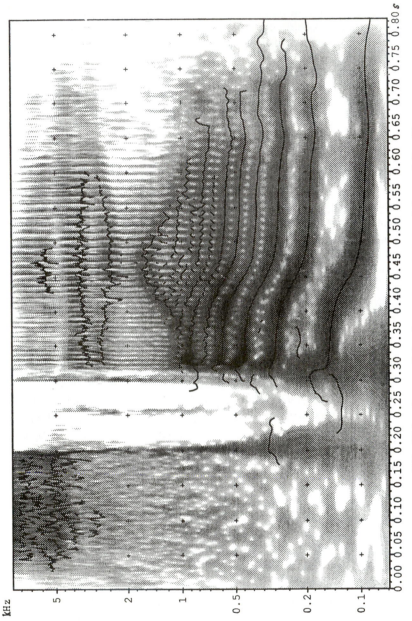

FIG. 13.2c. Constant Q log-frequency spectrogram of the word "spoil".

(1984), who showed that if the harmonic partials of three synthetic vowel sounds are summed with no vibrato or amplitude motion, it is impossible for the human ear to separate and recognise them; yet if those of any group are given some coherent frequency motion, they will fuse into a separate recognisable vowel sound. The effect is especially strong if the motion also causes amplitude change, as when partials are being independently modified by steeply shaped resonances.

It seems that sound from a natural vibrating system conveys a signature in the form of micro-perturbations—amplitude and frequency modulations that distinguish its partials from those of other sources. We observe with characteristic hindsight that when instrument makers of the mid-1500's experimented on the early viol with motion-inducing enhancements (removal of frets to permit vibrato; an ornate body for steeper resonances) they "invented" the modern violin (aurally more separable, the future vehicle of the concerto). We also note that when two strings are driven by the same bow, the coupling is still loose enough to impart two distinct perturbation patterns to the mix.

Signal separation is a complex problem, and the challenge of emulating what the human ear does so well (both in and out of the concert hall) has been squarely confronted by researchers in the emerging field of Computational Auditory Scene Analysis. The most effective techniques first divide the signal into energy strands (using roughly constant Q-filters), find the local energy peaks amongst neighbouring frequencies (block voting), then group the energy tracks into clusters which likely stem from a single source (exhibit common onset time, integer frequency ratios, and co-modulation of frequency, amplitude and phase) (Ellis, 1994). These techniques are showing much progress, and will eventually allow computers to do things like polyphonic pitch tracking and multi-timbral identification with the confidence of skilled musicians.

In the meantime, we cannot simply ignore the polyphonic problem. Although music in some cultures is primarily melodic (e.g. Native-American chant with slow drum accompaniment), that of most cultures incorporates multi-source strands in which the interpretation of one strand (either rhythmic or harmonic) is informed by its relation to events in another. Such powerful influences need some kind of representation and this remains one of our goals, even though machine separation of a polyphonic web is still inferior to that of the average music listener. We can see this most easily in the rhythmic domain.

Events and Event Patterns

What is a musical event, how is it encoded, and what induces the hierarchy of events that we describe as musical rhythm? We can look to neurophysiology for some initial assistance. While investigating auditory-nerve firing rates due to simple tone-bursts at different energy levels, Delgutte (1980) found a two-stage encoding process that appeared to treat event onsets and their steady-state continuation in quite different ways. During event onsets the neural firing rate at first exhibits a very rapid increase, then a rapid adaptation, after which it eventually settles on a steady state acknowledgement of the event's continued presence. Significantly, the energy level (note intensity) was encoded almost entirely in the onset flash (lasting about 10 milliseconds); a second adaptation (50 milliseconds) and the steady state continuation gave only mild recognition to the intensity of the event. In subsequent research (Smith, Brachman & Goodman, 1983) it was found that an event with a slow onset receives a compromise encoding; the peak firing rate depends on the slope of the envelope and its target intensity.

What do these two neurophysiological results suggest for computational music cognition? The first can be taken almost literally. We have always known that note attacks are important: if one builds an electronic 'pipe' organ with no simulated acoustic chiff at each onset it simply fails to support the literature; and we see that composers annotate the important with fortepiano (fp) markings and percussive doublings. Consequently, a simple event detector and rhythm interpreter might encode Delgutte-like onset-only pulses (the louder the stronger), then look for patterns. But the second result above (slow onsets) suggests that something else is going on. To investigate that we turn to perceptual psychology.

Any perceived event tends to have a persistence in the perceiver. Persistence (impulse response) can model phenomena as distinct as two-tone forward masking and the perception of accents in equitone sequences. This latter was studied by Povel and Okkerman (1981), who presented subjects with equitone sequences (same frequency, intensity, timbre) with slightly different inter-onset intervals. When the inter-onset intervals (alternating long and short) differed from each other by less than 8%, the first of each adjacent note-pair seemed louder. Yet when the difference was increased beyond 8%, the accent seemed to move from the first of the pair to the second (as in a 6/8 lilt). In no case was any physical accent actually present.

So what is happening here? Presumably at least two things. The first effect can be attributed to incomplete recovery from adaptation, making the second note of each group appear softer. But what of the second effect? Given its shorter inter-onset interval, the effect is apparently due to the time we initially need to estimate the energy in a tonal stimulus. The energy of a single pulse is integrated over some 200–300 milliseconds, and when the integration is interrupted by the arrival of another pulse the tail of the first integration is lost. The amount of loss depends on the inter-onset interval, and its significance here apparently exceeds that of incomplete recovery going into the second note. In related research by Zwislocki and Sokolich (1974), when the tones are of different frequency but in the same critical band, the tail of the first actually enhances the integration of the second, suggesting that integrators are perhaps "warmed up" by a nearby preceding tone. But either way the effect is the same: our perception of a lilting sequence is that the first of the adjacent pair is at a lower intensity than the second.

This seemingly simple effect is one of the prime generators of human-perceived rhythm and meter. For within the window of our preferred beat size (about 600 milliseconds), there is a perceptual mechanism that artificially weights the sub-events so that the longer ones seem louder than the shorter ones. Of course, performers know about this: if asked to impart a dotted rhythm so the audience will perceive the beat on the short note, they know they must reverse this effect by giving the short note extra stress (about 4dB according to Povel and Okkerman, 1981). The energy integration curve is not a simple one. To a first approximation it is roughly exponential. A multiple time-constant has been advocated (Todd, 1994), although this possibly involves perceptual/motor constructs. Moreover, in preliminary experiments conducted by the present author the time constant differs widely amongst individuals; it is also frequency dependent, but has not yet been adequately mapped over this domain. About all we can safely say about energy integration is that it is widespread, and has a very large influence on how we hear musical patterns. And it does not occur naturally in machines.

So how can a machine possibly hear musical rhythms the way we hear them? Somehow we need to build the above effect into the collecting mechanism of our musical machine. We could elect to develop a "rule system" that would recognise the condition that causes loudness weighting, then apply some algorithmic modification of the physical signal measurement to simulate the human auditory bias. Imagine the overload, however, when the rule set is applied to a large mass of polyphonic music: would the computer have time to find the beat? A less beleaboured way would be to build this auditory bias into the way spectral analysis filters encode intensity. We have examined two effects above, one in which sudden intensity is encoded in a short-lived firing-rate flash (Delgutte, 1980), the other in which slow-rising intensity and successive pulses demonstrate persistence in the ensuing central auditory system (Povel & Okkerman, 1981; Smith et al., 1983). In all cases the important thing seems to be positive change; note releases and decays do not disturb this system in any significant way. Moreover, short-term adaptation and response to an increasing stimulus each appear to be additive, wherein the increased response is independent of the state of adaptation (Smith & Zwislocki, 1975), and several computational models have been assessed for adherence to this empirical data and for suitability as front-ends to speech recognisers (Hewitt & Meddis, 1991).

However, these can get to be computationally expensive. In order that we might have enough computational power remaining for higher-level realtime polyphonic processing on affordable machines, we might prefer to identify only the most salient causes of the above effects (although one must be vigilant of approximation errors that are amplified by later stages). We could look for a simple representation that combined positive change with impulse response (persistence) in each frequency channel to capture the essence of these auditory effects in a single step. We will use the notion of a Positive Difference Spectrum convolved with an Impulse Response in the representation developed below.

Meanwhile, there has been effective research into computer methods of assessing rhythmic pattern, meter, tempo and place, some using acoustic input and others using MIDI keyboard data. In an early example of realtime acoustic sensing (Vercoe, 1984) a flute was tracked using a combination of optical key sensors and realtime acoustic analysis, and the resulting event sequence compared to a predefined score. The comparison was then used to direct a realtime accompaniment to remain in sync with the soloist, who could speed up or slow down the duo performance at will. The beat tracking used both pitch and timing data, including phase locking onto the metre at two hierarchical levels, and the results were sufficiently stable to be used in public concert performances. Auditory input is also the stimulus for a beat induction model using sensory-motor filters (Todd & Lee, 1994). Two separate filters are tuned to the most natural periods for beats (600ms) and body sway (about 5 seconds), within which events are grouped by temporal proximity, and relative accent is derived from the relative and absolute distance between events.

MIDI keyboard performance data is the source for a connectionist analysis using formal models of entrainment (Large & Kolen, 1994). The event onsets serve to perturb the phase and period of a nonlinear oscillator, variably open to disturbance at certain times during its cycle. This produces a robust beat given complex metrically structured input, but the single oscillator model experiences difficulty when the input is highly expressive and contains heavy rubato.

Extracting expressive content involves a multiple task of identifying a metric grid and tempo, while also discerning the temporal warping of that grid (and oftentimes of polyphonic deviations from it) as parallel channels of communicative information. These channels are charged with expressive power, and true artists are skilled at their manipulation. In a detailed analysis of the renowned Cuban percussion ensemble Los Munequitos de Matanzas (Bilmes, 1993), it was shown that the minute deviations that constitute expressive content are themselves built from tiny temporal atoms (which the author called a Tatum), and that a computer could systematically remove and reinsert these various layers for reinterpreted performance. This line of research shows that computer analysis and representation can go beyond that for which we have either a written notation or even a fully conscious listening sense.

It will be some time before we have computer encoding of the full auditory musical experience. The point of present-day representations is two-fold: to help systematise that which we already know, and to form a basis for more exploratory research. The most demanding test of how well we are doing is de-representation (music performance based on the encoding), and some of the above techniques are happily being developed in this demanding forum. We will next examine an encoding method that is embedded in a system designed for realtime audio signal analysis and synthesis, one in which the critical performance check is always available.

COMPUTER REPRESENTATIONS

We now describe a comprehensive environment for realtime audio processing in which the concepts introduced above can be embodied as processes operating on data. Csound is a software audio processing system with a rich array of processing modalities and the capacity to do its work in realtime (Vercoe & Ellis, 1990). It is widely distributed as freeware to research communities, is well documented, and has a large community of users who lend mutual assistance through various networks. The examples given below can be run on the standard distribution. They are not intended to prove a theory, but rather to demonstrate a unified system for modelling music perception and cognition using acoustic-only input. The reader is invited to test these and develop them further (see Appendix 7: Adding your own Cmodules to Csound, in (Vercoe, 1995)).

Using acoustic input, we will first develop a model for encoding auditory processes that exhibits human-like response to rhythmic structure—the phenomenon resulting from the interaction of perceptual grouping and higher-level preference rules. We will then use the structure to extract a tempo which can drive other parts of this realtime system. As a convenient guide to where we are, we will also include a pitch tracker. The overall plan is outlined in Fig. 13.3, and the program that implements it is shown in Fig. 13.4. The program syntax is a simple one: the central column describes a sequence of operations on data; the input data (if any) is on its right and the results of an operation are assigned to its left. Results appearing on the left of an operation are then available as input to any subsequent operation. There are three types of results, distinguishable by name: those beginning with "a" are audio signals, names beginning with "w" are spectral data types, and names beginning with "k" are control signals. Audio signal rates are set to carry high-fidelity audio, and control signal rates are set to convey data at roughly the speed of neural communication (about 1KHz).

Given acoustic input (a segment of Keith Jarret's performance of Bach's G minor Fugue from Book I of the WTC), accessing the signal is programmed by the monaural input operator 'in', which places audio data into 'asig'. To get a spectral representation we pass 'asig' to a spectrum analyser 'spectrum', which divides the signal into 96 bands (8 octaves, 12 bands per octave) to simulate nerve fibre transmission (each "fibre" corresponds to one semitone on a piano). The filters are constant Q with a Q of 8 (CF/bandwidth), and their output in decibels is reported as a new spectrum 'wsig1' every 0.01 seconds. Since it is known that the human auditory periphery biases its loudness assessment along Fletcher-Munson curves (due to the outer-middle ear transfer function and the non-linear spread of response along the basilar membrane), we employ the 'specscal' unit to reshape our spectral data in similar fashion. We could have

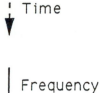

Time

Frequency

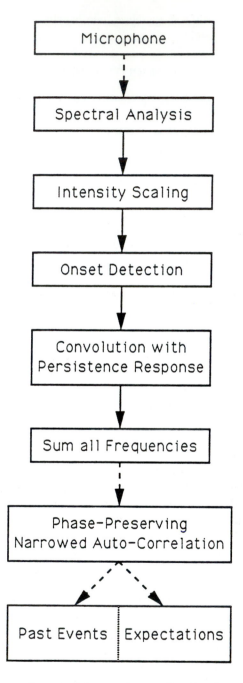

FIG. 13.3. Sequence of audio operations needed to perform auditory-based analysis of rhythmic acoustic input.

320

```
              sr = 32000
              kr =  1000
              ksmps = 32

              instr   1
asig          in
wsig1         spectrum asig,  .01,  8,  12,  8,  0,  1,  0
wsig2         specscal wsig1,  3,  4
wsig3         specdiff wsig2
wsig4         specfilt wsig3,  5
              specdisp wsig1,  .04,  0
              specdisp wsig3,  .04,  0
              specdisp wsig4,  .04,  0
ksum4         specsum   wsig4,  1
ktempo        tempest   ksum4,.01,.1,3,1,30,.005,.5,90,2,.04,1
koct,ka       specptrk  wsig1,  1.3,  7.4,  8.9,  8.1,  25,  3,  .5
koct          =         (koct > 7.4 ?   koct-7.4 : 0)
              display   koct,  .04,  72
              out       asig
              endin
```

FIG. 13.4. Csound program to perform auditory-based analysis of rhythmic acoustic input.

done this prior to spectral filtering, but prefer to do it here because the data is now in decibels and we can use a log frequency mapping across the spectral data.

The program of Fig. 13.4 is also seen to contain three spectral display requests ('specdisp'), which are projected in this case using X11 windows on an SGI monitor. The output of these are shown in Fig. 13.5a, b, and c, but to interpret them we must first understand something of the way time is handled in this realtime program. As stated above, the 'spectrum' opcode derives a new spectral cross-section every 0.01 seconds, which is thus the rate at which the 'wsig' cells are refreshed with new information. Each unit receiving a refreshed 'wsig' cell then has work to do. The 'specdisp' units, however, are asked to display only every 0.04 seconds (or 25 times a second), and the screen images are therefore downsampled snapshots of the 0.01 spectral cross-sections. The three spectra of Fig. 13.5 are thus snapshots of momentary spectra at a specific point in the acoustic signal, that point being made clear in Fig. 13.6a, b, and c, all three of which are time displays. In Fig. 13.6a the point is labelled "now", and in Fig. 13.6c the point is the onset of the final D4 of the treble fugal entry.

Returning to the spectral processing, Fig. 13.5a is a snapshot of the momentary decibel values emanating from the 96 filters. The output is visibly smooth, due to the broad-band filters used. This would have been even smoother had we used strict 1/3-octave filters (Q of 4), but our choice of 1/6 octave (Q of 8) for our sparse, symmetric filters is to acknowledge the very steep cutoff of human auditory filters (the cochlea has about 400 overlapping bands/octave in this region, and its filters are asymetric with a cutoff on one side of hundreds of db per

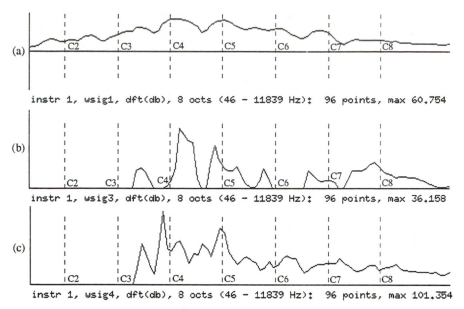

instr 1, wsig1, dft(db), 8 octs (46 - 11839 Hz):   96 points, max 60.754

instr 1, wsig3, dft(db), 8 octs (46 - 11839 Hz):   96 points, max 36.158

instr 1, wsig4, dft(db), 8 octs (46 - 11839 Hz):   96 points, max 101.354

FIG. 13.5. (a) Constant Q spectral snapshot of the F3/D4 dyad of the Bach excerpt (piano). (b) Positive difference spectrum (PDS) reflecting the spectral changes currently occurring in (a). (c) Spectral output of persistence filters following the injection of all PDS data up to the moment of 13.5b.

octave). As implied above, the spectrum of Fig. 13.5a will be Fletcher-Munson scaled before being passed to the next unit.

The task of onset detection is performed by 'specdiff'. As shown earlier, neural firing rates become intensely active during event onsets, and we have theorised that representing the onset slope by a sequence of positive changes (and ignoring the negatives) might capture this sensitivity. 'Specdiff' creates a new spectrum, comprised of just the positive changes seen in each filter channel from one spectral cross-section to the next (every 0.01 seconds). The resulting positive difference spectrum (PDS) can be seen in Fig. 13.5b. Also evident in this figure is the energy just being received from the pitches of the newest notes F3/D4.

We now inject the PDS into a set of persistence filters using 'specfilt'. These are simple recursive filters, one per spectral channel, with individual rates of sustaining new input specified in half-life values (the period for which any new input is reduced to one-half the original). The values are kept in a table (no. 5), and were set by running experiments in the style of Povel and Okkerman, extended to include frequency dependence. The effect of injecting PDS impulses into the filters is to accumulate and prolong the perceptual life of events. The result of this step can be seen in Fig. 13.5c, where the latest PDS of Fig. 13.5b has just been added to the persistence mix.

The energy in the total spectrum is now estimated by summing across the frequency bins of 'wsig4' using 'specsum'. This approximates the summation that occurs when humans assess the loudness of complex tones; there has been much work done on this (Zwicker & Fastl, 1990), and we could develop more accurate methods that incorporate frequency-related suppression. However, the real goal of our summing is to compare energies across time, so we will accept the approximation. Next, the sequence of energy estimates in 'ksum' is examined over small time-intervals using 'tempest'. We use a window size of three seconds to loosely relate it to echoic memory, but the real point of "tempest" is to detect the presence of regular patterns and to estimate the tempo of their recurrence.

The display generated by 'tempest' (Fig. 13.6a) gives the best view of its operation. Unlike the above, this display is time-based, and information is seen moving across the entire window as time passes. The display is in two parts, separated by a vertical line that represents 'now'. The data to its left is the three-second echoic memory, and information that begins at the 'now' (coincident with what you hear) moves increasingly left over this period, gradually decaying

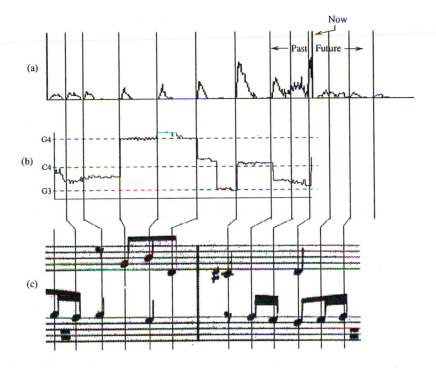

FIG. 13.6. (a) Time-magnitude representation of the perceptual importance of events emerging from the summed persistence filters. The 3-second windows on either side of the central "now" represent the immediate past (left) and the expected future (right). (b) Pitch analysis of the events of 13.6a. (c) Score fragment of Bach Fugue used as acoustic input for the spectral, rhythmic and pitch analysis of Figures 13.5 and 13.6.

to zero as it leaves the screen. The data on the right is a prediction of the future; information beginning small at its right will gather strength as it moves left towards the "now". There is interaction between the perceptual past and the anticipated future: as each expected event hits the "now" some portion of it is rolled into what becomes "perceived". Conversely, the pattern of already perceived events contributes via a feed-forward network to the growth of expectations.

The feed-forward network within 'tempest' is a variant of the Narrowed Auto-Correlation (NAC) algorithm developed by Brown and Puckette (1989). There is growing evidence that the auditory system uses autocorrelation in post-peripheral processing (Hartman, 1989), but the once-popular method lost favour because it did not account for the high resolutions and small JND's evident in practice. Narrowed auto-correlations do not have this problem. The general function is defined by:

$$\left|S_N(\tau)\right|^2 = <\left|f(t)+f(t-\tau)+f(t-2\tau)....+f(t-\overline{N-1}\tau)\right|^2$$

and the peaks have a width of 2T/N, where T is the period (2PI/w), and N the number of terms used. The NAC method has recently been used to sharpen the analysis of auditory-nerve firing patterns (de Cheveigne, 1989). Our use of it here for echoic memory pattern recognition is of course on a very different time scale, but the technique appears equally useful and extendable.

The problem with auto-correlations is that the resulting function is zero-phase. In order that our rhythmic analysis can preserve its placement in time, and can develop expectations about the future, we have developed a Phase-Preserving Narrowed Autocorrelation (PPNAC). The result is not only a sharpened account of past rhythmic activity, but a gradual formation of expected events (Fig. 13.6a). As the expectations move into current time, they are confirmed by the arrival of new peaks in the auditory analysis; if the acoustic source fails to inject new energy, the expectations will atrophy over the same short-term memory interval. Implementation of this as chain of cognitive processes devoted to temporal event patterns is not hard to imagine.

A musically interesting feature falls out as a simple property of PPNAC analysis: the additive combination of multiple terms will also tender reports at frequencies that are the harmonics of the actual stimuli. That is to say, a regular pulse of quarter-notes will induce a weak prediction of eighth-note activity, and a weaker expectation of triplet-eighths, sixteenths, and so on. The listener perceiving a quarter-note phrase is thus already prepared for its natural sub-divisions. It is important to realise that this listener need not be experienced, nor even paying much attention. But the grid for rhythmic hierarchy is already there.

Finally, the acoustic input is scanned for identifiable pitches by the unit "specptrk", and a scaled version of its output is displayed in Fig. 13.6b. As seen in the program, the pitch tracker uses the same spectral data as the event and tempo detectors, and its response is reasonably accurate. On close examination, the treble B-flat is at first accurately estimated then quit in favour of the G below. In fact the performer had articulated this phrase with a very short B-flat; the G is an octave error of the lower sounding G (which the tracker does get when the performer also releases the next D).

All the elements of Fig. 13.5a, b, c and Fig.13.6a, b were generated and displayed in realtime by the program of Fig. 13.4, with acoustic input direct from a CD.

CONCLUSION

We have shown that acoustic input can be the stimulus for computational models of an entire range of processes involved in the perception and cognition of music, and the prospect of how to organise this is now receiving serious thought (Leman, 1994). Parsing an acoustic signal for hierarchical rhythmic content is a case of determining the relative auditory importance of the acoustic events. A computer representation of the auditory processes involved can lead to confirmation of theories; it can also lead to systems for automatic sensing and interactive performance. It is clear that the auditory system has evolved some elegant solutions to the various problems, and a big challenge in computer representation is to match that elegance. The example of spectral formants quickly inducing wholesale synchrony across large groups of auditory fibres (Secker-Walker & Searle, 1990) is a model for that cause.

The questions we would like to pose are of the form "how do pitch and rhythmic hierarchies arise, how do they operate, how do they achieve flexibility and robustness, and how much computation do they take?" The above model is computationally efficient (it runs in realtime), but does not readily accommodate things like tempo modulation. When the metrical stimulus changes pace, both the PPNAC and expectations become time-smeared. Although this permits adequate tracking of slow tempo changes, it does not handle the extreme changes in tempo rubato that we have successfully modelled elsewhere (Vercoe & Puckette, 1985). If focused listening begins from the model we have outlined above, it must also be paying attention to short-time transforms, from which it can construct other representations that are strongly tempo-variable. This can be investigated using other facets of the Csound processing language, but that work still remains to be done.

The purpose of representing musical processes by computer should however be clear. The approach is one that permits theories of music cognitive processes to be posed, tested, and incrementally explored. The goal is to find how complex musical data is represented and processed by the human auditory-cognitive system. Only then will we understand why the music that exploits this capacity has the structure it does.

REFERENCES

Bilmes, J. (1993). *Timing is of the Essence: Perceptual and Computational Techniques for Representing, Learning, and Reproducing Expressive Timing in Percussive Rhythm.* (MS Thesis, Media Lab, Mass. Inst. Technology).

Brown, J., & Puckette, M. (1989). Calculation of a Narrowed Autocorrelation Function. *Journal of the Acoustical Society of America, 85*(4), 1595–1601.

de Cheveigne, A. (1989). Pitch and the narrowed autocoincidence histogram. *Proceedings of the 1st International Conference on Music Perception and Cognition* (pp. 67–70).

Delgutte, B. (1980). Representation of speech-like sound in the discharge patterns of auditory nerve fibers. *Journal of the Acoustical Society of America, 68*(3), 843–857.

Ellis, D. (1994). A computer implementation of psychoacoustic grouping rules. *Proceedings of the 12th International Conference on Pattern Recognition* (C108–C112). Jerusalem, Israel.

Hartman, W. (1989). Auditory grouping and the auditory periphery. *Proceedings of the 1st International Conference on Music Perception and Cognition* (pp. 299–304).

Hewitt, M., & Meddis, R. (1991). An evaluation of eight computer models of mammalian inner hair-cell function. *Journal of the Acoustical Society of America, 90*(2), 904–917.

Large, E., & Kolen, J. (1994). Resonance and the Perception of Musical Meter. *Connection Science, 6,* 177–208.

Leman, M. (1994). Signals, images, schemata, and mental representations. In I. Deliège, (Ed.), *Proceedings of the 3rd International Conference for Music Perception and Cognition* (pp. 203–204). Liège, Belgium: European Society for the Cognitive Sciences of Music.

McAdams, S. (1984). *Spectral fusion, spectral parsing, and the formation of auditory images.* (Ph.D. dissertation, Stanford University).

Povel, D., & Okkerman, H. (1981). Accents in equitone sequences. *Perception & Psychophysics, 30,* 565–572.

Richard, D.M. (1994). Name that tune: the Turing test revisited. In I. Deliège, (Ed.), *Proceedings of the 3rd International Conference for Music Perception and Cognition* (pp. 175–176). Liège, Belgium: European Society for the Cognitive Sciences of Music.

Secker-Walker, H., & Searle, C. (1990). Time-domain analysis of auditory-nerve-fiber firing rates. *Journal of the Acoustical Society of America, 88,* 1427–1436.

Smith, R., Brachman, M., & Goodman, D. (1983). Adaptation in the auditory periphery. In Parkins & Anderson, (Eds.), *Cochlear prosthesis. Annals of New York Academy of Sciences, Vol 405,* 79–93.

Smith, R., & Zwislocki, J. (1975). Short-term adaptation and incremental responses of single auditory nerve fibers. *Biological Cybernetics, 17,* 169–182.

Todd, N. (1994). The auditory primal sketch. *Journal of New Music Research, 23*(1), 25–70.

Todd, N., & Lee, C. (1994). An Auditory-Motor Model of Beat Induction. *Proceedings of the International Computer Music Conference.*

Vercoe, B. (1984). The Synthetic Performer in the Context of Live Performers. *Proceedings of the International Computer Music Conference* (pp.199–200).

Vercoe, B. (1995). *Csound: A manual for the Audio Processing System and Supporting Programs with Tutorials.* Cambridge, Mass: Media Lab, MIT.

Vercoe, B., & Ellis, D. (1990). Realtime Csound: Software Synthesis with Sensing and Control. *Proceedings of the International Computer Music Conference* (pp.209–211).

Vercoe, B., & Puckette, M. (1985). Synthetic Rehearsal: Training the Synthetic Performer. *Proceedings of the International Computer Music Conference* (pp.275–278).

Zwicker, E., & Fastl, H. (1990). *Psychoacoustics.* Berlin: Springer-Verlag.

Zwislocki, J., & Sokolich, W. (1974). On loudness enhancement of a tone burst by a preceding tone burst. *Perception and Psychophysics, 16,* 87–90.

V Structural Approaches

14 Tonal relations

Lola L. Cuddy
Department of Psychology, Queen's University, Kingston, Canada

An important development for music perception and cognition in the last few decades is the flourishing interaction between experimental and music-theoretic approaches to systematic issues. According to Krumhansl (1995), the current psychological literature contains many and varied instances of the exchange urged in the 1950s in the writings of Meyer (1956) and Francès (1958/1988). Empirical studies of tonal relations, for example, have led to quantitative descriptions of listeners' implicit knowledge of music-theoretic constructs; these descriptions portray the consistency and reliability of the internal representation of traditional tonal-harmonic structures. Moreover, and more recently, proposed theoretical structures for contemporary music have been subjected to experimental test, and the results have informed both analysis of psychological processes and critical evaluation of the theory. A particularly strong test of psychological proposals for music perception and cognition is offered when proposals are evaluated in the context of contemporary music (or composed excerpts with specially controlled properties).

In this chapter, I will provide an overview of the research issues engaged in our study of tonal relations (Cuddy, 1991, 1994), and will illustrate some connections between empirical results and music-theoretic constructs. I will first comment on the role of quantification and will illustrate research methods directed toward the quantification of the tonal hierarchy, taking the approach of Krumhansl and colleagues (Krumhansl, 1990). Next I will note convergence of the description of the tonal hierarchy that emerges from research findings with the description of stability conditions in Lerdahl's (1988a, 1988b, 1989) extension of his tonal theory with Jackendoff (Lerdahl & Jackendoff, 1983). These considerations lead to questions about the constraints that are implied by the study of tonal relations within the Western tonal-harmonic system. I will then pursue the notion that principles of tonal relations, from both empirical and music-theoretic perspectives, may be applied to the study of listeners' sensitivity to nontonal music structures.

QUANTIFICATION OF THE TONAL HIERARCHY

The study of tonality requires the analysis of complexity at many different levels, and is a challenge far beyond the scope of this chapter. I will deal primarily with elementary levels of description—the levels where the greatest control of experimental contexts can be obtained. This focus does not, however, mean that the findings are musically and psychologically trivial. On the contrary, the study of elementary levels conveys rich information about the delicate interface and interplay between the psychological processes of music perception and cognition. When musical elements as simple as scales and chord progressions engage a sense of tonality, we have evidence for many processes— the detection of raw acoustic attributes, detection of intervallic relationships, classification and categorisation, abstraction of a hierarchy of functions, and the application of knowledge. To illustrate: given the simple element C E G, a sense of the key of C depends on the input of sensory pitch information from the three sounded tones, the processing of relative information among the intervals formed by these tones, the detection of a tonal centre, C, from the pattern formed by the intervals, the assignment of function to the other tones sounded, and, finally, the assignment of function to tones not sounded. For example, once the key of C is established, our knowledge of tonal relations establishes the function of F even if F has not been sounded.

The above description is straight-forward, but detailed understanding of the nature, timing, and availability of the psychological processes engaged is not. To conduct research on these issues, a means of quantifying listeners' sense of tonality is needed. With a quantitative approach, we can evaluate listeners' sensitivity under different conditions, and examine how sensitivity changes with relationship to factors such as musical context, attention, learning, age, experience, and culture. Quantification provides a tool for testing the predictions of various theoretical formulations.

An important methodological contribution to the issue of quantification, called the probe-tone technique, was initiated in the late 1970's by C. L Krumhansl and R. N. Shepard (see Krumhansl & Shepard, 1979); subsequent developments are summarised in Krumhansl (1990). Two versions have been constructed, the single-probe and the double-probe technique. In the single-probe technique, a listener is presented with a musical context followed by a probe tone, one of the 12 tones of the chromatic scale. In a typical paradigm, the listener is asked to rate how well the probe tone fits the context in a musical sense. The set of 12 probe-tone ratings for a context is called the probe-tone profile for that context. In the double-probe technique, the listener is presented with a musical context followed by two probe tones, a pair of tones selected from the 12 tones of the chromatic scale. The listener is asked to judge the musical relationship, or similarity of function, of the first tone to the second tone, given the context.

Figure 14.1 displays standardised probe-tone profiles, collected by the single-probe technique, for the keys of C major and C minor (Krumhansl & Kessler, 1982). Profiles were obtained for contexts consisting of tonic triads, and chord cadences, and then averaged to form the standardised profiles shown in Fig. 14.1. The averaging of profiles is an important point to note; the standardised profiles are not intended to reflect local variation dependent on specific context, but, rather, reflect the overall regularity contained in profiles obtained from key-defining contexts. Thus, they provide a standard against which specific profiles, obtained in specific cases, can be compared.

Inspection of Fig. 14.1 reveals that the standardised profiles capture the hierarchy of function described by traditional music theory: the tonic receives the highest rating, followed by the other tones of the tonic triad, followed by the other scale tones, followed, finally, by the tones outside the scale.

The reliability and validity of tonal hierarchy measures collected by the probe-tone technique have been repeatedly demonstrated in our laboratory and elsewhere. One example is research conducted in collaboration with Willi Steinke (Steinke, Cuddy, & Holden, 1993; Steinke, Cuddy, & Peretz, 1994). Probe-tone ratings for musical contexts consisting of cadences in both the major and minor keys and a tonal melody in the major key were collected from a large sample of participants (n = 100) over a wide range of age, formal education, and music training. Reliability was demonstrated in the finding that the ratings for all contexts reflected the levels of the tonal hierarchy recovered in the standardised profiles.

Moreover, validity was demonstrated in the finding that participants' abilities to produce the levels of the tonal hierarchy in the probe-tone profiles were intercorrelated with other tests of sensitivity to tonal relations. These other tests included judgement of melodic endings, discrimination of tonal from atonal melodies, and discrimination of tonally conventional from non-conventional chord progressions. All tests involved ranking the most to least tonal stimulus along a continuum of tonality. Further analyses revealed that the intercorrelations could not be completely explained in terms of amount of musical training or in terms of performance on intelligence measures or other nonmusic tests of cognitive ability (e.g. standardised tests of abstraction, vocabulary, and memory).

At Liège, we reported the results of factor analyses and model testing of these data (Steinke, Cuddy, & Peretz, 1994). A principle-components analysis

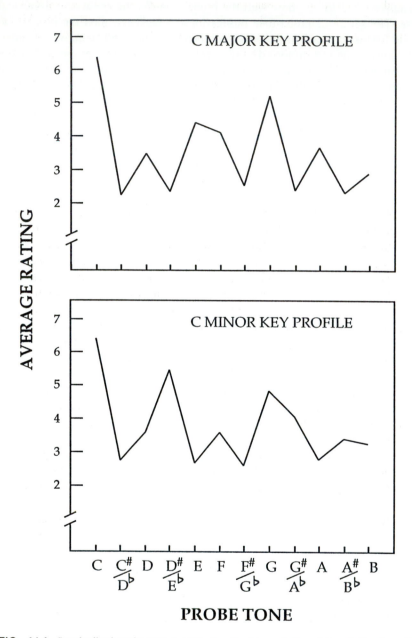

FIG. 14.1. Standardised probe-tone profiles for the keys of C major and C minor. From *Tracing the dynamic changes in perceived tonal organization in a spatial representation of musical keys* by C. L. Krumhansl and E. J. Kessler, 1982, *Psychological Review, 89*, p. 343. Copyright 1982 by the American Psychological Association. Redrawn with permission.

revealed a dissociation between the music tests and the nonmusic tests; music tests loaded on one factor and the nonmusic tests on a second factor. Model testing ruled out alternative solutions, including dissociation between abstraction vs nonabstraction tests, auditory vs nonauditory tests and linguistic vs nonlinguistic tests.

In addition, we reported the data from a neurologically impaired individual, CN, who had a history of bilateral temporal-lobe surgery. CN had been classified as amusic but not aphasic (Peretz & Kolinsky, 1993). Compared to controls matched for age, gender, formal education and musical background, CN scored much lower on the music tests, but scored much the same on the nonmusic tests. Her data were consistent with the notion that there is functional specificity for certain music abilities; in the present instance there was a specific loss of tonal encoding of musical pitch.

Another validation of the tonal hierarchy measure recovered by the probe-tone technique has been obtained from studies of sensitivity to key shifts or modulations in a musical passage. Krumhansl and Kessler (1982) constructed chord sequences in which the type of modulation contained in each sequence was derived from Piston's (1987) table of harmonic progressions. Probe-tone profiles were collected for each successive chord in each sequence. The findings outline how a sense of the first key of the sequence becomes established and then changes, over time, to a sense of the second key. Comparison of the findings for the different modulation types (e.g. near vs distant) were interpretable in terms of music-theoretic expectations, and also informed psychological descriptions of the unfolding processes tracking key movement in time.

Bill Thompson and I have pursued the application of probe-tone techniques to track the shifting sense of key in excerpts from Bach chorales (Cuddy & Thompson, 1992). More recently, we have been studying listeners' sensitivity to modulations in harmonised sequences based on melodies composed by Hindemith (1968). In the course of this work, we have been analysing the performance expression for the sequences provided by an expert pianist (Thompson & Cuddy, 1994, in press), and we presented some of these data at Liège.

Judgements of key movement were obtained for harmonised sequences presented without performance expression in one experiment, and with performance expression provided by the pianist in a second experiment. Sequences contained modulations of either 0, 2, 4 or 6 steps around the cycle of fifths. When performance expression was provided, judgements of key movement conformed more closely to predictions based on models of key-relatedness (Krumhansl & Kessler, 1982) than when performance expression was absent.

Next we examined the expressive variations introduced by the pianist (coded as MIDI data) and compared the variations with the values of the standardised profiles for the keys of the sequences. This comparison revealed that the pianists's variations in loudness and timing were correlated with the tonal hierarchies of the keys of the sequences. Notes that were tonally stable within a key tended to be played for longer duration in the soprano and bass voices, and softer in the bass voice. The performance thus contained cues about tonal hierarchies that may have influenced listeners' judgements of key and key movement.

THE TONAL HIERARCHY AND STABILITY CONDITIONS

The concept of the tonal hierarchy described above is a summary of response patterns obtained in experimental data—a summary that depicts the relative importance of pitch classes within a key as an abstract hierarchical representation. Arguing from a music-theoretic rather than an empirical perspective, Lerdahl (1988a) proposed a model of tonal pitch space in which the tonal hierarchy, pitch space, and stability conditions are treated as equivalent. Lerdahl's concepts of basic pitch space and stability conditions will next be briefly reviewed.

The basic pitch space proposed by Lerdahl is shown in Fig. 14.2. Lerdahl (1988a), citing Deutsch and Feroe (1981), describes "different pitch 'alphabets'—chiefly the chromatic, diatonic, and triadic—that the listener 'highly overlearns' from previously heard musical surfaces. . . . These alphabets are hierarchically related . . . where each level elaborates into more pcs [pitch classes] at the next smaller level. . . . Level *a* is octave space, *b* 'open fifth' space, *c* triadic space, *d* diatonic space, and *e* chromatic space. Pcs at larger levels are more stable than pcs at smaller levels." (p.320).

Lerdahl (1988a) then introduces the concept of "depth of embedding" which is the count of the number of levels down (from level *a*) that a pitch class first appears. A visual comparison of Figs. 14.1 and 14.2 readily reveals the relationship between the standardised ratings for tones in the probe-tone profile for C major in Fig. 14.1 and the depth of embedding of tones in Fig. 14.2. Tones assigned high ratings in the standardised profile appear at larger levels of the basic space. Tones assigned low ratings in the standardised profile appear at smaller levels—that is, they are deeply embedded in the pitch space.

Stability conditions are identified with tonal hierarchies as "nontemporal mental" schemata (Lerdahl, 1988a, p. 316) for tonal music. The stability conditions are an extended component (Lerdahl, 1988a, 1988b, 1989) of the generative theory of tonal music (Lerdahl & Jackendoff, 1983). Their function, according to the theory, is to provide a distance metric—distances between pitch events—that is referenced by the ongoing processes that infer the temporal structure of music.

In the generative theory of tonal music, the temporal structure of a piece is achieved through reduction of the musical surface. The theory outlines two

level *a*:	C							G				(C)
level *b*:	C							G		A	B	(C)
level *c*:	C				E			G		A	B	(C)
level *d*:	C		D		E	F		G	Ab	A	B	(C)
level *e*:	C	Db	D	Eb	E	F	F#	G	Ab	Bb	B	(C)

The basic space, oriented to I/I.

level *a*:	0											
level *b*:	0							7				
level *c*:	0				4			7				
level *d*:	0		2		4	5		7		9		b
level *e*:	0	1	2	3	4	5	6	7	8	9	a	b

A numerical representation of the basic space, oriented to I/I.

FIG. 14.2. The basic tonal pitch space. From *Tonal pitch space* by F. Lerdahl, 1988, *Music Perception*, 5, p. 321. Copyright 1988 by the Regents of the University of California. Redrawn with permission.

reduction components—*"time-span reduction,* which expresses the relative structural importance of events as heard within rhythmic units; and *prolongational reduction,* which expresses recursive patterns of tension and relaxation among events" (Lerdahl, 1988a, p. 316). Reduction is hypothesised to arise from a listener's efforts "to organize all the pitch-events of a piece into a single coherent structure, such that they are heard in a hierarchy of relative importance" (Lerdahl & Jackendoff, 1983, p. 106).

Bigand (1993) has summarised experimental work supporting the psychological reality of the proposed reduction components. Palmer and Krumhansl (1987a, 1987b), for example, obtained listeners' judgements of the structural importance of the final event of musical excerpts, and found that the judgements corresponded to predictions based on time-span reductions. Bigand's own work, (e.g. Bigand, 1990, 1993), found that listeners' perceptions of tension and relaxation in musical fragments corresponded to descriptions of prolongational structures for the fragments. More recently, Large, Palmer, and Pollack (1995) found support for time-span reduction in their analyses of musicians' improvisations. Improvised variations on melodies tended to preserve the events of greatest structural importance in the time-span reductions.

Figure 14.3 shows the relation of stability conditions to the reduction components. The distinction between stability conditions and the reduction components in the theory has been likened by Lerdahl (1988a) to Bharucha's (1984a, 1984b) distinction between tonal hierarchies and event hierarchies, respectively. Stability conditions and tonal hierarchies are specific to a particular musical idiom—for example, the tonal-harmonic idiom of the classical era—and are representative of all pieces written in the idiom. An event hierarchy, on the other hand, is a temporal schema for the specific sequence of events in a piece of music. In general, event hierarchies are the proposed form in which the musical events of a piece are encoded and remembered (Deutsch & Feroe, 1981; Simon & Sumner, 1968). Thus, they reflect the listener's understanding of a specific piece.

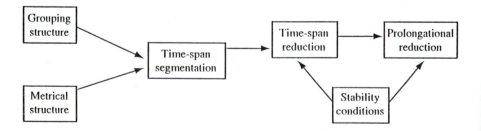

FIG. 14.3. The form of generative music theory. From *Tonal pitch space* by F. Lerdahl, 1988, *Music Perception, 5,* p. 317. Copyright 1988 by the Regents of the University of California. Redrawn with permission.

What is particularly important in the elaboration of the stability conditions provided by Lerdahl (1988a, 1988b, 1989) is the role ascribed to these conditions. A strong claim is made: "Listeners cannot infer complex event hierarchies without having access to [stability] conditions . . . An event hierarchy cannot be constructed without such a schema" (Lerdahl, 1988a, pp. 316–317). Event hierarchies "depend for their operation on *stability conditions* among pitch configurations as considered 'out-of-time' . . . and brought to bear on the in-time event sequences . . ."(Lerdahl, 1988b, p. 238). In other words, understanding a piece of tonal music depends, in part, on the availability and accessibility of a listener's knowledge of tonal relations.

ARE CONSTRAINTS IMPLIED BY STABILITY CONDITIONS?

There is a considerable body of research supporting the idea that abstract knowledge of tonal relations influences perception and memory for musical materials (see reviews by Bigand, 1993; Cuddy, 1993; Dowling & Harwood, 1986; Francès, 1958/1988; Handel, 1989; Jones, 1982; Krumhansl, 1983, 1990). Three examples are detection of a pitch alteration in a melody, accuracy of melody recognition, and accuracy of melodic dictation; all are dependent on the degree of tonal structure present in a melodic pattern and the listener's ability to detect that structure. The critical role of the tonal hierarchy is, therefore, readily demonstrated. The question that arises, however, is: To what degree can there be music understanding if stability conditions are absent? If a musical piece does not contain the pitch structures of the conventional tonal-harmonic idiom, can an unfamiliar pitch structure nevertheless be detected?

Lerdahl (1989) puts the question this way: "Atonal music almost by definition does not have stability conditions. Its pitch space is flat; sensory consonance and dissonance do not have any syntactic counterpart. . . . Listeners to atonal music do not have at their disposal a consistent, psychologically relevant set of principles by which to organize pitches at the musical surface. . . . How then is pitch reduction to be developed?" (p. 73 and p. 84). Lerdahl then makes the following proposal: "Atonal music may not have stability conditions, but it does project the relative salience of events. The absence of stability conditions makes salience cognitively all the more important. I argue that listeners organise atonal surfaces by means of it." (p. 73). A provisional list of salience conditions is provided; these include both global (motivic) and local (surface) factors.

Deliège has proposed a compatible notion in a series of articles (see, for example, Deliège, 1989, 1993, 1995, 1996; Deliège, Mélen, Stammers & Cross, 1994; Mélen & Deliège, 1995). Deliège's work has shown the importance of musical cues in recognition and categorisation for tonal contexts, and particularly for atonal ones. Cues are distinctive features that are automatically preserved (Mélen & Deliège, 1995). "Cue extraction is peripheral and perceptual, here suggested to be a modular system . . . [cues] permit structures to be identified and become a reference for the processes of classification and comparison" (Deliège, 1995, p. 63). Different types of cues may be selected depending on the musical context. These may be motivic (e.g. themes and rhythms) or local properties of the musical surface (e.g. changes in pitch register or textural densities). Listeners are sensitive to the regularities expressed by the cues.

The question whether listeners are sensitive to pitch structure in the musical surface when the structure does not conform to conventional tonality is an ongoing project in our laboratory. The work that I will review below was done in collaboration with Nicholas Oram (Cuddy & Oram, 1996; Oram, 1989; Oram & Cuddy, 1995). As will be seen, we began from a perspective different from that of Lerdahl—that of experimental psychology. We argue, however, that our findings relate to, and support, Lerdahl's (1989) notion of salience conditions and the notion that listeners may pick up pitch structure from the structure available at the musical surface.

This further suggests that, if there is pitch structure in the musical surface, and if this structure is detectable, the listener has an additional and potentially powerful resource for music understanding. Salience conditions provide a means of drawing connections or relations, not merely within temporal groupings but also between temporally distant musical events. As expressed by Deliège in the work cited above, salient events may provide reference points about which other events may be hierarchically categorised.

For these reasons, our research focused on the question of whether listeners are indeed sensitive to salience conditions. As outlined in the next section, previous experimental research and theory suggested different answers to the question.

THE RESEARCH QUESTION

In a series of experiments, we examined whether listeners were sensitive to surface cues to pitch structure when the cues conflicted with the properties of the familiar tonal hierarchy. The surface cue that we examined most closely was the relative frequency with which tones in a musical pattern were sounded. The listeners' sensitivity was assessed by means of the probe-tone technique. Different outcomes were predicted, and these predictions reflected different presuppositions about the rigidity and inflexibility of tonal schema once acquired.

Consider, for example, the evidence supporting the precocity of tonal knowledge, emphasised by Peretz and Morais (1989). Infants less than one year of age can discriminate intervals of the tonal system and can discriminate the major from the augmented triad (for reviews see Trehub 1993; Trehub & Trainor, 1993). Evidence of tonal knowledge has been obtained from very young children, and the full properties of the tonal hierarchy by early school years (Cuddy & Badertscher, 1987; Hargreaves, 1986; Krumhansl & Keil, 1982;

Zenatti, 1993). We cannot conclude that these sensitivities are innate, but we can conclude that there is an early affinity for the regularities of the acoustic structure of the physical world.

Moreover, the music to which both children and adults are exposed in our culture consistently provides instances of tonal structure. For example, the frequency with which tones are sounded in tonal-harmonic music is correlated with relative stability of the tones in the tonal hierarchy (Krumhansl, 1987, 1990). Thus, in day-to-day musical encounters the internal schema for the tonal hierarchy is regularly activated, and becomes highly overlearned. It makes sense to conclude that the tonal schema functions as a perceptual filter facilitating the abstraction of pitch relationships (Lynch, Eilers, Oller, & Urbano, 1991) and, further, that the schema assimilates conflicting information to its structure (Dowling, 1978; Jordan & Shepard, 1987).

Therefore, one possible prediction is that, when listeners encounter for the first time a melody or melody-like pattern with an unfamiliar pitch structure, this structure is undetected. Perhaps only those elements that conform approximately to the tonal hierarchy convey meaning to the listener.

On the other hand, there is also reason to suppose that listeners flexibly and appropriately disengage the tonal hierarchy when the musical context is unfamiliar and attend to surface properties of the music (Deliège, 1989, 1993). Moreover, the results of two probe-tone studies in which tone sequences presented to Western listeners were abstracted from nonWestern idioms support this alternative. For tone sequences derived from the music of north India (Castellano, Bharucha, & Krumhansl, 1984) and of Bali (Kessler, Hansen, & Shepard, 1984), listeners based their probe-tone ratings on the distribution of pitches in the sequences. The more frequent tones—the tones that occupied the greatest number of beats—were rated as better fitting than less frequent tones. These findings suggest considerable listener adaptability to the surface cues of unfamiliar musical contexts.

As noted above, our research is investigating the sensitivity of Western adults to frequency of occurrence of tones in musical contexts where the frequency of occurrence does not conform to the usual conventions of the tonal system. We are also concerned with possible differences in sensitivity between musically trained and untrained listeners. It might reasonably be assumed that the internalised tonal schema of the musically trained listener is more fully developed than that of the untrained listener. Thus influences of the schema on perceptions might be most evident for the musically trained listener.

EXPERIMENTS WITH ABSTRACT SEQUENCES

I will next describe a example taken from Oram and Cuddy (Experiment 1, 1995) which illustrates a direct attack on the research question and the general nature of our experimental approach. In this study 24 listeners were tested; 12 had attained a proficiency level of conservatory training in at least one musical instrument or voice (approximately university entrance standards for a music programme), and 12 reported having no formal musical training.

The sequences that were presented to the listeners were generated from one of two toneset types—diatonic or nondiatonic. The tones of each toneset, ordered by pitch height, are shown in Fig. 14.4. The diatonic toneset comprised the members of the C major scale. Each of the nondiatonic tonesets differed from the diatonic toneset by three tones. These tones were selected so that none of the nondiatonic tonesets conformed to any major or minor scale. (This was checked by comparing the distribution of all intervals contained in the toneset against the distribution of intervals contained in the major and minor keys.) The nondiatonic tonesets, however, were contained within the same or nearly the same pitch range as the diatonic toneset.

Each nondiatonic toneset was paired with the diatonic toneset to form a sequence set; there were four sequence sets in all. Within each set, the same ordinal positions in terms of pitch height were selected to be the tones that would occur more frequently than others. Eight sequences are shown in Fig. 14.5. Four of the sequences were generated from the diatonic toneset. The other four sequences were generated from the nondiatonic tonesets. In each sequence in Fig. 14.5, one tone occurs eight times, two tones occur four times, and four tones occur once each. The order in which the tones were presented was fixed as shown in the figure, and this order distributed the more frequent tones throughout the sequence (i.e. they could not all occur in a "clump" at the end).

Pitch height order	1	2	3	4	5	6	7
Diatonic toneset							
C Major	C	D	E	F	G	A	B
Nondiatonic tonesets							
1	C	C#	E	F	F#	A#	B
2	C	D#	F	F#	G	A	A#
3	C	C#	E	F#	G	A#	B
4	C	C#	D#	F	F#	A	B

FIG. 14.4. The tones of the diatonic and the nondiatonic tonesets ordered by pitch height. From *Responsiveness of Western adults to pitch-distributional information in melodic sequences* by N. Oram and L. L. Cuddy, 1995, *Psychological Research/Psychologische Forschung, 57*, p. 106. Reprinted with permission.

Figure 14.6 shows the events of a single trial according to the probe-tone technique. Each tone in a sequence was a pure tone 200ms in duration with 22ms rise and fall times. Between adjacent tones in the sequence there was a 50ms gap. The probe tones were 12 pure tones of the chromatic scale from C4 to B4. Each probe tone was 1s in duration with 22ms rise and fall times. There was a 1s gap between the probe tone and the last tone in the sequence. There was a 4s response period between trials for the listeners to make their ratings. The probe tone was selected randomly without replacement; the order was independently randomised for each listener and each sequence tested.

The listeners were asked to rate how well, in a musical sense, the probe tone fitted the tone sequence that preceded the probe tone. These ratings were made on a 7-point scale that ranged from "1", fits very poorly, to "7", fits very well. The listeners were encouraged to use the full range of this 7-point scale.

The stimuli were realised by a DMX-1000 real-time digital synthesiser controlled by a minicomputer (LSI 11/23). The relative amplitude of each of the tones was adjusted to equal loudness. The subjects heard the tones through

Temporal order of tones

Sequence Set 1

Diatonic																			
G	F	C	F	B	A	F	C	F	B	E	F	C	F	B	D	F	C	F	B

Nondiatonic																			
A#	F	C	F	B	F#	F	C	F	B	E	F	C	F	B	C#	F	C	F	B

Sequence set 2

Diatonic																			
B	F	E	F	G	C	F	E	F	G	D	F	E	F	G	A	F	E	F	G

Nondiatonic																			
A#	F#	F	F#	G	C	F#	F	F#	G	D#	F#	F	F#	G	A	F#	F	F#	G

Sequence set 3

Diatonic																			
G	D	E	D	B	A	D	E	D	B	C	D	E	D	B	F	D	E	D	B

Nondiatonic																			
G	C#	E	C#	B	A#	C#	E	C#	B	C	C#	E	C#	B	F#	C#	E	C#	B

Sequence set 4

Diatonic																			
B	A	D	A	F	E	A	D	A	F	C	A	D	A	F	G	A	D	A	F

Nondiatonic																			
B	A	C#	A	F	D#	A	C#	A	F	C	A	C#	A	F	F#	A	C#	A	F

FIG. 14.5. The temporal order of the tones in each sequence. From Responsiveness of Western adults to pitch-distributional information in melodic sequences by N. Oram and L. L. Cuddy, 1995, *Psychological Research/Psychologische Forschung, 57*, p. 106. Reprinted with permission.

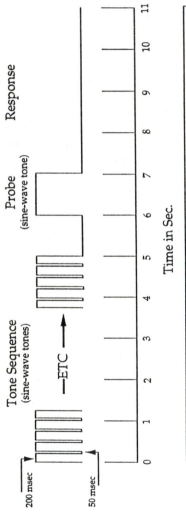

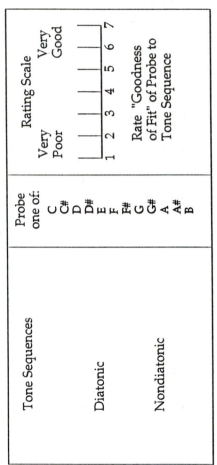

FIG. 14.6. The events of a single trial.

Sennheiser headphones (HD 242) in a sound-attenuated room. The overall sound pressure level was set at a level judged comfortable by the listener and was in the range 60 to 70dB SPL.

Figure 14.7 shows the mean rating at each level of frequency of occurrence for each toneset type (diatonic and nondiatonic) and for each level of musical training. Data are shown averaged for the diatonic sequences on the lefthand side of the figure, and averaged for the nondiatonic sequences on the righthand side of the figure. The x-axis represents frequency of occurrence of the probe tones in the sequence, (8, 4, 1, and 0), and the y-axis represents the mean rating given to each category of frequency of occurrence. The standard error of each mean rating is also shown in this figure.

Each panel in the figure suggests a regular decrease in mean rating as frequency of occurrence decreases. This effect was highly significant statistically (beyond the 0.0001 level) and was supported by significant orthogonal contrasts (beyond at least the 0.001 level). There are also two significant interactions in this figure. First, the effect of frequency of occurrence was more pronounced for musically trained than for untrained listeners. Second, the effect of frequency of occurrence was more pronounced for diatonic than for nondiatonic sequences. These interactions were significant beyond the 0.0001 level.

These, then, were the main findings of the experiment, but there were subsidiary findings of further interest. There were significant differences in mean rating among the tones that occurred an equal number of times. This finding suggests that, as well as responding to frequency of occurrence, listeners were responding to other characteristics of the sequences. To uncover the presence of other influences on listeners' ratings, statistical procedures of hierarchical and multiple regression were applied to the data.

These analyses revealed that, although listeners' ratings were primarily influenced by frequency of occurrence, there were two additional influences. First, pitch distance (closest to furthest) of the probe tone from the final tone of the sequence was reflected in the ratings. Proximal tones were rated higher than those more distant. This influence of pitch proximity is consistent with the bottom-up principle of proximity in Narmour's (1990) theory of melodic expectancy. Second, for diatonic sequences, the tonal hierarchy was also reflected in the ratings for musically trained listeners. Within a given level of frequency of occurrence, listeners tended to weight the probe-tone ratings in accordance with the values for the standardised profile for the key (Krumhansl & Kessler, 1982).

This experiment provided evidence that both musically trained and untrained listeners are responsive to frequency of occurrence information in both diatonic and nondiatonic sequences. It suggests that listeners can adaptively respond to distributional information in melodic sequences. In addition, there are interesting implications for the involvement of tonal resources.

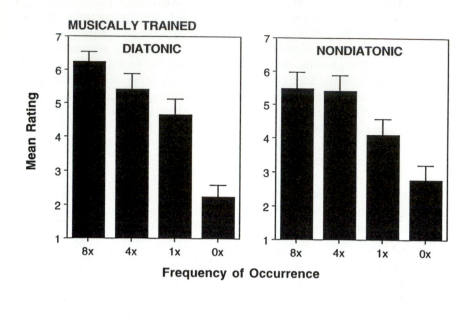

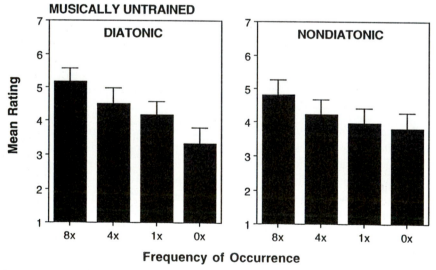

FIG. 14.7. The mean rating of "goodness of musical fit" at each level of frequency of occurrence for each toneset type and each level of musical training. From Responsiveness of Western adults to pitch-distributional information in melodic sequences by N. Oram and L. L. Cuddy, 1995, *Psychological Research/Psychologische Forschung, 57*, p. 107. Reprinted with permission.

344

Tonal resources were expected to be strongest in the condition in which musically trained listeners were tested with diatonic sequences (upper left hand panel of Fig. 14.7). If the tonal-harmonic schema actively interferes with the processing of unfamiliar pitch structures, this condition should produce the poorest sensitivity to frequency of occurrence information. Quite the reverse occurred: this condition produced the highest sensitivity. The implication, therefore, is that music exposure to tonal systems leads to enhanced appreciation of the structure of novel idioms—possibly because generalised strategies for listening to surface cues have been acquired.

EXPERIMENTS WITH COMPOSED MELODIES

The experiments conducted with abstract melodic sequences allowed precise control of pitch content. Other parameters such as duration and dynamics were held constant, so that the experimental effects could be directly attributed to the manipulation of pitch content. The contexts were not, of course, music, and so I wondered whether similar results would be obtained with a musical context—not sequential arrays of sine tones, but to short melodic compositions.

I first considered going to the music literature, but discussions with colleagues at the School of Music at Queen's University led to the agreement that a more controlled study would result if the musical compositions to be tested in the experiment embodied the pitch constraints of the earlier studies. The colleagues offered to compose flute melodies incorporating the hierarchy of relative importance of tones for a sequence tested in the earlier experiments. None of the composers had participated in the experiments with abstract sequences, and they were not told the exact nature of the results. (They did figure out, not surprisingly, that the purpose of the research had something to do with listeners' responses to frequency and duration.)

The composers agreed to follow the following constraints: they were to write a short diatonic melody that could be realised by a flute. The durations of the notes within the melody were to sum to 20 seconds. Durational biases for seven diatonic pitch classes were assigned as follows: eight seconds was to be allotted to the pitch class F, four seconds each to the pitch classes C and B, and 1 second was to be allotted to the pitch classes D, E, G, and A (compare Diatonic Set 1 in Fig. 14.5). In order to make the composition task reasonably challenging, and to allow each composer freedom to exercise his personal style, other constraints from the earlier experiments were relaxed. Specifically, composers were allowed to vary the frequency of occurrence of each tone within its assigned duration. They were free to vary temporal groupings, metric structures, and dynamic structures, and they were free to use the entire pitch register of the normal range of the instrument.

The composers worked independently over several weeks. They all reported that it was a more difficult task than they initially envisaged. Four melodies were produced. The melodies were realised on a Yamaha TX-802 synthesiser using the preset flute voice (Bank A no. 23), under control of a Zenith IBM-AT compatible microcomputer. After each melody had been entered into the computer from the composer's notation, the composer visited the laboratory and "finetuned" the dynamics to fit his intended performance. An example of a melody is shown in Fig. 14.8.

A second version of each melody was constructed by translating each melody to a nondiatonic toneset. Since the selection of pitch classes and durational biases for the original melodies was based on Diatonic Set 1 of the abstract sequences, the translation of each melody was based on Nondiatonic Set 1. Thus, the pitch classes D, G, and A were replaced by C#, F#, and A#.

The basic procedure was similar to that of the experiment just described. Listeners rated the "goodness of fit" of each of 12 probe tones to a musical context. The context in this case was one of the flute melodies. Two groups of musically trained listeners were tested, 12 listeners in each group. One group was tested with diatonic melodies, the other with nondiatonic melodies. Apart from the change from abstract melodic sequences to composed melodies in this experiment, there were two procedural changes that should be noted. Probe tones were not sine tones, but three-octave equivalents of single flute tones—that is, for example, the probe tone for pitch class C contained flute tones C4, C5, and C6 played simultaneously. The timbre of the probe tones was somewhat "organ-like" and louder than the average level of the melody. This was done to emphasise that listeners should pay attention to the pitch class of the probe tone, not to pitch height or melodic continuity. Finally, melodies were transposed up or down one semitone between blocks of trials so that no two successive blocks of melodies contained the same absolute pitches.

The results were similar to those found with abstract sequences. Regression analyses showed a very close relation between mean probe-tone rating and pitch-class duration. Duration accounted for a high proportion of variance in both diatonic and nondiatonic melodies. Also, as in the experiments with

FIG. 14.8. An example of the stimulus materials in the experiments with composed melodies.

abstract sequences, a small but significant amount of variance in the probe-tone ratings could be accounted for by the tonal hierarchy. For example, for both diatonic and nondiatonic melodies, higher ratings were given to the pitch class C than to B, although the total duration for the two pitch classes was the same. Hierarchical regression showed that, after prediction based on pitch-class duration had been taken into account, there was a significant contribution of a predictor based on the standardised profile derived by Krumhansl and Kessler (1982) for the key of C major.

Further experimental studies have been conducted with the flute melodies as musical contexts. The purpose was to explore and extend the musical implications of the study just reported. In a subsequent study, we asked whether the tone with the greatest total duration acted as a central reference point for the melody, with the other durationally biased tones acting as secondary reference points. This question may be addressed experimentally through the use of the double-probe technique.

For the double-probe technique, the melody was followed on each trial by a pair of probe tones and the listener was asked to judge how related was the first to the second tone of the pair with respect to the melody. The established finding for tonal-harmonic contexts is that judgements depend on the order of the tones of the pair (Krumhansl, 1979, 1990). For the same pair of two probe tones, judgements of relatedness are higher for the order in which the tone of less stability in the traditional tonal hierarchy is presented first and followed by the tone of greater stability (e.g. a nontriad tone is followed by the tonic) than for the reverse order. These data reflect that the proposition that each tone is drawn toward, or expected to resolve to, a tone of greater stability in the tonal hierarchy. Perceived relatedness is higher when this expectation is fulfilled.

The data that we obtained for the flute melodies also showed that judgements of relatedness were dependent on order. These judgements, however, did not correspond to predictions based on the tonal hierarchy. Judgements of relatedness were predictable from the durational biases in the melody. They were higher for the order in which a tone of less total duration was followed by a tone of greater total duration rather than the reverse. Thus, it may be proposed that the durationally biased tones acted as reference anchors for the unbiased tones. The direction of the dependence on order corresponded to relative salience according to durational bias, not stability in the tonal hierarchy.

CONCLUDING COMMENTS

The research project illustrated above with two specific examples is providing a consistent answer to the research question posed: listeners are indeed sensitive to surface cues to pitch structure in melodies and melody-like sequences. Moreover, listeners are remarkably sensitive to surface properties even when these properties violate the conventions of the tonal-harmonic idiom. Listeners appear to be able to disengage the pitch schemata acquired for tonal-harmonic music and are able to build new schemata as to accommodate the pitch structure available at the surface. Music training appears to facilitate, rather than interfere with, this process. One effect of music training may be the development of general-purpose strategies that foster listening to both conventional and nonconventional musical idioms.

The surface cues that we have studied in detail are the frequency and the duration with which tones are sounded in melodies. The selection of these cues was motivated by the report by Krumhansl (1987, 1990) of the close correspondence between the distribution of pitches in Western tonal compositions and the tonal hierarchy. This correspondence is, of course, a correlation, and cannot be interpreted as implying a causal relationship. However, the correspondence allows the possibility that listeners may use pitch regularities in music to develop an internal representation of its organisation (see also Bregman, 1990). Our data support the notion that listeners can and do abstract pitch regularities and are not entirely dependent on long-term exposure to a particular idiom in order to be able to so.

The cues of frequency and duration were chosen from psychological considerations. The cues also may be defined in terms of music-theoretic considerations—the salience conditions defined by Lerdahl (1989). Salience conditions isolate the most prominent event within a time-span of an atonal passage, and leave other, less salient, events to be reduced out. The cues of frequency and duration may be identified with the salience conditions of attack, relative density, and relative duration. An event that is attacked within the region and occurs with relatively greater density or relatively greater length is more likely (other conditions being equal) to be selected as a salient event.

Of course, the application of our experimental results to the complexities of music-theoretic proposals is limited. We do not know, for example, the degree to which our findings would generalise to harmonic as opposed to melodic processes, to pitch systems that do not embody octave equivalence and discrete categories within octaves, or to large-scale musical forms. Also, we do not know how listeners might respond if salience conditions conflicted—that is, how listeners would interpret the musical surface if different salience conditions pointed to different organisations. There may be cognitive constraints, yet to be explicated, on listeners' abilities to track regularities in the acoustic world.

These limitations do not, however, mask the important implications of the obtained convergence of the empirical findings and the music-theoretic proposals described above. It has been demonstrated that for the types of musical contexts studied to date—where the principles of tonal stability do not apply— a sense of hierarchical organisation or structure may be attained through the principle of relative salience. As noted, relative salience is a surface cue—the type of cue that experiments have shown influences listeners' memories (Krumhansl, 1991), and facilitates grouping and temporal schemata (Deliège, 1989, 1993) for atonal idioms. It will be exciting to further explore the implications for the flexibility and adaptability of the musical mind.

In this chapter, I have illustrated a contribution to the growing literature in which music-theoretic and experimental approaches are seen as compatible and mutually beneficial. This type of interaction introduces strenuous demands. The music-theoretic proposals must be articulated with precision sufficient to allow translation to empirical hypotheses. The experimental methods must be reliable and, importantly, valid in a musical context. In the ideal case, (Krumhansl, 1995), the research questions must be amenable to investigation both with abstract contexts where experimental control is paramount, and also with more ecologically valid musical contexts where the degree of control is relaxed. The present projects were oriented to meet these demands. By so doing, the picture of listeners' sensitivities to tonal relations could drawn from multiple perspectives, each perspective adding rich detail to the view.

ACKNOWLEDGEMENTS

I thank C. L. Krumhansl for advice, encouragement, and support, and for thoughtful comments on the present chapter. I acknowledge the many contributions of past and present members of the Acoustical Laboratory at Queen's University, especially W. F. Thompson and N. Oram, and the editorial comments of M. G. Wiebe. The composers who willingly donated their skill and time to provide the contexts for the flute-melody study were John Burge, Ted Dawson, and David Keane; John Burge also drafted Fig. 14.8. The research was supported by a grant to L. L. Cuddy from the Natural Sciences and Engineering Research Council of Canada.

REFERENCES

Bharucha, J. J. (1984a). Anchoring effects in music: The resolution of dissonance. *Cognitive Psychology*, *16*, 485–518.

Bharucha, J. J. (1984b). Event hierarchies, tonal hierarchies, and assimilation. *Journal of Experimental Psychology: General*, *113*, 421–425.

Bigand, E. (1990). Abstraction of two forms of underlying structure in a tonal melody. *Psychology of Music*, *18*, 45–59.

Bigand, E. (1993). Contributions of music to research on human auditory cognition. In S. McAdams & E. Bigand (Eds.), *Thinking in sound: The cognitive psychology of human audition* (pp. 231–277). Oxford: Clarendon.

Bregman, A. S. (1990). *Auditory scene analysis: The perceptual organization of sound.* Cambridge, Mass: The M.I.T. Press.

Castellano, M. A., Bharucha, J. J., & Krumhansl, C. L. (1984). Tonal hierarchies in the music of north India. *Journal of Experimental Psychology: General*, *113*, 394–412.

Cuddy, L. L. (1991). Melodic patterns and tonal structure: Converging evidence. *Psychomusicology*, *10*, 107–126.

Cuddy, L. L. (1993). Melody comprehension and tonal structure. In T. T. Tighe & W. J. Dowling (Eds.), *Psychology and music: The understanding of melody and rhythm* (pp. 19–38). Hillsdale, NJ: Erlbaum.

Cuddy, L. L. (1994). Tone distributions in melody: influences on judgments of salience and similarity. In I. Deliège (Ed.), *Proceedings of the 3rd International Conference for Music Perception and Cognition* (pp. 225–226). Liège, Belgium: ESCOM.

Cuddy, L. L., & Badertscher, B. (1987). Recovery of the tonal hierarchy: Some comparisons across age and levels of musical experience. *Perception & Psychophysics*, *41*, 609–620.

Cuddy, L. L., & Oram, N. (1996). *Pitch structure for nontonal melodies: the influence of tone distribution on judgments of salience and similarity.* (Manuscript in preparation).

Cuddy, L. L., & Thompson, W. F. (1992). Asymmetry of perceived key movement in chorale sequences: Converging evidence from a probe-tone analysis. *Psychological Research/ Psychologische Forschung, 54,* 51–59.

Deliège, I. (1989). A perceptual approach to contemporary musical forms. *Contemporary Music Review, 4,* 213–230.

Deliège, I. (1993). Mechanisms of cue extraction in memory for musical time. *Contemporary Music Review, 9,* 191–205.

Deliège, I. (1995). The two steps of the categorization process in music listening: An approach of the cue extraction mechanism as modular system. In R. Steinberg (Ed.), *Music and the mind machine: The psychophysiology and psychopathology of the sense of music* (pp. 63–73). Berlin: Springer-Verlag.

Deliège, I. (1996). Cue abstraction as a component of categorisation processes in music listening. *Psychology of Music, 24,* 131–156.

Deliège, I., Mélen, M., Stammers, D., & Cross, I. (1994). Musical schemata in real-time listening. In I. Deliège (Ed.), *Proceedings of the 3rd International Conference for Music Perception and Cognition* (pp. 271–272). Liège, Belgium: ESCOM.

Deutsch, D., & Feroe, J. (1981). The internal representation of pitch sequences in tonal music. *Psychological Review, 88,* 503–522.

Dowling, W. J. (1978). Scale and contour: Two components of a theory of memory for melodies. *Psychological Review, 85,* 341–354.

Dowling, W. J., & Harwood, D. L. (1986). *Music cognition.* Orlando, Florida: Academic Press.

Francès, R. (1988). *The perception of music.* (W. J. Dowling, Trans.). Hillsdale, NJ: Erlbaum. (Original work published 1958)

Handel, S. (1989). *Listening: An introduction to the perception of auditory events.* Cambridge, Mass: The M.I.T. Press.

Hargreaves, D. J. (1986). *The developmental psychology of music.* Cambridge: Cambridge University Press.

Hindemith, P. (1968). *A concentrated course in traditional harmony: Book 1* (rev. ed.). New York: Schott.

Jones, M. R. (1982). Music as a stimulus for psychological motion: Part II. An expectancy model. *Psychomusicology, 2*(1), 1–13.

Jordan, D. S., & Shepard, R. N. (1987). Tonal schemas: Evidence obtained by probing distorted musical scales. *Perception & Psychophysics, 41,* 489–504.

Kessler, E. J., Hansen, C., & Shepard, R. N. (1984). Tonal schemata in the perception of music in Bali and in the West. *Music Perception, 2,* 131–165.

Krumhansl, C. L. (1979). The psychological representation of musical pitch in a tonal context. *Cognitive Psychology, 11,* 346–374.

Krumhansl, C. L. (1983). Perceptual structures for tonal music. *Music Perception, 1,* 28–62.

Krumhansl, C. L. (1987). Tonal and harmonic hierarchies. In J. Sundberg (Ed.), *Harmony and tonality* (pp. 13–32). Stockholm, Sweden: Royal Swedish Academy.

Krumhansl, C. L. (1990). *Cognitive foundations of musical pitch.* Oxford: Oxford University Press.

Krumhansl, C. L. (1991). Memory for musical surface. *Memory & Cognition, 19,* 401–411.

Krumhansl, C. L. (1995). Music psychology and music theory: Problems and prospects. *Music Theory Spectrum, 17,* 53–80.

Krumhansl, C. L., & Keil, F. C. (1982). Acquisition of the hierarchy of tonal functions in music. *Memory & Cognition, 10,* 243–251.

Krumhansl, C. L., & Kessler, E. J. (1982). Tracing the dynamic changes in perceived tonal organization in a spatial representation of musical keys. *Psychological Review, 89,* 344–368.

Krumhansl, C. L., & Shepard, R. N. (1979). Quantification of the hierarchy of tonal functions within a diatonic context. *Journal of Experimental Psychology: Human Perception & Performance, 5,* 579–594.

Large, E. W., Palmer, C., & Pollack. J. B. (1995). Reduced memory representations for music. *Cognitive Science, 19,* 53–96.

Lerdahl, F. (1988a). Tonal pitch space. *Music Perception, 5,* 315–350.

Lerdahl, F. (1988b). Cognitive constraints on compositional systems. In J. A. Sloboda (Ed.), *Generative processes in music* (pp. 231–259). Oxford: Clarendon.

Lerdahl, F. (1989). Atonal prolongational structure. *Contemporary Music Review, 4,* 65–87.

Lerdahl, F., & Jackendoff, R. (1983). *A generative theory of tonal music.* Cambridge, Mass: The M.I.T. Press.

Lynch, M. P., Eilers, R. E., Oller, D. K., & Urbano, R. (1991). Influences of acculturation and musical sophistication on perception of native and nonnative musical scales. *Journal of Experimental Psychology: Human Perception & Performance, 17,* 967–975.

Mélen, M., & Deliège, I. (1995). Extraction of cues or underlying harmonic structure: Which guides recognition of familiar melodies? *European Journal of Cognitive Psychology, 7,* 81–106.

Meyer, L. B. (1956). *Emotion and meaning in music.* Chicago: University of Chicago Press.

Narmour, E. (1990). *The analysis and cognition of basic melodic structures: The implication-realization model.* Chicago: The University of Chicago Press.

Oram, N. (1989). *The responsiveness of Western adult listeners to pitch distributional information in diatonic and nondiatonic melodic sequences.* Unpublished doctoral dissertation, Queen's University, Kingston, Ontario.

Oram, N., & Cuddy, L. L. (1995). Responsiveness of Western adults to pitch distributional information in melodic sequences. *Psychological Research/Psychologische Forschung, 57,* 103–118.

Palmer, C., & Krumhansl, C. L. (1987a). Independent temporal and pitch structures in determination of musical phrases. *Journal of Experimental Psychology: Human Perception & Performance, 13,* 116–126.

Palmer, C., & Krumhansl, C. L. (1987b). Pitch and temporal contributions to musical phrase perception: Effects of harmony, performance timing, and familiarity. *Perception & Psychophysics, 41,* 505–518.

Peretz, I., & Kolinsky, R. (1993). Boundaries of separability between melody and rhythm in music discrimination: A neurological perspective. *Quarterly Journal of Experimental Psychology, 46,* 301–325.

Peretz, I., & Morais, J. (1989). Music and modularity. *Contemporary Music Review, 4,* 277–291.

Piston, W. (1987). *Harmony* (Revised and expanded by M. DeVoto). New York: Norton.

Simon, H. A., & Sumner, R.K. (1968). Pattern in music. In B. Kleinmutz (Ed.), *Formal representation of human judgment.* New York: Wiley.

Steinke, W. R., Cuddy, L. L., & Holden, R. R. (1993). Perception of musical tonality as assessed by the probe-tone method. *Canadian Acoustics, 21,* 85–86.

Steinke, W. R., Cuddy, L. L., & Peretz, I. (1994). Dissociation of music and cognitive abstraction abilities in normal and neurologically impaired subjects. In I. Deliège (Ed.), *Proceedings of the 3rd International Conference for Music Perception & Cognition* (pp. 425–428). Liège, Belgium: ESCOM.

Thompson, W. F., & Cuddy, L. L. (1994). Schemata for key expressed in musical performance. In I. Deliège (Ed.) *Proceedings of the 3rd International Conference for Music Perception and Cognition* (pp. 77–78). Liège, Belgium: ESCOM.

Thompson, W. F., & Cuddy, L. L. (in press). Music performance and the perception of key. *Journal of Experimental Psychology: Human Perception & Performance.*

Trehub, S. E. (1993). The music listening skills of infants and young children. In T. T. Tighe & W. J. Dowling (Eds.), *Psychology and music: The understanding of melody and rhythm* (pp. 161–176). Hillsdale, NJ: Erlbaum.

Trehub, S. E., & Trainor, L. J. (1993). Listening strategies in infancy: the roots of music and language development. In S. McAdams & E. Bigand (Eds.), *Thinking in sound: The cognitive psychology of human audition* (pp. 278–327). Oxford: Clarendon.

Zenatti, A. (1993). Children's musical cognition and taste. In T. T. Tighe & W. J. Dowling (Eds.), *Psychology and music: The understanding of melody and rhythm* (pp. 177–196). Hillsdale, NJ: Erlbaum.

15 Pitch schemata

Ian Cross
Cambridge University, UK

INTRODUCTION

The identity of a piece of Western tonal music is ordinarily assumed to derive from the way that pitch is organised within it. This is evident in the fact that the vernacular terms most commonly employed to refer to music are "tune" and "melody", both of which can be defined as "a succession of notes varying in pitch and having a recognisable musical shape" (Penguin New Dictionary of Music, 1972). In addition, most music-theoretic or music-analytic writings of the last two hundred years have focused on the elucidation of music's harmonic and melodic dimensions (see Bent, 1980; Palisca, 1980), exploring these primarily in terms of configurations of pitches and their inter-relations as scales, keys and modes under the banner of tonality.

The accounts of musical pitch—of melody and harmony—that these writings provide often appear as prescriptive rules and definitions which sanction the forms that musical pitch structure may take. They will describe: (1) what collections of notes belong together (in defining major and minor scales); (2) which notes from these collections are more important than others and are thus likely to occur at the beginning or end of successions of notes, or melodies (in defining the tonal functions—tonic, dominant etc.—of the different scale notes); (3) which notes from the collections may occur simultaneously with others (in defining triadic chord configurations); (4) which simultaneities are functionally similar (in defining inversional and substitutive equivalence of chords); (5) which keys are more closely, and which are more remotely, related;

353

(6) the ways in which the tonal function of notes in a melody determines which notes will succeed one another (as in the rules of voice-leading); and (7) the ways in which principles of combining notes in chords and melodies will interact.

It would seem logical that the highly elaborated theories about pitch organisation expounded in these writings should have played a major role in explorations of the psychology of music from the outset. However, the prevailing view of musical pitch within the psychology of music through the first half of this century appears highly reductionist, and can be summarised in Seashore's (1938/1967) statements that (p. 17) "The terms 'frequency' . . . 'cycles' and 'waves' are synonymous, and may be used interchangeably to designate frequency *and pitch*." [my italics] and that (p. 384) "When we have measured the sense of pitch, that is, pitch discrimination, in the laboratory with high reliability and we know that pitch was isolated from all other factors, no scientist will question but that we have measured pitch."[1] In other words, pitch as a psychological phenomenon was to be equated with the acoustical phenomenon of frequency; while phenomena not easily explicable in terms of acoustics (such as the tendency of performers to flatten or sharpen particular notes of the scale in particular melodic contexts) were recognised and investigated (see, e.g. Francès, 1958/1988), the rationales that were advanced for their existence generally remained unsystematic.

Nevertheless, music theory describes relations between sets of pitches (such as transposition, inversion, and even reduction) which can lead to two different sets being regarded as more or less similar even although their constituent frequencies are quite different. Musical pitch is commonly discussed in terms of melodies, themes, motifs and keys; many of these concepts prove to be remarkably intractable when an attempt is made to account for them in terms of relations between frequencies. Thus, if an understanding of the psychology of musical pitch is simply equated with an understanding of frequency so that, for example, two pitches are different only if they correspond to different frequencies, it becomes difficult—if not impossible—to account for many of the notions that are taken for granted in music theory (although it may be questioned whether these notions have any "reality" outside music theory, a possibility considered later in this chapter). However, everyday musical experience, together with the results of many experimental studies, indicate that pitches or patterns of pitches may be perceived as similar even when a frequency-based account would indicate that they should be experienced as being quite different, and any scientific account of the experience of musical pitch must confront this issue.

With the development of cognitive psychology in the 1950s and 1960s a new concern to account for the psychological mechanisms underlying the cognition of musical pitch became evident. Over the last twenty years a vast body of research has grown that seeks to reconcile an understanding of the experience of musical pitch with its rich description in the musicological literature. Much of this research has focused on the development and empirical testing of a range of functionalist models of musical pitch cognition that can account for the diverse capacities exhibited by listeners and performers in respect of a wide variety of musical materials and circumstances. While most of these models are symbolic or sub-symbolic, being intended to reproduce cognitive capacities with no particular reference to specific neurophysiological structures, a few are more closely based on determinate properties of the auditory system. This chapter will outline the course of this recent research and will describe the different strands that comprise it in an attempt to provide a clear picture of the development of current views of musical pitch in cognition.

MUSICAL PITCH IN COGNITION: INITIAL APPROACHES

An early attempt to explain the perception of some commonly accepted aspects of musical pitch that are difficult to account for in terms of simple frequency relations is that of Deutsch (1969). She proposed a model that could underlie the perception of equivalence between equivalent musical intervals and chords under both transposition and inversion (see Fig. 15.1, which illustrates a particular configuration of the mechanism for abstracting equivalence information for intervals and chords). Elements of this model were further developed in Deutsch (1981) and Deutsch and Feroe (1981), where a formal set of procedures that might underlie perception of and memory for complexly structured melodic sequences was described and experimentally tested (see Deutsch, 1982, for a summary account of the model). This formal set of procedures (which shares several features with that proposed by Simon and Sumner, 1968) was intended to be capable of modelling the cognitive processes involved in abstracting information about various aspects of melodic structure and explicitly sought to represent the effects of scale-membership, melodic contour and repetition of melodic patterns on the memorability and perceptual integrity of melodies.

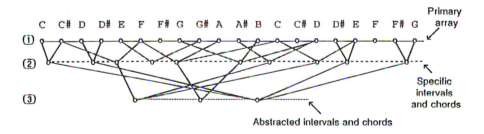

FIG. 15.1. A particular configuration of Deutsch's (1969) system for abstracting equivalence information for musical intervals and chords. Individual pitches are represented on level 1; intervals and chords formed between specific pitches are represented on level 2; and classes of intervals and chords are represented on level 3.

An alternative and more elaborate account is provided by Christopher Longuet-Higgins, who in a series of papers (Longuet-Higgins, 1962a and b, 1976, 1979) proposed a formal model of "tonal space" intended to elucidate the perception of pitch relations in music. Longuet-Higgins' model represents pitches as points on an infinite two-dimensional plane, single steps being perfect fifths within one dimension and major thirds in the other. Diatonic major scales thus constitute asymmetrical and uninvertible L-shaped blocks formed by groups of seven proximate pitches (see Fig. 15. 2). In this way movement between notes within a key and movement between keys can be represented as shifts within and between regions of the two-dimensional plane.

Longuet-Higgins intends his model to constitute a component of a formal, computational, "competence theory" of tonal musical pitch: that is, a theory that makes explicit the rules and processes that underlie a listener's experience of tonal musical works. As such he has not sought to test the model experimentally; however, as we shall see, his model has many similarities to that of Balzano (1980, 1982), which has been the focus of extensive experimental investigation.

A different model is suggested by Dowling (1982), whose concern with generalisability has led him to propose a system within which the regularities of

A	C#	F	A'	C#'	F'	A"	C#"	F"	A"'
D	F#	A#	D'	F#'	A#'	D"	F#"	A#"	D"'
G	B	D#	G'	B'	D#'	G"	B"	D#"	G"'
C	E	G#	C'	E'	G#'	C"	E"	G#"	C"'
F	A	C#	F'	A'	C#'	F"	A"	C#"	F"'
Bb	D	F#	Bb'	D'	F#'	Bb"	D"	F#"	Bb"'
Eb	G	B	Eb'	G'	B'	Eb"	G"	B"	Eb"'
Ab	C	E	Ab'	C'	E'	Ab"	C"	E"	Ab"'

FIG. 15.2. Longuet-Higgins' model representing pitches as points on an infinite two-dimensional plane: single steps are perfect fifths in the y-dimension and major thirds in the x-dimension. The diatonic major scale on C is shown as an asymmetrical and uninvertible L-shaped region.

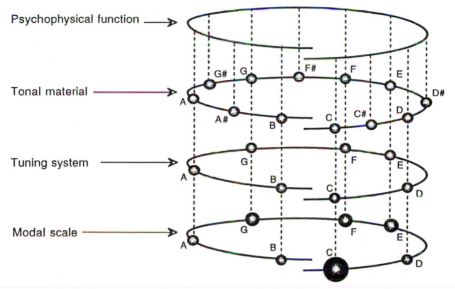

Psychophysical function ⟶

Tonal material ⟶

Tuning system ⟶

Modal scale ⟶

FIG. 15.3. Dowling's four levels of analysis of musical pitch in cognition.

musical pitch in cognition can be represented in a way that may be applied to music of many different cultures. Dowling suggests four "levels of analysis" of musical scales: the first, the *psychophysical pitch function* maps pitches to frequencies; the second, the level of *tonal material* incorporates all the available pitches within a culture's music; the third, the *tuning system* is a subset of the pitches from the tonal material that is employed within sets of melodies; whilst at the level of the fourth, the *modal scale*, pitches of the tuning system are hierarchically organised to reflect the way in which pitches are used in an actual melody, with certain pitches being in some way "more important" than others (see Fig. 15.3).

Each level within Dowling's model is formed by selecting pitches out of the next higher level, or by conferring different types of properties on them. Dowling intends this model to be capable of accounting for a range of sensitivities to pitch organisation, while being sufficiently general to be applicable to the cognition of pitch structure in different types of music and in the music of a wide range of cultures.

THE COGNITIVE-STRUCTURALIST APPROACH

The view of musical pitch that has given rise to one of the most influential research programmes (after Lakatos, 1970) within music cognition over the last fifteen years is the *cognitive-structural* approach, developed initially by Shepard and Krumhansl (see Shepard, 1982) and elaborated and extended by the latter. This approach is explicitly intended to investigate questions that approaches based on a one-to-one correspondence between pitch and frequency appear incapable of answering. It addresses itself to issues such as "why do melodies within which notes are in the same scale sound more coherent than melodies within which notes are not?", or "why are some notes in melodies apparently more important than others?", or "why do some chords seem more closely related than others ?", and "why do chords seem to fall into more or less closely related groups?". In asking these questions, Shepard and Krumhansl suggest that underlying our perceptions or judgements of pitches and pitch relations is some form of mental model or schema. A schema is a mental structure that organises the information received from our senses and is itself altered by that information (see Neisser, 1976), that shapes our interpretations of what we encounter and determines the nature of our experiences.

Shepard proposed that this schema for musical pitch is best conceived of in terms of some multi-dimensional spatial representation. An early version of this representation (Shepard, 1964) took the form of a simple spiral (enabling representation of octave-equivalence). Shepard's more sophisticated 1982 version of the cognitive-structural model aims to account for many different types of perceived musical pitch relations in terms of the proximity of pitches within a complex spatial representation; spatial proximity is intended to model the degree to which pitches might be perceived as similar within a variety of musical contexts. This model makes use of three components, one being unidimensional (and correlating with differences in adjudged pitch height) and two being two-dimensional (taking the forms of the circle of fifths and the chroma circle). The circle of the fifths simply consists of the notes of the equal-tempered chromatic scale laid out in a circle so that each pitch forms the enharmonic musical interval of a perfect fifth with the notes on either side of it, while the chroma circle is produced by treating octave-related notes as functionally identical, and consists of the notes of the equal-tempered chromatic scale laid out in a circle so that each pitch forms the musical interval of a semitone with the notes on either side of it.

Shepard points out that as well as representing octave equivalence, his model has other properties that appear musically significant; these are most easily described in terms of the three-dimensional structure formed by the pitch height and circle of fifths components, which takes the form of a double helix on the surface of a regular cylinder (see Fig. 15.4a). In this representation the notes of any major diatonic key can be divided from the notes not in that key by passing a plane through the central axis of the double helix. Moreover, transposition into the most closely-related keys is achieved by the smallest angles of rotation of the dividing plane about the central axis. A further aspect of the representation, obtained by combining the (two-dimensional) pitch chroma component with the circle of fifths component to produce a four-dimensional torus, is shown in Fig. 15.4(b). Shepard (1982) states that the five-dimensional structure that

Figure 4(a)

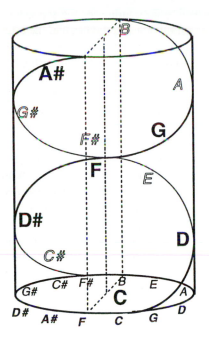

Figure 4(b)

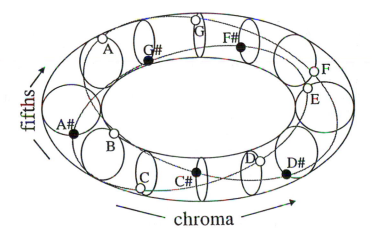

fifths

chroma

FIG. 15.4. (a) Regular cylinder produced by combining pitch height and circle of fifths dimension. (b) Torus produced by combining the chroma circle and circle of fifths dimensions.

results from adding both two-dimensional components and the unidimensional pitch height component can account for perceived similarity of pitches which are close in pitch height, heightened similarity of pitches at the octave and the perfect fifth, as well as accounting for the separability of the pitches within the major diatonic key from non-key pitches and the rotational proximity of closely-related keys.

In this way Shepard provides an *imagistic* structural representation of musical pitch. It is intended to provide an account of the ways in which our cognitive mechanisms may function when we experience music; it is being proposed that the ways in which we represent musical pitch relations in our cognitions—our mental models, or tonal schemata—have properties similar to the model that he proposes. It integrates many of the features of perceived relations between pitches that experiments have shown to be significant; it would seem to be capable of explaining many of the observed judgemental and memory abilities of Western musical listeners. The model provides a coherent and logical basis for cross-octave chroma identity, for the "privileged" status that notes within a scale or key have in respect of one another, and for the idea of key-distance relations. Moreover, Shepard suggests that the model could be adjusted while retaining its fundamental attributes if the experimental evidence so required, e.g. by weighting different dimensions to account for the perception of tones and semitones as being equivalent in certain musical contexts (as experiments such as those of Dowling, 1978, appear to indicate).

COGNITIVE-STRUCTURALISM: THEORY AND EXPERIMENT

Krumhansl and her collaborators have developed and refined the cognitive-structural approach, extending its theoretical basis and grounding it in a wide-ranging programme of empirical studies. The course of this work is described in Krumhansl (1990), which summarises the research central to the development of the approach. A cornerstone of Krumhansl's research programme is the *probe-tone* technique, in which listeners are presented with some sort of musical fragment—a *musical context*—and required to make judgements about tones immediately following the fragment. From close and complex analyses of the patterns of listeners' responses, formal models of the structures and processes that are embodied in listeners' perceptions and cognitions have been inferred.

A hypothesis central to the approach is the idea that listeners make use of a cognitive representation of pitch organisation within which different pitches can be said to be differently *stable*. *Stability* is accounted for in terms of the degree to which a pitch can be said to be representative of a class or category of pitches. The idea of categorisation is an instance of a general principle that has been shown to operate in many cognitive domains (Rosch, 1978) and which contributes significantly to efficiency of cognitive functioning.

Krumhansl (1990, p. 19) suggests that "the relative stability of a tone will depend to some degree on its treatment within a particular compositional context. However, it is presumed that there is a more abstract, invariant hierarchy of stability that is typical of a musical style more generally, and that this more abstract hierarchy is an important characteristic contributing to the perceived stability of each tone within a complex musical sequence." Listeners brought up within a particular musical culture will progressively form this "tonal hierarchy" as they are exposed more and more to the music of their culture, as well as in the course of any formal musical training they undergo. The formation of the "tonal hierarchy" is thus held to depend both on processes of acculturation—most likely non-conscious—and on explicit and conscious learning.

A range of empirical studies conducted by Krumhansl and others supports the idea of a hierarchy of stability for pitches in cognition. Following major and minor scalic passages as well as triadic arpeggios and major and minor cadences as contexts, subjects were asked to give a numerical rating of how well subsequent single pitches—"probe tones"—fitted the contexts. It was found that subjects were highly consistent in the ratings that they accorded to particular pitches following particular contexts; the note that could be construed as the context's tonic would be likely to be rated most highly, next highest-rated were the dominant or mediant (depending on whether the context was, respectively, major or minor), then the other notes diatonic in respect of the context, and finally (and rated lowest) the non-diatonic notes (see Fig. 15.5). Most significantly, these findings were replicated in a number of studies (for summary accounts see Krumhansl, 1990).

Krumhansl (1990, Ch. 3) suggests two possible factors as giving rise to the tonal hierarchy: consonance and statistical distribution of tones. The former is taken as deriving from the degree to which two or more tones interact in the peripheral auditory sense-organs and hence give rise to a greater or lesser sensation of "roughness" or "sensory dissonance", while the latter derives from statistical analyses of pitch distribution in various corpuses of tonal music. It was found that tonal hierarchy rating profiles correlated strongly with statistical predictions based on frequency of pitch occurrence in tonal music, and (less strongly) with predictions based on sensory dissonance calculations; this finding implies that learning—whether formal, or by enculturation—is a stronger determinant of the tonal hierarchy than is the nature of the sensory-transductive mechanisms. Briefly, the cognitive-structuralist programme would suggest that the tonal hierarchy owes more to nurture than to nature (although nature's paternity cannot be disproved nor its contribution discounted).

A slightly different form of experimental study (Krumhansl, 1990, Chapter 5) sheds further light on the nature of the cognitive representation of the tonal hierarchy. In this, subjects heard two pitches preceded by a variety of contexts and judged how similar the first pitch was to the second. This afforded the possibility of providing a geometric model of listeners' cognitive

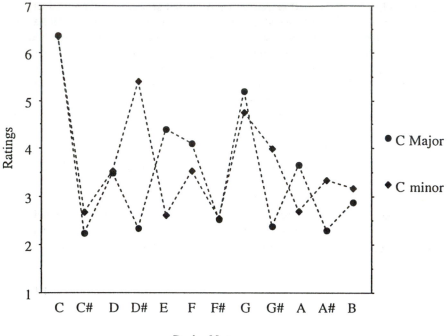

FIG. 15.5. The "tonal hierarchies" evident in subjects' ratings of probe notes following major or minor contexts.

representations of tonal relations between pitches, wherein pitches that were adjudged to be highly similar were represented by points close together within a multi-dimensional space, dissimilar pitches being far apart. Krumhansl (1990, p. 119) acknowledges that an imagistic model (such as that proposed by Shepard, above) might be problematic in the strong assumptions that it makes about the satisfaction of metric axioms (see Tversky, 1977). She provides an alternative propositional version (Krumhansl, 1990, p.130), which enables her to account for the finding that the order of presentation of a pair of pitches that differ in their stability in respect of the preceding context affected the similarity judgements made. If the first pitch of a pair was less stable than the second (e.g. the pitches B then C in the context of a C major scale), it was judged to be more similar to the second pitch than if the order of presentation of the pitch-pair was reversed.

Krumhansl and her collaborators have extended the idea of a tonal hierarchy for pitches in cognition to chords and to keys, altering the probe-tone paradigm by changing the elements to be rated to triadic chords. In these experiments it should be noted that the tones used were synthesised so as to contain only octave-related partials and were spectrally-scaled so that if a single ascending chromatic octave were to be played repeatedly, the effect of an infinite ascent would be perceived (*Shepard-tones*). This was done so as avoid any putative effects of voice-leading between chords of a context and probe chords on adjudged fit, or, in Krumhansl's (1990) own words, to "minimise the effect of pitch height differences between the context and probe tones" (p. 26) and to "minimise the effects of melodic motion" (p. 170). A hierarchical representation of harmonic function of single chords in tonal contexts was again found, but one with a structure different from that found for single notes (see Fig. 15.6). Chords that function in the same key were found to be perceived as more closely related than chords that function in different keys even in the absence of contexts. Within the resulting "harmonic hierarchy", chords on the tonic, dominant and subdominant were found to be most highly rated, although Krumhansl suggests that these results show strong interdependencies between the three levels of musical structure: tones, chords and keys, an interdependence of the sort that Lerdahl's (1988) model seeks to express in formal terms.

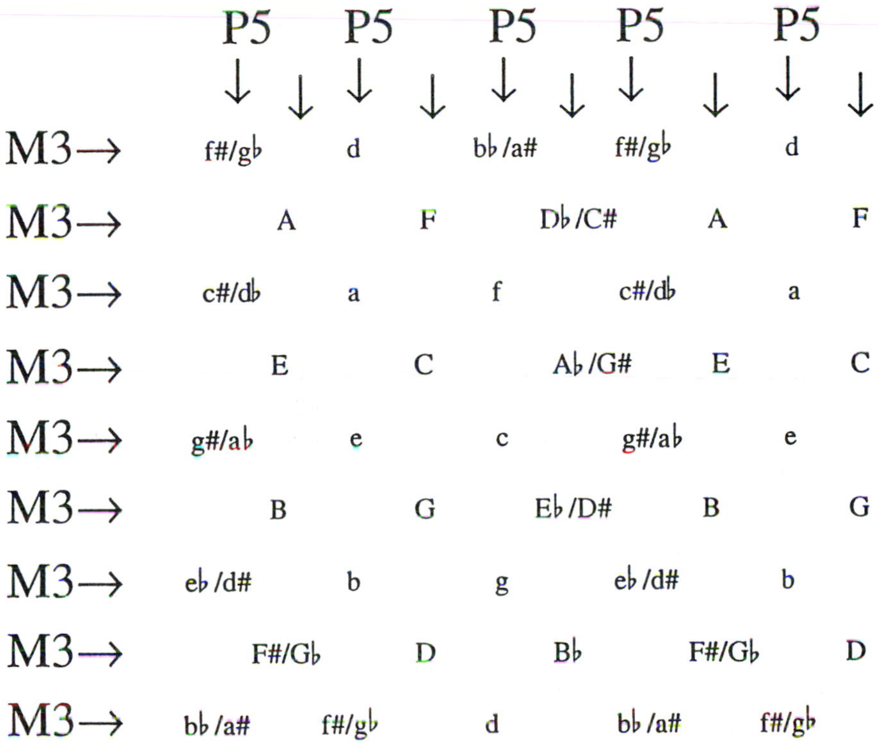

	P5 ↓	↓	P5 ↓	↓	P5 ↓	↓	P5 ↓	↓	P5 ↓	↓
M3→	f#/gb		d		bb/a#		f#/gb		d	
M3→		A		F		Db/C#		A		F
M3→	c#/db		a		f		c#/db		a	
M3→		E		C		Ab/G#		E		C
M3→	g#/ab		e		c		g#/ab		e	
M3→		B		G		Eb/D#		B		G
M3→	eb/d#		b		g		eb/d#		b	
M3→		F#/Gb		D		Bb		F#/Gb		D
M3→	bb/a#		f#/gb		d		bb/a#		f#/gb	

FIG. 15.6. "Harmony-space" derived from subjects' ratings of chords in harmonic contexts.

Further studies conducted by Krumhansl have again modified the probe-tone technique, employing more complex contexts such as modulatory, bitonal or serial sequences, or short pieces of North Indian music. The results of the experiments on modulatory chord sequences were shown to be predictable from the results of earlier studies on the harmonic hierarchy in cognition, as they demonstrated that subjects developed a sense of key by integrating the possible harmonic functions of the individual chords over time. The results of the experiment on the perception of tonal structure in a bitonal context were more complex, indicating that subjects might well have employed aspects of the octatonic set (see van den Toorn, 1983) in their judgements. The experiment employing serial contexts (Krumhansl, Sandell & Sergeant, 1987) again found that listeners adapted the bases of their judgements of the "fittingness" of notes to suit the contexts. However, the ratings of a group of listeners familiar with serial music correlated *negatively* with local key implications, indicating that listeners inverted the normal tonal hierarchy to reflect the denial of key structures that they expected to be associated with twelve-tone, serial music. Interestingly, the responses of a group of listeners with very limited experience of atonal music did appear to show that these listeners were making use of some tonal hierarchy in their judgements; these listeners had apparently acquired an interpretive strategy and continued to apply it even when it might not be wholly appropriate.

The experiment employing North Indian contexts (Castellano, Bharucha & Krumhansl, 1984) used listeners who were placed into two matched groups according to whether or not they had extensive experience with Indian and with Western music or only with Western music. This experiment employed short pieces of music as contexts, and examined the relation between subjects' ratings of subsequent pitches and the theoretical hierarchies of pitches that characterise the heptatonic modal structures called thaats. Thaats can be grouped in a circle so that adjacent thaats differ in their make-up by one single pitch. The context pieces were pre-existing compositions that had been categorised as belonging to different thaats. It was found that the relative durations with which the various tones were sounded in the context pieces strongly affected listeners' responses. However, only the listeners with extensive prior exposure to Indian music showed any sensitivity to thaat structure in their responses; this sensitivity was structured in such a way that their responses to different pitches in the context of different compositions could be mathematically scaled so as to demonstrate the "circle of thaats" as underlying those responses.

COGNITIVE-STRUCTURALISM: PROCESS

This difference in responses between Indian and Western listeners was clarified by Bharucha (1984), who invoked the concepts of event hierarchy and tonal hierarchy. If the tonal hierarchy is taken to be a time-independent abstraction, the event hierarchy corresponds to a time-dependent dynamic state of organisation that occurs during listening and reflects the structure and function of pitches in the piece being heard. The Western subjects were thus responding to the event hierarchies of the contexts that they had heard, while the Indian subjects were integrating their experience of the event hierarchies of these contexts into their pre-existing, schematic knowledge of pitch organisation within North Indian music.

Bharucha has further elucidated the processes that underlie listeners' sensitivity to pitch organisation through a series of experiments (Bharucha & Stoeckig, 1986, 1987) and by the development of a connectionist account of the perception of tonal structure (Bharucha 1987, 1991; Bharucha & Todd, 1991; Bharucha, 1994). Bharucha and Stoeckig's experiments demonstrated that even Western listeners with no formal training in music theory are sensitive to the tonal context of pitches; they showed that the speed and accuracy of processing a chord are greater when it is related to the preceding context than when it is unrelated, and explain this in terms of a process whereby the context generates expectancies, or "primes" the subject to expect that a related chord will follow.

Bharucha explains this phenomenon, and the fact that it appears to arise through processes of enculturation ("passive exposure"), in terms of the capacities of a distributed or connectionist representation of relations between pitches in cognition. He suggests (1987, 1991) that a neural net model (of which Deutsch's 1969 model can be seen as an early instance) should be able to exhibit the sensitivities to pitch structure shown by listeners through a process of unsupervised learning, and outlines just such a system, MUSACT. This model presupposes multiple levels of pitch representation; these range from the "spectral" level (reflecting many of the characteristics of the acoustical signal) to the "invariant pitch-class" level (a highly abstract level of representation in which pitch-classes are differentiated by tonal function). In this respect Bharucha addresses some of the issues that prompted Dowling's account (see above).

The MUSACT network as described in Bharucha (1991) consists of units representing pitch classes, chords and keys (see Fig. 15.7) that acquire their functions through a process of competitive self-organisation during exposure to musical pitches, whether presented as single pitches or as chords. The resulting network will then exhibit patterns of activation of its constituent units that reflect many of the characteristics evident in the perception of musical pitch. For example, a given chord unit may be activated by the activation of either all or just some of its component pitch class units; this latter case may derive from "top-down" activation by a parent key unit that has itself been activated by a preceding context, thus modelling the way in which inferences about tonal identity and function can be made on the basis of partial evidence. Bharucha (1994) sketches a further refinement of this model that builds on the work of Gjerdingen (1994) in order to account for the temporal dimension inherent in the idea of dissonance and resolution.

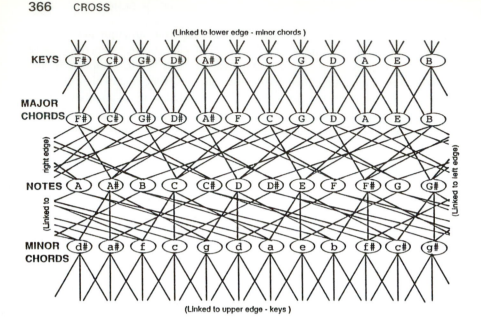

FIG. 15.7.   Units and links in Bharucha's MUSACT system

COGNITIVE-STRUCTURALISM: DEVELOPMENT

The cognitive-structuralist programme is intended to provide explicit representations of the sensitivities to pitch structure exhibited by adult listeners (even those who have received no formal training in music). The account is supplemented by the research of Krumhansl and Keil (1982) who put forward an account of the time-course of the development of these sensitivities. They investigated the capacities of three different age groups of children (7, 9 and 11), who were presented with a "key-defining" context of an arpeggiated major tonic triad followed by pairs of probe notes. Their resultant rating profiles indicated an orderly progression in the acquisition of a sense of tonality; younger children showed a sensitivity to diatonic scale membership, whereas older children appeared able to recognise more subtle patterns of differential stability of scale notes. These results appear to indicate a process of progressive differentiation between pitches on the basis of their musical function as age increases that steers a more-or-less orderly course from what Dowling describes as the tuning system level (here, effectively, the diatonic scale) to the modal scale level (where different scale notes are perceived as differently stable).

However, two further sets of experiments using the probe-tone technique appear to contradict these findings. Using contexts of complete ascending and descending major diatonic scales, Speer and Meeks (1985) found that children of ages 8 and 11 were able to make all the distinctions that were made by musically *experienced* adults in earlier studies such as Krumhansl and Shepard (1979). They concluded that tonal features that are salient to children may differ from those which are salient to musically *inexperienced* adults, a conclusion echoed by the findings of a similar study (Cuddy & Badertscher, 1987) which again conflict with Krumhansl and Keil's earlier results. Using contexts of an arpeggiated major triad, a complete ascending major scale, and a diminished triad, Cuddy and Badertscher found no apparent developmental change in patterns of judgements. The factor of context-type in this instance appeared to be more influential; the major triad context evoked a profile corresponding to that of a key of which the root of the triad could be assumed to be the tonic, the major scale produced a less defined profile (with the tonic the only note strongly preferred) and the diminished triad an essentially flat profile. Cuddy and Badertscher concluded that the triad is the most effective determinant of Western tonality.

THE STRUCTURE OF THE DIATONIC SCALE

These contradictory results throw into relief an issue that appears to have played only a limited role within the cognitive-structuralist programme, that of a rationale for the specific forms that scales and keys take within the models that it proposes. These could, of course, be taken as cultural "givens"; abstraction of the regularities of the music to which a listener had been exposed could then suffice (through the operation of something like Bharucha's MUSACT model) to actualise a sensitivity to scale and key structures as manifested within the culture's music. However, it has been suggested that particularities evident if pitch organisation is construed within a group-theoretic framework might in part determine the specific structure of the scales and keys that are employed in the musics of a number of different cultures; the empirical exploration of these particularities has served as the basis for an account of musical pitch in cognition that is explicitly intended as an alternative to that provided by the cognitive-structuralists[2].

It may be recalled that Shepard's model can depict the notes of a diatonic scale as a "connected region" of his multi-dimensional space. This property arises because Shepard's model is directly analogous in some of its characteristics to another method of representing musical pitch relations: Balzano's group–theoretic model of musical pitch relations (Balzano, 1982). Balzano treats the notes of the chromatic scale as analogous to the cyclic group of order 12 (i.e. the set of numbers 1 to 12, or 0 to 11). Within this approach, all octave-related notes are treated as functionally identical. This enables the notes of the chromatic scale—or chromatic set—to be depicted in two different circular, or cyclical, forms; these are directly analogous to the chroma circle and to the circle of fifths (see Fig. 15.8). This approach also relies on the idea that sets of notes can be regarded as functionally identical at the level of pitch class set if one set can be transformed into another by means of an operation such as

Figure 8(a)

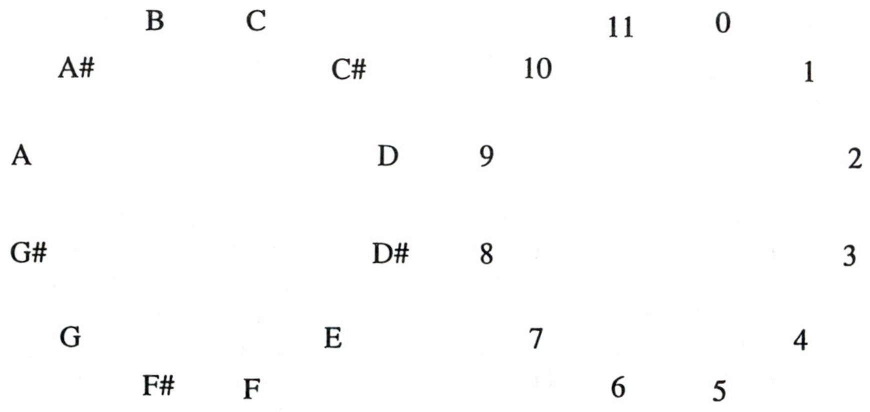

```
        B       C                              11      0
   A#                      C#              10                  1

 A                          D       9                              2

   G#                       D#      8                              3

     G              E                7                    4
        F#     F                                  6     5
```

Figure 8(b)

```
        F       C                               5      0
   A#                      G               10                 7

 D#                        D       3                              2

   G#                      A       8                              9

     C#             E                1                    4
        F#     B                                  6     11
```

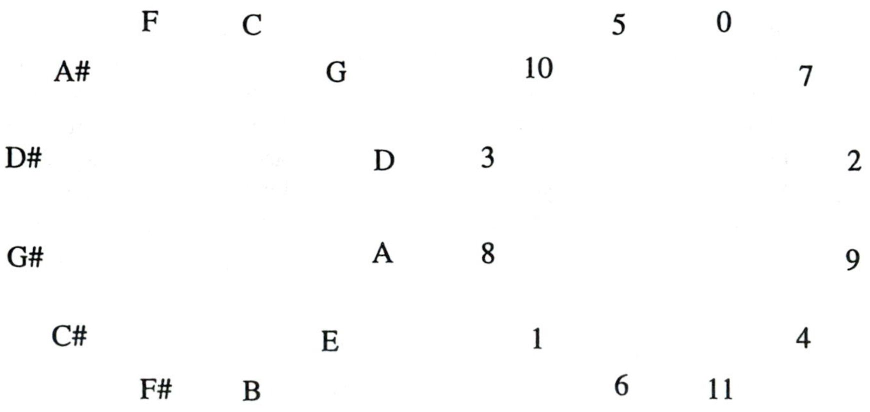

FIG. 15.8. (a) The chroma circle as note-names and as integers. (b) The circle of fifths as note-names and as integers.

368

transposition (and, in Forte's (1973) formulation, transposition together within inversion). Pitch class sets are unordered, being regarded as identical if they have the same membership irrespective of the order in which the members of the pitch class set are laid out. To give an example, the set [2,0,7]—or D, C, G—would be regarded as identical to the set [0,2,7], and to the set [2,4,9]. That is, within the group-theoretic representation of musical pitch, two sets of notes or pitch classes are identical when the same structural relations can be shown to hold for each set.

Balzano points out that within the group-theoretic representation, the pitch class set—or set of notes—corresponding to the notes of the diatonic scale has a number of special properties: it has the property of uniqueness, in that each pitch class can be differentiated from every other pitch class by the set of intervals that it forms with all other pitch classes of the set; it has the property of simplicity, in that each diatonic scale or diatonic set may be transformed into another such set by changing only one pitch class, the relation between the initial set and the transforming element being the same for all equivalent forms of the diatonic set; and it has the property of coherence in that the sum of any two intervals formed between three adjacent pitch classes or notes of the set will be greater than any single interval occurring between adjacent pitch classes. Coherence and uniqueness can be thought of as conferring possible advantages in perception, in that the notes of a diatonic melody will be differentiable by the intervals that they form with other notes irrespective of their order of occurrence, and any major or minor interval within the melody will correspond to a given number of diatonic scale steps enabling a listener to judge the size of movement that it constitutes within the underlying scale (with the sole exception of the tritone). The diatonic set is the only set within the group-theoretic representation of musical pitch that exhibits all these particular properties.

Balzano (1980) presents a further, more complex two-dimensional model based on intervals of major and minor thirds that is essentially analogous to that proposed by Longuet-Higgins (see above), except that Balzano's model requires enharmonic pitch identity (i.e. for the purposes of the model B♭ is functionally identical to A#). Within this more complex model, based on the direct-product group representation of the cyclic group of order 12, diatonic scales are compact entities formed by overlapping major and minor triads (see Fig. 15.9), with closely related keys lying adjacent within the space (cf. Fig. 15.6, Krumhansl's "harmony space"). In fact, all the unique properties of the diatonic set that are evident in the chroma and fifths circles are evident in the direct-product representation, with the addition that scales can also be seen as agglomerations of triadic structures, affording the possibility of easily representing both melodic and harmonic relations.

Possible implications of these properties of the diatonic set for perception have been further explored by Browne (1981). He suggests that diatonic set structure uniquely facilitates cognitive activities which he describes as position finding and pattern matching. Position finding involves questions concerning

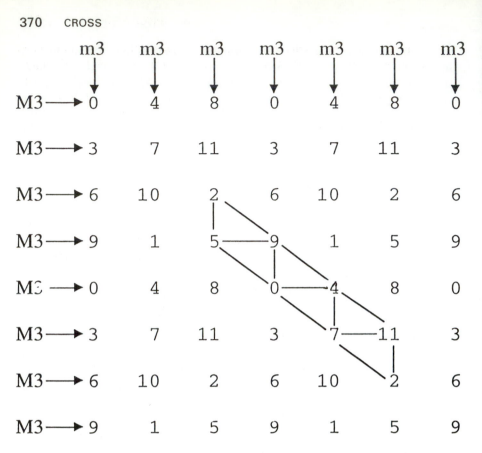

FIG. 15.9. Balzano's direct product group. Single steps are minor thirds in the y-dimension and major thirds in the x-dimension. A diatonic major set is shown based around C as an asymmetrical region. (Note that this two-dimensional representation constitutes an "unrolling" of a toroidal structure on the surface of which all points of the same integer are coincident.)

orientation and reference, such as "where are we?" (in respect of tonal space) and of "how long should I hear what happens in terms of note x?". So the identification of the tonic (or other structural notes) within a passage, or the tracking of modulations between tonal regions, could both be described as position finding processes. Pattern matching involves questions of similarity and belongingness, such as "is this the same as that?", or "does this belong to the same thing as that?".

Browne points out that within the diatonic set, intervals and subsets of the diatonic set (a diatonic subset is a set formable between any members of the diatonic set) can be regarded as either more rare or more common (i.e. can have a low or a high multiplicity). Thus the interval of a semitone occurs in only two positions within the set, while the interval of a perfect fourth occurs in six positions. Similarly the pitch class set [5,7,11]—equivalent to the set of notes F, G and B—can only occur in the one position within the set (low multiplicity), the pitch class [0,5,7]—C, F, G—can occur in five positions (see Fig. 15.10), while the pitch class set [0,2,5]—equivalent to C, D and F, or, (if inverted around the central pitch class) to the notes E, D and B—can occur in eight different positions (high multiplicity). Browne suggests that rare intervals (such as the tritone and semitone) or rare diatonic subsets such as [0,2,6] may fulfil position finding functions in cognition involving differentiation between notes within the diatonic set so as to specify a tonal hierarchy. On the other hand, common intervals or high multiplicity subsets such as [0,2,5] may help to effect pattern matching functions in cognition involving association and integration of notes as members of the set. Thus Browne proposes that the *structure* of the diatonic set —which, in Shepard's model, seems quite static, and rather "grid-like"—may play a dynamic role in the cognition of musical pitch and pitch relations.

PITCH STRUCTURE IN COGNITION: AN ALTERNATIVE ACCOUNT

The possibility that the type of diatonic structure described by Balzano (corresponding to Dowling's "tuning system" level of representation) might have some privileged status for Western listeners was tested by Cross, Howell and West (1983), who showed that even subjects who were not musically trained were sensitive to diatonic pitch structure. They algorithmically generated random melodic sequences that differed only in the number of consecutive notes they contained that could derive from any single diatonic major scale; for example, in the "least scalar" sequences any two, but no more than two, consecutive notes could derive from a single scale, while in the "most scalar" sequences all notes derived from a single scale. They asked subjects to rate these for preference (giving no explicit directions as to the features upon which subjects were to base their judgements). They found that subjects' preferences were linked to number of consecutive scale notes; the greater the number of consecutive diatonic notes contained in a sequence, the more subjects were likely to prefer that sequence.

A subsequent series of experiments (Howell, West & Cross, 1984) tested the bases for subjects' judgements about the degree to which pitches fitted in melodic sequences by asking subjects to identify wrong (i.e. "out-of-scale") notes in ongoing sequences. Their findings indicated that subjects were more likely to identify notes as wrong when the preceding pitches constituted a pitch-class set that was common within the diatonic set (i.e. constituted a set of type that Browne implicates in pattern-matching processes) than when the preceding pitches constituted a more scale-specific (position-finding) set. A further series of experiments (West, Cross & Howell, 1991) clarified these results by asking subjects to rate the fit of "out-of scale" probe notes following three-note

Figure 10(a)

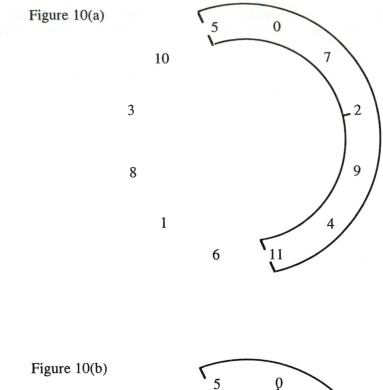

Figure 10(b)

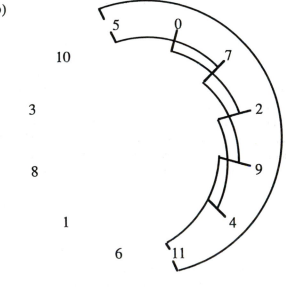

FIG. 15.10. Rareness and ubiquity of pitch-class sets within the diatonic set.
(a) Sets of the type [5, x, 11] can be formed in only a few positions within the diatonic set
(that shown is the set [5, 2, 11]).
(b) Sets of the type [5, 0, 7] occur in five positions within the diatonic set.

372

sequences that varied according to their diatonic commonness or multiplicity; it was found that high multiplicity sets such as the set [0,2,5] led to lower ratings for the probes than did low multiplicity sets, indicating that diatonically common sets were evoking a stronger sense of diatonic structure than were diatonically rare (but scale-specific) sets. A feature of these results was that even the tonally-referential triad set [0,3,7] was less efficacious than higher multiplicity sets in evoking a sense of diatonic structure. Overall, these findings suggest that Western listeners, whether musically trained or not, employ a schematic representation of musical pitch in listening within which diatonic structure has a privileged position and in which sets of pitches that are common within the diatonic set constitute the most potent activators of a "diatonic schema", fulfilling a pattern-matching function of the type suggested by Browne.

Exploration of Browne's concept of position-finding, together with a dissatisfaction with aspects of the cognitive-structuralist programme, have led Brown and Butler to put forward an account of musical pitch in cognition that differs significantly from the cognitive-structuralist version. Butler (1989) suggests that cognitive-structuralist findings can be accounted for largely by local pattern implications or by short-term memory processes. For example, the finding that diatonic notes are rated more highly than non-diatonic notes following a context of an ascending diatonic major scale might derive from a bias towards rating highly those notes of which traces persist in short-term memory rather than from the application of any schematic representation within longer-term memory. Similarly, a tendency to rate the tonic most highly following an ascending scalar context spanning a complete octave might derive from the saliency accorded to the tonic because it starts and ends the context (cf. Divenyi & Hirsh, 1978) rather than from operations based on a cognitive representation of the tonal hierarchy. Or it could be proposed that a tendency to rate the tonic highly following presentation of an *incomplete* ascending scale (i.e. rising from the tonic to the leading-note) could derive from local pattern implications of good continuation (see Bregman, 1990) rather than from global considerations of tonal hierarchy. In other words, Butler and Brown are proposing that the tonal hierarchy is an experimental artefact; they suggest that the perception of musical pitch is mediated by processes that are both more dynamic than those implicated in the cognitive-structuralist theories and more closely tied to structural potentials of patterns of pitches.

Brown and Butler (1981) showed that listeners exhibited a high degree of accuracy (87%) in producing a feasible tonic when presented with a three-note context consisting of two notes separated by a tritone plus one other note, irrespective of the order of the notes in the context. This finding sits well with Browne's (1981) suggestion that rare diatonic intervals (such as the tritone) are well-suited to play a position-finding role. However, a further study involving the identification of tonal centres (Butler, 1983) found that the efficacy of four-note diatonic subsets containing a tritone between two members (e.g. the set [0,1,5,6]) in acting as contexts that unequivocally specified a tonic for listeners was dependent on the order in which the notes of the context were presented. While the set is a good cue to the identity of a tonic for listeners when presented in the order [0,1,5,6], when presented in the order [0,5,1,6]—an order in which the diatonically-rare intervals in the set (semitones and a tritone) are not explicitly present—the efficacy of the context in cueing a tonic decreases.

Building on these findings, a study by Brown (1988) used nine categories of tonal *content* and four categories of tonal *context*, and required musically-trained listeners to sing appropriate tonics following brief contexts. The variable tonal content ordered the context sets according to the degree to which their structure unambiguously specified a tonic, while the variable tonal context classified context sets on the basis of the salience of diatonically-rare intervals within each context. She found that both variables, as well as their interaction, affected the performance of her subjects in identifying a tonic, and concluded that her subjects were sensitive to both time-independent and time-dependent functional relationships between pitches, these relationships being most easily perceived in the presence of rare intervals in "optimal" temporal orderings.

Recent papers by Butler (1989) and by Brown, Butler and Jones (1994) have extended and clarified these findings in presenting and testing the intervallic rivalry model, which is intended to counter many of the problematic aspects of the cognitive-structuralist account. The intervallic rivalry model rests on three related hypotheses: (1) that listeners assume the first pitch of a sequence is the tonal centre until a better candidate arrives (the primacy hypothesis); (2) that listeners rely upon rare intervals more than common intervals in deriving a sense of tonal centre, as these provide more reliable key information by unambiguously correlating with a single diatonic set; and (3) that listeners are more accurate in determining key when a rare interval appears in a temporal order implying goal-oriented harmonic motion of a type common in tonal music. They suggest (p. 377) that "the intervallic rivalry model assumes that enculturated listeners respond to incoming context by engaging in an active discovery process oriented toward identifying a tonal centre over the course of the music".

They tested the intervallic rivalry model in two "probe-tone" experiments, using a range of different types of context and employing listeners grouped according to level of musical training. Their first experiment set out to replicate the findings of Cuddy and Badertscher (1987) using adult listeners and to account for these findings in terms of the degree of ambiguity in the presented contexts when interpreted according to the intervallic rivalry model. It used three different contexts to precede probes (an ascending major diatonic scale, and arpeggiations of the major triad and diminished triad), predicting that the particular pitches used would act together with their temporal ordering so as to elicit the tonal hierarchy in subjects' responses (except that the responses to the diminished triad were expected to indicate no advantage for any particular pitch). The results of this experiment were closely in line with those of Cuddy and Badertscher, except that the tonic received a higher than expected rating following the diminished triad. While noting that this latter aspect of their results did not unambiguously favour either the intervallic rivalry or the tonal hierarchy theory, Brown, Butler and Jones claim that the intervallic rivalry theory is better able to account for most of their findings.

Their second experiment was designed explicitly to test the degree to which temporal and structural features of the contexts could be manipulated according to the intervallic rivalry theory so as to steer listeners towards particular interpretations of the contexts. Contexts with the same pitch content as in the previous experiment were employed; however, these were internally re-ordered so as to cue different responses. The major triad context was ordered so as to "favour" the subdominant (being presented as tonic, dominant, mediant, tonic) and the diminished triad was intended to favour the tonic (being ordered as leading-note, subdominant, supertonic, leading-note). The scalar contexts were presented in random order, the likelihood being that subjects would produce essentially flat responses as no particular note was being accorded primacy. The results of this experiment did not unambiguously support the intervallic rivalry theory; despite the randomisation the tonal hierarchy emerged in the responses following the scalar context. However, in accordance with the predictions of their theory the reordered major triad favoured the putative subdominant, while the diminished context led to responses favouring tonic as well as the submediant and the leading-note.

Butler and Brown's research indicates that temporal and structural factors that are generally neglected in the cognitive-structuralist approach can play a major role in the perception of musical pitch, even for listeners with little musical training; as Brown, Butler and Jones state (1994, p. 406) "key discovery and responsiveness to tonal implications is not the preserve of specially trained musicians". The role that Browne's theory allows for diatonically rare intervals and sets in pitch perception is confirmed, and they are identified as one component of the processes involved in key identification.

A COMPARISON OF THEORIES

The cognitive structuralists and the intervallic rivalry theorists thus propose two different mechanisms to account for musical pitch in cognition. The cognitive-structuralist research suggests that the primary processes involved in the perception of musical pitch are largely based on the pickup of information about the frequency distributions of pitches in the music of the perceiver's culture, both in terms of the "event hierarchies" of individual pieces and the "aggregate event hierarchies" of the totality of the music to which the perceiver has been exposed, or tonal hierarchy. Pickup of frequency distribution information thus leads to the formation of schemata within which pitches are functionally differentiated within keys in terms of their relative stabilities. By contrast, the intervallic rivalry theory suggests that processes of musical pitch perception are likely to be based on both order-information and on structural relations between pitches, emphasising the active, discovery-oriented nature of the processes involved. Such processes rely on the application of schemata embodying information about the functional characteristics of intervals and sets of pitches—in particular, their diatonic multiplicity and their harmonic implications—in the listening process.

It is notable that both cognitive-structural and intervallic rivalry theories incorporate schemata that embody diatonic structure. For the cognitive-structuralists, such a schema presumably arises through exposure to diatonic music within which the divergent frequency distributions of pitches that are differentiated by their positions within the diatonic scale—their scale-step aspect—give rise to different degrees of stability inhering in the cognitive representations of those pitches. Here, diatonic structure constitutes a given, and appears to be grid-like and static. On the other hand, within intervallic rivalry theory the schema embodies information about the structural characteristics of intervals and sets of pitches within diatonicism that can be employed to identify location within the scale. In this theory, diatonic structure is a dynamic feature of the listening process, and could be construed as an emergent property of the intervals and pitch-sets encountered in listening to music (cf. Cross, West & Howell, 1991).

The differences between the two theories can be interpreted as a difference in focus rather than in fact. Both theories acknowledge the role of order information in determining the "stability" of pitches in perception, and as we have seen, both rely on some representation of diatonicism. However, while the cognitive-structuralist theory focuses on the differential frequency distributions of pitches within music as an operational characteristic in perception, the intervallic rivalry theorists emphasise the role of diatonic multiplicity. This divergence between the two models can be interpreted as deriving from their focus on different perceptual stages and strategies in the perception of musical pitch. Brown, Butler and Jones (1994) themselves suggest as much in stating that the two models accentuate different aspects of tacit knowledge about tonality; the intervallic rivalry model centres on process of key discovery, the cognitive-structuralist account on reinforcement of tonal function, but both processes are necessary for a listener to follow tonal music in real time.

This suggestion, that the two theories reflect different stages or strategies in listening, is given force by the findings of both Castellano, Bharucha and Krumhansl (1984) (in which Western listeners responded to the event structures of the unfamiliar, North Indian, contexts while the responses of Indian listeners reflected "tonal hierarchical" relations appropriate to the music) and a recent study by Cuddy (1994). The latter conducted probe-tone experiments where diatonic contexts were specially composed so as to have frequency distributions of pitches (a component of the event structure) that differed from the tonal 'norm'. She found that subjects' responses to this unfamiliar music directly reflected the frequency-distribution aspect of the contexts' event-structures. This could be taken to imply that when the detail of the flow of events in a piece is unfamiliar it is likely that listeners will respond to global statistical characteristics such as the frequency distribution of events, while in listening to pieces that conform more to cultural norms prior knowledge concerning functional characteristics of intervals and pitch sets can employed in interpreting the music's structure. In other words, when presented with music in an unfamiliar but "followable" idiom in which structural relations between notes are employed in unexpected ways, expectations based on abstractions of structure (prior tonal knowledge) will be abrogated and attention directed towards the holistic properties of the music rather than to the detailed "argument" of its unfolding.

COOK AND THE CHARGE OF "THEORISMS"

Despite the advances in our understanding of musical pitch that these theories present, there is the possibility that both cognitive-structuralist and intervallic rivalry theories could be entirely misleading; as noted at the outset of this chapter, the possibility exists that the ideas of music theory, upon which many of the premises of both theories rest, do not encapsulate any of the characteristics of pitch cognition. Indeed Cook (1994) has attacked the notion of employing music-theoretic concepts in the investigation of music cognition (with particular reference to the cognitive-structuralist research programme); he asserts that studies of music cognition are unsatisfactory as studies of musical listening because "they begin with the premise that people hear music in terms of music-theoretical categories", an approach that he labels "theorism". He argues that such categories may well play a role in the perceptions of trained musicians, and claims that the study of music cognition, in relying on those theoretical entities, has produced not a "psychology of music" but a "psychology of ear training", instancing the findings of his own (1987) study as evidence for this[3].

Certain aspects of Cook's charge are undoubtedly worth considering. His contention that studies of music cognition, in relying on music theory, have undermined the validity of their results as accounts of the listening experience might well be applied as a criticism to some of Krumhansl's work; after all, in describing her study with Kessler (Krumhansl & Kessler, 1982) in her 1990 book, she states (p.26) that ". . . in order to decrease the chance that non-musical response strategies would be adopted, listeners had to have an average of 5 years of formal instruction in music", appearing to fall into the trap of identifying "musical" response strategies with those prescribed by music theory.

However, Cook's refutation of the utility of all studies of music cognition—or even of all Krumhansl's studies—as accounts of the listening experience does not stand up to scrutiny. It can scarcely be argued that those many studies that employ musically untrained listeners as subjects, and require them to make judgements that do not rely on any overt use of music-theoretic concepts or labels in their responses, fall into the error that Cook condemns. Indeed, it is evident that one of the studies that he criticises most harshly[4]—that of Castellano, Bharucha and Krumhansl (1984)—employs just such a group of listeners among its subjects (Western subjects with no prior experience of North Indian music), and that their results greatly illuminate the processes involved in listening to music in an unfamiliar but "followable" idiom.

In general, Cook's claims stand as a warning to (rather than a proscription of) research in music cognition. His criticisms may indeed stand as a valid reproach to many studies of ostensibly "musical" listening; however, there are many studies that do not make the assumption that music-theoretic entities and elements accurately encapsulate the varieties of musical experience, but use such entities simply because they offer ways of controlling and manipulating musical materials (much in the way that they are used in practical music within a literate culture: see Cross, 1985). Moreover, when the results of an experimental study suggest that aspects of these music-theoretic entities are operational in the cognitions of untrained listeners, this surely indicates either (1) that the experimental procedures involved were so over-determining that their potential findings must necessarily reflect an "artefactual" effect of these music-theoretic entities (a problem which should become evident through careful examination of the operational definitions employed, and of the experimental design) or (2) that these music-theoretic entities actually do capture something about the music as experienced (as one presumes many music-theoretic entities and principles must, for music theory to be anything other than an idiosyncratically deconstructionist fantasia). Indeed, as suggested at the outset of this chapter, the concepts of music theory can themselves be regarded as phenomena that the empirical study of music cognition must seek to investigate.

THE PSYCHOACOUSTICAL PERSPECTIVE

While Cook's charge of theorism might be applicable to a few of the studies cited above, almost all these studies could be charged legitimately with neglect of what would seem to be a fundamental aspect of the perception of musical pitch: that of how the physical signal and its mental depiction are interrelated. This is an issue which Shepard intended his original formulation of the cognitive-structuralist programme to exclude from explanations of musical pitch in cognition by his strictures on the unsatisfactory nature of a psychoacoustically-based theory of musical pitch perception (Shepard, 1982). Shepard suggests that psychophysical theories that are predicated on one-to-one correspondences between values in a physical domain and values in a psychological domain (such as are implicit in the statements by Seashore quoted at the outset of this chapter) cannot capture the complexity of perceived relations between pitches in a musical context. However, Shepard's criticisms are simply not applicable to certain recent psychoacoustical accounts of pitch perception.

The most developed of these accounts, that of Parncutt (1989), which partly derives from that of Terhardt (see Terhardt, Stoll & Seewann, 1982), provides an explanation for the way that chords and chordal successions are heard that derives both from the processes whereby the ear analyses out components of complex waveforms and from the processes whereby these components are integrated into some unitary percept are heard. Parncutt has produced an algorithmic version of his theory that is intended as a formal model of the ways that our perceptual systems function in musical perception; it is not intended to be a model of the actual neural processes involved.

Parncutt proposes that chords are heard as having unitary identities or roots because listeners have learned to hear complex periodic waveforms as having unitary pitches (generally correlatable with the fundamental frequency of the complex waveform). When a complex periodic sound is encountered, it is generally experienced as one pitch (see Fig. 15.11a); this occurs through a process of analysis of the waveform and its re-integration as a percept by the auditory system. Parncutt suggests that a similar process governs the perception of chords in music. Thus, a sounding triad—major or minor—can be heard as being one thing rather than three notes sounding together. However, Parncutt states that chords may be heard either synthetically or analytically, i.e. that individual chord components may be "heard out", on a similar basis to the processes involved in "hearing out" the components of a complex periodic waveform (see Fig. 15.11b). He suggests that the same factors constrain perception of single pitches and of chords. These factors derive, among other things, from the frequency-resolving power of the inner ear, the latency-period of the auditory nerve, and the establishment of a system of pattern-recognition based on "best fit" to the harmonic series. Thus he holds that the sensory processes involved in perception of single pitches govern the perception of chords.

The input to Parncutt's algorithmic model of the auditory system may be either a complex periodic waveform or a chord. The output, in response to the former, would not be one single "perceived pitch", but a set of probable perceived pitches, weighted according to the likelihood of their being "heard" in response to the input (see Fig. 15.11b). The output in response to a chord would similarly be either a set of possible weighted chord roots as in Fig. 15.11c or a set of chord components that are weighted according to their likelihood of being noticed. The set of chord roots would, Parncutt suggests, provide an index of the chord's perceptual stability, and hence of the likelihood of its being used in some referential way; if one root is much more highly weighted than the others the chord is probably stable—a major triad would be likely to have a fairly unambiguous root—while if several different roots are given the same

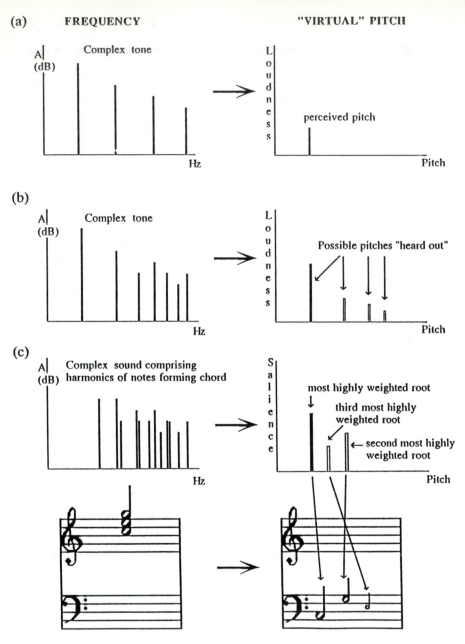

FIG. 15.11.

(a) Unitary pitch percept corresponding to fundamental frequency evoked by harmonic complex tone.

(b) Pitch evoked by harmonic complex tone constituting either a unitary percept ("virtual" pitch, shown as solid bar) or a cluster of "spectral" pitches corresponding to higher spectral components (shown as dotted bars).

(c) Possible "roots" of a triadic chord.

weighting, then the chord is likely to be perceived as unstable (e.g. the *Tristan* chord, which generates several equally likely roots).

In this way, this algorithmic account provides a rationale for harmonic stability or instability—functionally, consonance and dissonance—that is rooted in the nature of the sensory processes involved in hearing. Hence, Parncutt's theory can provide an explanation of why certain sets of notes should sound well together as chords and why others should sound unpleasant, as well as providing reasons for why chords such as major or minor triads should end a passage (their roots being relatively unambiguous, and the chords therefore stable) while others such as the *Tristan* chord sound "incomplete" (because its root is ambiguous it appears unstable).

This account can be seen as complementary rather than antithetical to the cognitive approaches outlined above, in that it addresses an issue—that of the relation between physical signal and the experience of musical sound—that they do not, and hence fills what could have been a theoretical lacuna. Indeed, Parncutt admits of the need for a theory at the pitch-class level (such as is embodied in most of these cognitive approaches) in order to account for aspects of musical perception that remain outside his theory. In fact, the bases of Parncutt's account have been disputed by some psychoacousticians who consider that the experimental evidence points to the operation of periodicity-sensitive mechanisms (see Moore, 1989) rather than to the spectral-abstraction processes upon which Parncutt's (and Terhardt's) theory relies. Patterson (1986) has proposed an account of musical pitch in cognition that relies on detection and abstraction of periodicities in the physical signal to structure our perceptions of pitch. He puts forward a complex "spectro-temporal" model for the perception of musical pitch, and suggests that the structure of the scales employed within Western tonal music, and hence their efficacy in music cognition, can be accounted for on the basis of properties of this model. However, his model relies on occurrence of low-integer relations between scale notes, leading him to accord a pre-eminent role to the "Just" scale form that cannot be supported by the historical record (see, e.g. Lloyd & Boyle, 1963).

Notwithstanding these caveats, it is evident that any theory of the perception of musical pitch must consider the processes that link the physical signal and the experience of musical sound as operational factors in determining the nature of that experience. It may be that such factors play a more potent role in shaping the tuning systems upon which Western music relies than in determining our sensitivities to structure in musical pitch (as suggested in Burns & Ward, 1982); it may be that they play quite different roles in musical perception within different cultures (as hinted at in Kubik, 1985). In the limit, they constitute constraints on our experience of musical pitch that cannot be ignored, and Parncutt's theory represents the most comprehensive attempt to date to explore this issue.

CONCLUSIONS

In summary, this Chapter has outlined the most influential recent research on the cognition of musical pitch. Following a brief description of the theories of Deutsch, Longuet-Higgins and Dowling, Shepard's formulation of the cognitive-structuralist approach is summarised. The empirical and theoretical development and refinement of cognitive-structural research programme by Krumhansl, Bharucha and others are then delineated in some detail. Following a brief reference to problematic issues in that research, the theories of Balzano and Browne are described; an account of the intervallic rivalry theory of Butler and Brown is then provided, and an attempt is made to compare and integrate the theories and findings of these two principal strands of current research on musical pitch in cognition. Cook's accusation that much of the research described here is invalidated by its "theorism" is addressed, and a brief account is given of current psychoacoustically-based approaches to the perception of musical pitch.

Given the primacy accorded to pitch in music theory and in casual discourse about music it is unsurprising that the cognition of musical pitch has been the focus of so much research interest. This research has resulted in the formation of coherent and robust accounts of the factors and processes that determine our experience of musical pitch. Nevertheless, pitch is but one aspect of music; however coherent a cognitive theory of musical pitch may be, it remains at best a partial account of the experience of music. Recent experimental work has begun to explore the perception of music by treating pitch as one amongst several interacting musical dimensions (see, for example, Monahan & Carterette, 1985; Boltz, 1993; Schmuckler & Boltz, 1994; Thompson, 1993, 1994; Thompson & Cuddy, 1992). Other research has focused on the global experience of music, in the process seeking to elucidate the role of pitch within the whole by examining the impact on subjects' responses of different types of pitch organisation (see Bigand, 1993; Deliège, 1987; Deliège & El Ahmadi, 1990).

In the last fifteen years the complexities of musical experience have been assailed by a number of researchers, notably Lerdahl and Jackendoff (1983) and Narmour (1989, 1992), who have put forward theories that purport to account for the global experience of music. Theories of pitch that are more or less compatible with those outlined above constitute significant components of these accounts (see, e.g. Lerdahl, 1988), and the theories that are outlined in this chapter can be expected to play a significant role in future research that is aimed at explicating the richness of the global experience of music.

NOTES

1. There were always exceptions to this equation of musical pitch with physical frequency. Indeed, Helmholtz, who, in laying much of the groundwork for an acoustical and psychoacoustical understanding of music might be thought to have been a proto-reductionist, explicitly defended his inclusion of "room ... for the action of artistic

invention and esthetic inclination" in his *Theory of Music* in the preface to the third German edition of his *"Die Lehre von den Tonempfindungen"* (1870).

2. Although Shepard (1982) and Krumhansl (1988, 1990) both agree that these particularities are likely to play a role in shaping the organisation of musical pitch in cognition.
3. Although Brown (1994) provides a concise and convincing reinterpretation of this study that renders this aspect of his case at best "not proven".
4. This criticism appears to arise from a misinterpretation of the concepts of "event hierarchy" and "tonal hierarchy" as evident in the combined and separate analyses of the responses of Indian and western subjects.

REFERENCES

Balzano, G. (1980). The group-theoretic representation of 12-fold and microtonal pitch systems. *Computer Music Journal, 4*, 66–84.

Balzano, G. (1982). The pitch set as a level of description for studying musical perception. In M. Clynes, (Ed.), *Music Mind and Brain*. New York: Plenum.

Bent, I. (1980). Analysis. Entry in S. Sadie (Ed.), *Grove's Dictionary of Music*. London: Macmillan.

Bharucha, J. J. (1984). Event hierarchies, tonal hierarchies, and assimilation: a reply to Deutsch and Dowling. *Journal of Experimental Psychology: General, 113*, 421–25.

Bharucha, J. J. (1987). Music Cognition and Perceptual Facilitation: a Connectionist Framework. *Music Perception, 5*, 1–30.

Bharucha, (1991). Pitch, harmony and neural nets: a psychological perspective. In P. Todd & D. G. Loy (Eds.), *Music and connectionism*. Cambridge, Mass.: MIT Press.

Bharucha, (1994). Mental tonal structures. In I. Deliège (Ed.), *Proceedings of the 3rd International Conference on Music Perception and Cognition*, (pp. 79–80). Liège, Belgium: European Society for the Cognitive Sciences of Music.

Bharucha, J. J., & Stoeckig, K. (1986). Priming of chords: spreading activation or overlapping frequency spectra? *Perception & Psychophysics, 41*, 519–524.

Bharucha, J. J., & Stoeckig, K. (1987). Priming of chords: spreading activation or overlapping frequency spectra? *Perception & Psychophysics, 41*, 519–524.

Bharucha, J. J., & Todd, P. (1991). Modelling the perception of tonal structure with neural nets. In P. Todd & D. G. Loy (Eds.), *Music and connectionism*. Cambridge, Mass.: MIT Press.

Bigand, E. (1993). Contributions of music to research on human auditory cognition. In S. McAdams & E. Bigand (Eds.), *Thinking in sound: the cognitive psychology of human audition*. Oxford: Oxford University Press.

Boltz, M. G. (1993). The generation of temporal and melodic expectancies during musical listening. *Perception & Psychophysics, 53* (6), 585–600.

Bregman, A.S. (1990). *Auditory Scene Analysis: the Perceptual Organisation of Sound*. Cambridge, Mass: M.I.T. Press.

Brown, H. (1988). The interplay of set content and temporal context in a functional theory of tonality perception. *Music Perception, 5*, 219–250.

Brown, H. (1994). Theories of perception of tonal harmony—musical psychoacoustical and cognitive: what do we really know about what we hear ? In I. Deliège (Ed.), *Proceedings of the 3rd International Conference on Music Perception and Cognition*, (pp. 71–72). Liège, Belgium: European Society for the Cognitive Sciences of Music.

Brown, H., & Butler, D. (1981). Diatonic trichords as minimal cue-cells. *In Theory Only, 5*, 39–55.

Brown, H. Butler, D., & Jones, M. R. (1994). Musical and temporal influences on key discovery. *Music Perception, 11* (4), 371–407.

Browne, R. (1981). Tonal implications of the diatonic set. *In Theory Only, 5*, 3–21.

Burns, E. M., & Ward, W. D. (1982). Intervals, scales and tuning. In D. Deutsch, (Ed.), *The psychology of music.* D. Deutsch (Ed.), London: Academic Press.

Butler, D. (1983). The initial identification of tonal centers in music. In J. Sloboda & D. Rogers (Eds.), *The acquisition of symbolic skills.* New York: Plenum Press.

Butler, D. (1989). Describing the perception of tonality in music: a critique of the tonal hierarchy theory and a proposal for a theory of intervallic rivalry. *Music Perception, 6,* 219–242.

Castellano, M. A., Bharucha J. J., & Krumhansl C. L. (1984). Tonal hierarchies in the music of North India. *Journal of Experimental Psychology: General, 113,* 394–412.

Cook, N. (1987). The perception of large-scale tonal closure. *Music Perception, 5* (2), 197–205.

Cook, N. (1994). Perception: a perspective from music theory. In R. Aiello with J. Sloboda, (Eds.), *Musical perceptions.* Oxford: Oxford University Press.

Cross, I. (1985). Music and Change. In P. Howell, I. Cross, & R. West (Eds.), *Musical Structure and Cognition.* London: Academic Press.

Cross, I., Howell, P. & West, R. (1983). Preferences for scale structure in melodic sequences. *Journal of Experimental Psychology: Human Perception and Performance, 9* (3), 444–460.

Cross, I., West, R., & Howell, P. (1991). Cognitive correlates of tonality. In P. Howell, R. West & I. Cross, (Eds), *Representing musical structure.* London: Academic Press.

Cuddy, L. L. (1994). Tone distributions in melody: influence on judgments of salience and similarity. In I. Deliège (Ed.), *Proceedings of the 3rd International Conference on Music Perception and Cognition,* (pp. 225–226). Liège, Belgium: European Society for the Cognitive Sciences of Music.

Cuddy, L. L. & Badertscher, B. (1987). Recovery of the Tonal Hierarchy. *Perception & Psychophysics, 41,* 609–620.

Deliège, I. (1987). Grouping conditions in listening to music: An approach to Lerdahl & Jackendoff's grouping preference rules. *Music Perception, 4,* 325–360.

Deliège, I., & El Ahmadi, A. (1990). Mechanisms of cue extraction in musical groupings: A study of perception on *Sequenza VI* for viola solo by L. Berio. *Psychology of Music, 18,*(1), 18–44.

Deutsch, D. (1969). Music recognition. *Psychological Review, 76,* 300–307.

Deutsch, D. (1981). The processing of structured and unstructured tonal sequences. *Perception and Psychophyics, 28,* 381–389.

Deutsch (1982). In D. Deutsch (Ed.), *The Psychology of Music.* London: Academic Press.

Deutsch, D. & Feroe, J. (1981). The Internal Representation of Pitch Sequences in Tonal Music. *Psychological Review, 88,* 503–522.

Divenyi, P. L., & Hirsh, I. J. (1978). Some figural properties of auditory patterns. *Journal of the Acoustical Society of America, 64,* 1369–1386.

Dowling, W. J. (1978). Scale and contour: two components of a theory of memory for melodies. *Psychological Review, 85,* 341–354.

Dowling, W. J. (1982). Musical scales and psychophysical scales: their psychological reality. In T. Rice and R. Falck (Eds.), *Cross-cultural perspectives on music.* Toronto: University of Toronto Press.

Forte, A. (1973) *The structure of Atonal Music.* New Haven: Yale University Press.

Francès, R. (1988). *The perception of music.* (trans. W. J. Dowling). Hove: Lawrence Erlbaum Associates Ltd. (Original work published, 1958).

Gjerdingen, R. O. (1994). Apparent motion in music. *Music Perception, 11* (4) 335–370.

Howell, P., West, R. & Cross, I. (1984). The detection of notes incompatible with scalar structure. *Journal of the Acoustical Society of America, 76* (6), 1682–1689.

Krumhansl, C. L. (1988). Tonal and harmonic hierarchies. In Sundberg, J. (Ed.), *Harmony and Tonality*. Stockholm: Royal Swedish Academy of Music.

Krumhansl, C. L. (1990). *The cognitive foundations of musical pitch*. Oxford: Oxford University Press.

Krumhansl, C. L., & Keil, F. C. (1982). Acquisition of the hierarchy of tonal functions in music. *Memory and Cognition, 10*, 243–51.

Krumhansl, C. L & Kessler, E. J. (1982). Tracing the Dynamic Changes in Perceived Tonal Organization in a Spatial Representation of Musical Keys. *Psychological Review, 89*, 334–368.

Krumhansl, C. L., Sandell, G. J. & Sergeant, D. C. (1987). The perception of tone hierarchies and mirror forms in twelve-tone serial music. *Music Perception, 5*, 31–78.

Krumhansl, C.L. & Shepard, R.N. (1979). Quantification of the hierarchy of tonal functions within a diatonic context. *Journal of Experimental Psychology: Human Perception and Performance, 5*, 579–594.

Kubik, G. (1985). African tone-systems: a re-assessment. *Yearbook for traditional music, 17*, 31–63.

Lakatos, I. (1970). Falsification and the methodology of scientific research programmes. In I. Lakatos & A. Musgrave (Eds.), *Criticism and the growth of knowledge*. C.U.P., Cambridge.

Lerdahl, F. (1988). Tonal pitch space. *Music Perception, 5*, 315–350.

Lerdahl, F., & Jackendoff, R. (1983). *A generative theory of tonal music*. Cambridge, Mass: MIT Press.

Lloyd, Ll. S., & Boyle, H. (1963). *Intervals, scales and temperaments*. London: Macmillan.

Longuet-Higgins, C. H. (1962a and b). Two letters to a musical friend. *The Music Review*, 244–248, 271–280.

Longuet-Higgins, C. H. (1976). The perception of melodies. *Nature, 263*, 646–653.

Longuet-Higgins, C. H. (1979). The perception of music. *Proceedings of the Royal Society, London, Series B, 205*, 307–322.

Monahan, C. B., & Carterette, E. C. (1985). Pitch and duration as determinants of musical space. *Music Perception, 3* (1), 1–32.

Moore, B C J. (1989). *Introduction to the Psychology of Hearing*. (3rd edn). London: Academic Press.

Narmour, E. (1989). *The analysis and cognition of basic melodic structures*. London: University of Chicago Press.

Narmour, E. (1992) *The analysis and cognition of melodic complexity*. London: University of Chicago Press.

Neisser, U. (1976). *Cognition and Reality*. New York: WH Freeman & Co.

Palisca, C. V. (1980). Theory. Entry in S. Sadie (Eds.), *Grove's Dictionary of Music*. London: Macmillan.

Parncutt, R. (1989). *Harmony: a psychoacoustical approach*. London: Springer-Verlag.

Patterson, R. D. (1986). Spiral detection of periodicity and the sprial form of musical scales. *Psychology of Music, 14* (1), 44–61.

Rosch, E. (1978). Principles of categorization. In E. Rosch & B. B. Lloyd (Eds.), *Cognition and categorization*. Hillsdale, NJ.: Erlbaum.

Schmuckler, M. A. & Boltz, M. G. (1994). Harmonic and rhythmic influences on musical expectancy. *Perception & Psychophysics, 56* (3), 313–325.

Seashore, C. E. (1938/1967). *Psychology of Music*. Dover: New York (original work published 1938).

Shepard, R. N. (1964). Circularity in judgments of relative pitch. *Journal of the Acoustical Society of America, 36*, 2346–2353.

Shepard, R. N. (1982). Structural representations of musical pitch. In D. Deutsch (Ed.), *The Psychology of Music*. London: Academic Press.

Simon, H.A., & Sumner, R.K. (1968). Pattern in music. In B Kleinmuntz (Ed.), *Formal representations of human judgment*. New York: Wiley.

Speer, J. R. & Meeks, P. U. (1985). School Children's Perception of Pitch in Music. *Psychomusicology, 5,* 49–56.

Terhardt, E., Stoll, G., & Seewann, M. (1982). Algorithm for extraction of pitch and pitch salience from complex tonal signals. *Journal of the Acoustical Society of America, 71,* 679–688

Thompson, W. F. (1993). Modelling perceived relationships between melody, harmony, and key. *Perception & Psychophysics, 53* (1), 13–24.

Thompson, W. F. (1994). Sensitivity to combinations of musical parameters—pitch with duration, and pitch pattern with durational pattern. *Perception & Psychophysics, 56,* 3, 363–374.

Thompson, W. F., & Cuddy, L. L. (1992). Perceived key movement in 4-voice harmony and single voices. *Music Perception, 9* (4), 427–438.

Tversky, A. (1977). Features of similarity. *Psychological Review, 84,* 327–352.

van den Toorn, P. C. (1983). *The music of Igor Stravinsky*. London: Yale University Press.

West, R., Cross, I. & Howell, P. (1991). Activation of schemas in perception—the case of musical scale conformance. *Psychologica Belgica, 31* (2), 197–216.

16 Cue abstraction in the representation of musical form[1]

Irène Deliège and Marc Mélen

Unité de Recherche en Psychologie de la Musique
Centre de Recherches et de Formation Musicale, de Wallonie
Université de Liège

INTRODUCTION

Until now, research in the psychology of music has rarely aimed to apprehend how a listener may grasp musical form. Nevertheless, this seems to be an urgent task if the discipline wishes to open up new perspectives. Most approaches generally present very brief stimuli of which the musical structure is very simple, being conceived so as to vary one dimension (rhythm, melody, . . .) while keeping the others constant. These simplifications are based on a legitimate desire to control the variables as in any experimental science. However, such an approach is unable to address the cognitive processes implied in listening to a complete piece of real music. The understanding of the perception of musical form needs to be based on appropriate musical objects, and interpretation of responses must be related to a close analysis of the musical structures employed. Thus, such approaches must be based on material taken from the existing repertoire, even if such materials provide few controllable and replicable dimensions.

Several generative models of music have been proposed (Deutsch & Feroe, 1981; Lerdahl & Jackendoff, 1983; Tenney & Polansky, 1980; Winograd, 1968). These models have several limitations. First, they are dedicated to tonal music. Moreover, they are not "real-time" models of ongoing music perception but rather "post hoc" accounts of the representations that might be formed after listening to a piece of music. In respect of Lerdahl and Jackendoff's *Generative Theory of Tonal Music*, Imberty put this idea in other words while drawing the attention to the fact that it is a theory of "the final stages of cognitive processing implied by the activity of listening and auditory analysis (. . .) which does not take into account cognitive processes which occur during listening, in the real time of actual listening" (Imberty, 1993, p.327). This remark, without doubt, could be extended to Tenney and Polansky's or Deutsch and Feroe's model, as these are much less developed than that of Lerdahl and Jackendoff. Moreover, that of Deutsch and Feroe is not strongly supported by empirical evidence (Boltz & Jones, 1986).

Lerdahl and Jackendoff's model is probably one of the most quoted by music psychologists. Paradoxically, very few experimental studies have been undertaken to test the validity of the rules underlying the model. The grouping preference rules (Deliège, 1987 b) and the metrical structures (Palmer & Krumhansl, 1987) have been for a long time the only aspects of the *Generative Theory of Tonal Music* that had been empirically approached. Recently, however, Bigand, Lerdahl & Pineau (1994) studied each of the four components of this theory: grouping structure, metrical structure, time-span reductions, and prolongational reductions. The theoretical structures of two pieces—the *St Antoni* chorale of Brahms and the chorale *Christus, der ist mein Leben*—were compared to the structures perceived by musicians and non-musicians. Only the grouping rules were empirically confirmed, several important discrepancies being observed between the perceived and the theoretical structures of the music in respect of the other components of the model.

This chapter aims to propose a model of the cognitive processes involved in attentive listening to a piece of music. "Attentive listening" should be understood as the situation in which the listener is devoting maximal cognitive resources to engage with the structure of the piece in an active listening process. Imberty (1981) has proposed similar ideas in an attempt to explain the temporal structuring of a musical work by both listener and performer. The main principle of this proposal lies in the perception of qualitative changes, which is the basic principle of segmentation of the musical information. These changes accentuate the elements that confer directionality on the piece,which come to constitute the dynamic vectors that progressively take on the weight of the successive changes during listening. Simultaneously they determine the style and the global schema of the work, i.e. the macrostructure (to adopt the term suggested by Kintsch and van Dijk (1978) in the context of text-comprehension). The organisation of the segmentations, reiterated at different hierarchical levels, permits the structure of the musical piece to be grasped. Two types of hierarchical organisation are postulated according to the perceptual salience of the changes encountered: when changes are few but very clear, they lead to a strong hierarchy; when segmentations are numerous and easily perceptible but are all of similar salience, they result in a weak hierarchy. The notions of schemata of order and schemata of order-relation are linked to these two types of organisation: schemata of order are formed by simple successions and juxtapositions and embrace both proximate and distant relations (increase, decrease, repetition and imitation); schemata of order-relation involve the organic relations that enable the establishment of relations between temporally-adjacent elements (theme, variation of the theme, syntactical or rhetorical relations, . . .). Schemata of order are more numerous within weak hierarchies—a situation often encountered in twentieth century works—while schemata of order relation can give rise to strong hierarchies, which are much more common in pieces from the tonal repertoire. It must be remembered, however, that what may be observed is the dominance of one organisational type or the other that changes according to the historical period (Imberty, 1985, p. 113).

Lerdahl (1989) suggested that in atonal music the hierarchies of alternations of tensions and relaxations should be replaced by hierarchies of salience of auditory events. Recently, Imberty (1991, 1993) extended this suggestion to any music, whether tonal or atonal; he proposes that perceptual organisation must constitute a "hierarchy of saliencies" before it can be a syntactic functional hierarchy. Nevertheless, according to Imberty, in the cognition of tonal music perceptual stability coincides with structural stability, in contrast to what happens in atonal music (Imberty, 1991).

THE PRESENT MODEL: OVERVIEW

To summarise, the model put forth here sees auditory analysis as a schematisation process, i.e. a reduction or even a simplification of the objective content of the material to be perceived, based on particular events picked up from the musical surface by the listener. A first sketch of this model was proposed in Deliège (1987 a) and has been progressively extended and experimentally studied. The main stages of the model are as follows.

The musical surface is first segmented into sections of various lengths. The cue abstraction mechanism, on the one hand, the principle of sameness and the principle of difference, on the other hand, offer the basis for the processes operating at this level, allowing segmentation of the temporal flow (Deliège, 1989) and the categorisation of musical structures (Deliège, 1991a; Deliège, 1996). In a later stage, the traces left by the reiterations of the cues lead to the formation of imprints in the long-term memory. The latter are forms of prototypes that integrate the main features of the style of the piece and enable an evaluation of the structures throughout listening. It is probably worth noting that analogous concepts have been quite recently proposed independently in the domain of visual art (Changeux, 1994).

Several experimental procedures have been employed to test the functional elements of the model, and will be outlined jointly with an explanation of the components of the model. The abstraction of cues has been assessed using a segmentation procedure; the mental line procedure and the segment-pair relation procedure show how cues may act as reference points during long time-spans; as a counterexample the puzzle procedure indicates that subjects without previous musical training (i.e. having thus poor declarative memory of what a musical construct is) are unable to organise musical fragments so as to construct a piece without previous listening during which they could have abstracted cues; the categorisation procedure specifies the classification and evaluation processes underlying the segmentation involved in listening; the imprint procedure, while showing also the effect of cues, clarified the cumulative effect of varied repetitions during the listening processes.

It seems reasonable to conceive of active listening as a schematisation process. Except in the case of exceptional memory (e.g. Sloboda, Hermelin, & O'Connor, 1985), a listener cannot remember all the details of a musical work. What kind of schematisation process can be hypothesised? A simple answer would be one based on processes of reduction, an idea with which musicians and music analysts, in particular, are familiar.

However, it should be noted that the processes of perceptual reduction proposed here as underlying the formation of a cognitive representation of a work are not directly analogous to the processes of reduction that are employed in the sphere of musical analysis (see Mélen & Deliège, 1995). The type of reduction engendered by the cues embodies, by definition, surface elements. It is in these surface elements that the most immediately identifiable reference points lie; the idea of cue-based reduction may thus be generalisable to any musical system since the model has its foundation in general cognitive mechanisms. It would be impracticable, however, to consider that the listener employs psychological mechanisms in listening that are specific to the type of music to which he is listening, the more so in that it would appear that identical processes mediate the treatment of stimuli of different origins (Deliège, 1992c). Psycho-linguistic studies can help us to imagine how a schematisation can operate. When one wishes to grasp the contents of a discourse, for example, one does not focus entirely on the literal text but rather on certain salient elements which summarise the meaning of a given section of the text. These elements can constitute the starting point for a kind of schematisation (Bartlett, 1932). Given that music, unlike a literary text, does not have an unequivocal semantic extension, the tools whereby a schema might be derived cannot be semantic. It can be argued that a general model of schematisation of music must be founded on elements coming from the musical surface, i.e. the cues.

The idea of cue

A cue always contains rare but striking attributes that link it to that which it cues (see Fig. 16.1) in order that the latter may be recognised (C. Peirce, 1974). A cue is a kind of conspicuous point that becomes fixed in memory by virtue of its relevance and by repetition (Deliège, ibid.). What might constitute a cue depends on the cultural and historical provenance of a given piece. For example, "motifs", i.e. local structures whose identity is reinforced by forms of repetition and/or variation, appeared in Western music only in the fifteenth century. Thus from this period until the end of the period of common tonal practice, cues may well be provided principally by motivic elements. In more recent periods—and most likely, in other cultures—other types of musical elements (acoustic, instrumental or temporal parameters) may operate to fulfill this role (Deliège, 1992d). (see below for further details).

The process of cue-abstraction could well have physiological correlates: Rötter (1994) recorded electrodermal responses while subjects segmented the final movement of the fourth *Brandeburgisches Konzert* by Bach, and found that peaks in skin resistance coincided with the different occurrences of the theme of the fugue, indicating an orientation reflex towards this structure.

The Cue as a Tool Underlying Processes of Discourse Segmentation

As in any other perceptual domain (in the domain of visual perception, for example, see Kubovy & Pomerantz, 1981), the formation of a representation of music requires at the outset the segmentation of the information; the object to be represented must be divided into small units. As far as music is concerned, this process (which is the perception of the rhythmic pulse of music) assembles the sounds in groups on the basis of their temporal and/or acoustic properties. Several experimental programmes have been devoted to the study of grouping processes (for a review see Deliège, 1987b; Deutsch, 1982), generally interpreting their results in the context of Gestalt principles, mainly the principles of proximity and similarity.

FIG. 16.1. A leitmotif, *Riesen-Motif*, from *Das Reingold* by Wagner, indicating examples of different durations of musical material that may be held to constitute cues in perception. (adapted from Deliège 1992, reprinted by permission from the publisher)

THE SEGMENTATION PROCEDURE

Two principles can be thought of as even more general than proximity and/or similarity, and are responsible for processes of grouping and of integration of groups: the principle of sameness and the principle of difference (Deliège, 1989). Elements will be attributed to a given group as long as they are not considered too different from the preceding elements (principle of sameness), although a certain degree of tolerance is accepted and a boundary between two groups will be only established when a contrast is perceived between two regions (principle of difference). [see also Deliège (1991b)].

Grouping is generally conceived of as a means to avoid overloading memory. This assumption is probably true in a very large number of situations. However, given that a piece of music generally extends over a long time-span, local groupings do not seem to be adequate to the task of representing an entire piece economically. In other words, the accumulation in memory of small rhythmic units concatenated in a long series of groups is unlikely to constitute an appropriate means of deriving an acceptable cognitive representation (Deliège, 1991a, 1992a). The cue-abstraction mechanism suggested by Deliège (1987a, 1989) seems to offer an appropriate alternative mechanism for encoding the information contained in groups recorded successively over long periods of time.

Instead of storing each group in memory, it is suggested that the listener selects salient cues that are themselves incorporated in the groups. Because of their special temporal and/or acoustic features, these cues are picked up from the musical surface and stored by the listener in working memory. The cues contain the *invariants* of the musical discourse. As such they are the starting point for processes of comparison between old and new entries in working memory on the basis of the principles of sameness and difference. Thus cues intervene at all stages of the grouping process and become principal factors in the integration of groups at different hierarchical levels of listening (i.e. the grouping process will persist as long as similar kinds of invariants are recognised).

The role of the principles of sameness and difference based on the invariants contained in the cues were investigated by requiring subjects to segment a piece of music in order to delineate the most important sections of pieces (using Berio's *Sequenza VI* for viola solo and Boulez's *Eclat* as stimuli; see Deliège, 1989, 1991 a & b). In both experiments, the subjects listened to the piece three times. During the first hearing (given for familiarisation) subjects could write down, if they wished, any observations which might help them to complete the task; during the second and the third hearings they gave their responses. Subjects could follow the elapsed time (in minutes and seconds) on the screen of a computer, and marked off the sections of the pieces by pressing a key of the computer. The segmentations of Berio's piece were compared with two auditory analyses provided by two young composers who served as experts (see Fig. 16.2). Both experts divided Berio's piece into six sections (for further description of the piece see Deliège, 1989). It was predicted that subjects would not mark off a section as having ended as long as the same invariant (a cue) was perceived, i.e. that subject's segmentations would coincide with the main sections of the piece. This prediction was supported by the results: many more subjects segmented at the boundaries of sections indicated by the experts than at other places. Inside of these main sections, internal segmentations were also recorded but these did not contradict the cue-abstraction hypothesis, being always less frequent and being motivated by perception of a local contrast. A similar tendency was evident in the experiment on Boulez's *Eclat*, which was undertaken in order to replicate the previous experiment and to test the cue abstraction hypothesis itself in a different musical context. Indeed, whereas Berio's writing in *Sequenza VI* is mainly concerned with intense processes of development based on invariant structures—which should favour integration of groups based on the sameness principle, and consequently generate results that should favour the cue-abstraction hypothesis—Boulez, in *Eclat*, takes a completely different approach where invariance is not a dominating

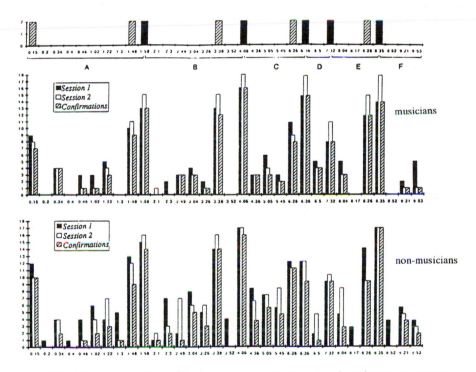

FIG. 16.2. The segmentations of Berio's *Sequenza VI* (the entire piece) by two composers, 18 musicians, and 18 non-musicians, in the two experimental sessions. "Confirmations" indicate the number of subjects who had segmented at the same place in both sessions (source, Deliège 1989, reprinted by permission from the publisher).

compositional principle. In *Eclat*, the listener is faced with relatively independent sound-states separated by long temporal breaks, and as a consequence, cue abstraction should be less operative and contradicted in the segmentation process by the presence of important rests.

Surprisingly, the results corresponded with those recorded for the Berio piece: it appeared that the temporal gaps were progressively less effective after about three minutes listening, and strong main segmentations were again perceived by musician subjects as well as non-musicians', leading to a division of the piece into five main sections (see Fig. 16.3). Non-musicians sensitivity to temporal disjunctions lead them to segment in shorter groups than musicians. The latter result was previously observed in Deliège (1987 b) and again recently by Bigand et al. (1994) in a segmentation study of a piece by Brahms.

These two experiments indicate that cues are key elements in the schematisation of musical discourse. As groups become integrated into larger structures, there is a dynamic interaction between the cues that have been developed. Most are likely to succeed and become the landmarks of the

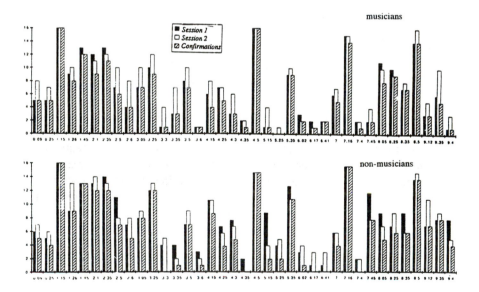

FIG. 16.3. The segmentations of Boulez's *Eclat* (the entire piece) by 16 musicians, and 16 non-musicians, in the two experimental sessions. "Confirmations' indicate the number of subjects who had segmented at the same place in both sessions (source, Deliège 1989, reprinted by permission from the publisher).

discourse. A mental representation of the musical form progressively develops on the basis of the abstracted cues which simultaneously organises the "same-different" testing. According to Guyau (1890), the discrimination of similarities and differences is the "first condition of the idea of time" (p. 22). That is precisely the role played by the cues in the course of listening: the elements that the cues integrate and represent are, by definition, frequently reiterated and permeate the whole form of the work, its entire architecture. They are figures around which a musical process is built up. The choice of contemporary pieces of music and the comparison of the responses of musicians (professionals involved in performing contemporary music who had received a complete tuition in harmony and music analysis) with those of non-musicians (who had never received any formal tuition and were not acculturated to new music) allowed the degree of generality of the cue-abstraction mechanism to be tested. It seems that musicians and non-musicians do use identical means to process music, differences between the two groups being largely attributable to the efficiency of their use of these processes. Cues collected by musicians tend to be richer, broader, and more relevant than cues picked up by non-musicians.

The Cues as Reference Points for Long Time Spans: Three Research Procedures

The foregoing was intended to indicate how cues mediate in the processes of segmentation of a piece. However, the cues also have another function. Each cue can be though of as an encodable label which summarises and gives access to the whole group (Deliège, 1987a, 1989). In other words, a further function of the cues is to generate abbreviations of self-organised units which reduce the amount of information to be stored in memory. Such abbreviations are thus a simple and effective way of processing large quantities of data (ibid). They would act primarily as reference points which help subjects to represent the time course of the piece. Accordingly, it was hypothesised that the representation of the temporal course of a piece could be symbolised in the form of a mental line (Deliège, 1991a, 1993) along which the structures labelled by the cues would progressively take their place. Delineating identifiable temporal regions, the cues would orient attention while a representation of the architecture of the work is built. Processes of cue abstraction would give rise to a "feeling" of the time that had elapsed between two events, and to an idea of the location of the similar structures in the work. As noted by Deliège (1991a, 1992b), this notion has some kinship with ideas developed by Fraisse (1967), Michon (1979), Richelle and Lejeune (1988). Other affinities exist with the notion of cognitive maps formulated by Tolman (1948) and expanded by Pailhous (1970) in his work on the representation of the urban space. The function of cues as reference points has been studied through the mental line and puzzle procedures, with some evidence being provided by the segment pair relation procedure.

THE MENTAL LINE PROCEDURE

In this procedure subjects listened to a piece three times and were then presented with segments which they had to locate precisely in the piece. Three different versions of this procedure have been applied. In the first, subjects were informed that the piece contained X sections and that they would be presented with a large number of segments to be located in their original section. The second version was more demanding as the subjects received fewer segments to be located on a horizontal line divided into X boxes which symbolised the complete duration of the piece. ("X" corresponds to the number of segments to be expected by the subject in the task). They were told to write in one of the boxes the number of the segment (i.e. the number corresponding to the order of its occurrence in a random presentation) that they considered to be the first segment heard in the piece, in a second box the number of the second-heard segment, etc. They were not obliged to fill all the boxes and were allowed to insert a segment between two segments already positioned. An additional task was incorporated in the third version of the procedure by giving the subjects the opportunity to listen to the "piece" which resulted from their own ordering and to correct their errors if possible.

The different versions of the procedure have been applied in respect of a number of different pieces: Berio's *Sequenza VI* (Deliège & El Ahmadi, 1990), Boulez's *Eclat* (Deliège, 1991a; 1993), Schubert's *Valse sentimentale* D779 (Deliège, Mélen, Stammers, & Cross, 1994), Haydn's *Menuet* Hob IX;12(8) (Cross, Stammers, Mélen, & Deliège, 1996). Broadly similar results have been obtained in respect of the different pieces. In the first application of the mental-line approach (in its first version), after having performed the segmentation experiment on Berio's piece subjects were presented with about forty extracts. They were told that the piece was divided into six main sections and had listened to a performance in which the boundaries of the sections were signalled by an external tone. Subjects then heard all the extracts in a random order and were asked to assign each of them to the appropriate section. Interestingly, some extracts were mislocated when similar cues appeared in different sections, nevertheless it was less the case for musicians. This result is a first indication of an imprint effect (see later discussion) as the confusions generally occurred for segments belonging to temporal locations based on similar invariant structures.

In Boulez's *Eclat*, using the second version of the procedure, subjects were not presented with all the segments of the piece. The experiment would have been too long as the task took place immediately after the segmentation experiment (reported above) in which the subjects had not been warned that they had to make any particular effort to memorise the piece. Fifteen segments (including the first and last) were chosen so as to present a variety of local cues. They were taken from the different sections. Subjects (musicians and non-musicians) had to order the fifteen segments on a line made of fifteen boxes symbolising the full length of the piece. In musicians' responses, the first segment received a mean location of 1.7 (actual location = 1) and the last segment a mean location of 14.7 (actual location = 15). For the non-musicians, the mean locations were situated between 6 and 12.1 (see Table 16.1). Thus the temporal frame was narrower for non-musicians than for musicians. The mode of the frequency distribution of each segment-placement in musicians' responses coincided almost perfectly with the actual position of the segments in the piece. The errors were more frequent for segments located at the middle of the piece. Musicians exhibited a primacy and a recency effect: the initial segment and those from the final section were remarkably well localised. The non-musicians evidenced a greater disparity between the actual positions of the segment and the adjudged position, and their results did not appear to show either a recency or a primacy effect. The mean correlation between the actual order and the perceived order was r = 0.62 for musicians and r = 0.30 for non-musicians. The correlation was negative for some non-musician subjects, indicating a confusion between the beginning and the end of the piece. Such confusions never occurred for musicians. Clustering analyses showed that the perceived proximities between the segments in the mental schemata of the subjects, either musicians or non-musicians, corresponded with the actual proximities of the segments in the piece to a high degree.

The third version of the mental line procedure was employed only with non-musicians (Deliège et al., 1994). This experiment was based on a very simple and short piece by Schubert (*Valse sentimentale* D779) divided into eight two-bar segments according to Lerdahl & Jackendoff's (1983) grouping rules (it should be noted that segments 5 and 6 were exact repetitions, see Fig. 16.4). Subjects

FIG. 16.4. Schubert's *Valse sentimentale*, D 779, Op. 50 No. 6 and the partitioning into eight segments used in the experiment.

TABLE 16.1
Mode (**) and Mean Localisation Judgement Observed
in the Subjects' Responses

extract	MUSICIANS		NON-MUSICIANS	
	mode	mean	mode	mean
1	**1**	1,7	**1**	6
2	**2**/5	5,1	**2**/12	7,8
3	**6**/4	6,3	**11**/12-5(*)	8,1
4	**5**/2-9	7,2	**3**/7 (*)	7,2
5	**5**/7	7,7	**12**/5-3	7,9
6	**6**	6,2	2-5 (*)	6,3
7	**9** (*)	9,3	**9**/7	8,9
8	7-8-9-10	9,5	4-6 (*)	8,9
9	**4**/9	7,3	**3** (*)	6,5
10	**12**/7-3	8,5	**10**/5-8	7,5
11	**11**/10	9,9	**9**/11	9,3
12	**12**	10,5	**9**/12-10	9,4
13	**13**	10,7	13-6	10,7
14	**14**	13,3	**15**/14	12,1
15	**15**	14,7	**15**/14	11,3

(*) = extracts for which the modes do not reflect their actual localisation.

(**) figure in bold = principal mode; ordinary figures = secondary mode, i.e. the most frequent response after the principal mode. The numbers separated by a hyphen are the cases where 2 extracts were equally located in that position.

(from Deliège, 1993, adapted by permission from the publisher).

had to reorder the eight segments after three hearings of the piece, the task being carried out twice. For segments 1, 5 and 8, the mode of the frequency distribution of segments localisation corresponded to their actual occurrence in the piece, although for segments 5 and 8 these modes appeared to be rather weak. Moreover, analyses of mean distances between actual location and the position attributed by subjects produced significant differences for all segments except segment 1, showing a real discrepancy between the expected results and the observed responses. It seems that the function of the first segment was the only one generally well understood. Segment 4 was often localised near its actual position on both trials, but the mode of the frequency distribution of placement did not correspond to its actual location. Thus it seems that the subjects were clearly sensitive to the central position of this segment but not to its order in relation to the exact centre of the piece. Both segments 5 and 6 were generally placed in the right position on the second trial: in the first trial this was the case for only one of these segments.

As far as the frequency distribution of the positions attributed to the segments is concerned (see Table 16.2), subjects' representations of the piece improved in accuracy on the second hearing; for five segments out of eight (segments 1, 2, 5, 6, and 8) the mode corresponded to the actual location. Moreover it should be noted that on the second trial modes were recorded that had at least four or five responses. Nevertheless, this apparent increase in accuracy in the second trial is hypothetical: the effect of trial, and of the interaction between segments and trials, did not reach significance.

THE PUZZLE PROCEDURE

If the cues collected during listening enable subjects to construct a mental representation of the piece, thanks to their function as temporal landmarks, it should be very difficult, at least for non-musicians, to build a piece starting from separated chunks without having created any references by prior listening. In order to test this hypothesis, subjects were required to recreate the most coherent piece possible within a given time using the "kit" of segments prepared for the previous procedure. All segments were visually symbolised by identical icons that had no relationship to their content. They were displayed simultaneously on the screen of a computer. Subjects built a piece simply by moving these icons so as to arrange them in a linear order. The segments were presented in a different random initial layout for each subject. Subjects could make as many changes as they liked during the thirty minutes allowed for the task. Before and during the task they could listen to the segments and to their constructed "piece" at will as often as they wished (Deliège et al., 1996).

In musicians' pieces the segments were generally in the correct position. In non-musicians' pieces, no segments were placed in a correct location: position 1 or 2 was generally assigned to segment 7; position 3 or 5 to segment 1; position 4 to segment 8; position 6 to segment 2; and position 7 or 8 to segments 5 and 6.

TABLE 16.2
Primary and secondary modes of location

Seg.	First trial					Second trial				
	Mode	Mean	Mean distance	t-value	p	Mode	Mean	Mean distance	t-value	p
1	1/3	2.19	1.19	2.10	.07	1/7	3.31	2.31	2.37	.04
2	2-7	3.94	2.19	2.99	.02	2/8	4.69	2.69	2.77	.02
3	2-3-5.5	4.50	2.00	3.09	.01	2/4	3.06	1.06	4.43	.003
4	**5.5**/4	4.87	1.62	3.39	.01	2-3-4-5.5	3.62	1.12	4.02	.002
5	**5.5**/4	4.56	1.56	2.78	.02	**5.5**/4	5.12	1.00	2.49	.04
6	8/1-7	5.69	2.44	4.53	.002	**5.5**/7	6.19	0.68	1.94	.09
7	7-5.5	5.25	2.00	3.09	.01	1-3-5.5	3.75	3.25	4.23	.003
8	8/5.5-4	5.75	2.25	3.13	.01	8	5.87	2.12	1.97	.08

The table indicates, for the eight segments in both trials, the primary (bold numbers) and secondary modes of location, the mean location chosen for each segment, the mean distance from the correct location and the comparison tests with significance levels for the results of the Experiment (non-musician subjects, on Schubert's *Valse*).

Nevertheless, analyses of the mean distances between the actual location and the position selected showed that some segments were less well located both by musicians and non-musicians: for musicians, segments 3 and to a lesser extent 2 and 5 were given more distant mean positions, while segment 4 received less distant mean positions. For non-musicians, segments 1 and 2 were given more distant locations while segment 3 received less distant mean positions. Again, for the non-musicians, a particular ordering of the segments was more frequent: they put a cadential segment at the mid-point of the piece and began the second part with a tonic segment. Nevertheless, in general they did not confer a well-formed structure on the piece, tending to use cadential segments too early which resulted in a dearth of cadential segments in the latter half of the piece. While it is worth emphasising that non-musicians never started the piece with a cadential segment, they could not enlarge the tension-relaxation relationships beyond a local level: for any increase in tension the need of an immediate relaxation is observed [Bigand et al. (1994) reported similar results for a piece of Brahms].

Even in the best cases, non-musicians' pieces were unbalanced and far from the classical model. Musicians were more sensitive to the structural functions while non-musicians' appeared to be only sensitive to local or immediate tonal structural relations. Nevertheless, the musicians' sensitivity to tonal functions was far from infallible: if they put generally the appropriate cadential segments into the correct locations, their representation of the tonal functions seems to be imprecise. Indeed, given the particularly trivial compositional plan of that piece, a better result would have been expected with formally trained subjects.

These results confirm that non-musicians' prior implicit knowledge of the tonal system is too vague to allow them to build a coherent piece. The reference to a set of memorised cues seems to be necessary. Let us emphasise that the comparison of the appropriateness of the locations was statistically better in the mental line experiment, where subjects had the opportunity to listen to the piece beforehand, allowing abstraction of cues. The puzzle procedure evidenced also, but *a contrario*, the usefulness of cues for the musicians: even if their pieces were closer to the original piece, they made, with such a simple material, errors which show that the implicit knowledge alone is insufficient to reach an accurate mental representation of a more complex piece of music.

Using a segment inversion method, a kind of puzzle imposed by the experimenter on the material, H. de la Motte (1994) reported results of related interests. The subject, in this case, is only listening to the patchwork made up before the task and is not required to reconstruct a piece. Sixty five professional musicians were presented with the first movement of the *Sonata op. 49 n° 1* by Beethoven in which the order of the exposition and recapitulation had been reversed. Only seven subjects noticed the inversion leading to her conclusion that "form perception is a conceptual act rather than a spontaneous perception" (ibid., p. 279). Of course, the inversion of the exposition and recapitulation does not violate tension-relaxation relationships existing at a local level, a result that seems to meet the observation made in the puzzle procedure experiments where it was shown that non-musicians were not able to extend tonal relationships beyond a local level. These results may also be regarded as indicating that a cognitively abstracted musical form does not necessarily coincide with the musical form as theoretically defined (see also Molino's tripartition, 1975).

THE SEGMENT-PAIR RELATION PROCEDURE

Further light is cast on the mental line hypothesis by results of experiments using a segment-pair relation procedure. If cues serve as reference points they should enhance subjects' capacities to judge the temporal position of each segment with regard to each other. In an initial experiment subjects listened to the piece by Schubert three times. They then heard every possible serial ordering of all pairs of different segments, presented in both correct (i.e. the order in which the segments had occured within the piece) and incorrect orders and were asked if the segments in each pair were correctly ordered or not (Cross et al., 1996).

A primacy effect was observed for musicians: performance was better when the first segment of the piece was included in the pair. They also appeared to perform better when a segment-pair could be identified as forming a phrase. Overall, the presentation of segment-pairs in the correct order positively influenced musicians' results, indicating that their mental representations incorporated temporal characteristics of the musical surface. On the contrary, non-musicians' performances remained largely opaque.

A further experiment modified the materials of the piece by excising the anacrusis (of three quavers) at the beginning of each phrase, which was intended to delineate more clearly the periodic structure of the piece. Musicians' responses did not appear to differ greatly from those found with the previous presentation; however, temporal characteristics of the musical surface were incorporated in representations formed by both musicians and non-musicians. The initial and terminal functions of segments were encoded in both musicians' and non-musicians' representations (both groups' results indicating primacy and/or recency effects). Moreover, as for musicians, non-musicians performed better when a segment-pair formed a phrase, especially when presented in correct order. It seems that the excision of the anacruses improved non-musicians' performance. This appears to indicate that non-musicians tended to abstract less efficient cues than musicians, a conclusion already evident in the results of experiments reported above: remember that limited similarities between segments mislead the non-musicians to a considerable extent. Such confusions, indicating the formation of an imprint, will appear clearly in the next procedure, as it is especially designed to study this process.

The Cue as Reference Point in a Categorisation Process: Two Procedures

The categorisation process in listening to music (Deliège, 1991a, 1995, 1996; Deliège & Dupont, 1994) is described here in relation to Rosch's model. Rosch (1975, 1978) defined two categorisation principles—horizontality and verticality—in connection with the concept of category. Horizontality is to be understood as the spreading out of different exemplars within the same unit in which the category is still identifiable no matter how far deviation from the original model occurs. Verticality, on the other hand, specifies relationships between categories, which leads to the idea of hierarchy of category levels. Rosch (ibid) defined three levels: the superordinate, the basic, and the subordinate levels. At the highest or superordinate level, the category is defined by its function. The intermediate, or basic level, contains the greatest number of specimens having common attributes. They belong to the functional category but remain independent of one another. The lowest level, the subordinate, is made up of all imaginable variations of the specimens from the basic level.

The notion of horizontality is exploited primarily in the listening process, since we are here concerned with the incidence of the set of variations that may be generated from one basic element (the cue). The application of the notion of verticality is not nearly so obvious. A simple transfer to music listening of hierarchical principles deriving from language, and hence referring back to precise semantic concepts and content, is not possible. Nevertheless, these principles could be extended to music in the following way. The idea of a basic level in categorisation in listening to music may be conceived of in terms of different cues being abstracted within the same work. Each of these cues will engender its own relationships of horizontality. They will each have their own function and create their own particular auditory image (Leipp, 1977) yet share a common reference: the style of the work. The superordinate level may then be conceived as inhering in the referential value that each cue confers on a group within the mental representation of the work. The subordinate level is characterised by the relationships between patterns having analogous auditory images, which falls within the concept of horizontality.

Rosch's notion of horizontality also touches on the concepts of typicality and prototype. Most cues are momentary and fugitive: if the memory trace left by a given cue is not "refreshed" by a simple or varied repetition, it is erased from the memory. The traces deposited by the accumulation of varied repetitions of cues are transformed into a sort of "résumé" of the main coordinates of a set of presentations around the same basic structure, i.e. the imprint. The notion of imprint is not, however, a set of fixed traces any more so than the reiterations of cues themselves are. Rather, it is a central yet moving and flexible tendency which either settles or readjusts depending on the particular presentation of the cues. One can see a direct kinship between the notion of imprint and the notion of prototype.

The concept of the imprint has a twofold application to listening to music. As a prototypical "résumé", it first acts in facilitating the recognition of musical patterns as well as the style of the work. The imprint does not exist prior to listening except in the case of works and styles known beforehand. As it develops, however, the imprint not only synthesises and integrates the co-ordinates of its own category but also those of the composition itself. It thereby becomes capable of detecting errors or stylistic deviations. Consequently, the notions of cues and imprint formation require that the musical architecture of a given work correspond to a system that is identifiable when heard: they are not applicable with random music.

THE CATEGORISATION PROCEDURE

The basic level (cue-abstraction) and superordinate level (integration of groups based on the principle of sameness) have been addressed by means of the segmentation procedure (see above). Starting again from the basic level, the subordinate level was studied by means of a categorisation procedure made up in four different tasks.

In the first task, subjects (musicians and non-musicians) listened to the "Allegro assai" of Bach's *First sonata for violin solo* in C major (Deliège, 1991a; Deliège, 1996). They then listened only once to the two main motives (reference motives A and B, see Fig 16.5) of that piece and were asked to evaluate their frequency of occurrence on a three points scale (from 1 = not frequent to 3 = very frequent). For the second task, motives A and B were presented eight times consecutively (plus one repetition of each to refresh memory), then all the motives derived from both reference motives (first degree derivatives, see Fig. 16.5) were presented randomly and had to be classified in the appropriate category (A or B). In the third task, subjects had to evaluate, on a seven point scale (with 0 = completely different and 6 = perfectly identical), the similarity between one of the main motives followed by one of its variations; each pair was presented three times in a different random order. Four problematic cases were included: two pairs whose elements shared a perfect similarity (A followed by A, or B followed by B) and two pairs whose elements did not share any similarity (A followed by B or the reverse). The fourth task was a new classification test where the subjects were presented with motives which had a less direct kinship with the main motives than those employed in the second and third tasks, i.e. second degree derivatives (see Fig. 16.5).

It has already been suggested that the different cues abstracted during listening to a piece represent the basic level of categorisation, since they engender their own relations of horizontality in the process of encoding their auditory image in the mental structures. The present procedure seems to give support to this hypothesis: for example, after one hearing, musicians' evaluation of the frequency of occurrence of the main motifs was perfect, while that of the non-musicians was nearly so. Musicians also performed perfectly on the first classification task, and non-musicians reached a good level of performance. However, non-musicians seemed to have a more rigid auditory image which reduced their ability to compare the patterns, as shown by several convergent results. Moreover, the range of relationships of horizontality, i.e. the boundary of a category engendered by a cue, can thus be seen as narrower for a non-musician (the segmentation procedure and the mental line procedure led to similar observations). Once again, familiarisation with the musical structures through repeated listening influenced the performance of non-musicians more than musicians: the accuracy of non-musicians' similarity judgements improved linearly with the number of auditions of the segments to be compared. A similar effect was found for the recognition of Wagnerian leitmotivs (Deliège, 1992 a): non-musicians required more repetitions of the leitmotivs but as soon as they were well memorised, non-musicians and musicians reached comparable levels of efficiency in identifying the numerous variations of these leitmotivs.

The second task—classification of first degree derivatives—yielded better results than any of the other tasks. This led to the hypothesis that categorisation is a two-stage mechanism, one stage involving automatic processes (cue-abstraction for classification), the other involving central processes (evaluation of occurrence and similarity judgements). In order to test this hypothesis, a similar experiment was undertaken with 9-to-11 years old children, musicians and non-musicians (Deliège and Dupont, 1994). It was suggested that this dissociation between stages of categorisation might be more readily observable before adulthood.

The fourth task—classification of the second degree derivatives—however, was excluded from the experiment with children: the first classification task was taken to be sufficient to test the hypothesis. Moreover, for subjects of this age the experiment would have been too long. It was predicted that children would encounter more difficulties than adults in the estimation of occurrences of the

FIG. 16.5. The "Allegro assai" of Bach's *First sonata for violin solo* in C major. The reference motifs A and B are underlined (from Deliège, 1991a; Deliège, 1996, adapted by permission from the publisher).

reference motives and in the evaluation of similarities. Three pieces were chosen: the *Ländler* n°10 D 145 by Schubert, the final "Rondo" of Diabelli's *Sonatine* n° 2 and the initial section of the "Allegro assai" of Bach's *Sonata for violin solo* in C major (measures 1-42). The results seem to provide support to the hypothesis: classification performance reached about 90 percent for Diabelli and Schubert, and about 75 percent for Bach; the estimation of frequency of occurrence was undertaken adequately only in respect of the most simple musical structure (i.e. Diabelli's piece). The similarity rating task led to poor results: children were more misled than adults by partial similarities or by hidden similarities.

THE IMPRINT PROCEDURE

Since the end of the 1960's, the notion of prototype has given rise to significant experimental studies within different areas of cognitive psychology (Bransford & Franks, 1971, 1972; Franks & Bransford, 1971; Posner, Goldsmith, & Welton, 1967; Posner & Keele, 1968; Solso & Raynis, 1982). A method similar to that used in these studies was adopted for the research reported here. This method is centred principally on the acquisition phase of material containing a number of items that can be identified as coming from a basic model, a prototype, followed by a recognition phase (the prototype is not presented among the items of the acquisition phase). The recognition phase then follows. All items to be recognised derive from the prototype. Some were presented during the acquisition phase, while others were not; the prototype is, however, presented in this phase. The subjects were then asked to report whether they had perceived the item during the acquisition phase or not, and to specify if possible the degree of certainty of their responses. The underlying hypothesis is that the *prototype would be erroneously felt as having been perceived during the acquisition phase* although it had not been presented during this phase.

The idea of imprint formation which is examined here is akin to the concept of prototype. In the mental line procedure (see above), subjects, mainly non-musicians, were confused about the localisation of segments which were more or less similar. This result was referred to an imprint. effect. Further investigations of this cognitive aspect of the information process are undertaken using an experimental procedure that follows a method similar to that described above. Subjects listened to the initial section of the "Allegro assai" of Bach's *First sonata for violin solo* in C major (Deliège, 1991a). They were then presented with 36 sequences divided in three conditions: (1) items which had been already heard; (2) items which belonged to the unheard section of the piece; (3) items incorporating some rhythmic modifications (see Fig. 16.6). Subjects had to decide whether the sequences had been heard or not in the section of the piece they had listened to. It was hypothesised that, in the second condition, items very similar to already-heard sequences from the initial section would be likely

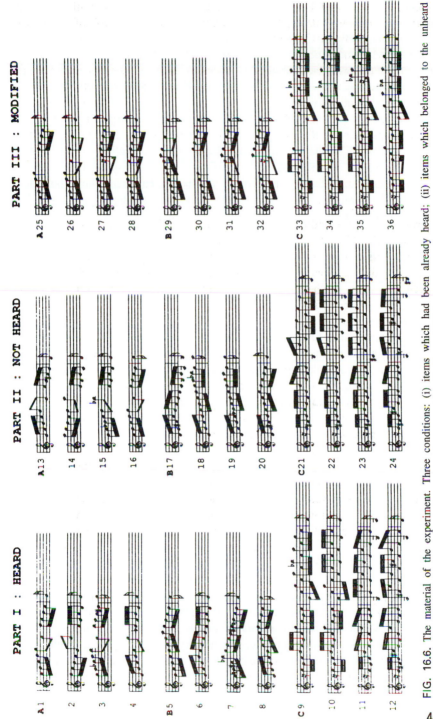

FIG. 16.6. The material of the experiment. Three conditions: (i) items which had been already heard; (ii) items which belonged to the unheard section of the piece; (iii) items with rhythmic modifications (from Deliège, 1991a).

to be accepted as already-heard. As for the last condition, errors and stylistic incongruities should be detected easily as the auditory image that constitutes an imprint will embody stylistic features of the piece. As expected, an imprint effect was observed in both non-musicians' *and* musicians' responses. For a great proportion of the responses, sequences pertaining to the non-heard section of the piece were accepted as having already been heard and sequences involving rhythmic modifications were massively rejected.

Accordingly, it is essential to consider the effects of imprints in relation to the stylistic characteristics of a work. Imprints seem to form relatively rapidly after cue-abstraction by means of repetition. These standard auditory images thus take on the role of analysers of the "musical scene", establishing the boundary between what is and what is not the norm within a given piece. The importance of rhythmic characteristics and their effect on the similarity perceived by listeners is here again demonstrated. As a final point, it can be stated that this research establishes a direct link with the concepts developed by Biederman (1981) in the analysis of visual scenes. It supports the idea of the existence of psychological constants underlying temporal experience in listening to music as well as in visual conditions.

CONCLUSIONS

To date there are very few psychologically plausible accounts of the cognitive representation of musical form. Psychology of music must find in this matter, as in others , a sort of middle way between two extreme positions (Sloboda, 1992). On the one hand, most of the suggestions proposed by music analysts or theoreticians are too general to be easily testable, formulating definitions of the musical form which are analogic in essence. H. de la Motte (1994) refers us to the concept of the musical form as an organism, an idea first evident in the works of Aristotle. Another and more contemporary example of such an analogy is proposed by Nicolas (1994), who suggests that musical form could be considered as a number. Such propositions may have some heuristic value but their discussion is beyond the scope of the present chapter. It suffices to note that they do not enable any experimental approach to the idea of musical form. On the other hand, most current psychological approaches are based on extreme simplifications of the musical material, rendering themselves irrelevant in the study of musical form. The experimental testability of *The generative theory of tonal music* is probably the main factor explaining its attraction among music psychologists. This model can be considered as falling in the middle way alluded to here. Nevertheless, empirical studies seem to indicate that its psychological plausibility is questionable, at least considered as a model of real-time listening to music. Furthermore, it is largely restricted to tonal music.

The present chapter is intended to put forward a plausible and testable model of real-time listening to music that is applicable to a broader repertoire. This model assumes that, in order to experience the form of a piece of music, a listener must abstract a mental representation of the given work. As such, music comprehension relies on processes which govern also the understanding of other conceptual objects. This assumption can sound very surprising as music is generally considered as having no direct semantic content. It must be remembered, however, that a concept, per se, is in fact a-modal, i.e. does not have a specified format (Rumelhart & Norman, 1985; Vauclair, 1994). Thus there may well be no obstacle to conceiving of music comprehension as a particular example of conceptual reasoning. In accordance with this basic postulate, it was assumed that the schematisation of the musical discourse underlined by the cue is similar to the schematisation arising in text comprehension; and that the idea of imprint, as a prototypical résumé, is similar to the prototype resulting from the numerous occurrences of different exemplars of a given object or individual.

The absence of semantic content in music obliges us, however, to focus on the role of the elements deriving from the musical surface. The present model assumes that a general theory of music understanding, i.e. a theory potentially relevant for any music or any listener, must show how the musical surface is progressively processed to form a mental representation. This proposal is not intended to "flatten out" the differences between musics of different origins, nor to neglect the differences between musicians and non-musicians. The analyses of results reported throughout this chapter prove aplenty that the particularities of the piece to be represented must be taken into account. The analyses show also that musicians and non-musicians do differ in their ability to understand music, but that the processes exhibited by both categories of listeners are not different, they are simply used more efficiently by musicians, as indicated by the effect of musical training on the memorisation of the musical structures. The cue-abstraction process has been observed by expert musicians and untrained listeners in different musical repertoires (Bach, Schubert, Wagner, Berio, Boulez, Reich, among others). Whatever the type of musical literature, the functional role of the mechanism has never been denied. The fundamental reason of the broad generalisability of the cue-abstraction process lies in the fact that this process is accompanied by the formation of the *imprint* which embodies the stylistical characteristics of the work in the course of listening. The cue-abstraction and the imprint formation orient the listener toward an "intelligent" auditory analysis. The auditory images of the structures are related to each other, establishing horizontality relationships characteristic of the subordinate level. and allowing the categorisation of these structures. These comparisons of structures and the evaluations of similarity organize the schema of the work.

The study of the representation of the musical form is for psychology of music a difficult topic, as it implies the use of musical material taken directly from the repertoire. Moreover it has to be underpinned by a theoretical framework not restricted to a limited period of the history or on the music of a particular culture.

In this sense, this model presented here may well offer a sufficiently generalisable tool for the investigation of these questions.

NOTE

1. The authors are profoundly indebted to Ian Cross for comments on an earlier draft of this paper and his supervision of the English writing. This research was supported by a grant from the Belgian Programs of Scientific Politics for an Interuniversity Pole of Attraction "Temporal reasoning and behavioral variability".

REFERENCES

Bartlett, F.C. (1932). *Remembering*. Cambridge (UK.), Cambridge University Press.

Biederman, I. (1981). On the semantics of a glance at a scene. In M. Kubovy and J.R. Pomerantz (Eds.), *Perceptual Organization*, pp. 213–253. Hillsdale, NJ, Lawrence Erlbaum.

Bigand, E., Lerdahl, F. & Pineau, M. (1994). Deux approches expérimentales des quatre composants de la Théorie Générative de la Musique Tonale. In I. Deliège (Ed.), *Proceedings of the 3rd International Conference on Music Perception and Cognition* pp. 259–260. Liège, Belgium: European Society for the Cognitive Sciences of Music.

Boltz, M., & Jones, M.R. (1986). Does rule recursion make melodies easier to reproduce? If not, what does? *Cognitive Psychology*, *18*, 389–431.

Bransford, J.D., & Franks, J.R. (1971). The abstraction of linguistic ideas. *Cognitive Psychology*, *2*, 331–350.

Bransford, J.D., & Franks, J.R. (1972). The abstraction of linguistic ideas: A review. *Cognition*, *1*, 211–249.

Changeux, J.P. (1994). *Raison et plaisir*. Paris: Odile Jacob.

Cross, I., Stammers, D., Mélen, M., & Deliège, I. (1996). The cognitive representation of tonal musical structure. In B. Pennycook & E. Costan-Giomi (Eds), *Proceedings of the 4th IPMPC* (pp. 59–63). Montreal, McGill University.

de la Motte, H. (1994). La perception de la forme musicale. In I. Deliège (Ed.), *Proceedings of the 3rd International Conference on Music Perception and Cognition* pp. 279–280. Liège, Belgium: European Society for the Cognitive Sciences of Music.

Deliège, I. (1987a). Le parallélisme, support d'une analyse auditive de la musique: vers un modèle des parcours cognitifs de l'information musicale. *Analyse musicale*, *6*, 73–79.

Deliège, I. (1987b). Grouping conditions in listening to music: An approach to Lerdahl & Jackendoff's grouping preference rules. *Music Perception*, *4*(4), 325–360.

Deliège, I. (1989). A perceptual approach to contemporary musical forms. In S. McAdams et I. Deliège (Eds.), Music and cognitive Sciences. *Contemporary Music Review*, *4*, 213–230.

Deliège, I. (1991a). *L'organisation psychologique de l'écoute de la musique. Des marques de sédimentation—indice, empreinte—dans la représentation mentale de l'œuvre*. Université de Liège. (Unpublished Doctoral Dissertation).

Deliège, I. (1991b). La perception de l'opposition Invariant /Variant. Etude expérimentale à partir de l'œuvre de Steve Reich: "Four Organs". *Psychologica Belgica*, *31*(2), 239–263.

Deliège, I. (1992a). Recognition of the Wagnerian Leitmotiv. Experimental Study based on an excerpt from *Das Rheingold*. *Jahrbuch für Musikpsychologie*, *9*, 25–54.

Deliège, I. (1992b). Analyse musicale et Perception: points de rencontre. *Analyse Musicale*, *26*, 7–14.

Deliège, I. (1992c). De l'activité perceptive à la représentation mentale de l'œuvre musicale. L'extraction d'indices: un parallèle entre les processus de compréhension de textes et l'écoute de la musique. *Analyse Musicale*, *28*, 29–36.

Deliège, I. (1992d). Paramètres psychologiques et processus de segmentation dans l'écoute de la musique. In R. Dalmonte and M. Baroni (Eds), *Actes du 2e Congrès Européen d'Analyse Musicale*, pp. 83–90. Trento, Italy: Universita' degli studi di Trento, Dipartimento di Storia della Civilta' Europea.

Deliège, I. (1993). Mechanisms of cue extraction in memory for musical time. In I. Cross and I. Deliège (Eds), Proceedings of the 2nd International Conference on Music and the Cognitive Sciences, Cambridge, September 1990. *Contemporary Music Review*, 9, 191–207.

Deliège, I. (1995). The two steps of the categorization process in music listening. An approach of the cue extraction mechanism as modular system. In R. Steinberg (Ed.), *Music and the mind machine. Psychophysiology and psychopathology of the sense of music*. Heidelberg: Springer Verlag, 63–73.

Deliège, I. (1996). Cue abstraction as a component of categorisation processes in music listening. *Psychology of Music*, 24, 131–156.

Deliège, I., & Dupont, M. (1994). Extraction d'indices et catégorisation dans l'écoute de la musique chez l'enfant: effet de l'âge, de la formation et du style sur la capacité à identifier, classer et comparer des structures musicales. In I. Deliège (Ed.), *Proceedings of the 3rd International Conference on Music Perception and Cognition* (pp. 287–288). Liège, Belgium: European Society for the Cognitive Sciences of Music.

Deliège, I., & El Ahmadi, A. (1990). Mechanisms of cue extraction in musical groupings: A study of perception on *Sequenza VI* for viola solo by L. Berio. *Psychology of Music*, *18*(1), 18–44.

Deliège, I., Mélen, M., Stammers, D., & Cross, I. (1994 a). Musical schemata in real time listening. In I. Deliège (Ed.), *Proceedings of the 3rd International Conference on Music Perception and Cognition* (pp. 271–272). Liège, Belgium: European Society for the Cognitive Sciences of Music.

Deliège, I., Mélen, M., Stammers, D., & Cross, I. (1996). Musical schemata in real time listening to music. *Music Perception*, *14*(2), 117–160.

Deutsch, D. (1982). Grouping mechanisms in music. In D. Deutsch (Ed.), *The psychology of Music* (pp. 99–134). New York, Academic Press.

Deutsch, D., & Feroe, J. (1981). The internal representation of pitch sequences in tonal music. *Psychological Review*, 88, 503–522.

Fraisse, P. (1956). *Les structures rythmiques*. Louvain, Belgium: Publications universitaires.

Fraisse, P. (1967). *La psychologie du temps*. Paris: Presses universitaires de France.

Franks, J.J., & Bransford, J.D. (1971). Abstraction of visual patterns. *Journal of Experimental Psychology*, 90, 65–74.

Guyau, J.M. (1890). *Genèse de l'idée de temps*. Paris: Alcan.

Imberty, M. (1981). *Les écritures du temps. Sémantique psychologique de la musique*. Tome 2. Paris: Dunod.

Imberty, M. (1985). La *Cathédrale Engloutie* de Claude Debussy: de la Perception au sens. *Revue de Musique des Universités Canadiennes*, 6, 90–160.

Imberty, M. (1991). Comment l'interprète et l'auditeur organisent-ils la progression temporelle d'une oeuvre musicale? *Psychologica Belgica*, *31*(2), 173–196.

Imberty, M. (1993). How do we perceive atonal music? Suggestions for a theoretical approach. *Contemporary music review*, 9, 325–338.

Kintsch, W., & van Dijk, T.A. (1978). Toward a model of text comprehension and production. *Psychological Review*, *85*(5), 363–394. French translation in Denhière, (Ed.), *Il était une fois . . . Compréhension et souvenir de récits* (pp. 85–142). Lille, France: Presses Universitaires.

Kubovy, M., & Pomerantz, J.R. (Edss) (1981). *Perceptual Organization*. Hillsdale, NJ: Lawrence Erlbaum.

Leipp, E. (1977). *La machine à écouter*. Paris, Masson.

Lerdahl, F. (1989). Atonal prolongation structure. *Contemporary music review*, *4*, 65–88.

Lerdahl, F., & Jackendoff, R. (1983). *A generative theory of tonal music*. Cambridge, Mass.: M.I.T. Press.

Mélen, M., & Deliège, I. (1995). Extraction of cues or underlying harmonic structure: Which guides recognition of familiar melodies? *European Journal of Cognitiive Psychology*, *7*, 81–106.

Michon, J.A. (1979). Le traitement de l'information temporelle. In P. Fraisse et al. (Eds), *Du temps biologique au temps psychologique* (pp. 255–287). Paris: Presses Universitaires de France.

Molino, J. (1975). Fait musical et sémiologie de la musique. *Musique en Jeu*, *17*, 37–62.

Nicolas, F. (1994). Nombre/lettre et œuvres musicales. In I. Deliège (Ed.), *Proceedings of the 3rd International Conference on Music Perception and Cognition* (pp. 91–92). Liège, Belgium: European Society for the Cognitive Sciences of Music.

Pailhous, J. (1970). *La représentation de l'espace urbain*. Paris, Presses Universitaires de France.

Palmer, C. & Krumhansl, C. L. (1987). Independent temporal and pitch structures in perception of musical phrases. *Journal of Experimental Psychology: Human Perception and Performance*, *13*, 116–26.

Peirce, Ch. S. (1974). *Collected Papers*. Cambridge, Mass.: Harvard University Press.

Posner, M.I., Goldsmith, R., & Welton, K.E. Jr. (1967). Perceived distance and the classification of distorted patterns. *Journal of Experimental Psychology*, *73*, 28–38.

Posner, M.I., & Keele, S.W. (1968). On the genesis of abstract ideas. *Journal of Experimental Psychology*, *77*, 353–363.

Richelle, M. & Lejeune, H. (1988). Le temps en psychologie. In A. Nysenhole & J.P. Boon (Eds), *Redécouvrir le temps* (pp. 103–115). Bruxelles, Belgium: Editions de l'U.L.B.

Rosch, E. (1975). Cognitive reference points. *Journal of Experimental Psychology: General*, *104*, 192–233.

Rosch, E. (1978). Principles of categorization. In E. Rosch & B. Lloyd (Eds.), *Cognition and categorization* (pp. 28–49). Hillsdale, NJ: Lawrence Erlbaum.

Rötter, G. (1994). The perception of form and its relation to emotional listening and physiological data. In I. Deliège (Ed.), *Proceedings of the 3rd International Conference on Music Perception and Cognition* (pp. 277–278). Liège, Belgium: European Society for the Cognitive Sciences of Music.

Rumelhart, D.E. & Norman, D.A. (1985). Representation of knowledge. In A.M. Aitkenhead & J.M. Slack (Eds), *Issues in cognitive modelling* (pp.15–62). Hillsdale, NJ: Lawrence Erlbaum.

Sloboda, J.A. (1992). Psychological structures in music: core research. In J. Paynter, T. Howell, R. Orton & P. Seymour (Eds), *Companion to contemporary musical thought*, vol. 2 (pp. 803–839). London: Routledge.

Sloboda, J.A., Hermelin, B., & O'Connor, N. (1985). An Exceptional Musical Memory. *Music Perception*, *3*(2), 155–170.

Solso, R.L., & Raynis, S.A. (1982). Transfer of prototypes based on visual, tactual and kinesthetic exemplars. *American Journal of Psychology*, *95*, 13–29.

Tenney, J. & Polansky, L. (1980). Temporal gestal perception in music. *Journal of Music Theory*, *24* (2), 205–241.

Tolman, E.C. (1948). Cognitive maps in rats and men. *Psychological Review*, *55*, 189–208.

Vauclair, J.A. (1994). Les représentations chez l'animal. In M. Richelle, J. Requin, M. Robert (Eds), *Traité de psychologie expérimentale*, vol. 2, pp. 226–270. Paris: Presses Universitaires de France.

Winograd, T. (1968). Linguistics and the computer analysis of tonal harmony. *Journal of Music Theory*, *12*(1), 2–49.

17

What is the pertinence of the Lerdahl-Jackendoff theory?

Jean-Jacques Nattiez
University of Montreal, Canada

By the "pertinence" of a particular musical theory, I mean ascertaining those aspects of the total musical fact which it is in a position to describe. Within the semiological perspective which I have adopted, it means knowing whether the theory describes the immanent structures of a piece of music, the compositional strategies which produced it, or the strategies of perception to which it gives rise. I am referring here to the semiological theory (Molino 1975, Nattiez 1987) which makes a distinction between three levels: the neutral, the poietic and the aesthesic.

A search for such pertinence is not restricted to these three dimensions. For example, in the case of the theory which I shall examine—that developed in Lerdahl and Jackendoff's *A Generative Theory of Tonal Music* of 1983—one could test out its parametrical pertinence: the work takes account of pitches, rhythms, metre and accents, but makes little of timbre, mass, texture; similarly, it neglects music's expressive dimension—musical semantics, to use the semiological term. I shall limit this inquiry to pertinence as defined by the theory of tripartition: the three levels.

For the sake of the clarity of what follows, before examining the *Generative Theory* from this point of view, two points need to be defined:

1. In seeking to establish the pertinence of a theory, it is useful to distinguish between what the author explicitly states and what the author really does.
2. In my own elaboration of the tripartite model, I distinguish between what I call the inductive poietic and the external poietic, and, symmetrically,

between the inductive aesthesic and the external aesthesic (Nattiez 1987 pp. 176-8).

An inductive analytical process is one which infers compositional or perceptual strategies from the observation of a piece's structure. In assigning structures a pertinence—poietic or aesthesic—one in fact proceeds to an *interpretation* of these structures, and in order to be able to proceed to this interpretation, it is necessary to have at one's disposal a *theory* of the poietic and a *theory* of the aesthesic which are kept separate from the methods for describing structures.

An external analytical process is one which, to determine the poietic or aesthesic pertinence of structures, has recourse to documents external to the piece under consideration: on the poietic side, letters, sketches, a series of other works; on the aesthesic side, accounts obtained from guinea-pig listeners in the context of an experiment.

The aesthesic pertinence of Lerdahl and Jackendoff's theory is clearly expressed from the book's very opening: "We take the goal of a theory of music to be a *formal description of the musical intuitions of a listener who is experienced in a musical idiom*" (1983 p. 1). In its explicit form, the theory's pertinence comes under the category of inductive aesthesic: *aesthesic*, because it concerns the description of the listeners' intuitive strategies; *inductive*, because the theory presents itself as formal, that is, its intention is to describe hypothetically, and with the help of rules, the predictable perceptual strategies which are linked with certain musical configurations observed in the score. This is why the theory envisages the verification of such rules by the expedient of the experimental process (ibid., p. 5). Certain of Irène Smismans-Deliège's works (1985) have focused upon this issue.

So, in this case, we have an inductive aesthesic pertinence. But is this *realm* what the authors are doing?

First, they define what they mean by an "experienced listener". This listener is presented as an "idealisation" and Lerdahl and Jackendoff add: "The concept of the "experienced listener" is no more than a convenient delimitation. Occasionally we will refer to the intuitions of a less sophisticated listener, who uses the same principles as the experienced listener in organising his hearing of music, but in a more limited way. In dealing with especially complex artistic issues, we will sometimes elevate the experienced listener to the status of a "perfect listener—that privileged being whom the great composers and theorists presumably aspire to address" (ibid., p. 3).

The difference between an inexperienced listener and, on the other hand, an ideal, perfect, listener (who is in some way omniscient) does not pose a serious theoretical problem, since the rules are given as hypothetical and subject to verification: in distinguishing between degrees of musical knowledge among subjects, the experimental process allows the authors to establish whether certain rules correspond more closely than others to different specific types of listener. And, as we know, most experiments nowadays take care to distinguish between different levels of musical knowledge among members of the group tested.

In the quotation I read, what causes problems is the fact that in referring to the supposed objectives of composers and theorists, the authors situate their model in the larger context of an implicit theory of musical communication which might be explained thus: in giving their theory the objective of describing not only the perceptual strategies of the ideal listener but the strategies of the perfect listener which the composer and the theorist seek to reach, the authors, even though they are theoretically aware of the "discrepancy" between the poietic and the aesthesic, seem, in practice, to place an "equals" sign between the description of perceptual strategies and the composer's ideal predictions regarding perception, which, themselves, refer to *compositional* strategies—what Varese called "the internal ear".

This idea brings with it three consequences:

1. It means that the proposed model of perception acquires, equally, a poietic pertinence, since it is clear that the composer's predictions of perception form a part of compositional strategies. In so doing, the model destroys the distinction between the poietic and the aesthesic, inasmuch as the authors put forward the hypothesis ("presumably", they say) that the composer's objective is to address an ideal listener.
2. Therefore, the model implies an implicit idea of musical communication and composition in which compositional and perceptual strategies must correspond, and in which the composer *must* create according to his listeners. It has, therefore, a normative dimension. Moreover, this is what the reflections on composition in Chapter 11 lead us to understand: "We believe that our theory is relevant to compositional problems, in that it focuses detailed attention on the facts of hearing. To the extent that a composer cares about his listeners, this is a vital issue" (ibid., p. 300).
3. Even if it presents itself as pertinent in terms of perception, the model turns out to be equally *structural* in nature, to the extent that, positing analytical description as pertinent a priori in relation to perceptual strategies and a composer's perceptual predictions it reduces the description of works to a single dimension. In fact, most often, what the Lerdahl-Jackendoff theory offers is essentially a neutral-level description of musical structures, whose poietic and/or aesthesic pertinence has to be demonstrated later, case by case, aping either to a theory of the poietic or the aesthesic, or to external poietic givens, or to experiments in perception.

To summarise: Lerdahl and Jackendoff's theory puts forward structural descriptions whose pertinence is explicitly aesthesic following an inductive process, whilst also opening the door, in certain cases, to a poietic pertinence.

The difficulty arises because the authors do not, in their theory, thematise the distinction between poietic, neutral level and aesthesic. Explanation of the tripartite distinction would, in fact, permit them to take account of an incontrovertible fact: that composers' perceptual predictions and real perceptual strategies do not necessarily correspond. From the point of view of a theory of musical communication, it is exactly this discrepancy between the poietic and the aesthesic which is best turned into an axiom; otherwise, the theory founders on a *normative* prescription which could be defined thus: every musical composition must be constructed in such a way as to meet its listeners. To the extent that it is desirable for cognitive research to avoid the complete abstraction of aesthetic preoccupations, it is worth emphasising that the Lerdahl-Jackendoff theory is revealing of the postmodern age inasmuch as, by all accounts, one of its authors is a composer whose concern is to succeed in reaching his public—i.e. to integrate the greatest number of perceptual predictions into the composer's working method. This also explains why although the theory deals only with tonal music, its authors are constantly searching for universals of perception, that is to say, they try to put forward rules of perception (those in their book which do not have an asterisk (1983 pp. 345–52) which apply to all the world's musics, and therefore apply also to contemporary non-tonal musics.

It might be said, against Lerdahl and Jackendoff's position, that the fact of "communication" in music (correspondence between the poietic and the aesthesic) works only within strictly limited periods in music's history (the Classical era) or in specific cultural situations: those of microsocieties in which the roles of the producer of music and its listeners are interchangeable—such as the musics of certain African communities. Outside instances of this kind, the prevalent situation is one in which there is a discrepancy between the poietic and the aesthesic. If this is indeed the case, it is necessary to distinguish between the immanent analysis, on the one hand, and the poietic and perceptual strategies on the other, if one wishes to define the specific nature of each. In other words, one of the problems of the Lerdahl-Jackendoff theory is that it short-circuits immanent description and the definition of perceptual strategies on the one hand, and immanent description and poietic strategies on the other. Why? Because a musical structure to which one assigns a poietic pertinence is an *interpreted* structure.

There is an example of the first case at the point where the authors refuse to lay down perceptual rules describing the transformational distance between musical units which present similarities and differences: "When two passages are identical they count as parallel, *but how different can they be before they are judged as no longer parallel?* . . . It appears that a set of preference rules for parallelism must be developed, the most highly reinforced case of which is identity. But we are not prepared to go beyond this, and we feel that our failure to flesh out the notion of parallelism is a serious gap in our attempt to formulate a fully explicit theory of musical understanding. For the present we must rely on intuitive judgements to deal with this area of analysis in which the theory cannot make predictions" (ibid., pp. 52–3). Here, Lerdahl and Jackendoff commit the error of wanting to try, *straight away*, to put forward the evaluative rules of the distance between two comparable units. In fact, in order to establish such rules, it is necessary *first* to utilise an inventory of the so-called neutral level—that is to say without the aesthesic pertinence being defined a priori—which describes the relationships between similar units in order *then* to propose evaluative rules for these similarities. In this respect, musicological literature preceding Lerdahl and Jackendoff's book could have provided a good point of departure for their enterprise.

On the one hand, of course, we have Ruwet's propositions for paradigmatic analysis which allows one to proceed to a systematic inventory of related units (1972, Chaps 4 and 5). It is symptomatic that a good number of Lerdahl and Jackendoff' analyses actually use a paradigmatic analysis, without referring to it as such; this corresponds to the feeling which they themselves qualify as intuitive, as is the case each time they talk of parallelism, in particular in the analyses contained in Chapter 10. Particularly striking is Example 10.5 (Fig. 17.1 below), in which the authors have rewritten the opening of the minuet from Beethoven's Sonata Op. 22, in part according to the principle of paradigmatic rewriting, that is to say, in this particular case, by omitting from bars 10 and 11 the melodic elements which lie outside the paradigmatic continuity of bars 2–3 and 6–7.

10.5

FIG. 17.1. Ex. 10.5 (p.24 of L & J).

On the other hand, we have the rule proposed by Meyer, in *Explaining Music* (1973, p.49), for the evaluation of the distance between musical elements in what he calls "conformant relationships":

The greater the variety of intervening events and the greater the separation in time between two comparable events, the more patent the shape of the model must be if a conformant relationship is to be perceived. Or, to put the matter the other way round: the more regular and individual the pattern (and, of course, the more alike events are in interval, rhythm, etc.), the greater can be the temporal separation between model and variant and the greater the variety of intervening motives, with the conformant relationship still recognizable.

Here, certainly, is an excellent point of departure for anyone seeking to refine the cognitive rules of perception in the relationships of proximity and separation between related units. But in order to be able to develop such rules, it is first necessary to give oneself the paradigmatic tool, to separate the *description* of structures from the study of processes—here, aesthesic ones—and to assign an aesthesic *interpretation* to these structures by means of a perceptual theory analogous to Meyer's, which I have just cited. Lerdahl and Jackendoff justify their neglect of transformations by means of various considerations (1983 pp. 186–7), among which is the importance given, in their work, to the notion of hierarchies. Without meaning to make judgements based on assumptions, I wonder if they have not avoided the subject because their theory does not provide them with a descriptive tool for paradigmatic relationships.

The same problem—the absence of a distinction between the description of structures and their interpretation—is presented on the poietic side. On the subject of the celebrated metrical and rhythmic ambiguity of the theme from Mozart's Symphony in *G* minor, which is analysed several times in the course of their book, the authors record that the two analytical possibilities which they propose (Ex. 2.11, p. 24 of L & J, Fig. 17.2 below) correspond to the interpretations of Bruno Walter and Leonard Bernstein respectively. "We will refrain from choosing between these competing alternatives; suffice it to say that in such ambiguous cases the performer's choice, communicated by a slightly extra stress (in this case, at the downbeat of either bar 10 or bar 11), can tip the balance one way or the other for the listener" (1983 p. 25). The refusal to choose is significant. What are the authors proposing in their portrayal? Precisely, a neutral-level analysis of the two possibilities of analytical interpretation of the metrical structure. If the authors cannot choose, it is because the choice would correspond not to an aesthesic strategy—that is the conductor's job—but to a poietic interpretation of this structural ambiguity: it would allow us to know, *stylistically*, which of these structures corresponds to Mozart's compositional practices.

And to answer the question would require recourse to a stylistic and historical working method analogous to that which Meyer used to decide upon good phrasing in his analysis of Mozart's Piano Sonata in A major (1973, chap. 2)—an analysis put forward with musical interpretation in mind. But to do this it is once more necessary to have first effected the distinction between the description of structures and the analysis of processes—here, of a poietic and stylistic nature—which the authors explicitly refuse to do: "We are focusing on the listener because listening is a much more widespread musical activity than composing or performing" (1983 p. 7).

FIG. 17.2. Ex. 2.11 (p.24 of L & J).

To summarise: Lerdahl and Jackendoff's working method—against which, after all this criticism, it would be grudging not to stress that to my mind it represents one of the most remarkable developments of music theory since Schenker, suffers from not having quizzed itself on the functioning of a musical work as a symbolic form. The aporias of their model and the difficulties which they encountered in the course of its development could easily be resolved if (1) one accepts the necessity of distinguishing between an immanent description of structures and the interpretation of processes; if (2) within processes, one clearly separates poietic and aesthesic strategies; and if (3) one distinguishes, for both the poietic and the aesthesic, between an inductive and an external approach. But, in order to do this, it remains necessary to place the entire cognitive enterprise within the framework of a unified conception of musicology.

Translated by Katharine Ellis

REFERENCES

Lerdahl, F., Jackendoff, R. (1983). *A Generative Theory of Tonal Music*. Cambridge, Mass: The MIT Press.

Meyer, L.B. (1973). *Explaining Music*. Berkeley, Los Angeles: University of California Press.

Molino, J. (1975). Fait musical et sémiologie de la musique. *Musique en jeu*, *17*, 37–62.

Nattiez, J.-J. (1987). *Musicologie générale et sémiologie de la musique*. Paris: Christian Bourgois Editeur. Translated into English as *Music and Discourse*. Princeton: Princeton University Press, 1990.

Ruwet, N. (1972). *Langage, musique, poésie*. Paris: Editions du Seuil.

Smismans-Deliège, I. (1985). *Les règles préférentielles de groupement dans la perception musicale*. (Master of Psychology dissertation, Université libre de Bruxelles, Belgium).

18 Composing and listening: A reply to Nattiez

Fred Lerdahl
Columbia University

Nattiez (this volume) uses his and Molino's tripartite semiological model to develop a critique of aspects of Jackendoff's and my *A Generative Theory of Tonal Music* (GTTM). I shall respond rather freely to two issues raised by Nattiez: GTTM's alleged confusion of the poietic and aesthesic levels, and the status of the neutral level. If my remarks are more polemical than usual, it is Nattiez himself who is my inspiration, for I always respect and enjoy his lively engagement with the issues.

POIETIC CONTRA AESTHESIC

Nattiez aptly categorizes GTTM's intent as that of an inductive aesthesic theory. He claims that in reality, however, the theory intermingles compositional strategies (the poietic) with its modelling of heard structure (the aesthesic). This claim is incorrect. Though he does not state it as such, he is referring less to GTTM than to my article *Cognitive Constraints on Compositional Systems*, which, enlarging on section 11.6 of GTTM, confronts the gap in contemporary music between compositional method and heard result and proposes principles for narrowing the gap. While I believe that well developed theories of musical cognition can shed important light on contemporary music and that their implications for future compositional methods are profound, nowhere does the argument about composition affect the theory of listening. The influence flows only in the other direction.

Nattiez misreads my position when he says that I advocate an obligatory correspondence between perceptual and compositional strategies and concludes that GTTM has a normative dimension. I do not believe there must be such a correspondence, nor do I think there is a one-to-one relationship between the extent of such a correspondence and musical value. Any popular song is likely to exhibit a close correspondence, but that does not make it good (or bad). At the other extreme, certain highly valued works of art, such as Joyce's *Ulysses* or Bach's *Die Kunst der Fuge*, are created using techniques that make them difficult to apprehend in all their richness. Somewhere in between lie most works of art; they are moderately difficult to understand and they are judged as good or bad for all kinds of reasons.

My concern with the poietic-aesthesic relationship is not to judge individual works by some recipe but to shed light on the health of our musical languages. What if a work is constructed according to principles fundamentally foreign to the ways in which humans process music? *Ulysses*, after all, follows English syntax, and *Die Kunst der Fuge* elaborates on standard tonal syntax. The aesthetic of these works depends on a strong tension between the poietic and the aesthesic without breaking the connection. Yet it would easy to construct some arbitrary poietic device that generates patterns of words or notes that have nothing at all to do with how people comprehend them. The resulting "work" would be perceived as incoherent or nonsensical. There is, then, even in the most arcane of genuine artistic creations, a meaningful relationship (and sometimes a playful one) between the poietic and the aesthesic.

One might argue instead that all poietic methods are perceptually equal and that comprehension is just a matter of exposure. This empiricist position, which assumes that the mind is a *tabula rasa* that learns only by association, dates back to Locke and in its modern form has been espoused in a radical form by Skinnerian behaviorism. It was the dominant philosophical and psychological view in the 1940s and 1950s, adopted among composers explicitly by Babbitt and implicitly by the European serialists. (It was also an assumption of the Marxists, who believed that socio-economic forces alone mould human nature and history.) This view has since been powerfully challenged among philosophers and psychologists, beginning with Chomsky's (1959) review of Skinner's *Verbal Behavior*. Although there is ongoing debate within the cognitive and neural sciences regarding the structure and development of learning and behaviour, no one proposes going back to the assumption of an unstructured brain that is merely conditioned. The degree to which the mind/brain is modular, the ways in which its mechanisms require interaction with the environment, and the range of learning options that are available, are issues to be treated by a convergence of theory and experiment.

GTTM falls within this more recent cognitivist tradition. It is akin to linguistic and visual theories in providing a comprehensive yet detailed set of hypotheses about the structure of a mental module. That GTTM's point of departure is the classical tonal idiom is a consequence of the authors' joint expertise and does not reflect—contrary to Nattiez's impression—an a priori bias in the pursuit of psychological musical universals. (NB the search is for psychological, not necessarily cultural, universals.) In the ideal case, one could begin with any musical idiom and end up with the same theory of the musical module. In practice, of course, this cannot be the case. Just as in linguistics, comparative studies in music are needed to identify further principles and to rectify imbalances or mistaken claims.

As co-creator of GTTM and as a composer inevitably involved in issues of musical organisation, it has been natural for me to reflect on the implications of work in music theory and psychology for contemporary music. This theoretical side-activity hardly muddies the distinction between the poietic and the aesthesic. What it does do, I think, is threaten the mind-set of aesthetic modernists who believe that the artist is a high priest who breaks laws and creates new ones that advance civilisation. To hold such a conviction, one must tacitly embrace both behaviourist psychology and a Hegelian philosophy of history. That is, one must believe that the mind is unconstrained in what it can learn except by what it is exposed to, and that history is a river that flows ineluctably forward through dialectical stages that determine who or what is significant. The combination of Skinnerism and Hegelianism encourages the artist as commissar: manipulate what audiences are exposed to and claim the authority of history.

In my view there is an intimate connection between modernist ideology and the problems of contemporary music. The gap between how composers put their music together and what listeners actually hear (and yes, there will always be a poietic-aesthesic gap, since composing and listening are not identical activities) has become uniquely wide in this century, as a result of the self-conscious development of compositional grammars. Although this development was probably inevitable after the evolution from diatonic tonality into full chromaticism, early attempts at consciously constructed grammars failed because they were not based on explicit knowledge of the musical mind but were merely historically motivated. Modernist ideology drove composers in quest of innovation to stand on the shoulders of their predecessors and shoot their arrows into the future; if the aim was on target (that is, if the innovation influenced later composers), the composer was deemed important. But composers interpreted the historical imperative in irreconcilable ways; they broke different rules and built different systems. These tendencies led to private compositional codes, overall stylistic fragmentation, and alienation from most listeners, who were deprived of regular exposure to perceptually relevant structures. Eventually, by around 1960 (when Cage and Stockhausen were ascendant), there were in effect no more rules to break, and the path to the future became obscure. Musical "progress" ceased. Whether we like it or not, we now live in the postmodernist period that Meyer (1967) forecast, in which incompatible aesthetics and styles coexist in a fluctuating steady state. Modernist ideology, while still dominant in an institutional sense, has become old-fashioned. For a younger generation it embodies attitudes about human nature and history that are no longer credible and that have led to a stylistic dead end.

It is no coincidence that soon after this crisis became undeniable Boulez conceived the contemporary equivalent of Bayreuth, the *Institut de recherche et coordination acoustique/musique*. If the arrow of history had lost its way, might not technology propel the future of music? It is true that technology opens doors and that such prospects are exciting at present. But the digital revolution by itself cannot resolve the poietic-aesthesic gap that lies at the heart of the problem. We must think the problem through.

Nattiez denies the crisis by asserting that a large poietic-aesthesic gap is typical of music. On the contrary, I can think of only one period in the Western tradition where the gap has been even remotely comparable to that of this century: the late 14th century, with its isorhythmic techniques and complicated surface rhythms. It is not surprising that Messiaen and Boulez were attracted to this period. What attracts me is the following century: the *fauxbourdon* period, the time of Dunstable and Dufay, when surface complications gave way to euphony and structural richness. I predict that a similar development will eventually resolve our current dilemmas, and with the help of technology. For it has become clear in this age of computer modelling that most of the compositional grammars invented in this century have been musically arbitrary and intellectually trivial, and that a foundation in the exigencies of history does not suffice. We need to recognise that our natural capacities can be studied computationally and experimentally and that we can apply this knowledge to the future practice of music.

My *Cognitive Constraints* . . . offers guidelines, based on theoretical and psychological evidence from GTTM and elsewhere, toward constructing rich compositional systems that are transparent to perception. Contrary to what has sometimes been supposed, I do not presume to tell composers how to compose (how could I?). I just reveal some of the factors involved if they want their poietic methods to be aesthesically available. Composers with modernist ambitions do not like to face limitations of any kind, for they indulge in the naive romantic notion that their imaginations are unfettered. We are all constrained by our biology and by our experience. Acknowledging limitations does not mean a return to the past or even facing a future with narrow options. The possibilities for future musics that respect the nature of the musical mind are virtually infinite.

All of this is a far cry from Nattiez's statement that "one of [GTTM's] authors is a composer whose concern is to succeed in reaching his public." Serious composers, myself included, pay more attention to the work than to the audience. But if the attempt to create music that is original, expressive, elegantly crafted, sonically beautiful, formally unified, and aesthetically coherent also leads to success, so much the better. Success or not, public reception in an ordinary sense is not the issue, at least in anything that I have discussed. The issue is the relationship between the poietic and the aesthesic as viewed from the cognitive science of music.

The criterion of value that I advocate in *Cognitive Constraints . . .* has to do not with reaching the public but with a distinction between "complicatedness" and "complexity". Complicatedness is a function of the number and variety of events per unit time at the musical surface. Complexity is a function of the structural depth that the listener is able to infer from a surface (this is the "relational richness" of Meyer 1975). To these categories I would add a third: "simplicity" is the absence of both complicatedness and complexity. I prefer complexity and am neutral about complicatedness. I believe that complexity is achievable only if the relationship between the poietic and the aesthesic is relatively transparent. Many 20th-century composers, sensing the lack of complexity in their music no matter how ornate their poietic methods, have sought recompense in complicated surfaces. These surfaces have impressed some but estranged others, who in many cases have reacted by turning to minimalist simplicity.

It is amusing and perhaps instructive (in the vein of Isaiah Berlin's classification of writers as foxes or hedgehogs) to place composers in these pigeon holes. Mozart and Schubert are complex but not complicated. Bach, Brahms, and much of Wagner are both complex and complicated. Donizetti is simple. In the 20th century, Debussy, Stravinsky, and early Webern are complex but not complicated. Schoenberg is both complex and complicated. Carter, Babbitt, Xenakis, early Stockhausen, and the Boulez of *Le Marteau sans Maître* are complicated but not complex; the same holds for the composers of the "new complexity" such as Ferneyhough. Glass and Pärt are simple.

WHAT IS THE NEUTRAL LEVEL?

I have difficulty with Nattiez's central concept of the neutral level. To be sure, the poietic process creates an "object" to which the aesthesic process responds. But this object is inevitably a mental construct at the poietic or the aesthesic level. At first blush, one might suppose that the neutral level is the musical score. However, the score is just a notational means for embodying aspects of the poietic process and for enabling production of the aesthesic process. From a psychoacoustic standpoint, even the sonic events notated in a score constitute a perceptual organisation of enormous intricacy. It would be better, and in the spirit of Nattiez (1990), to say that the neutral level represents relations immanent in the events that the score symbolises. But which relations, and how "immanent"? There are innumerable ways of relating any two musical passages (or of transforming one into the other). As for "immanent", the term begs the issue. Musical relations are not inherent per se but are the result of constructive processes in composers, performers, and listeners.

Let me ground these remarks in an example. Along the lines of Nattiez's tripartition, I have been puzzled about the status of Forte's (1973) theory of pitch-class relations in atonal music. On the one hand, the theory's constructs have only a tangential connection to how atonal music was composed. On the other, they have little relationship to how this music is heard. Do the constructs then belong to the neutral level? In a sense, yes: assuming the notes on the page, certain set-theoretic properties can be adduced between pitch-class sets which have been selected by the analyst. But why these particular properties rather than others? Why octave and inversional equivalence, the various measures of similarity, the set complex, and so forth? Presumably because these formal properties yield "illuminating" analyses. But illuminating in what sense? If they do not illuminate how listeners spontaneously hear atonal music, are they meant to tell people how they *ought* to hear it? Schenkerian theory has such a normative dimension for tonal music; but since Forte has tried to cleanse Schenkerism of its problematic value system, it would seem unlikely that he would wish to infect his atonal theory in a similar way. Well then, to use Babbitt's term: do these particular properties yield "significant" relationships? Significant in what sense? And so on. Unless constrained poietically or aesthesically, the neutral level is left free to describe an infinite number of relationships immanent in the music, no matter how remote from perception. Status is assigned to a property or relationship because it is illuminating or significant (or "pertinent", to use semiotic vocabulary) in terms of musical experience; and precisely because it is in terms of experience (poietic or aesthesic), the property or relationship is no longer neutral.

A similar argument applies to musical parallelism, which is treated in Nattiez's work by the method of paradigmatic analysis (derived from Ruwet 1966). GTTM shows how parallelism impacts on the perception of hierarchical structures but fails to explicate how two passages are judged as parallel in the first place. This deficiency resulted from Jackendoff's and my recognition that, because parallelism is not bound by hierarchical well-formedness rules, such an explication would lie outside the framework of the other components of our theory and would be difficult to achieve with any precision. At the same time, the explication would have to incorporate the hierarchical components described in GTTM, for parallelism is a feature not just of the musical surface but of underlying structures as well (this is most obvious in the cases of classical variation form and of jazz improvisation on a tune). The Ruwet-Nattiez approach has made some progress on parallelism, but only in terms of surface relationships, since it does not have a theory of pitch reduction at its disposal. But is even this progress truly at the neutral level? Literal repetition no doubt counts as parallelism, but why is the relationship between two non-repeating passages labeled in one case as A and A' and in another as A and B? Since any mechanism can in principle be invoked at the neutral level for transforming one passage into another, what is it that privileges those particular transformations that count as parallel from those that do not? In actuality, the issue is decided by an implicit appeal to poietic or, more commonly, aesthesic processes. A successful paradigmatic analysis steps off its neutral pedestal in order to be musically relevant.

The chimerical nature of the neutral level perhaps explains why it is rarely invoked by other kinds of music theory and why it has no function in music psychology. The latter field is usually concerned with unconscious aesthesic processes, although a few attempts have been made with regard to poietic processes (as in Sloboda 1985). (The role of musical performance, the third area of psychological inquiry, does not fit comfortably within Nattiez's tripartition.)

Nattiez's discussion of GTTM is understandably general (as is this reply), but he does refer to two specific examples. The first, concerning the Minuet of Beethoven's Op. 22, rightly points out that Jackendoff and I use a form of paradigmatic analysis without mentioning it. The second, on competing metrical interpretations of the beginning of Mozart's G minor Symphony, makes the odd claim that we have provided a neutral-level analysis and that our inability to choose between Walter's and Bernstein's performances reflects our refusal to engage poietic processes. In fact our treatment takes place entirely at the aesthesic level. Each of the metrical preference rules registers a heard feature that, all else being equal, yields an unconscious preference for one metrical grid over another. When the rules reinforce one another, the music module selects a single grid; when they conflict, the module senses a metrical ambiguity that can be resolved by strengthening a given rule through performing interpretation. In the Mozart example at the metrical level in question, the rule applications are conflicting, so Walter's and Bernstein's contrasting interpretive stresses are able subtly to project contrasting grids. We did not choose one rendition over the other not because we lacked an opinion (I am partial to the Walter, perhaps because I grew up with his recordings of Mozart) but because our personal tastes were not to the point. The point was to illustrate how, in conflicting preference-rule situations, different performances tip the perceptual balance one way or the other.

More broadly, Nattiez says that most of GTTM's preference rules provide descriptions not at the aesthesic but at the neutral level, and that these descriptions must be "interpreted" at the aesthesic level. Thus he recommends two theoretical stages in place of GTTM's single stage. Although he is not explicit here, I would guess from his other writings (especially Nattiez 1990) that he means not "unconsciously interpreted" by the music module but "critically intepreted" according to various metatheoretical and comparative criteria. The combination of non-criterial logical system (any mechanism carried out at the neutral level) and subsequent evaluation by the analyst has the flavour of logical positivism (the philosophical counterpart of behaviourist psychology) plus a twist of literary theory. The affinity with positivism should come as no surprise, for Nattiez's predecessor Ruwet developed paradigmatic music analysis from the pre-generative, distributionalist linguistics of Harris (1951), which shared empiricist assumptions. In particular, Harris's method of "discovery procedures" that, he hoped, would automatically find grammars of unfamiliar languages bears some resemblance to the inventory tables employed, say, in Nattiez's (1975) analysis of Debussy's *Syrinx*. But a grammar discoverable by automatic methods is capable at best of revealing only simple surface features. Theories of real explanatory power, whether in the physical or the behavioural sciences, arise not through automatic procedures but through a combination of various strategies, including intuition and model building along with experimental evidence.

Origins aside, it should be apparent that I reject the neutral level as a working hypothesis, and that my psychological orientation leads me to an interest in unconscious over critical interpretation. The modelling of unconscious inter-pretation—that is, of the spontaneous operations of the music module in response to musical stimuli—takes place not as the second of two theoretical stages but through a unified set of rules that predict structures inferred by the listener. Therefore I do not accept Nattiez's recommendation for framing Jackendoff's and my theory in terms of his semiological tripartition. If I were to make a suggestion in return, it would be that he jettison the neutral level and concentrate on poietic or aesthesic structures. His most compelling work does this anyway.

REFERENCES

Chomsky, N. (1959). Review of B. F. Skinner's "Verbal Behavior". *Language, 35*, 26–58.

Forte, A. (1973). *The Structure of Atonal Music*. New Haven: Yale University Press.

Harris, Z. (1951). *Methods in Structural Linguistics*. Chicago: University of Chicago Press.

Lerdahl, F. (1988). Cognitive Constraints on Compositional Systems. In J. Sloboda, (Ed.), *Generative Processes in Music*. Oxford: Oxford University Press. Issued in French in *Contrechamps, 10*. Lausanne: Editions l'age d'homme.

Lerdahl, F., & Jackendoff, R. (1983). *A Generative Theory of Tonal Music*. Cambridge, Mass.: The MIT Press.

Meyer, L. B. (1967). *Music, the Arts, and Ideas*. Chicago: University of Chicago Press (2nd edition, 1994).

Meyer, L. B. (1975). Grammatical Simplicity and Relational Richness: The Trio of Mozart's G minor Symphony. *Critical Inquiry, II*(2), 693–761.

Nattiez, J.J. (1975). *Fondements d'une sémiologie de la musique*. Paris: Union Générale d'Editions.

Nattiez, J.J. (1990). *Music and Discourse: Toward a Semiology of Music*. English translation by C. Abbate. Princeton: Princeton University Press. (French edition, *Musicologie générale et sémiologie*. Paris: Christian Bourgois, 1987.)

Ruwet, N. (1966). Méthodes d'analyse en musicologie. *Revue Belge de Musicologie, 20*, 65-90.

Sloboda, J.A. (1985). *The Musical Mind*. Oxford: Oxford University Press.

19

Epistemic subject, historical subject, psychological subject: Regarding Lerdahl and Jackendoff's generative theory of tonal music

Michel Imberty
President of the University of Paris X - Nanterre, France

A RESPONSE TO J.-J. NATTIEZ

I should like to take up two points among Nattiez's remarks: the first concerns the fact that the Lerdahl and Jackendoff model is apparently a listener's model which, nonetheless, permits inductions regarding the compositional process; the second concerns the functioning of a musical work as a symbolic form.

The entire Chomskyan linguistic rests upon the hypothesis that in linguistic functioning there exists sufficient coincidence between the system of encoding capacity and the system of decoding capacity for indiction in the direction of one of the two systems from the description of the other to be possible. In practice, the theory of generative grammar explicitly avows itself to be a theory of the speaker's knowledge of the mother tongue. Such knowledge is itself thought of as a "knowledge of meaning", a knowledge of "how to decode": in effect, the grammar allows an explanation of how the speaker is able to comprehend an infinite number of phrases in his/her own language (i.e. the question of *competence*), whilst his or her *performance* (if you like, the element of production, of linguistic creativity) may remain limited.

My belief is that there is in fact an ambiguity here: the Chomskyan theory from which our authors openly take their inspiration is a "decoder's" or "perceiver's" theory and not that of a "producer" or an "inventor". I am capable of reading, understanding and interpreting Proust's entire output, yet I shall never produce as much, nor as well, as him.

As much in music as in language, this ambiguity of the two theories conveys itself by the fact that the first experimental verifications of such models have immediately focused upon the "psychological reality" of procedures and rules, the innately empirical reporting of "discrepancies" between their formal and rigorous use as foreseen within the framework of the theory, and the reality of behaviours which were sometimes considerably distant from those same theoretical expectations.

In short, in one case as in the other, the principal comparison has been between the ideal listener and the real listener, or the ideal speaker (in the function of reader or of listener) and the real speaker, these latter being nothing more than sociological, educational or historical variants—but in all respects "degraded" variants—of the ideal model. For a long time Chomsky has held a very low opinion of the interests, for linguistic theory in general, of studies relating to performance. We can thus say not only that such a perspective does not allow us to distinguish between the work's poietic and aesthesic levels, but that the aesthesic is conceptualised within, by means of the poietic, though the model does not really take this into account other than in a normative manner. Nattiez is correct to highlight the point.

I think, in fact, that this ambiguity, "significant of the postmodern era", is the result of a confusion, implied by the Chomskian procedure, between the structures and functioning of that which is "biologically determined"—we can call it the mental apparatus—on the one hand, and, on the other, the structures and functioning of the real behaviours *constructed* by the subject, listener or composer in different social and historical situations; in other words, a confusion between the epistemic subject and the psychological subject.

I shall pick up two important elements which show how this confusion underlies the work of Lerdahl and Jackendoff. Nattiez has already indicated the first: the authors embark directly upon a plan to provide a model of the problem of the degrees of distance which separate comparable musical units. It is the prime example of a problem which cannot, nevertheless, be addressed without recourse to (1) an inventory of the types of identifiable distances right up to the object's structure (a taxonomy of the neutral level); (2) a formal model which systematises the *transformational* rules of the units by placing them within a hierarchy (this is still no more than a reconstruction of the object and not an inference of the perceptual procedures of the subject); (3) an experimental verification of such formalisation at the level of the perception of these distances themselves, of their evaluation by varied groups of listeners (the aesthesic level); (4) only finally, a generalisation and a formalisation which would allow the construction of a real grammar of the units' transformations, predictive of the real behaviour of various systems, in various cultures—a universal grammar which would be that of an epistemic subject, that is to say, a subject resulting from an inductive construction of all the possible behavioural patterns of all possible real listeners.

At this point a second underlying confusion appears: the ideal subject, the epistemic subject—in as much as one has the means of constructing one—is that subject the composer? In their concern to base their work upon communication between this composer and the listener, Lerdahl and Jackendoff address this new ambiguity throughout their book. In fact, the epistemic subject is no more than the ideal, perfect, composing musician than s/he is the ideal listener, who exists nowhere. Their chosen example explains the problem: we hardly know, still, how the listener perceives the link between a theme and its variations. Nevertheless, we could imagine numerous and detailed experiments which would enable us to establish the point at which, and under what conditions and circumstances, a listener no longer experiences one musical sequence as a variation of another. We could study all the historical, educational, stylistic constraints imaginable. Equally, we still have very little precise knowledge of the process of the creation of a variation in relation to its theme; we cannot, from work on perception, say how the composer constructs (rather than perceives) the variation. For example, we can imagine that the listener has some notion of distance between theme and variation linked to the quantity or ornamentation "added" to the original outline (it would be necessary here to specify the meaning of "ornament"—and only an historically situated analysis on the neutral level would enable such a definition); but was it through the addition of ornamentation—by means of a cumulative procedure—that Beethoven constructed his 32 variations? We are well aware of the absurdity of such a suggestion. Was it not Berg who after explaining at length how he had written the *Lyric Suite*, hoped that the listener detects nothing of it?

Like any generative enterprise in linguistics, Lerdahl and Jackendoff's book on tonal music is actually dominated by the idea that structure and functioning of the human mind is biologically determined in a universal and innate manner—at least in part. Whilst such an hypothesis is undoubtedly true *on a very general plane*, that on which one could also imagine an epistemic subject, it ceases to be true from the moment that a psychological subject or an historical subject is linked to the study: all the research in the field of developmental psychology, as in the history of cultures, shows that the extent of the adaptation of processes to structures and of the overturning of structures under the influence of processes is considerable: in the first case (the adaptation of processes to structures) we could trace a history of musical perception and cognition which would doubtless show that the listener—even an ideal one—of the seventeenth century possibly did not decode the harmonic "audacities" of Monteverdi or Charpentier in the same way as we do, whilst to us they appear "filtered" through Romanticism and the post-tonality of the beginning of the twentieth century; in the second case (the overturning of structures under the influence of processes) we have, evidently, the entire history of musical creation itself, and the styles which it engenders.

This is exactly why Piaget, too, had given this distinction such emphasis earlier: the epistemic subject is only ever a *construction* of the scientific working method itself, which consists of a generalised induction of processes from systematic observations made on the level of the structures of real behaviour patterns and of the concrete strategies of the subjects in their cultural or historical situation. Moreover, according to Piaget, the structures of the behavioural patterns (or of the objects, or of the works—which is what concerns us here) are *observable features*, whilst the *co-ordinations* are inferred[1]. These latter have not only a developmental, extending character (going from a few "observations" to "all" the observable relationships), but are true constructions of purely reflexive relationships which go beyond the directly observable. They are thus interpretations[2].

And so I come briefly to the second point brough up by Nattiez: the musical work functioning as a symbolic form. My point follows directly, moreover, from everything I have said thus far, and is, in a way, no more than its ultimate consequence. For here again the chosen example is very significant: if, for a single passage in the Symphony in G minor, two neutral-level analyses are possible, it is because the observable structure not only admits of two different interpretations, but because the analyst's inferences, which ought to lead to the choice of the interpretation which is pertinent on the poietic plane, are constructions leading from the "intuitions" which this same analyst, in the guise of a psychological subject and an historical subject, may have of the work's reality and of its historical and cultural context.

Every structure demands interpretation, i.e. something beyond what a neutral-level analysis can describe, placed within a theory or a model of the listener on the one hand, of the composer on the other. To use an expression of Paul Veyne, taken up by J. Molino and J.-J. Nattiez, every structure thus induces the construction of a "plot" which includes the epistemic working within a "generalised psychological and historical relativity".

Translated by Katharine Ellis

NOTES

1. Piaget, J. (1976). *L'Equilibration des structures cognitives*. Paris: Presses   Universitaires de France (pp. 50–3).
2. Piaget, J. *Ibid.* (pp. 51-2). "For example, the anticipation of the fact that the shock of ball A hitting ball B will always be followed by a movement of ball B will not be called 'co-ordination', whilst this term will be applied to the hypothesis of transmission such that the thrust of A has passed to B, when no transmission of movement is itself observable."

Postscript

Intertwining of the objectivity of cognitive analysis and the subjectivity of the œuvre's interpretations

Michel Imberty
Professor at the University of Paris X
President of the ESCOM (1992–1994)

ON THE MOZARTIAN GRACE

At the end of a congress essentially dedicated to cognitive sciences in music and founded on an epistemology of experimental objectivity, I find it useful to consider this epistemology and its significance for the understanding of the musical phenomenon, which we have tried to analyse and break down in these few days, in order to apprehend its most subtle and secret aspects. Characterising our procedure may seem easy: it is based upon the principle of "objective"—that is, *falsifiable*—verification of sets of observable facts which can be repertoried, listed.

There is, in all the domains stimulating human curiosity, and particularly in the artistic fields, a quantity of facts that cannot be established without a considerable margin of uncertainty, or even about whose status as facts we may shed doubt; the minute we try to seize these facts, they vanish into complex and fleeting impressions, which refer us first to the cognisant subject himself. I shall start with an example which, although partial in relation to the whole of my presentation, is very significant. It is a passage from Ch. Rosens's book (1971/ 1978) on *The Classical Style: Haydn, Mozart and Beethoven.* Many other examples of the same type may be found in this remarkable book, which is capable even today of renewing our ideas about musical analysis. Rosen (1971 pp. 244–5) says:

"The controlled symmetry and the clear sense of movement are essential to the dramatic genius of Mozart. From this point of view, his first dramatic work of maturity is *La Finta Giardiniera*, which he wrote at the age of nineteen, and which possesses from end to end a dramatic power completely new for that period of time. It is particularly clear at the beginning of the finale of the first act, with the sensual and desperate cry of Sandrina. (. . . the musical citation follows). This seven-bar phrase is of an absolute though masked symmetry. The last three bars not only balance out the first three, with the fourth playing a pivot role, but also present essentially the same melodic profile. But in taking up this profile a second time in an ornamented form, he dresses it in a new, more agitated rhythm, and with a greater harmonic tension. The equilibrium and the symmetry are taken in the dramatic movement, at the same time giving it a certain stability which allows the drama to unroll as projected from inside.

This text examines a fact of structure (a very marked symmetry with a central pivot element), which turns out later, according to Rosen, to be a general principle of organisation of the Mozartian musical phrase. However, next to the presentation of this clearly defined fact which may be unambiguously recognised in the examples cited, we find what could be called an aesthetic justification, or a finalisation, or, even more generally, an interpretation. This interpretation refers this structure to Mozart's "dramatic genius", which makes us feel "the sensual and desperate cry", and even better, makes us suddenly understand the profound nature of Mozart's classicism in this dialectic of "movement" and "stability", taking into account the concentration and the interiority of the drama. In the pages preceding the example cited, we find the same subtle combination of the rigorous semiological demonstration and an aesthetic interpretative language articulated around complex and vague notions such as the "latent energy of the material" or the "the exposition's nervous energy" which shows us—or perhaps simply suggests—how in Mozart's music, "the symmetry of the whole is reflected in the symmetry of the details, in a way that despite the expressive violence which frequently defines Mozart's production, the music arrives at a constant equilibrium", and that finally "this symmetry is a condition of grace".

As a postscript to this book, this question seems very interesting, perhaps in its being a little impertinent: concerning Mozart's condition of grace, what is it objectively in face of the cognitive sciences of music? Analysis, psychology of memory or of perception, psychology of emotion—is the Mozartian grace definitely foreign to these domains? If it is, then to what purpose are our analyses and experiments?

I shall first note that Rosen's text is a text of limits. What I mean by this is that, within the arrangement of his own work, Rosen marks a moment in the act of knowing in which the distinction between fact and meaning-of-fact is blurred, where the limit between the objectivity of the established and of the proven and the subjectivity of the sensed (precisely by the person trying to show objectivity), crumbles. Basically, to simplify, I would say that these luminous and refined analyses teach us perhaps more about Charles Rosen as an interpreter of Mozart than about Mozart himself.

Or perhaps they teach us something about the Mozart that Charles Rosen alone could show us—could demonstrate to us. Something which participates in a Mozart which is no longer only the object of our analyses and of our demonstrations, but the object of a communication of personal or collective experiences of the interpreter-analyst or of the interpreter-musician from an analysable and analysed text in terms of structures (neutral level, in the Nattiez-Molino terminology, cf. Nattiez, (1987), and which is perceived and memorised in terms of knowledge and behaviors (aesthesic level in the same terminology). The act of analysis, instead of explaining Mozart's writing processes, instead of reducing them to "lists" of procedures and to simulation programs, enriches them, complexifies them, multiplies them as a function of the analyst's, the interpreter's, the listener's personal point of view. It is not just a mixture of facts and feelings, but a construction on several levels in which the (objective) facts are clarified by the (subjective) feelings, in which the (subjective) feelings contribute to the definition of the (objective) facts, in which, consequently, the sacro-saint scientific objectivity tumbles and is lost in a constant interaction between the knowing subject and the object of his knowing.

FROM OBJECTIVE TO SUBJECTIVE, OR THE TRAPS FROM THE MUSICIAN TO THE COGNITIVIST

Remaining on the matter of cognitive sciences applied to music, I will briefly analyse two problems which are complex enough, but which I will simplify for the sake of the efficacy of my presentation.

The first example is that of the perception of the correctness of intervals. We can obviously define "correctness" of an interval in a purely "objective" way, that is independent of any perceiving subject, through frequencies. However, numerous musical facts prove that the perception of "correctness" is something eminently "subjective", that is, it depends on the perceiving subject and on the context. Even temperament is no longer considered compromised within contrary and strongly felt acoustic constraints between the melodic and the harmonic structures. This was, however, the case in the 17th and 18th centuries when, as we know, this temperament was only universally adopted after many polemics and the trying out of many other temperaments. Likewise, we have for a long time played ancient music on instruments which were tuned according to even temperament, since it seemed to us impossible to tune them differently and have the music "sound right". Conversely, today, when the reinterpretation "in ancient style" is universally admitted, we find the performances on instruments tuned by the even temperament terribly flat. Besides, many experiments in psychology show how the perception of intervals depends on the musical context in which they are perceived. Thus, in 1958, R. Francès showed that the evaluation of correctness of the major third and of the leading tone depends on the subject's expectations, and in particular on the upward or downward direction of the melodic movement and the position of "false" notes in relation to their theoretical position in the scale.

Even if these facts are well known, we must also mention other examples which are even more significant; Balzano, in an article from 1989, shows how the appreciation of correctness of the blue third (which is situated between the minor third and the major third and cannot be defined in the usual tempered scales) is determined: when it is executed by a professional jazz singer, it is unanimously judged as correct; when it is executed by an amateur, it is judged as an awful dissonance even though no objective reference exists: the musical context, but also the social and cultural context of the intonation, completely transform the perception of the same physical reality.

These facts clearly show that the "subjectivity" of the perceived is as important a phenomenon as the perceived itself, and that the physical phenomena do not have an "objective" existence which the listener has to "decode" or detect by his own capacities. There is, in the contemporary cognitive sciences, a strong credo in the subject—world duality. The models used are all based on this duality, which separates the subject's variables from the object's variables, since the goal of research is to explain the univocal relations which may exist between the first and second, or put another way, to explain the subject's behaviour through the object's structures on one hand, and the subject's capacities to decode and memorise them on the other. The problems related to correctness evaluation show an interaction between subject and object, that the position of the subject, his "point of view", can modify the idea which he creates of the object, and that this idea may be more important for understanding the subject's behaviour than the structure of the object itself. To this we can add that, in the domain of cultural objects, the internal representation that the subject constructs of the object (a representation which is by nature moving and changing) can even modify the structure of the object itself when this structure is mediatised by the subject's action (an execution for example): this is the case in the execution of the blue third, or more generally in all sequences or musical pieces (Imberty, 1990). Moreover, the difference between the "good" and the "bad" execution of the blue third resides in a difference of interpretation in the strong sense of the term (and thus not only in a difference of execution), a difference of interpretation which covers complex and varied auditory, dynamic and cultural representations both in the interpreter and in the listener. From this stems the emotional subjective load of this interval, which the physical and psycho-acoustic parameters can in no way explain outside the act of interpretation and execution of the subject.

Another example of the problems that may be encountered in relation to the definition of the limits of the objective and the subjective is that of the memorisation of a musical sequence which is relatively long, or better, of a whole musical piece. More precisely, the issue is not of memorisation in itself, but the restitution of the memorised trace. In effect, we possess very sophisticated models which explain the organisation in musical memory (cf. Imberty, 1993), but these models, inspired by theories of tonal grammar, present the storage of the musical piece in the form of a set of sequences reduced and formed into a hierarchy. Thus a very static image is kept in memory. But the restitution of the musical piece is also, and above all, the restitution of a dynamic, of a movement, of a progression of a clear emotional character. How does the interpreter restore this temporal continuity, this unique flow of duration through the hierarchy of segmented sequences in memory?

I have tried to show in my own works (Imberty, 1981, 1985, 1991, 1993) that the dynamics of the form cannot be restored by a purely abstract mental reconstruction, but that it depends instead on one or more privileged moments when, suddenly, the form gains meaning both for the interpreter and for the listener, moments when, in an implicit manner, we suddenly feel the general schema, the essential direction, the goal towards which the composer wants to lead. These moments are not only determined by the musical structure, but also by the subject's mode of apprehension of the temporal continuity: he may modify the alternation of tension and release either as a function of the strict syntactic structure, or as a function of elements which are perceptively salient and marked by strong dynamic characters (accentuation, articulation, attack, intensity . . .), or as a function of emotionally invested elements outside any "objective" criteria. Most often it is a convergence of these three types of elements, and the restored dynamic organisation is, in relation to the text, both "objective" and "subjective" in being a construction of the temporal course of the piece through the intuitions both of the interpreter and of the listener.

I proposed an example of this through the comparison of two interpretations of the beginning of the *Symphonie Fantastique* by Berlioz: bars 15, 16 and 17 (1st beat) and the 1st movement which constitutes the fall—or in Lerdahlian terms, the structural conclusion of the motif which precedes bars 11 to 14. In one of the two interpretations chosen, Ozawa, in a relatively rapid tempo, only makes a global *decrescendo* without marking the *sforzandi*, which were nevertheless explicitly indicated by Berlioz: the fall of the tension is progressive, as strictly suggested by the deep tonal structure, the pivot of which appears in the low accentuated *sol* in bar 17. Karajan on the other hand stresses these *sforzandi*, with the result of holding a great tension until the end of the sequence, and thus the release does not really occur before the low *sol* of the cellos and the double basses. In Ozawa, the prolongational schema is, as I have shown (Imberty, 1991), conducted from the end of bar 10, where we already hear the fall on the dominant *sol*, whereas in Karajan, there is a new rupture creating new tension from bar 11. Thus, on the same deep tonal structure, that of the text which is hypothetically memorised and which organises the whole of musical information in memory, two different dynamic structures are built, modifying the perception of the prolongations and their effect of tension and loosening in the musical discourse, and which correspond to two different subjective visions of the piece.

FROM THE ROBOT TO THE INTERPRETER

I would now like to illustrate my presentation by the general considerations which touch the epistemological status of psychology and human sciences.

We should keep in mind that the confrontation of epistemologies of explanation and of verification on one hand, and epistemologies of interpretation on the other is essential when we deal with the field of cultural works. The work of art, and in particular the musical piece, cannot be reduced to its physical materiality and to its text (its written trace). This materiality or this text may be described in a way which may be exact or inexact; but this description does not remove the fundamental epistemological ambiguity of the work which makes it something other than what it is in this physical materiality, since it refers to an intention, or a "poietic project". This cannot directly be apprehended or explained, only reconstituted through a different procedure from the strict scientific one, a procedure which I call interpretation, and which is characterised by this fading of boundaries between objectivity and subjectivity which Rosen's text shows so well (Imberty, 1990).

Let us now examine matters more closely. I may consider that the "desperate sensuality" of Sandrina's cry is but a rhetoric effect of Rosen's pen, or at least consider that this indefinable quality is but a fugitive impression without importance, and in consequence eliminate it from the field of scientific study. Since I cannot formalise it, it is tempting to declare it unimportant for my knowledge of *La Finta Giardiniera*. There is but one small step from this to saying that the questions that cognitive sciences are incapable of dealing with are not scientifically interesting. However, I can also consider that this particular quality is essential since it constitutes the originality and the force of Mozart's music. But then, its formulation does not correspond to any rigorous scientific formulation, since it implies the mark of the person who designates it in a way which is particular to him and which he tries to share.

This type of language (communication, sharing, seduction, meaning) may seem strange. However, let us imagine, as Shaffer invites us to do in an article from 1989, a robot programmed to interpret a valse by Chopin: we can easily conceive that all sorts of precise details of the execution were programmed, up to the expression of nuances, the intensity of attacks, and the slowing down or accelerations of tempos to reproduce *rubati*. But still, even if this robot possesses a very high technical knowledge of the music, is he a worthy musician? Shaffer remarks that "the interpretation and its possible effects on the listener leave this robot indifferent" (op. cit., p. 546). The fact that the robot is not conscious of being an interpreter or of its feelings and sentiments makes it incapable of reacting in interaction with its audience, and with its own psychic state at the moment in which it is playing or with the previous states it may have known. The performance which it gives may be brilliant (technically perfect, and we know, at least virtually, how to program this perfection), but it is not musical, since it has no meaning for the robot—or for any one else. This reminds me exactly of what Furtwaengler said regarding the concert: it is minutely prepared by the repetitions, the aim of which is to put in place all the technical elements of the execution. But these repetitions' role should be such that, "during the concert, there is no more improvisation than is strictly indispensable. But—*no less either*—this also is very important" (Furtwaengler, 1953). This is like saying that the emotion which makes the music alive in its temporal dynamics is a given which is undoubtedly subjective but very predominant in the organisation of the piece's structures when it is executed. Our robot cannot be sensitive to this emotion which the music releases in the listeners or in interpreters, because it cannot share any of their experiences. It is true that if we try to "*objectively*" define what distinguishes the musical interpretation from the brilliant execution, we can always compare various parameters and present the observed differences as referring to the different qualities of the executions under consideration, differences which could very well be programmed in the robot. For pure cognitivists, it will seem futile to complicate the problem of interpretation by referring to so-called emotional or participational dimensions. However, it is unimaginable that the musician can pretend to feel an emotion during the execution: playing this emotion consists in an attempt to communicate a certain *lived experience of the piece* to the listener, and the listener is perfectly capable of distinguishing between the feigned and the felt and shared emotion. But nothing is more difficult for an authentic musician than to give an execution of a musical piece which is only brilliant and technical, without any feeling. This clearly shows that what the musical interpretation gives—and which cannot be programmed in the robot's electronics—is this dynamics, this movement, this unpredictable life which only exists in the interactive relation between the interpreter and the piece (and the composer), the public, with himself.

Better—and here we find the epistemological status of the interpretation: its essential connecting of the interpreting subject to the interpreted object through the listener—any musical interpretation is indeed a particular experience of the piece at the moment it is executed, in being the result of the interpreter's choice, a choice which corresponds first of all to his own vision of the piece, of the composer, of the period of time: his choices can in no way be formalised in terms of programs and execution procedures. They depend first of all on the subjectivity of the interpreter, that is what he is, his history, his intention which he projects as a function of his personality and the representations which he may have of the expectations of his public. The musical interpretation is first of all this identification of the interpreter with "the piece and the course of its development", an appropriation of the piece by the interpreter which will later allow this same appropriation by the listener. But this introjective penetration of the piece in the interpreter, this spiritual availability which it asks of him, what a demand of time, of patience and wisdom of which the robot is incapable! The musical interpreter arrives at the height of his art only with time, in a sort of impregnation which goes beyong the analytic knowledge of the piece's structures and of execution techniques.

I will cite here one more short example: two interpretations of the beginning of *Der Einsame im Herbst* from the *Chant de la Terre* by Mahler. The comparison is of the instrumental bars which precede the entrance of the woman-singer. The two interpretations considered are those of Karajan and Klemperer. If we carefully analyse the two versions, we can see that it is only the quality of the phrasing which separates them: in Karajan, in a very slightly faster tempo, the famous *legato* creates a remarkable poetic and narcissistic melancholy, in a total melodic continuity and a blending of timbres which is absolutely unique. In Klemperer, the phrasing seems totally fragmented, the accentuations, the *portamenti* clearly more emphasised, although reading of the music score while listening does not give the feeling that the *technical execution is very different from the previous one. But the psychological tension is different, the continuity of the temporal course is born through this discontinuity that the force of motion envelopes and forces into unity.* The result of this is not only the realease of a deep sadness, but a feeling of total and desperate solitude which places this version almost at the complete opposite of Karajan's hedonistic version. In summary, from such little technical differences, what differences in climate, emotion, what opposition in meaning, what gentleness on one hand, what violence on the other!

The model of the robot and the example which we have briefly examined clarify in what way interpretation goes beyond cognisance, as precise and detailed as we can imagine it: any interpretation is of course based on a text, with its meticulousness of details as well as its imprecision of writing, and which supposes an *analysis* as objective as possible which accumulates observations and historical, cultural and stylistic facts. All this belongs to cognition and we can imagine a complete model that the robot could simulate. But it is clear that two interpretations of the beginning of *Der Einsame im Herbst* of *Chant de la Terre*, in their profound opposition, contain this inevitable and necessary mark of the interpreter in his interpretation which, on one hand, operates choices in the structural complexity of the text and, on the other hand, transcends this work of discovery and knowledge of the score in learning and repetitions, in a sort of intuition, in a tussle with the piece.

Our sophisticated cognitive models, our computer programs, will allow us no doubt to deepen our knowledge of pieces, of the mental mechanisms, of the composer, of the interpreter and of the listener. They will allow us to create more perfected simulations, eliminating all the risks of failure typical of the human machine, and also to create types of music and of more and more refined executions. But will they be able to recreate this inexpressible terror of Mahler in face of solitude that Klemperer constructs, creates completely through his reading of the text? Will they be able to make us *feel* at the turning of a sensual and desperate cry, the grace and the unique gesture of the creative genius of Mozart? We may hope that this is impossible! If only because then we can still predict long and lovely days spent in the analysis of musical texts and the cognitive sciences of music.

Translated by Noémie Ziv

REFERENCES

Balzano, G.J. (1989). Exécution de commandes, commandes d'éxécution. In S. McAdams & I. Deliège, (Eds.), *La musique et les sciences cognitives* (pp. 613–627). Bruxelles, Belgium: Mardaga.

Francès, R. (1958). *La perception de la musique*. Paris: Vrin.

Furtwaengler, W. (1953). *Entretiens sur la musique*. Paris: A. Michel. French translation.

Imberty, M. (1981). *Les écritures du temps*. Paris: Dunod.

Imberty, M. (1985). *La cathédrale engloutie* de Claude Debussy: de la perception au sens. *Revue de Musique des Universités Canadiennes*, 6, 90–160.

Imberty, M. (1990). Les interprétations du sens en musique et en psychanalyse. *Convegno Internazionale: Tendenze e metodi nella ricerca musicologica*, Latina, Società Italiana di Musicologia, publ. in Atti del Convegno, Firenze, Olschki, 1995, 163–179.

Imberty, M. (1991). Comment l'interprète et l'auditeur organisent-ils la progression temporelle d'une oeuvre musicale? (Analyse, mémorisation et interprétation). *Psychologica Belgica, XXXI*(2), 173–195.

Imberty, M. (1993). Teorie della musica e teorie della memoria. In M. Imberty, M. Baroni, G. Pozzionato, *Memoria musicale e volori sociali*, Ricordi, 8–32.

Nattiez, J.J. (1987). *Musicologie générale et sémiologie*. Paris: Ch. Bourgois.

Rosen, Ch. (1971). *Le style classique: Haydn, Mozart, Beethoven*. French translation. Paris: Gallimard, 1978.

Shaffer, L.H. (1989). Cognition et affect dans l'interprétation musicale. In S. McAdams & I. Deliège, (Eds.), *La musique et les sciences cognitives* (pp. 537–550). Bruxelles, Belgium: Mardaga.

Author Index

444

Subject Index